# The 1994 Guide to France

Since 1934 Les Routiers have been recommending establishments that provide good quality food and accommodation, value for money and a warm and friendly welcome. The 1994 guide to France offers a superb choice of over 1,700 such establishments – just look out for the distinctive red and blue Les Routiers symbol!

## Contents

## Guide Entries

First published in the United Kingdom in 1994
Alan Sutton Publishing Ltd
Phoenix Mill · Far Thrupp · Stroud
Gloucestershire GL5 2BU

First published in the
United States of America in 1994
Alan Sutton Publishing Inc.
83 Washington Street
Dover · NH 03820

ISBN 0 7509 0547 6

Les Routiers inspectors visit each establishment anonymously and settle their bill before revealing their identity. Complimentary meals and/or accommodation are not accepted.

LES ROUTIERS: 25 Vanston Place, London SW6 1AZ

Tel: (071) 385 6644
Fax: (071) 385 7136

*Editor:* Malcolm Morris
*Maps:* Martin Latham and Kerry Chambler
*Cover illustration:* Gary Brazier

Typeset by Alan Sutton Publishing Limited.
Printed in Great Britain by
The Bath Press, Bath, Avon.

# Sixty Years of Tradition

In a country as discerning as France, no symbol could have possibly become such a household name as Les Routiers without representing the sort of standards that have stood the test of time. After sixty years, we think Les Routiers can confidently be said to have proved that it is an inspiration to those of you who share a high regard for food, value for money and hospitality.

For the traveller in France, the red and blue Les Routiers sign has become as much a part of the scenery as the poplars, châteaux and vineyards. The restaurants and hotels recommended by Les Routiers offer local cuisine, simple accommodation and a warm welcome – all at a price you can afford.

The Les Routiers Guide provides a reliable source of reference for all those looking for real French food, an authentic atmosphere and good value. All 'Relais Routiers' are regularly inspected to ensure they provide a warm welcome, serve good quality food, at least one fixed price menu, and observe rules of hygiene in kitchens, bedrooms and bathrooms.

The attractions of France are many – good food, fine wine, hospitable people. Indeed, the French have a unique respect for and love of food. Many visitors will find that where to eat dictates their entire holiday plans. With over 1,700 Les Routiers recommended establishments in France, ranging from family restaurants to local brasseries, your Les Routiers Guide offers plenty of choice.

By venturing off the motorway you will not only see the beauty of the French countryside, but will also avoid the motorway tolls and most congested routes. Let Les Routiers guide you through the vineyards of Burgundy or the sun-drenched villages of Provence. Taste the world-famous red and white wines and enjoy regional specialities such as *coq au vin* and *salade niçoise*.

As soon as you cross the Channel you will notice the different flavours and styles of cooking. The Les Routiers Guide is your assurance of finding a cheerful greeting, homely comfort and traditional food at good value for money. The following pages will explain how to get the best from your Guide and make the most of travelling in France.

**BON VOYAGE ET BON APPETIT!**

# When in France . . .

1. Take your Guide with you into restaurants and hotels – it will let the owners know that you have chosen their establishment by using the Guide, and that you expect a high standard of food and service.

2. There are two types of meals available – 'repas complet' and 'casse-croûte'. 'Repas complet' is a full meal and is served at set meal times. 'Casse-croûte', a snack meal, can be served at any time and usually consists of something simple, such as an omelette, a sandwich or a plate of cold meats.

3. Following a change in the laws in 1987, the service charge must be included in the price of a meal. Tips are rarely expected and are usually given by rounding up the bill.

4. The price quoted for accommodation will be for the room and not per person, but a small supplement will be charged if more than two people are sharing a room. This is usually minimal and a great help for families travelling on a budget. The price of the room is usually shown on a card on the back of the door, along with the price of breakfast.

5. French 'Hôtels de Tourisme' are officially classed on a star system. The stars provide a rating of 1–4 and 'luxe', and are usually displayed on a plaque by the main entrance. There are also many unclassified hotels where the standards are equally acceptable.

6. It is normal practice to view the room being offered before deciding to accept it. By doing so, you will be able to check on the level of cleanliness and comfort. However, should you wish to make an advance booking we strongly advise you to make your selection from the approved Relais Routiers 'Tourist Hotels'.

7. If you have booked a hotel room, try to arrive before 6.00pm. unless you have advised the hotel of your time of arrival. If you have been delayed, do try to contact the hotel. If you do not have a reservation the chances of finding a room are greatly improved if you arrive before 6.00pm.

8. Many small hotels will lock their doors quite early at night. If you wish to go out, remember to advise the proprietors who will probably make arrangements for you.

9. Many French people take their holiday between 14 July and 15 August and you may find some hotels and restaurants closed during this period. It is advisable to book accommodation well in advance if you wish to travel at this time.

# See Why Our Members Prefer Us

**BRITANNIA RESCUE**

# We Offer You the Choice

## Road Rescue – What price peace of mind?
## Answer –
## Less than you'd think!

For ten years Britannia Rescue has been providing a fast, efficient breakdown and recovery service, originally exclusively for members of the CSMA. But now, this excellent service is offered to buyers of the Les Routiers Guides to Britain and France. Britain's leading consumer testing magazine in their April 1992 issue, voted Britannia Rescue as their 'Best Buy' with an average callout time of 34 minutes, well ahead of the AA, RAC and National Breakdown.

## What services can you have?

### Superstart – a home start-up service from £26.50 per year

An economically priced service, ideal for drivers who use their cars infrequently or for shorter journeys. If your car will not start at home, or if you break down within half a mile of home, our agent will come to your assistance. If the car cannot be started you can be taken to a single destination of your choice (within 10 miles) while your car is transported to a local garage.

### Rescue Plus – roadside assistance and local recovery service from £40.00 per year

Designed to offer protection against minor breakdowns away from your home. If your problem can't be solved at

BRITANNIA RESCUE

the roadside we will transport you, your vehicle and up to five passengers to a nearby garage. We will also reimburse you up to £12 towards the cost of a taxi or other alternative transport.

## Standard Cover – roadside assistance and recovery to nearby garage or home or to an onward destination from £54.50 per year or £5.50 per month*

Cover offers protection from every breakdown situation while away from the vicinity of your home, both for your car and for you. We will endeavour to fix any minor problems on the spot as quickly as possible. If, however, this is not possible, our agent will transport you, your vehicle and up to five passengers home or to the destination of your choice.

## Comprehensive Cover – roadside assistance, recovery, attendance at home from £72.00 per year or £7.25 per month*

This cover gives you complete peace of mind. We cater for annoying non-start problems such as flat batteries and damp engines to roadside breakdowns and accident recovery. We also include Housecall, covering you at home or within half a mile radius of home. It should be noted that Housecall is not intended as a home maintenance service and we would not expect to attend to recurring faults.

## Deluxe Cover – roadside assistance, recovery, attendance at home, free car hire or hotel accommodation from £88.00 per year or £8.75 per month*

As the name suggests, this is the highest level of cover. You and your vehicle are not only catered for both at home and on the road, but if your car cannot be repaired the same day you can choose between a free replacement car (for up to 48 hours), or assistance with overnight hotel accommodation. Please note that car hire is subject to the terms and conditions of Britannia Rescue's car companies, minimum age of drivers must be 23 years.

## Personal Cover – £18.00 per year or £1.80 per month*

Whichever Britannia Rescue cover you choose, for just £18 we will extend the cover to include any car you or your spouse may drive.

## * Monthly Premiums

Monthly premiums are available on the top three levels of service – Standard, Comprehensive and Deluxe – when paying by Direct Debit.

# All Part of Our Service

### Legal advice and defence

We offer every member a 24 hour legal advice service. We can also provide representation in magistrates' courts.

### Assistance after theft and vandalism

In the case of vehicle immobilization, we will provide roadside repair or transport to a local garage or on to your destination.

### Relief driver

Britannia Rescue will arrange a relief driver to assist you in case of illness, injury or severe mental distress.

### Tyres and windscreens

We assist on less serious, but often annoying occasions, such as punctures, shattered windscreens, lack of fuel or even locking your keys in the car.

**BRITANNIA RESCUE**

### Caravans and trailers

These are covered free of charge (excluding Housecall).

# Why choose Britannia Rescue?

■ Dedicated to providing every member with a fast, caring road rescue service

■ 34 minutes average callout time

■ Over 3,000 trained personnel on call 24 hours a day 365 days a year

■ A BSI registered firm committed to consistent service quality

■ Value for money prices with easy payment methods

■ Recommended by Britain's leading consumer watchdog as 'Best Buy'

# How to apply for Britannia Rescue membership

Turn to pages 269 and 271 for an application form and direct debit mandate. Or if you wish to join immediately by telephone, simply ring FREE on 0800 591563 and quote your credit card number!

# Travelling abroad

Available to anyone, whether covered by Britannia Rescue in the UK or not, Britannia Continental is a superb emergency breakdown service, competitively priced, and designed to cover any mishap while travelling abroad. There are two types of cover, one for travel with a vehicle in Europe, and the other for travel anywhere in the world. Personal Insurance includes medical repatriation by air ambulance. For further details and a brochure, ring 0484 514848.

# Motoring Peace of Mind in France

Britannia Continental offers you, in France and elsewhere in Europe, the standards of road rescue assistance achieved by Britannia Rescue in the UK. Backed up by a 24-hour emergency helpline, Britannia Continental provides a truly comprehensive breakdown package for car, motor cycle, trailer/caravan and motor caravans.

## Real help just when you need it!

When an emergency arises abroad, the first thing you need is help from someone who will understand your problems. Our controllers will give you just that! They've met the problem before and they'll handle it with cool, calm efficiency so that the holiday you have looked forward to need not be spoiled.

## Summary of protection provided:

### Vehicle Cover

| | |
|---|---|
| Roadside assistance, towing and emergency repairs | £250 |
| Vehicle repatriation to the UK | vehicle market value |
| Car hire and continuation of journey | £800 |
| Repatriation of driver and passengers | Unlimited |
| Alternative driver | Unlimited |
| Hotel expenses | £150 p.p. |
| Spare parts delivery | Unlimited |
| Legal defence and claims recovery following motor accident | £50,000 |
| Advance for bail or Customs Duty | £1,000 |

## Personal Cover

| | Up to: |
|---|---|
| Medical and incidental expenses | *£2 million |
| Hospital inconvenience benefit | £300 |
| Delayed departure | £120 |
| Cancellation and curtailment | *£3,000 |
| Personal accident | £20,000 |
| Personal effects and baggage | *£1,500 |
| Personal legal liability | £1,000,000 |
| Replacement passport | £100 |
| Hijack, kidnap and detention | £1,000 |
| Missed departure | £500 |
| Personal money and travellers cheques | *£500 |
| Legal expenses | £10,000 |

*Under these sections the first £25 of each and every claim per person is excluded.

# Premiums:
## Vehicle Cover

| Period | Vehicles up to 6 years old | Vehicles 7 years to under 13 years | Vehicles 13 years and over |
|---|---|---|---|
| 3 days | 18.00 | 22.50 | 30.50 |
| 6 days | 27.75 | 34.75 | 47.25 |
| 9 days | 32.00 | 40.00 | 54.50 |
| 14 days | 37.75 | 47.25 | 64.25 |
| 19 days | 42.00 | 52.50 | 71.50 |
| 24 days | 46.00 | 57.50 | 78.25 |
| 31 days | 51.00 | 63.75 | 86.75 |
| Extra weeks | 8.50 | 10.50 | 14.50 |
| Caravan/trailer | 13.50 | 17.00 | 23.00 |
| Annual cover | 92.00 | 115.00 | 156.50 |

## Personal Cover

| Period not exceeding | Each person 16 years and over | Children aged 4 to 15 years |
|---|---|---|
| 3 days | 8.50 | 4.25 |
| 6 days | 12.75 | 6.50 |
| 9 days | 15.50 | 7.75 |
| 14 days | 17.50 | 8.75 |
| 19 days | 21.50 | 10.75 |
| 24 days | 23.25 | 11.75 |
| 31 days | 27.50 | 13.75 |
| Extra weeks | 6.00 | 3.00 |
| Annual cover | 45.00 | 38.00 |

For full details and an application form ring 0484 514848 and ask for the Britannia Continental Department.

Cover can be applied for by telephone by quoting your credit card number.

# How to Find a Relais Routiers

**1. You want to know whether there is a Relais Routiers in a certain locality.**
Look for the name of the town in question in the alphabetical index of towns. If the name is not present, there is no Relais Routiers in that town. Each establishment entry gives the name of the department and the number (the French equivalent of the county and postcode) as well as the map reference and a main road reference where possible.

**2. You are following an itinerary, and you want to know where to find a Relais Routiers.**
Turn to our list of maps of France, where you will find details of 19 maps covering the whole of the country. The motorways and main roads are shown on these maps and all the places where there are Relais Routiers are marked. Then all you have to do is turn to the alphabetical index of towns which will direct you to the entries for Relais Routiers on your route.

**3. You wish to find a hotel.**
Although the majority of Relais Routiers are restaurants, many of them also have accommodation. These are denoted in the guide by the hotel symbol, and on the maps by a triangle. However, as the standards in these may vary considerably, we have cited the official classification of Relais Routiers, as approved by the French Tourist Board. The classification is denoted by the number of stars at the top of the entry or see pages 41–4.

**4. What is a Casserole Relais?**
You will find a 'Casserole' symbol at the top of certain guide entries. This symbol distinguishes those Relais Routiers where particular care is taken to offer above-average meals with perhaps a special menu or specialities of the region. The 'Casserole' is the Les Routiers mark of excellence. A list of all 'Casseroles' can be found on pages 39–40.

# Symbols Used in this Guide

⊗ RESTAURANT
♀ BAR, CAFE, SNACKS
⌂ HOTEL – establishment with 4 or more rooms, bed and breakfast available.
☜ CASSEROLE – the Les Routiers mark of excellence awarded annually to those Relais Routiers where particular care is taken to offer above average meals.
☆ OFFICIAL CLASSIFICATION OF THE FRENCH TOURIST BOARD
– the number of stars (1–4) indicates the degree of comfort.

NB. All place-names given in the Guide indicate a Relais Routiers – but not its category. Do make sure you check the symbols so that on arrival at a Relais, you do not find a bar only, when what you require is a hotel.

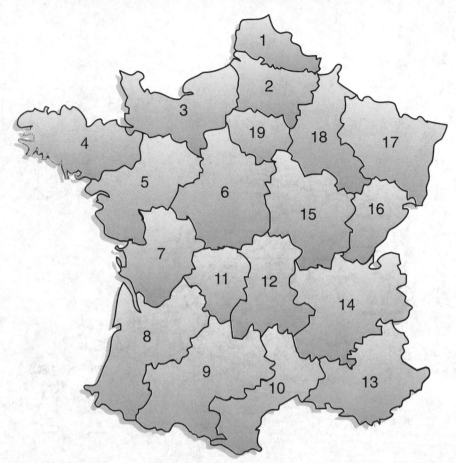

# List of Maps

## Key to Symbols

| | | | |
|---|---|---|---|
| food | | city | |
| food and accommodation | | motorway | |
| accommodation | | main road | |
| main town | | county boundary | |

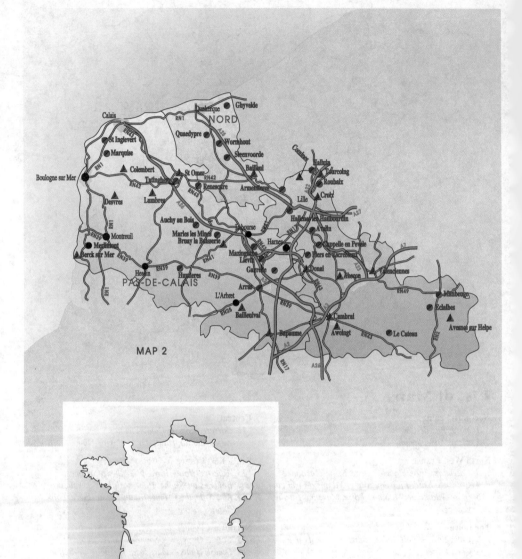

MAP 2

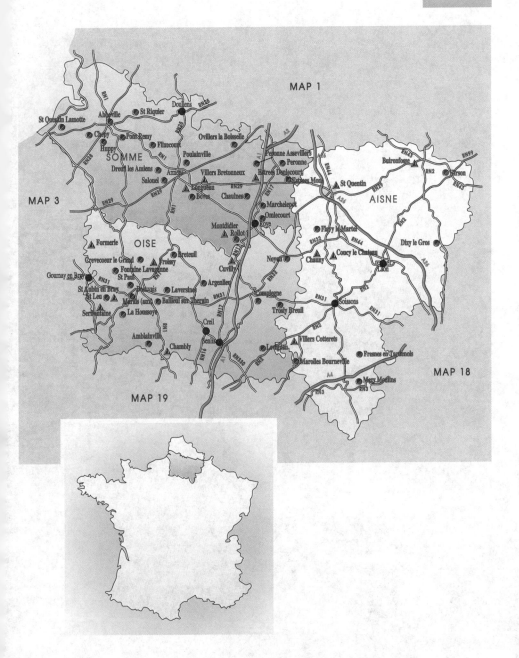

MAP 1

St Quentin Lamotte

Abbeville

St Riquier

Doullens

Chepy

Pont Remy

Flixecourt

Ovillers la Boisselle

Huppy

Poulainville

Péronne Asseviller

SOMME

Dreuil les Amiens

Amiens

Villers Bretonneux

Péronne

Buironfosse

Salouel

Longueau

Estrées Deniecourt

Estrées Mons

St Quentin

Bovès

Chaulnes

Marchelepot

Omiecourt

Roye

AISNE

MAP 3

Montdidier

Rollot

Flavy le Martel

Dizy le Gros

Formerie

OISE

Noyon

Chauny

Coucy le Chateau

Laon

Crevecoeur le Grand

Froissy

Breteuil

Fontaine Lavagenne

Cuvilly

Gournay en Bray

St Paul

Beauvais

Argenlieu

Compiegne

Soissons

St Aubin en Bray

St Leu

Laversines

Marais (and

Bailleul sur Therain

Trosly Breuil

Serifontaine

La Houssoye

Creil

Villers Cotterets

Amblainvilll

Senlis

Levignen

Fresnes en Tardenois

Chambly

Marolles Bourneville

MAP 18

Messy Moulins

MAP 19

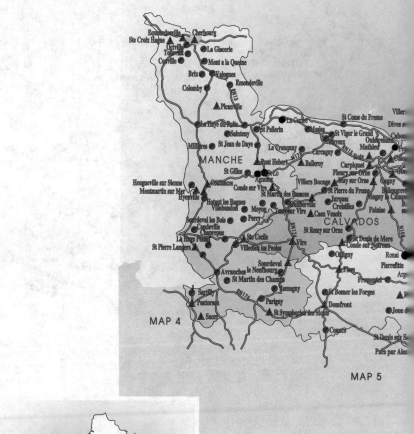

Equeurdreville · Cherbourg
Ste Croix Hague · Octeville
Tollevast
Couville · La Glacerie
Mont a la Quesne
Brix · Valognes
Colomby · Emondeville
Picauville
La Haye du Puits · St Pellerin · La Cambe
St Come du Freme · Viller
Dives s
Moules · St Vigor le Grand · Cabou
Sainteny · Oublrehains
Millières · St Jean de Daye · Le Vronguey · Carcagny · Mathiet · Edo
MANCHE · Pont Hebert · Balleroy · Carpiquet · Gou
St Gilles · St Lo · Villers Bocage · Fleury sur Orne · Ballengrev
Coutances · Agneau · May sur Orne · Maguy la Camps
Heugueville sur Sienne · Conde sur Vire · St Pierre du Fresne · Falaise
Montmartin sur Mer · St Martin des Besaces · Jurques · B
Hyesville · Gilberville · Crotelles · su
Hotant les Bagues · Moyon · Caen Venoix
Villebaudon · CALVADOS
Sourdeval les Bois · Percy · St Remy sur Orne
Condeville · Dang sur Vire
Chazrepus · St Denis de Mere
La Haye Pesnel · Ste Cecile · Conde sur Noireau
St Pierre Langers · Villedieu les Poeles · Vire · Ronai
Celigny · Pierrefitte
Flers · Arg
Sourdeval · Frument
Avranches le Neufbourg · St Bomer les Forges
Sartill · St Martin des Champs · Romagny · Donfront · Joue d
Pontorson · Parigny
Sacey · St Symphorien des Mon · St Denis sur S
Ceance · Pace par Alex
MAP 4

MAP 5

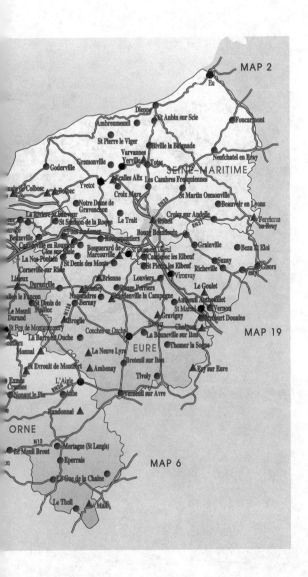

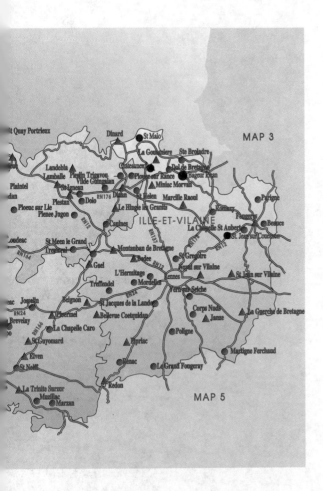

MAP 4

St Nicolas de Redon
Chateaubriant
LOIRE-ATLANTIQUE
Erbray
Vannes
St Gildas des Bois
Pontchateau
Rialle
Blain
Treillieres
Savenay Heric
Nort sur Erdre
Montoir de Bretagne
St Luce sur Loire
St Nazaire
Anetz
St Brevin les Pins
Ronans
St Sebastien sur Vertou
St Brevin l' Ocean
Basse Indre
Vallet
Les Sorinieres
Bouguenais
Chateauthebaud
Pont St Martin
St Germain sur
Bourgneuf en Retz
St Philbert de Grand Lieu
Machecoul
Mortagne sur
Beauvoir sur Mer
St Hilaire de Loulay
Legg
Les Herbiers
Chalian
VENDEE
Falleron
Herbergement
Fenouiller
Les Essarts
l' Aiguillon sur Vie
Landeronde
La Roche sur Yon
Nieul le Dolent
Bournez
Les Sables d'Olonne
St Jean de Beugne
Talmont St Hilaire
Mou
St Cyr en Talmondais
Morelli
Chaille les Marais

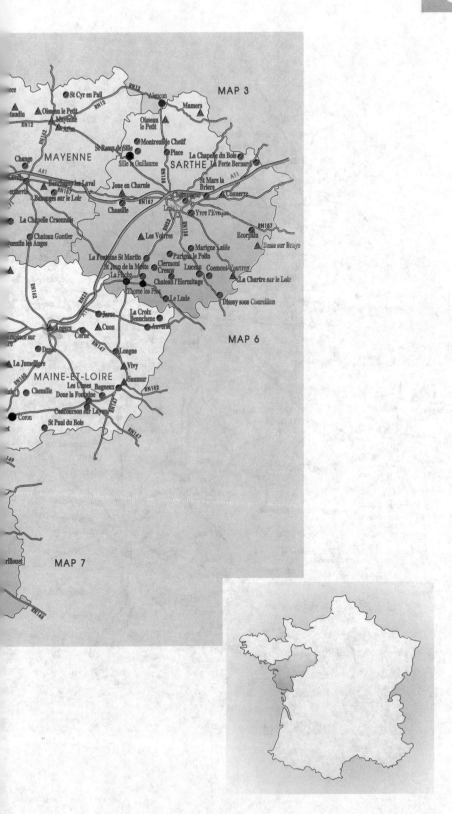

MAP 3

St Cyr en Pail

RN12

Alençon

Mamers

taudin

Oisseau le Petit

Mayenne

Oisseau
le Petit

RN12

Arso

Montreuille Chetif

St Rasuy de Sille

Place

La Chapelle du Bois

Change

MAYENNE

Sille le Guillaume

SARTHE

La Ferte Bernard

A81

Joue en Charnie

St Mars la
Brière

Bouchamp les Laval

Chaumpagne

Connerre

exhevill

RN167

Belanges sur le Loir

Le Ma

Yvre l'Eveque

La Chapelle Craonnaise

Chasslile

RN167

Ecorpain

Chateau Gontier

Les Voitres

Marigne Laille

Basse sur Braye

uentin les Anges

La Fontaine St Martin

Parigne le Polin

La Fleche

St Jean de la Motte

Clermont
Creans

Luceau

Coemont Vouvray

La Chartre sur le Loir

Chateau l'Hermitage

RN162

Thoree les Pin

Le Lude

Dissay sous Courcillon

Jarse

La Croix
Besuchene

Auverse

Cuon

MAP 6

alnglece sur

Corne

RN147

Longue

Deage

La Jumelliere

Vivy

RN160

MAINE-ET-LOIRE

Saumur

Les Ulmes

Bagneux

RN162

Chemille

Doue la Fontaine

Concourson sur Layon

RN147

Coron

St Paul du Bois

RN147

149

MAP 7

rillouet

MAP 5

RN148

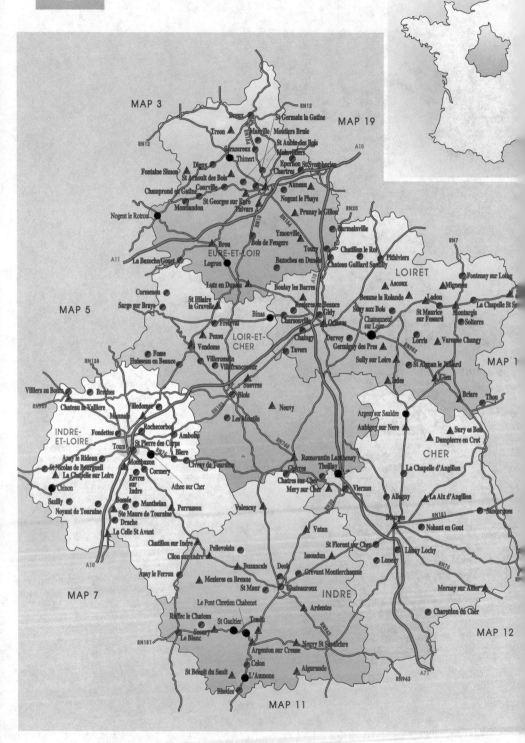

MAP 3

MAP 19

MAP 5

MAP 1

MAP 7

MAP 12

MAP 11

EURE-ET-LOIR

LOIR-ET-CHER

LOIRET

CHER

INDRE-ET-LOIRE

INDRE

Beauy
St Germain la Gatine
Treon
Manville Moutiers Brule
St Aubin des Bois
Mainvilliers
St Arnoult des Bois
Epernon St Symphorien
Thimert
Chartres
Digny
Fontaine Simon
Courville
Champrond en Gatine
St Georges sur Eure
Aunean
Montlandon
Thivars
Nogent le Phaye
Nogent le Rotrou
Prunay le Gillon
Germainville
Brou
Ymonville
Touty
Chatillon le Roi
Pithiviers
La Bezoche Gouet
Logron
Bois de Feugere
Bazoches en Dunois
Chateau Gaillard Sancilly
Fontenay sur Loing
Lutz en Dunois
Boulay les Barres
Ascoux
Mignieres
Cormenon
Beaune la Rolande
Ladon
La Chapelle St Se
St Hilaire la Gravelle
Rouvres en Beauce
Sary aux Bois
St Maurice sur Fessard
Montargis
Sarge sur Braye
Binas
Charsonville
Gidy
Chateauneuf sur Loire
Solterre
Freteval
Orleans
Lorris
Varennes Changy
Pezou
Chaingy
Darvoy
Vendome
Tavers
Germigny des Pres
St Aignan le Jaillard
Fosse
Villeromain
Sully sur Loire
Gien
Huisseau en Beauce
Villetrancoeur
Vades
Villiers au Bouin
Suevres
Briare
Thou
Breches
Blois
Chateau la Valliere
Villedomer
Neuvy
Argent sur Sauldre
Sury es Bois
Les Montils
Aubigny sur Nere
Damplerre en Crot
Mennau
Rochecorbon
Fondettes
Amboise
St Pierre des Corps
Romorantin Lanthenay
La Chapelle d'Angillon
Tours
Montbazon
Blere
Thelbay
Azay le Rideau
Cormery
Livray de Touraine
Chatres
La Aix d'Angillon
St Nicolas de Bourgueil
Eevres sur Indre
Chatres sur Cher
Vierzon
La Chapelle sur Loire
Mery sur Cher
Allogny
Chinon
Afhee sur Cher
Sazilly
Bossee
Manthelan
Perrusson
Valencay
Bourges
Saldurges
Noyant de Touraine
Ste Maure de Touraine
Vatan
Nohant en Gout
Drache
La Celle St Avant
St Florent sur Cher
Lissay Lochy
Chatillon sur Indre
Pellevoisin
Issoudun
Lunery
Clion sur Indre
Buzancais
Deols
Mornay sur Allier
Azay le Ferron
Crevant Moutierchaume
Mezieres en Brenne
St Maur
Chateauroux
Charenton du Cher
Le Pont Chretien Chabenet
Ardentes
Ruffec le Chateau
Tenan
St Gaultier
Seceny
Neuvy St Sepulchre
Le Blanc
Argenton sur Creuse
Celon
Algurande
St Benoit du Sault
L'Aumone
Rhedes

RN12
RN12
A10
RN20
RN7
A11
A10
RN138
RN727
RN143
RN152
RN7164
RN751
RN76
RN943
A71
A10
RN151
RN144

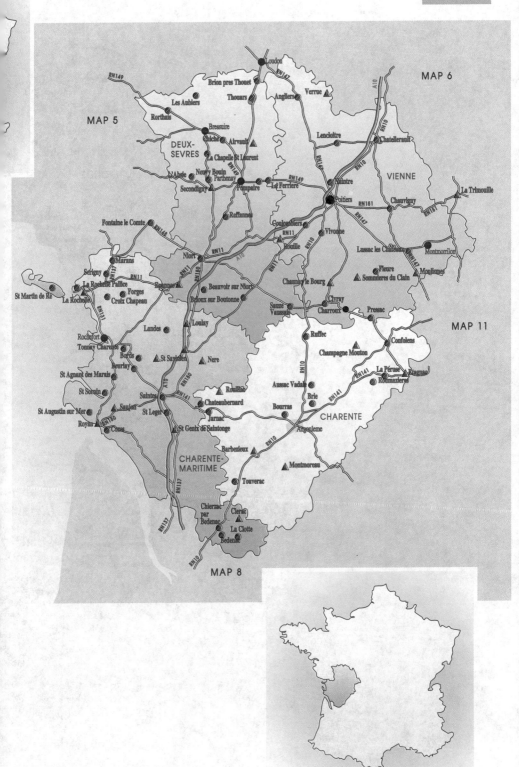

MAP 6

MAP 5

RN149

Loudon

Brion pres Thouet

Les Aubiers

Rorthais

Thouars

Angliers

Verrue

A10

Bressuire

Colche

Airvault

**DEUX-
SEVRES**

Lencloitre

Chatellerault

La Chapelle St Laurent

St'Abele

Neuvy Bouin

Secondigny

Parthenay

Pompaire

Le Ferriere

RN149

Saintre

Poitiers

RN151

Chauvigny

**VIENNE**

La Trimouille

Reffannes

Fontaine le Comte

RN148

Coulombiers

Rouille

Vivonne

RN11

Lussac les Chateaux

Montmorillon

Marans

Nlort

RN11

Serigny

La Rochelle Pallice

Epannes

Beauvoir sur Nlort

Chaunay le Bourg

Fleure

Sommieres du Clain

Moulismes

St Martin de Re

La Rochelle

Forges
Croix Chapeau

Brioux sur Boutonne

Sauze
Vaussais

Clvray

Charroux

Pressac

**MAP 11**

Landes

Loulay

Rochefort

Tonnay Charente

Bords

Neurlay

St Savinien

Nere

Ruffec

Champagne Mouton

Confolens

La Péruse

Etagnac

St Agnant des Marais

RN141

Roumazieres

St Soroln

Roullit

Aussac Vadala

Brie

Saintes

St Augustin sur Mer

Saujon

St Leger

Chateaubernard

Jarnac

Bourras

**CHARENTE**

Royan

Coze

St Genix de Saintonge

Angouleme

RN137

**CHARENTE-
MARITIME**

Barbezleux

RN10

Montmoreau

Touverac

RN137

Chierzac
par
Bedenac

Clerac

La Clotte

Bedenac

RN10

MAP 8

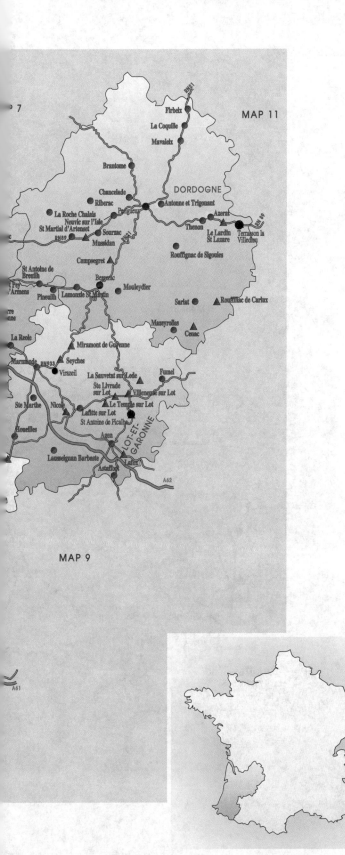

MAP 11

MAP 9

MAP 8

TARN-ET-GARO

GERS

HAUTES-
PYRENEES

Gou
St Germain d
Ca
Cahors Pern
St Paul de Loubre

Lauzderte
Moissac
Montauba
Castelsarrasin
Montech
B:
Grisolles

Ligardes

Valence sur Baise
Fleurance

Aucamvill
Selih

Marsan Aublet
Auch
L'Isle Jourdain
Toulo

Risde
Plaisance du Gers

Muret

Castelnau Riviere Basse

RN21

Maubourguet
Masseube

Carbonne
Les Bec

Vic en Bigorre

Mondanezan

Tarbe
Trie sur Baise

Lalombere
Sannemezan
Villeneuve de Riviere
Beauchelot

Lourdes

RN117

Pierrefitte Nestalas

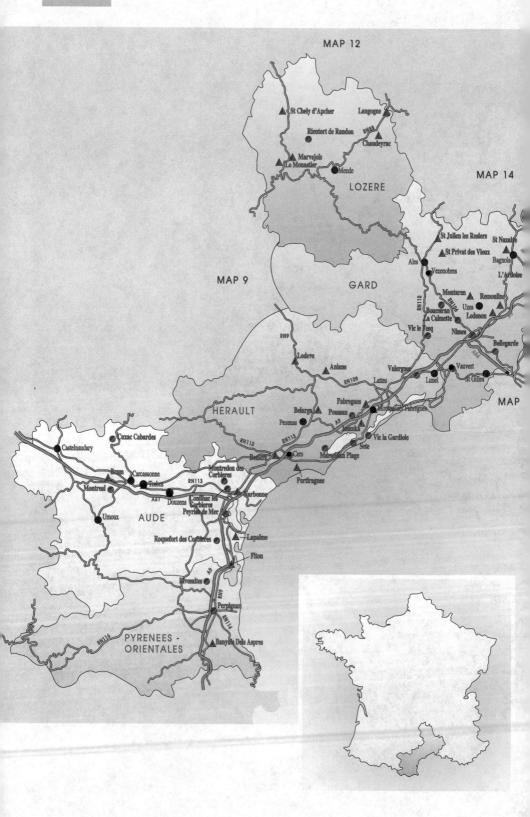

MAP 12

St Chely d'Apcher    Langogne

Rieutort de Randon

Chandeyrac

Marvejols
Le Monastier

Mende

LOZERE

MAP 14

St Julien les Rosiers

St Nazaire

St Privat des Vieux

Bagnols

Ales

Vezenobres

L'Ardoise

MAP 9

Montaren

Remoulins

GARD

Boucoiran
La Calmette

Uzes

Ledenon

Vic le Fesq

Nimes

Bellegarde

Lodeve

Aniane

Valergues

Vauvert

Lattes

Lunel

St Gilles

MAP

Fabregues

Montpellier Fabregues

Belarga

Poussan

Pezenas

Vic la Gardiole

HERAULT

Sete

Cuxac Cabardes

RN112

RN113

Beziers

Cers

Marseillan Plage

Castelnaudary

Braun

Montredon des
Corbieres

Carcassonne

Portiragnes

Montreal

Trebes

RN113

A61

Douzens

Conilhac les
Corbieres

Narbonne

Peyriac de Mer

Umoux

AUDE

Roquefort des Corbieres

Lapalme

Fitou

Rivesaltes

Perpignan

PYRENEES -
ORIENTALES

Banyuls Dels Aspres

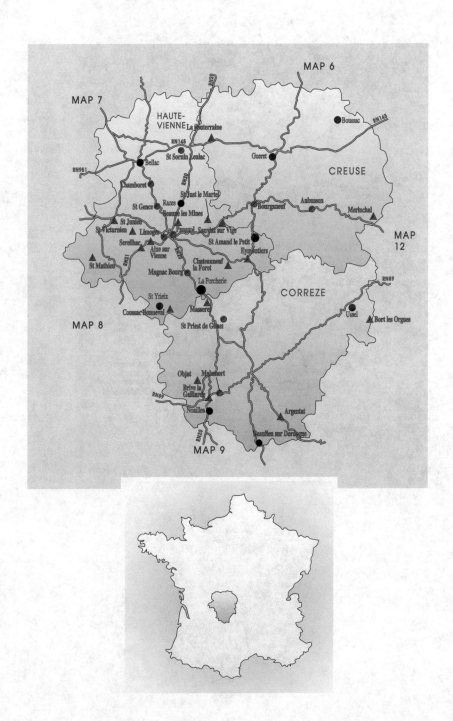

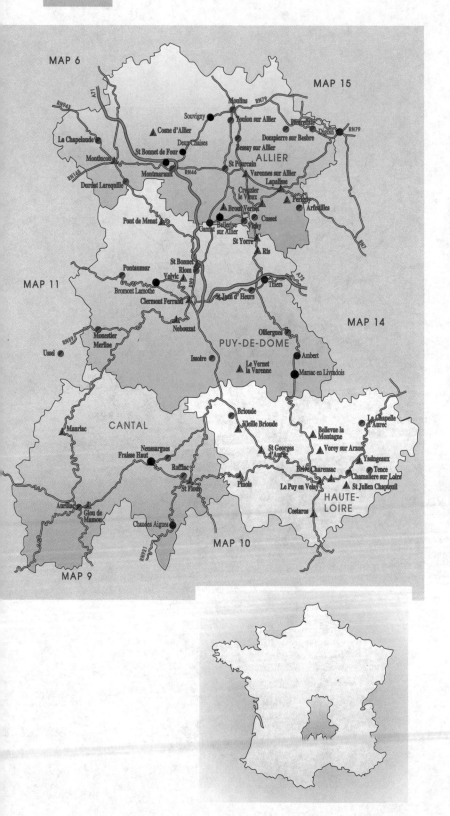

MAP 6

MAP 15

RN943

A71

Moulins
RN79

Souvigny

Toulon sur Allier

Cosne d'Allier

Neuville

Dompierre sur Besbre

RN79

La Chapelaude

Deux Chaises

Montlucon

St Bonnet de Four

Sessay sur Allier

ALLIER

Montmarault

St Pourcain

RN46

Varennes sur Allier

RM166

Durdot Larequille

Lapalisse

Creuzier
le Vieux

Périgny

Arfeuilles

Broni Vernet

Cusset

Pont de Menat

Bellerive
sur Allier

Vichy

Gannat

St Yorre

RN7

St Yorre

Ris

Pontaumur

St Bonnet
Riom

A72

Thiers

Volvic

Bromont Lamothe

St Jean d' Heurs

MAP 11

Clermont Ferrand

MAP 14

Nebouzat

Monestier
Merline

Olliergues

RN89

PUY-DE-DOME

MAP 10

Ussel

Issoire

Ambert

Le Vernet
la Varenne

Marsac en Livradois

Brioude

La Chapelle
d'Aurec

Mauriac

CANTAL

Kleille Brioude

Bellevue la
Montagne

Neussargues

St Georges
d'Aurac

Vorey sur Arzon

Fraisse Haut

Ysingeaux

Rouffiac

Brive Charensac

Tence

St Flour

Pinols

Chamalière sur Loire

Le Puy en Velay

St Julien Chapteuil

Aurillac

Giou de
Mamou

HAUTE-
LOIRE

Costaros

RNP21

Chaudes Aigues

MAP 10

MAP 9

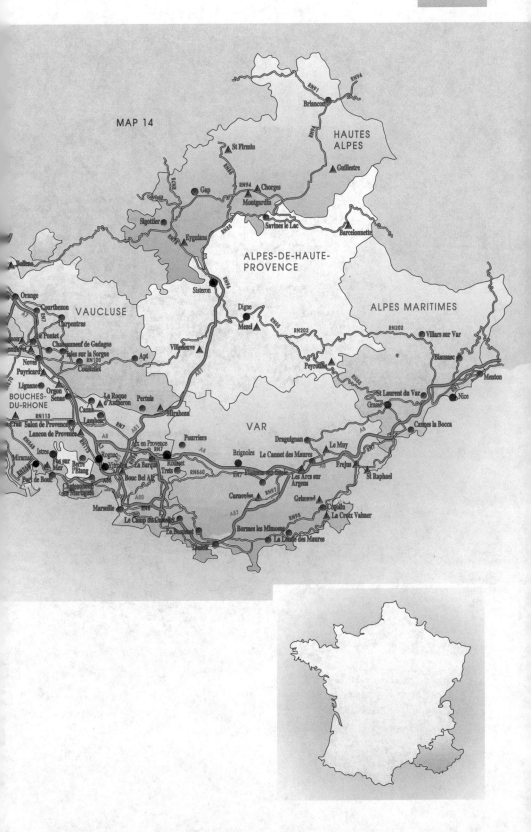

MAP 14

HAUTES
ALPES

Briançon

▲ St Firmin

▲ Guillestre

Gap ● RN94 ▲ Chorges
Montgardin

Sigottier ● Savines le Lac ▲ Barcelonnette

Eyguians

ALPES-DE-HAUTE-
PROVENCE

Sisteron

VAUCLUSE Digne

Mezel ▲ ALPES MARITIMES

Orange
Courthezon Villars sur Var
Carpentras
Le Pontet Villeneuve ▲ Peyrolle Blaussac
Chateauneuf de Gadagne
Isles sur la Sorgue Apt ● Menton
Novel Coustellet St Laurent du Var
Puyricard Grasse Nice
Lignane Pertuis
Orgon ● La Roque Mirabeau ▲ Cannes la Bocca
Senas d'Antheron
BOUCHES-
DU-RHONE Cazan Pourriers
Lambesc Draguignan Le Muy
Salon de Provence Le Cannet des Maures
Istres Lancon de Provence Brignoles Frejus
Miramas Aix en Provence VAR Les Arcs sur St Raphael
Rognac Argens
Berre Rousset
Port de Bouc l'Etang Trets
Vitrolles La Barque Carnoules Grimaud
Chateauneuf La Croix Valmer
les Martigues Bouc Bel Air Cogolin
Marseille Bormes les Mimosas
Le Camp du Castellet La Londe des Maures
Le Beausset

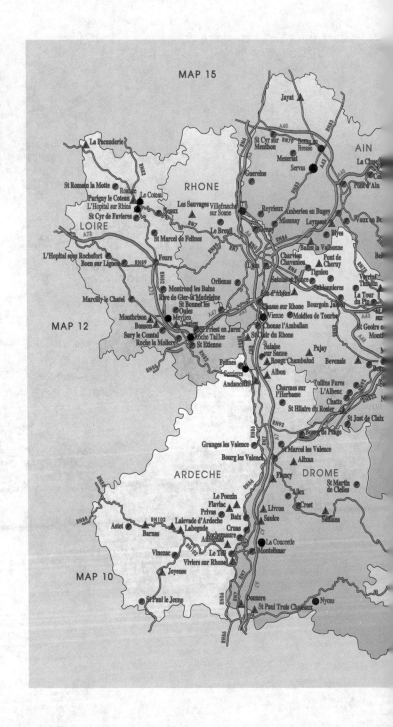

16

HAUTE-SAVOIE

RN1

A40
RN205 Bonneville
A40 Cluses
RN205
Domancy
Thones
Annecy
Megeve
Seynod
RN212

Chevelu
Albertville
RN90
Feissons sur Isere

La Ravoire
Chignin
Aiguebelle
La Rochette
SAVOIE
Pontcharra

St Jean de Maurienne

Modane
RN6

Roche Taillee

RN91

ISERE

MAP 13

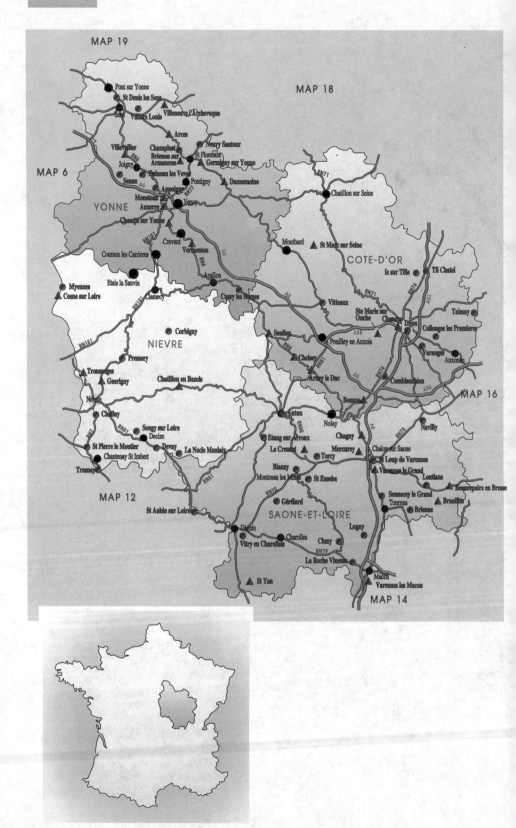

MAP 19

MAP 18

Pont sur Yonne
St Denis les Sens
Sens
Villiers Louis
Villeneuve l'Archevêque
Arces
Neuvy Sautour
Villevallier
Champlost
Brienon sur
Armancon
St Florentin
Germigny sur Yonne
Joigny
Senan
Epineau les Voves
Appoigny
Pontigny
Dannemoine
Chatillon sur Seine

MAP 6

YONNE
Moneteau
Auxerre
Vincy
Chassy sur Yonne

Cravant
Vermenton

Courson les Carrieres
Montbard
St Marc sur Seine
COTE-D'OR
Is sur Tille
Til Chatel

Avallon

Myennes
Etais la Sauvin
Cussy les Forges
Vitteaux
Ste Marie sur
Ouche
Chenove
Dijon
Talmay

Cosne sur Loire
Clamecy
Saulieu
Pouilley en Auxois
Collonges les Premieres

Corbigny
NIEVRE
Chelsey
Varanges
Auxonne

Premery
Chatillon en Bazols
Arnay le Duc
Comblanchien
MAP 16

Tronsanges
Guerigny
Beaune

Nevers
Challuy
Autun
Nolay
Navilly

Sougy sur Loire
Decize
Etang sur Arroux
Chagny
Chalon sur Saone

St Pierre le Moutier
Devay
La Nocle Maulaix
Le Creusot
Mercurey
St Loup de Varennes

Chantenay St Imbert
Torcy
Varennes le Grand
Loutlans

Tresnay
Blanzy
Montceau les Mines
St Eusebe
Senneccey le Grand
Beaurepaire en Bresse

MAP 12
Gergland
SAONE-ET-LOIRE
Tournus
Brienne
Brualtre

St Aubin sur Loire
Lugny

Digoin
Charolles
Cluny
La Roche Vineuse

Vitry en Charollais
Macon
Varennes les Macon

St Yan
MAP 14

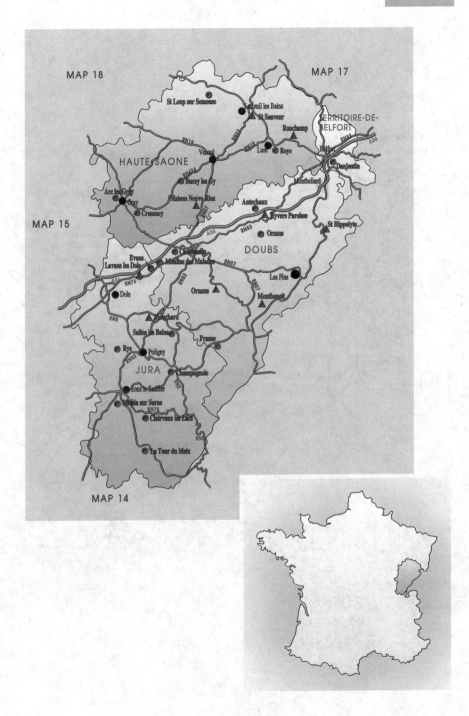

MAP 18

MAP 17

St Loup sur Semouse

Breuil les Bains
St Sauveur

Ronchamp

TERRITOIRE-DE-BELFORT

RN19

RN18

RN57A

HAUTE SAONE

Vesoul

Lure  Roye

Belfort

A36

RN83

Danjoutin

RN124

Bucey les Gy

Montbeliard

Arc les Gray

Maison Neuve Rioz

Antechaux

MAP 15

Gray

Cressancy

RN57

Ryvere Paroisse

St Hippolyte

RN83

Orsans

A36

DOUBS

Chatelay

Evans

Moulins des Malades

RN57

Les Fins

Lavans les Dole

RN73

RN49

A36

Ornans

Montbenoit

RN57

Dole

Mechard

RN5

Saline les Bains

Frasne

Rye

Poligny

RN83

JURA

Champagnole

RN78

Lons le Saulier

Messia sur Sorne

RN78

Clairvaux les Lacs

RN5

La Tour du Meix

MAP 14

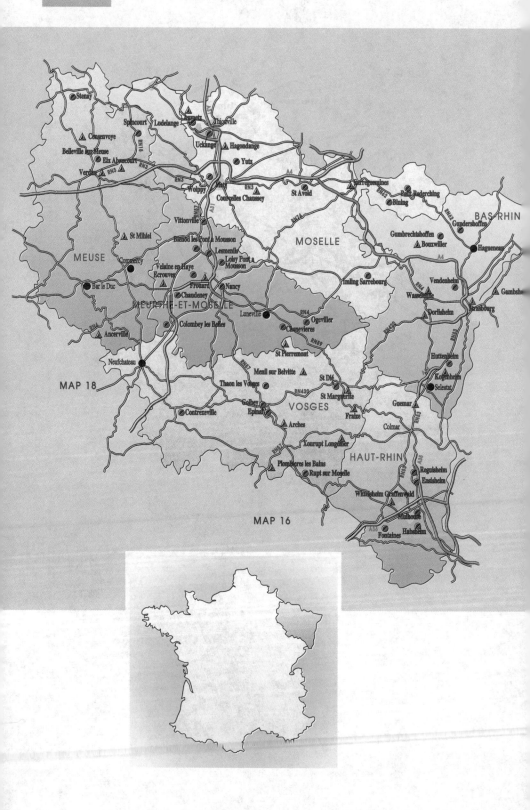

Stenay

Spincourt    Ludelange    Metz    Thionville

Consenvoye

Belleville sur Meuse    Uckange    Hagondange

Elx Abaucourt

Verdun    RN3    Yutz

Woippy    Metz    St Avold    Sarreguemines    Petit Raderching

Couscelles Chaussey    RN3    Bining

BAS-RHIN

Vittonville

St Mihiel    MOSELLE    Gumbrechtshoffen    Gundershoffen

Blenod les Pont a Mousson    Bouxwiller    Hagueneau

Lesmenils

MEUSE    Commercy    Loisy Pont a Mousson    Imling Sarrebourg    Vendenheim    Gambehm

Velaine en Haye    Wasselonne

Ecrouves    Dorlisheim    Strasbourg

Bar le Duc    Frouard    Nancy

Chaudeney

MEURTHE-ET-MOSELLE    Luneville    Ogeviller    Huttenheim

Ancerville    Colombey les Belles    Chenevieres    Kogenheim

RN69    Selestat

Neufchateau    St Pierremont

St Pierremont    Guemar

MAP 18    Menil sur Belvitte    St Dié    Colmar

Thaon les Vosges    St Marguerite

Golbey    VOSGES    Fraize

Contrexeville    Epinal

Arches    HAUT-RHIN

Xonrupt Longemer

Plombieres les Bains    Reguisheim

Rupt sur Moselle    Ensisheim

Wittelsheim Graffenwald

MAP 16    Mulhouse

Fontaines    Habsheim

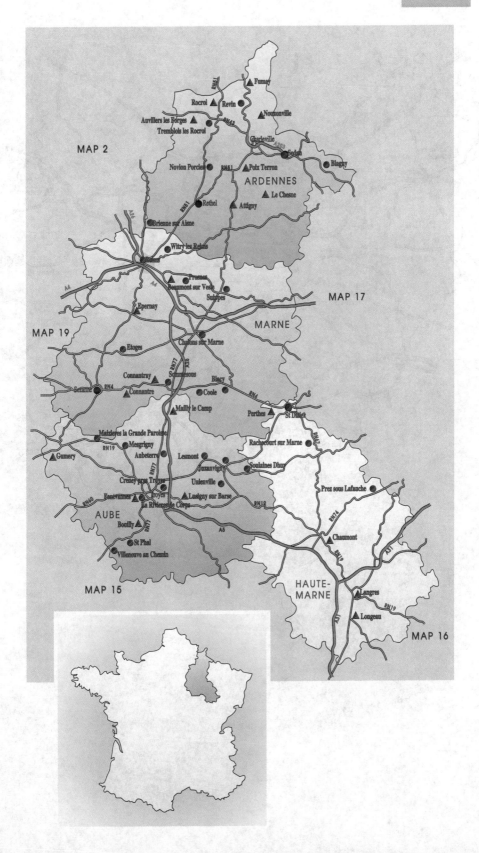

MAP 2

RN51

Fumay

Rocroi    Revin

Nouzonville

Auvillers les Forges    RN43

Tremblois les Rocroi

Charleville    A203    Sedan

Novion Porcien    RN51    Poix Terron    Blagny

ARDENNES

Le Chesne

RN51    Rethel

Attigny

Brienne sur Aisne

A4

Witry les Reims

Reims

MAP 17

Prosnes

Beaumont sur Vesle

Suippes

A4    A4

MARNE

Epernay

MAP 19

Etoges    Chalons sur Marne

RN77    A26

Connantray    Sommesous    Blacy

Sezanne    RN4    Connantre    Coole    RN4

Mailly le Camp    Perthes    St Dizier

Maizieres la Grande Paroisse    Rachecourt sur Marne    RN4

Mesgrigny    RN19

Gumery    Aubeterre    Lesmont

RN77    Juzanvigny    Soulaines Dhuys

Creney pres Troyes    Unienville    Prez sous Lafauche

RN60    Fontvannes    Troyes

la Riviere de Corps    Lusigny sur Barse    RN19

AUBE    RN77    A5

Bouilly

St Phal    Chaumont

Villeneuve au Chemin

RN74    A31

HAUTE-MARNE    RN19

A31    Langres

MAP 15    Longeau    RN19

MAP 16

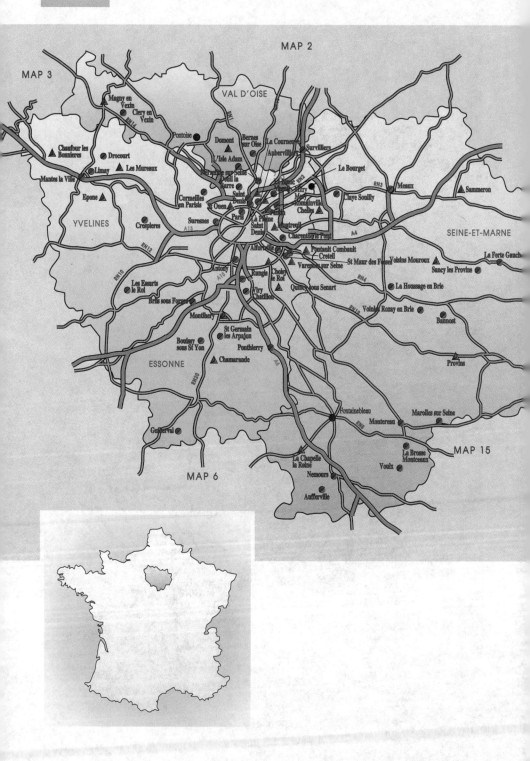

MAP 2

MAP 3

VAL D'OISE

Magny en Vexin

Clery en Vexin

Pontoise

Chaufour les Bonnieres

Drocourt

Domont

Bernes sur Oise

La Courneuve

Aubervilliers

Survilliers

Le Bourget

L'Isle Adam

Limay

Les Mureaux

Mantes la Ville

Cergy sur Oise

Pontoit la Garre

Saint Denis

Meaux

Sammeron

Epone

Cormeilles en Parisis

Ouen

Claye Souilly

Thiry

Romainville

Chelles

YVELINES

Crespieres

Suresnes

Paris

La Plaine Saint Denis

Montreuil

SEINE-ET-MARNE

Charenton le Pont

Alfortville

Fontsault Combault Creteil

Voisins Mouroux

La Ferte Gauch

Antony

Rungis

Varennes sur Seine

St Maur des Fosses

Sancy les Provins

Les Essarts le Rol

Choisy le Rol

Quincy sous Senart

La Houssage en Brie

Vitry Chatillon

Voinleu Rozay en Brie

Bannost

Bris sous Forges

Montlhery

St Germain les Arpajon

Ponthierry

Provins

Boulssy sous St Yon

Chamarande

ESSONNE

Fontainebleau

Marolles sur Seine

Montereau

Guillerval

La Brosse Monteaux

MAP 15

Voulx

La Chapelle la Reine

Nemours

MAP 6

Aufferville

# List of Casserole Relais Routiers

| TOWN | DEPARTMENT | ESTABLISHMENT |
|------|------------|---------------|
| | **Paris and Nearby** | |
| PIERREFITTE SUR SEINE | Seine-St-Denis 93380 | LE NORMANDIE |
| PROVINS | Seine-et-Marne 77160 | LE RELAIS DE LA CURE D'AIR |
| VOULX | Seine-et-Marne 77940 | LA BRUYERE |
| | **Northern France** | |
| NONE | | |
| | **North West France** | |
| BALLEROY | Calvados 14490 | LE RELAIS DE LA FORET |
| BAYEUX | Calvados 14400 | LA COLOMBE |
| BEDEE | Ille-et-Vilaine 35137 | HOTEL DU COMMERCE |
| CAST | Finistère 29150 | LE RELAIS ST GILDAS |
| DINAN | Côtes-du-Nord 22100 | LA MARMITE |
| DINARD | Ille-et-Vilaine 35800 | L'EPICURIEN |
| DOL DE BRETAGNE | Ille-et-Vilaine 35120 | LE RELAIS DE BELLE LANDE |
| DOMFRONT | Orne 61700 | LE RELAIS SAINT MICHEL |
| ELVEN | Morbihan 56250 | LE RELAIS DE L'ARGOUET |
| FERTE BERNARD (LA) | Sarthe 72400 | SARL CHEVAL BLANC |
| GUERCHE DE BRETAGNE (LA) | Ille-et-Vilaine 35130 | LE RELAIS DU PONT D'ANJOU |
| HAYE DU PUITS (LA) | Manche 50250 | RESTAURANT DES AMIS |
| HAYE PESNEL (LA) | Manche 50320 | LE RELAIS – Chez Armelle |
| HEUGUEVILLE SUR SIENNE | Manche 50200 | LE MASCARET |
| JALLAIS | Maine-et-Loire 49510 | LE GALANT VERT – LA CROIX VERTE |
| LAMBALLE | Côtes-du-Nord 22400 | LA TOUR D'ARGENT |
| LANDEVANT | Morbihan 56690 | LE RELAIS DU PELICAN |
| LANDIVISIAU | Finistère 29400 | HOTEL RESTAURANT LE TERMINUS |
| MONTAUBAN DE BRETAGNE | Ille-et-Vilaine 35360 | HOTEL DE FRANCE |
| MOUZEUIL ST MARTIN | Vendée 85370 | CENTRAL ROUTIERS |
| NONANT LE PIN | Orne 61240 | LE RELAIS DES HARAS |
| PLOUER SUR RANCE | Côtes-du-Nord 22490 | LE BON ACCUEIL |
| PONT AVEN | Finistère 29930 | CHEZ MELANIE ET MONIQUE |
| PONTCHATEAU | Loire-Atlantique 44160 | L'AUBERGE DU CALVAIRE |
| PONTCHATEAU | Loire-Atlantique 44160 | LE RELAIS DE BEAULIEU |
| REDON | Ille-et-Vilaine 35600 | LE RELAIS |
| RICHEVILLE | Eure 27420 | RESTAUROUTE LE BALTO |
| SAINT GILDAS DES BOIS | Loire-Atlantique 44530 | LES ROUTIERS |
| SAINT MARTIN DES BESACES | Calvados 14350 | LA RENAISSANCE |
| SAINT SYMPHORIEN DES MONTS | Manche 50640 | LE RELAIS DU BOIS LEGER |
| SAINTE LUCE SUR LOIRE | Loire-Atlantique 44980 | LA BOUGRIERE |
| SENE | Morbihan 56860 | RELAIS ROUTIERS |
| SIZUN | Finistère 29450 | HOTEL DES VOYAGEURS |
| VIRE | Calvados 14500 | HOTEL DE FRANCE |
| VIVY | Maine-et-Loire 49680 | RESTAURANT SAINT PAUL |
| | **North East France** | |
| AUXERRE | Yonne 89000 | LE SAINTE NITASSE |
| BEAUMONT SUR VESLE | Marne 51360 | LA MAISON DU CHAMPAGNE |
| BOUXWILLER | Bas-Rhin 67330 | AU SOLEIL |
| CLUNY | Saône-et-Loire 71250 | AUBERGE DU CHEVAL BLANC |
| COSNE SUR LOIRE | Nièvre 58200 | LES 3 COULEURS |
| HYEVRE PAROISSE | Doubs 25110 | RELAIS LA CREMAILLERE |
| NANCY | Meurthe-et-Moselle 54000 | RESTAURANT DU PORT |
| ORNANS | Doubs 25290 | HOTEL LE PROGRES |
| TOUR DU MEIX (LA) | Jura 39270 | AUBERGE DU PONT DE LA PYLE |
| VENDENHEIM | Bas-Rhin 67550 | LE RELAIS DE LA MAISON ROUGE |

### The Loire

| | | |
|---|---|---|
| ARGENTON SUR CREUSE | Indre 36200 | LE RELAIS |
| BARBEZIEUX SAINT HILAIRE | Charente 16120 | RELAIS DE LA BILLETTE |
| CHARROUX | Vienne 86250 | LA CROIX BLANCHE (RELAIS) |
| CHARTRES | Eure-et-Loir 28000 | RESTAURANT LE PALMIER |
| CHARTRES | Eure-et-Loir 28000 | RELAIS BEAUCERON |
| GERMIGNY DES PRES | Loiret 45110 | HOTEL DE LA PLACE |
| MAROLLES | Eure-et-Loir 28260 | AU RELAIS DE MAROLLES |
| NEUVY | Loir-et-Cher 41250 | LA CHEMINEE |
| SAINT EUGENE | Charente-Maritime 17520 | LES DEUX CHARENTES |
| SECONDIGNY | Deux-Sèvres 79130 | LES ROUTIERS |
| SOLTERRE | Loiret 45700 | AUBERGE DE LA ROUTE BLEUE |
| SUEVRES | Loir-et-Cher 41500 | LE RELAIS DE LA PROVIDENCE |
| SURY AUX BOIS | Loiret 45530 | LE RELAIS DU PONT DES BEIGNERS |
| THEILLAY | Loir-et-Cher 41300 | RELAIS DE LA LOGE |
| TRIMOUILLE (LA) | Vienne 86290 | L'AUBERGE FLEURIE |
| VILLEDOMER | Indre-et-Loire 37110 | LE RELAIS DES GRANDS VINS DE TOURAINE |

### Central France

| | | |
|---|---|---|
| BEAUNE LES MINES | Haute Vienne 87280 | LA TERRASSE DE BEAUNE |
| PONT DE MENAT | Puy-de-Dôme 63580 | CHEZ ROGER |
| SAINT FLOUR | Cantal 15100 | HOTEL LE PROGRES |
| SAINT JUST LE MARTEL | Haute-Vienne 87590 | LE PETIT SALE |
| VARENNES SUR ALLIER | Allier 03150 | LE RELAIS DES TOURISTES |

### South West France

| | | |
|---|---|---|
| BERTHOLENE | Aveyron 12310 | HOTEL BANCAREL |
| BRANTOME | Dordogne 24310 | LE GERGOVIE |
| CAMPSEGRET | Dordogne 24140 | LE RELAIS DES TAMARIS |
| CENAC SAINT JULIEN | Dordogne 24250 | LA PROMENADE |
| ESCOURCE | Landes 40210 | AU ROUTIER |
| GRAMAT | Lot 46500 | HOTEL DU CENTRE |
| LANGON | Gironde 33210 | RESTAURANT DARLOT |
| LAUSSEIGNAN BARBASTE | Lot-et-Garonne 47230 | LES PALMIERS |
| MOISSAC | Tarn-et-Garonne 82200 | RELAIS AUVERGNAT |
| MUSSIDAN | Dordogne 24400 | LE PERIGORD |
| ONET LE CHATEAU | Aveyron 12850 | LA ROCADE |
| REMOULINS | Gard 30210 | AUBERGE LES PLATANES |
| ROCHE CHALAIS (LA) | Dordogne 24490 | CAFE DU MIDI |
| ROUFFIGNAC DE SIGOULES | Dordogne 24240 | LA TAVERNE ALSACIENNE |
| SAINT PAUL DE LOUBRESSAC | Lot 46170 | RELAIS DE LA MADELEINE |
| SAINTE MARIE DE GOSSE | Landes 40390 | LE RELAIS ROUTIERS |
| SAINTE TERRE | Gironde 33350 | CHEZ REGIS |

### South East France

| | | |
|---|---|---|
| CORMORANCHE SUR SAONE | Ain 01290 | AUBERGE CHEZ LA MERE MARTINET |
| CORPS | Isère 38970 | RESTAURANT DU TILLEUL |
| EYGUIANS | Hautes-Alpes 05300 | HOTEL DE LA GARE |
| GUILLESTRE | Hautes-Alpes 05600 | HOTEL DE LA GARE |
| LIGNANE | Bouches-du-Rhône 13540 | LE RELAIS DE LIGNANE |
| MEGEVE | Haute-Savoie 74120 | CHALET DES FLEURS |
| PAJAY | Isère 38260 | MA PETITE AUBERGE |
| PIOLENC | Vaucluse 84420 | LE COMMERCE |
| ROCHETAILLEE | Isère 38520 | HOTEL BELLEDONNE |
| SAINT JEAN DE MAURIENNE | Savoie 73300 | BAR RESTAURANT RELAIS ROUTIERS |
| SAINT RAPHAEL | Var 83700 | LE BEL AZUR |
| THONES | Haute-Savoie 74230 | L'HERMITAGE |
| TOUR DU PIN (LA) | Isère 38110 | CHEZ BABETH |
| VIVIERS SUR RHONE | Ardèche 07220 | LE RELAIS DU VIVARAIS |

# List of Tourist Hotels

| STAR RATING | TOWN | DEPARTMENT | ESTABLISHMENT |
|---|---|---|---|
| | | **Paris and Nearby** | |
| * | CHAMARANDE | Essonne 91730 | RELAIS DE MONTFORT |
| * | MONTLHERY | Essonne 91310 | LE SOLOGNE |
| | | **Northern France** | |
| * | BAILLEUL | Nord 59270 | AUBERGE DU SEAU |
| * | BAPAUME | Pas-de-Calais 62450 | CHEZ BERNADETTE |
| * | BRUAY LA BUISSIERE | Pas-de-Calais 62700 | LA LOUETTE (formerly CHEZ MICHEL) |
| * | COMINES | Nord 59560 | RESTAURANT DE LA GARE |
| * | FORMERIE | Oise 60220 | CAFE DE LA PAIX |
| | | **North West France** | |
| * | BALLEROY | Calvados 14490 | LE RELAIS DE LA FORET |
| * | BEDEE | Ille-et-Vilaine 35137 | HOTEL DU COMMERCE |
| ** | BRIONNE | Eure 27800 | HOTEL DU HAVRE |
| * | CHATEAUBRIANT | Loire-Atlantique 44110 | S.A.R.L. PARIS-OCEAN |
| * | ELVEN | Morbihan 56250 | LE RELAIS DE L'ARGOUET |
| * | FOUGERES | Ille-et-Vilaine 35300 | AUX AMIS DE LA ROUTE |
| * | GRAND FOUGERAY (LE) | Ille-et-Vilaine 35390 | LE RELAIS DE LA BELLE ETOILE |
| * | HERBIERS (LES) | Vendée 85500 | L'OREE DES BOIS VERTS |
| ** | JALLAIS | Maine-et-Loire 49510 | LE VERT GALANT – LA CROIX VERTE |
| * | JOUE EN CHARNIE | Sarthe 72540 | LE CHEVAL BLANC |
| ** | LAMBALLE | Côtes-du-Nord 22400 | LA TOUR D'ARGENT |
| * | LANDIVISIAU | Finistère 29400 | HOTEL RESTAURANT LE TERMINUS |
| * | LANESTER | Morbihan 56600 | LA ROTONDE |
| * | LOUDEAC | Côtes-du-Nord 22600 | LES ROUTIERS |
| * | MALE | Orne 61260 | LA BELLE RENCONTRE |
| ** | MONT SAINT MICHEL (LE) | Manche 50116 | HOTEL MOTEL VERT – La Rôtisserie |
| ** | MONTAUBAN DE BRETAGNE | Ille-et-Vilaine 35360 | HOTEL DE FRANCE |
| ** | MONTAUBAN DE BRETAGNE | Ille-et-Vilaine 35360 | RELAIS DE LA HUCHERAIS |
| ** | MONTMARTIN SUR MER | Manche 50590 | HOTELLERIE DU BON VIEUX TEMPS |
| ** | MOREAC | Morbihan 56500 | LE RELAIS DU BARDERFF |
| * | PIPRIAC | Ille-et-Vilaine 35550 | HOTEL DE LA TOUR D'AUVERGNE |
| ** | PLOUAGAT | Côtes-du-Nord 22170 | CHEZ PIERRETTE |
| ** | PONTCHATEAU | Loire-Atlantique 44160 | L'AUBERGE DU CALVAIRE |
| * | REDON | Ille-et-Vilaine 35600 | LE RELAIS |
| ** | ROCHE SUR YON (LA) | Vendée 85000 | HOTEL SULLY |
| ** | SAINT BERTHEVIN | Mayenne 53940 | L'INTERNATIONAL |
| * | SAINT BRIEUC | Côtes-du-Nord 22000 | AU BEAUFEUILLAGE |
| * | SAINT GUYOMARD | Morbihan 56460 | LE RELAIS DES DOLMENS DE LANVAUX |
| ** | SAINT HILAIRE DE LOULAY | Vendée 85600 | LE RELAX |
| * | SAINT MARTIN DES BESACES | Calvados 14350 | LA RENAISSANCE |
| * | SAINT POL DE LEON | Finistère 29250 | LES ROUTIERS |
| ** | SAUMUR | Maine-et-Loire 49400 | HOTEL DE LA GARE |
| * | SENE | Morbihan 56860 | RELAIS ROUTIERS |
| * | SIZUN | Finistère 29450 | HOTEL DES VOYAGEURS |
| ** | TRINITE SURZUR (LA) | Morbihan 56190 | L'AUBERGE VIEILLE FONTAINE |
| * | VILLERS SUR MER | Calvados 14640 | LE NORMAND |
| ** | VIRE | Calvados 14500 | HOTEL DE FRANCE |
| * | VIVY | Maine-et-Loire 49680 | RESTAURANT SAINT PAUL |

## North East France

| | | | |
|---|---|---|---|
| * | ANCERVILLE | Meuse 55170 | LE RELAIS |
| * | ARCES | Yonne 89320 | RELAIS DE LA FORET D'OTHE |
| ** | ARCHES | Vosges 88380 | LA TRUITE RENOMMEE |
| * | AUXERRE | Yonne 89000 | LE SAINTE NITASSE |
| ** | BEAUMONT SUR VESLE | Mame 51360 | LA MAISON DU CHAMPAGNE |
| *** | BEAUNE | Côte-d'Or 21200 | RELAIS DE BEAUNE |
| * | BOUILLY | Aube 10320 | AU RELAIS MONTAIGU |
| ** | BOUXWILLER | Bas-Rhin 67330 | AU SOLEIL |
| ** | CHAMPS SUR YONNE | Yonne 89290 | L'ARCHE DE VENOY 1 |
| ** | CHAMPS SUR YONNE | Yonne 89290 | L'ARCHE DE VENOY EST |
| * | CHENOVE | Côte-d'Or 21300 | AU BON COIN |
| * | COSNE SUR LOIRE | Nièvre 58200 | LES 3 COULEURS |
| * | FUMAY | Ardennes 08170 | HOTEL LION |
| ** | GAMBSHEIM | Bas-Rhin 67760 | EUROPE RELAIS |
| *** | HYEVRE PAROISSE | Doubs 25110 | RELAIS LA CREMAILLERE |
| * | KOGENHEIM | Bas-Rhin 67230 | A L'ETOILE |
| * | MERCUREY | Saône-et-Loire 71640 | LE MERCUREY |
| ** | MONTBENOIT | Doubs 25650 | HOTEL RESTAURANT DES VOYAGEURS |
| * | ORNANS | Doubs 25290 | HOTEL LE PROGRES |
| * | PLOMBIERES LES BAINS | Vosges 88370 | LE RELAIS STRASBOURGEOIS |
| * | RONCHAMP | Haute-Saône 70250 | LE RELAIS DE LA POMME D'OR |
| ** | SAINT PIERREMONT | Vosges 88700 | LE RELAIS VOSGIEN |
| * | SAINTE MARGUERITE | Vosges 88100 | LE RELAIS DES AMIS |

## The Loire

| | | | |
|---|---|---|---|
| ** | AIGURANDE | Indre 36140 | LE RELAIS DE LA MARCHE |
| * | CHAMPAGNE MOUTON | Charente 16350 | HOTEL PLAISANCE |
| | CHAPELLE SUR LOIRE (LA) | Indre-et-Loire 37140 | LE RELAIS DE LA MAIRIE |
| ** | CHARTRES | Eure-et-Loir 28000 | RELAIS BEAUCERON |
| ** | CHATEAU LA VALLIERE | Indre-et-Loire 37330 | LE GRAND CERF |
| * | CHATILLON SUR INDRE | Indre 36700 | AUBERGE DE LA PROMENADE |
| * | CHAUNAY BOURG | Vienne 86510 | LE COMMERCE |
| * | CORME ROYAL | Charente-Maritime 17600 | LES TILLEULS |
| ** | ISSOUDUN | Indre 36100 | LE RELAIS |
| * | MOULISMES | Vienne 86500 | LA TABLE OUVERTE |
| * | ROCHELLE (LA) | Charente-Maritime 17000 | LA COTE VERTE |
| * | ROMORANTIN LANTHENAY | Loir-et-Cher 41200 | LES AUBIERS |
| * | SAINT GENIS DE SAINTONGE | Charente-Maritime 17240 | LE RELAIS DE SAINTONGE |
| * | SAINTE MAURE DE TOURAINE | Indre-et-Loire 37800 | L'ETOILE DU SUD |
| * | SAUJON | Charente-Maritime 17600 | HOTEL DE LA GARE |
| * | SULLY SUR LOIRE | Loiret 45600 | CAFE DE LA GARE – Chez Lionel |
| * | THEILLAY | Loir-et-Cher 41300 | RELAIS DE LA LOGE |
| * | YMONVILLE | Eure-et-Loir 28150 | A L'ETOILE |

## Central France

| | | | |
|---|---|---|---|
| * | CLERMONT FERRAND | Puy-de-Dôme 63000 | AUVERGNE PYRENEES–Les Routiers |
| * | CREUZIER LE VIEUX | Allier 03300 | CHEZ LA MERE RIBOULIN |
| ** | EYMOUTIERS | Haute-Vienne 87120 | LE SAINT PSALMET |
| * | LAPALISSE | Allier 03120 | LE CHAPON DORE |
| * | MAURIAC | Cantal 15200 | LES ROUTIERS |
| * | PERIGNY | Allier 03120 | LE RELAIS DE PERIGNY |
| ** | PUY EN VELAY (LE) | Haute-Loire 43000 | LA TAVERNE |
| ** | SAINT FLOUR | Cantal 15100 | HOTEL LE PROGRES |
| * | SAINT JULIEN CHAPTEUIL | Haute-Loire 43260 | AUBERGE DU MEYCAL |
| * | SAUVIAT SUR VIGE | Haute-Vienne 87400 | HOTEL DE LA POSTE |
| ** | VIEILLE BRIOUDE | Haute-Loire 43100 | LES GLYCINES |

## South West France

| | | |
|---|---|---|
| * | AIRE SUR L'ADOUR | Landes 40800 | LES ROUTIERS – Chez Pierrette |
| * | AMBRES | Tarn 81500 | AUBERGE DES POMMIERS |
| ** | AMOU | Landes 40330 | AU FEU DE BOIS |
| * | ANIANE | Hérault 34150 | LA CLAMOUSE |
| ** | BARAQUEVILLE | Aveyron 12160 | LE PALOUS |
| * | BERTHOLENE | Aveyron 12310 | HOTEL BANCAREL |
| * | CAMPSEGRET | Dordogne 24140 | LE RELAIS DES TAMARIS |
| * | CASTELSARRASIN | Tarn-et-Garonne 82100 | CHEZ MAURICE |
| * | CHAUDEYRAC | Lozère 48170 | HOTEL DE FRANCE |
| ** | CUQ TOULZA | Tarn 81470 | LE RELAIS CHEZ ALAIN |
| * | DENGUIN | Pyrénées-Atlantiques 64230 | RELAIS PYRENEES MONTAGNE OCEAN |
| * | ESPALION | Aveyron 12500 | RELAIS DES QUATRE ESPALION ROUTES |
| ** | FABREGUES | Hérault 34690 | L'ARCHE DE FABREGUES |
| * | FITOU | Aude 11510 | RELAIS LE PARADOR |
| * | GAGES | Aveyron 12630 | LE RELAIS DE LA PLAINE |
| ** | GRAMAT | Lot 46500 | HOTEL DU CENTRE |
| ** | ISSANKA | Hérault 34540 | LE GARRIGOU |
| * | LAFOX | Lot-et-Garonne 47270 | LE RELAIS TOULOUSAIN |
| * | LALOUBERE | Hautes-Pyrénées 65310 | HOTEL DES PYRENEES |
| * | LANGOGNE | Lozère 48300 | HOTEL DU LUXEMBOURG |
| * | LIBOURNE | Gironde 33500 | LE MOULIN BLANC |
| ** | MILLAU LARZAC | Aveyron 12230 | RELAIS ESPACE |
| ** | MIRAMONT DE GUYENNE | Lot-et-Garonne 47800 | LE RELAIS DE GUYENNE |
| * | MOISSAC | Tarn-et-Garonne 82200 | RELAIS AUVERGNAT |
| * | MONASTIER (LE) | Lozère 48100 | LES AJUSTONS |
| * | MONDAVEZAN | Haute-Garonne 31220 | LA FERMIERE |
| ** | NARBONNE | Aude 11100 | LA CAILLE QUI CHANTE |
| * | ONET LE CHATEAU | Aveyron 12850 | LA ROCADE |
| * | PAUILLAC | Gironde 33250 | LE YACHTING |
| ** | REMOULINS | Gard 30210 | AUBERGE LES PLATANES |
| * | RIEUPEYROUX | Aveyron 12240 | CHEZ PASCAL |
| * | RISCLE | Gers 32400 | RELAIS DE L'AUBERGE |
| ** | ROUFFILLAC DE CARLUX | Dordogne 24370 | AUX POISSONS FRAIS |
| * | SAINT LON LES MINES | Landes 40300 | HOTEL DU FRONTON |
| * | SAINT NAZAIRE | Gard 30200 | LES TERAILLES |
| * | SAINT PAUL DE LOUBRESSAC | Lot 46170 | RELAIS DE LA MADELEINE |
| * | SAINTE LIVRADE SUR LOT | Lot-et-Garonne 47110 | AU BON ACCUEIL |
| * | SAINTE MARIE DE GOSSE | Landes 40390 | LE RELAIS ROUTIERS |
| * | SAUVETERRE DE GUYENNE | Gironde 33540 | HOTEL DE GUYENNE |
| * | TARBES | Hautes-Pyrénées 65000 | LE VICTOR HUGO |

## South East France

| | | |
|---|---|---|
| ** | ALIXAN | Drôme 26300 | HOTEL ALPES PROVENCE |
| ** | AVIGNON | Vaucluse 84140 | RELAIS D'AVIGNON |
| * | BARCELONNETTE | Alpes-de-Hautes-Provence 04400 | LES SEOLANES |
| * | BONSON | Loire 42160 | RESTAURANT DES SPORTS |
| * | CHORGES | Hautes-Alpes 05230 | HOTEL DES ALPES |
| ** | CORMORANCHE SUR SAONE | Ain 01290 | AUBERGE CHEZ LA MERE MARTINET |
| ** | CORPS | Isère 38970 | RESTAURANT DU TILLEUL |
| * | DONZERE | Drôme 26290 | LE BOLO |
| * | EYGUIANS | Hautes-Alpes 05300 | HOTEL DE LA GARE |
| * | FREJUS | Var 83600 | LES TROIS CHENES |
| * | GENAY | Rhône 69730 | LA PETITE RIVE |
| * | GUILLESTRE | Hautes-Alpes 05600 | HOTEL DE LA GARE |
| ** | ISLE D'ABEAU | Isère 38080 | L'ARCHE DE L'ISLE D'ABEAU |
| * | JAYAT | Ain 01340 | LE RELAIS DE JAYAT |

| | | | |
|---|---|---|---|
| * | JOYEUSE | Ardèche 07260 | LES CEVENNES |
| * | LALEVADE D'ARDECHE | Ardèche 07380 | L'ESCHALLIER |
| ** | MEGEVE | Haute-Savoie 74120 | CHALET DES FLEURS |
| * | MONTFAVET | Vaucluse 84140 | RELAIS DE BONPAS |
| * | ORGON | Bouches-du-Rhône 13660 | RELAIS DES FUMADES |
| * | ROCHETAILLEE | Isère 38520 | HOTEL BELLEDONNE |
| * | SAINT FIRMIN | Hautes-Alpes 05800 | LE RELAIS DE LA TRINITE |
| * | SAINT RAPHAEL | Var 83700 | LE BEL AZUR |
| * | SEYNOD | Haute-Savoie 74600 | RELAIS SAINTE CATHERINE |
| * | THONES | Haute-Savoie 74230 | L'HERMITAGE |
| * | VEYRINS THUELLIN | Isère 38630 | L'ASTRAL |
| * | VIVIERS SUR RHONE | Ardèche 07220 | LE RELAIS DU VIVARAIS |

# A L'Hotel . . .

**Dear Sir**

Your hotel has been recommended to me by Les Routiers. I would be grateful if you would reserve me a single/double room with/without bathroom/shower on the . . . . . . for one night/from . . . . . . to . . . . . .

Please could you confirm this and let me know if a deposit is required.

Thanking you in advance.

Yours sincerely


**Monsieur,**

Votre hôtel m'a été recommandé par Les Routiers. Je vous prie de vouloir bien me retenir une chambre à un lit/pour deux personnes avec/sans salle de bain/douche pour la nuit . . . . . . /du . . . . . . jusqu'au . . . . . .

Soyez assez aimable de nous confirmer cette location et de nous dire s'il vous faut une caution.

Avec nos remerciements anticipés.

Veuillez agréer, Monsieur, nos sentiments les plus distingués.


| | |
|---|---|
| **Single room** | – une chambre à un lit |
| **Double room** | – une chambre pour deux personnes avec un grand lit |
| **Twin room** | – une chambre avec deux lits |
| **Bathroom** | – salle de bain |
| **Shower** | – douche |
| | |
| **Breakfast** | – le petit déjeuner |
| **Half board** | – demi-pension |
| **Full board** | – pension complète |

| | |
|---|---|
| **Je voudrais retenir/réserver . . .** | – I'd like to book/reserve . . . |
| **Combien coûte/vaut la chambre?** | – How much does the room cost? |

# Au Restaurant . . .

Choosing a restaurant and deciding what to eat can be one of the most enjoyable parts of your stay in France. One of the delights of eating in Relais Routiers lies in the discovery of authentic French cuisine and atmosphere. Providing the season is right, you can experiment with regional dishes and taste the true flavours of France. Here are a few useful points.

1. Note the difference between the 'set menu' and à la carte. The set menu is a complete three or four course meal and may or may not include drinks. Many restaurants will offer more than one set menu and the lunch-time menus will often cost less than those of the evening. Please note that you are not entitled to a reduction of the cost of the set menu if you do not eat all courses. Every Relais Routiers must state if drinks are included in the menu price. In these cases a 25 cl glass of wine will be about 6 Frs. The à la carte menu offers a full choice of dishes. The price of each dish is marked separately. A meal selected from the à la carte menu is always more expensive, even if it comprises the same dishes as the set menu.

2. Soft drinks are much more expensive in France than in Britain or Ireland. 'Sirops', which are mixed with water like a cordial, are a cheaper alternative to coke and lemonade.

3. Prices in cafés must be clearly displayed. Drinks are more expensive if you sit at a table as opposed to standing at the bar.

4. Tap water must be provided free by law. If you are unwilling to drink the tap water ask for 'l'eau minéral' but you will be charged for this.

5. 'Vin compris' on a menu means that a pichet (jug) of ordinary or house wine is included in the price. 'Boisson compris' means that 'a drink' is included. As this could be a pichet (jug) of wine, a beer, or a bottle of mineral water, do check what is available.

**BON APPETIT!**

# En Route . . .

Traffic rules in France are very similar to those in Britain and Ireland, with the obvious exception that in France you drive on the right. When leaving a restaurant after a relaxing lunch, setting off from your hotel early in the morning, or after using a one-way street, beware! Many experienced British and Irish drivers in France will have tales to tell about the times they have happily set off on the left-hand side of the road. Here are a few extra points.

1. Speed Limits – Dry Roads

50 km (approx. 30 miles per hour) – Built-up areas/towns
90 km (approx. 56 miles per hour) – Main roads
110 km (approx. 68 miles per hour) – Dual carriageways/non-toll motorways
130 km (approx. 80 miles per hour) – Toll motorways

Wet Roads

50 km – Built-up areas/towns
80 km – Main roads
100 km – Dual carriageways/non-toll motorways
110 km – Toll motorways

**New drivers must not exceed 90 km in the first year after passing their test. A minimum speed limit of 80 km (50 mph) applies on the outside lane of motorways, on level ground, with good visibility, during dry daylight hours.**

2. Motorways

France has over 3,000 miles of motorways, and tolls (péages) are charged on most of these. Usually a ticket is issued and a toll paid when you leave the motorway or at intermediate points during the motorway journey. Some motorway stretches have automatic collection points where you throw the change into a basket. If you do not have the correct change, use the marked separate lane. Travellers cheques are NOT accepted but Visa card can be used as an alternative. Toll charges vary according to route.

To escape the motorway tolls and the most congested roads follow the 'Green Arrow' routes (Itinéraires Bis). There should be less traffic and the routes are designed to provide the holiday-maker with a more attractive journey.

Free emergency telephones are available every 2 km on motorways; parking and resting areas every 10 km; 24-hour services can be found at regular intervals of about 40 km.

3. Insurance

Fully comprehensive cover is advisable. A green card will give you a better coverage than the minimum otherwise applicable in France. Europ Assistance do special schemes for motorists and passengers and discounts can be obtained through membership of Les Routiers' Club Bon Viveur (see page 00 for details of how to join).

## 4. Petrol – **L'ESSENCE**

NB **Pétrole** translates as crude oil or paraffin.

| | | | |
|---|---|---|---|
| Super | – **de super** | ordinary | – **d'ordinaire** |
| lead-free | – **sans plomb** | diesel | – **gazole** |

Diesel is considerably cheaper in France and unleaded petrol is widely available.

## 5. Speeding and drink-driving

Breath test limits are as for the UK (80 mg), but LOWER than the Republic of Ireland (100 mg). Tests are random. On-the-spot fines may be 2,000 to 3,000 Frs.

For speeding the minimum fine is 1,300 Frs. For not wearing a seat-belt a fine of between 450 and 1,100 Frs can be imposed.

The use of car telephones is prohibited, and you should affix a note to the unit indicating the prohibition.

You must carry the original vehicle registration document, a full valid national driving licence and current insurance certificate (plus a letter of authority from the owner if the vehicle is not registered in your name).

During August the southbound motorways are very busy with French families heading to the coast for their summer holiday, but most of the time French roads are relatively empty. If you equip yourself with a good map, driving in France can be an enjoyable part of your holiday.

## 6. Points to remember (to avoid hefty on-the-spot fines or worse)

1) Minimum driving age in France is 18 not 17.
2) No driving on a provisional licence.
3) Driver and front passenger must wear seat-belts (rear passengers also if belts are fitted).
4) Under 10s must travel in back.
5) Stop signs mean STOP. Come to a complete halt.
6) Don't stop on open roads unless the car is driven OFF the road.
7) Heavy penalties can be imposed for overtaking on a solid single white line.
8) Red warning triangle must be carried, unless car has hazard flashers. Warning triangles are COMPULSORY when towing a caravan or trailer.
9) Beams must be altered for right-hand drive using beam deflectors. Yellow tinted headlights are no longer compulsory. Sidelights are only permitted when stationary. Take a full kit of spare bulbs – you may be fined if driving with faulty lights.

# Useful Information for Travellers

**BRITISH EMBASSY**
Ambassade de Grande-Bretagne
16, rue d'Anjou, 75008 Paris, France
Tel: 42.66.38.10 (prefix 010-331 if dialling from the UK)

**IRISH EMBASSY**
12, avenue Foch, 75116 Paris, France
Tel: 45.00.20.87 (prefix 0033 if dialling from the Republic of Ireland)

**OFFICE DE TOURISME DE PARIS**
127, Champs–Elysées, 75008 Paris, France
Tel: 47.23.61.72

**INFORMATION OF ALL KEY EVENTS 1994**
Maison de la France
8, avenue de l'Opéra, 75001 Paris, France
Tel: 42.96.10.23

**FRENCH GOVERNMENT TOURIST OFFICE**

| | |
|---|---|
| 178, Piccadilly, London W1V 0AL | 35, Lower Abbey Street, Dublin 1 |
| Tel: 071–493 3480 | Tel: 01–7034046 |

**FRENCH NATIONAL PARKS**

**Parc National des Cévennes**
BP 4, 48400 Florac
Tel: 66.44.01.75

**Parc National de Port-Cross**
50, avenue Gambetta, 83400 Hyères
Tel: 94.65.32.98

**Parc National des Ecrins**
7, rue du Colonel-Roux, 05000 Gap
Tel: 92.51.40.71

**Parc National des Pyrénées Occidentales**
BP 300, 65000 Tarbes
Tel: 62.93.30.60

**Parc National Mercantour**
23, rue d'Italie, 06000 Nice
Tel: 93.87.86.10

**Parc National de la Vanoise**
135, rue du Docteur Julliand,
BP 705, 73007 Chambéry, Cedex
Tel: 79.62.30.54

# Club Bon Viveur
# The Ultimate Dining Scheme!

**CLUB BON VIVEUR** is an exciting National Dining Scheme operated by Les Routiers within the British Isles, which invites you to rediscover the 'Joie de Vivre' in hundreds of restaurants throughout the country, offering more than twenty-three types of international cuisine!

As a Club Bon Viveur cardholder, you are entitled to a range of substantial discounts and benefits, including reductions of up to 50% on food bills (subject to individual restaurants' restrictions) when dining with one or more guests. You can use your card as often as you wish, in any of the establishments listed in the 'Joie de Vivre' Directory. The directory will be sent to you with your members' pack when you join.

Membership of Club Bon Viveur costs just £30 per annum, which can very quickly be recouped through discounts.

**MEMBERSHIP BENEFITS INCLUDE:**

* **Discounted food prices when dining out.**
* **The 'Joie de Vivre' Directory for easy reference.**
* **Discounts on purchases of Les Routiers guidebooks and publications.**
* **Other promotional offers.**

To apply for your Club Bon Viveur membership, simply complete the application form (overleaf) and return it with your payment of £30 to:

**The Club Secretary**
**CLUB BON VIVEUR**
**25 Vanston Place**
**London SW6 1AZ**

# Application Form

If you use the Guide regularly then it would certainly be in your interest to join Club Bon Viveur and receive the exciting benefits on offer.

We are always pleased to hear your comments on any restaurants and hotels you have visited. On the next page there is opportunity to give your opinion.

To join Club Bon Viveur simply complete the form below and return it to us with the annual subscription fee of £30.

Name ................................................................................................................................

Address ..........................................................................................................................

..........................................................................................................................

I enclose a cheque for £—— (payable to Club Bon Viveur)
OR
Please debit my Access/Visa/Amex/Mastercard card for the amount of £——

Card Number ............................................................ Expiry Date ....................................

Return to: Club Bon Viveur, 25 Vanston Place, London SW6 1AZ.
Please allow 28 days for delivery.

# Your Opinion

Do you have a favourite pub, restaurant or hotel which you would like to recommend to us, which is not already Les Routiers recommended? If you feel it is worthy of nomination, please let us know on the form below so that, with the establishment's consent, we may arrange for an inspector to call.

Alternatively, if you are dissatisfied with an establishment, we would like to hear your comments.

With your help we can maintain Les Routiers standards, and all correspondence will be treated in the strictest of confidence.

Name of establishment: ...........................................................................................................

Address/Location: ...................................................................................................................

Type of establishment (please circle):

   Restaurant/Public House   Wine Bar/Bistro   Hotel    B&B

Nomination OR Complaint (please circle)

Comments:

# Glossary

The following list is not intended as a substitute for a phrase book or French dictionary, but as a quick and easy reference guide in a restaurant or hotel, or while travelling.

## GREETINGS/GENERAL CONVERSATION

| | |
|---|---|
| Good Morning | Bonjour |
| Goodbye | Au Revoir |
| Please | S'il vous plaît |
| Thank you | Merci |
| Do you speak English? | Parlez-vous anglais? |
| I don't understand. | Je ne comprends pas. |
| Sorry/Excuse me. | Je vous prie de m'excuser. |
| Yes, No | Oui, Non |
| I come from England | Je viens d'Angleterre |
| Scotland | d'Ecosse |
| Wales | du Pays de Galles |
| Ireland | d'Irelande |
| United States | des Etats-Unis |

## A L'HOTEL

| | |
|---|---|
| Can you recommend a good hotel? | Pouvez-vous m'indiquer un bon hôtel? |
| Do you have a room available? | Avez-vous une chambre libre? |
| I would like to reserve a twin room with bathroom. | Je voudrais réserver une chambre à deux lits avec salle de bains. |
| At what time is dinner? | A quelle heure servez-vous le dîner? |
| A table for four please? | Je voudrais une table pour quatre personnes? |
| Can I have the menu please? | Voulez-vous me donner le menu? |
| Where are the toilets? | Où sont les toilettes? |
| Could you prepare my bill please? | Pouvez-vous me préparer la note? |
| How much do I owe you? | Combien vous dois-je? |

## WHERE IS . . . ?

| | |
|---|---|
| Where is the police station? | Où se trouve la gendarmerie? |
| Where is . . . Road/Street? | Où se trouve la rue . . . ? |
| Where is the British Embassy? | L'ambassade de Grande Bretagne? |
| How do I get to the bank? | Comment aller à la banque? |
| How do I get to the Post Office? | Comment aller à la poste? |
| Where can I find a post-box? | Comment puis-je trouver une boîte aux lettres? |

## ACCIDENT/ILLNESS

| | |
|---|---|
| I have had an accident. | J'ai en un accident. |
| There are people injured. | Il y a des blessés. |
| Call an ambulance. | Appelez une ambulance. |
| Where can I find a doctor? | Où puis-je trouver un docteur? |
| Where is the nearest chemist? | Où est la pharmacie la plus proche? |
| I am ill. I have a temperature. | Je suis malade. J'ai de la fièvre. |
| Do you have any asprin? | Avez-vous des aspirines? |

## GETTING TO A GARAGE

| | |
|---|---|
| How far is the nearest garage? | A quelle distance se trouve le garage le plus proche? |
| Is it far? | Est-ce loin? |
| Do I go straight on? | Faut-il aller tout droit? |
| Turn around/Do a U-turn? | Faire demi-tour? |
| Do I have to turn left/right? | Dois-je tourner à gauche/à droite? |
| At which crossroads must I turn? | A quel croisement dois-je tourner? |
| At which traffic lights do I turn? | Je tourne à quel feu? |
| Fill her up, please. | Le plein, s'il vous plaît. |

## IN CASE OF BREAKDOWN

| | |
|---|---|
| I have broken down. | Je suis en panne. |
| I have a flat tyre. | J'ai un pneu crevé. |
| It's overheating. | Cela surchauffe. |
| The battery needs recharging. | Les batteries ont besoin d'être rechargées. |
| The . . . does not work. | Le/la . . . ne marche pas. |
| The . . . is broken. | Le/la . . . est cassé(e). |
| Will it take long? | Ce sera vite fait? |
| axle | essieu |
| battery | batterie |
| brake | frein |
| carburettor | carburateur |
| choke | starter |
| clutch | embrayage |
| distributor | allumeur |
| engine | moteur |
| exhaust-pipe | tuyau d'échappement |
| fan belt | courroie |
| fuel tank | réservoir de carburant |
| gear box | boîte de vitesses |
| headlight | phare |
| horn | avertisseur |
| ignition | allumage |
| indicator | (feu) clignotant |
| oil | huile |
| radiator | radiateur |
| silencer | silencieux |
| spark-plug | bougie |
| steering | direction |
| steering wheel | volant |
| suspension | suspension |
| tyre | pneu |
| wheel | roue |
| windscreen | pare-brise |
| windscreen-wiper | essuie-glace |

## UNDERSTANDING THE MENU

| Les Viandes | Meat |
|---|---|
| boeuf | beef |
| charolais | best cut |
| chateaubriand | double fillet steak |
| contrefilet | siloin |
| entrecôte | rib steak |
| faux filet | sirloin steak |
| filet | fillet |
| agneau | lamb |
| porc | pork |
| jambon | ham |
| jambon cru | raw smoked ham |
| veau | veal |
| foie | liver |
| foie gras | goose liver |
| ris | sweetbreads |
| rognons | kidneys |
| tripes | tripe |

| Volaille/Gibier | Poultry/Game |
|---|---|
| caille | quail |
| canard | duck |
| dindon | turkey |
| faisan | pheasant |
| lièvre | hare |
| oie | goose |
| perdreau | partridge |
| pintade | guineafowl |
| poulet | chicken |

| Les Poisons/Coquillages | Fish/Shellfish |
|---|---|
| calmar | squid |
| coquille St Jacques | scallop |
| crabe | crab |
| crevette | prawn |
| daurade | sea bream |
| ecrevisse | crayfish |
| flétan | halibut |
| fruits de mer | seafood |
| homard | lobster |
| huître | oyster |
| limande | lemon sole |
| lotte de mer | monkfish |
| maquereau | mackerel |
| morue | salt cod |
| moule | mussel |
| plie | plaice |
| raie | skate |

| | |
|---|---|
| saumon | salmon |
| seiche | cuttlefish |
| sole | sole |
| St Pierre | John Dory |
| thon | tuna |
| truite | trout |

| Les Fruits/Les Legumes Les Herbes/Epices | Fruit/Vegetables Herbs/Spices |
|---|---|
| ail | garlic |
| ananas | pineapple |
| aneth | dill |
| abricot | apricot |
| artichaut | artichoke |
| asperge | asparagus |
| avocat | avocado |
| banane | banana |
| basilic | basil |
| cassis | blackcurrant |
| cérise | cherry |
| champignon | mushroom |
| chou | cabbage |
| choufleur | cauliflower |
| ciboulette | chive |
| citron | lemon |
| citron vert | lime |
| concombre | cucumber |
| coriandre | coriander |
| cornichon | gherkin |
| courgette | courgette |
| cresson | watercress |
| echalotte | shallot |
| endive | chicory |
| epinards | spinach |
| estragon | tarragon |
| fenouil | fennel |
| fève | broad bean |
| fraise | strawberry |
| framboise | raspberry |
| gingembre | ginger |
| groseille | gooseberry |
| haricot vert | french bean |
| laitue | lettuce |
| menthe | mint |
| mûre | blackberry |
| muscade | nutmeg |
| myrtille | blueberry |
| oignon | onion |
| oseille | sorrel |

| | | | |
|---|---|---|---|
| pamplemousse | grapefruit | dégustation | tasting |
| pêche | peach | dentelle | lace |
| persil | parsley | dolmen | megalithic tomb |
| petit pois | pea | église | church |
| poire | pear | environs | surroundings |
| poireau | leek | étang | pond |
| poivre | pepper | fabrique | factory |
| poivron | green, red, yellow pepper | faïencerie | earthenware factory |
| pomme | apple | falaise | cliff |
| pomme de terre | potato | fouilles | excavations |
| prune | plum | fourrure | fur |
| pruneau | prune | gouffre | abyss, gulf |
| radis | radish | grotte | cave |
| raisin | grape | guerre | war |
| romarin | rosemary | haras | stud farm |
| safran | saffron | hôtel de ville | town hall |
| thym | thyme | marais | marsh |
| tomate | tomato | métier | trade, craft |
| truffe | truffle | mine d'argent | silver mine |
| | | moulin à vent | windmill |

## PLACES OF INTEREST

| | | | |
|---|---|---|---|
| | | pêche | fishing |
| abeille | bee | pierre sculptée | sculpted stone |
| barrage | dam | plage du débarquement | landing beach |
| beffroi | belfry | plage | beach |
| blindé | tank | pont | bridge |
| bord | bank (of a river) | poupée | doll |
| carrière | quarry | rapace | bird of prey |
| cascade | waterfall | sabotier | clog maker |
| cave | cellar | singe | monkey |
| corderie | rope-making factory | souffleur de verre | glass blower |
| | | tapisserie | tapestry |
| corniche | coast/cliff road | usine | factory |
| cristallerie | glass works | vieille ville | old town |
| croisière | cruise | | |

# Paris and Nearby

## ALFORTVILLE, Val-de-Marne, 94140

### LA TERRASSE
**Languages spoken:** English. **Restaurant:** Dinner served from midday until 8:00pm. Closed Sundays and in September. **Other points:** bar. **Address:** 173, rue Etienne Bolet.
MR BOUALEM BELAMRI
**Telephone:** 43.75.17.02
⊗ ⅋ Map 19

## ANTONY, Hauts-de-Seine, 92160

### LES ROUTIERS, RN 20
**Menu:** 50 Frs. **Restaurant:** Breakfast served from 7:30am. Lunch served from midday until 2:00pm. Closed Sundays. **Specialities:** home cooking. **Other points:** bar, car park, traditional decor. **Address:** 86, avenue de la Division Leclerc.
MME GINETTE LAURENCE
**Telephone:** 46.66.02.62
⊗ ⅋ Map 19

## AUBERVILLIERS, Seine-St-Denis, 93300

### AU RENDEZ VOUS DES CAMIONNEURS, Porte d'Aubervilliers
**Other points:** bar. **Address:** 17, rue de la Haie Coq.
MR AKLI AYADI
**Telephone:** 43.52.09.15
⊗ ⅋ Map 19

## AUFFERVILLE, Seine-et-Marne, 77570

### AUBERGE DE LA DILIGENCE, RD 403, between Nemours and Orléans
**Menu:** 55 to 75 Frs. **Accommodation:** 120 Frs. **Restaurant:** Breakfast served from 7:00am. Lunch served from 11:00am until 3:00pm. Dinner served from 6:00pm until 9:00pm. **Specialities:** home cooking. **Hotel:** 2 beds; 1 single room, 1 double room with shower, bath. **Other points:** bar, open to non-residents, children welcome, terraces, pets welcome – check for details, car park, traditional decor. **Address:** 9, Route Nationale.
MR BERNARD VINCENT
**Telephone:** 64.28.75.91
⊗ ⅋ Map 19

## BANNOST, Seine-et-Marne, 77970

### LE RELAIS DE LA GARE, RN 4
**Restaurant:** Closed Saturdays and in August. **Other points:** bar. **Address:** La Gare, Route Nationale 4.
MR GEORGES FONTAINE
**Telephone:** 64.01.02.07
⊗ ⅋ Map 19

## BERNES SUR OISE, Val-d'Oise, 95340

### LE BEL AIR
**Menu:** 54 Frs (wine included). **Restaurant:** Breakfast served from 5:00am. Lunch served from midday until 2:00pm. Dinner served from 8:00pm until 9:00pm. Closed Sundays. **Specialities:** home cooking. **Other points:** bar, children welcome, car park. **Address:** 1, rue de Creil.
MR HUBERT ANSEVIN
**Telephone:** 34.70.04.00, 30.34.17.49
⊗ ⅋ Map 19

## BLANC MESNIL, Seine-St-Denis, 93150

### LA TRAVERSEE DE L'ATLANTIQUE
**Languages spoken:** English, Italian and Portugese. **Menu:** 55 to 78 Frs. **Restaurant:** Lunch served from 11:30am until 2:30pm. Dinner served from 6:30pm until 10:00pm. **Other points:** bar. **Address:** 178, avenue du 8 Mai 1945.
MR BLAÏD MAKKEB
**Telephone:** 48.67.25.97
⊗ ⅋ Map 19

### LE BON ACCUEIL, RN 2, le Bourget
**Languages spoken:** English. **Restaurant:** Dinner served from midday until 9:00pm. Closed Sundays. **Specialities:** home cooking. **Other points:** bar, pets welcome – check for details, car park, modern decor. **Address:** 58, avenue du 8 mai 1945.
MR ANDRÉ SEBAN
**Telephone:** 48.67.19.88
⊗ ⅋ Map 19

## BOISSY SOUS ST YON, Essonne, 91790

### LE RELAIS DE TORFOU, RN 20
**Languages spoken:** English, German and Spanish. **Menu:** 51 Frs. **Accommodation:** 70 to 80 Frs. **Restaurant:** Breakfast served from 6:30am. Lunch served from midday

until 3:00pm. Dinner served from 7:00pm until 10:30pm. Closed Saturdays. **Specialities:** home cooking. **Hotel:** 4 beds. **Other points:** bar, open to non-residents, à la carte menu, children welcome, pets welcome – check for details, car park. **Address:** 52, avenue de Paris.
MR MOHAMED TOUFAHI
**Telephone:** 64.91.30.50
⊗ ♉ Map 19

## BOURGET (LE), Seine-St-Denis, 93350

### LE SPOUTNICK, RN 2
**Languages spoken:** English and Italian. **Menu:** 50 to 70 Frs. **Restaurant:** Breakfast served from 5:00am. Lunch served from 11:30am until 3:30pm. Dinner served from 7:30pm until 10:00pm. Closed Saturdays and in August. **Specialities:** home cooking. **Hotel:** 5 beds; 4 single rooms, 1 double room with shower, private WC. **Other points:** bar, open to non-residents, children welcome, pets welcome – check for details, car park, modern decor. **Address:** 70, rue de Verdun.
MR ROGER BRANKOVIC
**Telephone:** 48.38.32.97
⊗ ♉ 🏠 Map 19

## BRIIS SOUS FORGES, Essonne, 91640

### CAFETERIA DE LIMOURS, A 10
**Menu:** 55 to 85 Frs. **Restaurant:** Open 24 hours. **Other points:** bar, open to non-residents, children welcome, terraces, pets welcome – check for details, car park, modern decor. **Address:** A 10 Aire de Limours Janvry, sens Paris/Bordeaux.
MR STÉPHANE DUVOTY
**Telephone:** 64.90.77.18. **Fax:** 64.90.89.81
⊗ ♉ Map 19

## BROSSE MONTCEAUX (LA), Seine-et-Marne, 77940

### LE PETIT PERICHOIS, RN 6, between Fontainebleau and Sens
**Languages spoken:** German and English. **Menu:** 56 to 140 Frs. **Restaurant:** Breakfast served from 5:00am. Lunch served from 11:00am until 3:00pm. Dinner served from 7:00pm until 11:00pm. **Specialities:** regional menu, home cooking. **Other points:** bar, open to non-residents, à la carte menu, children welcome, terraces, pets welcome – check for details, car park, modern decor. **Address:** 33, rue de la Vallée.
MR AIMÉ VOLLEREAU
**Telephone:** 60.96.25.75. **Fax:** 64.70.29.41
⊗ ♉ Map 19

## CHAMARANDE, Essonne, 91730

### RELAIS DE MONTFORT, RN 20, between Arpajon and Etampes
**Languages spoken:** English. **Menu:** 48 Frs (drink included). **Accommodation:** 70 to 180 Frs. **Restaurant:** Breakfast served from 3:30am. Lunch served from midday until 3:00pm. Dinner served from 7:30pm until 11:00pm. Closed Saturdays, in August and the last week in December. **Specialities:** home cooking. **Hotel:** 34 beds; 13 single rooms, 21 double rooms with shower, private WC. **Other points:** bar, open to non-residents, car park, modern decor. **Address:** Route Nationale 20.
MR DANIEL COTTIN
**Telephone:** 60.82.20.80
⊗ ♉ 🏠 ☆ Map 19

## CHAPELLE LA REINE (LA), Seine-et-Marne, 77760

### LA SALAMANDRE, RN 152, the main road between Fontainebleau and Orleans
**Menu:** 58 to 80 Frs. **Accommodation:** 150 to 180 Frs. **Restaurant:** Breakfast served from 6:30am. Lunch served from 11:30am until 2:30pm. Dinner served from 7:00pm until 9:00pm. Closed Saturdays and between Christmas Day and New Year's Day. **Specialities:** home cooking. **Hotel:** 6 beds; 1 single room, 5 double rooms with shower. **Other points:** bar, open to non-residents, children welcome, pets welcome – check for details, car park, traditional decor. **Address:** 5, rue du Docteur Battesti.
MME MICHELINE BOURLIER
**Telephone:** 64.24.30.03
⊗ ♉ 🏠 Map 19

## CHARENTON LE PONT, Val-de-Marne, 94220

### L'ALLIANCE
**Menu:** 61 Frs. **Restaurant:** Breakfast served from 6:30am. Lunch served from midday until 2:30pm. Closed Wednesdays and in August. **Other points:** bar, open to non-residents, à la carte menu, traditional decor. **Address:** 121, rue de Paris.
MR ALBERT SERIES
**Telephone:** 43.68.03.71
⊗ ♉ Map 19

### LE PARIS/LISBONNE
**Languages spoken:** Spanish and Portugese. **Menu:** 50 Frs. **Restaurant:** Breakfast served from 10:00am. Lunch served from midday until 3:00pm. Dinner served from 7:00pm until 11:00pm. Closed in August. **Specialities:** regional menu. **Other points:** bar, open to non-residents, à la carte menu, modern decor. **Address:** 195, rue de Paris.
MR JACINTO DUARTE
**Telephone:** 43.68.32.29
⊗ ♉ Map 19

## CHAUFOUR LES BONNIERES, Yvelines, 78270

### AU BON ACCUEIL, RN 13, the main road between Paris and Deauville

**Menu:** 60 to 165 Frs. **Accommodation:** 110 to 200 Frs. **Restaurant:** Breakfast served from 5:30am. Lunch served from 11:30am until 2:30pm. Dinner served from 7:55pm until 10:00pm. Closed Saturdays and from 15 July to 15 August. **Specialities:** regional menu, home cooking. **Hotel:** 15 beds; 10 single rooms, 5 double rooms with shower, private WC. **Other points:** bar, open to non-residents, à la carte menu, children welcome, pets welcome – check for details, car park, traditional decor. **Address:** Route Nationale 13.
MR GÉRARD MAGNE
**Telephone:** 34.76.11.29
⊗ ♻ 🏠 Map 19

## CHELLES, Seine-et-Marne, 77500

### RELAIS DE LA PETITE VITESSE, RN 34
**Restaurant:** Closed Sundays. **Hotel:** 7 beds. **Other points:** bar. **Address:** 32, avenue du Marais.
MR MICHEL CHÉA
**Telephone:** 64.21.09.47
⊗ ♻ 🏠 Map 19

## CHOISY LE ROI, Val-de-Marne, 94600

### LE STADE, RN 186
**Restaurant:** Closed Saturdays and Sundays. **Other points:** bar. **Address:** 134, avenue de Villeneuve-Saint-Georges.
MR JEAN-CLAUDE VILLECHENOUX
**Telephone:** 48.90.90.55
⊗ ♻ Map 19

## CLAYE SOUILLY, Seine-et-Marne, 77410

### LE RELAIS DE LA ROSEE, CD 212
**Menu:** 57 Frs (wine included). **Restaurant:** Breakfast served from 10:00am. Dinner served from midday until 10:00pm. Closed Saturdays. **Specialities:** home cooking. **Other points:** bar, open to non-residents, terraces, pets welcome – check for details, car park, traditional decor. **Address:** Chemin Départemental 212.
MR CLAUDE BLOM
**Telephone:** 60.26.17.74. **Fax:** 60.27.02.28
⊗ ♻ Map 19

## CLERY EN VEXIN, Val-d'Oise, 95420

### AUBERGE DE CLERY EN VEXIN
**Restaurant:** Closed Saturdays and Sundays. **Other points:** bar, car park. **Address:** 4, Route Nationale 14.
MR JEAN-GUY DEGOUL
**Telephone:** 34.67.44.15
⊗ ♻ Map 19

## CORMEILLES EN PARISIS, Val-d'Oise, 95240

### LE BON ACCUEIL, RN 192

**Languages spoken:** Polish and Russian. **Menu:** 52,50 Frs (¼ carafe wine included). **Restaurant:** Breakfast served from 6:45am. Lunch served from 11:30am until 3:00pm. Closed Saturdays. **Specialities:** home cooking. **Other points:** terraces, pets welcome – check for details, car park, traditional decor. **Address:** 76, boulevard du Maréchal Joffre.
PATRICK ET EWA GRANDAY-RICHARD-NAM
**Telephone:** 39.78.83.24
⊗ Map 19

## COURNEUVE (LA), Seine-St-Denis, 93120

### L'AUBERGE DES SEPT COEURS, Porte de la Villette à Paris, exit Porte de la Villette
**Languages spoken:** English, Italian and Arabic. **Menu:** 55 Frs. **Restaurant:** Breakfast served from 6:30am. Lunch served from midday until 3:00pm. Dinner served from 7:30pm until midnight. Closed Sundays. **Specialities:** home cooking. **Hotel:** 14 beds; with shower, bath, private WC. **Other points:** bar, open to non-residents, à la carte menu, children welcome, terraces, pets welcome – check for details, traditional decor. **Address:** 27, avenue Jean Jaurès.
MR KHALED NAÏET LIMAN
**Telephone:** 48.36.43.78
⊗ ♻ 🏠 Map 19

## CRESPIERES, Yvelines, 78121

### AUBERGE DES ROUTIERS, RN 307
**Menu:** 60 to 80 Frs. **Restaurant:** Breakfast served from 7:30am. Lunch served from 11:30am until 2:30pm. Dinner served from 7:00pm until 9:00pm. Closed Saturdays. **Specialities:** regional menu, home cooking. **Other points:** bar, à la carte menu, children welcome, terraces, pets welcome – check for details, car park, traditional decor. **Address:** Route Nationale 307.
MME MAGDELEINE GLATIGNY
**Telephone:** 30.54.44.28
⊗ ♻ Map 19

## CRETEIL, Val-de-Marne, 94000

### LE MIRABELLIER, A 86, the main road between Paris/Metz/Nancy
**Menu:** 53 Frs (13th meal free). **Restaurant:** Breakfast served from 6:00am. **Specialities:** home cooking. **Other points:** bar, open to non-residents, children welcome, pets welcome – check for details, car park, modern decor. **Address:** Aire de Service de Pompadour.
**Telephone:** 48.99.77.00. **Fax:** 48.99.04.97
⊗ ♻ Map 19

## DEUIL LA BARRE, Val-d'Oise, 95170

### AU COQ HARDI, RN 328, towards Saint Denis Taverny
**Menu:** 50 to 60 Frs (wine and coffee included).

Restaurant: Breakfast served from 9:00am. Lunch served from 11:30am until 3:00pm. Closed Saturdays and in August. Specialities: home cooking. Other points: bar, open to non-residents. Address: 62, avenue de la Division Leclerc.
MR GÉRARD LANTINIER
Telephone: 39.64.16.81
⊗ ⟟ Map 19

## DOMONT, Val-d'Oise, 95330

### LA VIEILLE AUBERGE
Languages spoken: Spanish. Menu: 55 Frs.
Accommodation: 115 to 160 Frs. Restaurant: Breakfast served from 6:00am. Lunch served from 11:30am until 2:30pm. Closed Saturdays, Sundays and in August. Specialities: home cooking. Hotel: 6 beds; with shower. Other points: bar, pets welcome – check for details, car park, traditional decor. Address: 7, rue de l'Europe.
MR ROGER BADAIRE
Telephone: 39.91.01.66
⊗ ⟟ ⌂ Map 19

## DROCOURT, Yvelines, 78440

### AU RELAIS DU NORD, RN 183, between Mantes la Jolie and Magny en Vexin
Menu: 55 Frs. Restaurant: Breakfast served from 7:00am. Lunch served from midday until 2:00pm. Closed Sundays. Specialities: home cooking. Other points: bar, open to non-residents, à la carte menu, children welcome, pets welcome – check for details, car park, traditional decor. Address: 15, rue Nationale.
MR DANIEL TIROUARD
Telephone: 34.76.71.23
⊗ ⟟ Map 19

## EPONE, Yvelines, 78680

### REST'AU VERT, RN 13, motorway for west Paris/Caen, exit Epône towards Gargenville
Languages spoken: Italian. Menu: 60 Frs.
Accommodation: 120 Frs. Restaurant: Breakfast served from 6:00am. Lunch served from 11:30am until 3:00pm. Dinner served from 7:00pm until 10:00pm. Closed Saturdays. Specialities: home cooking. Hotel: 14 beds; 3 single rooms, 11 double rooms with telephone. Other points: bar, open to non-residents, children welcome, lounge area, terraces, pets welcome – check for details, car park. Address: Route de Gargenville.
MME ASSUNTA ARTIER
Telephone: 30.95.60.20
⊗ ⟟ ⌂ Map 19

## ESSARTS LE ROI (LES), Yvelines, 78690

### A LA GRACE DE DIEU, RN 10, the main road between Paris and Chartres

Menu: 50 to 55 Frs. Restaurant: Breakfast served from 5:00am. Lunch served from 11:30am until 3:00pm. Dinner served from 6:30pm until 10:30pm. Closed Saturdays and in August. Specialities: home cooking. Other points: bar, open to non-residents, children welcome, pets welcome – check for details, car park. Address: Route Nationale 10.
MR DANIEL BIGOT
Telephone: 30.41.60.04
⊗ ⟟ Map 19

### LE RELAIS D'ARCOAT, RN 10, between Rambouillet and Paris
Languages spoken: English. Menu: 53 Frs.
Restaurant: Breakfast served from 6:00am. Lunch served from midday until 3:00pm. Dinner served from 7:00pm until 10:00pm. Closed Saturdays, public holidays and in July. Specialities: home cooking. Other points: bar, open to non-residents, car park, traditional decor. Address: 39, Route Nationale 10.
SARL ARCOAT
Telephone: 30.41.60.53
⊗ ⟟ Map 19

## FERTE GAUCHER (LA), Seine-et-Marne, 77320

### LE CONTRE-TEMPS, RN 34, Sézanne
Languages spoken: English. Menu: 60 to 120 Frs.
Restaurant: Lunch served from midday until 2:30pm. Dinner served from 7:30pm until 10:00pm. Closed Saturdays. Specialities: home cooking. Other points: bar, open to non-residents, à la carte menu, terraces, pets welcome – check for details, car park, traditional decor. Address: 4, avenue de la Gare.
MR HERVÉ LANGLE
Telephone: 64.04.01.90
⊗ ⟟ Map 19

## GUILLERVAL, Essonne, 91690

### RELAIS DE MONDESIR, RN 20
Languages spoken: Spanish and Portuguese. Menu: 50 to 60 Frs. Restaurant: Breakfast served from 6:00am. Closed Sundays Specialities: regional menu, home cooking. Other points: bar, open to non-residents, à la carte menu, children welcome, pets welcome – check for details, car park, traditional decor. Address: Hameau de Mondésir.
MR JEAN PICQ
Telephone: 64.95.60.76
⊗ ⟟ Map 19

## HOUSSAYE EN BRIE (LA), Seine-et-Marne, 77610

### AUBERGE DU COUCOU, RN 36
Languages spoken: English. Other points: bar.
Address: La Haute-Gonière.

MR CHRISTIAN BROUST
**Telephone:** 64.07.40.75
⊗ ♀ Map 19

## ISLE ADAM (L'), Val-d'Oise, 95290

### AU RALLYE, RN 322

**Restaurant:** Closed Saturday evenings, Sunday evenings and in August. **Other points:** bar. **Address:** 71, rue de Pontoise.
MME PAULETTE COMBES
**Telephone:** 34.69.08.24
⊗ ♀ Map 19

## LIMAY, Yvelines, 78520

### LA MARMITE

**Menu:** 55 to 70 Frs. **Restaurant:** Lunch served from 11:30am until 4:00pm. Dinner served from 7:30pm until 10:30pm. Closed Saturdays. **Specialities:** home cooking. **Other points:** bar, open to non-residents, children welcome, pets welcome – check for details, car park. **Address:** 1, route de Meulan.
MR MICHEL BLANCHARD
**Telephone:** 34.78.65.52
⊗ ♀ Map 19

## MAGNY EN VEXIN, Val-d'Oise, 95420

### HOTEL DE LA GARE

**Accommodation:** 150 to 160 Frs. **Restaurant:** Dinner served from midday until 10:00pm. Closed Sundays and from 23 December to 1 January. **Specialities:** Couscous, home cooking. **Hotel:** 10 beds; 5 single rooms, 5 double rooms with shower. **Other points:** bar, à la carte menu, pets welcome – check for details, car park. **Address:** 65, rue de Beauvais.
MME FABIENNE DEGOUL ALVES
**Telephone:** 34.67.20.70
⊗ ♀ ⌂ Map 19

## MANTES LA VILLE, Yvelines, 78200

### LA DEMIE LUNE, Autoroute Paris/Rouen, exit Mantes south, towards Beauvais

**Languages spoken:** English, Spanish and Italian.
**Menu:** 50 to 80 Frs. **Restaurant:** Breakfast served from 7:00am. Lunch served from 11:30am until 3:00pm. Dinner served from 7:00pm until 9:00pm. Closed Sundays. **Specialities:** home cooking. **Other points:** bar, open to non-residents, à la carte menu, children welcome, pets welcome – check for details, car park, modern decor. **Address:** 51, boulevard Roger Salengro.
MRE STÉPHANE WARNIEZ
**Telephone:** 34.77.03.66
⊗ ♀ Map 19

### LE HOUDAN BAR, RN 13, Houdan

**Languages spoken:** English. **Menu:** 52 Frs. **Restaurant:** Breakfast served from 8:30am. Lunch served from

midday. Dinner served until 2:00am. **Specialities:** home cooking. **Other points:** bar, open to non-residents, à la carte menu, terraces, traditional decor. **Address:** 43, route de Houdan.
MR HOCINE OUHAB
**Telephone:** 34.77.06.11
⊗ ♀ Map 19

## MAROLLES SUR SEINE, Seine-et-Marne, 77130

### AU RENDEZ-VOUS DES PECHEURS ET DES CHASSEURS

**Restaurant:** Dinner served from midday until 8:30pm. Closed Sundays. **Other points:** bar. **Address:** 70, Grande Rue.
MME BODIC
**Telephone:** 64.31.32.20
⊗ ♀ Map 19

## MEAUX, Seine-et-Marne, 77100

### RESTAURANT DE LA MARNE, RN 3, the main road between Paris and Châlons sur Marne

**Languages spoken:** English. **Menu:** 39 to 138 Frs. **Restaurant:** Breakfast served from 8:30am. Closed Sundays. **Specialities:** home cooking. **Other points:** bar, open to non-residents, children welcome, pets welcome – check for details, car park. **Address:** 3, avenue Foch.
MR ALAIN RAMY
**Telephone:** 64.34.06.31
⊗ ♀ Map 19

## MONTEREAU, Seine-et-Marne, 77130

### LES ROUTIERS, RN 105

**Restaurant:** Closed Sundays and in July. **Other points:** bar. **Address:** Route Nationale 105.
MME PICARD
**Telephone:** 64.32.44.93
⊗ ♀ Map 19

## MONTLHERY, Essonne, 91310

### LE SOLOGNE

**Menu:** 49,50 Frs. **Accommodation:** 120 to 180 Frs. **Restaurant:** Breakfast served from 7:00am. Lunch served from 11:30am until 2:00pm. Dinner served from 7:30pm until 9:00pm. Closed Sundays and in August. **Specialities:** home cooking. **Hotel:** 7 beds; 5 single rooms, 2 double rooms with shower, telephone. **Other points:** bar, open to non-residents, pets welcome – check for details, car park, traditional decor. **Address:** 65, route d'Orléans.
MR JACQUES CHERON
**Telephone:** 69.01.00.98, 69.01.20.76
⊗ ♀ ⌂ ☆ Map 19

## MONTREUIL, Seine-St-Denis, 93100

### LE RELAIS DES ROUTIERS
**Restaurant:** Closed Sundays and in August. **Other points:** bar. **Address:** 70, rue de Lagny.
MMES SOL ET PUECH
**Telephone:** 48.51.54.41
⊗ ☂ Map 19

## MUREAUX (LES), Yvelines, 78130

### LE RELAIS ICI ON COUPE SOIF, RD 14
**Restaurant:** Closed Sundays and in August. **Hotel:** 7 beds. **Other points:** bar. **Address:** 102, avenue du Maréchal Foch.
MME SUZANNE COMPAGNON
**Telephone:** 34.74.05.04
⊗ ☂ ⌂ Map 19

## NEMOURS, Seine-et-Marne, 77140

### RELAIS DE NEMOURS, A 6, bridge which spans motorway
**Restaurant:** Open 24 hours. **Specialities:** regional menu. **Other points:** à la carte menu, children welcome, terraces, pets welcome – check for details, car park. **Address:** Aire de Service de Darvault, dans les deux sens.
**Telephone:** 64.28.11.97
⊗ Map 19

## PANTIN, Seine-St-Denis, 93500

### RESTODEM, de Porte de Pantin, take the CD 115 as far as the SNCF bridge
**Menu:** 50 Frs. **Restaurant:** Breakfast served from 7:00am. Lunch served from 11:30am until 3:00pm. Closed Saturdays. **Specialities:** home cooking. **Other points:** bar, open to non-residents, à la carte menu, lounge area, terraces, pets welcome – check for details, car park, modern decor. **Address:** 110, avenue du Général Leclerc.
MR ANDRÉ DEMOUGIN
**Telephone:** 48.44.75.84. **Fax:** 49.91.07.45
⊗ ☂ Map 19

## PARIS, Paris, 75000

### AUX ROUTIERS, Porte de la Chapelle
**Menu:** 60 to 83 Frs. **Restaurant:** Breakfast served from 7:30am. Lunch served from midday until 2:15pm. Dinner served from 7:15pm until 10:15pm. Closed Sundays. **Specialities:** couscous, paëlla, choucroute, home cooking. **Other points:** bar, open to non-residents, traditional decor. **Address:** 50, rue Marx Dormoy.
MR BERNARD DUBREUIL
**Telephone:** 46.07.93.00
⊗ ☂ Map 19

### CHEZ LEON
**Restaurant:** Dinner served from midday until 9:00pm. Closed Sundays and in August. **Other points:** bar. **Address:** 5, rue de l'Isly.
MME GRANGE
**Telephone:** 43.87.42.77
⊗ ☂ Map 19

## PIERREFITTE SUR SEINE, Seine-St-Denis, 93380

### LE NORMANDIE, RN 1, Porte de la Chapelle, towards Beauvais
**Menu:** 57 Frs. **Restaurant:** Breakfast served from 6:00am. Lunch served from 11:30am until 3:00pm. Dinner served from 7:00pm until 9:00pm. Closed Sundays and in September. **Specialities:** confit de canard, paëlla, escalope normande, home cooking. **Other points:** bar, children welcome, pets welcome – check for details, car park, modern decor. **Address:** 105, avenue du Général Gallièni.
MME MARCELLINE VIDAL
**Telephone:** 48.26.55.62
⊗ ☂ ⌣ Map 19

## PLAINE SAINT DENIS (LA), Seine-St-Denis, 93210

### LE CHRISTAL, Porte de la Chapelle
**Languages spoken:** English. **Menu:** 50 to 86 Frs. **Restaurant:** Breakfast served from 7:00am. Lunch served from midday until 4:00pm. Dinner served from 7:00pm until 11:00pm. Closed Sundays. **Other points:** open to non-residents, à la carte menu, children welcome, pets welcome – check for details, modern decor. **Address:** 101, avenue du Président Wilson.
MR CLAUDE AGNIER
**Telephone:** 42.43.75.58
⊗ Map 19

## PONTAULT COMBAULT, Seine-et-Marne, 77340

### LE RELAIS DU PAVE
**Languages spoken:** German, English and Portugese. **Menu:** 60 Frs (drink included). **Restaurant:** Lunch served from midday until 3:00pm. Dinner served from 7:00pm until 11:00pm. Closed Sundays. **Specialities:** regional menu, home cooking. **Hotel:** 44 beds; with shower, bath, private WC, television, telephone. **Other points:** bar, open to non-residents, à la carte menu, children welcome, lounge area, car park. **Address:** 9, route de Paris.
MR ALBANO MOTA DOS SANTOS
**Telephone:** 60.28.00.21
⊗ ☂ ⌂ Map 19

## PONTHIERRY, Seine-et-Marne, 77310

### AUX TROIS MARCHES, RN 7

**Menu:** 52 Frs (wine included). **Restaurant:** Breakfast served from 6:00am. Lunch served from midday until 2:00pm. Dinner served from 8:00pm until 9:00pm. Closed Sundays and in August. **Specialities:** home cooking. **Other points:** bar, car park, traditional decor. **Address:** 7, rue de la Saussaie.
MME ODETTE POTHIER
**Telephone:** 60.65.77.67
⊗ ⍩ Map 19

## PROVINS, Seine-et-Marne, 77160

### LE RELAIS DE LA CUR D'AIR, RN 19

**Restaurant:** Closed Fridays and the 2nd fortnight in July. **Hotel:** 8 beds. **Other points:** bar. **Address:** 54, avenue du Général de Gaulle.
MR AMROUN
**Telephone:** 64.00.03.21
⊗ ⍩ ⌂ ⌣ Map 19

## QUINCY SOUS SENART, Essonne, 91480

### A LA BONNE TABLE, RN 6

**Menu:** 48 to 75 Frs. **Accommodation:** 90 to 120 Frs. **Restaurant:** Breakfast served from 5:30am. Lunch served from 11:30am until 2:30pm. Dinner served from 7:45pm until 9:30pm. Closed Sundays and in February. **Specialities:** regional menu, home cooking. **Hotel:** 5 beds; with shower, bath. **Other points:** bar, open to non-residents, à la carte menu, children welcome, terraces, pets welcome – check for details, car park, modern decor. **Address:** 3, avenue Henri Chasles.
MR PIERRE WALTER
**Telephone:** 69.00.93.81
⊗ ⍩ ⌂ Map 19

## ROMAINVILLE, Seine-St-Denis, 93230

### LE REFUGE – CHEZ ANNA

**Languages spoken:** Spanish, Portugese and Yugoslavian. **Menu:** 56, 50 Frs. **Restaurant:** Lunch served from 11:30am until 3:30pm. Closed Sundays. **Address:** 79, boulevard Henri Barbusse.
MME MARIA VUKO
**Telephone:** 48.91.04.85
⊗ Map 19

## RUNGIS, Val-de-Marne, 94595

### GRAND COMPTOIR DE RUNGIS, RN 7

**Menu:** 64, 60 to 110 Frs. **Restaurant:** Breakfast served from 5:30am. Closed Saturdays. **Specialities:** home cooking. **Other points:** bar, open to non-residents, à la carte menu, terraces, pets welcome – check for details, car park, modern decor. **Address:** Place St-Hubert, Halles de Rungis.
MR MAX LEMOINE
**Telephone:** 46.86.29.30. **Fax:** 46.87.82.30
⊗ ⍩ Map 19

## SAINT DENIS, Seine-St-Denis, 93200

### L'ARRET DES CHAUFFEURS, Portes de la Chapelle and de Clignancourt

**Menu:** 49 Frs. **Restaurant:** Breakfast served from 7:00am. Closed Saturdays and in August. **Specialities:** home cooking. **Other points:** bar, à la carte menu, pets welcome – check for details. **Address:** 47, boulevard de la Libération.
MME MICHELINE SAHUT
**Telephone:** 48.20.13.81
⊗ ⍩ Map 19

### LE RELAIS DU FRET – CHEZ DANIEL, Portes de la Chapelle and de Clignancourt

**Languages spoken:** English. **Menu:** from 58 Frs. **Restaurant:** Dinner served from midday until midnight. Closed Saturdays. **Specialities:** regional menu, home cooking. **Hotel:** with shower. **Other points:** bar, open to non-residents, children welcome, lounge area, traditional decor. **Address:** 53, avenue du Président Wilson, la Plaine Saint Denis.
MR DANIEL DAHAN
**Telephone:** 48.09.41.22, 48.09.38.51
⊗ ⍩ Map 19

## SAINT GERMAIN LES ARPAJON, Essonne, 91180

### A L'AS DE TREFLE, RN 20, Orléans

**Languages spoken:** English. **Menu:** 58 Frs. **Restaurant:** Breakfast served from 4:30am. Lunch served from 11:45am until 2:15pm. Dinner served from 7:00pm until 8:45pm. Closed Sundays. **Specialities:** home cooking. **Other points:** bar, open to non-residents, pets welcome – check for details, car park, traditional decor. **Address:** 7–11, Route Nationale 20, 'La Petite Folie'.
MR GUY BERGOUGNOUX
**Telephone:** 64.90.02.24
⊗ ⍩ Map 19

## SAINT MAUR DES FOSSES, Val-de-Marne, 94100

### LA PASSERELLE

**Languages spoken:** Portugese. **Menu:** 52 Frs. **Restaurant:** Closed Sundays and between Christmas Day and New Year's Day. **Specialities:** home cooking. **Other points:** bar, terraces, pets welcome – check for details, car park, modern decor. **Address:** 45, boulevard du Général Férrié.
MR JEAN DIAS
**Telephone:** 42.83.21.71
⊗ ⍩ Map 19

## SAINT OUEN, Seine-St-Denis, 93400

### *AUX ROUTIERS SYMPAS, bridge at Saint Ouen*

**Menu:** 48 Frs (wine included). **Accommodation:** 90 Frs. **Restaurant:** Breakfast served from 6:00am. Lunch served from 11:45am until 3:00pm. Dinner served from 6:30pm until 8:00pm. Closed Saturdays and in August. **Specialities:** home cooking. **Hotel:** 9 beds; 3 single rooms, 6 double rooms with shower, bath. **Other points:** bar, pets welcome – check for details, traditional decor. **Address:** 93, boulevard Victor Hugo.
MR BERNARD DELOUVRIER
**Telephone:** 40.11.00.31
⊗ 🍷 🏠 Map 19

## SAMMERON, Seine-et-Marne, 77260

### *LES CIGOGNES, RN 3*

**Languages spoken:** Portugese. **Menu:** 60 to 70 Frs. **Accommodation:** 95 to 130 Frs. **Restaurant:** Breakfast served from 6:30am. Lunch served from midday until 3:00pm. Dinner served from 7:00pm until 9:00pm. Closed Sundays and in August. **Specialities:** home cooking. **Hotel:** 5 beds; 2 single rooms, 3 double rooms with shower. **Other points:** bar, open to non-residents, à la carte menu, children welcome, car park. **Address:** 2, rue de Metz.
MME GLORIA BENTO
**Telephone:** 60.22.79.40
⊗ 🍷 🏠 Map 19

## SANCY LES PROVINS, Seine-et-Marne, 77320

### *LE RELAIS DE SANCY, RN 4*

**Menu:** 55 Frs. **Restaurant:** Breakfast served from 4:00am. Closed Saturdays. **Specialities:** home cooking. **Other points:** bar, open to non-residents, car park, modern decor. **Address:** Route Nationale 4.
MR PHILIPPE SAVAGE
**Telephone:** 64.01.92.07
⊗ 🍷 Map 19

## SURESNES, Hauts-de-Seine, 92150

### *LES ECLUSES, Porte de St Cloud.*

**Restaurant:** Breakfast served from 5:30am. Closed Sundays and in August. **Specialities:** home cooking. **Other points:** bar. **Address:** 30, quai Galliéni.
MR HENRI BODIN
**Telephone:** 45.06.11.48
⊗ 🍷 Map 19

## SURVILLIERS, Val-d'Oise, 95470

### *LE COQ CHANTANT, RN 17, Senlis*

**Languages spoken:** German. **Menu:** 53, 50 or 90 Frs. **Restaurant:** Breakfast served from 6:00am. Lunch served from midday until 2:30pm. Dinner served from 7:00pm until 10:15pm. Closed Fridays. **Specialities:** home cooking. **Other points:** bar, open to non-residents, pets welcome – check for details, car park, traditional decor. **Address:** Route Nationale 17.
MME EDITH RESSLEN
**Telephone:** 34.68.24.65
⊗ 🍷 Map 19

### *RELAIS ILE DE FRANCE, A 1, accessible from either side via pedestrian footbridge*

**Languages spoken:** German and English. **Restaurant:** Open 24 hours. **Specialities:** regional menu. **Other points:** children welcome, terraces, pets welcome – check for details, car park. **Address:** Aire de service de Vemars, dans les deux sens.
**Telephone:** 34.68.39.20
⊗ Map 19

## VARENNES SUR SEINE, Seine-et-Marne, 77130

### *SARL LE PETIT FOSSARD, RN 6, the main road between Paris and Sens*

**Languages spoken:** Portuguese. **Menu:** 57 to 80 Frs. **Accommodation:** 100 to 120 Frs. **Restaurant:** Breakfast served from 4:30am. Lunch served from 11:30am until 3:00pm. Dinner served from 7:00pm until 11:00pm. Closed Sundays and in August. **Specialities:** home cooking. **Hotel:** 6 beds; 5 single rooms, 1 double room. **Other points:** bar, open to non-residents, à la carte menu, pets welcome – check for details, car park, traditional decor. **Address:** Route Nationale 6.
MR JOSÉ DA SILVA
**Telephone:** 64.32.17.47
⊗ 🍷 🏠 Map 19

## VIRY CHATILLON, Essonne, 91170

### *LES ROUTIERS, RN 7 and RD 91, exit Viry Chatillon or Grigny*

**Restaurant:** Breakfast served from 6:30am. Lunch served from 11:30am until 2:00pm. Dinner served from 7:00pm until 9:00pm. Closed Saturdays, public holidays and in August. **Specialities:** home cooking. **Other points:** bar. **Address:** 100, route de Fleury.
MR FERNAND GADREAU
**Telephone:** 69.05.28.46
⊗ 🍷 Map 19

## VOINSLES ROZAY EN BRIE, Seine-et-Marne, 77540

### *RELAIS DE VOINSLES, RN 4*

**Restaurant:** Closed Saturdays.
MARTINE ET PATRICE KLEIN-RENAUDIN
**Telephone:** 64.07.75.20
⊗ Map 19

## VOISINS MOUROUX, Seine-et-Marne, 77120

### LE RELAIS DU SOMMET

**Menu:** 55 Frs (drinks included). **Restaurant:** Breakfast served from 7:00am. Closed Saturdays and in August. **Specialities:** home cooking. **Hotel:** 7 beds; with shower, bath. **Other points:** bar, open to non-residents, pets welcome – check for details. **Address:** 968, rue du Général de Gaulle.
MR JACQUES SANTERRE
**Telephone:** 64.03.05.47
⊗ 𝖸 ⌂ Map 19

## VOULX, Seine-et-Marne, 77940

### LA BRUYERE, RD 219, after Montereau, towards Montargis

**Menu:** 90 to 125 Frs. **Restaurant:** Dinner served from midday until 9:30pm. Closed Sundays, from 16 to 28 February and from 16 to 31 August. **Specialities:** Huitres, escargots, tête de veau, grillades, home cooking. **Other points:** bar, à la carte menu, children welcome.
**Address:** 72, Grande Rue.
MR ALBAN BALDRAN
**Telephone:** 64.31.92.41
⊗ 𝖸 ⌣ Map 19

# Northern France

## ABBEVILLE, Somme, 80100

### AU CHEVAL NOIR, RN 25
Restaurant: Closed from Friday afternoons to Saturday afternoons and the last week of August. Other points: bar. Address: Route Nationale 25, Petit Miannay.
MR BERNARD LAFARGUE-FORTIER
Telephone: 22.24.20.17
⊗ ♀ Map 2

### AUBERGE FLEURIE, RN 1, between Abbeville and Dunkerque
Menu: 54 Frs. Restaurant: Breakfast served from 5:00am. Lunch served from 11:30am until 3:00pm. Dinner served from 7:00pm until 11:00pm. Closed Saturdays. Specialities: home cooking. Other points: bar, children welcome, pets welcome – check for details, car park, traditional decor. Address:. 294, côte de la Justice.
MR MICHEL RUBIN
Telephone: 22.24.88.80, 22.24.88.22
⊗ ♀ Map 2

### CHEZ GILBERT, RN 1, between Boulogne and Calais
Menu: 50 to 80 Frs. Restaurant: Breakfast served from 7:00am. Lunch served from midday until 2:00pm. Dinner served from 7:30pm until 9:30pm. Closed Saturdays. Specialities: home cooking. Other points: bar, open to non-residents, pets welcome – check for details, car park. Address: 5, Route Nationale, Buigny Saint Maclou.
MR MARC CARON
Telephone: 22.24.20.47
⊗ ♀ Map 2

## ABSCON, Nord, 59215

### LE MOULIN D'OR, RN 45, between Douai and Denain
Accommodation: 60 to 90 Frs. Restaurant: Closed in August. Specialities: home cooking. Hotel: 16 beds; 10 single rooms, 6 double rooms. Other points: bar, open to non-residents, car park, traditional decor. Address: 17, place de Gaulle
MME MONIQUE BAUDUIN
Telephone: 27.36.30.33
⊗ ♀ ⌂ Map 1

## AMBLAINVILLE, Oise, 60110

### CHEZ MARIE-ODILE, RN 327
Restaurant: Closed Sundays. Other points: bar.
Address: 40, rue Nationale.
MME MARIE-ODILE PRUNIER
Telephone: 44.52.03.10
⊗ ♀ Map 2

## ARMENTIERES, Nord, 59280

### AUBERGE DE LA LYS, RN 42, the main road between Lille and Dunkerque
Menu: 50 to 60 Frs. Restaurant: Breakfast served from 7:00am. Lunch served from midday until 2:30pm. Dinner served from 7:30pm until 9:30pm. Closed Sundays. Specialities: regional menu. Other points: bar, open to non-residents, à la carte menu, children welcome, car park, traditional decor. Address: 110, rue des Résistants.
MME JACQUELINE LEFLON
Telephone: 20.77.21.83
⊗ ♀ Map 1

### LA TERRASSE, RN 42, opposite customs, near to Hem
Menu: 37 Frs. Restaurant: Lunch served from 11:30am until 3:30pm. Dinner served from 6:00pm until 11:00pm. Specialities: home cooking. Other points: bar, terraces, pets welcome – check for details, car park. Address: 112, rue des Résistants.
MME JOCELYNE DUBAR
Telephone: 20.35.44.80
⊗ ♀ Map 1

## ARRAS, Pas-de-Calais, 62000

### LE POINT DU JOUR, RN 25
Languages spoken: English. Menu: 50 to 100 Frs.
Restaurant: Breakfast served from 4:00am. Closed Sundays. Specialities: regional menu, home cooking. Other points: bar, open to non-residents, à la carte menu, children welcome, pets welcome – check for details, car park. Address: 13, avenue Michonneau.
MME SYLVIE KELLE
Telephone: 21.59.96.42
⊗ ♀ Map 1

**RELAIS DE L'ARTOIS,** *A 1, accessible from either side via pedestrian footbridge* **Languages spoken:** English. **Restaurant:** Open 24 hours. **Specialities:** regional menu. **Other points:** children welcome, lounge area, terraces, pets welcome – check for details, car park. **Address:** Aire de Service de Wancourt, dans les deux sens. **Telephone:** 21.55.97.83

⊗  Map 1

## AUCHY AU BOIS, Pas-de-Calais, 62190

**LE VERT DRAGON,** *between Bruay la Buissière and Saint Omer* **Languages spoken:** German and English. **Menu:** 55 Frs. **Restaurant:** Breakfast served from 7:00am. **Specialities:** home cooking. **Other points:** bar, open to non-residents, children welcome, pets welcome – check for details, car park, modern decor. **Address:** Chaussée Brunehaut. MME PATRICIA GODET **Telephone:** 21.26.64.29

⊗  ☖  Map 1

## AVELIN, Nord, 59710

**A L'EMBUSCADE,** *RD 949, exit Seclin, towards Valenciennes* **Menu:** 35 to 70 Frs. **Restaurant:** Breakfast served from 6:00am. Lunch served from 11:30am until 3:00pm. Dinner served from 7:00pm until 9:00pm. Closed Saturdays. **Specialities:** home cooking. **Other points:** bar, open to non-residents, à la carte menu, children welcome, pets welcome – check for details, car park, traditional decor. **Address:** 14, route de Seclin. MME GENEVIÈVE LEMOINE **Telephone:** 20.32.90.33

⊗  ☖  Map 1

## AVESNES SUR HELPE, Nord, 59440

**CAFE MARGUERITTE – AU ROUTIERS,** *RN 2, the main road between Maubeuge and Paris* **Menu:** 48 to 55 Frs. **Accommodation:** 60 Frs. **Restaurant:** Breakfast served from 7:00am. Lunch served from midday until 2:00pm. Closed the 1st fortnight of August. **Specialities:** home cooking. **Hotel:** 6 beds; 6 single rooms. **Other points:** bar, pets welcome – check for details, car park, traditional decor. **Address:** 20, avenue de la Gare. MME MARGUERITTE SORRIAUX **Telephone:** 20.61.17.88

⊗  ☖  ☖  Map 1

## AWOINGT, Nord, 59400

**AUX CHANTS DES OISEAUX,** *RN 39*

**Restaurant:** Closed Saturdays and in August. **Hotel:** 12 beds. **Other points:** bar. **Address:** 3, route du Cateau. MR JEAN-PIERRE PLOUQUET **Telephone:** 27.78.77.05

⊗  ☖  ☖  Map 1

## BAILLEUL, Nord, 59270

**AUBERGE DU SEAU,** *CD 933, Autoroute for Lille exit no 9 – Dunkerque exit no 12* **Accommodation:** 130 to 200 Frs. **Restaurant:** Lunch served from midday until 2:30pm. Dinner served from 7:00pm until 10:00pm. **Specialities:** Steack de veau de la mer, home cooking. **Hotel:** 11 beds; 3 single rooms, 8 double rooms with shower, bath, private WC, television, telephone. **Other points:** bar, open to non-residents, à la carte menu, children welcome, terraces, pets welcome – check for details, car park, traditional decor. **Address:** Chemin Départemental 933, le Seau. MR JOËL DEQUIDT **Telephone:** 20.48.62.00

⊗  ☖  ☖  ☆  Map 1

**CHEZ ANDRE,** *RD 933* **Restaurant:** Dinner served from midday until 9:00pm. **Other points:** bar. **Address:** Route Nationale 4671, route de Lille. MR ANDRÉ NOORENBERGHE **Telephone:** 28.49.29.14

⊗  ☖  Map 1

## BAILLEUL SUR THERAIN, Oise, 60930

**L'ALOUETTE,** *between Beauvais and Mouy* **Menu:** 56 Frs (wine and coffee included). **Restaurant:** Breakfast served from 6:00am. Closed Saturdays. **Specialities:** home cooking. **Other points:** bar, open to non-residents, children welcome. **Address:** 3, rue de Villers. MLLE VALÉRIE DUCLOS **Telephone:** 44.07.55.62

⊗  ☖  Map 2

## BAILLEULVAL, Pas-de-Calais, 62123

**RELAIS BAC DU SUD,** *RN 25, between Arras and Doulens* **Languages spoken:** Dutch. **Menu:** 60 Frs (wine and coffee included). **Accommodation:** 120 to 170 Frs. **Restaurant:** Breakfast served from 5:30am. Lunch served from midday until 2:30pm. Dinner served from 7:00pm until 10:00pm. Closed Sundays, 15 days in August and 1 week at Christmas. **Specialities:** home cooking. **Hotel:** 6 beds; 6 double rooms with shower. **Other points:** bar, open to non-residents, à la carte menu, children welcome, terraces, pets welcome – check for details, car park, modern decor. **Address:** Route Nationale 25.

MR YVES SANSON
**Telephone:** 21.58.79.12
⊗ ⚲ ⌂ Map 1

## BAPAUME, Pas-de-Calais, 62450

### CHEZ BERNADETTE, RN 17, the main road between Cambrai and Amiens

**Menu:** 53 Frs. **Accommodation:** 100 to 200 Frs. **Restaurant:** Breakfast served from 6:00am. Lunch served from midday until 2:30pm. Dinner served from 8:00pm until 9:30pm. Closed Saturdays. **Specialities:** home cooking. **Hotel:** 9 beds; 3 single rooms, 6 double rooms with shower, bath, private WC, telephone. **Other points:** bar, open to non-residents, pets welcome – check for details, car park, traditional decor. **Address:** 45, faubourg de Péronne.
MME BERNADETTE MOLLE
**Telephone:** 21.07.12.78
⊗ ⚲ ⌂ ☆ Map 1

## BERCK SUR MER, Pas-de-Calais, 62600

### RELAIS D'ARTOIS

**Specialities:** home cooking. **Hotel:** 14 beds. **Other points:** bar, open to non-residents, car park. **Address:** 20, rue Alfred Lambert.
MR RAOUL POSTEL
**Telephone:** 21.09.29.35
⊗ ⚲ ⌂ Map 1

## BOVES, Somme, 80440

### LA GRENOUILLERE, RN 334, via the motorway Amiens–Roye

**Languages spoken:** English. **Menu:** 55 to 68 Frs. **Restaurant:** Breakfast served from 6:00am. Lunch served from 11:00am until 3:00pm. Closed Sundays and in August. **Specialities:** home cooking. **Other points:** open to non-residents, children welcome, terraces, pets welcome – check for details, car park, traditional decor. **Address:** Route Nationale 334.
MR BOUHOU OUANNOUNE
**Telephone:** 22.09.31.26, 22.09.24.14
⊗ Map 2

## BRETEUIL, Oise, 60120

### AUBERGE DU MARAIS, RN 16, on the road to Clermont

**Menu:** 57,50 (wine included) to 85 Frs. **Restaurant:** Breakfast served from 8:00am. Lunch served from midday until 3:00pm. Dinner served from 7:00pm until 10:00pm. Closed Sundays. **Specialities:** home cooking. **Other points:** bar, open to non-residents, à la carte menu, children welcome, terraces, pets welcome – check for details, car park, traditional decor. **Address:** 38, rue de Paris.

JOSIANE ET JEAN-PAUL CLÉMENT
**Telephone:** 44.80.12.21
⊗ ⚲ Map 2

## BRUAY LA BUISSIERE, Pas-de-Calais, 62700

### LA LOUETTE, between Béthune and Saint Pol sur Ternoise

**Languages spoken:** German and English. **Menu:** 60 Frs – Plat du jour 35 Frs. **Accommodation:** 85 to 140 Frs. **Restaurant:** Breakfast served from 5:00am. Lunch served from 11:30am until 2:30pm. Dinner served from 7:00pm until 9:00pm. **Specialities:** home cooking. **Hotel:** 15 beds; 1 single room, 14 double rooms with shower, bath, private WC. **Other points:** bar, open to non-residents, children welcome, pets welcome – check for details, car park, traditional decor. **Address:** 114, rue Raoul Briquet.
MR PHILIPPE CHEVALIER
**Telephone:** 21.53.42.07
⊗ ⚲ ⌂ ☆ Map 1

## BUIRONFOSSE, Aisne, 02620

### AUX AMIS DE LA ROUTE, RN 29, between Saint Quentin and la Capelle

**Menu:** 58 Frs (wine included). **Accommodation:** 90 to 110 Frs. **Restaurant:** Breakfast served from 7:00am. Closed Sundays. **Specialities:** home cooking. **Hotel:** 5 beds; 3 single rooms, 2 double rooms. **Other points:** bar, open to non-residents, children welcome, terraces, pets welcome – check for details, car park, traditional decor. **Address:** Route Nationale 29.
MME DANIELLE DOUCHEZ
**Telephone:** 23.97.24.05
⊗ ⚲ ⌂ Map 2

## CAMBRAI, Nord, 59400

### AU RELAIS, RN 39, Charleville

**Menu:** 50 Frs. **Restaurant:** Breakfast served from 7:00am. Lunch served from midday until 2:00pm. Dinner served from 7:00pm until 8:00pm. Closed Sundays and in August. **Specialities:** home cooking. **Hotel:** 4 beds. **Other points:** pets welcome – check for details, traditional decor. **Address:** 1084, avenue du Cateau.
MR ROGER GUISGAND
**Telephone:** 27.81.35.82
⊗ Map 1

### CHEZ ROGER

**Menu:** 58 Frs. **Accommodation:** 65 to 95 Frs. **Restaurant:** Breakfast served from 6:15am. Lunch served from midday until 3:00pm. Dinner served from 7.30pm until 10:30pm. Closed Saturdays and in August. **Specialities:** home cooking. **Hotel:** 6 beds; 4 single rooms, 2 double rooms with shower, television, telephone. **Other points:** bar, open to non-residents,

children welcome, pets welcome – check for details, car park, traditional decor. **Address:** 10, rue des Docks.
MR ROGER LEPRINCE
**Telephone:** 27.83.26.05
⊗ ⅋ ⌂ Map 1

### LA GARGOTE, *A 2 and A 23, along the canal*

**Menu:** 60 Frs. **Restaurant:** Breakfast served from 7:00am. Lunch served from midday until 3:00pm. Dinner served from 7:00pm until 11:00pm. Closed Sundays and in August. **Specialities:** home cooking. **Other points:** bar, open to non-residents, terraces, pets welcome – check for details, car park, modern decor. **Address:** 136, boulevard Jean Bart.
MR JEAN BEDU
**Telephone:** 27.81.07.18
⊗ ⅋ Map 1

## CAPPELLE EN PEVELE, Nord, 59242

### L'AS VEGAS, *RN 393*

**Restaurant:** Dinner served from midday until 8:00pm. Closed Sundays. **Other points:** bar. **Address:** 13, rue de l'Obeau.
MME ELIANE DUQUESNOY
**Telephone:** 20.61.83.10
⊗ ⅋ Map 1

## CATEAU (LE), Nord, 59360

### SARL L'ESCALE, *the main road between Charleville Mézières and Cambrai*

**Menu:** 40 to 55 Frs. **Restaurant:** Breakfast served from 6:00am. Closed Sundays. **Specialities:** regional menu, home cooking. **Other points:** bar, open to non-residents, pets welcome – check for details, car park. **Address:** 65, route de Bazuel.
MME ELISABETH MASSON
**Telephone:** 27.84.25.50
⊗ ⅋ Map 1

## CHAMBLY, Oise, 60230

### LE RELAIS DE CHAMBLY, *RN 1, the main road between Paris and Beauvais via Beaumont en Oise*

**Menu:** 65 Frs (wine and coffee included).
**Accommodation:** 130 Frs to 280 Frs. **Restaurant:** Breakfast served from 7:00am. Lunch served from midday until 3:30pm. Dinner served from 7:00pm until 8:30pm. Closed Saturdays and from 20 December to 20 January. **Specialities:** home cooking. **Hotel:** 15 beds; with bath, private WC, television. **Other points:** bar, open to non-residents, children welcome, lounge area, terraces, pets welcome – check for details, car park, modern decor. **Address:** 660, avenue Aristide Briand.
MME FRANÇOISE VIOLETTE
**Telephone:** 34.70.50.37
⊗ ⅋ ⌂ Map 2

## CHAULNES, Somme, 80320

### L'ESCALE DES ROUTIERS, *RN 17, exit Roye or Péronne*

**Menu:** 55 to 65 Frs. **Restaurant:** Breakfast served from 5:30am. Lunch served from 11:30am until 2:30pm. Dinner served from 7:00pm until 10:00pm. Closed Saturdays and in August. **Specialities:** home cooking. **Other points:** bar, open to non-residents, pets welcome – check for details, car park, traditional decor. **Address:** Route Nationale 17, Fresnes.
Mr JEAN-CLAUDE GUERQUIN
**Telephone:** 22.85.28.50
⊗ ⅋ Map 2

## CHAUNY, Aisne, 02300

### LE CASAMANCE, *RN 83, between Noyon and Soissons*

**Languages spoken:** English. **Menu:** 55 Frs (wine included). **Accommodation:** 90 to 110 Frs. **Restaurant:** Breakfast served from 7:00am. Lunch served from 11:30am until 2:30pm. Dinner served from 6:30pm until 9:30pm. Closed Sundays. **Specialities:** home cooking. **Hotel:** 4 beds; 3 single rooms, 1 double room. **Other points:** bar, open to non-residents, à la carte menu, children welcome, pets welcome – check for details, car park, traditional decor. **Address:** 92, rue de la Chaussée.
MME CATHERINE GAUBEN
**Telephone:** 23.52.16.33
⊗ ⅋ Map 2

### LE VAN GOGH

**Languages spoken:** English. **Menu:** 55 to 120 Frs. **Restaurant:** Breakfast served from 8:30am. Lunch served from midday until 2:00pm. Dinner served from 7:00pm until 8:30pm. Closed Sundays. **Specialities:** home cooking. **Other points:** bar, open to non-residents, pets welcome – check for details, car park, traditional decor. **Address:** 37, rue A. Ternynck.
MME CHRISTINE HAUDIQUET
**Telephone:** 23.39.40.32
⊗ ⅋ Map 2

## CHEPY, Somme, 80210

### RELAIS SAS BOIRE, *RD 29, between le Tréport and Oisemont*

**Menu:** 55 to 120 Frs. **Restaurant:** Breakfast served from 6:00am. Lunch served from 11:30am until 2:30pm. Dinner served from 7:00pm until 10:00pm. Closed Tuesdays and in August. **Specialities:** Confits, garbure, regional food, home cooking. **Other points:** bar, open to non-residents, à la carte menu, children welcome, terraces, pets welcome – check for details, car park, traditional decor. **Address:** 40, route de Oisemont, la Croix de Pierre.
MR JACKY SUEUR
**Telephone:** 22.26.26.67
⊗ ⅋ Map 2

## COLEMBERT, Pas-de-Calais, 62142

### CAFE DU COMMERCE
**Menu:** 56 Frs. **Accommodation:** 130 to 130 Frs.
**Restaurant:** Breakfast served from 6:00am. Closed
Saturdays. **Hotel:** 9 beds. **Other points:** bar, car park.
**Address:** Route Nationale.
MME MARIE PIERRE
**Telephone:** 21.33.31.11
⊗ ℙ 🏠 Map 1

## COMINES, Nord, 59560

### RESTAURANT DE LA GARE, Lille
**Languages spoken:** German, English, Spanish, Italian.
**Menu:** 38 to 105 Frs. **Accommodation:** 132 Frs
(breakfast included). **Restaurant:** Breakfast served from
10:00am. Lunch served from midday until 2:30pm.
Dinner served from 6:00pm until midnight. Closed
Sundays. **Specialities:** regional menu, home cooking.
**Hotel:** 10 beds; 10 single rooms with shower, private
WC. **Other points:** bar, open to non-residents, children
welcome, traditional decor. **Address:** 81–3, avenue du
Général Leclerc.
MME YVETTE DESIÉTER
**Telephone:** 20.39.45.78
⊗ ℙ 🏠 ☆ Map 1

## COMPIEGNE, Oise, 60200

### BAR DE LA MARINE
**Restaurant:** Breakfast served from 6:00am. Closed
Saturdays. **Other points:** bar. **Address:** 17, rue de
l'Estacade.
MR AIMÉ LOGGHE
**Telephone:** 44.40.26.37
⊗ ℙ Map 2

## COUCY LE CHATEAU, Aisne, 02380

### LE LION ROUGE, RN 1, between Soissons and Saint Quentin
**Languages spoken:** German and English. **Menu:** 52 to
174 Frs. **Accommodation:** 86 to 92 Frs. **Restaurant:**
Breakfast served from 7:00am. Lunch served from midday
until 2:30pm. Dinner served from 7:00pm until 9:30pm.
**Specialities:** regional menu, home cooking. **Hotel:** 13
beds; 3 single rooms, 10 double rooms. **Other points:** bar,
open to non-residents, à la carte menu, children welcome,
lounge area, terraces, pets welcome – check for details, car
park, traditional decor. **Address:** 62, avenue Altenkessel.
Mr Patrick Clavet
**Telephone:** 23.52.70.13
⊗ ℙ 🏠 Map 2

## CREVECOEUR LE GRAND, Oise, 60360

### LE REFLAX, RN 30 and RD 93
**Restaurant:** Closed Sundays. **Other points:** bar.
**Address:** 12, rue de Breteuil.
MR MICHEL DUBOIS
**Telephone:** 44.46.87.65
⊗ ℙ Map 2

## CROIX, Nord, 59170

### LE RELAIS CHEZ ALIAN, RD 14, motorway Lille–Tourcoing, near station for Croix-Wasquehal
**Languages spoken:** Spanish. **Menu:** 35 to 60 Frs.
**Accommodation:** 100 to 150 Frs. **Restaurant:**
Breakfast served from 4:00am. Lunch served from
midday until 3:00pm. Dinner served from 7:00pm until
10:00pm. Closed Sundays. **Specialities:** home cooking.
**Hotel:** 9 beds; 5 single rooms, 4 double rooms with
shower, private WC, television, telephone. **Other
points:** bar, open to non-residents, à la carte menu,
children welcome, lounge area, car park, traditional
decor. **Address:** 53, avenue Georges Hannart.
MME GEORGETTE CAUFRIEZ
**Telephone:** 20.72.59.08
⊗ ℙ 🏠 Map 1

## CUVILLY, Oise, 60490

### LA CAMPAGNARDE, RN 17, the main road between Paris and Lille
**Languages spoken:** English. **Menu:** 47 to 60 Frs.
**Accommodation:** 90 to 150 Frs. **Restaurant:**
Breakfast served from 5:00am. Lunch served from
11:00am until 3:00pm. Dinner served from 7:00pm
until 10:30pm. Closed Sundays. **Specialities:** home
cooking. **Hotel:** 9 beds; 9 double rooms with shower,
bath, private WC. **Other points:** bar, open to non-
residents, children welcome, pets welcome – check for
details, car park, modern decor. **Address:** 5, route des
Flandres.
DANIEL ET ANNE-MARYSE HILLION NICOL
**Telephone:** 44.85.00.30
⊗ ℙ 🏠 Map 2

## DESVRES, Pas-de-Calais, 62240

### LE RELAIS DE LA BELL CROIX, RN 342, between Boulogne en Mer and Longfossé
**Languages spoken:** English. **Menu:** 45 to 70 Frs.
**Accommodation:** 60 Frs (per person). **Restaurant:**
Breakfast served from 7:00am. Closed Sundays.
**Specialities:** regional menu. **Hotel:** 5 beds; 2 single
rooms, 3 double rooms with shower. **Other points:** bar,
open to non-residents, à la carte menu, children
welcome, terraces, pets welcome – check for details, car
park, modern decor. **Address:** 1, rue du Bidet.
MR JEAN-CLAUDE GRUMELART
**Telephone:** 21.91.65.81, 21.87.46.93
⊗ ℙ 🏠 Map 1

## DIZY LE GROS, Aisne, 02340

### LES ROUTIERS FRANCE EUROPE, RD 366, Reims/Vervins/Belgique

**Menu:** 54 Frs. **Restaurant:** Breakfast served from 6:00am. Lunch served from 11:00am until 2:00pm. Dinner served from 7:00pm until 9:00pm. Closed Saturdays and from 15 to 30 August. **Other points:** bar, open to non-residents, pets welcome – check for details, car park, traditional decor. **Address:** 78, Grande Rue.
MR JEAN-CLAUDE DUBOIS
**Telephone:** 23.21.23.15
⊗ ♈ Map 2

## DOUAI, Nord, 59500

### A L'EPI D'OR, RN 17 and 34

**Restaurant:** Breakfast served from 4:30am. Dinner served from midday until midnight. Closed Saturdays from 3pm and Sundays. **Hotel:** 7 beds. **Other points:** bar. **Address:** 38, Faubourg d'Aras, Lambres.
MR MICHEL BARJOU
**Telephone:** 27.87.04.56
⊗ ♈ ⌂ Map 1

## DREUIL LES AMIENS, Somme, 80730

### CHEZ JEAN-MARIE ET CHRISTIANE, RN 235, Pic Quigny

**Menu:** 52 Frs. **Restaurant:** Breakfast served from 6:30am. Lunch served from 11:45am until 2:00pm. Dinner served from 7:30pm until 9:00pm. Closed Sundays and in August. **Specialities:** home cooking. **Other points:** pets welcome – check for details, car park, traditional decor. **Address:** 285, avenue Pasteur.
MR JEAN-MARIE DUMEIGE
Telephone: 22.54.10.72
⊗ Map 2

## ECLAIBES, Nord, 59330

### LE ROBINSON, RN 2

**Other points:** bar. **Address:** Route Nationale 2.
MR EL HADI MANSEUR
**Telephone:** 27.57.81.26
⊗ ♈ Map 1

## ESTREES DENIECOURT, Somme, 80200

### AUBERGE DE LA MAIRIE, RN 336, exit A 1 Péronne, on the right, towards Amiens

**Menu:** 55 to 65 Frs. **Accommodation:** 100 to 225 Frs. **Restaurant:** Dinner served from 7:00pm until 11:00pm. Closed Saturdays and in August. **Specialities:** home cooking. **Hotel:** 7 beds; 5 single rooms, 2 double rooms with shower, private WC. **Other points:** bar, open to non-residents, à la carte menu, lounge area, terraces, pets

welcome – check for details, car park. **Address:** Route Nationale 336.
MME CLAUDETTE DEMUYNCK DEHENRY
**Telephone:** 22.85.20.16
⊗ ♈ ⌂ Map 2

## ESTREES MONS, Somme, 80200

### A LA POMME D'API, RN 29, exit Péronne, towards Saint Quentin

**Menu:** 60 Frs. **Restaurant:** Breakfast served from 6:30am. Lunch served from 11:30am until 2:30pm. Dinner served from 7:00pm until 9:30pm. Closed Sundays and in August. **Specialities:** home cooking. **Other points:** bar, open to non-residents, children welcome, lounge area, terraces, pets welcome – check for details, car park, traditional decor. **Address:** 28 Route Nationale.
MR ALBERT GRAS
**Telephone:** 22.85.60.04
⊗ ♈ Map 2

## FLAVY LE MARTEL, Aisne, 02520

### LE RELAIS DES ROUTIERS

**Restaurant:** Dinner served from midday until 9:00pm. Closed Saturdays. **Specialities:** home cooking. **Other points:** bar. **Address:** 17, rue André Brulé.
MR JEAN-PAUL BRIÈRE
**Telephone:** 23.52.51.31
⊗ ♈ Map 2

## FLERS EN ESCREBIEUX, Nord, 59128

### AU BON CASSE CROUTE, RN 43

**Menu:** 55 Frs. **Restaurant:** Breakfast served from 6:00am. Closed Saturdays. **Specialities:** home cooking. **Other points:** car park, traditional decor. **Address:** 59, Route Nationale 43.
MR RAYMOND DUFOUR
**Telephone:** 27.88.69.41
⊗ Map 1

## FLIXECOURT, Somme, 80420

### LES FLONFLONS DU BAL, RN 1, between Amiens and Abbeville

**Languages spoken:** English. **Menu:** 45 to 100 Frs. **Restaurant:** Breakfast served from 6:00am. **Specialities:** regional menu, home cooking. **Other points:** bar, à la carte menu, children welcome, terraces, pets welcome – check for details, car park, traditional decor. **Address:** 16, rue Georges Clémenceau.
MR JEAN-MARC ROHAUT
**Telephone:** 22.51.36.34
⊗ ♈ Map 2

## FONTAINE LAVAGANNE, Oise, 60690

*LE BIENVENU, RN 901, between Beauvais and Abbeville*

**Menu:** 60 Frs (coffee included). **Restaurant:** Breakfast served from 8:00am. Closed Wednesdays. **Specialities:** home cooking. **Other points:** bar, open to non-residents, à la carte menu, children welcome, terraces, pets welcome – check for details, car park, modern decor. **Address:** Route Nationale 901.
MR MAURICE LELONG
**Telephone:** 44.46.25.84
⊗ ☙ Map 2

## FORMERIE, Oise, 60220

*CAFE DE LA PAIX, between Beauvais and Forges les Eaux*

**Menu:** 50 to 65 Frs. **Accommodation:** 50 Frs. **Restaurant:** Breakfast served from 4:30am. Lunch served from 11:30am until 3:00pm. Dinner served from 7:30pm until 9:00pm. Closed Sundays. **Specialities:** home cooking. **Hotel:** 5 beds; with shower, bath. **Other points:** bar, open to non-residents, children welcome, pets welcome – check for details. **Address:** 8, rue Dornat.
MME FRANÇOISE MERLIN
**Telephone:** 44.46.17.08
⊗ ☙ 🏠 ☆ Map 2

## FRESNES EN TARDENOIS, Aisne, 02130

*RELAIS DU TARDENOIS, A 4, accessible from either side via pedestrian footbridge*

**Languages spoken:** German and English. **Restaurant:** Breakfast served from 6:30am. **Specialities:** regional menu. **Other points:** children welcome, lounge area, terraces, pets welcome – check for details, car park. **Address:** Aire de Service du Tardenois, dans les deux sens.
**Telephone:** 23.70.23.16
⊗ Map 2

## FROISSY, Oise, 60480

*LE BEAUVAIS BRETEUIL, RN 1, between Beauvais (10km) and Amiens*

**Menu:** 52 to 95 Frs. **Accommodation:** 100 to 150 Frs. **Restaurant:** Breakfast served from 7:00am. Lunch served from midday until 3:00pm. Dinner served from 7:00pm until 10:00pm. Closed Saturdays, 4 weeks in August and 15 days at Christmas. **Specialities:** home cooking. **Hotel:** 5 beds; 3 single rooms, 2 double rooms. **Other points:** bar, open to non-residents, à la carte menu, children welcome, pets welcome – check for details, car park, traditional decor. **Address:** 5, rue du Bois Saint Martin, Abbeville Saint Lucien.
MR RAYMOND JULEN
**Telephone:** 44.79.13.09
⊗ ☙ 🏠 Map 2

## GAVRELLE, Pas-de-Calais, 62580

*RELAIS DE LA CHAUMIERE, RN 50, A 1 exit Fresnes-les-Montauban*

**Languages spoken:** English. **Menu:** 45 Frs. **Restaurant:** Breakfast served from 7:00am. **Specialities:** home cooking. **Other points:** bar, open to non-residents, à la carte menu, pets welcome – check for details, car park, traditional decor. **Address:** 21 Route Nationale.
MR FRANCK COURCELLE
**Telephone:** 21.58.16.99
⊗ ☙ Map 1

## GHYVELDE, Nord, 59254

*LE SAINT SEBASTIEN, RN 947, on the right before the Belgian border*

**Languages spoken:** Dutch. **Menu:** 45 to 180 Frs. **Restaurant:** Breakfast served from 7:30am. Lunch served from 11:00am until 4:00pm. Closed Tuesdays and in August. **Specialities:** Flamandes, regional food, home cooking. **Other points:** bar, open to non-residents, à la carte menu, children welcome, pets welcome – check for details, car park. **Address:** 161, rue Nationale.
MME EDITH MARIE-RUBBEN
**Telephone:** 28.26.61.95
⊗ ☙ Map 1

## HALLENNES LEZ HAUBOURDIN, Nord, 59320

*AUX DE LA ROUTE, RN 41, exit la Bassé*

**Menu:** 60 Frs. **Restaurant:** Breakfast served from 6:00am. Lunch served from 11:00am until 3:30pm. Dinner served from 7:00pm until 10:00pm. Closed Saturdays and in August. **Specialities:** home cooking. **Other points:** children welcome. **Address:** 329, rue du Général de Gaulle.
MR DOMINIQUE DELECLUSE
**Telephone:** 20.07.14.24
⊗ Map 1

## HALLUIN, Nord, 59250

*Au Routier, RD 945, in the industrial zone of le Col Bras*

**Languages spoken:** Dutch, Polish and Yugoslavian. **Menu:** 61,20 Frs. **Restaurant:** Breakfast served from 6:30am. Lunch served from 11:30am until 2:00pm. Dinner served from 7:00pm until 9:00pm. Closed Saturdays and in August. **Specialities:** home cooking. **Other points:** bar, open to non-residents, pets welcome – check for details, car park, traditional decor. **Address:** 196, rue de la Lys.
MR RICHARD KOZIOR
**Telephone:** 20.23.88.20
⊗ ☙ Map 1

## HIRSON, Aisne, 02500

### JUPITER, RN 43, at the exit of Hirson, towards Paris or Lille

**Places of interest:** Fontainebleau (23km), Château-Landon (11km), Nemours (9km), musée de la préhistoire, forêt de Poligny. Parc des Oiseaux à Villars, musées, caves de beaujolais, Roche de Solutré, Pérouge (village médiéval). **Languages spoken:** English and Italian. **Menu:** 53 Frs. **Restaurant:** Breakfast served from 6:00am. Lunch served from 11:30am until 5:00pm. Dinner served from 5:00pm until 10:00pm. Closed Sundays and in August. **Specialities:** home cooking. **Other points:** bar, open to non-residents, à la carte menu, children welcome, pets welcome – check for details, car park, modern decor. **Address:** 151, avenue Joffre.
MR GUILIO CORSINI
**Telephone:** 23.58.14.03
⊗ ♟ Map 2

## HOUSSOYE (LA), Oise, 60390

### LE CHEVAL BLANC, RN 181

**Languages spoken:** English. **Menu:** 60 Frs. **Accommodation:** 100 Frs. **Restaurant:** Lunch served from 11:30am until 2:30pm. Dinner served from 7:00pm until 9:30pm. Closed Saturdays. **Hotel:** 3 beds. **Other points:** bar, pets welcome – check for details, car park, traditional decor. **Address:** 5, route de Gisors.
MME LILIANE HEYTHUYZEN
**Telephone:** 44.81.40.40
⊗ ♟ Map 2

## HOUSSOYE (LA), Somme, 80800

### LE RELAIS DE LA HOUSSOYE, RD 929, between Amiens and Albert

**Menu:** 56 Frs. **Restaurant:** Breakfast served from 6:45am. **Specialities:** home cooking. **Other points:** bar, children welcome, terraces, pets welcome – check for details, car park, traditional decor. **Address:** 300, Route Nationale.
MME CHRISTINE SACHOT
**Telephone:** 22.40.57.29
⊗ ♟ Map 2

## HUMIERES, Pas-de-Calais, 62130

### LES ROUTIERS, RN 39

**Menu:** 48 Frs. **Restaurant:** Breakfast served from 5:00am. Lunch served from midday until 2:00pm. Dinner served from 7:00pm until 9:00pm. Closed Sundays and beginning of September. **Specialities:** home cooking. **Other points:** bar, open to non-residents, pets welcome – check for details, car park, modern decor. **Address:** Route Nationale 39.
MME BERTHE TERNISIEN
**Telephone:** 21.41.85.77
⊗ ♟ Map 1

## HUPPY, Somme, 80140

### LE RELAIS DU BEL AIR, RN 28, between Rouen and Abbeville

**Menu:** 55 to 85 Frs. **Restaurant:** Breakfast served from 6:00am. Closed Sundays. **Specialities:** home cooking. **Other points:** bar, à la carte menu, children welcome, terraces, pets welcome – check for details, car park. **Address:** 42, Route Nationale.
MME NADINE MARTEL
**Telephone:** 22.28.47.75
⊗ ♟ Map 2

## LAVERSINES, Oise, 60510

### LE RELAIS ROUTIER, RN 31, between Reims and Rouen

**Menu:** 58 Frs (wine included) to 70 Frs. **Restaurant:** Breakfast served from 6:00am. Lunch served from 11:30am until 2:30pm. Dinner served from 7:30pm until 9:30pm. Closed Saturdays, the 2nd fortnight of August and 1 week at Christmas. **Specialities:** home cooking. **Other points:** bar, open to non-residents, pets welcome – check for details, car park, traditional decor. **Address:** 90, rue Saint Germain.
MR MARCEAU FORESTIER
**Telephone:** 44.07.75.80
⊗ ♟ Map 2

## LEVIGNEN, Oise, 60800

### RELAIS DE LA IL, RN 2, the main road between Paris and Soisson

**Menu:** 53 to 70 Frs. **Restaurant:** Breakfast served from 5:00am. Lunch served from 11:30am until 3:00pm. Dinner served from 7:00pm until 10:30pm. **Specialities:** home cooking. **Other points:** bar, open to non-residents, à la carte menu, pets welcome – check for details, car park. **Address:** Route Nationale 2.
MR JACQUES CARRIER
**Telephone:** 44.94.21.01
⊗ ♟ Map 2

## LIEVIN, Pas-de-Calais, 62800

### LE ZOLA, A 26

**Menu:** 55 Frs. **Restaurant:** Breakfast served from 6:00am. Lunch served from midday until 3:00pm. Dinner served from 7:00pm until 10:00pm. Closed Sundays and in August. **Specialities:** home cooking. **Other points:** bar, open to non-residents, à la carte menu, children welcome, traditional decor. **Address:** 215, rue Emile Zola.
MR ANDRÉ CLÉMENT
**Telephone:** 21.29.29.72
⊗ ♟ Map 1

## LONGUEAU, Somme, 80330

### LE RELAIS DE L'HOTEL DE VILLE, RN 35

**Languages spoken:** English and Arabic. **Restaurant:** Closed Sundays. **Hotel:** 10 beds. **Other points:** bar. **Address:** 105, avenue Henri Barbusse.
MR KONIDER BELLAREDJ
**Telephone:** 22.46.16.14
⊗ ♉ 🏠 Map 2

## LUMBRES, Pas-de-Calais, 62380

### HOTEL MODERNE, opposite the station

**Restaurant:** Dinner served from midday until 9:00pm. Closed Sundays and August. **Hotel:** 6 beds. **Other points:** bar. **Address:** 18, rue François Cousin.
MR PIERRE FICHAUX
**Telephone:** 21.39.62.87
⊗ ♉ 🏠 Map 1

## MARAIS (AUX), Oise, 60000

### AU GRAND R, RN 981, between Mantes and Gisors

**Menu:** 54 Frs. **Restaurant:** Breakfast served from 5:30am. Dinner served from midday until 9:30pm. Closed Sundays and in August. **Specialities:** home cooking. **Other points:** bar, open to non-residents, children welcome, car park, traditional decor. **Address:** 12, route de Gisors.
MR MARCEL BOUTOILLE
**Telephone:** 44.48.18.66
⊗ ♉ Map 2

## MARCHELEPOT, Somme, 80200

### RESTAURANT DE PARC, RN 17, between Roye and Péronne

**Menu:** 55 Frs. **Restaurant:** Closed Saturdays. **Specialities:** home cooking. **Other points:** bar, open to non-residents, children welcome, pets welcome – check for details, car park, traditional decor. **Address:** Route Nationale 17.
EMILE ET ANGELIQUE JOVANOVIC
**Telephone:** 22.83.90.85
⊗ ♉ Map 2

## MARLES LES MINES, Pas-de-Calais, 62540

### AU 74, between Lens and Lillers via Bruay la Buissière

**Menu:** 59 Frs. **Restaurant:** Breakfast served from 7:00am. Closed Saturdays, Sundays and from 15 to 30 August. **Specialities:** home cooking. **Other points:** bar, open to non-residents, pets welcome – check for details, car park. **Address:** 74, rue Jean Jaurès.
MME NICHOLE COINTRE
**Telephone:** 21.65.53.71
⊗ ♉ Map 1

## MAROLLES BOURNEVILLE, Oise, 60890

### LES ROUTIERS, RD 936

**Menu:** 60 to 75 Frs. **Restaurant:** Breakfast served from 7:00am. **Specialities:** home cooking. **Other points:** bar, open to non-residents, pets welcome – check for details, traditional decor. **Address:** 7, rue de Meaux.
MME HUGUETTE PICARD-MATHIAS
**Telephone:** 23.96.72.11
⊗ ♉ Map 2

## MARQUISE, Pas-de-Calais, 62250

### A LA DESCENTE DES VOYAGEURS, between Marquise and Guines

**Menu:** 58 to 120 Frs. **Accommodation:** 100 Frs (half board 160 Frs – full board 190 Frs). **Restaurant:** Breakfast served from 7:00am. Lunch served from midday until 2:00pm. Dinner served from 7:00pm until 8:30pm. **Specialities:** home cooking. **Hotel:** 4 beds; 3 single rooms, 1 double room. **Other points:** bar, open to non-residents, modern decor. **Address:** 17, rue du 8 mai.
MME NELLY BRISBOUT
**Telephone:** 21.92.85.55
⊗ ♉ Map 1

## MAUBEUGE, Nord, 59600

### LE BERLOIZ, RN 2

**Menu:** 55 Frs. **Restaurant:** Breakfast served from 7:15am. Closed Sundays. **Other points:** bar, car park. **Address:** 27, avenue de la Gare.
MR PHILIPPE CAPPELIEZ
**Telephone:** 27.64.68.79
⊗ ♉ Map 1

## MAZINGARBE, Pas-de-Calais, 62670

### AU RELAIS DES ROUTIERS, RN 43, between Lens and Béthune

**Languages spoken:** German and Polish. **Menu:** 55 Frs. **Restaurant:** Breakfast served from 8:00am. Lunch served from midday until 2:30pm. Closed Sundays and in August. **Specialities:** home cooking. **Other points:** bar, children welcome, lounge area, car park, modern decor. **Address:** 85, Route Nationale 43.
MME GENEVIÉVE MARCINKOWSKI
**Telephone:** 21.72.00.09
⊗ ♉ Map 1

## MEZY MOULINS, Aisne, 02650

### RESTAURANT DE CHEVAL NOIR, RN 3, between Dormans and Château-Thierry

**Menu:** 55 to 90 Frs. **Restaurant:** Breakfast served from 7:00am. Lunch served from midday until 2:30pm. Dinner served from 7:00pm until 10:30pm. Closed Sundays and in September. **Other points:** bar, open to

non-residents, à la carte menu, children welcome, terraces, pets welcome – check for details, car park, traditional decor. **Address:** 25, avenue de Champagne.
MME MARTINE CARON
**Telephone:** 23.71.91.30
⊗ 🍸 Map 2

## MONTDIDIER, Somme, 80500

### *LE RELAIS DU MOUTON D'OR*

**Restaurant:** Breakfast served from 7:00am. Lunch served from midday until 2:00pm. Dinner served from 7:00pm until 9:00pm. Closed Sundays and in August. **Specialities:** home cooking. **Hotel:** 5 beds. **Other points:** bar, open to non-residents, pets welcome – check for details, car park, modern decor. **Address:** 10, boulevard Debeney.
MR CHRISTIAN PARMENTIER
**Telephone:** 22.78.03.43
⊗ 🍸 Ⓗ Map 2

## NOYON, Oise, 60400

### *LE VESUVE*

**Menu:** 55 to 90 Frs. **Restaurant:** Closed Saturdays. **Other points:** bar, à la carte menu, car park. **Address:** 1, avenue Jean Jaurès.
CORINNE ET PHILIPPE DELET
**Telephone:** 44.44.19.56
⊗ 🍸 Map 2

## OMIECOURT PAR CHAULNES, Somme, 80320

### *AU BON ACCUEIL, RN 17, between Péronne and Roye*

**Languages spoken:** Arabic. **Menu:** 56 to 85 Frs. **Restaurant:** Open 24 hours. **Specialities:** regional menu, home cooking. **Other points:** bar, open to non-residents, children welcome, terraces, pets welcome – check for details, car park. **Address:** Route Nationale 17.
MR ALLAOUA BETROUNE
**Telephone:** 22.85.42.49
⊗ 🍸 Map 2

## OVILLERS LA BOISSELLE, Somme, 80300

### *LE POPPY, RD 329, between Bapaume and Albert*

**Menu:** 50 to 95 Frs. **Restaurant:** Breakfast served from 6:30am. Lunch served from midday until 3:00pm. Dinner served from 7:00pm until 10:30pm. Closed Saturdays and in August. **Specialities:** home cooking. **Other points:** bar, open to non-residents, children welcome, terraces, car park, traditional decor. **Address:** 4, route de Bapaume.
MR GEORGES VANDENBULKE
**Telephone:** 22.75.45.45. **Fax:** 22.74.75.65
⊗ 🍸 Map 2

## PERONNE, Somme, 80200

### *LA CHAPELETTE – CHEZ CLAUDE ET NICHOLE, RN 17, between Roye and Péronne*

**Menu:** 55 Frs. **Restaurant:** Breakfast served from 7:00am. Closed Saturdays. **Specialities:** home cooking. **Other points:** bar, open to non-residents, à la carte menu, children welcome, pets welcome – check for details, car park, traditional decor. **Address:** 61, route de Paris.
CLAUDE ET NICOLE CHARPENTIER
**Telephone:** 22.84.10.82
⊗ 🍸 Map 2

## PERONNE ASSEVILLERS, Somme, 80200

### *L'ARCHE D'ASSEVILLERS, A 1*

**Restaurant:** Open 24 hours. **Specialities:** home cooking. **Other points:** open to non-residents, children welcome, terraces, pets welcome – check for details, car park. **Address:** A 1 Aire d'Assevillers Ouest, sens Lille/Paris.
**Telephone:** 22.85.20.35. **Fax:** 22.85.24.11
⊗ Map 2

## PONT REMY, Somme, 80580

### *LE CONTINENTAL*

**Restaurant:** Closed in August. **Other points:** bar. **Address:** 9, rue Robert Bordeux.
MME GINETTE THÉRASSE
**Telephone:** 22.27.12.89
⊗ 🍸 Map 2

## POULAINVILLE, Somme, 80260

### *LE RELAIS DE POULAINVILLE, RN 25, between Amiens and Arras*

**Menu:** 58 Frs. **Restaurant:** Breakfast served from 6:00am. Lunch served from midday until 3:00pm. Dinner served from 7:00pm until 10:00pm. Closed Saturdays and in August. **Specialities:** home cooking. **Other points:** bar, open to non-residents, children welcome, pets welcome – check for details, car park. **Address:** 2, Route Nationale.
MR JEAN-PIERRE HENNEBERT
**Telephone:** 22.43.05.00
⊗ 🍸 Map 2

## QUAEDYPRE, Nord, 59380

### *L'GITANT, CD 916, the main road between Lille and Dunkerque, exit no 16 Cassel*

**Menu:** 35 to 160 Frs. **Restaurant:** Breakfast served from 7:00am. Lunch served from midday until 3:00pm. Dinner served from 7:00pm until 10:00pm. Closed Saturdays and the 1st fortnight of August. **Specialities:**

regional menu, home cooking. **Other points:** bar, open
to non-residents, children welcome, pets welcome –
check for details, car park, traditional decor. **Address:**
Chemin Départemental 916.
MR JOSÉ LERMYTTE
**Telephone:** 28.68.69.87
⊗ ♀ Map 1

## RENESCURE, Nord, 59173

### LA CLE DES CHAMPS, RN 42, between Saint Omer and Hazebrouck

**Menu:** 40 Frs. **Restaurant:** Lunch served from 11:30am
until 2:00pm. Closed Saturdays. **Specialities:** home
cooking. **Other points:** pets welcome – check for
details, car park, traditional decor. **Address:** Lieu dit 'La
Clé des Champs', 89, route de Saint Omer.
MME MARLÈNE DEMAN-LAMIAUX
**Telephone:** 28.49.81.12
⊗ Map 1

## ROLLOT, Somme, 80500

### LE RELAIS DE LA MADELEINE, RD 935, between Compiègne and Amiens

**Menu:** 48 to 70 Frs. **Restaurant:** Breakfast served from
8:00am. Closed Mondays and in August. **Specialities:**
home cooking. **Other points:** bar, à la carte menu,
children welcome, terraces, pets welcome – check for
details, car park, traditional decor. **Address:** 88, rue de
la Madeleine.
MME CAROLINE PRIOU
**Telephone:** 22.78.02.81
⊗ ♀ Map 2

## ROUBAIX, Nord, 59100

### LE CALAIS

**Languages spoken:** German, English and Dutch. **Menu:**
50 Frs (wine included). **Restaurant:** Breakfast served
from 6:00am. Lunch served from midday until 2:30pm.
Dinner served from 7:30pm until 10:30pm. Closed
Saturdays, in August and end of December. **Specialities:**
home cooking. **Other points:** bar, open to non-residents,
pets welcome – check for details, car park, modern
decor. **Address:** 2, quai de Calais.
MME JOSETTE VAZE
**Telephone:** 20.26.00.35
⊗ ♀ Map 1

## SAINT AUBIN EN BRAY, Oise, 60650

### RELAIS DES FONTAINETTES

**Menu:** 55 Frs. **Accommodation:** 85 Frs. **Restaurant:**
Breakfast served from 4:30am. Lunch served from
11:30am until 2:00pm. Dinner served from 7:30pm until
9:00pm. Closed Sundays. **Hotel:** 6 beds. **Other points:**
bar, car park, modern decor. **Address:** Lieu dit
'Fontainettes', 20, rue des Fontainettes.

MR GÉRARD PARPAILLON
**Telephone:** 44.80.50.26
⊗ ♀ ⌂ Map 2

## SAINT INGLEVERT, Pas-de-Calais, 62250

### LA MURAILLE, RN 1, bypass for Calais/Boulogne

**Languages spoken:** a little English. **Menu:** 62 Frs
(drink and coffee included). **Restaurant:** Breakfast
served from 6:30am. Lunch served from 11:45am until
2:30pm. Dinner served from 7:30pm until 9:00pm.
Closed Saturdays and 2 to 3 weeks during August.
**Specialities:** home cooking. **Other points:** open to non-
residents, pets welcome – check for details, car park,
modern decor. **Address:** Route Nationale 1.
MME JOCELYNE SALMON
**Telephone:** 21.33.75.44
⊗ Map 1

## SAINT LEU, Oise, 60850

### RELAIS DE SAINT LEU, RN 31, between Beauvais and Gournay

**Languages spoken:** English. **Menu:** 50 to 75 Frs.
**Restaurant:** Breakfast served from 6:30am. Closed
Sundays. **Specialities:** home cooking. **Other points:**
bar, open to non-residents, children welcome, terraces,
pets welcome – check for details, car park, traditional
decor. **Address:** 20, rue de Saint Leu, Cuigy en Bray.
MR JEAN-CLAUDE LAUDE
**Telephone:** 44.82.53.17
⊗ ♀ Map 2

## SAINT OMER, Pas-de-Calais, 62500

### LE RENAISSANCE, RN 43

**Languages spoken:** English and a little German. **Menu:**
50 Frs. **Accommodation:** 105 to 120 Frs. **Restaurant:**
Breakfast served from 6:30am. Lunch served from
midday until 2:00pm. Dinner served from 8:00pm until
9:00pm. Closed Saturdays and 3 weeks in August.
**Specialities:** regional menu, home cooking. **Hotel:** 18
beds; 8 single rooms, 10 double rooms. **Other points:**
bar, open to non-residents, à la carte menu, pets
welcome – check for details, car park, traditional decor.
**Address:** 10, place du 11 Novembre.
VANYPER SARL
**Telephone:** 21.38.26.55
⊗ ♀ ⌂ Map 1

## SAINT PAUL, Oise, 60650

### LE RELAIS SAINT PAUL, RN 31, Beauvais–Rouen–le Havre

**Menu:** 55 Frs. **Restaurant:** Breakfast served from
5:00am. **Specialities:** home cooking. **Other points:** bar,
open to non-residents, children welcome, terraces, pets
welcome – check for details, car park, traditional decor.

**Address:** Route Nationale 31.
MME JEANNE-LISE FAURE
**Telephone:** 44.82.20.19
⊗ ♉ Map 2

## SAINT QUENTIN, Aisne, 02100

### LE VASCO DE GAMA
**Places of interest:** Château de Montrond. **Languages spoken:** German, English and Dutch. **Menu:** 50 Frs. **Accommodation:** 85 to 98 Frs. **Restaurant:** Breakfast served from 6:00am. Lunch served from midday until 3:00pm. Dinner served from 7:00pm until 10:00pm. **Specialities:** regional menu, home cooking. **Hotel:** 11 beds; 10 single rooms, 1 double room with shower, television, telephone. **Other points:** bar, open to non-residents, children welcome, car park, modern decor. **Address:** 30, place Cordier.
MME ALICE MARIÉ
**Telephone:** 23.68.22.84
⊗ ♉ 🏠 Map 2

## SAINT QUENTIN LAMOTTE,
Somme, 80880

### A GROS JACQUES, RD 925, between Eu and Abbeville
**Menu:** 52 to 62 Frs. **Restaurant:** Breakfast served from 7:00am. Lunch served from midday until 2:30pm. Closed Sundays and from 20 August to 5 September. **Specialities:** home cooking. **Other points:** bar, open to non-residents, lounge area, terraces, pets welcome – check for details, modern decor. **Address:** Route Départemental 925.
MME JEANINE DECAYEUX
**Telephone:** 22.60.41.14
⊗ ♉ Map 2

## SAINT RIQUIER, Somme, 80135

### LE CENTULOIS
**Restaurant:** Closed Wednesdays. **Other points:** bar. **Address:** 70, rue du Général de Gaulle.
MME LILI COLINET
**Telephone:** 22.28.88.15
⊗ ♉ Map 2

## SALOUEL, Somme, 80480

### AUBERGE DU TROU NORMAND, RN 29
**Languages spoken:** German and English. **Restaurant:** Lunch served from midday until 3:00pm. Dinner served from 7:00pm until 9:00pm. Closed Saturdays and from 2 to 26 August. **Specialities:** home cooking. **Other points:** bar, open to non-residents, children welcome, traditional decor. **Address:** 75, route de Rouen.
MR JEAN-MICHEL PICARD
**Telephone:** 22.95.53.90
⊗ ♉ Map 2

## SERIFONTAINE, Oise, 60590

### LE RELAIS FLEURI, between Gournay en Bray and Gisors
**Menu:** 62,50 to 90 Frs. **Accommodation:** 90 to 160 Frs. **Restaurant:** Lunch served from midday until 2:00pm. Dinner served from 7:00pm until 9:00pm. Closed Saturdays. **Specialities:** home cooking. **Hotel:** 9 beds; 3 single rooms, 6 double rooms with shower, bath, private WC. **Other points:** bar, open to non-residents, car park, modern decor. **Address:** 22, rue Hacque.
MME ANNICK FONTAINE
**Telephone:** 44.84.89.17
⊗ ♉ 🏠 Map 2

## STEENVOORDE, Nord, 59114

### CAFETERIA DE STEENVOORDE, A 25
**Restaurant:** Open 24 hours. **Other points:** open to non-residents, terraces, pets welcome – check for details, car park, modern decor. **Address:** Aire de Saint-Laurent, dans les deux sens.
MR MICHEL JAMINION
**Telephone:** 28.49.71.33, 28.49.71.88
⊗ Map 1

## TATINGHEM, Pas-de-Calais, 62500

### LE TRUCK WASH, RN 42, between Boulogne and Saint Omer
**Languages spoken:** English. **Menu:** 55 Frs (coffee included). **Restaurant:** Breakfast served from 7:00am. Lunch served from midday until 2:30pm. Dinner served from 7:30pm until 9:00pm. Closed Saturdays, in August and in December. **Specialities:** home cooking. **Other points:** bar, open to non-residents, children welcome, terraces, pets welcome – check for details, car park, modern decor. **Address:** Zone Artisanale.
JACQUES ET CHRISTINE LEROY
**Telephone:** 21.98.45.45
⊗ ♉ Map 1

## TOURCOING, Nord, 59200

### AU SIGNAL D'ARRET, exit Tourcoing le Francs, right at the lights
**Menu:** 56 Frs. **Accommodation:** 85 to 135 Frs. **Restaurant:** Breakfast served from 6:30am. Lunch served from 11:30am until 3:00pm. Dinner served from 7:30pm until 9:30pm. Closed Saturdays and the 2nd fortnight of August. **Specialities:** home cooking. **Hotel:** 5 beds; 3 single rooms, 2 double rooms with shower, bath, private WC, television. **Other points:** bar, children welcome, lounge area, pets welcome – check for details, car park, traditional decor. **Address:** 28, rue des Francs.
MR MICHEL GUILBERT
**Telephone:** 20.26.56.74
⊗ ♉ 🏠 Map 1

## TROSLY BREUIL, Oise, 60350

### LA TERRASSE, RN 31, between Compiègne and Soissons

**Languages spoken:** German and Italian. **Menu:** 55 Frs (drink included). **Restaurant:** Breakfast served from 4:00am. Dinner served from midday until 10:00pm. Closed Fridays and 15 days in July. **Specialities:** regional menu, home cooking. **Other points:** bar, open to non-residents, terraces, pets welcome – check for details, car park, modern decor. **Address:** 47, route de Reims.
MR ENSO DAL SACCO
**Telephone:** 44.85.70.39
⊗ ⍙ Map 2

## VALENCIENNES, Nord, 59300

### AUBERGE DE LA POTERNE, RN 29, exit Valenciennes south

**Menu:** 55 Frs. **Accommodation:** 90 to 160 Frs. **Restaurant:** Breakfast served from 7:00am. Lunch served from midday until 2:00pm. Dinner served from 7:30pm until 9:30pm. Closed Sundays and between Christmas Day and New Year's Day. **Specialities:** home cooking. **Hotel:** 12 beds; 6 single rooms, 6 double rooms. **Other points:** bar, open to non-residents, pets welcome – check for details, car park, modern decor. **Address:** 9, boulevard Eisen.
MR JEAN DEMOLLE
**Telephone:** 27.46.44.98
⊗ ⍙ ⌂ Map 1

## VILLERS BRETONNEUX, Somme, 80380

### LE MELBOURNE, RN 29, the main road between Amiens and Saint Quentin

**Languages spoken:** English. **Menu:** 55 Frs (coffee included). **Accommodation:** 70 to 100 Frs. **Restaurant:** Breakfast served from 7:00am. Lunch served from midday until 2:30pm. Dinner served from 7:00pm until 10:00pm. Closed Sundays and in August. **Specialities:** home cooking. **Hotel:** 8 beds; 2 single rooms, 6 double rooms. **Other points:** bar, open to non-residents, children welcome, pets welcome – check for details, car park. **Address:** 2, rue de la Gare.
MR SÉBASTIEN MANSION
**Telephone:** 22.48.00.14
⊗ ⍙ ⌂ Map 2

## VILLERS COTTERETS, Aisne, 02600

### AU BOUT DU MONDE, RD 936, Meaux

**Places of interest:** Albi, Cordes sur Ciel, Monestiers. **Menu:** 53,50 to 150 Frs. **Restaurant:** Breakfast served from 6:30am. Lunch served from 11:30am until 3:00pm. Dinner served from 7:00pm until 10:00pm. Closed Sundays, 15 days at Christmas and 15 days in August. **Specialities:** confit, Pierre gourmande, regional food, home cooking. **Hotel:** 5 beds; 2 single rooms, 3 double rooms with shower. **Other points:** bar, open to non-residents, à la carte menu, children welcome, lounge area, terraces, pets welcome – check for details, car park, traditional decor. **Address:** Route de la Ferté Milon.
MME MICHÈLE DORGE
**Telephone:** 23.96.07.12
⊗ ⍙ ⌂ Map 2

## WORMHOUT, Nord, 59470

### CAFE DE LA FORGE, Dunkerque

**Languages spoken:** Flemish. **Menu:** 50 Frs. **Restaurant:** Breakfast served from 6:00am. Lunch served from midday until 2:00pm. Dinner served from 7:00pm until 9:00pm. Closed from 15 to 31 August. **Specialities:** home cooking. **Other points:** bar, open to non-residents, children welcome, traditional decor. **Address:** 84, Grand Place.
MR GUY DEPRIESTER
**Telephone:** 28.65.62.33
⊗ ⍙ Map 1

# North West France

## AIGUILLON SUR VIE (L'), Vendée, 85220

### RELAIS LA GREVE, between Challans and les Sables d'Olonne

**Languages spoken:** English. **Menu:** 50 Frs (wine included) to 65 Frs. **Restaurant:** Breakfast served from 6:30am. Lunch served from 11:30am until 3:00pm. Dinner served from 7:00pm until 10:00pm. Closed Sundays. **Specialities:** home cooking. **Other points:** bar, open to non-residents, children welcome, lounge area, terraces, pets welcome – check for details, car park, traditional decor. **Address:** 5, rue des Sables.
MR JEAN-PIERRE ALFONSI
**Telephone:** 51.22.86.23
⊗ ⵎ Map 5

## AMBENAY, Eure, 27250

### HOTEL DE LA RISLE, RD 830, between Evreux and l'Aigle

**Menu:** 50 Frs. **Restaurant:** Breakfast served from 6:00am. Lunch served from midday until 2:00pm. Dinner served from 7:30pm until 10:00pm. Closed Sundays. **Specialities:** home cooking. **Hotel:** 6 beds. **Other points:** bar, open to non-residents, traditional decor. **Address:** 9, rue Guy Lacombe.
MR JEAN-LOUIS MARCILLY
**Telephone:** 32.24.63.45
⊗ ⵎ ⌂ Map 3

## AMBREUMESNIL, Seine-Maritime, 76550

### LE TORTILLARD, RD 152

**Menu:** 50 Frs. **Specialities:** provençales, home cooking. **Other points:** bar, open to non-residents, à la carte menu, children welcome, pets welcome – check for details, car park, modern decor. **Address:** Hameau Ribeuf.
MME GILBERTE DOLBEC
**Telephone:** 35.83.17.00
⊗ ⵎ Map 3

## ANETZ, Loire-Atlantique, 44150

### LE RELAIS DE LA BARBINIERE, RN 23, the main road between Angers and Nantes

**Languages spoken:** English. **Menu:** 46, 50 Frs.

**Accommodation:** 70 Frs. **Restaurant:** Breakfast served from 6:00am. Lunch served from 11:00am until 2:00pm. Dinner served from 7:00pm until 9:30pm. Closed Saturdays, Sundays and 1 week from 15 August. **Specialities:** home cooking. **Hotel:** 4 beds; 2 single rooms, 2 double rooms with shower. **Other points:** bar, open to non-residents, pets welcome – check for details, car park, traditional decor. **Address:** La Barbinière, Route Nationale 23.
MME SYLVIE DRONET
**Telephone:** 40.83.11.25
⊗ ⵎ Map 5

## ANGERS, Maine-et-Loire, 49100

### CHEZ JEAN-CLAUDE, the main road between Paris and Nantes, exit Saint Serge

**Menu:** 54 Frs (wine included). **Accommodation:** 120 Frs. **Restaurant:** Breakfast served from 5:00am. Lunch served from 11:30am until 2:30pm. Dinner served from 7:30pm until 11:00pm. Closed Saturdays, in July and in December. **Specialities:** Paté aux pommes de terre, magrets de canard, home cooking. **Hotel:** 10 beds; 8 single rooms, 2 double rooms with shower, private WC, television. **Other points:** bar, open to non-residents, children welcome, lounge area, pets welcome – check for details, car park, modern decor. **Address:** 7, boulevard Ayrault, Place Saint Serge.
MR JEAN-CLAUDE DEROUET
**Telephone:** 41.43.88.99, 41.43.82.43
⊗ ⵎ ⌂ Map 5

### LE RELAIS DE L'ARCEAU

**Languages spoken:** English. **Menu:** 54 Frs. **Restaurant:** Breakfast served from 6:00am. Lunch served from 11:30am until 3:00pm. Closed Sundays. **Specialities:** home cooking. **Other points:** bar, open to non-residents, children welcome, terraces, pets welcome – check for details, car park, traditional decor. **Address:** 47, rue Guillaume Lekeu.
MR BRUNO HÉRANT
**Telephone:** 41.43.86.25
⊗ ⵎ Map 5

## AUBE, Orne, 61270

### LE PETIT QUEBEC, RN 26, between l'Aigle and Argentan

**Languages spoken:** English and Spanish. **Menu:** 50

Frs. **Restaurant:** Breakfast served from 5:00am. Lunch served from 11:00am until 2:00pm. Dinner served from 7:00pm until 9:00pm. Closed Saturdays, Sundays and the 1st fortnight of August. **Specialities:** home cooking. **Other points:** bar, terraces, pets welcome – check for details, car park, traditional decor. **Address:** 47, route de Paris.
MR JEAN-CLAUDE RIALLAND
**Telephone:** 33.24.55.34
⊗ ♈ Map 3

## AUTHEUIL AUTHOUILLET, Eure, 27490

### CHEZ PIERROT, RD 316 and 836, exit Gaillon, towards Evreux
**Restaurant:** Breakfast served from 6:30am. Lunch served from midday until 2:00pm. Dinner served from midday until 9:00pm. Closed Sundays and mid-August. **Specialities:** home cooking. **Other points:** bar, open to non-residents, terraces, car park, traditional decor. **Address:** 17, rue de Pacy.
MR PIERRE DENOITTE
**Telephone:** 32.34.67.67
⊗ ♈ Map 3

## AUVERSE, Maine-et-Loire, 49490

### CHEZ NANOU, RD 766, the main road between Angers and Tours
**Languages spoken:** English. **Menu:** 53 to 63 Frs. **Restaurant:** Breakfast served from 6:30am. Lunch served from midday until 2:00pm. Dinner served from 7:00pm until 9:00pm. Closed Sundays and from mid-September to mid-October. **Specialities:** home cooking. **Other points:** bar, open to non-residents, pets welcome – check for details, car park, traditional decor. **Address:** Route de Noyant, le Bourg.
MLLE VÉRONIQUE CHASSEAU
**Telephone:** 41.82.20.13
⊗ ♈ Map 5

## AVRANCHES, Manche, 50300

### LES ROUTIERS, RN 176
**Menu:** 45 Frs. **Restaurant:** Breakfast served from 9:00am. Closed Sundays and in September. **Specialities:** home cooking. **Other points:** bar, open to non-residents. **Address:** 70, rue de la Constitution.
MR GEORGES HIPPOLYTE
**Telephone:** 33.58.01.13
⊗ ♈ Map 3

## BAGNEUX, Maine-et-Loire, 49400

### RELAIS DE BOURNAN, RN 160, between Chôlet und Niort
**Menu:** 55 Frs. **Restaurant:** Breakfast served from

6:30am. Lunch served from 11:30am until 2:00pm. Closed Saturdays. **Specialities:** home cooking. **Other points:** bar, open to non-residents, children welcome, pets welcome – check for details, car park, traditional decor. **Address:** 288, rue du Pont Fouchard.
MME JEANINE SANZAY
**Telephone:** 41.50.18.02
⊗ ♈ Map 5

## BALLEROY, Calvados, 14490

### LE RELAIS DE LA FORET, RD 572, between Bayeux and Saint Lo
**Menu:** 52 to 158 Frs. **Accommodation:** 180 to 190 Frs. **Restaurant:** Breakfast served from 5:00am. Lunch served from 11:30am until 3:00pm. Dinner served from 7:00pm until midnight. **Specialities:** home cooking. **Hotel:** 10 beds; 4 single rooms, 6 double rooms with shower, private WC, television, telephone. **Other points:** bar, open to non-residents, à la carte menu, children welcome, terraces, pets welcome – check for details, car park, traditional decor. **Address:** 288, rue du Pont Fouchard.
MR CHRISTIAN DESOBEAUX
**Telephone:** 31.21.39.78. **Fax:** 31.21.44.19
⊗ ♈ 🏠 ⬤ ☆ Map 3

## BARRE EN OUCHE (LA), Eure, 27330

### CHEZ JACKY ET CORINNE, RN 833, the main road between Paris and Evreux
**Menu:** 52 Frs. **Restaurant:** Breakfast served from 7:30am. Lunch served from 11:30am until 3:00pm. Dinner served from 7:00pm until 9:00pm. Closed Sundays, 15 days in August and 15 days in December. **Specialities:** home cooking. **Other points:** bar, open to non-residents, children welcome, pets welcome – check for details, car park, traditional decor. **Address:** Grande Rue.
MR JACKY SCIPION
**Telephone:** 32.44.35.28
⊗ ♈ Map 3

## BASSE INDRE, Loire-Atlantique, 44610

### HOTEL RESTAURANT BRETON, RD 107, Saint Herblain
**Menu:** 47 Frs. **Accommodation:** 90 Frs. **Restaurant:** Breakfast served from 6:30am. Lunch served from 11:30am until 2:00pm. Dinner served from 7:30pm until 9:00pm. Closed weekends and in August. **Specialities:** home cooking. **Hotel:** 12 beds; 2 single rooms, 10 double rooms with shower, private WC. **Other points:** bar, terraces, pets welcome – check for details, car park. **Address:** 10, quai Langlois.
MR YANNICK JAHENY
**Telephone:** 40.86.01.65
⊗ ♈ 🏠 Map 5

## BAYEUX, Calvados, 14400

### LA COLOMBE, RN 13, Cherbourg

**Menu:** 48 to 130 Frs. **Restaurant:** Breakfast served from 7:00am. Lunch served from midday until 3:00pm. Dinner served from 5:00pm until 9:00pm. Closed Saturdays. **Specialities:** regional menu, home cooking. **Other points:** bar, open to non-residents, à la carte menu, children welcome, lounge area, terraces, pets welcome – check for details, car park, modern decor. **Address:** 13, route de Caen.
MR GÉRARD HARDY
**Telephone:** 31.92.13.65
⊗ ⅋ 🍽 Map 3

## BAZOUGES SUR LE LOIR, Sarthe, 72200

### AUBERGE DU SOLEIL LEVANT, RN 23, between la Flèche and Angers

**Languages spoken:** English. **Menu:** 48 to 62 Frs. **Restaurant:** Breakfast served from 7:00am. Lunch served from midday until 2:00pm. Dinner served from 7:00pm until 9:00pm. Closed Saturdays and 15 days in November. **Specialities:** home cooking. **Other points:** bar, open to non-residents, à la carte menu, children welcome. **Address:** 79, rue du Maine.
MR DENIS BORÉE
**Telephone:** 43.45.33.47
⊗ ⅋ Map 5

## BEAUCE, Ille-et-Vilaine, 35133

### AUX BECS FINS, RN 12, the main road between Paris and Brest, 3km before Fougères

**Menu:** 50 Frs. **Restaurant:** Breakfast served from 6:30am. Lunch served from midday until 2:00pm. Dinner served from 7:30pm until 9:30pm. Closed Sundays and in August. **Specialities:** home cooking. **Other points:** bar, open to non-residents, à la carte menu, children welcome, pets welcome – check for details, car park, traditional decor. **Address:** 19, route de Paris.
MR PIERRICK ROUX
**Telephone:** 99.99.08.00
⊗ ⅋ Map 4

## BEAUVOIR EN LYONS, Seine-Maritime, 76220

### RELAIS NORMAND – CHEZ FRANÇOISE ET JULIEN, RN 31, the main road between Rouen and Reims

**Menu:** 54,50 Frs (coffee included). **Restaurant:** Breakfast served from 5:00am. Lunch served from 11:00am until 2:30pm. Dinner served from 7:00pm until 9:00pm. Closed Saturdays, the 1st week of May and the last of December. **Specialities:** home cooking. **Other points:** bar, open to non-residents. **Address:** Les Carreaux, Route Nationale 31.
MR JULIEN JUE
**Telephone:** 35.90.17.20
⊗ ⅋ Map 3

## BEAUVOIR SUR MER, Vendée, 85230

### AU RELAIS DU GOIS, RN 148, between Noirmoutier and le Gois

**Menu:** 55 to 160 Frs. **Restaurant:** Lunch served from midday until 2:00pm. Closed in December. **Specialities:** regional menu. **Other points:** bar, à la carte menu, children welcome, terraces, pets welcome – check for details, car park, traditional decor. **Address:** Route Nationale 148.
MR GILLES GRONDIN
**Telephone:** 51.68.70.31
⊗ ⅋ Map 5

## BEDEE, Ille-et-Vilaine, 35137

### HOTEL DU COMMERCE, RN 12, between Rennes and Saint Brieuc

**Languages spoken:** English. **Menu:** 558 to 105 Frs. **Accommodation:** 100 to 138 Frs. **Restaurant:** Breakfast served from 6:30am. Lunch served from midday until 2:00pm. Dinner served from 7:30pm until 9:00pm. Closed Saturdays and 3 weeks in August. **Specialities:** Coquilles Saint-Jacques à la Bretonne, Gibelotte au cidre, home cooking. **Hotel:** 22 beds; 1 single room, 21 double rooms with shower, bath, private WC, television, telephone. **Other points:** bar, open to non-residents, à la carte menu, pets welcome – check for details, car park, modern decor. **Address:** 14, place de l'Eglise.
MR JEAN-LOUIS RIGOREAU
**Telephone:** 99.07.00.37, 99.07.00.76
⊗ ⅋ ⌂ 🍽 ☆ Map 4

## BEIGNON, Morbihan, 56380

### LES ROUTIERS, RN 24, between Rennes and Lorient

**Restaurant:** Breakfast served from 6:30am. Lunch served from midday until 2:00pm. Dinner served from 7:00pm until 9:30pm. Closed Saturdays. **Specialities:** home cooking. **Hotel:** 6 beds. **Other points:** bar, open to non-residents, à la carte menu, children welcome, car park, traditional decor. **Address:** Place de l'Eglise.
MME BERTHE-SIMONE LABBÉ
**Telephone:** 97.75.74.37
⊗ ⅋ ⌂ Map 4

## BELLENGREVILLE, Calvados, 14370

### LES ROUTIERS, RN 13

**Menu:** 50 Frs. **Restaurant:** Breakfast served from 7:00am. Closed Sundays. **Other points:** bar. **Address:** 16, rue de Paris.

MR DÉSIRÉ DESMEULLES
**Telephone:** 31.23.61.50
⊗ ♈ Map 3

# BELLEVUE COETQUIDAN,
Morbihan, 56380

## L'UNION
**Menu:** 42 to 50 Frs. **Accommodation:** 90 to 130 Frs.
**Restaurant:** Breakfast served from 7:00am. Lunch
served from midday until 2:00pm. Dinner served from
7:00pm until 9:00pm. Closed Sundays and in August.
**Specialities:** home cooking. **Hotel:** 5 beds; with shower.
**Other points:** bar, open to non-residents, children
welcome, pets welcome – check for details, car park,
modern decor. **Address:** 3, avenue Brocéliande.
MR OLIVIER GUÉRIN
**Telephone:** 97.75.71.46
⊗ ♈ 🏠 Map 4

# BERNAY, Eure, 27300

## L'ESCARBILLE, RN 138, the main road between Alençon and Rouen
**Languages spoken:** English. **Menu:** 35 to 90 Frs.
**Restaurant:** Breakfast served from 5:00am. Lunch
served from midday until 2:00pm. Dinner served from
7:00pm until 9:30pm. Closed Sundays. **Specialities:**
home cooking. **Other points:** bar, open to non-residents,
à la carte menu, children welcome, pets welcome –
check for details, car park, modern decor. **Address:** 29,
boulevard Dubus.
MME CHANTAL VERDONCK
**Telephone:** 33.43.60.43
⊗ ♈ Map 3

## L'ESCALE, RN 13
**Menu:** 52 Frs. **Accommodation:** 100 Frs. **Restaurant:**
Breakfast served from 4:30am. Dinner served from
7:00pm until 9:00pm. Closed Saturdays and in July.
**Specialities:** home cooking. **Hotel:** 6 beds; 1 single
room, 5 double rooms with shower, television. **Other
points:** bar, open to non-residents, children welcome,
pets welcome – check for details, car park. **Address:**
Carrefour de Malbrouck.
MR MICHEL SILLIAU
**Telephone:** 32.44.79.99
⊗ ♈ 🏠 Map 3

# BESSE SUR BRAYE, Sarthe, 72310

## LES ROUTIERS, RN 817
**Menu:** 46,50 to 50 Frs. **Accommodation:** 130 to 165
Frs. **Restaurant:** Breakfast served from 8:00am. Lunch
served from midday until 2:00pm. Dinner served from
7:00pm until 9:30pm. Closed Sundays, in August and
beginning of September. **Specialities:** home cooking.
**Hotel:** 12 beds; 8 single rooms, 4 double rooms with
shower, bath, private WC, television, telephone. **Other**

**points:** bar, open to non-residents, pets welcome – check
for details, car park, traditional decor. **Address:** 19,
avenue de la Gare.
MME NADINE LENOIR
**Telephone:** 43.35.30.22, 43.35.59.34
⊗ ♈ 🏠 ☆ Map 5

# BEUZEVILLE, Eure, 27210

## CAFE DE L'ESPERANCE, Honfleur or Caen
**Languages spoken:** English. **Menu:** 48 Frs.
**Restaurant:** Closed Saturdays and 15 days in August.
**Specialities:** home cooking. **Other points:** bar, pets
welcome – check for details, traditional decor. **Address:**
4, rue Pasteur.
MME DENISE DEGUINE
**Telephone:** 32.57.70.60
⊗ ♈ Map 3

# BEZU SAINT ELOI, Eure, 27660

## AUBERGE DE LA LEVRIERE, between Gisors and Rouen
**Menu:** 50 Frs. **Restaurant:** Breakfast served from
6:30am. Lunch served from midday until 3:00pm.
Dinner served from 7:00pm until 9:30pm. Closed
Saturdays and in August/September. **Specialities:**
regional menu, home cooking. **Other points:** bar, open
to non-residents, à la carte menu, children welcome, pets
welcome – check for details, car park, traditional decor.
**Address:** 42, route de Gisors.
MR YVES ROQUAIN
**Telephone:** 32.55.07.12
⊗ ♈ Map 3

# BIVILLE LA BAIGNADE, Seine-Maritime, 76890

## LA CUILLERE EN BOIS, RN 27
**Restaurant:** Closed Wednesdays. **Other points:** bar.
MME YVETTE GUERILLON
**Telephone:** 35.32.88.81
⊗ ♈ Map 3

# BLAIN, Loire-Atlantique, 44130

## LE RELAIS DU CHATEAU, RN 171, between Saint Nazaire (40km) and Rennes (80km)
**Menu:** 48 Frs (wine included). **Restaurant:** Breakfast
served from 5:30am. Closed Sundays. **Specialities:**
home cooking. **Other points:** bar, open to non-residents,
pets welcome – check for details, car park. **Address:**
Lieu dit 'Le Gravier'.
MLLE FRANCESCA BONHOMME
**Telephone:** 40.79.97.11
⊗ ♈ Map 5

## BOISNEY, Eure, 27800

### CHEZ BILL, RN 13, the main road between Evreux and Lisieux

**Menu:** 50 Frs. **Restaurant:** Breakfast served from 5:00am. Closed Saturdays. **Specialities:** home cooking. **Other points:** bar, open to non-residents, children welcome, pets welcome – check for details, car park, traditional decor. **Address:** Route Nationale 13.
MR JEAN-JACQUES BILLY
**Telephone:** 32.46.23.43
⊗ ♈ Map 3

## BOLBEC, Seine-Maritime, 76210

### AUBERGE NORMANDE

**Menu:** 53 Frs. **Accommodation:** 90 Frs. **Restaurant:** Breakfast served from 5:45am. Lunch served from 11:30am until 2:30pm. Dinner served from 7:00pm until 9:30pm. Closed Saturdays, 15 days in August and 15 in December. **Specialities:** home cooking. **Hotel:** 5 beds; 3 single rooms, 2 double rooms with shower, bath. **Other points:** bar, open to non-residents, terraces, pets welcome – check for details, car park, modern decor. **Address:** Route Nationale 15, Trouville-Alliquerville.
MR GÉRARD BAUDRIBOS
**Telephone:** 35.31.15.21
⊗ ♈ 🏠 Map 3

## BONNEVILLE SUR ITON (LA), Eure, 27190

### LE CAFE DES SPORTS, RN 830, Conches via Vallée de la Iton

**Menu:** 48 Frs. **Restaurant:** Breakfast served from 6:30am. Closed between Christmas Day and New Year's Day. **Specialities:** home cooking. **Other points:** bar, children welcome, car park. **Address:** 45, rue Jean Maréchal.
MR ROLAND FONTAINE
**Telephone:** 32.37.10.16
⊗ ♈ Map 3

## BOSGUERARD DE MARCOUVILLE, Eure, 27520

### AUBERGE DE LA TETE D'OR, RN 138, Alençon

**Languages spoken:** English. **Menu:** 50 to 170 Frs. **Accommodation:** 140 to 180 Frs. **Restaurant:** Breakfast served from 6:00am. Closed Sundays. **Specialities:** home cooking. **Hotel:** 12 beds; with shower, television, telephone. **Other points:** bar, open to non-residents, à la carte menu, children welcome, terraces, pets welcome – check for details, car park, traditional decor. **Address:** Nationale 138.
MME COLETTE FOURNIER
**Telephone:** 35.87.60.24
⊗ ♈ 🏠 Map 3

## BOUGUENAIS, Loire-Atlantique, 44340

### A LA FERME, RN 751, industrial zone of Cheviré (near the port)

**Menu:** 47 to 51 Frs (wine and coffee included). **Restaurant:** Breakfast served from 7:00am. Closed Saturdays. **Specialities:** home cooking. **Other points:** bar, pets welcome – check for details, car park, traditional decor. **Address:** 65, rue de la Pierre.
MR YVON BURLOT
**Telephone:** 40.65.23.58
⊗ ♈ Map 5

## BOURG BEAUDOUIN, Eure, 27380

### AU PECHE MIGNON, RN 14, 20km from Rouen, towards Pontoise

**Menu:** 53 to 60 Frs. **Restaurant:** Breakfast served from 7:00am. Lunch served from 11:00am until 4:00pm. Dinner served from 7:00pm until 11:00pm. Closed Sundays. **Specialities:** home cooking. **Other points:** bar, open to non-residents, children welcome, lounge area, car park. **Address:** 19, route de Paris.
MR PASCAL LENOIR
**Telephone:** 32.49.05.20
⊗ ♈ Map 3

## BOURGNEUF EN MAUGES, Maine-et-Loire, 49290

### RELAIS DE LA BOULE D'OR, RD 762

**Menu:** 45 to 140 Frs. **Accommodation:** 100 to 150 Frs. **Restaurant:** Breakfast served from 6:30am. Lunch served from midday until 2:00pm. Dinner served from 7:00pm until 8:00pm. Closed Wednesdays. **Specialities:** home cooking. **Hotel:** 5 beds; with shower, bath, private WC. **Other points:** bar, open to non-residents, pets welcome – check for details, car park, traditional decor. **Address:** 6, rue Notre Dame.
MR THIERRY VÉRON
**Telephone:** 41.78.03.61
⊗ ♈ 🏠 Map 5

## BOURNEZEAU, Vendée, 85480

### LE RELAIS DU CHEVAL BLANC, RD 949 and 948, la Roche sur Yon/Fontenay le Comte

**Languages spoken:** Spanish. **Menu:** 47 Frs. **Restaurant:** Dinner served from midday until 10:00pm. **Specialities:** home cooking. **Other points:** bar, à la carte menu, children welcome, terraces, pets welcome – check for details, car park, traditional decor. **Address:** 29, rue Jean Grolleau.
MME SYLVIA DEMESY
**Telephone:** 51.40.71.54
⊗ ♈ Map 5

## BRECE, Mayenne, 53120

### LE DOMINO

**Menu:** 50 Frs. **Restaurant:** Breakfast served from 8:00am. Lunch served from midday until 2:00pm. Dinner served from 7:00pm until 9:00pm. **Specialities:** home cooking. **Other points:** bar, pets welcome – check for details, car park, traditional decor. **Address:** 1, rue du Lavoir.
MME JANINE CARLIN
**Telephone:** 43.08.62.72
⊗ ♆ Map 5

## BRECOURT DOUAINS, Eure, 27120

### LE PACY VERNON, RN 181, between Pacy en Eure and Vernon

**Menu:** 55 Frs. **Restaurant:** Breakfast served from 5:30am. Closed Saturdays and 1 week from 14 July. **Specialities:** home cooking. **Other points:** bar, open to non-residents, pets welcome – check for details, car park, traditional decor. **Address:** Route Nationale 181.
MR ALAINE COTE
**Telephone:** 32.52.44.67
⊗ ♆ Map 3

## BRETEUIL SUR ITON, Eure, 27160

### CHEZ CLAUDE, RD 833

**Menu:** 52 Frs (wine and coffee included). **Restaurant:** Breakfast served from 7:00am. Lunch served from midday until 2:00pm. Closed Sundays and in August. **Specialities:** home cooking. **Other points:** bar, terraces, pets welcome – check for details, car park, traditional decor. **Address:** Le Chesnay, Condé sur Iton.
MR CLAUDE BLANFUNÉ
**Telephone:** 32.29.89.27
⊗ ♆ Map 3

### LE RELAIS DES MARES, RD 840, Rouen

**Menu:** 52 Frs. **Restaurant:** Breakfast served from 5:00am. Lunch served from 11:00am until 3:00pm. Dinner served from 7:30pm until 10:00pm. Closed Saturdays. **Specialities:** regional menu. **Other points:** bar, open to non-residents, pets welcome – check for details, car park, traditional decor. **Address:** Le Chesne.
MR DANICK GUIOT
**Telephone:** 32.29.85.09, 32.34.88.24
⊗ ♆ Map 3

## BRETTEVILLE SUR DIVES, Calvados, 14170

### LE BRETTEVILLAIS, RD 16, Crèvecoeur – Auge/Saint Pierre sur Dives

**Menu:** 53 Frs. **Restaurant:** Breakfast served from 6.00am. Closed Sundays. **Specialities:** home cooking. **Other points:** bar, open to non-residents, children welcome, terraces, pets welcome – check for details, car park.
MME PATRICIA DUFAILLY
**Telephone:** 31.20.13.31
⊗ ♆ Map 3

## BRIONNE, Eure, 27800

### HOTEL DU HAVRE, the main road between Bernay and Rouen

**Menu:** 50 Frs. **Accommodation:** 180 to 240 Frs. **Restaurant:** Breakfast served from 6:00am. Dinner served from midday until midnight. Closed from 24 December to 2 January. **Specialities:** Plats en sauce, regional food, home cooking. **Hotel:** 32 beds; with shower, bath, private WC, television. **Other points:** bar, à la carte menu, children welcome, lounge area, terraces, car park. **Address:** 13, rue de la Soie.
MR JACKY PANET
**Telephone:** 32.44.80.28
⊗ ♆ 🏠 ☆☆ Map 3

## BRIX, Manche, 50700

### LE CLOS NORMAND, RN 13

**Other points:** bar
MME JOSIANE GERMAIN
**Telephone:** 33.41.94.35
⊗ ♆ Map 3

## BROGLIE, Eure, 27270

### LES TOURISTES ET LES ROUTIERS, RN 138, the main road between Rouen and Bordeaux

**Menu:** 55 to 78 Frs. **Accommodation:** 100 to 140 Frs. **Restaurant:** Breakfast served from 10:00am. Lunch served from midday until 2:00pm. Dinner served from 7:30pm until 10:00pm. Closed Wednesdays. **Specialities:** regional menu, home cooking. **Hotel:** 5 beds; 4 single rooms, 1 double room with shower. **Other points:** bar, open to non-residents, à la carte menu, children welcome, pets welcome – check for details, traditional decor. **Address:** 47, rue Augustin Fresnel.
MR JEAN-LOUIS BUNEL
**Telephone:** 32.44.60.38
⊗ ♆ 🏠 Map 3

## CABOURG, Calvados, 14390

### LE COLOMBIER, RD 513, between Caen and Cabourg

**Menu:** 55 Frs. **Restaurant:** Breakfast served from 6:30am. Lunch served from 11:30am until 2:30pm. Closed Sundays and from 20 December to 6 January. **Specialities:** home cooking. **Other points:** bar, traditional decor. **Address:** Petiville.
MR GÉRARD BAUDEL
**Telephone:** 31.78.00.67
⊗ ♆ Map 3

## CAEN VENOIX, Calvados, 14350

### LE VELODROME, RN 175, on the road to Vire, towards Mont Saint Michel

**Menu:** 50 Frs. **Accommodation:** 110 Frs (60 Frs for extra bed). **Restaurant:** Breakfast served from 7:00am. Lunch served from 11:30am until 2:00pm. Dinner served from 7:00pm until 8:30pm. Closed Saturdays and in August. **Specialities:** home cooking. **Hotel:** 5 beds; 5 single rooms with shower. **Other points:** bar, open to non-residents, pets welcome – check for details. **Address:** 9, avenue Henry Cheron.
MR DANIEL LEVIGOUREUX
**Telephone:** 31.74.40.71
⊗ ℣ ⌂ Map 3

## CAGNY, Calvados, 14630

### HOTEL DE LA POSTE, RN 13, between Caen and Lisieux

**Menu:** 48 Frs. **Accommodation:** 120 to 150 Frs. **Restaurant:** Breakfast served from 6:00am. Dinner served from 7:00pm until 8:30pm. Closed Saturdays. **Specialities:** regional menu, home cooking. **Hotel:** 5 beds; 3 single rooms, 2 double rooms with shower. **Other points:** bar, open to non-residents, pets welcome – check for details, car park, modern decor. **Address:** 32, route de Paris.
MME ANNICK ROBENARD
**Telephone:** 31.23.41.26
⊗ ℣ ⌂ Map 3

## CALIGNY, Orne, 61100

### RELAIS DU PONT DE VERE, RD 962, Caen

**Menu:** 52 to 55 Frs. **Restaurant:** Breakfast served from 7:00am. Lunch served from 11:30am until 2:30pm. Dinner served from 7:00pm until 9:30pm. Closed Saturdays and 3 weeks in August. **Specialities:** home cooking. **Other points:** bar, open to non-residents, car park, modern decor. **Address:** Le Pont de Vère.
MR HENRI VIVIER
**Telephone:** 33.65.65.60
⊗ ℣ Map 3

## CALLAC DE BRETAGNE, Côtes-du-Nord, 22160

### LE KERGUIVIOU, RD 787, between Guingamp and Carhaix

**Menu:** 49,50 to 120 Frs. **Restaurant:** Breakfast served from 6:30am. **Specialities:** regional menu, home cooking. **Other points:** bar, open to non-residents, à la carte menu, children welcome, lounge area, terraces, pets welcome – check for details, car park, modern decor. **Address:** Zone Artisanale.
MME MURIEL AUBRY
**Telephone:** 96.45.92.08
⊗ ℣ Map 4

## LES ROUTIERS, between Guingamps and Carhaix

**Menu:** 47 Frs. **Accommodation:** 90 to 150 Frs. **Restaurant:** Breakfast served from 7:30am. Lunch served from midday until 2:00pm. Dinner served from 7:00pm until 8:30pm. Closed Sundays and the 2nd fortnight of August. **Specialities:** home cooking. **Hotel:** 11 beds; 9 single rooms, 2 double rooms. **Other points:** bar, open to non-residents, children welcome, car park, traditional decor. **Address:** 21, rue de la Gare.
MME MARIE-YVONNE RICHARD
**Telephone:** 96.45.51.10
⊗ ℣ ⌂ Map 4

## CAMBRES FRESQUIENNES (LES), Seine-Maritime, 76570

### LES AMIS DE LA ROUTE, RN 27, the main road between Rouen and Dieppe

**Languages spoken:** English. **Menu:** 53 Frs. **Restaurant:** Breakfast served from 6:30am. Lunch served from 11:30am until 3:00pm. Closed Saturdays. **Specialities:** home cooking. **Other points:** bar, open to non-residents, children welcome, terraces, pets welcome – check for details, car park, modern decor. **Address:** Route Nationale 27.
MR LUC LEDRAIT
**Telephone:** 35.32.51.98
⊗ ℣ Map 3

## CARCAGNY, Calvados, 14740

### AUX JOYEUX ROUTIERS, Ancienne RN 13, between Caen and Bayeux

**Languages spoken:** English and Italian. **Menu:** 50 Frs. **Restaurant:** Breakfast served from 7:30am. Lunch served from 11:45am until 2:00pm. Dinner served from 7:00pm until 9:00pm. Closed Saturdays. **Specialities:** regional menu, home cooking. **Other points:** bar, open to non-residents, children welcome, pets welcome – check for details, car park, traditional decor. **Address:** Le Hameau Saint Léger.
MR MICHEL PACARY
**Telephone:** 31.80.22.01
⊗ ℣ Map 3

## CARENTAN, Manche, 50500

### LE DERBY, RN 13, between Bayeux and Caen

**Menu:** 45 to 49 Frs. **Restaurant:** Breakfast served from 6:00am. Dinner served from 7:30pm until 9:00pm. Closed Saturdays, 2 weeks beginning of May and 3 weeks end of September. **Specialities:** tripes maison; tripes maison, home cooking. **Other points:** bar, open to non-residents, children welcome, pets welcome – check for details, car park. **Address:** 21, rue de la 101 Airborne.
MR MAURICE LEGUELINEL
**Telephone:** 33.42.04.77
⊗ ℣ Map 3

## CARHAIX PLOUGUER, Finistère, 29270

### AU CHEVAL BRETON, RN 164
**Restaurant:** Closed Saturdays and in August.
**Specialities:** home cooking. **Hotel:** 10 beds. **Other points:** bar, open to non-residents, pets welcome – check for details. **Address:** 2, boulevard de la République.
MR LOUIS LE MIGNON
**Telephone:** 98.93.01.38
⊗ ⚲ ⌂ Map 4

## CARPIQUET, Calvados, 14650

### LE POURQUOI PAS, between Caen le Madeleine and Cherbourg
**Menu:** 46 Frs (drink and coffee included). **Restaurant:** Breakfast served from 6:30am. Lunch served from 11:30am until 2:00pm. Dinner served from 6:30pm until 8:30pm. Closed Saturdays and 8 days in August.
**Specialities:** home cooking. **Hotel:** 4 beds; with shower. **Other points:** bar, open to non-residents, car park, traditional decor. **Address:** 33, route de Bayeux.
MR DIDIER PREMPAIN
**Telephone:** 31.73.84.84
⊗ ⚲ Map 3

## CAST, Finistère, 29150

### LE RELAIS SAINT GILDAS, between Châteaulin and Douarnenez
**Languages spoken:** English. **Menu:** 46 to 195 Frs.
**Accommodation:** 120 to 190 Frs. **Restaurant:** Breakfast served from 7:00am. Lunch served from midday until 2:30pm. Dinner served from 7:00pm until 9:30pm. Closed Saturdays and in November.
**Specialities:** Fruits de mer, couscous maison, regional food, home cooking. **Hotel:** 15 beds; 8 single rooms, 7 double rooms with shower. **Other points:** bar, open to non-residents, à la carte menu, children welcome, lounge area, terraces, pets welcome – check for details, car park, traditional decor. **Address:** 11–13, rue du Kreisker.
MARIE ET PATRICE PHILIPPE
**Telephone:** 98.73.54.76, 98.73.55.43
⊗ ⚲ ⌂ ⬭ Map 4

## CAUDAN, Morbihan, 56850

### LE BOUTON D'OR, RD 81, via the motorway Quimper/Nantes, exit Lorient
**Languages spoken:** English. **Menu:** 41 to 45 Frs.
**Restaurant:** Breakfast served from 7:00am. Lunch served from 11:30am until 3:00pm. Closed Saturdays and in August. **Specialities:** regional menu, home cooking. **Other points:** bar, open to non-residents, lounge area, terraces, car park, modern decor. **Address:** ZA Kergoussel.
MME JOËLLE LE BAIL
**Telephone:** 97.81.16.01
⊗ ⚲ Map 4

## CAUDEBEC LES ELBEUF, Seine-Maritime, 76320

### LE TIVOLI BAR, Elbeuf, on the road to Pont l'Arche
**Menu:** 50 Frs (wine included). **Restaurant:** Breakfast served from 6:00am. Lunch served from 11:30am until 2:30pm. Dinner served from 6:30pm until 8:00pm. Closed Sundays. **Specialities:** home cooking. **Other points:** bar, open to non-residents, modern decor. **Address:** 43, rue Félix Faure.
MME CLAUDETTE TOUCHARD
**Telephone:** 35.77.19.54
⊗ ⚲ Map 3

## CAULNES, Côtes-du-Nord, 22350

### LES ROUTIERS
**Restaurant:** Dinner served from midday until 10:00pm.
**Other points:** bar. **Address:** 40, rue de la Gare.
MME MARIE THÉRÉSE GAUDREL
**Telephone:** 96.83.94.14
⊗ ⚲ Map 4

## CAUVERVILLE EN ROUMOIS, Eure, 27350

### LE MEDINE, RN 175, crossroads for Médine Pont Audemer
**Menu:** 49 to 52 Frs (wine included). **Restaurant:** Breakfast served from 6:00am. Lunch served from 11:00am until 5:00pm. Closed Saturdays and in August. **Specialities:** choucroute, pizzas, couscous, home cooking. **Other points:** bar, open to non-residents, children welcome, pets welcome – check for details, car park, traditional decor. **Address:** Route Nationale 175.
MR JEAN-PIERRE FERRETTE
**Telephone:** 32.57.01.55
⊗ ⚲ Map 3

## CEAUCE, Orne, 61330

### LE RELAIS DE L'ETAPE, RD 962, the main road between Caen/Laval, Laval/Angers
**Menu:** 49 Frs. **Restaurant:** Breakfast served from 7:30am. Lunch served from 11:30am until 2:30pm. Closed Sundays. **Specialities:** moules, poissons, regional food. **Other points:** bar, open to non-residents, children welcome, terraces, pets welcome – check for details, car park, traditional decor. **Address:** 21, rue de Domfront.
MME MICHÈLE GÉRAULT
**Telephone:** 33.30.84.04
⊗ ⚲ Map 3

## CHAIGNES, Eure, 27120

*AUBERGE MA NORMANDIE, RN 13, the main road between Paris and Lisieux*
**Languages spoken:** English. **Menu:** 58 to 75 Frs.
**Restaurant:** Breakfast served from 4:30am. Lunch served from 11:00am until midday. Dinner served from midday until 11:00pm. Closed Saturdays. **Specialities:** regional menu, home cooking. **Hotel:** 14 beds. **Other points:** bar, open to non-residents, à la carte menu, lounge area, pets welcome – check for details, car park. **Address:** Route Nationale 13.
MR YVES HOLLIGER
**Telephone:** 32.36.95.52
⊗ ♀ 🏠 Map 3

## CHAILLE LES MARAIS, Vendée, 85450

*AU CHTI-MI, RN 137, the main road between Nantes and la Rochelle*
**Languages spoken:** English. **Menu:** 52 to 62 Frs.
**Restaurant:** Breakfast served from 5:00am. Lunch served from 11:30am until 2:30pm. Dinner served from 7:00pm until 9:00pm. Closed Saturdays. **Specialities:** home cooking. **Other points:** bar, open to non-residents, children welcome, pets welcome – check for details, car park, traditional decor. **Address:** 13, rue Principale, le Sableau.
MR JEAN-PIERRE TISON
**Telephone:** 51.56.70.87
⊗ ♀ Map 5

## CHALLANS, Vendée, 85300

*RELAIS DE LA NOUE, RN 148*
**Menu:** 43, 30 to 50 Frs. **Restaurant:** Breakfast served from 7:00am. Lunch served from 11:30am until 2:30pm. Dinner served from 7:30pm until 9:00pm. Closed Saturdays and 3 weeks in August **Specialities:** home cooking. **Other points:** bar, open to non-residents, children welcome, pets welcome – check for details, car park, traditional decor. **Address:** Place Victor Charbonnel.
MME MONIQUE MENEZ
**Telephone:** 51.93.20.20
⊗ ♀ Map 5

## CHAMBRETAUD, Vendée, 85500

*AUBERGE BEL'AIR, RN 160, between les Herbiers (7km) and Chôlet (18km)*
**Menu:** 55 to 150 Frs. **Restaurant:** Breakfast served from 7:00am. Lunch served from midday until 3:00pm. Dinner served from 7:00pm until 10:00pm. **Specialities:** regional menu, home cooking. **Other points:** open to non-residents, à la carte menu, children welcome, terraces, pets welcome – check for details, car park, traditional decor. **Address:** Route du Puy du Fou.
MME JACQUELINE MARTIN
**Telephone:** 51.67.51.61
⊗ Map 5

## CHAMPAGNE, Sarthe, 72470

*LE RELAIS DES FOUGERES, RN 157, between le Mans and Saint Calais*
**Menu:** 49,50 to 85 Frs. **Restaurant:** Breakfast served from 6:00am. Lunch served from 11:30am until 2:00pm. Dinner served from 6:30pm until 8:00pm. Closed Saturdays. **Specialities:** home cooking. **Other points:** bar, open to non-residents, à la carte menu, terraces, pets welcome – check for details, car park, traditional decor. **Address:** Route de Saint Calais.
MR ANTOINE MICHELIC
**Telephone:** 43.89.50.96
⊗ ♀ Map 5

## CHAMPTOCE SUR LOIRE, Maine-et-Loire, 49170

*HOTEL LES RIVETTES, the main road between Angers and Nantes*
**Languages spoken:** English and Spanish. **Menu:** 43 Frs. **Accommodation:** 100 to 145 Frs. **Restaurant:** Breakfast served from 8:00am. Lunch served from 11:45am until 3:00pm. Dinner served from 7:00pm until 8:30pm. Closed Saturdays and 3 weeks beginning of August. **Specialities:** tripes à l'Angevine, canard sauce muscade, regional food, home cooking. **Hotel:** 4 beds; 4 double rooms with shower. **Other points:** bar, children welcome, terraces, pets welcome – check for details, car park, traditional decor. **Address:** Route de Montjean.
MME AGNÈS CHÊNE
**Telephone:** 41.39.91.75
⊗ ♀ Map 5

## CHANGE, Mayenne, 53810

*LE RELAIS DE NIAFLES, A 81, exit no 3, towards Laval*
**Menu:** 52 Frs. **Restaurant:** Breakfast served from 5:00am. Lunch served from 11:00am until 2:30pm. Dinner served from 6:30pm until 10:30pm. Closed Saturdays. **Specialities:** home cooking. **Other points:** bar, open to non-residents, pets welcome – check for details, car park, traditional decor. **Address:** Niafles.
MR PIERRE DADET
**Telephone:** 43.53.76.15
⊗ ♀ Map 5

## CHANGE LES LAVAL, Mayenne, 53810

*CHEZ CHRISTIANE, RN 30, motorway A 81, exit no 4, towards Fougères, (2km)*
**Menu:** 50 Frs. **Accommodation:** 100 to 150 Frs. **Restaurant:** Breakfast served from 6:00am. Lunch served from midday until 2:30pm. Dinner served from 7:00pm until 10:30pm. Closed only evenings of public holidays. **Specialities:** home cooking. **Hotel:** 7 beds; 5 single rooms, 2 double rooms with bath, private WC.

**Other points:** bar, open to non-residents, children welcome, pets welcome – check for details, car park, traditional decor. **Address:** Les Chênes Secs.
MME CHRISTIANE POUTEAU
**Telephone:** 43.02.39.26, 43.56.16.06
⊗ ▽ ⌂ Map 5

## CHAPELLE CARO (LA), Morbihan, 56460

### HOTEL DE LA GARE, RN 166, Vannes
**Restaurant:** Breakfast served from 7:00am. Lunch served from 11:00am until 3:00pm. Dinner served from 7:00pm until 10:00pm. Closed from 25 December to 2 January. **Specialities:** home cooking. **Hotel:** 4 beds. **Other points:** bar, open to non-residents, children welcome. **Address:** La Gare.
MME MARIE-CLAIRE BOULVAIS
**Telephone:** 97.74.93.47
⊗ ▽ Map 4

## CHAPELLE CRAONNAISE (LA), Mayenne, 53230

### CAFE DES SPORTS, RN 171, the main road between Châteaubriant/Laval/Nantes
**Menu:** 45 Frs. **Restaurant:** Breakfast served from 7:30am. **Other points:** bar, children welcome, terraces, pets welcome – check for details, car park, modern decor. **Address:** Le Bourg.
MR JEAN-FRANÇOIS LITTÉE
**Telephone:** 43.98.81.80
⊗ ▽ Map 5

## CHAPELLE DU BOIS (LA), Sarthe, 72400

### LE RELAIS, RD 59, between Mamers and la Ferté Bernard
**Restaurant:** Breakfast served from 7:30am. Lunch served from 11:30am until 3:00pm. Dinner served from 7:00pm until 9:00pm. Closed Sundays. **Other points:** bar, open to non-residents, lounge area, pets welcome – check for details, car park, modern decor. **Address:** 3, rue de la Poste.
MR JEAN-CLAUDE LHÉRAULT
**Telephone:** 43.93.18.69. **Fax:** 43.71.29.30
⊗ ▽ Map 5

## CHAPELLE SAINT AUBERT (LA), Ille-et-Vilaine, 35140

### LE RELAIS PARIS/BREST, RN 12, between Fougères and Rennes
**Menu:** 46 to 75 Frs. **Restaurant:** Breakfast served from 7.00am. Closed Sundays. **Specialities:** home cooking. **Other points:** bar, open to non-residents, children welcome, pets welcome – check for details, car park. **Address:** Lieu dit 'La Salorgue'.

MR DENIS POTREL
**Telephone:** 99.98.82.04
⊗ ▽ Map 4

## CHARTRE SUR LE LOIR (LA), Sarthe, 72340

### RESTAURANT JEANNE D'ARC
**Menu:** 42 to 70 Frs. **Accommodation:** 100 Frs. **Restaurant:** Breakfast served from 8:00am. Lunch served from midday until 2:30pm. Dinner served from 7:00pm until 9:00pm. Closed Sundays. **Specialities:** home cooking. **Hotel:** 5 beds; 4 single rooms, 1 double room with shower. **Other points:** bar, open to non-residents, children welcome, pets welcome – check for details, car park, traditional decor. **Address:** 23, place Carnot.
MR JACQUES OLIVIER
**Telephone:** 43.44.41.14
⊗ ▽ ⌂ Map 5

## CHASSILLE, Sarthe, 72540

### LE PETIT ROBINSON, RN 157, the main road between le Mans and Laval
**Menu:** 50 Frs. **Accommodation:** 90 to 110 Frs. **Restaurant:** Breakfast served from 5:30am. Lunch served from midday until 2:00pm. Dinner served from 7:00pm until 10:00pm. Closed Saturdays and in August. **Specialities:** home cooking. **Hotel:** 4 beds; 3 single rooms, 1 double room. **Other points:** bar, open to non-residents, car park, traditional decor. **Address:** Le Petit Robinson.
MR OLIVIER FOURNIGAULT
**Telephone:** 43.88.92.01
⊗ ▽ Map 5

## CHATEAU GONTIER, Mayenne, 53200

### L'ETOILE, RN 162, the main road between Angers and Laval
**Menu:** 46 Frs (wine included). **Restaurant:** Breakfast served from 8:00am. Lunch served from 11:45am until 2:30pm. Dinner served from 7:00pm until 9:00pm. Closed Sundays and in August. **Specialities:** home cooking. **Other points:** bar, open to non-residents, children welcome, pets welcome – check for details, car park, modern decor. **Address:** 43, rue Garnier.
MR NORBERT CORVÉ
**Telephone:** 43.07.20.80
⊗ ▽ Map 5

## CHATEAU L'HERMITAGE, Sarthe, 72510

### LA BELLE CROIX, RD 307, le Lude
**Menu:** 47,50 Frs. **Restaurant:** Breakfast served from 7:00am. Closed Sundays. **Specialities:** home cooking. **Other points:** bar, open to non-residents. **Address:** La Belle Croix.

MR BRUNO DAVID
Telephone: 43.46.35.73
⊗ ⟁ Map 5

## CHATEAUBRIANT, Loire-Atlantique, 44110

### CAFE DE LA POSTE, RN 171, the main road between Laval and Paris

Restaurant: Lunch served from midday until 2:00pm. Closed Mondays and in August. Specialities: home cooking. Other points: bar, open to non-residents, pets welcome – check for details, car park. Address: 7, place Talhouët.
MR CLAUDE FRUCHARD
Telephone: 40.28.62.36
⊗ ⟁ Map 5

### SARL LE TUGNY, RN 171, Châteaubriant/Saint Nazaire

Restaurant: Breakfast served from 8:00am. Closed Sundays. Specialities: home cooking. Other points: bar, open to non-residents, children welcome, lounge area, terraces, pets welcome – check for details, car park, modern decor. Address: Rue du Général Eisenhower, ZI, Centre Leclerc.
MR JEAN-LOUIS BOISGARD
Telephone: 40.28.29.58
⊗ ⟁ Map 5

### SARL PARIS/OCEAN, Route for Laval, last stop

Languages spoken: English and Spanish. Menu: to 35 to 115 Frs. Accommodation: 85 to 100 Frs. Restaurant: Breakfast served from 6:30am. Lunch served from midday until 3:00pm. Dinner served from 7:30pm until 11:00pm. Specialities: regional menu. Hotel: 7 beds; 4 single rooms, 3 double rooms. Other points: bar, open to non-residents, à la carte menu, children welcome, terraces, pets welcome – check for details, car park, modern decor. Address: 25, rue d'Ancenis.
MR PATRICK GELÉE
Telephone: 40.81.21.79
⊗ ⟁ ⌂ ☆ Map 5

## CHATEAUTHEBAUD, Loire-Atlantique, 44690

### LA SAUCISSE VOLANTE, RN 137, La Rochelle/Bordeaux/Niort

Languages spoken: English. Menu: 52 to 67, 50 Frs. Accommodation: 85 Frs. Restaurant: Breakfast served from 5:00am. Lunch served from midday until 2:30pm. Dinner served from 7:00pm until 10:30pm. Closed Saturdays and in July or in August. Specialities: home cooking. Hotel: 5 beds; 1 single room, 4 double rooms. Other points: bar, open to non-residents, children welcome, terraces, car park, traditional decor. Address: Route de la Rochelle, le Butay.

MR SERGE VIOLEAU
Telephone: 40.06.63.55
⊗ ⟁ ⌂ Map 5

## CHEMILLE, Maine-et-Loire, 49120

### SARL L'ESCALE, RN 160, the main road between Chôlet and Angers

Menu: 52 to 65 Frs. Restaurant: Breakfast served from 6:00am. Lunch served from 11:45am until 2:30pm. Dinner served from 7:30pm until 10:30pm. Closed Saturdays. Specialities: home cooking. Other points: bar, open to non-residents, children welcome, lounge area, pets welcome – check for details, car park, modern decor. Address: Rue du Foirial.
MR BERNARD ROUTHIAU
Telephone: 41.30.63.79
⊗ ⟁ Map 5

## CHERBOURG, Manche, 50100

### LES ROUTIERS, RN 13

Languages spoken: English and Spanish. Other points: bar. Address: 10, rue de l'Onglet.
MME VIVIANE COUVRIE
Telephone: 33.53.08.15
⊗ ⟁ Map 3

## CHOLET, Maine-et-Loire, 49300

### HOTEL RESTAURANT LES ROUTIERS, RN 160

Menu: 47 Frs. Accommodation: 75 to 97 Frs. Restaurant: Breakfast served from 6:45am. Lunch served from midday until 2:00pm. Dinner served from 7:30pm until 9:00pm. Closed Saturdays and from 10 July to 10 August. Specialities: home cooking. Hotel: 19 beds; 13 single rooms, 6 double rooms. Other points: bar, open to non-residents, pets welcome – check for details, car park, modern decor. Address: 13, place de la République.
MR MICHEL DUBILLOT
Telephone: 41.62.11.09
⊗ ⟁ ⌂ Map 5

### LE RELAIS DES PRAIRIES, RN 160, opposite the aérodrome

Languages spoken: German and English. Menu: 45 to 155 Frs. Restaurant: Breakfast served from 6:30am. Lunch served from midday until 2:00pm. Dinner served from 7:30pm until 9:00pm. Closed Saturdays and from 25 December to 2 January. Specialities: Onglet à l'échalotte, côte de boeuf, tête de veau, home cooking. Other points: bar, open to non-residents, à la carte menu, children welcome, terraces, pets welcome – check for details, car park. Address: 3, boulevard du Pont de Pierre, Parc des Prairies.
MR CLAUDE ALBERT
Telephone: 41.58.09.39
⊗ ⟁ Map 5

## CLERMONT CREANS, Sarthe, 72200

### LE CREANS, RN 23, le Mans/Angers/ Saumur

**Menu:** 52 Frs. **Restaurant:** Breakfast served from 5:00am. Closed Sundays. **Specialities:** home cooking. **Other points:** bar, open to non-residents, children welcome, terraces, pets welcome – check for details, car park, modern decor. **Address:** 19, rue Nationale.
MME MARIE-FRANCE ROUALT
**Telephone:** 43.45.20.13
⊗ ⵁ Map 5

## COEMONT-VOUVRAY, Sarthe, 72500

### LE BON COIN, RN 158

**Restaurant:** Breakfast served from 7:00am. Lunch served from 11:30am until 3:00pm. Closed Sundays and in August. **Specialities:** home cooking. **Other points:** bar, children welcome, terraces, pets welcome – check for details, car park, traditional decor.
MME JOUANNEAU
**Telephone:** 43.44.04.17
⊗ ⵁ Map 5

## COLOMBELLES, Calvados, 14460

### LES VIKINGS, RD 513

**Menu:** 51 to 90 Frs. **Accommodation:** 95 to 130 Frs. **Restaurant:** Breakfast served from 6:30am. Dinner served from 7:00pm until 9:30pm. Closed Sundays and in August. **Specialities:** home cooking. **Hotel:** 32 beds; with shower, private WC. **Other points:** bar, open to non-residents. **Address:** 3, route de Cabourg.
MR JEAN-CLAUDE MUSSON
**Telephone:** 31.72.18.83, 31.72.40.40
⊗ ⵁ 🏠 Map 3

## COLOMBY, Manche, 50700

### CHEZ MEMENE, RD 2, Valognes/Avranche

**Menu:** 48 Frs (two choices). **Restaurant:** Closed Mondays. **Other points:** bar, car park. **Address:** Le Bourg, Valognes.
MME GERMAINE DELACOTTE
**Telephone:** 33.40.10.59
⊗ ⵁ Map 3

## COLPO, Morbihan, 56390

### AUX DELICES DE L'OCEAN, the main road between Vannes and Saint Brieuc

**Languages spoken:** English and Spanish. **Menu:** 44 to 150 Frs. **Accommodation:** 89 Frs. **Restaurant:** Breakfast served from 8:00am. Lunch served from midday until 2:30pm. Dinner served from 7:30pm until 9:00pm. Closed Sundays and in July. **Specialities:** home cooking. **Hotel:** 10 beds; 5 single rooms, 5 double rooms with shower. **Other points:** bar, open to non-residents, à la carte menu, children welcome, lounge area, pets welcome – check for details, car park, traditional decor. **Address:** 1, avenue de la Princesse.
MR JEAN-CLAUDE LE GUILLAN
**Telephone:** 97.66.82.21
⊗ ⵁ 🏠 Map 4

## CONCOURSON SUR LAYON, Maine-et-Loire, 49700

### AUBERGE DU HAUT LAYON, RD 160, the main road between Tours and Nantes

**Languages spoken:** English. **Menu:** 54 to 75 Frs. **Restaurant:** Breakfast served from 6:30am. Lunch served from midday until 2:30pm. Dinner served from 7:00pm until 9:00pm. Closed Sundays. **Specialities:** home cooking. **Other points:** bar, open to non-residents, à la carte menu, children welcome, pets welcome – check for details, car park, traditional decor. **Address:** 7 Route Nationale.
MR BERNARD BATTAIS
**Telephone:** 41.59.27.60
⊗ ⵁ Map 5

## CONDE SUR HUISNE, Orne, 61110

### L'EUROPEENNE, RN 23, between Chartes and le Mans

**Languages spoken:** English, Spanish and Italian. **Menu:** 50 Frs. **Restaurant:** Lunch served from midday until 2:00pm. Dinner served from 6:00pm until 10:00pm. Closed Sundays and from 20 December to 6 January. **Specialities:** home cooking. **Other points:** open to non-residents, terraces, pets welcome – check for details, car park, traditional decor. **Address:** La Fourche.
SARL L'EUROPÉENNE
**Telephone:** 37.52.53.18
⊗ Map 3

## CONDE SUR NOIREAU, Calvados, 14110

### HOTEL LES PROMENADES, RD 562, the main road between Caen/Flers/Laval

**Menu:** 47 to 115 Frs. **Accommodation:** 120 to 150 Frs. **Restaurant:** Breakfast served from 6:30am. Lunch served from midday until 1:30pm. Dinner served from 7:00pm until 8:30pm. Closed Sundays and in August. **Specialities:** home cooking. **Hotel:** 6 beds; 4 single rooms, 2 double rooms with shower, bath. **Other points:** bar, open to non-residents, à la carte menu, children welcome, terraces, pets welcome – check for details, car park. **Address:** 2, rue Motte de Lutre, Angle Rue Saint Martin.
MR MICHEL JUMAT
**Telephone:** 31.69.03.36
⊗ ⵁ 🏠 Map 3

## CONDE SUR VIRE, Manche, 50890

### HOTEL DES ROCHES

**Languages spoken:** English. **Restaurant:** Dinner served from midday until 8:00pm. Closed Sundays and August. **Hotel:** 7 beds. **Other points:** bar. **Address:** 12, rue Alfred Duros.
MR ACHOUR MOHABEDDINE
**Telephone:** 33.55.20.82
⊗ ☖ ⚏ Map 3

## CONNERRE, Sarthe, 72160

### LA BICHE DOREE, RN 23, the main road between le Mans and Paris

**Languages spoken:** English and a little German. **Menu:** 50 Frs. **Accommodation:** 90 to 130 Frs. **Restaurant:** Breakfast served from 5:00am. Lunch served from midday until 2:30pm. Dinner served from 7:00pm until 10:00pm. Closed Saturdays. **Specialities:** home cooking. **Hotel:** 10 beds; 6 single rooms, 4 double rooms with shower, bath. **Other points:** bar, open to non-residents, pets welcome – check for details, car park. **Address:** Route Nationale 23, la Belle Inutile.
MR DOMINIQUE HÉRAULT
**Telephone:** 43.76.70.45
⊗ ☖ ⚏ Map 5

## CORBON, Calvados, 14340

### AUBERGE LE CARREFOUR SAINT JEAN, RN 13, between Lisieux and Caen

**Menu:** 50 Frs. **Restaurant:** Breakfast served from 6:00am. **Specialities:** home cooking. **Other points:** bar, open to non-residents, children welcome, pets welcome – check for details, car park, traditional decor. **Address:** Route Nationale 13, Carrefour Saint Jean.
MR JEAN-HUGUES NEVEU
**Telephone:** 31.63.05.33
⊗ ☖ Map 3

## CORNE, Maine-et-Loire, 49250

### LE RELAIS DE LA CROIX BLANCHE, RN 147, the main road between Tours and Nantes via Saumur

**Menu:** 52 Frs. **Restaurant:** Breakfast served from 6:30am. Lunch served from midday until 1:30pm. Dinner served from 7:30pm until 9:00pm. Closed Saturdays, 1 week in August and between Christmas Day and New Year's Day. **Specialities:** home cooking. **Other points:** bar, terraces, pets welcome – check for details, car park, traditional decor. **Address:** Route Nationale 147.
MR JEAN-NOËL PIGNARD
**Telephone:** 41.45.01.82
⊗ ☖ Map 5

## CORNEVILLE SUR RISLE, Eure, 27500

### RELAIS DU BOULANGARD, RN 180, between Pont Audemer and Rouen or Brionne

**Menu:** 49,50 and 55 Frs. **Restaurant:** Breakfast served from 7:30am. Closed Saturdays. **Specialities:** home cooking. **Other points:** bar, open to non-residents, children welcome, pets welcome – check for details, car park.
MR FRANCIS EGRET
**Telephone:** 32.57.01.27
⊗ ☖ Map 3

## CORPS NUDS, Ille-et-Vilaine, 35150

### LES ROUTIERS, RN 163, the main road between Rennes and Châteaubriant

**Menu:** 43 Frs. **Restaurant:** Breakfast served from 7:00am. Lunch served from midday until 1:30pm. Closed Saturdays and in August. **Specialities:** home cooking. **Other points:** bar. **Address:** 7, place de l'Eglise.
MME SOLANGE PIEL
**Telephone:** 99.44.00.25
⊗ ☖ Map 4

## COUDEVILLE, Manche, 50290

### LA POMME D'ARGENT, between Coutance and Granville

**Languages spoken:** English. **Menu:** 55 to 95 Frs – Plat du jour 40 Frs. **Restaurant:** Breakfast served from 8:00am. Lunch served from midday until 2:30pm. Dinner served from 7:00pm until 9:30pm. **Specialities:** home cooking. **Other points:** bar, à la carte menu, children welcome, terraces, pets welcome – check for details, car park, traditional decor. **Address:** Lieu dit 'La Plesse'.
MR ABDEL BEN MUSTAPHA
**Telephone:** 33.90.03.33
⊗ ☖ Map 3

## COUTANCES, Manche, 50202

### LE RELAIS DU VIADUC, RN 171, between Granville and Saint Lo

**Languages spoken:** English. **Menu:** 45 to 220 Frs. **Accommodation:** 90 to 220 Frs. **Specialities:** langouste gratinée, tripes maison, gigot d'agneau, regional food. **Hotel:** 7 beds. **Other points:** bar, children welcome, car park. **Address:** 25, avenue de Verdun.
MR JEAN-MARC HARAU
**Telephone:** 33.45.02.68
⊗ ☖ ⚏ Map 3

## SARL CLOSERIE DES LILAS

**Menu:** 50 Frs. **Accommodation:** 118 to 130 Frs.
**Restaurant:** Breakfast served from 6:30am. Closed
Saturdays. **Specialities:** regional menu, home cooking.
**Hotel:** 16 beds; 11 single rooms, 5 double rooms.
**Other points:** bar, open to non-residents, children
welcome, terraces, pets welcome – check for details,
car park, traditional decor. **Address:** 1, rue des
Abattoirs.
MR GILLES LETOURNEUR
**Telephone:** 33.45.53.23
⊗ ☗ ⌂ Map 3

## COUVILLE, Manche, 50690

### LE BOURG NEUF, between Cherbourg and Valognes

**Menu:** 48 to 55 Frs. **Restaurant:** Breakfast served from
6:00am. Lunch served from midday until 4:00pm.
Dinner served from 7:00pm until 10:00pm. Closed
Tuesdays and in August. **Specialities:** home cooking.
**Other points:** bar, open to non-residents, à la carte
menu, children welcome, traditional decor. **Address:** Le
Bourg Neuf.
MR YVES ANQUETIL
**Telephone:** 33.52.01.76. **Fax:** 33.52.01.76
⊗ ☗ Map 3

## CROISILLES, Calvados, 14220

### RELAIS DE LA FORGE, RD 962, the main road between Caen and Flers

**Menu:** 48 Frs. **Restaurant:** Breakfast served from
6:00am. Lunch served from 11:00am until 3:00pm.
Closed Sundays. **Specialities:** home cooking. **Other
points:** bar, open to non-residents, children welcome,
car park, modern decor. **Address:** Le Bourg à
Cambro.
MME MONIQUE GIBON
**Telephone:** 31.79.71.80
⊗ ☗ Map 3

## CROISY SUR ANDELLE, Seine-Maritime, 76780

### LE RELAIS DU COMMERCE, RN 31, the main road between Rouen and Beauvais

**Menu:** 55 to 80 Frs. **Restaurant:** Breakfast served from
5:00am. Lunch served from 11:00am until 3:00pm.
Dinner served from 7:00pm until 10:30pm. Closed
Sundays and the Christmas period. **Specialities:** home
cooking. **Other points:** bar, open to non-residents,
children welcome, terraces, pets welcome – check for
details, car park, modern decor. **Address:** Route
Nationale 31.
MME COLETTE BELIÈRE
**Telephone:** 35.23.61.82
⊗ ☗ Map 3

## CROIX BEAUCHENE (LA), Maine-et-Loire, 49490

### RELAIS DE LA CROIX BEAUCHENE, RD 767, between le Lude and Noyant

**Menu:** 48,50 Frs. **Restaurant:** Breakfast served from
6:00am. **Specialities:** home cooking. **Other points:**
bar, open to non-residents, children welcome,
terraces, pets welcome – check for details, car park,
traditional decor. **Address:** Route Départementale
767.
MR JEAN-LOUIS METZGER
**Telephone:** 41.82.14.63
⊗ ☗ Map 5

## CROIX MARE, Seine-Maritime, 76190

### LE BON ACCUEIL, RN 15, between Rouen and Yvetot

**Menu:** 55 Frs. **Restaurant:** Breakfast served from
4:00am. Closed Saturdays, 15 days in May and 15 in
winter. **Specialities:** home cooking. **Other points:** bar,
children welcome, terraces, pets welcome – check for
details, car park, traditional decor. **Address:** Route
Nationale 15.
MR CHRISTIAN LEMAITRE
**Telephone:** 35.91.25.86
⊗ ☗ Map 3

## CUON, Maine-et-Loire, 49150

### LA POMM'DE PIN, RN 938

**Menu:** 48 to 118 Frs. **Restaurant:** Lunch served from
11:30am until 2:30pm. Dinner served from 7:30pm
until 10:00pm. Closed Mondays and the last 3 weeks
of August. **Specialities:** home cooking. **Hotel:** 4 beds;
2 single rooms, 2 double rooms with shower, bath,
private WC. **Other points:** bar, open to non-residents,
à la carte menu, children welcome, lounge area,
terraces, pets welcome – check for details, car park,
traditional decor. **Address:** Route Nationale 938, le
Bourg.
MME YVETTE PÉCOT
**Telephone:** 41.82.75.74
⊗ ☗ Map 5

## DENEE, Maine-et-Loire, 49190

### LE PENALTY

**Languages spoken:** German. **Restaurant:** Dinner
served from midday until 10:00pm. Closed Sunday
afternoons and from Christmas Day to New Year's Day.
**Other points:** bar. **Address:** Place Muller.
MR ALAIN SAULGRAIN
**Telephone:** 41.78.72.03
⊗ ☗ Map 5

## DIEPPE, Seine-Maritime, 76200

### CAFE DE L AVENIR, RN 15

**Menu:** 51 Frs. **Restaurant:** Breakfast served from 4:30am. Lunch served from 11:00am until 2:00pm. Closed Sundays and in August. **Specialities:** home cooking. **Other points:** bar, pets welcome – check for details, car park, traditional decor. **Address:** 10, cours de Dakar, Port de Commerce.
MR BENOÎT PAN
**Telephone:** 35.84.18.10
⊗ ⅋ Map 3

## DINAN, Côtes-du-Nord, 22100

### LA MARMITE, RN 176, Saint Brieuc

**Languages spoken:** English. **Menu:** 45 to 75 Frs. **Accommodation:** 115 to 180 Frs. **Restaurant:** Breakfast served from 7:00am. Lunch served from midday until 2:00pm. Dinner served from 7:30pm until 9:00pm. Closed Saturdays, 3 weeks in July and 1 week at Christmas. **Specialities:** regional menu, home cooking. **Hotel:** 5 beds; 3 single rooms, 2 double rooms. **Other points:** bar, open to non-residents, children welcome, pets welcome – check for details, car park, modern decor. **Address:** 91, rue de Brest.
MR GÉRARD BOUILLET
**Telephone:** 96.39.04.42
⊗ ⅋ ⌂ ⌣ Map 3

## DINARD, Ille-et-Vilaine, 35800

### L'EPICURIEN

**Menu:** 50 to 100 Frs. **Accommodation:** 105 to 170 Frs. **Restaurant:** Breakfast served from 10:00am. Lunch served from midday until 2:30pm. Dinner served from 7:30pm until 10:00pm. Closed Saturdays, 15 days in February and 15 days in October. **Specialities:** home cooking. **Hotel:** 9 beds; 5 single rooms, 4 double rooms. **Other points:** bar, à la carte menu, children welcome, pets welcome – check for details, car park, traditional decor. **Address:** 28, rue de la Corbinais.
MR MARC ARNOULT
**Telephone:** 99.46.10.84
⊗ ⅋ ⌂ ⌣ Map 4

## DISSAY SOUS COURCILLON, Sarthe, 72500

### RELAIS MAINE TOURAINE, RN 138

**Restaurant:** Dinner served from midday until 10:00pm. **Specialities:** regional menu. **Other points:** bar, open to non-residents, traditional decor. **Address:** Route Nationale 138.
MME COLETTE PETIT
**Telephone:** 43.44.09.08
⊗ ⅋ Map 5

## DIVES SUR MER, Calvados, 14160

### LE BON GITE

**Menu:** 45 to 120 Frs. **Restaurant:** Breakfast served from 6:30am. Lunch served from midday until 2:30pm. Dinner served from 7:00pm until 10:30pm. Closed Sundays and from 25 to 31 December. **Specialities:** couscous, paëlla. **Other points:** bar. **Address:** 71, rue du Général de Gaulle.
MR ALAIN BELKACEMI
**Telephone:** 91.91.24.39
⊗ ⅋ Map 3

## DOL DE BRETAGNE, Ille-et-Vilaine, 35120

### LE RELAIS DE BELLE LANDE, RN 12

**Menu:** 47 to 90 Frs. **Restaurant:** Dinner served from midday until 9:00pm. **Specialities:** moules marinières bouchots de la baie, home cooking. **Other points:** bar, à la carte menu. **Address:** 23, bis rue de Rennes.
MR JEAN-YVES BEUBRY
**Telephone:** 99.48.06.14
⊗ ⅋ ⌣ Map 4

## DOLO, Côtes-du-Nord, 22270

### CHEZ PAULETTE, RN 12, between Rennes and Saint Brieuc

**Languages spoken:** English. **Menu:** 47 Frs. **Restaurant:** Breakfast served from 5:30am. Lunch served from 11:30am until 3:00pm. Dinner served from 7:00pm until 11:00pm. Closed Sundays. **Specialities:** regional menu, home cooking. **Other points:** bar, open to non-residents, children welcome, pets welcome – check for details, car park, traditional decor. **Address:** Les Vallées.
MME PAULETTE HERVÉ RENONCOURT
**Telephone:** 96.31.64.62
⊗ ⅋ Map 3

## DOMFRONT, Orne, 61700

### LA CROIX DES LANDES, RD 908, la Ferté Macé

**Languages spoken:** English and Spanish. **Menu:** 53 Frs. **Accommodation:** 90 to 165 Frs. **Restaurant:** Breakfast served from 5:30am. Lunch served from 11:00am until 2:30pm. Dinner served from 7:00pm until 10:00pm. Closed Saturdays. **Specialities:** home cooking. **Hotel:** 8 beds; with shower, bath, telephone. **Other points:** bar, open to non-residents, children welcome, pets welcome – check for details, car park, traditional decor. **Address:** Route de la Ferté Macé.
MR CLAUDE LEVEAU
**Telephone:** 33.38.51.35
⊗ ⅋ ⌂ Map 3

## DOUE LA FONTAINE, Maine-et-Loire, 49700

### CHEZ PAUL, *Poitiers on leaving Angers, or Chôlet on leaving Saumur*
**Languages spoken:** English. **Menu:** 54 Frs (weekdays) and 57 Frs (week-ends) **Restaurant:** Breakfast served from 4:30am. Lunch served from 11:00am until 3:00pm. Dinner served from 6:30pm until 10:00pm. Closed Sundays and the 1st 3 weeks of August. **Specialities:** home cooking. **Other points:** bar, open to non-residents, children welcome, terraces, pets welcome – check for details, car park, modern decor. **Address:** Zone Industrielle, Route de Montreuil.
SARL TYPE-BASSANT
**Telephone:** 41.59.03.33. **Fax:** 41.59.00.34
⊗ ♟ Map 5

## DOZULE, Calvados, 14430

### CHEZ MICHEL, *RN 175*
**Menu:** 60 Frs. **Restaurant:** Breakfast served from 5:30am. Lunch served from midday until 3:00pm. Dinner served from 7:30pm until 10:00pm. Closed Saturdays and from 7 or 8 to 24 August. **Specialities:** home cooking. **Other points:** bar, open to non-residents, children welcome, car park. **Address:** Route de Rouen, Putot en Auge.
MR MICHEL MARTIN
**Telephone:** 31.79.20.29
⊗ ♟ Map 3

## DURANVILLE, Eure, 27230

### LES ARCADES, *RN 13, between Evreux and Lisieux*
**Menu:** 50 to 60 Frs. **Restaurant:** Breakfast served from 5:30am. Lunch served from 11:30am until 3:30pm. Dinner served from 7:00pm until midnight. Closed from Saturdays after 3pm to Sundays 10pm. **Specialities:** home cooking. **Other points:** bar, open to non-residents, children welcome, pets welcome – check for details, car park, modern decor. **Address:** Route Nationale 13.
MME GENEVIÈVE BOGA
**Telephone:** 32.46.83.01
⊗ ♟ Map 3

## ECALLES ALIX, Seine-Maritime, 76190

### AUBERGE DE LA FOURCHE, *RN 15 Bis, Rouen-le Havre*
**Restaurant:** Breakfast served from 6:00am. Lunch served from midday until 3:00pm. Dinner served from 7:00pm until 10:00pm. Closed from Saturdays (1:30pm) to Mondays (6:00am) and from 15 December to the 1st week of January. **Specialities:** regional menu. **Hotel:** 3 beds; 2 single rooms, 1 double room with shower, private WC. **Other points:** bar, open to non-residents, à la carte menu, children welcome, car park, traditional decor. **Address:** Hameau de Loumare.

MR SERGE VANNIER
**Telephone:** 35.95.45.01, 35.56.45.90
⊗ ♟ Map 3

## ECARDENVILLE LA CAMPAGNE, Eure, 27170

### AUBERGE DU RELAIS, *RN 13, the main road between Paris/Lisieux/Caen*
**Menu:** 55 to 95 Frs. **Accommodation:** 90 to 110 Frs. **Restaurant:** Breakfast served from 5:00am. Lunch served from 11:00am until 2:00pm. Dinner served from 6:30pm until 10:00pm. Closed Saturdays, Saturday evenings (in season) and Christmas Day. **Specialities:** home cooking. **Hotel:** 10 beds; 7 single rooms, 3 double rooms with shower. **Other points:** bar, open to non-residents, pets welcome – check for details, car park, traditional decor. **Address:** Route Nationale 13.
MR JEAN-CLAUDE LOTHON
**Telephone:** 32.35.05.32
⊗ ♟ 🏠 Map 3

## ECORPAIN, Sarthe, 72120

### LE RELAIS DE LA JAGOTIERE, *RN 157, between Bouloire and Saint Calais*
**Menu:** 50 Frs. **Restaurant:** Breakfast served from 6:00am. Lunch served from midday until 2:00pm. Dinner served from 7:00pm until 9:00pm. **Specialities:** home cooking. **Other points:** bar, open to non-residents, terraces, pets welcome – check for details, car park, traditional decor. **Address:** La Jagotière.
MME MIREILLE GABORIT
**Telephone:** 43.35.12.00
⊗ ♟ Map 5

## ELVEN, Morbihan, 56250

### LE RELAIS DE L'ARGOUET, *RN 166*
**Languages spoken:** English. **Menu:** 49 to 130 Frs. **Accommodation:** 110 to 160 Frs. **Restaurant:** Lunch served from midday until 2:30pm. Dinner served from 7:30pm until 10:00pm. Closed Saturdays and the 1st fortnight of October. **Specialities:** fruits de mer et poissons, regional food. **Hotel:** 12 beds; 7 single rooms, 5 double rooms. **Other points:** bar, open to non-residents, à la carte menu, children welcome, terraces, pets welcome – check for details, car park, modern decor. **Address:** 36, avenue de l'Argouet.
MR ANDRÉ LE DOUARIN
**Telephone:** 97.53.32.98, 97.53.30.27
⊗ ♟ 🏠 🍲 ☆ Map 4

## EMONDEVILLE, Manche, 50310

### LE COUP DE FREIN, *RN 13, Cherbourg*
**Menu:** 54,50 Frs (coffee included). **Restaurant:** Breakfast served from 6:30am. Lunch served from

11:30am until 2:30pm. Dinner served from 7:30pm until 10:30pm. Closed Saturdays and 3 weeks in August. **Specialities:** home cooking. **Hotel:** 4 beds; 1 single room, 3 double rooms with television. **Other points:** bar, open to non-residents, car park, modern decor. **Address:** Route Nationale 13.
MME ALBERT JEAN
**Telephone:** 33.41.22.74
⊗ ♈ Map 3

## EPERRAIS, Orne, 61400

### LA PETITE VALLEE, RD 938, between Mortagne and Bellême
**Languages spoken:** English. **Menu:** 45 to 58 Frs. **Restaurant:** Breakfast served from 8:00am. Closed Sundays, from 15 to 30 June and from mid-December to mid-January. **Specialities:** regional menu, home cooking. **Other points:** bar, open to non-residents, à la carte menu, children welcome, terraces, pets welcome – check for details, car park, traditional decor. **Address:** La Petite Vallée.
MME MONIQUE GERMOND
**Telephone:** 33.83.91.34
⊗ ♈ Map 3

## EQUEURDREVILLE, Manche, 50120

### RESTAURANT DE LA HAGUE, RD 901
**Languages spoken:** English. **Menu:** 42 Frs. **Accommodation:** 100 to 200 Frs. **Restaurant:** Breakfast served from 6:30am. Lunch served from midday until 2:30pm. Dinner served from 7:30pm until 8:45pm. Closed Saturdays and the 2nd fortnight of August. **Specialities:** home cooking. **Hotel:** 20 beds; 13 single rooms, 7 double rooms with shower, bath. **Other points:** bar, pets welcome – check for details, car park. **Address:** 120, rue de la Paix.
MR CLAUDE LAMY
**Telephone:** 33.93.88.46
⊗ ♈ 🏠 Map 3

## ERBRAY, Loire-Atlantique, 44110

### LE SAINT HUBERT, between Châteaubriant and Angers
**Menu:** 48 Frs (wine included) to 120 Frs. **Restaurant:** Breakfast served from 5:30am. Lunch served from 11:00am until 2:30pm. Dinner served from 7:00pm until 10:30pm. **Specialities:** regional menu, home cooking. **Hotel:** 8 beds; 8 double rooms with shower, bath, private WC, television, telephone. **Other points:** bar, open to non-residents, children welcome, lounge area, terraces, pets welcome – check for details, car park, modern decor. **Address:** 1, place du Calvaire, la Touche.
MR BERNARD BELLANGER
**Telephone:** 40.55.08.37
⊗ ♈ 🏠 Map 5

## ESSARTS (LES), Vendée, 85140

### LE RELAIS DU PINIER, RN 160, la Roche sur Yon
**Menu:** 48 to 60 Frs. **Restaurant:** Breakfast served from 7:00am. Lunch served from midday until 2:30pm. Dinner served from midday until 9:00pm. Closed Saturdays. **Specialities:** home cooking. **Other points:** bar, open to non-residents, à la carte menu, children welcome. **Address:** Route Nationale 160.
MME JACQUELINE DUPONT
**Telephone:** 51.62.81.69
⊗ ♈ Map 5

## EXMES, Orne, 61310

### HOTEL DU COMMERCE, CD 14, the main road between Rouen and Granville
**Menu:** 53 to 85 Frs. **Restaurant:** Breakfast served from 7:00am. Lunch served from 11:00am until 2:00pm. **Specialities:** home cooking. **Hotel:** 4 beds; 2 single rooms, 2 double rooms with shower, bath. **Other points:** bar, open to non-residents, à la carte menu, children welcome. **Address:** Grande Rue.
MME FERNANDE SIMON
**Telephone:** 33.39.93.04
⊗ ♈ Map 3

## EZY SUR EURE, Eure, 27530

### HOTEL TERMINUS – CHEZ ANNIE
**Menu:** 54 to 100 Frs (drink included). **Accommodation:** 100 to 110 Frs. **Restaurant:** Breakfast served from 6:30am. Lunch served from midday until 2:00pm. Dinner served from 7:00pm until 8:30pm. Closed Saturdays and in August. **Specialities:** home cooking. **Hotel:** 11 beds; 8 single rooms, 3 double rooms with shower, private WC. **Other points:** bar, open to non-residents, terraces, pets welcome – check for details, car park, modern decor. **Address:** 16, boulevard Ulysse Lavertue.
MME ANNIE VEISEN
**Telephone:** 37.64.73.24
⊗ ♈ 🏠 Map 3

## FALAISE, Calvados, 14700

### L'ESCALE, between Argentan and Caen
**Menu:** 54 Frs (all included). **Restaurant:** Breakfast served from 6:00am. Dinner served from midday until 8:30pm. Closed Sundays. **Specialities:** home cooking. **Other points:** bar, open to non-residents, children welcome, pets welcome – check for details, car park, modern decor. **Address:** 16, rue du Pavillon.
MR CLAUDE RUSSEAU
**Telephone:** 31.90.12.67
⊗ ♈ Map 3

### LE RELAIS DES ROUTIERS, *RN 158, exit Caen, towards le Mans*

**Menu:** 46 Frs. **Accommodation:** 100 to 140 Frs.
**Restaurant:** Breakfast served from 6:30am. Lunch
served from midday until 2:00pm. Dinner served from
7:30pm until 8:30pm. Closed Sundays and in July.
**Specialities:** home cooking. **Hotel:** 5 beds; 3 single
rooms, 2 double rooms with shower. **Other points:** bar,
open to non-residents, children welcome, pets welcome
– check for details, car park, traditional decor. **Address:**
33, avenue D'Hastings.
MR CHRISTIAN DURAND
**Telephone:** 31.90.04.67
⊗ ♗ ⌂ Map 3

## FALLERON, Vendée, 85670

### CHEZ MARLENE

**Menu:** 47 Frs. **Restaurant:** Lunch served from 11:00am
until 2:00pm. Dinner served from midday until 8:00pm.
Closed Sundays. **Specialities:** home cooking. **Other
points:** bar, open to non-residents, pets welcome – check
for details, car park, traditional decor. **Address:** 54, rue
Nationale.
MME MARLÈNE POTERLOT
**Telephone:** 51.35.50.22
⊗ ♗ Map 5

## FAOUET (LE), Morbihan, 56320

### LE RELAIS DES HALLES, *RN 782, between Lorient and Roscoff*

**Languages spoken:** English. **Menu:** 46 Frs.
**Accommodation:** 75 to 120 Frs. **Restaurant:**
Breakfast served from 7:00am. Lunch served from
midday until 2:00pm. Dinner served from 7:30pm until
9:00pm. Closed Sundays and in September.
**Specialities:** home cooking. **Hotel:** 8 beds; 6 single
rooms, 2 double rooms with shower, private WC,
telephone. **Other points:** bar, open to non-residents,
children welcome, pets welcome – check for details,
car park. **Address:** 19, rue du Soleil.
MR ARMEL LE PUIL
**Telephone:** 97.23.07.66
⊗ ♗ ⌂ Map 4

### LE TY GRAVIC, *RD 769, the main road between Lorient and Roscoff*

**Languages spoken:** English, Italian, Finnish and
Swedish. **Menu:** 46 Frs. **Restaurant:** Breakfast
served from 7:00am. Closed Sundays. **Specialities:**
home cooking. **Other points:** bar, open to non-
residents, children welcome, pets welcome – check
for details, car park, traditional decor. **Address:** Route
de Gourin.
MR ALAIN HALTER
**Telephone:** 97.23.07.04
⊗ ♗ Map 4

### FENOUILLER (LE), Vendée, 85800

### LA MADELON, *RN 754, Saint Gilles Croix de Vie, towards Nantes*

**Languages spoken:** English. **Menu:** 49 to 110 Frs.
**Accommodation:** 90 to 210 Frs. **Restaurant:** Breakfast
served from 8:00am. Lunch served from midday until
2:00pm. Dinner served from 7:30pm until 9:00pm.
Closed in January. **Specialities:** home cooking. **Hotel:**
15 beds; 11 single rooms, 4 double rooms with shower,
bath. **Other points:** bar, open to non-residents, à la carte
menu, children welcome, lounge area, pets welcome –
check for details, car park, traditional decor. **Address:**
64, rue du Centre.
MME CHRISTINE POUPART
**Telephone:** 51.55.17.37, 51.55.05.35
⊗ ♗ ⌂ Map 5

## FERRIERES EN BRAY, Seine-Maritime, 76220

### HOTEL DU CHEMIN DE FER, *RN 31, Rouen or Beauvais*

**Menu:** 46 Frs. **Accommodation:** 90 to 140 Frs.
**Restaurant:** Breakfast served from 7:00am. Lunch
served from midday until 3:00pm. Dinner served from
7:30pm until 10:30pm. Closed Saturdays and 15 days in
May. **Specialities:** home cooking. **Hotel:** 10 beds; 4
single rooms, 6 double rooms with shower. **Other
points:** bar, open to non-residents, pets welcome – check
for details, car park, traditional decor. **Address:** 26,
avenue de la Gare.
MR JEAN-SERGE FERET
**Telephone:** 35.90.01.61
⊗ ♗ ⌂ Map 3

## FERTE BERNARD (LA), Sarthe, 72400

### L'ARCHE DE LA FERTE BERNARD, *A 11*

**Menu:** 59 Frs. **Restaurant:** Open 24 hours. **Other
points:** open to non-residents, à la carte menu, children
welcome, terraces, pets welcome – check for details, car
park. **Address:** A 11 Aire de Villaines la Gonais, dans
les deux sens.
MR GASTON BISSON
**Telephone:** 43.93.41.02. **Fax:** 43.93.42.58
⊗ Map 5

### SARL CHEVAL BLANC, *RN 23, between la Ferté Bernard and Nogent le Rotrou*

**Languages spoken:** English. **Menu:** 50 to 180 Frs.
**Restaurant:** Breakfast served from 5:00am.
**Specialities:** home cooking. **Other points:** bar, open to
non-residents, à la carte menu, children welcome, lounge
area, terraces, pets welcome – check for details, car
park, modern decor. **Address:** Lieu dit 'La Grange'.
MR PATRICK DELANNÉE
**Telephone:** 43.93.17.05
⊗ ♗ ⌱ Map 5

## FLERS, Orne, 61100

### HOTEL DES TOURISTES

**Menu:** 43 to 60 Frs. **Accommodation:** 80 to 100 Frs. **Restaurant:** Breakfast served from 7:00am. Lunch served from midday until 4:00pm. Dinner served from 7:00pm until 10:00pm. Closed Sundays and 3 weeks in August. **Specialities:** home cooking. **Hotel:** 12 beds. **Other points:** bar, open to non-residents, à la carte menu, children welcome, traditional decor. **Address:** 80, rue de Paris. MR MAURICE DUPONT **Telephone:** 33.65.25.57 ⊗ 🍷 🏠 Map 3

## FLEURY SUR ORNE, Calvados, 14123

### LA POMME D'OR, RD 562, Caen/Flers, towards Laval

**Menu:** 48 to 50 Frs. **Restaurant:** Breakfast served from 7:00am. Lunch served from midday until 3:00pm. Closed Sundays and in August. **Specialities:** home cooking. **Other points:** bar, pets welcome – check for details, car park, modern decor. **Address:** 20, route d'Harcourt. MME EMILIENNE FRANÇOIS **Telephone:** 31.82.36.87 ⊗ 🍷 Map 3

## FONTAINE SAINT MARTIN (LA), Sarthe, 72330

### LE CHENE VERT, RN 23, Nantes

**Menu:** 55 to 65 Frs. **Restaurant:** Breakfast served from 7:00am. Lunch served from 11:00am until 3:00pm. Dinner served from 7:00pm until 10:00pm. Closed Saturdays and in August. **Specialities:** home cooking. **Other points:** bar, open to non-residents, à la carte menu, pets welcome – check for details, traditional decor. **Address:** Le Chêne Vert. MME MARIE-LOUISE FLAMEYGH **Telephone:** 43.87.80.84, 43.87.24.84 ⊗ 🍷 Map 5

## FOUCARMONT, Seine-Maritime, 76340

### CLUB ARLEQUIN, RN 28, between Neufchâtel en Bray and Blangy sur Bresle

**Menu:** 50 Frs. **Restaurant:** Lunch served from midday until 3:00pm. Closed Saturdays. **Specialities:** home cooking. **Other points:** bar, open to non-residents, terraces, car park, traditional decor. **Address:** 28 Route Nationale. MME RÉGINE BÉNARD **Telephone:** 35.93.91.50 ⊗ 🍷 Map 3

## FOUGERES, Ille-et-Vilaine, 35300

### AUX AMIS DE LA ROUTE, RN 12, the main road between Rennes and Saint Malo

**Languages spoken:** English and German. **Menu:** 60 Frs (drink included). **Accommodation:** 140 to 150 Frs. **Restaurant:** Breakfast served from 7:00am. Lunch served from midday until 2:00pm. Dinner served from 7:30pm until 9:00pm. Closed Sundays and Saturdays (in season). **Specialities:** regional menu, home cooking. **Hotel:** 12 beds; 6 single rooms, 6 double rooms with shower, bath, private WC. **Other points:** bar, open to non-residents, children welcome, lounge area, terraces, car park. **Address:** 6, boulevard Saint Germain. MR MICHEL BASTIEN **Telephone:** 99.99.07.62 ⊗ 🍷 🏠 ☆ Map 4

## GAEL, Ille-et-Vilaine, 35290

### LES ROUTIERS, the main road between Dinan and Lorient

**Places of interest:** Cuisses de grenouilles. **Menu:** 46 Frs. **Accommodation:** 83 to 126 Frs. **Restaurant:** Breakfast served from 7:00am. Lunch served from 11:30am until 2:30pm. Dinner served from 7:00pm until 9:00pm. Closed Fridays. **Specialities:** paëlla (to order), regional food, home cooking. **Hotel:** 5 beds; 1 single room, 4 double rooms with shower, private WC, telephone. **Other points:** bar, open to non-residents, children welcome, lounge area, pets welcome – check for details, car park, traditional decor. **Address:** Place des Tilleuls. MME ANNICK REBILLARD **Telephone:** 99.07.72.39 ⊗ 🍷 🏠 Map 4

## GISORS, Eure, 27140

### BAR DE L'AVENUE, RN 15, between Dieppe and Gournay

**Languages spoken:** English. **Menu:** 60 Frs. **Accommodation:** 120 to 160 Frs. **Restaurant:** Breakfast served from 7:00am. Closed Sundays and in August. **Specialities:** home cooking. **Hotel:** 9 beds; with shower, private WC, television. **Other points:** bar, children welcome, terraces, car park. **Address:** Route de Dieppe. MR ROUSSEL **Telephone:** 32.27.19.45 ⊗ 🍷 🏠 Map 3

## GLACERIE (LA), Manche, 50470

### LE RELAIS DE LA GLACERIE, RN 13, Cherbourg

**Menu:** 50 Frs. **Restaurant:** Breakfast served from 6:00am. Lunch served from midday until 2:00pm. Dinner served from 7:30pm until 9:00pm. Closed Saturdays and from 20 July to 8 August. **Specialities:** home cooking. **Other points:** bar, open to non-residents, à la carte menu, children welcome, lounge area, terraces, pets welcome – check for details, car park, modern

decor. **Address:** Route Nationale 13.
MR PAUL ROUPSARD
**Telephone:** 33.44.13.54
⊗ ♥ Map 3

## GLOS SUR RISLE, Eure, 27290

### RELAIS DE LA FORGE, RD 130, between Montfort and Brionne

**Menu:** 35 to 50 Frs. **Restaurant:** Breakfast served from 6:30am. Dinner served from 7:00pm until 8:30pm. Closed Sundays and 8 days in February. **Specialities:** home cooking. **Other points:** bar, children welcome, pets welcome – check for details, car park, traditional decor. **Address:** La Forge.
MR SERGE LANGLOIS
**Telephone:** 32.56.16.34
⊗ ♥ Map 3

## GODERVILLE, Seine-Maritime, 76110

### RELAIS DE SAINT SAUVEUR, CD 925, between le Havre and Fécamp

**Menu:** 50 to 55 Frs. **Restaurant:** Breakfast served from 6:30am. Closed Saturdays **Specialities:** home cooking. **Other points:** bar, open to non-residents, terraces, pets welcome – check for details, car park. **Address:** Saint Sauveur d'Emalleville.
MR PHILIPPE GUÉRIN
**Telephone:** 35.27.21.56
⊗ ♥ Map 3

## GOUESNIERE (LA), Ille-et-Vilaine, 35350

### LE RELAIS ROUTIERS, the main road between Rennes and Saint Malo

**Places of interest:** Center Parc, Verneuil sur Avre. **Menu:** 50 Frs. **Accommodation:** 130 to 165 Frs. **Restaurant:** Breakfast served from 7:00am. Lunch served from midday until 2:00pm. Dinner served from 7:00pm until 10:00pm. Closed Sundays and in August. **Specialities:** home cooking. **Hotel:** 14 beds; 9 single rooms, 5 double rooms with shower. **Other points:** bar, open to non-residents, children welcome, car park. **Address:** 2, rue d'Halet.
MME MARIE-THÉ BOURGALAIS
**Telephone:** 99.58.80.57, 99.58.89.33
⊗ ♥ 🏠 Map 4

## GOULET (LE), Eure, 27950

### LE TERMINUS, RN 15, the main road between Vernon and Rouen

**Menu:** 55 Frs. **Accommodation:** 120 to 150 Frs. **Restaurant:** Breakfast served from 6:00am. Lunch served from 11:30am until 3:00pm. Dinner served from 7:30pm until 8:30pm. Closed Saturdays, 3 weeks in August and 1 at Christmas. **Specialities:** home cooking. **Hotel:** 18 beds; 6 single rooms, 12 double rooms with shower, bath. **Other points:** bar, open to non-residents,

children welcome, pets welcome – check for details, car park, traditional decor. **Address:** 30, route de Rouen.
MR CLAUDE HARD
**Telephone:** 32.52.50.07
⊗ ♥ 🏠 Map 3

## GOUSTRANVILLE, Calvados, 14430

### LE RELAIS DU BON ACCUEIL, RN 175

**Languages spoken:** English and Spanish. **Menu:** 50 Frs. **Restaurant:** Breakfast served from 6:30am. Closed Sundays and the last week of the August. **Specialities:** home cooking. **Other points:** bar, open to non-residents, children welcome, terraces, pets welcome – check for details, car park.
SARL CHORNET/LARDOUX
**Telephone:** 31.79.21.90
⊗ ♥ Map 3

## GRAINVILLE, Eure, 27380

### LE RELAIS DE GRAINVILLE, RN 14, the main road between Paris/Rouen/le Havre

**Menu:** 50 Frs. **Restaurant:** Breakfast served from 5:00am. Lunch served from 11:30am until 2:30pm. Closed Saturdays and 1 week between Christmas Day and New Year's Day. **Specialities:** home cooking. **Other points:** bar, open to non-residents, pets welcome – check for details, car park, traditional decor. **Address:** 40, Route Nationale.
MME EDWIGE LEGATT
**Telephone:** 32.48.06.28
⊗ ♥ Map 3

## GRAND FOUGERAY (LE), Ille-et-Vilaine, 35390

### LE RELAIS DE LA BELLE ETOILE, RN 137

**Languages spoken:** English. **Restaurant:** Closed Sundays. **Other points:** bar. **Address:** La Belle Etoile.
MR ROLAND PIROT
**Telephone:** 99.08.42.59
⊗ ♥ ☆ 🏠 Map 4

## GRAVIGNY, Eure, 27930

### HOTEL DES SPORTS

**Languages spoken:** English, Spanish and Arabic. **Menu:** 49 Frs. **Accommodation:** 80 Frs. **Restaurant:** Breakfast served from 7:00am. Lunch served from midday until 2:30pm. Dinner served from 7:30pm until 9:30pm. Closed Sundays. **Hotel:** 7 beds; 4 single rooms, 3 double rooms with shower, bath, private WC. **Other points:** bar, open to non-residents, children welcome, terraces, pets welcome – check for details, car park, modern decor. **Address:** 109, avenue Aristide Briand.
MR TARIK SENOUCI
**Telephone:** 32.33.16.19
⊗ ♥ 🏠 Map 3

## GREMONVILLE, Seine-Maritime, 76970

### *LA CHAUMIERE, RN 15, the main road between Rouen and Saint Valéry en Caux*

**Languages spoken:** English. **Menu:** 45 Frs. **Restaurant:** Dinner served from midday until 9:00pm. Closed Tuesdays. **Specialities:** home cooking. **Other points:** bar, children welcome, terraces, pets welcome – check for details, car park, traditional decor. **Address:** Place de l'Eglise, Motteville.
MR CHRISTIAN LE MASURIER
**Telephone:** 35.56.45.65
⊗ 🍸 Map 3

## GUE DE LA CHAINE (LE), Orne, 61130

### *LE GUE ROUTIER, between Mamers and Bellèmes*

**Menu:** 55 to 58 Frs. **Restaurant:** Breakfast served from 6:30am. **Specialities:** home cooking. **Other points:** bar, children welcome, pets welcome – check for details, car park, modern decor. **Address:** 3, route de Mamers.
MME MARYLÈNE DISZTL
**Telephone:** 33.73.02.66
⊗ 🍸 Map 3

## GUENIN, Morbihan, 56150

### *LE RELAIS DE BON VALLON*

**Languages spoken:** English. **Restaurant:** Dinner served from midday until 11:00pm. **Other points:** bar, car park. **Address:** ZI de Bon Vallon.
MR JOËL LE HAZIF
**Telephone:** 97.39.10.40
⊗ 🍸 Map 4

## GUERCHE DE BRETAGNE (LA), Ille-et-Vilaine, 35130

### *LE RELAIS DU PONT D'ANJOU, RN 176, the main road between Rennes and Angers*

**Menu:** 44,50 to 125 Frs. **Restaurant:** Breakfast served from 6:45am. Lunch served from 11:00am until 3:00pm. Dinner served from 7:00pm until 10:00pm. Closed Sundays. **Specialities:** Fruits de Mer, couscous, paëlla, regional food, home cooking. **Hotel:** 12 beds. **Other points:** bar, open to non-residents, à la carte menu, children welcome. **Address:** 11, faubourg d'Anjou.
MR ANDRÉ MOUSSU
**Telephone:** 99.96.23.10
⊗ 🍸 🏠 ☆ Map 4

## GUILBERVILLE, Manche, 50160

### *RESTAURANT LE POTEAU, RN 175*

**Languages spoken:** German and English. **Restaurant:** Dinner served from midday until midnight. Closed Saturdays, Sundays and vacation periods at Christmas. **Other points:** bar, car park. **Address:** Le Poteau.
MR FRÉDY MENANT
**Telephone:** 33.56.73.10
⊗ 🍸 Map 3

## GUIPAVAS, Finistère, 29490

### *PMU – LE RELAIS DU LION D'OR, CD 712*

**Other points:** bar. **Address:** 52, rue de Paris.
MME TROADEC
**Telephone:** 98.28.00.33
⊗ 🍸 Map 4

## GURUNHUEL, Côtes-du-Nord, 22390

### *CHEZ GILBERTE, RN 787*

**Restaurant:** Breakfast served from 7:30am. Closed in July. **Other points:** bar. **Address:** Kérambellec.
MR YVES GEORGELIN
**Telephone:** 96.21.81.00
⊗ 🍸 Map 4

## HAVRE (LE), Seine-Maritime, 76600

### *AU TELEPHONE, in the area of Eure*

**Languages spoken:** English. **Menu:** 54 Frs (wine included). **Restaurant:** Breakfast served from 7:00am. Closed Saturdays and in July. **Specialities:** home cooking. **Other points:** bar, open to non-residents, pets welcome – check for details, car park, traditional decor. **Address:** 173, boulevard Amiral Mouchez.
MR JEAN-CLAUDE BOUILLON
**Telephone:** 35.53.24.76, 35.53.24.74
⊗ 🍸 Map 3

### *LE P'TIT COMPTOIR, in the area of Saint François*

**Menu:** 56 to 78 Frs. **Restaurant:** Breakfast served from 8:00am. Lunch served from midday until 2:15pm. Dinner served from 7:15pm until 9:30pm. Closed Sundays and from 20 December to 15 January. **Specialities:** home cooking. **Other points:** open to non-residents, children welcome. **Address:** 31, rue du Général Faidherbe.
MR BERNARD RONDEL
**Telephone:** 35.42.78.72
⊗ Map 3

### *LE RELAIS, Autoroute towards le Havre, 1st left at the lights*

**Languages spoken:** English. **Menu:** 55 to 120 Frs. **Restaurant:** Breakfast served from 6:30am. Lunch served from 11:45am until 2:30pm. Dinner served from 6:45pm until 10:30pm. Closed Sundays. **Specialities:** regional menu. **Other points:** bar, open to non-residents, à la carte menu, children welcome, lounge area, pets welcome – check for details, car park, traditional decor. **Address:** 128, boulevard de Graville.

MR DIDIER EUDES
**Telephone:** 35.24.54.48
⊗ ♉

## LE RELAIS DES ROUTIERS, *RN 15*

**Menu:** 50 Frs. **Restaurant:** Breakfast served from 7:00am. Lunch served from 11:30am until 4:00pm. Dinner served from 7:00pm until 11:00pm. Closed Fridays and from 23 December to 7 January. **Specialities:** home cooking. **Other points:** bar, children welcome, car park, traditional decor. **Address:** 57, rue Marceau.
MME MARIE-PIERRE PRISER
**Telephone:** 34.74.06.32
⊗ ♉ Map 3

## LE WELCOME, *RN 13 Bis*

**Accommodation:** 90 to 180 Frs. **Restaurant:** Lunch served from midday until 3:00pm. Dinner served from 7:00pm until 1:00am. **Specialities:** regional menu. **Hotel:** 8 beds; with shower, bath, private WC, telephone. **Other points:** bar, à la carte menu, car park, modern decor. **Address:** 55–7, quai de Southampton.
MME MARIE-PIERRE PRISER
**Telephone:** 35.43.17.84
⊗ ♉ ⌂ Map 3

# HAYE DU PUITS (LA), Manche, 50250

## RESTAURANT DES AMIS, *RN 800, Cherbourg*

**Menu:** 48 to 80 Frs. **Restaurant:** Breakfast served from 7:00am. Closed Saturdays. **Specialities:** home cooking. **Other points:** bar, open to non-residents, à la carte menu, terraces, pets welcome – check for details, car park. **Address:** 16, rue du Château.
MR LOUIS LE FILLASTRE
**Telephone:** 33.46.03.42
⊗ ♉ ⌣ Map 3

# HAYE PESNEL (LA), Manche, 50320

## CHEZ ARMELLE

**Languages spoken:** English. **Menu:** 54 to 90 Frs. **Restaurant:** Breakfast served from 8:00am. Dinner served from midday until 10:00pm. Closed Saturdays and in December. **Specialities:** regional menu, home cooking. **Other points:** bar, open to non-residents, à la carte menu, children welcome, terraces, pets welcome – check for details, car park, traditional decor. **Address:** Rue de la Libération.
MME ARMELLE JACQUETTE
**Telephone:** 33.61.50.83, 33.61.58.94
⊗ ♉ ⌣ Map 3

# HERBERGEMENT (L'), Vendée, 85260

## LES ROUTIERS, *RD 763, between Nantes und la Roche sur Yon*

**Menu:** 48 Frs. **Restaurant:** Breakfast served from 7:30am. Lunch served from 11:45am until 2:30pm. Closed Thursdays and in August. **Specialities:** home cooking. **Other points:** bar, children welcome, car park.
**Address:** 17, rue Georges Clémenceau.
MR MICHEL BRETIN
**Telephone:** 51.42.80.71
⊗ ♉ Map 5

# HERBIERS (LES), Vendée, 85500

## L'OREE DES BOIS VERTS, *RN 160, between Angers and les Sables d'Olonne*

**Menu:** 45 Frs. **Accommodation:** 110 to 210 Frs. **Restaurant:** Breakfast served from 7:00am. Lunch served from midday until 2:00pm. Dinner served from 5:30pm until 9:00pm. Closed Sundays, for All Saints and the 1st fortnight in May. **Specialities:** home cooking. **Hotel:** 11 beds; 8 single rooms, 3 double rooms with shower, bath, private WC, television, telephone. **Other points:** bar, open to non-residents, lounge area, terraces, pets welcome – check for details, car park, traditional decor. **Address:** Route des Sables.
MR RENÉ JOULIN
**Telephone:** 51.91.00.18
⊗ ♉ ⌂ ☆ Map 5

# HERIC, Loire-Atlantique, 44810

## LE BIEF, *RN 137, the main road between Nantes and Rennes*

**Languages spoken:** English and Italian. **Menu:** 56 Frs (drink and coffee included). **Restaurant:** Breakfast served from 6:00am. Lunch served from midday until 2:00pm. Dinner served from 7:00pm until 9:30pm. Closed Sundays and the 2nd fortnight of August. **Specialities:** home cooking. **Other points:** bar, open to non-residents, children welcome, lounge area, pets welcome – check for details, car park, traditional decor. **Address:** Lieu dit 'Bout de Bois', Route Nationale 137.
MR DIDIER CRÉTEAU
**Telephone:** 40.57.60.54
⊗ ♉ Map 5

# HERMITAGE (L'), Ille-et-Vilaine, 35590

## LE VILLAGE

**Menu:** 49 to 60 Frs. **Restaurant:** Breakfast served from 7:00am. Lunch served from 11:00am until 2:00pm. Dinner served from 7:30pm until 9:00pm. Closed Sundays and in August. **Specialities:** regional menu. **Other points:** bar, open to non-residents, children welcome, pets welcome – check for details, car park, traditional decor. **Address:** 23, rue de Rennes.
MR MICHEL BOISSEL
**Telephone:** 99.64.03.31
⊗ ♉ Map 4

# HEUGUEVILLE SUR SIENNE, Manche, 50200

## LE MASCARET, *Cherbourg*

Menu: 50 to 120 Frs. Restaurant: Closed Tuesdays. Specialities: regional menu. Other points: bar, open to non-residents, terraces, pets welcome – check for details, car park, traditional decor.
MR GILBERT DESLANDES
Telephone: 33.45.86.09
⊗ ॰ ᗏ Map 3

## HINGLE LES GRANITS (LE),
Côtes-du-Nord, 22100

### LES ROUTIERS, RN 166
Languages spoken: English. Menu: 44 Frs.
Restaurant: Breakfast served from 6:30am. Lunch served from 11:45am until 2:00pm. Closed Saturdays and in August. Specialities: home cooking. Hotel: 6 beds. Other points: bar, open to non-residents, car park.
Address: Rue de la Gare.
MR RÉMY PESSEL
Telephone: 96.83.58.45
⊗ ॰ ⌂ Map 4

## HONFLEUR, Calvados, 14600

### LE MERLE BLANC
Languages spoken: English. Restaurant: Dinner served from midday until midnight. Closed Saturdays and August and from 20 to 31 December. Other points: bar. Address: Honfleur.
MME DENISE RENAULT
Telephone: 31.89.11.98
⊗ ॰ Map 3

## HOPITAL CAMFROUT (L'),
Finistère, 29460

### LES ROUTIERS, RN 170, motorway Brest/Quimper, exit Daoulas
Menu: 47 to 150 Frs. Restaurant: Breakfast served from 8:00am. Lunch served from midday until 2:00pm. Closed Mondays. Specialities: fruits de mer, regional food, home cooking. Other points: bar, open to non-residents, à la carte menu, pets welcome – check for details, car park, traditional decor. Address: 68, rue Emile Salaun.
MR BERNARD HAMERY
Telephone: 98.20.01.21, 98.20.05.34
⊗ ॰ Map 4

## HOTTOT LES BAGUES, Calvados, 14250

### LE RELAIS DE LA MANCHE
Menu: 48 Frs. Restaurant: Breakfast served from 6:00am. Lunch served from 11:30am until 2:00pm. Closed Saturdays in June and in September. Specialities: home cooking. Other points: bar, open to non-residents, terraces, traditional decor. Address: Route de Caumont.

MR ROLAND JEANNE
Telephone: 31.80.81.72
⊗ ॰ Map 3

## HYENVILLE, Manche, 50660

### LE RELAIS DE LA SIENNE, RD 971, between Coutances and Granville
Languages spoken: English. Menu: 50 to 85 Frs. Accommodation: 90 to 150 Frs. Restaurant: Breakfast served from 6:00am. Closed Sundays. Specialities: home cooking. Hotel: 7 beds; 1 single room, 6 double rooms with shower. Other points: bar, open to non-residents, à la carte menu, terraces, pets welcome – check for details, car park, traditional decor. Address: Le Pont.
MME ELIANE MAYOR
Telephone: 33.07.56.03
⊗ ॰ ⌂ Map 3

## JALLAIS, Maine-et-Loire, 49510

### LE VERT GALANT – LA CROIX VERTE
Languages spoken: English. Menu: 100 Frs. Accommodation: 180 to 250 Frs. Restaurant: Breakfast served from 7:00am. Lunch served from midday until 2:00pm. Dinner served from 7:00pm until 10:00pm. Specialities: salade rillauds d'anjou chauds, pavé boeuf au Chinon, regional food. Hotel: 27 beds; with shower, bath, private WC, television, telephone. Other points: bar, open to non-residents, à la carte menu, children welcome, lounge area, pets welcome – check for details, car park, traditional decor. Address: Place de la Mairie.
MR PIERRE GAILLARD
Telephone: 41.64.20.22. Fax: 41.64.15.17
⊗ ॰ ⌂ ᗏ ☆☆ Map 5

## JANZE, Ille-et-Vilaine, 35150

### HOTEL RESTAURANT BAR METAYER, RN 777
Accommodation: 140 to 160 Frs. Restaurant: Breakfast served from 7:00am. Lunch served from midday until 1:00pm. Dinner served from 7:00pm until 8:30pm. Specialities: home cooking. Hotel: 7 beds; with shower, private WC, television, telephone. Other points: bar, open to non-residents, car park, modern decor. Address: 5, rue Jean-Marie Lacire.
MR MICHEL MÉTAYER
Telephone: 99.47.05.10
⊗ ॰ ⌂ Map 4

## JARZE, Maine-et-Loire, 49140

### LE MOULINET, RN 766, Angers Tours via Seiches/Loir-Baugé
Menu: 46 Frs and 70 to 120 Frs. Restaurant: Lunch served from 11:30am until 2:30pm. Dinner served from 6:30pm until 9:30pm. Closed Sundays. Specialities:

fruits de mer. **Other points:** bar, car park. **Address:** Route Nationale 766.
MR DANIEL DOMAS
**Telephone:** 41.95.47.52
⊗ ♀ Map 5

## JOSSELIN, Morbihan, 56120

### *LA ROCHETTE – LES ROUTIERS*
**Languages spoken:** English. **Menu:** 43 to 70 Frs. **Restaurant:** Breakfast served from 8:00am. Lunch served from midday until 2:00pm. Dinner served from 7:00pm until 9:30pm. Closed Saturdays. **Specialities:** home cooking. **Other points:** bar, open to non-residents, children welcome, terraces, pets welcome – check for details, traditional decor. **Address:** 128, rue Glatinier.
MME ANNIE LE CORRE
**Telephone:** 97.22.27.29
⊗ ♀ Map 4

## JOUE DU BOIS, Orne, 61320

### *LE RELAIS DU MANOIR, RN 12, Alençon*
**Languages spoken:** English and Yugoslavian. **Menu:** 48 to 90 Frs. **Restaurant:** Breakfast served from 7:00am. Lunch served from 11:30am until 2:30pm. Dinner served from 7:00pm until 10:00pm. Closed Mondays. **Specialities:** regional menu. **Other points:** bar, open to non-residents, à la carte menu, terraces, pets welcome – check for details, car park, traditional decor. **Address:** Le Bourg.
MME VIOLAINE VULOVIC
**Telephone:** 33.37.48.54
⊗ ♀ Map 3

## JOUE EN CHARNIE, Sarthe, 72540

### *LE CHEVAL BLANC, RN 157, the main road between le Mans and Laval*
**Languages spoken:** English. **Menu:** 48 to 130 Frs. **Accommodation:** 90 to 190 Frs. **Restaurant:** Breakfast served from 7:00am. Lunch served from midday until 2:30pm. Dinner served from 7:00pm until 9:00pm. Closed Saturdays. **Specialities:** regional menu, home cooking. **Hotel:** 10 beds; 4 single rooms, 6 double rooms with shower, bath, private WC. **Other points:** bar, open to non-residents, à la carte menu, children welcome, terraces, pets welcome – check for details, car park, traditional decor. **Address:** Le Bourg.
MR DOMINIQUE BOURGON
**Telephone:** 43.88.42.13
⊗ ♀ ⌂ ☆ Map 5

## JUMELLIERE (LA), Maine-et-Loire, 49120

### *LA BOULE D'OR, RD 961, the main road between Chôlet and Angers, exit Chemillé, 5km on the left*

**Menu:** 49 to 170 Frs. **Accommodation:** 100 to 170 Frs. **Restaurant:** Breakfast served from 7:15am. Lunch served from 11:45am until 2:00pm. Dinner served from 7:00pm until 8:15pm. Closed Sundays. **Specialities:** home cooking. **Hotel:** 6 beds; 3 single rooms, 3 double rooms with shower, bath, private WC. **Other points:** bar, open to non-residents, children welcome, terraces, pets welcome – check for details, car park, traditional decor. **Address:** 2, rue du Val de Loire.
MME JANINE SÉCHER
**Telephone:** 41.64.33.23
⊗ ♀ ⌂ Map 5

## JURQUES, Calvados, 14260

### *AU BON ACCUEIL, RD 577, exit at slip road for Caen, via interchange of Vire*
**Menu:** 50 Frs (wine included). **Restaurant:** Lunch served from 11:45am until 2:00pm. Dinner served from 7:00pm until 9:30pm. Closed Sundays. **Specialities:** regional menu, home cooking. **Other points:** bar, à la carte menu, children welcome, car park. **Address:** Route de Vire.
MR CHRISTIAN LESAGE
**Telephone:** 31.77.81.17
⊗ ♀ Map 3

## KERFAVEN, Finistère, 29230

### *RESTAURANT DE KERFAVEN, RD 712, between Landivisiau and Landernau*
**Languages spoken:** English. **Menu:** 50 Frs (coffee included). **Restaurant:** Breakfast served from 6:00am. Closed Saturdays, 15 days in July and 1 week in August. **Specialities:** home cooking. **Other points:** bar, open to non-residents, children welcome, lounge area, terraces, pets welcome – check for details, car park.
MR VINCENT PRONOST
**Telephone:** 98.20.41.26
⊗ ♀ Map 4

## KERGONAN LANGUIDIC, Morbihan, 56440

### *LE RELAIS ROUTIER, RN 24, the main road between Lorient and Rennes*
**Menu:** 42 Frs. **Restaurant:** Breakfast served from 7:00am. Lunch served from 11:30am until 2:00pm. Closed Saturdays and in December. **Specialities:** home cooking. **Other points:** bar, open to non-residents, children welcome, terraces, pets welcome – check for details, car park, modern decor. **Address:** 9, rue du Commerce.
MR ANDRÉ LE GARREC
**Telephone:** 97.85.90.69
⊗ ♀ Map 4

## KERHOSTIN, Morbihan, 56510

### LA CHALOUPE, Quiberon

**Menu:** 50 to 75 Frs. **Accommodation:** 100 to 130
Frs. **Restaurant:** Breakfast served from 8:00am.
Lunch served from midday until 2:00pm. Dinner
served from 7:00pm until 8:30pm. Closed Saturdays
and from 15 October to 15 November. **Specialities:**
home cooking. **Hotel:** 6 beds; 1 single room, 5 double
rooms with shower. **Other points:** bar, open to non-
residents, à la carte menu, terraces, pets welcome –
check for details, car park, traditional decor. **Address:**
10, rue Hoche.
MLLE CHRISTIANE BOUVRANDE
**Telephone:** 97.30.91.54
⊗ ♀ 🏠 Map 4

## LAMBALLE, Côtes-du-Nord, 22400

### LA TOUR D'ARGENT, RD 12, between
### Rennes and Saint Brieuc

**Languages spoken:** English. **Menu:** 55 to 180 Frs.
**Accommodation:** 180 to 350 Frs. **Restaurant:**
Breakfast served from 7:00am. Lunch served from
midday until 2:30pm. Dinner served from 7:00pm until
9:30pm. Closed Saturdays and the 2nd fortnight in June.
**Specialities:** crevettes grillées, canard à l'orange, blancs
de seiches, regional food, home cooking. **Hotel:** 31
beds; 2 single rooms, 29 double rooms with shower,
bath, private WC, television, telephone. **Other points:**
bar, open to non-residents, à la carte menu, children
welcome, lounge area, terraces, pets welcome – check
for details, car park. **Address:** 2, rue du Docteur
Lavergne.
MR CLAUDE MOUNIER
**Telephone:** 96.31.01.37. **Fax:** 96.31.37.59
⊗ ♀ 🏠 ⌣ ☆☆ Map 4

## LANDEBIA, Côtes-du-Nord, 22130

### AU RENDEZ-VOUS DES AMIS, RD 768,
### between Plancoët and Lamballe

**Menu:** 45 Frs. **Accommodation:** 90 to 180 Frs.
**Restaurant:** Breakfast served from 7:00am.
**Specialities:** home cooking. **Hotel:** 12 beds; 3 single
rooms, 9 double rooms with shower. **Other points:** bar,
open to non-residents, children welcome, terraces, pets
welcome – check for details, car park, modern decor.
**Address:** 17, rue de la Gare.
MME MICHÈLE ABBÉ
**Telephone:** 96.84.48.22
⊗ ♀ 🏠 Map 4

## LANDERONDE, Vendée, 85150

### L'HORTENSE, RN 160, between la Roche
### sur Yon and les Sables d'Olonne

**Menu:** 47 Frs (wine included) to 170 Frs. **Restaurant:**
Breakfast served from 7:00am. Lunch served from

midday until 3:00pm. Dinner served from 7:00pm until
9:00pm. Closed Mondays. **Specialities:** regional menu,
home cooking. **Other points:** bar, open to non-residents,
à la carte menu, children welcome, terraces, pets
welcome – check for details, car park, traditional decor.
**Address:** Lieu dit 'Les Loges', Route Nationale 160.
MR MICHEL MIGRAN
**Telephone:** 51.34.22.81
⊗ ♀ Map 5

## LANDEVANT, Morbihan, 56690

### LE RELAIS DU PELICAN, RN 165

**Restaurant:** Closed Monday evenings, Tuesdays and
October. **Other points:** bar. **Address:** 14, Route
Nationale.
MR BOURN
**Telephone:** 97.56.93.12
⊗ ♀ ⌣ Map 4

## LANDIVISIAU, Finistère, 29400

### HOTEL RESTAURANT LE TERMINUS,
### RN 12, Brest

**Languages spoken:** English. **Menu:** 58 to 100 Frs.
**Accommodation:** 95 to 130 Frs. **Restaurant:** Breakfast
served from 6:00am. Lunch served from 11:00am until
3:00pm. Dinner served from 7:30pm until 10:00pm.
Closed Saturdays and in August. **Specialities:** fruits de
mer, home cooking. **Hotel:** 25 beds; 17 single rooms, 8
double rooms with shower. **Other points:** bar, open to
non-residents, à la carte menu, children welcome, lounge
area, car park, modern decor. **Address:** 94, avenue Foch.
MR RAYMOND FLOCH
**Telephone:** 98.68.02.00
⊗ ♀ 🏠 ⌣ ☆ Map 4

## LANESTER, Morbihan, 56600

### LA ROTONDE, RN 24, Lorient

**Menu:** 40 to 60 Frs. **Accommodation:** 90 to 140 Frs.
**Restaurant:** Breakfast served from 7:00am. Lunch
served from midday until 2:00pm. Dinner served from
7:00pm until 9:00pm. Closed Saturdays, 15 days at end
of August and 15 days at Christmas. **Specialities:** home
cooking. **Hotel:** 14 beds; 12 single rooms, 2 double
rooms with shower, private WC. **Other points:** bar,
open to non-residents, à la carte menu, pets welcome –
check for details, car park, traditional decor. **Address:**
120, rue Jean Jaurès.
MME CÉCILE MERCIER
**Telephone:** 97.76.06.37
⊗ ♀ 🏠 ☆ Map 4

### LE RELAIS DU PONT DU BONHOMME,
### RN 24, between Lorient and Carnac

**Restaurant:** Breakfast served from 7:00am. Lunch
served from 11:30am until 2:30pm. Closed in August.
**Specialities:** regional menu, home cooking. **Other**

**points:** bar, à la carte menu, children welcome.
**Address:** Avenue du Pont du Bonhomme.
MR LUCIEN PHILIPPE
**Telephone:** 97.76.51.23
⊗ ⋎ Map 4

## LANISCAT, Côtes-du-Nord, 22570

### AUBERGE DU DAOULAS, RN 164, between Rostrenen and Mur de Bretagne
**Menu:** 46 Frs. **Accommodation:** 120 to 175 Frs.
**Restaurant:** Breakfast served from 6:30am. Lunch
served from 11:30am until 2:30pm. Dinner served from
7:00pm until 9:00pm. **Specialities:** home cooking.
**Hotel:** 7 beds; 3 single rooms, 4 double rooms. **Other
points:** bar, open to non-residents, children welcome,
lounge area, terraces, pets welcome – check for details,
car park, traditional decor. **Address:** Rue de Bon Repos.
MME MARIE-CLAUDE QUEMENER
**Telephone:** 96.24.81.78
⊗ ⋎ ⌂ Map 4

## LANNION, Côtes-du-Nord, 22300

### LA CROIX ROUGE, on the road to Morlaix
**Menu:** 48 to 145 Frs. **Restaurant:** Lunch served from
11:30am until 3:00pm. Dinner served from 7:00pm until
9:30pm. Closed the 2nd fortnight of August.
**Specialities:** home cooking. **Hotel:** 15 beds. **Other
points:** bar, open to non-residents, pets welcome – check
for details, car park. **Address:** La Croix Rouge
Ploumilliau.
MR CLAUDE BROZEC
**Telephone:** 96.35.45.08
⊗ ⋎ ⌂ Map 4

## LAVAL, Mayenne, 53000

### BAR DE LA GARE, RN 162 and RD 53
**Restaurant:** Breakfast served from 7:00am. Closed
Mondays. **Other points:** bar, open to non-residents,
terraces, pets welcome – check for details, traditional
decor. **Address:** 107, avenue Robert Buron.
MME CLAUDIA HELBERT
**Telephone:** 43.53.94.88
⋎ Map 5

## LEUE (LA), Vendée, 85210

### LES ROUTIERS, RN 137
**Menu:** 59 Frs. **Accommodation:** 60 to 120 Frs.
**Restaurant:** Breakfast served from 6:00am. Lunch served
from midday until 2:00pm. Dinner served from 7:30pm
until 10:00pm. Closed Saturdays and in July. **Specialities:**
home cooking. **Hotel:** 8 beds; 7 single rooms, 1 double
room. **Other points:** bar, open to non-residents, car park,
traditional decor. **Address:** Route Nationale 137.
SARL CHARBONNEAU-DAVIET
**Telephone:** 51.94.41.46
⊗ ⋎ ⌂ Map 5

## LIGNOL, Morbihan, 56160

### RELAIS DES VOYAGEURS, RD 782, the main road between Pontivy and Quimper via le Faouet
**Menu:** 50 Frs. **Accommodation:** 85 to 100 Frs.
**Restaurant:** Breakfast served from 7:00am. Lunch
served from midday until 2:00pm. Dinner served from
7:00pm until 9:00pm. Closed Mondays. **Specialities:**
home cooking. **Hotel:** 7 beds; 4 single rooms, 3 double
rooms. **Other points:** bar, open to non-residents,
children welcome, pets welcome – check for details,
car park, traditional decor. **Address:** 4, rue de la
Mairie.
MR BERNARD LE SOLLIEC
**Telephone:** 97.27.03.48
⊗ ⋎ ⌂ Map 4

## LISIEUX, Calvados, 14100

### LE PARIS/CHERBOURG, RN 13, the main road between Caen and Lisieux
**Menu:** 50 Frs. **Accommodation:** to 120 Frs (extra bed
30 Frs). **Restaurant:** Breakfast served from 6:30am.
**Specialities:** home cooking. **Hotel:** 6 beds; 1 single
room, 5 double rooms with shower. **Other points:** bar,
open to non-residents, à la carte menu, children
welcome, terraces, pets welcome – check for details, car
park, modern decor. **Address:** 113, avenue du 6 juin.
MR JOËL LOUIS
**Telephone:** 31.62.63.38
⊗ ⋎ ⌂ Map 3

## LOCMARIA GRAND CHAMPS, Morbihan, 56390

### LA MARMITE, RD 767, 10km from Vannes, towards Pontivy
**Menu:** 45 to 200 Frs. **Restaurant:** Breakfast served
from 5:30am. Lunch served from 11:30am until 3:00pm.
Dinner served from 6:30pm until 10:00pm. **Specialities:**
regional menu. **Other points:** bar, open to non-residents,
à la carte menu, children welcome, pets welcome –
check for details, car park, modern decor. **Address:**
Collec.
MR JEAN-PIERRE JOULAUD
**Telephone:** 97.66.66.80
⊗ ⋎ Map 4

## LOIRE, Maine-et-Loire, 49440

### AU RENDEZ-VOUS DES ROUTIERS
**Restaurant:** Breakfast served from 6:30am.
**Specialities:** home cooking. **Other points:** bar, open to
non-residents, children welcome. **Address:** 24, rue de la
Libération.
MR PHILIPPE AUDOUIN
**Telephone:** 41.94.10.83
⊗ ⋎ Map 5

## LONGUE, Maine-et-Loire, 49160

### LE RELAIS DES SOUVENETS, RN 147

**Restaurant:** Breakfast served from 7:30am. Closed Saturdays and end of August. **Specialities:** home cooking. **Other points:** bar, open to non-residents, pets welcome – check for details, car park. **Address:** Les Souvenets.
MME RÉJANE TAUGOURDEAU
**Telephone:** 41.52.13.86
⊗ ♉ Map 5

### SARL LE RELAX, RN 147, between Saumur (15km) and Anger (40km)

**Menu:** 55 (wine included) to 135 Frs. **Restaurant:** Breakfast served from 6:00am. Closed Sundays. **Specialities:** regional menu, home cooking. **Other points:** bar, open to non-residents, à la carte menu, children welcome, terraces, pets welcome – check for details, car park. **Address:** Route Nationale 147.
MR CHEVRÉ
**Telephone:** 41.52.68.81
⊗ ♉ Map 5

## LORIENT, Morbihan, 56100

### L'ALBATROS

**Menu:** 45 Frs (wine included). **Restaurant:** Breakfast served from 9:00am. Lunch served from 11:00am until 3:30pm. Dinner served from 7:00pm until 11:00pm. Closed Sundays. **Specialities:** home cooking. **Other points:** bar, open to non-residents, children welcome, pets welcome – check for details, traditional decor. **Address:** 56, avenue de la Perrière.
MME MARIE LEGOUIC
**Telephone:** 97.37.55.76
⊗ ♉ Map 4

## LOUARGAT, Côtes-du-Nord, 22540

### LE CONCORDEOU, RN 12, between Guingamp and Morlaix

**Menu:** 48 to 90 Frs. **Restaurant:** Breakfast served from 8:00am. Closed the 2nd fortnight in December. **Specialities:** home cooking. **Other points:** bar, children welcome, lounge area, terraces, pets welcome – check for details, car park. **Address:** 34, rue Prunus.
MME PAULETTE ENTZMANN
**Telephone:** 96.43.13.75
⊗ ♉ Map 4

## LOUDEAC, Côtes-du-Nord, 22600

### LE STOP, RN 164, Rennes

**Languages spoken:** English. **Menu:** 45 to 75 Frs. **Restaurant:** Breakfast served from 6:00am. Closed Sundays. **Other points:** bar, traditional decor. **Address:** Le Haut-Breuil.
MR YVES GICQUEL
**Telephone:** 96.28.01.76
⊗ ♉ Map 4

## LES ROUTIERS, RN 164

**Languages spoken:** English. **Menu:** 45 to 55 Frs. **Accommodation:** 75 to 130 Frs. **Restaurant:** Breakfast served from 7:00am. Lunch served from midday until 2:00pm. Dinner served from 7:00pm until 9:00pm. Closed Sundays. **Specialities:** fruits de mer, regional food, home cooking. **Hotel:** 44 beds; with shower, bath, private WC, television, telephone. **Other points:** bar, open to non-residents, pets welcome – check for details, car park. **Address:** 7, rue Lavergne.
MR DOMINIQUE LE COZANNET
**Telephone:** 96.28.01.44
⊗ ♉ ⌂ ☆ Map 4

## LOUVIERS, Eure, 27400

### L'ARCHE DE VIRONVAY, A 13, between Gaillon and Rouen

**Languages spoken:** English. **Menu:** 60 Frs. **Restaurant:** Breakfast served from 6:00am. Lunch served from 10:00am until 6:00pm. Dinner served from 6:00pm until 11:00pm. **Specialities:** home cooking. **Other points:** open to non-residents, children welcome, terraces, pets welcome – check for details, car park, traditional decor. **Address:** A 13 Aire de Vironvay, accessible dans les deux sens.
MR PASCAL LEGAL
**Telephone:** 32.40.21.51. **Fax:** 32.25.20.04
⊗ Map 3

### LE RELAIS DES ROUTIERS, RN 154

**Restaurant:** Dinner served from midday until 1:00am. **Other points:** bar. **Address:** 13, rue de Paris.
MME GUYLAINE QUESNEY
**Telephone:** 32.40.29.22
⊗ ♉ Map 3

## LUCEAU, Sarthe, 72500

### LA CROIX DE PAILLE, RN 138, between le Mans and Tours

**Restaurant:** Dinner served from midday until 1:00am. Closed Sundays and in August. **Specialities:** home cooking. **Other points:** bar, open to non-residents. **Address:** Route du Mans, Château du Loir.
MR JACQUES-YVES MOREAU
**Telephone:** 43.44.05.50
⊗ ♉ Map 5

## LUDE (LE), Sarthe, 72800

### LE RELAIS DES PECHEURS, RD 307

**Menu:** 55 to 65 Frs. **Restaurant:** Breakfast served from 7:30am. Lunch served from midday until 2:30pm. Dinner served from 6:45pm until 8:00pm. Closed Sundays and end of August/beginning of September. **Specialities:** regional menu, home cooking. **Other points:** bar, open to non-residents, children welcome, terraces. **Address:** 14, boulevard de l'Hospice.

MR GILBERT MOIRE
Telephone: 43.94.61.03
⊗ 𝟈 Map 5

## MACHECOUL, Loire-Atlantique, 44270

### LA BICYCLETTE D'ARGENT
Languages spoken: English. Restaurant: Dinner
served from midday until 9:00pm. Closed Saturday
afternoons, Sunday afternoons, from 18 to 25 February
and from 22 December to 1 January. Hotel: 9 beds.
Other points: bar, car park. Address: 6, place du Pont.
MME MARIE-JOSEPH BAUDRY
Telephone: 40.78.50.48
⊗ 𝟈 ⌂ Map 5

## MAGNY LA CAMPAGNE, Calvados, 14270

### LA VALLEE D'AUGE, RD 40, between Caen and Saint Pierre sur Dives
Menu: 50 to 105 Frs. Restaurant: Breakfast served
from 7:30am. Closed Tuesdays and in January.
Specialities: regional menu. Other points: open to non-
residents, à la carte menu, children welcome, pets
welcome – check for details, car park, traditional decor.
MME MARIE-THÉRÉSE SEVIN
Telephone: 31.20.04.20
⊗ Map 3

## MALE, Orne, 61260

### LA BELLE RENCONTRE, RN 23, the main road between Paris and le Mans
Menu: 48 Frs. Accommodation: 95 to 190 Frs.
Restaurant: Breakfast served from 6:00am. Dinner
served from 7:00pm until 10:00pm. Closed Sundays and
in August. Specialities: home cooking. Hotel: 17 beds;
5 single rooms, 12 double rooms with shower, private
WC, television. Other points: bar, open to non-
residents, children welcome, terraces, car park,
traditional decor. Address: Le Gibet.
MR ANDRÉ CARLE
Telephone: 37.49.68.85
⊗ 𝟈 ⌂ ☆ Map 3

## MAMERS, Sarthe, 72600

### LES ROUTIERS TABAC, RN 155
Restaurant: Dinner served from midday until 10:00pm.
Closed August. Hotel: 12 beds. Other points: bar.
MME CHRISTIANE CHAPELLIER
Telephone: 43.97.74.10
⊗ 𝟈 ⌂ Map 5

## MARCILLE RAOUL, Ille-et-Vilaine, 35560

### LES ROUTIERS, the main road between Combourg and Vitré

Menu: 45 to 75 Frs. Accommodation: 85 to 105 Frs.
Restaurant: Breakfast served from 7:00am. Lunch served
from 11:30am until 2:00pm. Dinner served from 7:30pm
until 9:00pm. Specialities: home cooking. Hotel: 7 beds;
2 single rooms, 5 double rooms with shower, bath. Other
points: bar, open to non-residents, à la carte menu,
children welcome, pets welcome – check for details, car
park, traditional decor. Address: Le Bourg.
MR CHRISTIAN BELLEPERCHE
Telephone: 99.73.62.14
⊗ 𝟈 ⌂ Map 4

## MARIGNE LAILLE, Sarthe, 72220

### AUBERGE DU BON ACCUEIL, RN 138, the main road between le Mans and Tours
Menu: 49 to 150 Frs. Restaurant: Breakfast served
from 7:00am. Lunch served from midday until 2:30pm.
Dinner served from 7:00pm until 9:30pm. Closed
Wednesdays. Specialities: home cooking. Other points:
bar, open to non-residents, à la carte menu, pets
welcome – check for details, car park. Address: Route
Nationale 138, Laillé.
MR JEAN-LOUIS LOUDIÈRE
Telephone: 43.42.12.01
⊗ 𝟈 Map 5

## MARTIGNE FERCHAUD, Ille-et-Vilaine, 35640

### LE POT D'ETAIN, RN 178
Restaurant: Closed Saturdays and 3 weeks in August.
Specialities: home cooking. Other points: bar, pets
welcome – check for details, car park, traditional decor.
Address: 10, Grande Rue.
MME YVONNE BOUTEILLER
Telephone: 99.47.90.12
⊗ 𝟈 Map 4

## MARZAN, Morbihan, 56130

### LES RIVES DE VILAINE, RN 165, Vannes, on the right after the bridge for la Roche Bernard
Menu: 42 to 140 Frs. Restaurant: Breakfast served
from 7:30am. Lunch served from midday until 2:00pm.
Dinner served from 7:00pm until 8:00pm. Specialities:
regional menu, home cooking. Other points: bar, open
to non-residents, children welcome, terraces, pets
welcome – check for details, car park, traditional decor.
Address: 13, rue de la Fontaine.
MR GILLES JOUAN
Telephone: 99.90.63.22
⊗ 𝟈 Map 4

## MATHIEU, Calvados, 14920

### RELAIS DE LA COTE DE NACRE, RD 7, exit Douvres la Délivrande

**Menu:** 51 to 60 Frs. **Restaurant:** Breakfast served from 7:00am. Lunch served from midday until 3:00pm. Dinner served from 7:30pm until 9:00pm. Closed Sundays and from 20 December to 5 January. **Specialities:** home cooking. **Hotel:** 2 beds; 1 single room, 1 double room. **Other points:** bar, open to non-residents, traditional decor. **Address:** 4, rue Augustin Fresnel.
MR MARC BEDEAU DE L'ECOCHÈRE
**Telephone:** 31.44.10.17
⊗ ♀ Map 3

## MAY SUR ORNE, Calvados, 14320

*L'AMMONITE, RD 562, the main road between Caen and Laval (8km from Caen)*
**Languages spoken:** English. **Menu:** 50 to 127 Frs. **Accommodation:** 120 Frs. **Restaurant:** Breakfast served from 8:00am. Lunch served from 11:30am until 2:30pm. Dinner served from 7:30pm until 9:30pm. Closed Sundays. **Specialities:** regional menu, home cooking. **Hotel:** 7 beds; 5 single rooms, 2 double rooms with bath, private WC. **Other points:** bar, open to non-residents, children welcome, terraces, pets welcome – check for details, car park, traditional decor. **Address:** 2, rue du Canada.
MME MARYVONNE HOREL
**Telephone:** 31.79.80.27
⊗ ♀ 🏠 Map 3

## MAYENNE, Mayenne, 53100

*L'ESCALE, CD 35, le Mans*
**Menu:** 49,50 Frs (wine included). **Accommodation:** 92 Frs. **Restaurant:** Breakfast served from 5:30am. Lunch served from 11:00am until 2:00pm. Dinner served from 7:00pm until 9:00pm. Closed Saturdays. **Specialities:** home cooking. **Hotel:** 13 beds; 2 single rooms, 11 double rooms. **Other points:** bar, open to non-residents, children welcome, terraces, pets welcome – check for details, car park, traditional decor. **Address:** Route du Mans.
MR DOMINIQUE FORTIN
**Telephone:** 43.04.19.14
⊗ ♀ 🏠 Map 5

*LE RELAIS DES BRUYERES, RN 12, between Alençon and Mayenne*
**Languages spoken:** German. **Menu:** 55 to 138 Frs. **Accommodation:** 120 to 180 Frs. **Restaurant:** Breakfast served from 5:00am. Closed Saturdays and in August. **Specialities:** regional menu, home cooking. **Hotel:** 9 beds; 7 single rooms, 2 double rooms with shower, bath, television. **Other points:** bar, open to non-residents, à la carte menu, children welcome, lounge area, terraces, pets welcome – check for details, car park, traditional decor. **Address:** Route d'Alençon.
MR JEAN-PIERRE BORDAS
**Telephone:** 43.04.13.64
⊗ ♀ 🏠 Map 5

## MELLAC, Finistère, 29300

*TI LANIG, RN 165, via the crossroads Lorient/Quimper*
**Languages spoken:** English. **Menu:** 48 to 120 Frs. **Restaurant:** Breakfast served from 6:00am. Closed Sundays **Specialities:** regional menu, home cooking. **Other points:** bar, open to non-residents, à la carte menu, children welcome, lounge area, terraces, pets welcome – check for details, car park, modern decor. **Address:** ZA de Keringant.
MR ALAIN MINEC
**Telephone:** 98.39.16.07
⊗ ♀ Map 4

## MENIL BROUT (LE), Orne, 61250

*CHEZ GHISLAINE, RN 12, between Alençon and Dreux*
**Menu:** 53 Frs. **Accommodation:** 100 to 120 Frs. **Restaurant:** Closed Saturdays. **Specialities:** home cooking. **Hotel:** 8 beds; 6 single rooms, 2 double rooms with shower, bath, private WC. **Other points:** bar, open to non-residents, children welcome, pets welcome – check for details, car park, modern decor. **Address:** Route Nationale 12.
MME GHISLAINE GAUTIER
**Telephone:** 33.27.10.03
⊗ ♀ 🏠 Map 3

## MESNIL DURAND (LE), Calvados, 14140

*LE RELAIS DE LA FORGE, RD 579, between Lisieux and Livarot*
**Menu:** 52 Frs. **Restaurant:** Breakfast served from 5:00am. Closed Sundays. **Specialities:** home cooking. **Other points:** bar, children welcome, terraces, pets welcome – check for details, car park, traditional decor. **Address:** Les Forges Mézières.
MME CHANTALE LE ROSIER
**Telephone:** 31.63.52.79
⊗ ♀ Map 3

## MILLIERES, Manche, 50190

*RELAIS DES TOURISTES, the main road between Lessay and Saint Lo, between Perriers and Lessay*
**Languages spoken:** English. **Restaurant:** Dinner served from midday until 9:00pm. Closed Sundays. **Specialities:** coq à la bière ou au vin, home cooking. **Other points:** bar, children welcome, terraces, pets welcome – check for details, car park. **Address:** La Bezanterie.
MR GÉRARD LUNEL
**Telephone:** 33.46.71.12
⊗ ♀ Map 3

## MINIAC MORVAN, Ille-et-Vilaine, 35540

### L'HOTEL DE LA GARE, between Rennes and Saint Malo

**Places of interest:** Château d'Ansouis, de Lourmarin et de la Tour d'Aigues, étang de la Bonde. **Languages spoken:** English. **Menu:** 48 Frs. **Accommodation:** 110 to 220 Frs. **Restaurant:** Breakfast served from 6:00am. Lunch served from 11:30am until 3:00pm. Dinner served from 7:30pm until 9:30pm. **Specialities:** home cooking. **Hotel:** 9 beds; 6 single rooms, 3 double rooms. **Other points:** bar, pets welcome – check for details, car park. **Address:** La Costardais.
MR DANIEL CLÉRO
**Telephone:** 99.58.58.14
⊗ ♈ ⌂ Map 4

## MONNAI, Orne, 61470

### LE CHEVAL BAI, RN 138

**Restaurant:** Dinner served from midday until 11:00pm. Closed Sundays. **Hotel:** 6 beds. **Other points:** bar. **Address:** Route Nationale 138.
MR GILBERT ROUSSEL
**Telephone:** 33.39.42.00
⊗ ♈ ⌂ Map 3

## MONT SAINT MICHEL (LE), Manche, 50116

### HOTEL MOTEL VERT – LA RÔTISSERIE, RN 776, last crossroads before the dyke

**Languages spoken:** German and English. **Menu:** 55 to 198 Frs. **Accommodation:** 200 to 465 Frs. **Restaurant:** Lunch served from midday until 1:30pm. Dinner served from 7:00pm until 9:00pm. Closed in December and in January. **Specialities:** regional menu. **Hotel:** 113 beds; with shower, bath, private WC, television, telephone. **Other points:** bar, open to non-residents, à la carte menu, children welcome, modern decor. **Address:** Route du Mont Saint Michel.
MR PHILIPPE FRANÇOIS
**Telephone:** 33.60.09.33. **Fax:** 33.68.22.09
⊗ ♈ ⌂ ☆☆ Map 3

## MONTAUBAN DE BRETAGNE, Ille-et-Vilaine, 35360

### HOTEL DE FRANCE, RN 12 and 164 Bis, town centre

**Languages spoken:** English and Spanish. **Menu:** 58 to 150 Frs. **Accommodation:** 110 to 205 Frs. **Restaurant:** Breakfast served from 7:00am. Lunch served from 11:30am until 2:00pm. Dinner served from 7:00pm until 9:30pm. Closed Mondays and from 20 December to 20 January. **Specialities:** fruits de mer, coq au Muscadet, far breton, poissons, regional food. **Hotel:** 12 beds; 8 single rooms, 4 double rooms with shower, bath, private WC,

television, telephone. **Other points:** bar, open to non-residents, à la carte menu, children welcome, lounge area, pets welcome – check for details, car park, traditional decor. **Address:** 34, rue du Général de Gaulle.
MR GABRIEL LE METAYER
**Telephone:** 99.06.40.19
⊗ ♈ ⌂ 🐾 ☆☆ Map 4

### RELAIS DE LA HUCHERAIS, RN 12 and 164 Bis

**Languages spoken:** English. **Accommodation:** 100 to 170 Frs. **Restaurant:** Dinner served from midday until 10:00pm. Closed Sundays. **Hotel:** 14 beds. **Other points:** bar, pets welcome – check for details, car park. **Address:** La Hucherais.
MR ALAIN MEHEUS
**Telephone:** 99.06.40.29
⊗ ♈ ⌂ ☆☆ Map 4

## MONTAUDIN, Mayenne, 53220

### HOTEL DE PARIS, RN 799

**Languages spoken:** English. **Menu:** 44 to 48 Frs. **Accommodation:** 135 to 185 Frs. **Restaurant:** Breakfast served from 7:00am. Dinner served from midday until 9:00pm. Closed Mondays and in August. **Specialities:** home cooking. **Hotel:** 5 beds; 3 single rooms, 2 double rooms with shower, private WC, television. **Other points:** bar, open to non-residents, children welcome, terraces, pets welcome – check for details, car park, modern decor. **Address:** Route d'Ernée.
MR DANIEL DOUDARD
**Telephone:** 43.05.30.79
⊗ ♈ ⌂ Map 5

## MONTMARTIN SUR MER, Manche, 50590

### HOTELLERIE DU BON VIEUX TEMPS, RD 20, Granville

**Languages spoken:** English. **Menu:** 60 to 200 Frs. **Accommodation:** 135 to 340 Frs. **Restaurant:** Breakfast served from 7:30am. Lunch served from midday until 2:00pm. Dinner served from 7:30pm until 9:30pm. Closed Sundays. **Specialities:** regional menu. **Hotel:** 20 beds; 15 single rooms, 5 double rooms with shower, bath, private WC, telephone. **Other points:** bar, open to non-residents, à la carte menu, children welcome, pets welcome – check for details, car park, traditional decor.
MR ERICK BOURBONNAIS
**Telephone:** 33.47.54.44. **Fax:** 33.46.27.12
⊗ ♈ ⌂ ☆☆ Map 3

## MONTOIR DE BRETAGNE, Loire-Atlantique, 44550

### LES NOES, RN 171, via the motorway Nantes/Saint Nazaire

**Menu:** 50 Frs. **Restaurant:** Breakfast served from 6:30am. Lunch served from 11:45am until 2:00pm. Dinner served from 7:00pm until 9:00pm. Closed Saturdays. **Specialities:** home cooking. **Other points:** bar, open to non-residents, terraces, pets welcome – check for details, car park. **Address:** Route Nationale 171, les Noës.
MME BRIGITTE LIBERGE
**Telephone:** 40.45.55.67
⊗ ⍩ Map 5

### RELAIS DU BOSCO, between Nantes and Saint Nazaire
**Menu:** 48 Frs. **Restaurant:** Breakfast served from 6:00am. Dinner served from midday until 10:00pm. Closed Saturdays. **Specialities:** home cooking. **Other points:** bar, open to non-residents, children welcome, lounge area, pets welcome – check for details, car park, modern decor. **Address:** Centre International de Frêt.
MR JEAN-MICHEL VALAIN
**Telephone:** 40.90.18.80
⊗ ⍩ Map 5

## MONTREUIL LE CHETIF, Sarthe, 72130

### AU RENDEZ-VOUS DES CHASSEURS, RD 310, Sillé le Guillaume, at Fresnay on the edge of the forest
**Menu:** 48 to 80 Frs. **Restaurant:** Breakfast served from 7:00am. Lunch served from midday until 2:00pm. Dinner served from 7:00pm until 9:00pm. **Specialities:** regional menu, home cooking. **Other points:** bar, open to non-residents, à la carte menu, children welcome, terraces, pets welcome – check for details, car park, traditional decor. **Address:** Le Grand Gué.
MME FRANÇOISE BORDEAU
**Telephone:** 43.33.39.90
⊗ ⍩ Map 5

## MORDELLES, Ille-et-Vilaine, 35310

### LE RELAIS, RN 24, between Renne and Lorient
**Menu:** 50 Frs. **Restaurant:** Breakfast served from 7:30am. Lunch served from midday until 3:00pm. Closed Saturdays and in August. **Specialities:** home cooking. **Other points:** bar, car park, modern decor. **Address:** La Croix Ignon.
MR MICHEL CAVELIER
**Telephone:** 99.60.02.50
⊗ ⍩ Map 4

## MOREAC, Morbihan, 56500

### LE RELAIS DU BARDERFF, RN 24, between Rennes and Lorient or Vannes and Saint Brieuc
**Languages spoken:** English. **Menu:** 45 to 85 Frs.

**Accommodation:** 220 to 360 Frs. **Restaurant:** Breakfast served from 5:00am. Lunch served from midday until 2:00pm. Dinner served from 7:00pm until 10:00pm. Closed Sundays. **Specialities:** regional menu, home cooking. **Hotel:** 20 beds; 20 double rooms with shower, private WC, television, telephone. **Other points:** bar, open to non-residents, à la carte menu, children welcome, lounge area, car park, modern decor. **Address:** ZI du Barderff.
MR JEAN LAMOUR
**Telephone:** 97.60.18.60. **Fax:** 97.60.25.55
⊗ ⍩ ⌂ ☆☆ Map 4

## MOREILLES, Vendée, 85450

### LE CHEVAL BLANC, RN 137, the main road between Nantes and Bordeaux
**Menu:** 59 Frs. **Accommodation:** 95 to 130 Frs. **Restaurant:** Breakfast served from 6:00am. Lunch served from 11:30am until 2:00pm. Dinner served from 7:00pm until 10:00pm. Closed Sundays and from 28 December to 17 January. **Specialities:** regional menu, home cooking. **Hotel:** 5 beds; 1 single room, 4 double rooms. **Other points:** bar, open to non-residents, children welcome, terraces, pets welcome – check for details, car park, modern decor. **Address:** 9, Route Nationale.
MR CHRISTIAN SARRAUD
**Telephone:** 51.56.11.02
⊗ ⍩ ⌂ Map 5

## MORTAGNE (SAINT LANGIS), Orne, 61400

### HOTEL DE LA GARE, the main road between le Mans/Bellême/Mortagne
**Menu:** 45 Frs. **Restaurant:** Breakfast served from 6:00am. Lunch served from 11:30am until 2:30pm. Dinner served from 7:00pm until 9:30pm. Closed Saturdays. **Specialities:** home cooking. **Other points:** bar, open to non-residents, terraces, pets welcome – check for details, car park, traditional decor. **Address:** Avenue de la Gare.
MR LEROUL
**Telephone:** 33.25.16.10
⊗ ⍩ Map 3

## MORTAGNE SUR SEVRE, Vendée, 85290

### LE PUY NARDON, RN 149, the main road between Nantes and Poitiers
**Languages spoken:** English. **Menu:** 46 Frs (wine included). **Restaurant:** Breakfast served from 6:00am. Lunch served from 11:30am until 2:30pm. Dinner served from 7:00pm until 9:30pm. **Specialities:** home cooking. **Other points:** bar, open to non-residents, à la carte menu, children welcome, terraces, pets welcome – check for details, car park, modern decor. **Address:** ZA du Puy Nardon, Route de Poitiers.

MR GÉRARD DUVAL
**Telephone:** 51.65.19.14. **Fax:** 51.65.19.12
⊗ ⑨ Map 5

### LE RELAIS DE LA GARE, *RN 160*

**Restaurant:** Closed Saturdays and August. **Other points:** bar. **Address:** 52, route de Chôlet.
MR JEAN-LUC ARROUET
**Telephone:** 51.65.11.56
⊗ ⑨ Map 5

## MORTREE, Orne, 61570

### LE POINT DU JOUR, *RN 158, between Argentan and Sées*

**Languages spoken:** English. **Menu:** 53 to 80 Frs.
**Restaurant:** Breakfast served from 7:00am. Lunch served from 11:45am until 2:00pm. Dinner served from 7:00pm until 9:00pm. Closed from Saturday afternoons to Sundays (except groups) and in August. **Specialities:** regional menu, home cooking. **Other points:** bar, open to non-residents, à la carte menu, children welcome, terraces, pets welcome – check for details, car park, traditional decor. **Address:** 139, Grande Rue.
FABIENNE ET JACKY HUETTE
**Telephone:** 33.35.35.22
⊗ ⑨ Map 3

## MOSLES, Calvados, 14400

### RESTAURANT DE LA POSTE, *RN 13, the main road between Bayeux and Cherbourg*

**Menu:** 50 to 70 Frs. **Restaurant:** Breakfast served from 6:00am. Lunch served from 11:00am until 3:00pm. Dinner served from 7:00pm until 10:00pm. Closed Saturdays. **Specialities:** home cooking. **Other points:** bar, open to non-residents, car park, modern decor. **Address:** Route Nationale 13.
MR JACQUES LEROSIER
**Telephone:** 31.22.33.79
⊗ ⑨ Map 3

## MOUZEUIL SAINT MARTIN, Vendée, 85370

### CENTRAL ROUTIERS, *RN 148, between Niort and les Sables d'Olonne*

**Menu:** 50 to 140 Frs. **Accommodation:** 90 to 220 Frs.
**Restaurant:** Breakfast served from 7:00am. Lunch served from midday until 3:00pm. Dinner served from 8:00pm until 10:00pm. **Specialities:** regional menu, home cooking. **Hotel:** 9 beds; with shower, bath, private WC, television. **Other points:** bar, open to non-residents, children welcome, lounge area, terraces, pets welcome – check for details, car park, modern decor.
**Address:** 33, rue Louis Anraille.
MR JEAN-MARIE GUILBAUD
**Telephone:** 51.28.72.44
⊗ ⑨ ⌂ ⌣ Map 5

## MOYON, Manche, 50860

### EUROGRIL – CARREFOUR PARIS, *CD 999, the main road between Carentan/Saint Lo/Avranches*

**Languages spoken:** English. **Menu:** 40 to 120 Frs.
**Restaurant:** Breakfast served from 6:00am. Closed Fridays. **Specialities:** pied de veau, regional food. **Other points:** bar, open to non-residents, children welcome, terraces, pets welcome – check for details, car park.
**Address:** 1, Carrefour Paris.
MR JEAN-ROBERT FÉCAN
**Telephone:** 33.05.59.74. **Fax:** 33.05.05.52
⊗ ⑨ Map 3

## MUZILLAC, Morbihan, 56190

### LA CLE DES CHAMPS, *RN 165, between Vannes and la Roche Bernard*

**Languages spoken:** German, English and Spanish.
**Menu:** 48 Frs. **Restaurant:** Breakfast served from 7:00am. **Specialities:** regional menu, home cooking.
**Other points:** bar, open to non-residents, à la carte menu, children welcome, lounge area, terraces, pets welcome – check for details, car park, modern decor.
**Address:** Route de Vannes.
MME ANNICK MELLOUL
**Telephone:** 97.41.68.74.
⊗ ⑨ Map 4

## NANTES, Loire-Atlantique, 44200

### A L'ANCRE D'OR, *RN 43*

**Menu:** 43 to 53 Frs. **Accommodation:** 75 to 130 Frs.
**Restaurant:** Breakfast served from 4:30am. Lunch served from 6:30am until 2:30pm. Dinner served from 7:00pm until 9:30pm. Closed Saturdays, Sundays and in August. **Specialities:** home cooking. **Hotel:** 5 beds; 2 single rooms, 3 double rooms with shower. **Other points:** bar, à la carte menu, car park, modern decor.
**Address:** 55, boulevard Gustave Roch.
MR SERGE DESMORTIERS
**Telephone:** 40.35.39.30
⊗ ⑨ ⌂ Map 5

### AU RENDEZ-VOUS DES SPORTIFS, *RN 43*

**Menu:** 42 to 55 Frs. **Restaurant:** Breakfast served from 6:00am. Lunch served from 11:00am until 4:00pm. Dinner served from 6:00pm until 9:00pm. Closed Saturdays. **Specialities:** Paëlla, couscous, home cooking. **Other points:** bar, open to non-residents, à la carte menu, pets welcome – check for details, car park, modern decor. **Address:** 40, quai de Malakoff.
MR BERNARD ALBERT
**Telephone:** 40.47.75.39
⊗ ⑨ Map 5

**L'AVENIR,** *RN 23, on the banks of the Loire*
**Restaurant:** Breakfast served from 5:30am. Lunch served from 11:30am until 2:30pm. Dinner served from 7:00pm until 10:00pm. Closed Saturdays and mid-December. **Specialities:** home cooking. **Other points:** bar, car park, traditional decor. **Address:** 1, rue de la Pompe.
MME VIVIANE BARON
**Telephone:** 40.43.46.03
⊗ ϒ Map 5

# NASSANDRES, Eure, 27550

**LE PARIS CAEN CHERBOURG INTERNATIONAL,** *RN 13*
**Restaurant:** Dinner served from midday until 1:00am. Closed Saturdays. **Other points:** bar, pets welcome – check for details. **Address:** 11, Route Nationale 13.
MR PATRICE BOUTEL
**Telephone:** 32.45.00.26
⊗ ϒ Map 3

# NEUFBOURG (LE), Manche, 50140

**LES ROUTIERS,** *between Vire Sourdeval and Mortain*
**Menu:** 50 Frs (coffee included). **Restaurant:** Breakfast served from 8:00am. Lunch served from 11:30am until 2:30pm. Dinner served from 7:00pm until 10:00pm. Closed Mondays and in July. **Specialities:** home cooking. **Other points:** bar, open to non-residents, children welcome, terraces, pets welcome – check for details, car park, modern decor. **Address:** 13, route de Vire.
MME ANNIE GUERRIER
**Telephone:** 33.59.00.59
⊗ ϒ Map 3

# NEUFCHATEL EN BRAY, Seine-Maritime, 76270

**RELAIS DES HAYONS,** *RN 28, the main road between Paris and Dieppe*
**Menu:** 45 to 70 Frs. **Restaurant:** Breakfast served from 5:30am. Lunch served from 11:30am until 3:00pm. Dinner served from 6:30pm until 11:00pm. Closed Sundays. **Specialities:** home cooking. **Other points:** bar, open to non-residents, à la carte menu, children welcome, lounge area, pets welcome – check for details, car park, traditional decor. **Address:** Esclavelles.
MR JEAN-CLAUDE PIEDNOËL
**Telephone:** 35.93.13.15
⊗ ϒ Map 3

# NEUVE LYRE (LA), Eure, 27330

**LE RELAIS DES AMIS,** *between Evreux and l'Aigle*
**Accommodation:** 49 Frs. **Restaurant:** Breakfast served from 6:30am. Closed Sundays and 15 days beginning of August. **Specialities:** home cooking. **Hotel:** 5 beds; with shower. **Other points:** bar, open to non-residents, children welcome, terraces, pets welcome – check for details, car park. **Address:** Hameau de Chagny.
MR JEAN-CLAUDE GUYOT
**Telephone:** 32.30.50.60
⊗ ϒ ⌂ Map 3

# NIEUL LE DOLENT, Vendée, 85430

**CHEZ JACQUES,** *RD 36, between la Roche sur Yon and la Tranche sur Mer*
**Menu:** 45 to 55 Frs. **Restaurant:** Breakfast served from 7:30am. Lunch served from 11:30am until 2:30pm. Closed Sundays. **Specialities:** home cooking. **Other points:** bar, open to non-residents, pets welcome – check for details, car park, traditional decor. **Address:** 8, rue de Lattre de Tassigny.
MR JACQUES PINEL
**Telephone:** 51.07.93.71
⊗ ϒ Map 5

# NOE POULAIN (LA), Eure, 27560

**CHEZ MANU ET JOJO,** *CD 810, between Pontaumer and Bernay*
**Menu:** 52 Frs. **Restaurant:** Dinner served from midday until 10:00pm. Closed Saturdays **Specialities:** home cooking. **Other points:** bar, open to non-residents, car park, modern decor.
MME EMMANUEL LANGIN
**Telephone:** 32.57.90.35
⊗ ϒ Map 3

# NONANT LE PIN, Orne, 61240

**LE RELAIS DES HARAS,** *RN 26, Argentan*
**Menu:** 50 Frs. **Restaurant:** Breakfast served from 6:30am. Lunch served from 11:00am until 3:00pm. Dinner served from 7:30pm until 10:00pm. Closed Sundays and in August. **Specialities:** home cooking. **Other points:** bar, open to non-residents, children welcome, pets welcome – check for details, traditional decor. **Address:** Grande Rue.
MR JACQUES LAMPIN
**Telephone:** 33.39.93.35, 33.39.93.39
⊗ ϒ ⊂ Map 3

# NORT SUR ERDRE, Loire-Atlantique, 44390

**LES 3 MARCHANDS**
**Menu:** 48 to 78 Frs. **Accommodation:** 90 to 130 Frs. **Restaurant:** Breakfast served from 6:30am. Lunch served from 11:30am until 3:00pm. Dinner served from 6:30pm until 9:30pm. Closed Sundays. **Specialities:** home cooking. **Hotel:** 9 beds; 6 single rooms, 3 double rooms with shower, bath, television. **Other points:** bar, open to non-residents, children welcome, pets welcome – check for details, car park, traditional decor. **Address:**

3, place du Champ de Foire.
MR YANNICK BRIAND
**Telephone:** 40.72.20.34
⊗ ⍑ ⌂ Map 5

## NOTRE DAME DE GRAVENCHON, Seine-Maritime, 76330

*AU COUP DE FREIN, town centre, towards Norville*
**Menu:** 42 Frs. **Restaurant:** Breakfast served from 6:30am. Lunch served from 11:30am until 2:30pm. Dinner served from 7:00pm until 9:30pm. Closed Saturdays. **Specialities:** home cooking. **Hotel:** 4 beds. **Other points:** open to non-residents, pets welcome – check for details, car park, modern decor. **Address:** Rue Claude Bernard.
MME MARIE JOSÉE DAVID
**Telephone:** 35.38.61.35
⊗ Map 3

## NOYAL SUR VILAINE, Ille-et-Vilaine, 35530

*LE RELAIS 35, RN 157, on the old road for Paris/Rennes*
**Languages spoken:** English. **Menu:** 48 Frs. **Accommodation:** 100 to 115 Frs. **Restaurant:** Lunch served from 11:00am until 3:00pm. Dinner served from 6:00pm until 10:00pm. Closed Saturdays and 1 week from 15 August. **Specialities:** home cooking. **Hotel:** 13 beds; 13 double rooms. **Other points:** bar, open to non-residents, à la carte menu, children welcome, terraces, pets welcome – check for details, car park, modern decor. **Address:** 20, avenue du Général de Gaulle.
MME PASCALE SEFELIN
**Telephone:** 99.00.51.20
⊗ ⍑ ⌂ Map 4

## OCTEVILLE, Manche, 50130

*LE VENT D'AMONT, RN 3 and 900*
**Languages spoken:** English. **Restaurant:** Closed Mondays. **Other points:** bar, car park. **Address:** 1, rue Jules Ferry.
MR JACKY TRAVERS
**Telephone:** 33.52.16.16
⊗ ⍑ Map 3

## OISSEAU LE PETIT, Sarthe, 72610

*HOTEL DE L'ESPERANCE, RN 138, between le Mans and Alençon*
**Menu:** 48 to 60 Frs. **Restaurant:** Breakfast served from 6:00am. Lunch served from midday until 2:00pm. Dinner served from 7:30pm until 9:00pm. Closed Saturdays and in August. **Specialities:** home cooking. **Hotel:** 4 beds. **Other points:** bar, open to non-residents, children welcome, pets welcome – check for details, car park.

MME ANDRÉE BESNARD
**Telephone:** 33.26.81.97
⊗ ⍑ Map 5

## OUISTREHAM, Calvados, 14150

*AU COIN DU PORT*
**Menu:** 50 to 198 Frs. **Restaurant:** Breakfast served from 7:30am. Lunch served from midday until 3:00pm. Dinner served from 7:00pm until 10:30pm. Closed Sundays and from 20 to 31 December. **Specialities:** home cooking. **Other points:** bar, open to non-residents, à la carte menu, children welcome, modern decor. **Address:** 90, avenue Michel Cabieu.
CLAUDE ET ANDRÉE MORIN NOTAMY
**Telephone:** 31.97.15.22
⊗ ⍑ Map 3

## PACE PAR ALENCON, Orne, 61250

*LE RELAIS DU CHENE, RN 12, between Alençon and Mayenne*
**Menu:** 49 Frs. **Restaurant:** Breakfast served from 5:00am. Closed Saturdays and 1 week at Christmas. **Specialities:** home cooking. **Other points:** bar, open to non-residents, children welcome, pets welcome – check for details, car park, traditional decor. **Address:** Route Nationale 12.
MR GILLES BOUTINON
**Telephone:** 33.27.72.06
⊗ ⍑ Map 3

*LE RELAIS DES ROUTIERS, RN 12, Saint Malo/Rennes/Alençon*
**Menu:** 60 to 120 Frs. **Restaurant:** Breakfast served from 6:30am. Lunch served from 11:30am until 3:00pm. Dinner served from 7:00pm until 9:00pm. Closed Saturdays. **Specialities:** regional menu. **Other points:** bar, open to non-residents, à la carte menu, pets welcome – check for details, car park. **Address:** Damigni.
MR MARCEL BRUNEAU
**Telephone:** 33.27.70.69
⊗ ⍑ Map 3

## PARIGNE, Ille-et-Vilaine, 35133

*LE FRANCK'ELLE, RD 108, Flers, exit Fougères*
**Menu:** 51 to 120 Frs. **Restaurant:** Breakfast served from 8:00am. Lunch served from midday until 3:00pm. Dinner served from 7:00pm until 9:00pm. Closed Mondays and 15 days beginning of August. **Specialities:** regional menu. **Other points:** bar, open to non-residents, children welcome, pets welcome – check for details, car park, traditional decor. **Address:** 12, rue de la Mairie.
MR FRANCK ROUSSET
**Telephone:** 99.97.22.90
⊗ ⍑ Map 4

## PARIGNE LE POLIN, Sarthe, 72330

### LA CHESNAIE

**Menu:** 50 Frs. **Restaurant:** Breakfast served from
5:00am. Lunch served from 11:15am until 2:00pm.
Dinner served from 7:00pm until 9:45pm. Closed
Saturdays. **Specialities:** home cooking. **Other points:**
open to non-residents, pets welcome – check for details,
car park. **Address:** Route Nationale 23.
MME CHANTAL MARY
**Telephone:** 43.87.90.70
⊗ Map 5

## PARIGNY, Manche, 50600

### HOTEL DU CHEMIN DE FER, RD 977, the main road between Caen and Rennes, between Mortain and Saint Hilaire

**Menu:** 48 Frs. **Accommodation:** 98 to 120 Frs.
**Restaurant:** Breakfast served from 6:45am. Lunch served
from 1:00pm until 3:00pm. Dinner served from 7:00pm
until 9:30pm. Closed Sundays and 15 days in August.
**Specialities:** regional menu, home cooking. **Hotel:** 4 beds;
3 single rooms, 1 double room with shower, bath, private
WC, television. **Other points:** bar, open to non-residents, à
la carte menu, children welcome, pets welcome – check for
details, car park, modern decor. **Address:** La Gare.
MR GILBERT LECORNU
**Telephone:** 33.49.10.55
⊗ ♉ Map 3

## PEDERNEC, Côtes-du-Nord, 22540

### LE MAUDEZ, Lannion

**Menu:** 36 to 85 Frs. **Restaurant:** Breakfast served from
6:45am. Lunch served from 11:30am until 2:00pm.
Dinner served from 7:00pm until 9:00pm. Closed
Sundays and 15 days in August. **Specialities:** home
cooking. **Other points:** bar, open to non-residents, à la
carte menu, children welcome. **Address:** Maudez.
MR DENIS DUTILLET
**Telephone:** 96.45.31.28
⊗ ♉ Map 4

## PERCY, Manche, 50410

### LE RELAIS DE LA GARE, RD 999, on the left entering Percy from Saint-Lo

**Menu:** 45 Frs (midday) and 55 Frs (evenings).
**Accommodation:** 80 to 100 Frs. **Restaurant:** Lunch
served from midday. Dinner served from 7:00pm until
10:00pm. Closed Sundays and from 15 to 28 February.
**Specialities:** home cooking. **Hotel:** 4 double rooms with
shower, private WC. **Other points:** bar, pets welcome –
check for details, car park, modern decor. **Address:** 4,
rue de l'Ancienne Gare.
MR BERNARD GUILLOTTE
**Telephone:** 33.61.20.96, 33.61.94.60
⊗ ♉ Map 3

## PERROS GUIREC, Côtes-du-Nord, 22700

### CHEZ CHARLY

**Menu:** 50 to 70 Frs. **Accommodation:** 130 to 180 Frs.
**Restaurant:** Lunch served from midday until 3:00pm.
Dinner served from 7:00pm until 10:00pm. **Hotel:** 7
beds. **Other points:** bar. **Address:** 41, boulevard
Clémenceau.
MR CHARLES HUON
**Telephone:** 96.23.20.65
⊗ ♉ 🏠 Map 4

## PIACE, Sarthe, 72170

### LES DEUX RENARDS, RN 138, between Alençon (20km) and le Mans (30km)

**Menu:** 47 to 54 Frs. **Restaurant:** Breakfast served from
5:00am. Lunch served from 11:00am until 2:30pm.
Dinner served from 7:00pm until 10:00pm. Closed
Saturdays. **Specialities:** home cooking. **Other points:**
bar, open to non-residents, children welcome, car park.
**Address:** Route Nationale 138, Le Bourg.
MR JÉRÔME BRILLIET
**Telephone:** 43.97.02.16
⊗ ♉ Map 5

## PICAUVILLE, Manche, 50360

### HOTEL DES VOYAGEURS, RN 13, Cherbourg

**Languages spoken:** English. **Menu:** 47 to 115 Frs.
**Accommodation:** 85 to 135 Frs. **Restaurant:**
Breakfast served from 6:30am. Lunch served from
midday until midday. Dinner served from 7:30pm
until midday. Closed Sundays and 15 days end of
December. **Specialities:** home cooking. **Hotel:** 9 beds.
**Other points:** bar, open to non-residents, à la carte
menu, children welcome, pets welcome – check for
details, car park, traditional decor. **Address:** 43, rue
de Périers.
MME FABIENNE FRANÇOISE
**Telephone:** 33.41.00.59
⊗ ♉ 🏠 Map 3

## PIERREFITTE, Orne, 61160

### LE PIERREFITTE, RN 158, the main road between Caen and Argentan

**Menu:** 52 Frs. **Restaurant:** Breakfast served from
6:30am. Closed Saturdays, 15 days in January and 15
days end of August. **Specialities:** home cooking. **Other
points:** bar, children welcome, pets welcome – check for
details, car park, traditional decor. **Address:** Route
Nationale 158.
MR YVES DELAUNAY
**Telephone:** 33.35.95.06
⊗ ♉ Map 3

## PIPRIAC, Ille-et-Vilaine, 35550

### HOTEL DE LA TOUR D'AUVERGNE, RD 777

**Menu:** 50 to 180 Frs. **Accommodation:** 100 to 150 Frs (extra bed for children). **Restaurant:** Breakfast served from 7:00am. Lunch served from midday until 2:00pm. Dinner served from 7:00pm until 9:30pm. Closed Mondays and 15 days in February. **Specialities:** poissons au beurre blanc, regional food. **Hotel:** 10 beds; 8 single rooms, 2 double rooms with shower, private WC, television, telephone. **Other points:** bar, open to non-residents, terraces, car park, traditional decor. **Address:** 7, rue de l'Avenir.
MR MICHEL GÉRARD
**Telephone:** 99.34.41.34
⊗ ⦆ 🏠 ☆ Map 4

## PLAINTEL, Côtes-du-Nord, 22940

### LE SEBASTOPOL, RD 700, on the road to Loudéac

**Languages spoken:** English. **Menu:** 50 to 150 Frs. **Restaurant:** Breakfast served from 8:00am. **Specialities:** regional menu, home cooking. **Other points:** bar, à la carte menu, children welcome, pets welcome – check for details, car park, traditional decor. **Address:** Route de Sébastopol.
MR THIERRY PODEUR
**Telephone:** 96.32.15.74
⊗ ⦆ Map 4

## PLENEE JUGON, Côtes-du-Nord, 22640

### RELAIS DES GARENNES, RN 12, between Rennes and Brest

**Languages spoken:** English and Dutch. **Menu:** 47 Frs. **Restaurant:** Breakfast served from 5:00am. Lunch served from 11:45am until 3:00pm. Dinner served from 7:00pm until 11:30pm. Closed Saturdays. **Specialities:** truite farcie aux cèpes, pëlla, couscous, cassoulet, home cooking. **Other points:** bar, open to non-residents, children welcome, pets welcome – check for details, car park, traditional decor.
MR GRANT SHANNOD
**Telephone:** 96.34.52.11
⊗ ⦆ Map 4

## PLESLIN TRIGAVOU, Côtes-du-Nord, 22490

### LE MILL'PATT

**Menu:** 40 to 50 Frs. **Restaurant:** Breakfast served from 7:00am. Closed Sundays. **Specialities:** regional menu. **Other points:** bar, à la carte menu, modern decor. **Address:** Le Bourg.
MR LOÏC RENAULT
**Telephone:** 96.27.84.14
⊗ ⦆ Map 4

## PLESTAN, Côtes-du-Nord, 22640

### HOTEL DU CENTRE, RN 12, Saint Brieuc

**Places of interest:** Nancy, Metz, abbaye des Remontrés, Pont à Mousson, Château d'Auneau. **Menu:** 48 Frs. **Accommodation:** 105 to 135 Frs. **Restaurant:** Breakfast served from 7:00am. Lunch served from 11:30am until 3:00pm. Dinner served from 7:00pm until 11:00pm. Closed Sundays. **Specialities:** home cooking. **Hotel:** 11 beds; with shower, bath, private WC. **Other points:** bar, open to non-residents, à la carte menu, children welcome, pets welcome – check for details, car park, traditional decor. **Address:** 5, rue de Penthièvre.
MME VIOLETTE MÉLINE
**Telephone:** 96.34.10.96
⊗ ⦆ 🏠 Map 4

## PLEUMEUR GAUTIER, Côtes-du-Nord, 22740

### CHEZ CINDY, CD 33, route of Tréguier/ Paimpol

**Menu:** 50 to 90 Frs. **Restaurant:** Breakfast served from 9:00am. Lunch served from midday until 2:00pm. Dinner served from 7:00pm until 9:00pm. Closed Saturdays and 3 weeks in August. **Specialities:** home cooking. **Other points:** bar, open to non-residents, à la carte menu, children welcome, terraces, pets welcome – check for details, car park, traditional decor. **Address:** La Croix Neuve.
MR HERVÉ LE FOLL
**Telephone:** 96.92.42.19
⊗ ⦆ Map 4

## PLEYBEN, Finistère, 29190

### HOTEL DES VOYAGEURS, between Quimper and Brest

**Menu:** 70 Frs. **Accommodation:** 100 to 150 Frs. **Restaurant:** Breakfast served from 7:00am. Lunch served from midday until 2:00pm. Dinner served from 7:30pm until 9:00pm. Closed Sundays and the last 3 weeks of August. **Specialities:** fruits de mer, couscous, home cooking. **Hotel:** 7 beds; 5 single rooms, 2 double rooms. **Other points:** bar, open to non-residents, à la carte menu, children welcome, pets welcome – check for details, car park, traditional decor. **Address:** 17, place Charles de Gaulle.
MR JEAN-YVES MARZIN
**Telephone:** 98.26.61.06
⊗ ⦆ 🏠 Map 4

## PLOERMEL, Morbihan, 56800

### LES ROUTIERS, RN 24, after the roundabout entering Ploermel

**Menu:** 50 to 130 Frs. **Accommodation:** 90 to 150 Frs. **Restaurant:** Dinner served from midday until 10:00pm. Closed Saturdays and in September. **Specialities:** home

cooking. **Hotel:** 11 beds. **Other points:** bar, open to non-residents, children welcome, car park. **Address:** Route de Rennes.
MME SOLANGE RIO
**Telephone:** 97.74.00.48
⊗ ♸ 🏠 Map 4

## PLOEUC SUR LIE, Côtes-du-Nord, 22150

### LE RELAIS DU SQUARE, RN 168
**Restaurant:** Dinner served from midday until 9:00pm. Closed Saturdays and in August. **Other points:** bar **Address:** 5, rue d'Enfer.
MME SYLVIANE LAFON-SAGORY
**Telephone:** 96.28.70.47
⊗ ♸ Map 4

## PLOUAGAT, Côtes-du-Nord, 22170

### CHEZ PIERRETTE, RN 12, exit Quintin/Châtelaudren
**Menu:** 56 Frs (wine and coffee included). **Accommodation:** 170 Frs to 200 Frs. **Restaurant:** Breakfast served from 5:00am. Lunch served from 11:30am until midday. Dinner served from 7:00pm until 11:00pm. Closed Saturdays. **Specialities:** home cooking. **Hotel:** 12 beds; with shower, bath, private WC, television, telephone. **Other points:** bar, open to non-residents, children welcome, lounge area, pets welcome – check for details, car park, modern decor. **Address:** ZA de Fournello.
MR PIERRE DROUIN
**Telephone:** 96.74.28.13, 96.74.25.35. **Fax:** 96.74.25.42
⊗ ♸ 🏠 ☆☆ Map 4

## PLOUEDERN, Finistère, 29800

### LE RELAIS KERIEL, RN 12, the main road between Paris and Brest
**Languages spoken:** English. **Menu:** 52 Frs (drink and coffee included). **Restaurant:** Breakfast served from 6:30am. Lunch served from 11:30am until 2:00pm. Dinner served from 7:00pm until 9:00pm. Closed end of September. **Specialities:** regional menu, home cooking. **Other points:** bar, open to non-residents, children welcome, lounge area, pets welcome – check for details, car park, modern decor. **Address:** Keriel-Landerneau.
MME MARIE GAC
**Telephone:** 98.20.92.53, 98.20.88.22
⊗ ♸ Map 4

## PLOUER SUR RANCE, Côtes-du-Nord, 22490

### LE BON ACCUEIL, RD 366, between Dinan and Saint Malo
**Menu:** 50 to 180 Frs. **Restaurant:** Breakfast served from 7:30am. Lunch served from midday until 2:00pm. Closed Mondays and in August. **Specialities:** regional

menu, home cooking. **Other points:** bar, open to non-residents, à la carte menu, terraces, pets welcome – check for details, car park. **Address:** La Gourbanière.
MR THÉOPHILE YRIS
**Telephone:** 96.86.91.67
⊗ ♸ 🍲 Map 4

## PLOUGOUMELEN, Morbihan, 56400

### LE KENYAH, RN 165, the main road between Vannes and Lorient
**Languages spoken:** English. **Menu:** 50 Frs (all included). **Restaurant:** Breakfast served from 6:00am. Lunch served from midday until 2:00pm. Dinner served from 7:00pm until 10:00pm. Closed Saturdays. **Specialities:** regional menu, home cooking. **Other points:** bar, open to non-residents, terraces, pets welcome – check for details, car park, modern decor. **Address:** Zone Commerciale du Kenyah.
MR JOËL BORILLER
**Telephone:** 97.56.25.37
⊗ ♸ Map 4

## PLOUHINEC, Finistère, 29780

### RESTO-GRILL 'L'AN DAOL MEN', RD 784, after Quimper, road for Audierne
**Languages spoken:** English. **Menu:** 49 to 120 Frs. **Restaurant:** Lunch served from midday until 2:00pm. Dinner served from 7:00pm until 9:00pm. Closed Sundays. **Specialities:** home cooking. **Other points:** open to non-residents, à la carte menu, children welcome, pets welcome – check for details, car park, traditional decor. **Address:** 3, rue du Général Leclerc.
MR DANIEL OGOR
**Telephone:** 98.70.76.20
⊗ Map 4

## PLOUIGNEAU, Finistère, 29610

### BAR DES SPORTS, RN 12, towards the town centre
**Menu:** 50 to 180 Frs. **Restaurant:** Breakfast served from 7:00am. Lunch served from midday until 2:30pm. Dinner served from 7:00pm until 10:00pm. Closed Sundays and in August. **Specialities:** regional menu, home cooking. **Other points:** bar, open to non-residents, à la carte menu, children welcome, car park, traditional decor. **Address:** 18, rue du 9 août.
MR JEAN-PAUL TALGUEN
**Telephone:** 98.67.71.37, 98.67.71.81
⊗ ♸ Map 4

## PLOUNEVEZ MOEDEC, Côtes-du-Nord, 22810

### AUX ROUTIERS – RELAIS DU BEG AR C'HRA, RN 12, between Morlaix and Guingamp

**Menu:** from 50 Frs. **Accommodation:** 110 to 160 Frs. **Restaurant:** Breakfast served from 6:30am. Lunch served from midday until 2:00pm. Dinner served from 7:30pm until 10:00pm. Closed Saturdays, from 1 to 10 May and mid-August to mid-September. **Specialities:** home cooking. **Hotel:** 11 beds; with shower, bath, private WC. **Other points:** bar, open to non-residents, pets welcome – check for details, car park.
MR JEAN-MARIE RUBEUS
**Telephone:** 96.38.61.08
⊗ ♥ ⌂ Map 4

## PLOUNEVEZ QUINTIN, Côtes-du-Nord, 22110

### LES ROUTIERS, RN 790, Saint Brieuc
**Menu:** 50 to 120 Frs. **Restaurant:** Breakfast served from 7:00am. Lunch served from 11:30am until 1:30pm. Dinner served from 7:00pm until 9:00pm. Closed Saturdays and in September. **Specialities:** home cooking. **Other points:** bar, open to non-residents, children welcome, pets welcome – check for details, car park, modern decor. **Address:** 1, place de l'Eglise.
MME GILDAS MARTIN
**Telephone:** 96.24.54.05
⊗ ♥ Map 4

## PLOURAY, Morbihan, 56770

### LE RELAIS DES SPORTS
**Other points:** bar. **Address:** 2, rue de l'Ellé.
MME LÉANDRE LE LAIN
**Telephone:** 97.23.90.18
⊗ ♥ Map 4

## POLIGNE, Ille-et-Vilaine, 35320

### LE TIROUANEZ, RN 137, between Rennes and Nantes
**Languages spoken:** English. **Menu:** 45 Frs. **Restaurant:** Breakfast served from 6:30am. Closed Sundays and in August. **Specialities:** home cooking. **Other points:** bar, open to non-residents, children welcome, pets welcome – check for details, car park, modern decor.
MME MARYLÈNE GUILLARD
**Telephone:** 99.43.73.06
⊗ ♥ Map 4

## PONT AUDEMER, Eure, 27500

### AU RENDEZ-VOUS DES CHAUFFEURS, RN 180
**Restaurant:** Closed Sundays. **Hotel:** 3 beds. **Other points:** bar. **Address:** 4, rue Notre Dame du Pré.
MR RENAUD PIERREL
**Telephone:** 32.41.04.36
⊗ ♥ Map 3

### RELAIS DE SAINT PAUL, RN 180, between Pont Audemer and Bernay
**Menu:** 52 Frs. **Restaurant:** Breakfast served from 7:30am. Lunch served from 11:30am until 1:00pm. Closed Saturdays and the 1st fortnight of August. **Specialities:** home cooking. **Other points:** bar, open to non-residents, car park, traditional decor. **Address:** Route de Saint-Paul, les Saulniers.
MR CLAUDE VIRFOLLET
**Telephone:** 32.41.16.17
⊗ ♥ Map 3

## PONT AVEN, Finistère, 29930

### CHEZ MELANIE ET MONIQUE, RN 783
**Restaurant:** Closed Mondays and in September. **Other points:** bar. **Address:** Lieu dit 'Croissant-Kergos'.
MME LE GOC
**Telephone:** 98.06.03.09
⊗ ♥ ⌣ Map 4

## PONT HEBERT, Manche, 50880

### LE MADRILENE
**Menu:** 55 Frs. **Accommodation:** 90 to 110 Frs. **Restaurant:** Breakfast served from 7:00am. Lunch served from midday until 2:00pm. Dinner served from 7:00pm until 9:00pm. Closed Sundays. **Specialities:** home cooking. **Hotel:** 7 beds; with shower, bath. **Other points:** bar, open to non-residents, pets welcome – check for details, car park. **Address:** Quartier du Pont la Meauffe.
MME MARIE-THÉRÈSE HAMET
**Telephone:** 33.56.44.18
⊗ ♥ ⌂ Map 3

## PONT SAINT MARTIN, Loire-Atlantique, 44860

### LE RELAIS COTE OUEST, the main road between Nantes and la Roche sur Yon
**Menu:** 50 to 168 Frs. **Restaurant:** Breakfast served from 6:15am. Lunch served from midday until 2:30pm. Dinner served from 7:00pm until 9:30pm. Closed Sundays. **Specialities:** home cooking. **Other points:** bar, open to non-residents, à la carte menu, children welcome, terraces, pets welcome – check for details, car park, modern decor. **Address:** Parc d'Activité de Viais.
MR JEAN-LOUIS VRIGNAUD
**Telephone:** 40.32.72.40
⊗ ♥ Map 5

## PONTCHATEAU, Loire-Atlantique, 44160

### L'AUBERGE DU CALVAIRE, RD 33, 4km from the centre of Pontchâteau, towards Herbignac

Languages spoken: English. Menu: 60 to 120 Frs.
Accommodation: 180 to 250 Frs. Restaurant:
Breakfast served from 9:00am. Lunch served from
midday until 2:00pm. Dinner served from 7:00pm until
9:00pm. Specialities: regional menu, home cooking.
Hotel: 12 beds; 12 double rooms with shower, bath,
private WC, television, telephone. Other points: bar,
open to non-residents, à la carte menu, children
welcome, terraces, pets welcome – check for details, car
park, modern decor. Address: Lieu dit 'Le Calvaire',
6, route de la Brière.
MME GABRIELLE COUVRAND
Telephone: 40.01.61.65. Fax: 40.01.64.68
⊗ ⍾ ⌂ ⌲ ☆☆ Map 5

## LE RELAIS DE BEAULIEU, RN 165, the main road between Nantes and Vannes

Languages spoken: English and Italian. Menu: 65 to 155
Frs. Accommodation: 120 to 270 Frs. Restaurant:
Breakfast served from 5:00am. Lunch served from
midday until 3:00pm. Dinner served from 7:00pm until
10:00pm. Closed Saturdays. Specialities: anguilles au
cidre, saumon grillé au beurre blanc, langoustes, regional
food, home cooking. Hotel: 15 beds; 7 single rooms, 8
double rooms with shower, private WC. Other points:
bar, open to non-residents, à la carte menu, children
welcome, pets welcome – check for details, car park.
MME LOUISETTE PRAUD
Telephone: 40.01.60.58. Fax: 40.45.60.82
⊗ ⍾ ⌂ ⌲ Map 5

# PONTORSON, Manche, 50170

## LE RENOVE, RN 175

Menu: 48 to 120 Frs. Accommodation: 130 to 220 Frs.
Restaurant: Breakfast served from 7:00am. Lunch
served from midday until 3:00pm. Dinner served from
7:00pm until 10:00pm. Closed Sundays. Specialities:
home cooking. Hotel: 10 beds; 5 single rooms, 5 double
rooms with shower, private WC. Other points: bar,
open to non-residents, à la carte menu, children
welcome, pets welcome – check for details, car park,
modern decor. Address: 4, rue de Rennes.
MME MARIE-CLAIRE PÉPIN
Telephone: 33.60.00.21
⊗ ⍾ ⌂ Map 3

# QUEVEN, Morbihan, 56530

## LE RELAIS DE LA MAIRIE, RD 6

Hotel: 8 beds. Other points: bar. Address: Rue Principale.
MME YVONNE LEGALLIC
Telephone: 97.05.07.50
⊗ ⍾ ⌂ Map 4

# QUIMPERLE, Finistère, 29300

## LA FOURCHE, Quimperlé, exit Kerfleury

Menu: 50 Frs. Restaurant: Breakfast served from
6:30am. Lunch served from midday until 2:00pm. Dinner

served from 7:30pm until 9:30pm. Closed Sundays and
the 1st fortnight in September. Specialities: choucroute,
couscous, andouillette, home cooking. Other points: bar,
open to non-residents, pets welcome – check for details,
car park, traditional decor. Address: Route de Lorient.
MME SOLANGE LE GALL
Telephone: 98.39.11.45
⊗ ⍾ Map 4

# RANDONNAI, Orne, 61190

## HOTEL DU GRAND CERF, between l'Aigle and Nogent le Rotrou

Menu: 46 to 60 Frs. Accommodation: 100 to 120 Frs.
Restaurant: Breakfast served from 7:00am. Lunch
served from 11:30am until 3:00pm. Dinner served from
7:00pm until 10:00pm. Closed Tuesdays and the 1st
fortnight in June. Specialities: langue sauce piquante,
rognons au madère, home cooking. Hotel: 6 beds; 4
single rooms, 2 double rooms with shower, private WC.
Other points: bar, open to non-residents, children
welcome, pets welcome – check for details, car park,
traditional decor. Address: 5, route Sainte Anne.
MR DANIELI MILLIÈRE
Telephone: 33.34.20.03
⊗ ⍾ ⌂ Map 3

# RANES, Orne, 61150

## HOTEL DU PARC, RN 916, between Mont Saint Michel and Bretagne

Menu: 60 to 160 Frs. Accommodation: 140 to 260 Frs.
Restaurant: Breakfast served from 7:30am. Lunch
served from midday until 2:00pm. Dinner served from
7:00pm until 9:00pm. Closed Sundays. Specialities:
regional menu, home cooking. Hotel: 7 beds; 4 single
rooms, 3 double rooms with shower, bath, private WC,
television. Other points: bar, open to non-residents, à la
carte menu, children welcome, terraces, pets welcome –
check for details, car park, traditional decor. Address: 9,
rue du Parc.
MR ROGER CANTIN
Telephone: 33.39.73.85
⊗ ⍾ ⌂ Map 3

# REDON, Ille-et-Vilaine, 35600

## LE RELAIS, Rennes

Places of interest: Arrière pays et plage. Languages
spoken: English. Menu: 43 to 170 Frs.
Accommodation: 120 Frs. Restaurant: Lunch served
from midday until 2:00pm. Dinner served from 7:30pm
until 9:30pm. Hotel: 18 beds; 9 single rooms, 9 double
rooms with shower. Other points: bar, open to non-
residents, à la carte menu, children welcome, lounge
area, pets welcome – check for details, car park.
Address: Route de Rennes.
MR NOËL FRANÇOIS
Telephone: 99.71.46.54
⊗ ⍾ ⌂ ⌲ ☆ Map 4

## RENAC, Ille-et-Vilaine, 35660

### RESTAURANT CREPERIE BEAUREGARD, RD 177, between Rennes and Redon

**Menu:** 45 to 80 Frs. **Restaurant:** Breakfast served from 9:00am. Lunch served from midday until 2:00pm. Dinner served from 6:00pm until 9:00pm. Closed Mondays and 8 days in February. **Specialities:** ecrevisses, homarde, home cooking. **Other points:** open to non-residents, à la carte menu, pets welcome – check for details, car park, traditional decor. **Address:** Beauregard.
MME MARIE-ANNICK BONNO
**Telephone:** 99.72.07.83
⊗ Map 4

## RIAILLE, Loire-Atlantique, 44440

### AU RENDEZ-VOUS DES PECHEURS, D 178 and 33

**Menu:** 44 to 91 Frs. **Restaurant:** Lunch served from 11:45am until 2:30pm. Dinner served from 7:00pm until 9:00pm. Closed Wednesdays and from 28 July to 15 August. **Specialities:** home cooking. **Other points:** bar, open to non-residents, à la carte menu, children welcome, terraces, car park, traditional decor. **Address:** Place du champ de foire.
MR JOËL ASPOT
**Telephone:** 40.97.80.95
⊗ ♟ Map 5

## RICHEVILLE, Eure, 27420

### RESTAUROUTE LE BALTO, RN 14, the main road between Paris and Rouen

**Languages spoken:** English. **Menu:** 46 to 117 Frs. **Restaurant:** Breakfast served from 5:00am. Dinner served from 6:30pm until 9:00pm. Closed Sundays and in August. **Specialities:** home cooking. **Other points:** bar, open to non-residents, à la carte menu, children welcome, pets welcome – check for details, car park, traditional decor. **Address:** 4, Route Nationale 14.
MR PIERRE SADOK
**Telephone:** 32.27.10.55
⊗ ♟ ✌ Map 3

## RIVIERE ST SAUVEUR (LA), Calvados, 14600

### LES OISEAUX DE MER, in the industrial zone

**Menu:** 49 Frs (drink included). **Restaurant:** Breakfast served from 5:30am. Lunch served from 11:00am until 6:00pm. Dinner served from 6:00pm until 9:00pm. Closed Sundays and in August. **Specialities:** home cooking. **Other points:** bar, open to non-residents, children welcome, pets welcome – check for details. **Address:** 28, route des 4 Francs.

MR PASCAL QUESNEY
**Telephone:** 31.89.11.62
⊗ ♟ Map 3

## ROCHE SUR YON (LA), Vendée, 85000

### HOTEL SULLY, RN 137

**Languages spoken:** English and Spanish. **Accommodation:** 165 to 300 Frs. **Restaurant:** Breakfast served from 6:00am. Lunch served from midday until 3:00pm. Dinner served from 7:00pm until 11:00pm. **Specialities:** jambon de Vendée et haricots blancs, home cooking. **Hotel:** 34 beds; 14 single rooms, 20 double rooms with shower, bath, private WC, television, telephone. **Other points:** bar, à la carte menu, children welcome, lounge area, pets welcome – check for details, car park. **Address:** Boulevard Sully.
MME NATHALIE MALIDIN
**Telephone:** 51.37.18.21, 51.37.54.02
⊗ ♟ 🏠 ☆☆ Map 5

## ROMAGNY, Manche, 50140

### AUBERGE DES CLOSEAUX, RD 977, between Rennes and Caen towards Saint Hilaire du Harcouet

**Languages spoken:** a little English. **Menu:** 54 to 135 Frs. **Accommodation:** 170 to 220 Frs. **Restaurant:** Dinner served from midday until 8:30pm. Closed Sundays. **Specialities:** pintade au cidre, crutacés, poissons, regional food. **Hotel:** 10 beds; 10 double rooms with shower, bath, private WC, television, telephone. **Other points:** bar, à la carte menu, children welcome, lounge area, terraces, car park, modern decor. **Address:** Les Closeaux.
MR BERNARD CLOUARD
**Telephone:** 33.59.01.86. **Fax:** 33.69.41.02
⊗ ♟ 🏠 ☆☆ Map 3

## ROMAZY, Ille-et-Vilaine, 35490

### LE RELAIS, RN 175, between Rennes and Mont Saint Michel

**Places of interest:** Musée Claude Monet (Giverny), Château Bizy et Gaillon, musée et collégiale de Vernon. Evian, Genève, et nombreuses promenades en montagne. **Menu:** 50 Frs. **Restaurant:** Breakfast served from 6:30am. Lunch served from 11:00am until 2:30pm. Dinner served from 7:00pm until 10:00pm. Closed Saturdays. **Specialities:** home cooking. **Other points:** bar, open to non-residents, pets welcome – check for details, car park. **Address:** Le Bourg.
MR JEAN-CLAUDE MONCEL
**Telephone:** 99.39.50.83
⊗ ♟ Map 4

## ROSPORDEN, Finistère, 29140

### LES ROUTIERS, RN 165, Quimper

**Menu:** 48 Frs. **Accommodation:** 130 to 160 Frs.

Restaurant: Breakfast served from 6:00am. Lunch served from midday until 1:30pm. Dinner served from 7:30pm until 8:15pm. Closed Saturdays and in August (restaurant only). Specialities: home cooking. Hotel: 17 beds. Other points: bar, open to non-residents, pets welcome – check for details, car park. Address: 9, pont Biais.
MME MARYVONNE MICHAL
Telephone: 98.59.20.40
⊗ ⌁ ⌂ Map 4

## ROTS, Calvados, 14980

### LE RELAIS DU COUP DE POMPE, RN 13, Cherbourg
Languages spoken: English and Spanish. Restaurant: Breakfast served from 6:30am. Lunch served from midday until 2:00pm. Dinner served from 7:00pm until 9:30pm. Closed Saturday afternoons and Sundays. Specialities: home cooking. Hotel: 5 beds; 2 single rooms, 3 double rooms. Other points: bar, open to non-residents. Address: 22, route de Caen.
MR VALENTIN CASTANDER
Telephone: 31.26.63.56
⊗ ⌁ ⌂ Map 3

## ROUANS, Loire-Atlantique, 44640

### LA CHAUSSEE LE RETZ, Paimboeuf
Menu: 51 to 150 Frs. Accommodation: 130 to 160 Frs. Restaurant: Breakfast served from 7:00am. Lunch served from midday until 3:00pm. Dinner served from 7:30pm until 10:00pm. Closed Saturdays. Specialities: home cooking. Hotel: 7 beds; 2 single rooms, 5 double rooms with shower, private WC. Other points: bar, open to non-residents, à la carte menu, children welcome, terraces, pets welcome – check for details, car park, modern decor. Address: La Chaussée le Retz.
MME CLAUDETTE BITON
Telephone: 40.64.22.23
⊗ ⌁ ⌂ Map 5

## ROUEN, Seine-Maritime, 76100

### LES PLATANES, RN 13 bis and 14
Restaurant: Closed Saturdays and from 24 December to 2 January. Hotel: 20 beds. Other points: bar. Address: 57, avenue du Mont Riboudet.
MR ROGER SANNIER
Telephone: 35.71.01.52
⊗ ⌁ ⌂ Map 3

### RELAIS 207 – CHEZ JOËLLE ET PATRICK, RN 13 bis and 14
Restaurant: Closed Saturdays. Other points: bar. Address: 46, quai Cavelier de la Salle.
MR MEBARKI
Telephone: 35 73 18 55
⊗ ⌁ Map 3

## ROUGE PERRIERS, Eure, 27110

### LE RELAIS DU PONT DE L'EURE, RD 137, between le Neubourg and Brionne
Languages spoken: English. Menu: 50 to 85 Frs. Restaurant: Breakfast served from 7:00am. Lunch served from midday until 2:30pm. Dinner served from 7:00pm until 9:00pm. Closed Mondays. Specialities: home cooking. Other points: bar, open to non-residents, children welcome, terraces, pets welcome – check for details, car park. Address: 3, route d'Harcourt.
MME COLETTE LEPRINCE
Telephone: 32.35.05.00
⊗ ⌁ Map 3

## ROUGEMONTIER, Eure, 27350

### LE LUDO, RN 175, the main road between Rouen and Caen
Menu: 52 Frs. Restaurant: Breakfast served from 4:30am. Dinner served from midday until 9:30pm. Closed Saturdays and in August. Specialities: home cooking. Other points: bar, open to non-residents, à la carte menu, pets welcome – check for details, car park, modern decor. Address: 175 Route Nationale.
MR JEAN-CLAUDE DUBOC
Telephone: 32.56.85.22
⊗ ⌁ Map 3

## SABLES D'OLONNE (LES), Vendée, 85100

### AU COQ HARDI, RD 949, la Rochelle
Menu: 52 to 85 Frs. Accommodation: 160 to 200 Frs. Restaurant: Breakfast served from 8:30am. Lunch served from midday until 2:00pm. Dinner served from 7:00pm until 8:30pm. Closed Saturdays and from 20 September to 10 October. Specialities: home cooking. Hotel: 8 beds; 3 single rooms, 5 double rooms. Other points: bar, open to non-residents, terraces, traditional decor. Address: 7, avenue Alcide Cabaret.
MLLE FRANÇOISE PAJOT
Telephone: 51.32.04.62
⊗ ⌁ ⌂ Map 5

### LES VOYAGEURS, RN 160 and 149
Menu: 44 to 130 Frs. Accommodation: 180 to 220 Frs. Restaurant: Breakfast served from 7:00am. Lunch served from midday until 2:00pm. Dinner served from 7:15pm until 9:00pm. Closed Fridays and 3 weeks at Christmas. Specialities: home cooking. Hotel: 15 beds; 10 single rooms, 5 double rooms with shower, private WC, television, telephone. Other points: bar, open to non-residents, à la carte menu, pets welcome – check for details, car park, traditional decor. Address: 17, rue de la Baudière.
MR CLÉMENT PACORY
Telephone: 51.95.11.49. Fax: 51.21.50.21
⊗ ⌁ ⌂ Map 5

## SACEY, Manche, 50170

### *LES VOYAGEURS, the main road between Pontorson/Rennes/Fougères*

**Menu:** 48 to 120 Frs. **Accommodation:** 130 to 185 Frs. **Restaurant:** Breakfast served from 6:00am. Lunch served from midday until 3:00pm. Dinner served from 7:00pm until 10:00pm. **Specialities:** home cooking. **Hotel:** 7 beds; 3 single rooms, 4 double rooms. **Other points:** bar, open to non-residents, children welcome, terraces, pets welcome – check for details, car park, traditional decor. **Address:** Le Bourg.
MME MARCELLE BELAN
**Telephone:** 33.60.15.11
⊗ 🍷 Ⓗ Map 3

## SAINT AUBIN SUR SCIE, Seine-Maritime, 76550

### *CHEZ FRANCOISE*

**Restaurant:** Closed Sundays and in August. **Other points:** bar. **Address:** Rue du Gouffre.
MME FRANÇOISE SOICHET
**Telephone:** 35.85.91.09
⊗ 🍷 Map 3

## SAINT BERTHEVIN, Mayenne, 53940

### *L'INTERNATIONAL, RN 157, Rennes*

**Menu:** 53 to 110 Frs. **Accommodation:** 100 to 145 Frs. Accessible for handicapped. **Restaurant:** Breakfast served from 6:00am. Lunch served from midday until 3:00pm. Dinner served from 7:30pm until 11:00pm. Closed Sundays. **Specialities:** home cooking. **Hotel:** 22 beds; 16 single rooms, 6 double rooms with shower, bath, private WC, television, telephone. **Other points:** bar, opèn to non-residents, à la carte menu, children welcome, lounge area, terraces, pets welcome – check for details, car park, modern decor. **Address:** Lieu dit 'L'Aulne', Route Nationale 157.
MR HENRI GARNIER
**Telephone:** 43.69.31.74, 43.68.22.75
⊗ 🍷 Ⓗ ☆☆ Map 5

## SAINT BOMER LES FORGES, Orne, 61700

### *LE SAINT BOMER, RD 962, between Flers and Domfront*

**Menu:** 45 to 100 Frs. **Restaurant:** Breakfast served from 7:30am. Lunch served from 11:00am until 3:00pm. Dinner served from 7:00pm until 9:00pm. Closed Mondays. **Specialities:** regional menu. **Other points:** bar, open to non-residents, à la carte menu, children welcome, pets welcome – check for details, car park, traditional decor. **Address:** Le Bourg.
MR PIERRE JANNIARD
**Telephone:** 33.37.61.66
⊗ 🍷 Map 3

## SAINT BRANDAN, Côtes-du-Nord, 22800

### *RELAIS JACOB, RD 190, on the road to Saint Brieuc*

**Menu:** 50 to 80 Frs. **Restaurant:** Breakfast served from 8:00am. Lunch served from 11:00am until 3:00pm. Dinner served from 7:00pm until 10:00pm. Closed Saturdays and in August. **Specialities:** regional menu, home cooking. **Other points:** bar, open to non-residents, à la carte menu, children welcome, car park, traditional decor. **Address:** 47, rue de Launay.
MR PIERRE JACOB
**Telephone:** 96.74.88.19
⊗ 🍷 Map 4

## SAINT BREVIN L'OCEAN, Loire-Atlantique, 44250

### *LA DUCHESSE ANNE*

**Languages spoken:** English. **Menu:** 52 to 95 Frs. **Restaurant:** Open 24 hours. **Specialities:** home cooking. **Other points:** bar, open to non-residents, à la carte menu, pets welcome – check for details, car park. **Address:** 82, avenue du Président Roosevelt.
MR JACQUES LALOUE
**Telephone:** 40.27.23.38
⊗ 🍷 Map 5

## SAINT BREVIN LES PINS, Loire-Atlantique, 44250

### *LA GUINGUETTE, between Saint Nazaire and la Baule or Pornic*

**Menu:** 50 Frs (winter) and 74 Frs (during the season). **Restaurant:** Breakfast served from 6:00am. Lunch served from midday until 2:00pm. Dinner served from 7:00pm until 10:00pm. Closed Saturdays and from Christmas Day to New Year's Day. **Specialities:** home cooking. **Other points:** bar, open to non-residents, à la carte menu, children welcome, terraces, pets welcome – check for details, car park, traditional decor. **Address:** 137, avenue du Maréchal Foch, La Courance.
MME PIERRETTE GIRAULT
**Telephone:** 40.27.21.95
⊗ 🍷 Map 5

## SAINT BRIEUC, Côtes-du-Nord, 22000

### *AU BEAUFEUILLAGE, RN 12*

**Restaurant:** Closed Sundays and from 8 August to 1 September. **Hotel:** 29 beds. **Other points:** bar. **Address:** 2, rue de Paris.
MR CLAUDE ANDRIEUX
**Telephone:** 96.33.09.16
⊗ 🍷 Ⓗ ☆ Map 4

# SAINT COME DU FRESNE,
Calvados, 14960

## LE SANTA DE A
**Menu:** 45 to 85 Frs. **Restaurant:** Breakfast served from 8:00am. **Specialities:** regional menu, home cooking. **Other points:** bar, open to non-residents, à la carte menu, children welcome, pets welcome – check for details, car park, modern decor. **Address:** 3, rue Panoramique.
MME ANDRÉA BOQUET
**Telephone:** 31.21.15.70
⊗ ⵀ Map 3

# SAINT CYR EN PAIL, Mayenne, 53140

## LES ROUTIERS, RN 12, between Alençon and Mayenne
**Menu:** 48 to 50 Frs. **Restaurant:** Breakfast served from 6:30am. Lunch served from 11:30am until 2:30pm. Dinner served from 6:30pm until 9:00pm. Closed Sundays and in August. **Specialities:** home cooking. **Other points:** bar, open to non-residents, children welcome, pets welcome – check for details, car park, traditional decor. **Address:** Le Bourg.
Mme ANTOINETTE DUPONT
**Telephone:** 43.03.03.21
⊗ ⵀ Map 5

# SAINT CYR EN TALMONDAIS,
Vendée, 85540

## RESTAURANT DU CENTRE, RD 949, between Fontenay le Comte and les Sables d'Olonne
**Places of interest:** Château de la Roche Guyon (8km), jardin de Claude Monet à Giverny (20km), Collégiale de Mantes la Jolie (9km). **Menu:** 55 to 120 Frs. **Restaurant:** Breakfast served from 7:30am. Lunch served from midday until 3:00pm. Dinner served from 7:00pm until 9:00pm. Closed Thursdays and 8 days in January. **Specialities:** home cooking. **Other points:** bar, open to non-residents, à la carte menu, children welcome, car park, traditional decor. **Address:** Route Départementale 949, Au Bourg.
MR JEAN-CLAUDE VAUCELLE
**Telephone:** 51.30.82.84
⊗ ⵀ Map 5

# SAINT DENIS DE MAILLOC,
Calvados, 14100

## LA FORGE, RD 579, between Lisieux and Orbec
**Menu:** 50 Frs. **Restaurant:** Breakfast served from 6:45am. Lunch served from 11:00am until 2:30pm. Dinner served from 6:00pm until 8:30pm. Closed Saturdays and in August. **Specialities:** home cooking.

**Other points:** bar, open to non-residents, terraces, pets welcome – check for details, car park, traditional decor. **Address:** Lisieux.
MR YVAN LEROY
**Telephone:** 31.63.73.19
⊗ ⵀ Map 3

# SAINT DENIS DE MERE, Calvados, 14110

## LE RELAIS DES LANDES, RD 562, between Caen and Flers
**Menu:** 49 Frs. **Restaurant:** Breakfast served from 6:00am. **Specialities:** home cooking. **Other points:** bar, terraces, car park, traditional decor. **Address:** Route Départementale 562.
MR GÉRARD DEVRIÈSE
**Telephone:** 31.69.07.06
⊗ ⵀ Map 3

# SAINT DENIS DES MONTS, Eure, 27520

## LE LAMA, RN 138, between Rouen and Brionne
**Menu:** 52 Frs. **Restaurant:** Breakfast served from 6:00am. Lunch served from 11:00am until 3:00pm. Closed Saturdays, 3 weeks in August and 10 days at Christmas. **Specialities:** home cooking. **Other points:** bar, open to non-residents, children welcome, pets welcome – check for details, car park, traditional decor. **Address:** Route Nationale 138.
MR CHRISTIAN CHUETTE
**Telephone:** 32.42.60.10
⊗ ⵀ Map 3

# SAINT DENIS SUR SARTHON, Orne, 61420

## HOTEL DE LA GARE – LES AMIS DES ROUTIERS, RN 12
**Restaurant:** Closed Sundays. **Other points:** bar. **Address:** La Gare.
MR GUY ELLIEN
**Telephone:** 33.27.30.03
⊗ ⵀ Map 3

# SAINT ERBLON, Ille-et-Vilaine, 35230

## CHEZ MICHEL ET SYLVIE, RD 82, motorway Rennes/Nantes
**Languages spoken:** English. **Menu:** 47 Frs. **Restaurant:** Breakfast served from 9:00am. Lunch served from 11:30am until 2:00pm. Closed Sundays and 3 weeks in August. **Specialities:** regional menu, home cooking. **Other points:** bar, open to non-residents, children welcome, pets welcome – check for details, car park, traditional decor. **Address:** ZA, 3, allée des Leuzières.

MR MICHEL MARTIN
**Telephone:** 99.52.28.40, 99.00.44.69
⊗ ♀ Map 4

## SAINT ETIENNE DE BRILLOUET, Vendée, 85210

### LE STEPHANOIS, RN 148, Niort/Saint Hermine/Nantes

**Languages spoken:** English. **Menu:** 55 Frs (wine and coffee included). **Restaurant:** Breakfast served from 6:30am. Lunch served from 11:30am until 3:00pm. Dinner served from 6:00pm until 11:00pm. Closed Tuesdays. **Specialities:** regional menu, home cooking. **Other points:** bar, open to non-residents, à la carte menu, children welcome, lounge area, terraces, pets welcome – check for details, car park, traditional decor. **Address:** Route Nationale 148.
MME MARIE-THÉRÈSE RAGON
**Telephone:** 51.27.63.37
⊗ ♀ Map 5

## SAINT EVARZEC, Finistère, 29170

### AU BON REPOS, RD 783, between Quimper and Concarneau

**Menu:** 60 to 100 Frs. **Accommodation:** 130 to 200 Frs. **Restaurant:** Breakfast served from 6:30am. Lunch served from midday until 2:00pm. Dinner served from 7:00pm until 8:30pm. Closed Saturdays and in December. **Specialities:** Coquilles Saint-Jacques; Coquilles Saint-Jacques, home cooking. **Hotel:** 20 beds; with shower, bath, private WC, television, telephone. **Other points:** bar, open to non-residents, terraces, pets welcome – check for details, car park, traditional decor. **Address:** Poullogoden.
MR ROGER GUILLOU
**Telephone:** 98.56.20.09, 98.56.20.29
⊗ ♀ ⌂ Map 4

## SAINT EVROULT DE MONTFORT, Orne, 61230

### HOTEL DU RELAIS, RN 138, between Rouen and Alençon

**Menu:** 47 Frs. **Accommodation:** 80 to 150 Frs. **Restaurant:** Breakfast served from 7:00am. Lunch served from 11:00am until 3:00pm. Dinner served from 7:00pm until 10:00pm. Closed Sundays. **Specialities:** home cooking. **Hotel:** 5 beds; 2 single rooms, 3 double rooms with shower. **Other points:** bar, open to non-residents, car park. **Address:** Le Bourg.
MR DANIEL CONAN
**Telephone:** 33.35.60.58
⊗ ♀ ⌂ Map 3

## SAINT GERMAIN SUR MOINE, Maine-et-Loire, 49230

### LE TAILLIS DU VERGER, RN 249, edge of motorway 249, Nantes/Cholet

**Menu:** 55 Frs (coffee included). **Restaurant:** Breakfast served from 6:30am. Lunch served from 11:30am until 2:30pm. Dinner served from 7:00pm until 10:00pm. Closed Sundays. **Specialities:** regional menu, home cooking. **Other points:** bar, children welcome, terraces, pets welcome – check for details, car park, modern decor. **Address:** Carrefour du Petit Lapin, route de la Renaudière.
MR PAUL ERAUD
**Telephone:** 41.64.64.61
⊗ ♀ Map 5

## SAINT GILDAS DES BOIS, Loire-Atlantique, 44530

### RELAIS CASSEROLE LES ROUTIERS, RD 773, between Redon and Pontchâteau

**Menu:** 65 to 350 Frs. **Accommodation:** 120 to 130 Frs. **Restaurant:** Breakfast served from 7:30am. Lunch served from 2:00pm until 2:30pm. Dinner served from 8:00pm until 9:30pm. **Specialities:** plateau de fruits de mer, homard grillé, regional food. **Hotel:** 10 beds; 10 single rooms with television. **Other points:** bar, open to non-residents, à la carte menu, children welcome, terraces, pets welcome – check for details, car park, modern decor. **Address:** 27, rue du Pont.
MR MICHEL GAIDANO
**Telephone:** 40.01.42.15
⊗ ♀ ⌂ ⌒ Map 5

## SAINT GILLES, Manche, 50180

### CARREFOUR SAINT GILLES, RD 77, between Saint Lo and Coutance

**Menu:** 50 Frs. **Restaurant:** Breakfast served from 6:30am. Closed Saturdays. **Specialities:** home cooking. **Other points:** bar, open to non-residents, children welcome, terraces, pets welcome – check for details, car park, modern decor. **Address:** Le Bourg.
MR YANNIK TOUTAIN
**Telephone:** 33.05.24.50
⊗ ♀ Map 3

## SAINT GILLES, Ille-et-Vilaine, 35590

### LE RELAIS, RN 12

**Languages spoken:** German and English. **Restaurant:** Dinner served from midday until 1:00am. Closed Saturdays and from 1 to 15 August. **Other points:** bar, car park. **Address:** 23, rue de Rennes.
MME JEANINE ABIVEN
**Telephone:** 99.64.63.04
⊗ ♀ Map 4

## SAINT GREGOIRE, Ille-et-Vilaine, 35760

### RESTAURANT DE L'ETANG

**Menu:** 46 to 200 Frs. **Restaurant:** Breakfast served from 7:30am. Lunch served from 11:30am until 3:00pm. Dinner served from 7:00pm until 9:00pm. Closed Saturdays. **Specialities:** home cooking. **Other points:** bar, open to non-residents, pets welcome – check for details, car park, traditional decor. **Address:** Rue de l'Etang au Diable.
MR MICHEL HUBERT
**Telephone:** 99.38.49.43
⊗ ☶ Map 4

## SAINT GUYOMARD, Morbihan, 56460

### LE RELAIS DES DOLMENS DE LANVAUX, RN 166, between Ploermel and Vannes

**Menu:** 50 to 72 Frs. **Accommodation:** 130 to 150 Frs. **Restaurant:** Breakfast served from 6:30am. Lunch served from 11:45am until 2:00pm. Dinner served from 7:00pm until 9:00pm. Closed Saturdays. **Specialities:** home cooking. **Hotel:** 7 beds; 1 single room, 6 double rooms with shower, private WC. **Other points:** bar, open to non-residents, à la carte menu, children welcome, terraces, pets welcome – check for details, car park, traditional decor. **Address:** Lieu dit 'Le Passoir'.
MR PIERRE LEGRAND
**Telephone:** 97.93.81.05
⊗ ☶ ⌂ ☆ Map 4

## SAINT HELEN, Côtes-du-Nord, 22100

### RELAIS DE LA CROIX DU FRENE

**Restaurant:** Breakfast served from 7:00am. Lunch served from 11:30am until 2:30pm. Dinner served from 7:00pm until 10:30pm. Closed Saturdays and public holidays. **Specialities:** home cooking. **Other points:** bar. **Address:** La Croix du Frene.
MR GUY GABILLARD
**Telephone:** 96.83.25.02
⊗ ☶ Map 4

## SAINT HILAIRE DE LOULAY, Vendée, 85600

### LE RELAX, RN 137, between Nantes and la Rochelle, 30km from Nantes

**Languages spoken:** a little German and English. **Menu:** 60 to 144 Frs. **Accommodation:** 180 to 210 Frs. **Restaurant:** Breakfast served from 6:00am. Lunch served from 11:30am until 3:00pm. Dinner served from 7:00pm until midnight. Closed Saturdays and 15 days in July. **Specialities:** Grillades au feu de bois, poissons au beurre blanc, regional food. **Hotel:** 11 beds; 11 double rooms with shower, private WC, television, telephone. **Other points:** bar, open to non-residents, à la carte menu, children welcome, terraces, pets welcome – check

for details, car park, modern decor. **Address:** Les Landes de Roussais.
MR LUC VAN WANGHE
**Telephone:** 51.94.02.44, 51.06.39.41. **Fax:** 51.94.27.25
⊗ ☶ ⌂ ☆☆ Map 5

## SAINT IGNEUC, Côtes-du-Nord, 22270

### LES 4 ROUTES, RN 76, between Lamballe and Dinan

**Menu:** 47 Frs. **Restaurant:** Breakfast served from 5:00am. Closed Sundays. **Specialities:** home cooking. **Other points:** bar, open to non-residents, children welcome, pets welcome – check for details, car park. **Address:** Route Nationale 76.
MME CHANTAL DURAND
**Telephone:** 96.31.68.40
⊗ ☶ Map 4

## SAINT JACQUES DE LA LANDE, Ille-et-Vilaine, 35136

### LA GAITE, RD 177, exit for 'La Gaité' on the road to Redon

**Languages spoken:** English. **Menu:** from 46 Frs. **Accommodation:** 140 to 180 Frs. **Restaurant:** Breakfast served from 7:00am. Lunch served from midday until 2:30pm. Dinner served from 7:30pm until 10:00pm. Closed Saturdays and public holidays (except reservation from groups). **Specialities:** regional menu. **Hotel:** 3 beds; with shower. **Other points:** bar, open to non-residents, à la carte menu, pets welcome – check for details, car park. **Address:** 26, boulevard Roger Dodin.
MR YANNICK ECHELARD
**Telephone:** 99.31.27.56
⊗ ☶ Map 4

## SAINT JEAN BREVELAY, Morbihan, 56661

### LE SAINT-YANN, between Vannes and Josselin

**Languages spoken:** English and Spanish. **Menu:** 45 Frs (wine included). **Restaurant:** Breakfast served from 6:30am. Lunch served from 11:45am until 2:30pm. Dinner served from 8:00pm until 10:00pm. **Specialities:** home cooking. **Other points:** bar, open to non-residents, children welcome, pets welcome – check for details, car park, traditional decor. **Address:** 21, rue de Rennes.
MR RÉMI VERDEAU
**Telephone:** 97.60.30.10. **Fax:** 97.60.38.67
⊗ ☶ Map 4

## SAINT JEAN DE BEUGNE, Vendée, 85210

### L'OASIS, RN 137, the main road between la Rochelle and Nantes

Menu: 53 Frs. Restaurant: Breakfast served from 5:00am. Lunch served from 11:30am until 2:30pm. Dinner served from 6:30pm until 11:00pm. Closed Sundays. Specialities: regional menu, home cooking. Other points: bar, open to non-residents, à la carte menu, children welcome, terraces, pets welcome – check for details, car park, traditional decor. Address: 61, Route Nationale 137.
MME LOUISETTE LE JONCOUR
Telephone: 51.27.38.80
⊗ ⍟ Map 5

## SAINT JEAN DE COUESNON, Ille-et-Vilaine, 35140

### LA JUHUELLERIE, RN 12, between Fougères and Rennes
Languages spoken: English, Spanish and Italian. Menu: 47 Frs. Restaurant: Breakfast served from 7:00am. Closed Sundays. Specialities: home cooking. Other points: bar, pets welcome – check for details, car park, modern decor. Address: Route Nationale 12.
MR JOSEPH VERLISIER
Telephone: 99.39.11.85
⊗ ⍟ Map 4

## SAINT JEAN DE DAYE, Manche, 50620

### BAR DES SPORTS, RN 174, between Saint Lo and Carentan
Languages spoken: English. Menu: 48 Frs (weekdays) and 55 Frs (week-ends). Restaurant: Dinner served from midday until 9:00pm. Closed Sundays. Specialities: home cooking. Other points: bar, open to non-residents, à la carte menu, pets welcome – check for details, car park, modern decor. Address: 9, rue de la Libération.
MME MARYVONNE TILLARD
Telephone: 33.55.42.46
⊗ ⍟ Map 3

### LE PETIT TROT, RN 174, between Saint Lo and Carentan
Menu: 55 to 110 Frs. Restaurant: Breakfast served from 8:00am. Specialities: home cooking. Other points: bar, open to non-residents, children welcome, terraces, pets welcome – check for details, car park.
Address: Rue de la Libération.
EURL LEROUX
Telephone: 33.55.48.00
⊗ ⍟ Map 3

## SAINT JEAN DE LA MOTTE, Sarthe, 72510

### CHEZ BÉATRICE, RN 23, between le Mans and Anger
Languages spoken: English. Restaurant: Breakfast served from 6:00am. Lunch served from 11:30am until 2:30pm. Dinner served from 7:00pm until 10:30pm. Closed Sundays. Specialities: home cooking. Other points: bar, children welcome, car park, traditional decor. Address: Route Nationale 23.
MME BÉATRICE COLLIN
Telephone: 43.45.72.02
⊗ ⍟ Map 5

## SAINT JEAN SUR VILAINE, Ille-et-Vilaine, 35220

### LE RELAIS DU CHEVAL BLANC, RN 157
Hotel: 10 beds. Other points: bar. Address: 4, rue de Rennes.
MR ALAIN BELLEVIN
Telephone: 99.00.32.67
⊗ ⍟ 🏠 Map 4

## SAINT JULIEN LE FAUCON, Calvados, 14140

### LE CAFE DE LA GARE, RD 511, between Lisieux and Saint Pierre sur Dives
Menu: 49,50 Frs. Restaurant: Breakfast served from 7:00am. Closed Sundays and in August. Specialities: home cooking. Other points: bar, open to non-residents, children welcome, pets welcome – check for details, car park, traditional decor.
MR ROBERT GALLAIS
Telephone: 31.63.62.91
⊗ ⍟ Map 3

## SAINT MARS LA BRIERE, Sarthe, 72680

### AUBERGE DU MARAIS, RN 157, between le Mans and Orléans
Menu: 50 Frs. Restaurant: Breakfast served from 6:00am. Closed Saturdays. Specialities: home cooking. Other points: bar, terraces, pets welcome – check for details, car park, modern decor. Address: Route Nationale 157.
MR RÉMY TRESSY
Telephone: 43.89.87.30. Fax: 43.89.87.30
⊗ ⍟ Map 5

## SAINT MARTIN DES BESACES, Calvados, 14350

### LA RENAISSANCE, RN 175, between Avranches and Caen
Languages spoken: English. Menu: 55 to 75 Frs. Accommodation: 110 to 160 Frs. Restaurant: Breakfast served from 7:30am. Lunch served from midday until 2:30pm. Dinner served from 7:00pm until 9:30pm. Closed Mondays and in February. Specialities: regional menu. Hotel: 8 beds; 6 single rooms, 2 double rooms with shower, private WC. Other points: bar, open to non-residents, à la carte menu, terraces, pets

welcome – check for details, car park, modern decor.
**Address:** Route Nationale 175, Le Bourg.
MMEe RENÉE LEHERICEY
**Telephone:** 31.68.72.65
⊗ ♈ 🏠 ⌣ ☆ Map 3

## SAINT MARTIN DES CHAMPS,

Manche, 50300

*LE GRAND CHIEN, RN 175, between*
*Pontorson and Avranche*
**Menu:** 45 Frs (coffee included). **Restaurant:**
Breakfast served from 5:00am. Closed from 15 August
to 1 September. **Specialities:** home cooking. **Other**
**points:** bar, open to non-residents, children welcome,
pets welcome – check for details, car park, traditional
decor.
MR MICHEL BOITTIN
**Telephone:** 33.58.04.52
⊗ ♈ Map 3

## SAINT MARTIN OSMONVILLE,

Seine-Maritime, 76680

*LA GRANGE, RN 28, between Rouen and*
*Neufchâtel en Bray*
**Menu:** 50 Frs. **Restaurant:** Closed Sundays.
**Specialities:** home cooking. **Other points:** bar, à la
carte menu, children welcome, terraces, pets welcome –
check for details, car park, traditional decor. **Address:**
La Boissière.
MME DENISE DUBOIS
**Telephone:** 35.34.14.34
⊗ ♈ Map 3

## SAINT MEEN LE GRAND, Ille-et-

Vilaine, 35290

*LE RELAIS DU MIDI, RN 164, Rennes/*
*Vannes/Saint Malo/Loudéac*
**Menu:** 44 Frs (weekdays) and 48,50 Frs (Sundays).
**Restaurant:** Breakfast served from 8:00am. Lunch
served from midday until 2:00pm. Dinner served from
7:30pm until 9:00pm. Closed Saturdays and 15 days
from 15 August. **Specialities:** home cooking. **Hotel:** 3
beds; 3 single rooms with private WC, television,
telephone. **Other points:** bar, open to non-residents,
children welcome, pets welcome – check for details.
**Address:** 25, place Patton.
MR CHRISTIAN POSNIC
**Telephone:** 99.09.60.02
⊗ ♈ Map 4

## SAINT MESMIN, Vendée, 85700

*LE RELAIS, RD 960 Bis, la Roche sur Yon*
**Menu:** 47 Frs (wine included) to 80 Frs. **Restaurant:**
Breakfast served from 6:00am. Lunch served from
11:30am until 3:00pm. Dinner served from 7:00pm until

9:00pm. Closed Saturdays. **Specialities:** home cooking.
**Other points:** bar, open to non-residents, terraces, pets
welcome – check for details, car park. **Address:** La
Boutinerie.
MR HENRY THIBAULT
**Telephone:** 51.91.95.00
⊗ ♈ Map 5

## SAINT NICOLAS DE REDON,

Loire-Atlantique, 44460

*LES ROUTIERS, the main road between*
*Nantes and Redon or Rennes and Redon*
**Menu:** 45 to 80 Frs. **Restaurant:** Breakfast served from
7:00am. Lunch served from 11:45am until 3:00pm.
Dinner served from 7:00pm until 10:00pm. Closed
Sundays and in August. **Specialities:** home cooking.
**Other points:** bar, children welcome, modern decor.
**Address:** 84, avenue Jean Burel.
MME MARIE-ANNICK HEMERY
**Telephone:** 99.71.01.96
⊗ ♈ Map 5

## SAINT NOLFF, Morbihan, 56250

*LE RELAIS DE BELLEVUE, RN 164, via*
*the old road for Rennes*
**Menu:** 49 Frs (coffee included). **Restaurant:** Breakfast
served from 6:30am. Lunch served from 11:45am until
3:00pm. Dinner served from 7:00pm until 9:30pm.
Closed Sundays and in August. **Specialities:** home
cooking. **Other points:** bar. **Address:** Bellevue.
MME EDITH HUREAU
**Telephone:** 97.45.44.04
⊗ ♈ Map 4

## SAINT PAUL DU BOIS, Maine-et-Loire,

49310

*CHEZ GEGE ET MIMI, RN 748, between*
*Vihiers and Niort (6km)*
**Menu:** 45 to 135 Frs. **Restaurant:** Breakfast served
from 7:00am. Lunch served from 11:30am until 2:30pm.
Dinner served from 6:30pm until 9:00pm. Closed
Tuesdays. **Specialities:** home cooking. **Other points:**
bar, open to non-residents, à la carte menu, children
welcome, pets welcome – check for details, car park.
**Address:** La Réveillère.
MR GÉRARD BONNIN
**Telephone:** 41.75.81.44
⊗ ♈ Map 5

## SAINT PELLERIN, Manche, 50500

*LA FOURCHETTE, RN 13, the main road*
*between Caen and Cherbourg*
**Menu:** 50 to 70 Frs. **Restaurant:** Breakfast served from
6:00am. Closed Sundays. **Specialities:** pied de veau,
rillettes, tripes, home cooking. **Other points:** bar, à la

carte menu, children welcome, terraces, car park, traditional decor. **Address:** Carantan.
MME NICOLE LE ROUX
**Telephone:** 33.42.16.56
⊗ ♈ Map 3

## SAINT PHILBERT DE GRAND LIEU, Loire-Atlantique, 44310

### LA BOULOGNE, RD 18 Bis

**Menu:** 42 to 100 Frs. **Accommodation:** 65 to 120 Frs.
**Restaurant:** Breakfast served from 9:00am. Lunch served from midday until 2:00pm. Dinner served from 7:00pm until 8:30pm. Closed Saturdays and the 1st fortnight of August. **Specialities:** regional menu. **Hotel:** 6 beds; 1 single room, 5 double rooms with shower, private WC. **Other points:** bar, open to non-residents, children welcome, pets welcome – check for details, traditional decor. **Address:** 11, place de l'Abbatiale.
MR BERNARD ANDRÉ
**Telephone:** 40.78.70.55
⊗ ♈ 🏠 Map 5

## SAINT PIERRE DU FRESNE, Calvados, 14260

### CHEZ DOUDOU, RN 175, between Rennes and Dinan

**Languages spoken:** English. **Menu:** 50 to 70 Frs.
**Restaurant:** Breakfast served from 5:00am. Lunch served from 11:00am until 3:00pm. Dinner served from 7:00pm until 11:00pm. Closed Sundays. **Specialities:** home cooking. **Other points:** bar, open to non-residents, children welcome, pets welcome – check for details, car park, modern decor. **Address:** Les Haies Tigards.
MR LOÏC LELÈGARD
**Telephone:** 31.77.80.89
⊗ ♈ Map 3

## SAINT PIERRE LANGERS, Manche, 50530

### LA GRILLADE, RD 973, between Cherbourg and Avranches

**Languages spoken:** English. **Menu:** 50 to 60 Frs.
**Accommodation:** 110 to 160 Frs. **Restaurant:** Breakfast served from 6:00am. Closed Sundays and between Christmas and New Year's Day. **Hotel:** 8 beds; with shower, bath, private WC. **Other points:** bar, open to non-residents, children welcome, car park, traditional decor. **Address:** Hameau de la Havaudière.
MR MARC JOHAN
**Telephone:** 33.48.12.63
⊗ ♈ 🏠 Map 3

## SAINT PIERRE LE VIGER, Seine-Maritime, 76740

### CHEZ DIDIER, RD 142, between Veules les

### Roses and Rouen

**Menu:** 47 Frs. **Restaurant:** Breakfast served from 5:00am. Closed Sundays. **Specialities:** home cooking.
**Other points:** bar, open to non-residents, children welcome, pets welcome – check for details, car park.
**Address:** Route de Veules les Roses.
MR DIDIER MOUTON
**Telephone:** 35.97.43.29
⊗ ♈ Map 3

## SAINT PIERRE LES ELBEUF, Seine-Maritime, 76320

### LA SAUVAGINE

**Languages spoken:** English. **Restaurant:** Dinner served from midday until 11:00pm. Closed Sundays, 15 days in January/February and 3 weeks in August. **Other points:** bar. **Address:** 611, chemin du Halage.
MR PATRICK CLIVAZ
**Telephone:** 35.78.37.70
⊗ ♈ Map 3

## SAINT PIERRE SUR DIVES, Calvados, 14170

### LE PRESSOIR, RD 40

**Languages spoken:** English. **Menu:** 50 Frs.
**Restaurant:** Breakfast served from 7:30am. Lunch served from midday until 2:30pm. Dinner served from 7:00pm until 9:00pm. Closed Saturdays. **Specialities:** home cooking. **Other points:** bar, open to non-residents, car park, modern decor. **Address:** 17, route de Caen.
MR THIERRY BIGOT
**Telephone:** 31.20.56.03
⊗ ♈ Map 3

## SAINT POL DE LEON, Finistère, 29250

### LES ROUTIERS, 5km from the port of Roscoff

**Languages spoken:** German and English.
**Accommodation:** 120 to 160 Frs. **Restaurant:** Closed Sundays and in August (except the hotel). **Specialities:** home cooking. **Hotel:** 18 beds; with shower, private WC, television. **Other points:** bar, children welcome, pets welcome – check for details, car park. **Address:** 28, rue Pen Ar Pont.
MR JEAN-LOUIS FLOCH
**Telephone:** 98.69.00.52
⊗ ♈ 🏠 ☆ Map 4

## SAINT QUAY PORTRIEUX, Côtes-du-Nord, 22410

### LES ROUTIERS

**Menu:** 53 to 150 Frs. **Accommodation:** 110 to 150 Frs.
**Restaurant:** Breakfast served from 7:30am. Lunch served from midday until 3:00pm. Dinner served from 7:00pm until 9:00pm. Closed Sundays. **Specialities:**

couscous; couscous. **Hotel:** 9 beds; with shower. **Other points:** bar, terraces, pets welcome – check for details, car park. **Address:** 42, rue des 3 Frères Salaün.
MR CLAUDE BAILLEUL
**Telephone:** 96.70.40.19. **Fax:** 96.70.36.96
⊗ ℗ 🏠 Map 4

# SAINT QUENTIN LES ANGES,
Mayenne, 53400

*LE RELAIS, the main road between Rennes and Angers, between Craon and Segré*
**Languages spoken:** English. **Menu:** from 48 Frs. **Accommodation:** 85 to 125 Frs. **Restaurant:** Breakfast served from 7:00am. Lunch served from 11:30am until 3:00pm. Dinner served from 7:30pm until 9:30pm. Closed the last 3 weeks of August. **Specialities:** home cooking. **Hotel:** 9 beds; 6 single rooms, 3 double rooms with shower. **Other points:** bar, open to non-residents, children welcome, lounge area, pets welcome – check for details, car park, traditional decor. **Address:** Le Bourg.
MR HUBERT TROTTIER
**Telephone:** 43.06.10.62. **Fax:** 43.06.08.41
⊗ ℗ 🏠 Map 5

# SAINT REMY DE SILLE, Sarthe, 72140

*LA COQUE, RD 304, between le Mans and Sillé le Guillaume*
**Restaurant:** Breakfast served from 7:00am. Lunch served from midday until 3:00pm. Closed Sundays and in August. **Specialities:** home cooking. **Other points:** bar, open to non-residents, pets welcome – check for details, car park, traditional decor. **Address:** 11, bis route du Mans.
MR CLAUDE ROUZIER
**Telephone:** 43.20.11.84
⊗ ℗ Map 5

# SAINT REMY SUR ORNE, Calvados, 14570

*AU BON ACCUEIL, RD 562, between Condé sur Noireau and Thury Harcourt*
**Menu:** 48 Frs. **Restaurant:** Breakfast served from 6:00am. Closed Sundays **Specialities:** home cooking. **Other points:** bar, open to non-residents, children welcome, terraces, pets welcome – check for details, car park, traditional decor. **Address:** 11, bis route du Mans.
MME JOSETTE BENOIT
**Telephone:** 31.69.43.87
⊗ ℗ Map 3

# SAINT ROMAIN DE COLBOSC,
Seine-Maritime, 76430

*LE RELAIS DU FRESCOT, on the road for le Havre*

**Menu:** 48 Frs. **Restaurant:** Breakfast served from 5:30am. Lunch served from 11:30am until 2:30pm. Dinner served from midday until 9:00pm. Closed Sundays. **Specialities:** home cooking. **Hotel:** 7 beds. **Other points:** bar, à la carte menu, pets welcome – check for details, car park. **Address:** 18 Nationale.
MR JACQUES CHAPELET
**Telephone:** 35.20.15.09
⊗ ℗ 🏠 Map 3

# SAINT SAMSON DE LA ROQUE,
Eure, 27680

*RELAIS NORD BRETAGNE, RN 815 A*
**Languages spoken:** English and Spanish. **Restaurant:** Dinner served from midday until 11:00pm. Closed Saturdays **Other points:** bar. **Address:** Route du Pont de Tancarville.
MR MARCEL POIRAUD
**Telephone:** 32.57.67.30
⊗ ℗ Map 3

# SAINT SEBASTIEN SUR VERTOU, Loire-Atlantique, 44120

*CAFE RESTAURANT DE LA GARE, RN 149, between Clisson and Nantes – at Vertou station*
**Menu:** 46 Frs. **Restaurant:** Breakfast served from 6:00am. Lunch served from 11:30am until 2:00pm. Dinner served from 7:00pm until 8:30pm. Closed Saturdays. **Specialities:** home cooking. **Other points:** bar, open to non-residents, children welcome, pets welcome – check for details, car park, modern decor. **Address:** 10, avenue de la Gare.
MR NOËL GOHAUD
**Telephone:** 40.34.08.74
⊗ ℗ Map 5

# SAINT SYMPHORIEN DES MONTS, Manche, 50640

*LE RELAIS DU BOIS LEGER, RN 176, between Alençon and Mont Saint Michel*
**Languages spoken:** English. **Menu:** 46 to 90 Frs. **Accommodation:** 100 to 160 Frs. **Restaurant:** Breakfast served from 6:00am. Lunch served from midday until 2:00pm. Dinner served from 7:00pm until 9:00pm. Closed Sundays, 1 week in February and 3 in September. **Specialities:** pintade aux pommes, terrine du chef, regional food, home cooking. **Hotel:** 10 beds; 4 single rooms, 6 double rooms with shower, bath. **Other points:** bar, open to non-residents, à la carte menu, children welcome, lounge area, terraces, car park, traditional decor. **Address:** Route Nationale 176, le Bois Léger.
MR RAYMOND PINET
**Telephone:** 33.49.01.43
⊗ ℗ 🏠 🍽 Map 3

## SAINT THEGONNEC, Finistère, 29223

### RESTAURANT DU COMMERCE, RN 12, Brest via the motorway

**Menu:** 49 Frs. **Restaurant:** Breakfast served from 7:30am. Lunch served from 11:30am until 2:00pm. Closed Saturdays and beginning of August. **Specialities:** home cooking. **Other points:** bar, open to non-residents, à la carte menu, children welcome, car park, traditional decor. **Address:** 1, rue de Paris.
MR ALAIN MEVEL
**Telephone:** 98.79.61.07
⊗ ♀ Map 4

## SAINT VIGOR LE GRAND, Calvados, 14400

### CHEZ PEPONNE, between Bayeux and Cherbourg

**Menu:** 50 Frs. **Restaurant:** Breakfast served from 6:00am. Lunch served from 11:00am until 4:00pm. Dinner served from 6:00pm until 11:00pm. Closed Sundays, 1 week in February and 15 days in August. **Specialities:** home cooking. **Other points:** bar, open to non-residents, pets welcome – check for details, car park, modern decor. **Address:** 3, rue du Pont Trubert.
MME MARIE-ANNICK VICTOIRE
**Telephone:** 31.92.28.39
⊗ ♀ Map 3

## SAINTE BROLADRE, Ille-et-Vilaine, 35120

### LE FLORIDA, RD 797, between Pontorson and Saint Malo

**Menu:** 49 Frs. **Specialities:** home cooking. **Other points:** bar, children welcome, pets welcome – check for details, car park. **Address:** Le Bourg.
MME ELIANE LOAS
**Telephone:** 99.80.26.41
⊗ ♀ Map 4

## SAINTE CECILE, Manche, 50800

### LE CECILIA, RD 924

**Languages spoken:** English and German. **Restaurant:** Lunch served from midday until 1:30pm. Dinner served from 7:00pm until 8:30pm. Closed Saturdays. **Specialities:** home cooking. **Hotel:** 5 beds; with shower. **Other points:** bar, car park. **Address:** Le Bourg.
MR DANIEL LE HUBY
**Telephone:** 33.61.07.81
⊗ ♀ ⌂ Map 3

## SAINTE CROIX HAGUE, Manche, 50440

### LE PETIT BACCHUS, RD 908, between Cherbourg and Baumont Hague

**Accommodation:** Pension 170 Frs and half board 140 Frs. **Restaurant:** Breakfast served from 6:00am. Lunch served from midday until 3:00pm. Dinner served from 7:30pm until 9:30pm. Closed Saturdays. **Specialities:** home cooking. **Other points:** bar, children welcome, pets welcome – check for details, car park, modern decor. **Address:** Lieu dit 'Le Petit Bacchus'.
MR CLAUDE LE CAVELIER
**Telephone:** 33.52.77.53
⊗ ♀ Map 3

## SAINTE FOY DE MONTGOMMERY, Calvados, 14140

### LE RELAIS DE MONTGOMERY, RN 179

**Restaurant:** Closed Sundays. **Hotel:** 4 beds. **Other points:** bar.
MME PLANCKEEL
**Telephone:** 31.63.53.02
⊗ ♀ Map 3

## SAINTE LUCE SUR LOIRE, Loire-Atlantique, 44980

### LA BOUGRIERE, CD 68, A 11, exit Thouaré Sainte Luce centre

**Languages spoken:** English and Spanish. **Menu:** 47,70 to 175 Frs. **Restaurant:** Breakfast served from 6:30am. Lunch served from midday until 2:30pm. Dinner served from 7:00pm until 10:30pm. Closed Fridays, in August and 1 week between Christmas Day and New Year's Day. **Specialities:** Beurre blanc, grenouilles, anguilles, regional food, home cooking. **Other points:** bar, open to non-residents, à la carte menu, children welcome, terraces, pets welcome – check for details, car park, traditional decor. **Address:** 4, rue du Pavillon.
MR PIERRE PERTUE
**Telephone:** 40.25.60.84, 40.25.92.40
⊗ ♀ ⌣ Map 5

## SAINTENY, Manche, 50500

### LE RELAIS DES FORGES, CD 971

**Menu:** 45 Frs. **Restaurant:** Breakfast served from 7:30am. Lunch served from midday until 2:00pm. Dinner served from 7:00pm until 8:00pm. Closed Tuesdays and in August. **Specialities:** home cooking. **Other points:** bar, open to non-residents, pets welcome – check for details, car park. **Address:** Les Forges.
MME FRANCINE COUSIN
**Telephone:** 33.42.39.36
⊗ ♀ Map 3

## SARTILLY, Manche, 50530

### LE VIEUX LOGIS, between Avranches and Granville

**Languages spoken:** English. **Menu:** 53 Frs.

**Restaurant:** Breakfast served from 7:00am. Lunch served from midday until 1:30pm. Closed Sundays, 10 days beginning of March and 10 days end of October. **Specialities:** home cooking. **Other points:** bar, open to non-residents, pets welcome – check for details, car park, traditional decor. **Address:** Grande Rue.
MR GÉRARD CADIOT
**Telephone:** 33.48.80.31
⊗ ♀ Map 3

## SAUMUR, Maine-et-Loire, 49400

### *HOTEL RESTAURANT DE LA GARE,*
*opposite the SNCF station*
**Menu:** 60 to 120 Frs. **Accommodation:** 100 to 230 Frs. **Restaurant:** Breakfast served from 7:00am. Lunch served from midday until 2:00pm. Dinner served from 7:00pm until 9:00pm. Closed Mondays. **Specialities:** cuisses de poulet 'bonne femme', rôti à la saumuroise, regional food, home cooking. **Hotel:** 18 beds; 5 single rooms, 13 double rooms with shower, bath, private WC, telephone. **Other points:** bar, à la carte menu, children welcome, lounge area, pets welcome – check for details, car park, traditional decor. **Address:** 16, avenue David d'Angers.
MME THÉRÈSE LOISON
**Telephone:** 41.67.34.24
⊗ ♀ ⌂ ☆☆ Map 5

## SEGRE, Maine-et-Loire, 49500

### *LE RELAIS DU COMMERCE, RN 775, on the road to Chôlet*
**Restaurant:** Breakfast served from 6:30am. **Specialities:** home cooking. **Hotel:** 6 beds; 6 single rooms. **Other points:** bar, open to non-residents, children welcome, lounge area, terraces, car park. **Address:** 1, place de la Gare.
MR EMILE GEORGET
**Telephone:** 41.92.22.27
⊗ ♀ ⌂ Map 5

## SENE, Morbihan, 56860

### *RELAIS ROUTIERS, N 165, between Vannes and Lorient*
**Menu:** 45 to 160 Frs. **Accommodation:** 78 to 160 Frs. **Restaurant:** Breakfast served from 6:00am. Lunch served from midday until 3:30pm. Dinner served from 7:00pm until 9:30pm. Closed from 24 December to 2 January. **Specialities:** home cooking. **Hotel:** 42 beds; 28 single rooms, 14 double rooms with shower, bath, private WC, television. **Other points:** bar, open to non-residents, children welcome, pets welcome – check for details, car park, modern decor. **Address:** 46, route de Vannes, le Poulfanc.
SA PENRU
**Telephone:** 97.47.47.97, 97.42.48.50
⊗ ♀ ⌂ ⌣ ☆ Map 4

## SIZUN, Finistère, 29450

### *HOTEL DES VOYAGEURS, D 167*
**Languages spoken:** English. **Menu:** 55 to 85 Frs. **Accommodation:** 140 to 240 Frs. **Restaurant:** Breakfast served from 7:30am. Lunch served from midday until 1:45pm. Dinner served from 7:15pm until 8:45pm. Closed Saturdays and from 10 September to 4 October. **Specialities:** terrine de lapin, mousline de truite, fruits de mer, regional food, home cooking. **Hotel:** 28 beds; 1 single room, 27 double rooms with shower, bath, private WC, television, telephone. **Other points:** bar, open to non-residents, pets welcome – check for details, car park, modern decor. **Address:** 2, rue de l'Argoat.
MR JOSEPH CORRE
**Telephone:** 98.68.80.35. **Fax:** 98.24.11.49
⊗ ♀ ⌂ ⌣ ☆ Map 4

## SORINIERES (LES), Loire-Atlantique, 44840

### *LE RELAIS – CHEZ PIERRETTE ET JEAN, RN 137 and 178, on the road to la Roche sur Yon*
**Menu:** 41 to 110 Frs. **Accommodation:** 95 Frs. **Restaurant:** Breakfast served from 6:30am. Lunch served from midday until 3:00pm. Dinner served from 7:30pm until 10:00pm. Closed Sundays and from 20 December to 15 January. **Specialities:** home cooking. **Hotel:** 7 beds; 5 single rooms, 2 double rooms. **Other points:** bar, open to non-residents, à la carte menu, children welcome, terraces, pets welcome – check for details. **Address:** 16, rue du Général de Gaulle.
MR JEAN LOUIS BENOÎT
**Telephone:** 40.31.22.91
⊗ ♀ ⌂ Map 5

## SOURDEVAL, Manche, 50150

### *AU BON ACCUEIL – LES ROUTIERS, RD 977, the main road between Caen and Vire*
**Languages spoken:** English. **Menu:** 47 to 100 Frs. **Accommodation:** 80 to 120 Frs. **Restaurant:** Breakfast served from 6:00am. Dinner served from midday until 10:00pm. Closed Sundays. **Specialities:** home cooking. **Hotel:** 5 beds; 3 single rooms, 2 double rooms (2 with shower). **Other points:** bar, open to non-residents, à la carte menu, terraces, pets welcome – check for details, traditional decor. **Address:** 1, place du Champ de Foire.
MR DANIEL DELAUNAY
**Telephone:** 33.59.62.91
⊗ ♀ ⌂ Map 3

## SOURDEVAL LES BOIS, Manche, 50450

### *CHEZ COLETTE, RN 799*
**Menu:** 40 Frs. **Restaurant:** Breakfast served from

7:00am. Lunch served from midday until 2:00pm.
**Specialities:** home cooking. **Other points:** bar, open to
non-residents, pets welcome – check for details, car
park. **Address:** Lieu dit 'La Croix'.
MME COLETTE DUFOUR
**Telephone:** 33.61.77.99
⊗ ⛾ Map 3

## SUZAY, Eure, 27420

*LE RELAIS MODERNE, RN 14, the main
road between Paris and Rouen*
**Menu:** 55 to 60 Frs. **Restaurant:** Breakfast served
from 6:30am. **Specialities:** home cooking. **Other
points:** bar, open to non-residents, children welcome,
terraces, pets welcome – check for details, car park,
modern decor.
MR JEAN-CLAUDE LAURENT
**Telephone:** 32.55.65.01
⊗ ⛾ Map 3

## TALMONT SAINT HILAIRE,
Vendée, 85440

*HOTEL DU CENTRE, RD 949, les Sables
d'Olonne/Luçon*
**Accommodation:** 100 to 180 Frs. **Restaurant:** Dinner
served from midday until 9:00pm. Closed Saturdays and
in October. **Specialities:** fruits de mer, regional food,
home cooking. **Hotel:** 12 beds; with shower, private
WC, television, telephone. **Other points:** bar, à la carte
menu, children welcome, terraces, pets welcome – check
for details, car park. **Address:** 1, rue du Centre.
MR MICHEL LE BLOND
**Telephone:** 51.90.60.35
⊗ ⛾ ⌂ Map 5

## TESSY SUR VIRE, Manche, 50420

*LES ROUTIERS, RD 13, Granville*
**Menu:** 45 Frs. **Restaurant:** Lunch served from midday
until 3:00pm. Dinner served from 7:00pm until 8:30pm.
Closed Thursdays. **Specialities:** home cooking. **Other
points:** bar, open to non-residents, children welcome,
pets welcome – check for details, car park, traditional
decor. **Address:** Place du Marché.
MR MAURICE ROBERT
**Telephone:** 33.56.35.25
⊗ ⛾ Map 3

## THEIL (LE), Orne, 61260

*BAR DE L ARCHE*
**Restaurant:** Dinner served from midday until 1:00am.
**Other points:** bar. **Address:** La Rouge.
MR GÉRARD LEROUX
**Telephone:** 37.49.62.92
⊗ ⛾ Map 3

## THOMER LA SOGNE, Eure, 27240

*RELAIS 154, RN 154, between Evreux and
Dreux*
**Languages spoken:** English. **Menu:** 54 Frs.
**Restaurant:** Breakfast served from 5:00am. Lunch
served from 11:00am until 3:00pm. Dinner served from
7:00pm until 10:30pm. Closed Saturdays. **Specialities:**
home cooking. **Other points:** bar, open to non-residents,
pets welcome – check for details, car park, modern
decor. **Address:** Route d'Orléans.
MME NICOLE VANDECANDELAERE
**Telephone:** 32.67.41.00
⊗ ⛾ Map 3

## TIVOLY, Eure, 27320

*LE RELAIS EUROPEEN, RN 154, the main
road between Evreux and Dreux*
**Languages spoken:** English. **Menu:** 53 to 55 Frs.
**Restaurant:** Breakfast served from 5:00am. Closed
Saturdays. **Specialities:** home cooking. **Other points:**
bar, open to non-residents, children welcome, pets
welcome – check for details, car park, traditional decor.
**Address:** Route Nationale 154.
SNC LES RELAIS EUROPÉENS
**Telephone:** 32.58.31.75
⊗ ⛾ Map 3

## TOLLEVAST, Manche, 50470

*LES CHEVRES, RN 13*
**Languages spoken:** English. **Menu:** 50 Frs.
**Restaurant:** Open 24 hours. **Specialities:** home
cooking. **Other points:** bar, open to non-residents, pets
welcome – check for details, car park, traditional decor.
**Address:** Route Nationale 13.
MR CLAUDE YSSAMBOURG
**Telephone:** 33.43.77.92
⊗ ⛾ Map 3

## TOTES, Seine-Maritime, 76890

*LE NORMANDY, RN 27*
**Menu:** 55 to 85 Frs. **Restaurant:** Breakfast served from
7:00am. Closed Saturdays. **Specialities:** regional menu,
home cooking. **Other points:** bar, children welcome,
pets welcome – check for details, car park. **Address:**
Route d'Yvetôt.
MR ALAIN MONTIER
**Telephone:** 35.32.99.54
⊗ ⛾ Map 3

## TRAIT (LE), Seine-Maritime, 76580

*LE JEAN BART LES ROUTIERS, RD
982, between Duclair and Caudebec en Caux*
**Languages spoken:** German and English. **Menu:** 43

Frs. **Accommodation:** 80 Frs. **Restaurant:** Breakfast served from 5:30am. Lunch served from 11:30am until 3:30pm. Dinner served from 6:00pm until 10:00pm. Closed Sundays and the last 3 weeks of August. **Specialities:** regional menu, home cooking. **Hotel:** 3 beds; 1 single room, 2 double rooms with shower, private WC, television, telephone. **Other points:** bar, open to non-residents, à la carte menu, children welcome, terraces, pets welcome – check for details, car park, modern decor. **Address:** 488, rue Jean Bart.
MR JEAN MAHIER
**Telephone:** 35.37.22.47
⊗ ⅌ Map 3

## TREFFENDEL, Ille-et-Vilaine, 35380

### RELAIS ROUTIERS RN 24, between Rennes and Lorient
**Menu:** 45 Frs. **Restaurant:** Breakfast served from 6:00am. Lunch served from 11:30am until 3:00pm. Dinner served from 6:30pm until 10:30pm. Closed Saturdays. **Specialities:** home cooking. **Other points:** bar, open to non-residents, children welcome, pets welcome – check for details, car park. **Address:** La Gare.
MME YVETTE GUILLEMOT
**Telephone:** 99.61.00.62
⊗ ⅌ Map 4

## TREILLIERES, Loire-Atlantique, 44119

### LE PIGEON BLANC, RN 137 and D 537, Rennes
**Menu:** 51,50 to 120 Frs. **Accommodation:** 180 Frs. **Restaurant:** Breakfast served from 5:30am. Closed Sundays **Specialities:** home cooking. **Hotel:** 3 beds; with shower, private WC, television. **Other points:** bar, open to non-residents, children welcome, pets welcome – check for details, car park, traditional decor. **Address:** Lieu dit 'Le Pigeon Blanc'.
MME RÉGINE PLAT
**Telephone:** 40.94.67.22. **Fax:** 40.94.59.98
⊗ ⅌ Map 5

## TREMOREL, Côtes-du-Nord, 22230

### LES ROUTIERS – CHEZ SIMONE, RN 164 Bis, between Rennes and Loudéac
**Menu:** 45 Frs. **Restaurant:** Breakfast served from 7:00am. Lunch served from 11:00am until 4:00pm. Dinner served from 7:00pm until 9:00pm. Closed Mondays. **Specialities:** home cooking. **Other points:** bar, open to non-residents, children welcome, car park, modern decor. **Address:** Le Bourg.
MR SIMONE SOHIER
**Telephone:** 96.25.21.70
⊗ ⅌ Map 4

## TRINITE SURZUR (LA), Morbihan, 56190

### L'AUBERGE VIEILLE FONTAINE, between Muzillac and Vannes
**Languages spoken:** English. **Menu:** 45 to 120 Frs. **Accommodation:** 120 to 190 Frs. **Restaurant:** Breakfast served from 7:30am. Lunch served from midday until 2:00pm. Dinner served from 7:00pm until 9:30pm. **Specialities:** regional menu, home cooking. **Hotel:** 11 beds; 7 single rooms, 4 double rooms with shower, private WC, television, telephone. **Other points:** bar, open to non-residents, à la carte menu, children welcome, lounge area, terraces, pets welcome – check for details, car park, traditional decor. **Address:** La Vieille Fontaine.
MR DIDIER LE RAY
**Telephone:** 97.42.01.01
⊗ ⅌ ⌂ ☆☆ Map 4

## TRONQUAY (LE), Calvados, 14490

### AU ROUTIER SYMPA, RD 572, between Bayeux and Saint Lo
**Restaurant:** Breakfast served from 5:00am. Lunch served from 11:30am until 2:00pm. Dinner served from 6:30pm until 9:30pm. Closed Saturdays. **Specialities:** home cooking. **Other points:** bar, open to non-residents, à la carte menu, pets welcome – check for details, car park. **Address:** La Commune.
DANIEL ET CHRISTINE MERIEL
**Telephone:** 31.92.38.68
⊗ ⅌ Map 3

## ULMES (LES), Maine-et-Loire, 49700

### LA GRAPPE D'OR, RD 960, the main road between Chôlet and Saumur
**Menu:** 55 Frs. **Restaurant:** Breakfast served from 6:30am. **Specialities:** regional menu, home cooking. **Other points:** bar, children welcome, terraces, pets welcome – check for details, car park. **Address:** Lieu dit 'Le Moulin Cassé'.
MR PASCAL CONTE
**Telephone:** 41.67.03.31
⊗ ⅌ Map 5

## UROU ET CRENNES, Orne, 61200

### LE CLOS FLEURI, RN 26, the main road between Paris and Argentan
**Languages spoken:** English and German. **Menu:** from 49 Frs. **Accommodation:** 75 Frs. **Restaurant:** Breakfast served from 6:30am. Lunch served from 12:30pm until 2:00pm. Dinner served from 7:00pm until 9:30pm. Closed Saturdays. **Specialities:** home cooking. **Hotel:** 9 beds; 3 single rooms, 6 double rooms with shower, private WC. **Other points:** bar, open to non-residents,

children welcome, pets welcome – check for details, car park, traditional decor. **Address:** Route de Paris.
MR GILBERT ESTELLE
**Telephone:** 33.67.08.85
⊗ ⚲ 🏠 Map 3

## VALLET, Loire-Atlantique, 44330

### RESTAURANT DE LA GARE, RD 756 and 763, on the ring road, centre of Vallet
**Languages spoken:** English. **Menu:** 47 to 75 Frs.
**Accommodation:** 140 to 200 Frs. **Restaurant:**
Breakfast served from 6:00am. Lunch served from
11:30am until 2:30pm. Dinner served from 7:00pm until
9:30pm. Closed Sundays. **Specialities:** regional menu,
home cooking. **Hotel:** 25 beds; 14 single rooms, 11
double rooms with shower, private WC, television.
**Other points:** bar, open to non-residents, children
welcome, lounge area, terraces, pets welcome – check
for details, car park. **Address:** 43, rue Saint Vincent.
MR MICHEL JOUY
**Telephone:** 40.33.92.55
⊗ ⚲ 🏠 Map 5

## VALOGNES, Manche, 50700

### AU PETIT MONT ROUGE, RN 13
**Restaurant:** Breakfast served from 7:00am. Closed
Saturdays and in August. **Specialities:** home cooking. **Other**
points: bar, open to non-residents, pets welcome – check for
details, car park. **Address:** 14, boulevard de la Victoire.
MME MONIQUE LE BLOND
**Telephone:** 33.40.11.80
⊗ ⚲ Map 3

## VANNES, Morbihan, 56000

### LE RELAIS DE LUSCANEN, RN 165, motorway Nantes/Brest, exit Vannes
**Languages spoken:** English. **Menu:** 44 Frs (wine
included). **Accommodation:** 110 Frs. **Restaurant:**
Breakfast served from 6:00am. Lunch served from
11:30am until 3:00pm. Dinner served from 7:00pm until
11:00pm. Closed Sundays and 15 days in August.
**Specialities:** home cooking. **Hotel:** 24 beds; 12 single
rooms, 12 double rooms with shower, bath, private WC.
**Other points:** bar, open to non-residents, à la carte
menu, children welcome, lounge area, pets welcome –
check for details, car park, modern decor. **Address:**
Zone Artisanale de Luscanen.
MR JEAN-MARIE GITEAU
**Telephone:** 97.63.45.92, 97.63.15.77
⊗ ⚲ 🏠 Map 4

## VARVANNES, Seine-Maritime, 76890

### RELAIS DE VARVANNES, RN 29, between le Havre and Tôtes
**Menu:** 55 Frs. **Restaurant:** Breakfast served from

7:30am. Closed Sundays. **Specialities:** home cooking.
**Other points:** bar, terraces, pets welcome – check for
details, car park. **Address:** Le Clos de Varvannes.
MR GEORGES QUESTNEL
**Telephone:** 35.32.16.52
⊗ ⚲ Map 3

## VERN SUR SEICHE, Ille-et-Vilaine, 35770

### LE WELCOME BAR, RD 163, between Rennes and Angers
**Places of interest:** Les côtes bretonnes. **Menu:** 48 Frs.
**Restaurant:** Breakfast served from 7:30am. Lunch
served from 11:30am until 3:00pm. Dinner served from
7:00pm until 9:00pm. Closed Saturdays. **Specialities:**
home cooking. **Other points:** bar, open to non-residents,
children welcome, pets welcome – check for details, car
park, traditional decor. **Address:** Le Clos Berquet.
MR CLINARD
**Telephone:** 99.62.83.18
⊗ ⚲ Map 4

## VERNEUIL SUR AVRE, Eure, 27130

### RELAIS DE L ESPERANCE
**Other points:** bar. **Address:** 65, porte de Breteuil.
MR AGULLO
**Telephone:** 32.32.12.81
⊗ ⚲ Map 3

## VERNON, Eure, 27200

### LA BUISSONNIERE, the main road between Vernon and Paris
**Restaurant:** Breakfast served from 6:00am. Closed
Sundays. **Specialities:** home cooking. **Other points:**
bar, children welcome, car park, traditional decor.
**Address:** Le Petit Val.
MME MICHELLE BOURGAULT
**Telephone:** 32.51.08.41
⊗ ⚲ Map 3

### SARL DU HAMEAU FLEURI, RN 15, between Bonnières and Rouen
**Menu:** 48 to 76 Frs. **Restaurant:** Breakfast served from
7:00am. Lunch served from 11:30am until 2:30pm.
Dinner served from 7:00pm until 9:00pm. Closed
Saturdays. **Specialities:** home cooking. **Other points:**
bar, à la carte menu, children welcome, pets welcome –
check for details, car park, traditional decor. **Address:**
88–90, avenue de Rouen.
MMME CHANTAL DEKIMPE
**Telephone:** 32.51.84.69
⊗ ⚲ Map 3

## VESLY, Eure, 27870

### CHEZ JACKY, RD 181
**Menu:** 48 to 95 Frs. **Restaurant:** Breakfast served from

8:00am. Closed Mondays. **Specialities:** home cooking. **Other points:** open to non-residents, children welcome, car park. **Address:** 35, Grande Rue.
MR JACKY FRICHOT
**Telephone:** 32.55.00.53
⊗ Map 3

## VILDE GUINGALAN, Côtes-du-Nord, 22980

### LA BORGNETTE, the main road between Dinan and Saint Brieuc, 9km from Dinan
**Menu:** 45 Frs. **Restaurant:** Lunch served from 11:00am until 3:00pm. Dinner served from 7:00pm until 10:00pm. Closed Sundays. **Specialities:** home cooking. **Other points:** bar, children welcome, pets welcome – check for details, car park. **Address:** La Borgnette.
MR ALAIN LAMBARD – SARL MÉLODIE
**Telephone:** 96.27.61.10
⊗ ♈ Map 4

## VILLEBAUDON, Manche, 50410

### LES ROUTIERS, RD 999, the main road between Cherbourg and Rennes
**Menu:** 50 to 85 Frs. **Accommodation:** 100 to 150 Frs. **Restaurant:** Breakfast served from 6:00am. Lunch served from midday until 3:00pm. Dinner served from 7:00pm until 9:30pm. **Specialities:** home cooking. **Hotel:** 3 beds; 3 single rooms with shower, private WC. **Other points:** bar, open to non-residents, children welcome, terraces, car park, traditional decor.
MME AGNÈS OSOUF
**Telephone:** 33.61.20.52
⊗ ♈ Map 3

## VILLEDIEU LES POELES, Manche, 50800

### HOTEL DES VOYAGEURS, between Caen and Avranche
**Menu:** 50 Frs. **Accommodation:** 120 to 140 Frs. **Restaurant:** Breakfast served from 6:00am. Closed Sundays. **Specialities:** home cooking. **Hotel:** 6 beds; 3 single rooms, 3 double rooms. **Other points:** children welcome, terraces, car park, modern decor. **Address:** 36, avenue du Maréchal Leclerc.
MR BERNARD MAGUSTO
**Telephone:** 33.51.08.98
⊗ 🏠 Map 3

## VILLERS BOCAGE, Calvados, 14310

### HOTEL DE LA GARE, RN 175, the main road between Vire and Caen
**Languages spoken:** Spanish. **Menu:** 50 to 100 Frs. **Accommodation:** 160 to 260 Frs. **Restaurant:** Breakfast served from 6:30am. Lunch served from

11:00am until 3:00pm. Dinner served from 7:00pm until 10:00pm. **Specialities:** home cooking. **Hotel:** 9 beds; with shower, bath, private WC. **Other points:** bar, open to non-residents, à la carte menu, children welcome, terraces, pets welcome – check for details, car park. **Address:** 6, rue Foch.
MME MARTINE ECHIVARD
**Telephone:** 31.77.39.00
⊗ ♈ 🏠 Map 3

## VILLERS SUR MER, Calvados, 14640

### LE NORMAND, RD 813, the main road between Caen and Deauville
**Menu:** 52 to 89 Frs. **Accommodation:** 185 Frs. **Restaurant:** Breakfast served from 8:00am. Lunch served from midday until 2:00pm. Dinner served from 7:00pm until 9:00pm. Closed Sundays and from mid-September to mid-October. **Specialities:** regional menu, home cooking. **Hotel:** 8 beds; 8 double rooms with shower, television. **Other points:** bar, open to non-residents, à la carte menu, children welcome, pets welcome – check for details, car park, modern decor. **Address:** 44, rue du Maréchal Foch.
MR DOMINIQUE BRETEAU
**Telephone:** 31.87.04.23
⊗ ♈ 🏠 ☆ Map 3

## VIMOUTIERS, Orne, 61120

### HOTEL DE LISIEUX, RN 179
**Accommodation:** 75 to 105 Frs. **Restaurant:** Closed Saturdays and the 2nd fortnight of August. **Specialities:** home cooking. **Hotel:** 5 beds; 2 single rooms, 3 double rooms with shower. **Other points:** bar, modern decor. **Address:** 37, avenue Lyautey.
MME YVETTE LARIVIÈRE
**Telephone:** 33.39.02.62
⊗ ♈ 🏠 Map 3

## VIRE, Calvados, 14500

### HOTEL DE FRANCE, the main road between Caen and Rennes
**Languages spoken:** English. **Menu:** 60 to 90 Frs. **Accommodation:** 155 to 320 Frs. **Restaurant:** Breakfast served from 7:00am. Lunch served from midday until 2:00pm. Dinner served from 7:00pm until 9:30pm. Closed from end of December to 10 January. **Specialities:** ris de veau Vallée d'Auge, tarte aux pommes flambées au calvados, regional food. **Hotel:** 50 beds; 50 double rooms with shower, bath, private WC, television, telephone. **Other points:** bar, open to non-residents, à la carte menu, children welcome, lounge area, pets welcome – check for details, car park, modern decor. **Address:** 4, rue d'Aignaux.
MR ROGER CARNET
**Telephone:** 31.68.00.35. **Fax:** 31.68.22.65
⊗ ♈ 🏠 🍽 ☆☆ Map 3

## VIVY, Maine-et-Loire, 49680

### RESTAURANT SAINT PAUL, RN 147, between Saumur and le Mans via Baugé

**Languages spoken:** English. **Menu:** 55 to 165 Frs.
**Accommodation:** 120 to 215 Frs. **Restaurant:**
Breakfast served from 7:00am. Lunch served from
midday until 2:30pm. Dinner served from 5:30pm until
10:00pm. **Specialities:** brochet de Loire au beurre blanc,
regional food. **Hotel:** 25 beds; 2 single rooms, 23 double
rooms with shower, bath. **Other points:** bar, open to
non-residents, à la carte menu, children welcome, lounge
area, terraces, modern decor. **Address:** 30, rue
Nationale.
MME MARIE-LOUISE BIDET
**Telephone:** 41.52.50.13. **Fax:** 41.52.58.96
⊗ 🍷 ⌂ 🍳 ☆ Map 5

## VOIVRES (LES), Sarthe, 72210

### RELAIS LE TAMARIS, RD 23, exit le Mans south

**Menu:** 56 Frs. **Accommodation:** 82 Frs. **Restaurant:**
Breakfast served from 6:30am. Closed Saturdays and in
August. **Specialities:** home cooking. **Hotel:** 5 beds; 2
single rooms, 3 double rooms with shower, bath. **Other
points:** bar, open to non-residents, pets welcome – check
for details, car park, modern decor. **Address:** Route de la
Suze.
MR PATRICK LEGUY
**Telephone:** 43.88.52.60
⊗ 🍷 ⌂ Map 5

## YVRE L'EVEQUE, Sarthe, 72530

### LA MAISON DU BON CAFE, RN 23, le Mans east

**Menu:** 50 to 55 Frs. **Restaurant:** Breakfast served from
7:30am. Lunch served from midday until 2:00pm.
Dinner served from 7:00pm until 8:30pm. Closed
Wednesdays and in August. **Specialities:** home cooking.
**Other points:** bar, open to non-residents, children
welcome. **Address:** 25, route du Mans, Bener.
MME ANNICK SIMON
**Telephone:** 43.84.54.63
⊗ 🍷 Map 5

# North East France

## ANCERVILLE, Meuse, 55170

### LE RELAIS, RN 4, the main road between Paris and Strasbourg

**Languages spoken:** Italian and Polish. **Menu:** 55 to 75 Frs. **Accommodation:** 110 to 150 Frs. **Restaurant:** Breakfast served from 7:00am. Lunch served from midday until 2:00pm. Dinner served from 7:00pm until 9:00pm. Closed Saturdays and in September. **Specialities:** tête de veau, andouillettes, regional food, home cooking. **Hotel:** 12 beds; 6 single rooms, 6 double rooms with shower, bath, private WC. **Other points:** bar, open to non-residents, à la carte menu, children welcome, lounge area, terraces, car park, traditional decor. **Address:** 59, route de Saint Dizier.

MME RENÉE LANGE
**Telephone:** 29.75.30.13
⊗ ⵟ ⌂ ☆ Map 17

## APPOIGNY, Yonne, 89380

### STATION SERVICE SHELL – LE RELAIS DE L'AMITIE, RN 6, the main road between Sens and Paris

**Menu:** 60 Frs. **Restaurant:** Breakfast served from 7:00am. Lunch served from midday until 2:30pm. Dinner served from 7:00pm until 10:00pm. Closed Sundays and in August (restaurant only). **Specialities:** home cooking. **Other points:** car park, traditional decor. **Address:** 21, route d'Auxerre.

MR PHILIPPE SAUR
**Telephone:** 86.53.21.76
⊗ Map 15

## ARC LES GRAY, Haute-Saône, 70100

### LES ROUTIERS

**Restaurant:** Closed Sundays. **Other points:** bar. **Address:** 4, place Aristide Briand, la Croisée.

MME HENRIETTE DEMOULIN
**Telephone:** 84.65.37.23
⊗ ⵟ Map 16

## ARCES, Yonne, 89320

### RELAIS DE LA FORET D'OTHE, RD 905

**Hotel:** 8 beds. **Other points:** bar. **Address:** 15, place de l'Eglise.

MME YOLANDE MISURA
**Telephone:** 86.88.10.44
⊗ ⵟ ⌂ ☆ Map 15

## ARCHES, Vosges, 88380

### LA TRUITE RENOMMEE, Epinal-Remiremont

**Languages spoken:** English, German and Italian. **Menu:** 49 to 110 Frs. **Accommodation:** 190 to 210 Frs. **Restaurant:** Breakfast served from 6:00am. Lunch served from 12:00pm until 2:30pm. Dinner served from 7:00pm until 11:00pm. Closed Saturdays. **Specialities:** truite 'Fumée-Vosgien', regional food, home cooking. **Hotel:** 8 beds; 6 single rooms, 2 double rooms, with shower, bath, private WC, television, telephone. **Other points:** bar, open to non-residents, pets welcome – check for details, car park, traditional decor. **Address:** 1, rue d'Epinal.

MME JOSSELINE HAGENAUER
**Telephone:** 29.32.79.13
⊗ ⵟ ⌂ ☆☆ Map 17

## ARNAY LE DUC, Côte-d'Or, 21230

### RELAIS ROUTIERS LE SAINT PRIX, RN 6, towards Chalon sur Saône

**Languages spoken:** English and Italian. **Menu:** 54 to 70 Frs. **Accommodation:** 120 to 140 Frs. **Restaurant:** Breakfast served from 6:00am. Lunch served from 11:45am until 2:00pm. Dinner served from 7:30pm until 10:00pm. Closed Sundays. **Specialities:** home cooking. **Hotel:** 6 beds; with shower. **Other points:** bar, open to non-residents, terraces, car park, traditional decor. **Address:** Sivry.

MR ROBERT TONELLI
**Telephone:** 80.84.81.74
⊗ ⵟ ⌂ Map 15

## ATHIS, Marne, 51150

### AU BON ACCUEIL, between Châlons sur Marne and Epernay

**Menu:** 50 Frs. **Accommodation:** 70 to 140 Frs. **Restaurant:** Breakfast served from 6:30am. Lunch served from 11:30am until 2:30pm. Dinner served from 7:30pm until 9:00pm. Closed Sundays and in August. **Specialities:** home cooking. **Hotel:** 5 beds; 2 single

rooms, 3 double rooms with shower, private WC. **Other points:** bar, open to non-residents, terraces, pets welcome – check for details, car park, traditional decor. **Address:** 12, Route Départementale.
MR DANIEL BOURSCHEIDT
**Telephone:** 26.57.62.61
⊗ ♀ 🏠 Map 18

## ATTIGNY, Ardennes, 08130

### CHEZ NICOLE
**Menu:** 40 to 70 Frs. **Restaurant:** Breakfast served from 5:00am. Lunch served from 11:00am until 3:00pm. Dinner served from 7:30pm until 11:30pm. **Specialities:** home cooking. **Hotel:** 3 beds; 1 single room, 2 double rooms with shower, private WC. **Other points:** bar, open to non-residents, children welcome, pets welcome – check for details, car park. **Address:** 16, place Charlemagne.
MME NICOLE PIENNE
**Telephone:** 24.71.20.69
⊗ ♀ Map 18

## AUBETERRE, Aube, 10150

### LES TILLEULS, RN 77
**Menu:** 45 to 52 Frs. **Restaurant:** Dinner served from midday until 10:00pm. **Specialities:** home cooking. **Other points:** bar, à la carte menu, car park.
MR RAYMOND MIELLE
**Telephone:** 25.37.51.11
⊗ ♀ Map 18

## AUMETZ, Moselle, 57710

### CAFE DE LA POSTE, RN 52, the main road between Heyange and Longwy
**Languages spoken:** Italian. **Menu:** 45 to 65 Frs. **Accommodation:** 120 to 150 Frs. **Restaurant:** Breakfast served from 6:00am. Lunch served from 12:00pm until 3:00pm. Dinner served from 7:00pm until 9:00pm. Closed Tuesdays. **Specialities:** regional menu, home cooking. **Hotel:** 6 beds; 4 single rooms, 2 double rooms. **Other points:** bar, open to non-residents, à la carte menu, children welcome, pets welcome – check for details, car park, modern decor. **Address:** 15, rue Foch.
MME LINDA COSSA
**Telephone:** 82.91.91.71
⊗ ♀ 🏠 Map 17

## AUTECHAUX, Doubs, 25110

### RELAIS DE L'AUTOROUTE – CHEZ SIMONE, exit Baume le Dames, towards Lure Vesoul
**Languages spoken:** a little English and Spanish. **Menu:** 54 Frs (drink and coffee included). **Restaurant:** Breakfast served from 8:00am. Lunch served from 11:00am until 3:00pm. Dinner served from 7:00pm until midnight. Closed Sundays and 15 days in August. **Specialities:**

home cooking. **Other points:** bar, open to non-residents, children welcome, terraces, car park, traditional decor.
MME SIMONE COURTIAL
**Telephone:** 81.84.01.14
⊗ ♀ Map 16

## AUTUN, Saône-et-Loire, 71400

### LE CLUB
**Languages spoken:** German English Italian Spanish. **Menu:** 59 to 79 Frs. **Restaurant:** Breakfast served from 6:30am. Lunch served from 11:30am until 2:00pm. Dinner served from 7:00pm until 9:30pm. Closed Sundays and in August. **Specialities:** Italiennes; Italiennes, regional food, home cooking. **Other points:** bar, open to non-residents, à la carte menu, terraces, car park. **Address:** 13, route de Beaune.
MME EVA RIZZO
**Telephone:** 85.52.27.72
⊗ ♀ Map 15

## AUVILLERS LES FORGES, Ardennes, 08260

### L'ARRET DES ROUTIERS, Charleville-Mézières/Hirson
**Menu:** 50 Frs. **Accommodation:** 75 to 110 Frs. **Restaurant:** Breakfast served from 6:00am. Lunch served from midday until 3:00pm. Dinner served from 7:00pm until 9:00pm. Closed Saturdays. **Specialities:** home cooking. **Hotel:** 5 beds; with shower. **Other points:** bar, open to non-residents, lounge area, terraces, pets welcome – check for details, car park, modern decor.
MME NICOLE BONNAIRE
**Telephone:** 24.54.32.77
⊗ ♀ 🏠 Map 18

## AUXERRE, Yonne, 89000

### LE SAINTE NITASSE, RN 65, Auxerre south
**Languages spoken:** English. **Menu:** 55 to 85 Frs. **Accommodation:** 100 to 130 Frs. **Restaurant:** Breakfast served from 7:00am. Lunch served from 12:00pm until 2:30pm. Dinner served from 7:30pm until 10:30pm. Closed Saturdays. **Specialities:** home cooking. **Hotel:** 31 beds; 31 double rooms with bath, private WC. **Other points:** bar, open to non-residents, à la carte menu, pets welcome – check for details, car park, traditional decor. **Address:** Route de Chablis.
MME CORINNE COURAULT
**Telephone:** 86.46.95.07
⊗ ♀ 🏠 🍽 ☆ Map 15

## BEAUMONT SUR VESLE, Marne, 51300

### LA MAISON DU CHAMPAGNE, RN 44, between Reims and Châlons sur Marne

**Languages spoken:** German, English, Luxembourgeois. **Menu:** 69 to 180 Frs. **Accommodation:** 110 to 300 Frs. **Restaurant:** Breakfast served from 7:00am. Lunch served from midday until 2:15pm. Dinner served from 7:30pm until 9:00pm. Closed Sundays, 15 days in February and 15 days in October. **Specialities:** terrine du chef, rognons de veau au ratafia, canard aux griottes, regional food, home cooking. **Hotel:** 13 beds; 1 single room, 12 double rooms with bath, private WC, television, telephone. **Other points:** bar, open to non-residents, à la carte menu, children welcome, terraces, pets welcome – check for details, car park, traditional decor. **Address:** 2, rue du Port.
MR MARC BOULARD
**Telephone:** 26.03.92.45, 26.03.97.27. **Fax:** 26.03.97.59
⊗ ☐ ⌂ ⛾ ☆☆ Map 18

## BEAUNE, Côte-d'Or, 21200

### AUBERGE DE LA GARE, RN 74
**Restaurant:** Dinner served from midday until 8:00pm. Closed Sundays and in August. **Hotel:** 6 beds. **Other points:** bar. **Address:** 11, avenue des Lyonnais.
SARL AUBERGE DE LA GARE
**Telephone:** 80.22.11.13
⊗ ☐ ⌂ Map 15

### LE MALMEDY
**Menu:** 55 to 85 Frs. **Restaurant:** Breakfast served from 7:30am. Lunch served from 12:00pm until 2:00pm. Closed Sundays and in August. **Specialities:** coq au vin, boeuf bourguignon, regional food, home cooking. **Other points:** bar, pets welcome – check for details, car park, traditional decor. **Address:** 6, rue du Lieutenant Dupuis.
MME YVETTE PÉCOUT
**Telephone:** 80.22.14.74
⊗ ☐ Map 15

### RELAIS DE BEAUNE, A 6, via the bridge which spans the motorway
**Restaurant:** Open 24 hours. **Specialities:** regional menu. **Hotel:** 150 beds; with shower, bath, private WC, television, telephone. **Other points:** bar, à la carte menu, children welcome, lounge area, terraces, pets welcome – check for details, car park. **Address:** Aire de Service de Beaune, dans les deux sens.
**Telephone:** 80.21.46.24
⊗ ☐ ⌂ ☆☆☆ Map 15

### TRUCKSTORE CAFE, A 6, motorway Paris/Lyon, accessible from either side
**Languages spoken:** German, English and Spanish. **Menu:** 58 Frs. **Restaurant:** Open 24 hours. **Other points:** bar, à la carte menu, lounge area, terraces, pets welcome – check for details, car park, modern decor. **Address:** Aire de Service de Beaune Tailly.
**Telephone:** 80.21.40.78
⊗ ☐ Map 15

## BEAUREPAIRE EN BRESSE, Saône-et-Loire, 71580

### LE RELAIS DES PLATANES, RN 78, between Lons le Saunier and Louhans
**Languages spoken:** English. **Menu:** 55 Frs. **Accommodation:** 90 to 100 Frs. **Restaurant:** Breakfast served from 7:00am. Lunch served from 11:00am until 2:00pm. Dinner served from 7:00pm until 9:00pm. **Specialities:** regional menu, home cooking. **Hotel:** 6 beds; 1 single room, 5 double rooms with shower, private WC. **Other points:** bar, open to non-residents, à la carte menu, children welcome, terraces, car park.
MME THÉRESE CORNET
**Telephone:** 85.74.11.01
⊗ ☐ ⌂ Map 15

## BELLEVILLE SUR MEUSE, Meuse, 55430

### CHEZ DEDE, Charleville
**Languages spoken:** English and Italian. **Menu:** 50 Frs. **Restaurant:** Breakfast served from 5:00am. Lunch served from 11:30am until 3:00pm. Closed Sundays, public holidays and 8 days in September. **Specialities:** home cooking. **Other points:** bar, open to non-residents, pets welcome – check for details, car park, traditional decor. **Address:** 164, avenue du Général de Gaulle.
MR ANDRÉ BUFFELO
**Telephone:** 29.84.57.85
⊗ ☐ Map 17

## BINING, Moselle, 57410

### AUBERGE AU TILLEUL
**Languages spoken:** German and English. **Menu:** 58 to 120 Frs. **Restaurant:** Breakfast served from 8:00am. Lunch served from 12:00pm until 2:00pm. Dinner served from 7:00pm until 10:00pm. Closed Thursdays and the 2nd fortnight in September. **Other points:** bar, à la carte menu, children welcome, car park. **Address:** 2, rue du Tilleul.
MR GILLES EHRE
**Telephone:** 87.09.74.86
⊗ ☐ Map 17

## BLACY, Marne, 51300

### LE RELAIS DE LA MAISON BLANCHE, exit Vitry le François
**Menu:** 53 to 75 Frs. **Restaurant:** Breakfast served from 3:00am. Closed from Saturday 3:00pm to Monday midnight. **Specialities:** home cooking. **Other points:** bar, open to non-residents, à la carte menu, children welcome, pets welcome – check for details, car park, traditional decor. **Address:** 8, route de Paris.
MME CLAUDINE SIMIONI
**Telephone:** 26.74.44.98
⊗ ☐ Map 18

## BLAGNY, Ardennes, 08110

### RESTAURANT LES ROUTIERS, RN 43, between Sedan and Charleville-Mézières

**Menu:** 35 to 47 Frs. **Restaurant:** Breakfast served from 6:30am. Lunch served from 12:00pm until 2:00pm. Dinner served from 7:00pm until 9:00pm. Closed Saturdays and in August. **Specialities:** home cooking. **Other points:** bar, children welcome. **Address:** 37 Route Nationale.
SNC BIAGIO/PAILLEUX
**Telephone:** 24.22.00.23
⊗ ♈ Map 18

## BLANZY, Saône-et-Loire, 71450

### RELAIS DE LA GARE, exit la Fiolle, the Michelin factory

**Languages spoken:** English. **Restaurant:** Dinner served from midday until 10:00pm. **Specialities:** boeuf bourguignon, côtes de porc vigneronnes, regional food, home cooking. **Other points:** bar, terraces, pets welcome – check for details, car park, traditional decor. **Address:** 16, rue de la Gare.
MR BERNARD BOROWSKI
**Telephone:** 85.68.03.05
⊗ ♈ Map 15

## BLENOD LES PONT A MOUSSON, Meurthe-et-Moselle, 54700

### SARL CHEZ FERNANDE, RN 57, between Nancy and Metz

**Languages spoken:** German and Portugese. **Menu:** 50 Frs. **Accommodation:** 80 Frs (1 person) to 100 Frs (2 person). **Restaurant:** Breakfast served from 6:00am. Lunch served from 11:00am until 2:00pm. Dinner served from 7:00pm until 11:00pm. Closed Saturdays and in August. **Specialities:** couscous, paëlla, choucroute, home cooking. **Hotel:** 2 beds; with shower, private WC. **Other points:** bar, open to non-residents, à la carte menu, children welcome, terraces, pets welcome – check for details, traditional decor. **Address:** 88, avenue Victor Claude.
MME LOUISETTE PEREIRA
**Telephone:** 83.81.03.54
⊗ ♈ Map 17

## BOUILLY, Aube, 10320

### AU RELAIS MONTAIGU, RN 77, Auxerre

**Menu:** 50 to 80 Frs. **Accommodation:** 85 to 150 Frs. **Restaurant:** Breakfast served from 6:30am. Lunch served from midday until 2:00pm. **Specialities:** regional menu, home cooking. **Hotel:** 13 beds; 7 single rooms, 6 double rooms with shower, telephone. **Other points:** bar, children welcome, lounge area, terraces, pets welcome – check for details, car park, traditional decor. **Address:** 300, rue au Fébvres, Souligny.

MR RENÉ BRAUX
**Telephone:** 25.40.20.20
⊗ ♈ 🏠 ☆ Map 18

## BOUXWILLER, Bas-Rhin, 67330

### AU SOLEIL, RD 6 and 7

**Languages spoken:** German and English. **Menu:** 35 to 150 Frs. **Accommodation:** 130 to 250 Frs. **Restaurant:** Breakfast served from 8:00am. Lunch served from 11:30am until 2:15pm. Dinner served from 7:30pm until 9:15pm. Closed Wednesdays, beginning of July and school vacations in February. **Specialities:** choucroute, coq au Riesling, Sandre à l'oseille, regional food. **Hotel:** 16 beds; 2 single rooms, 14 double rooms with shower, bath, private WC, television, telephone. **Other points:** bar, open to non-residents, à la carte menu, pets welcome – check for details, car park. **Address:** 71, Grand Rue.
MR CHARLES JAEGER
**Telephone:** 88.70.70.06
⊗ ♈ 🏠 🍲 ☆☆ Map 17

## BRIENNE, Saône-et-Loire, 71290

### AUX AMIS DE LA ROUTE, RD 975, Bourg en Bresse

**Menu:** 65 to 100 Frs. **Restaurant:** Closed Sundays and in August. **Specialities:** home cooking. **Other points:** bar, à la carte menu, lounge area, terraces, pets welcome – check for details, car park, traditional decor. **Address:** Les Bas de Brienne, Cuisery.
MME ELSA BUSCA
**Telephone:** 85.40.04.18
⊗ ♈ Map 15

## BRIENNE SUR AISNE, Ardennes, 08190

### LES ROUTIERS

**Languages spoken:** English. **Menu:** 52 Frs. **Restaurant:** Breakfast served from 6:00am. **Specialities:** regional menu, home cooking. **Other points:** bar, car park. **Address:** 9, rue d'Obernai.
MR PASCAL RAMBEAUX
**Telephone:** 24.38.95.92
⊗ ♈ Map 18

## BRIENON SUR ARMANCON, Yonne, 89210

### LES ROUTIERS DE BOURGOGNE, the main road between Joigny and Saint Florentin

**Languages spoken:** English, Polish and Russian. **Menu:** 50 Frs. **Accommodation:** 80 to 100 Frs. **Restaurant:** Breakfast served from 5:00am. Closed Saturdays. **Specialities:** home cooking. **Hotel:** 9 beds; 7 single rooms, 2 double rooms with shower. **Other points:** bar, terraces, pets welcome – check for details, car park, traditional decor. **Address:** 21, route de Joigny.

MR CHRISTIAN DUSSART
TELEPHONE: 86.43.00.63
⊗ ♀ ⌂ Map 15

## BRUAILLES, Saône-et-Loire, 71500

### RELAIS DES QUATRE CHEMINS, RD 972
Menu: 50 to 120 Frs. Restaurant: Closed Wednesdays.
Specialities: home cooking. Hotel: 5 beds. Other
points: bar, à la carte menu. Address: Les Quatre
Chemins, Louhans.
MR THIERRY ROUSSE
Telephone: 85.75.15.81
⊗ ♀ ⌂ Map 15

## BUCEY LES GY, Haute-Saône, 70700

### CAFE DE LA GARE – LES ROUTIERS, RD 474, between Dijon and Vesoul
Menu: 60 Frs (drinks included). Restaurant: Breakfast
served from 5:00am. Lunch served from 11:30am until
2:00pm. Dinner served from 7:30pm until 9:30pm.
Closed Sundays. Specialities: home cooking. Other
points: bar, open to non-residents, children welcome,
pets welcome – check for details, car park, traditional
decor. Address: Rue de la Gare.
MME YVETTE BOLE-BESANÇON
Telephone: 84.32.92.02
⊗ ♀ Map 16

## CHAGNY, Saône-et-Loire, 71150

### HOTEL TERMINUS, RN 6, Beaune/Chalon sur Saône
Languages spoken: English. Menu: 60 Frs (wine and
coffee included) to 120 Frs. Accommodation: 90 to 160
Frs. Restaurant: Breakfast served from 6:30am. Lunch
served from midday until 2:30pm. Dinner served from
7:00pm until 10:00pm. Closed Saturdays. Specialities:
regional menu, home cooking. Hotel: 13 beds. Other
points: bar, open to non-residents, à la carte menu,
children welcome, pets welcome – check for details, car
park, traditional decor. Address: Avenue de la Gare.
MR SERGE SAVOYE
Telephone: 85.87.18.13
⊗ ♀ ⌂ Map 15

## CHALLUY, Nièvre, 58000

### RELAIS DU PONT CARREAU, RN 7
Hotel: 4 beds. Other points: bar..
MME FERNANDE TAILLEMITTE
Telephone: 86.21.00.02
⊗ ♀ Map 15

## CHALONS SUR MARNE, Marne, 51000

### AU MONT SAINT-MICHEL, RN 77, Troyes then A 26
Languages spoken: English, Spanish. Menu: 48 to 145
Frs. Restaurant: Breakfast served from 5:30am. Closed
Sundays. Specialities: regional menu, home cooking.
Other points: bar, open to non-residents, children
welcome, lounge area, pets welcome – check for details,
car park. Address: 31, route de Troyes, Route
Nationale 77.
SNC QUEIGE ET MAZEAU
Telephone: 26.68.05.08. Fax: 26.65.59.71
⊗ ♀ Map 18

## CHAMPAGNOLE, Jura, 39300

### LES ROUTIERS, the main road between Paris and Genève
Menu: 50 Frs. Restaurant: Lunch served from 12:00pm
until 2:00pm. Closed Sundays and 15 days in August.
Specialities: home cooking. Other points: bar, car park,
modern decor. Address: La Billaude, Commune du
Vaudioux.
MR GEORGES CHAGRE
Telephone: 84.51.60.33
⊗ ♀ Map 16

## CHAMPLOST, Yonne, 89210

### AU BON ACCUEIL, RD 905, between Sens and Dijon
Menu: 53 to 65 Frs. Restaurant: Breakfast served from
5:00am. Closed Sundays. Specialities: home cooking.
Other points: bar, car park. Address: 23, Route
Nationale 5.
SNC DUTERIEZ – LE LEUCH
Telephone: 86.43.14.71
⊗ ♀ Map 15

## CHAMPS SUR YONNE, Yonne, 89290

### L'ARCHE DE VENOY 1, A 6
Languages spoken: English. Menu: 55 to 80 Frs.
Accommodation: 255 to 295 Frs. Restaurant: Open 24
hours. Hotel: 74 beds; 52 single rooms, 22 double rooms
with shower, private WC, television, telephone. Other
points: open to non-residents, children welcome, lounge
area, terraces, pets welcome – check for details, car
park, modern decor. Address: A6 Aire de Grosse Pierre,
sens Paris/Lyon.
Telephone: 86.40.23.73. Fax: 86.40.31.79
⊗ ⌂ ☆☆ Map 15

### L'ARCHE DE VENOY EST, A 6
Languages spoken: English. Menu: 59 Frs.
Accommodation: 265 to 305 Frs. Restaurant: Open 24
hours. Specialities: home cooking. Hotel: 74 beds; 52
single rooms, 22 double rooms with shower, bath,
private WC, television, telephone. Other points: bar,
open to non-residents, à la carte menu, children
welcome, lounge area, terraces, pets welcome – check
for details, car park, modern decor. Address: A6 Aire

du Soleil Levant, sens Lyon/Paris.
ACCOR
**Telephone:** 86.40.35.52, 86.40.22.44. **Fax:** 86.40.23.73
⊗ ♈ ⌂ ☆☆ Map 15

## CHATELET SUR RETOURNE,
Ardennes, 08300

### LE RELAIS PONT ROYAL
**Menu:** 52 to 150 Frs. **Restaurant:** Breakfast served from
6:00am. Dinner served from midday until midnight. Closed
Tuesdays. **Specialities:** regional menu, home cooking.
**Other points:** bar. **Address:** Chatelet sur Retourne.
MR YVES DETRUISEAUX
**Telephone:** 24.38.93.27
⊗ ♈ Map 18

## CHATILLON EN BAZOIS, Nièvre,
58110

### HOTEL DU RELAIS, RD 978
**Restaurant:** Closed Sundays. **Hotel:** 7 beds. **Other
points:** bar.
MR JEAN-JACQUES CHARPRENET
**Telephone:** 86.84.13.79
⊗ ♈ ⌂ Map 15

## CHAUDENEY, Meurthe-et-Moselle, 54200

### LE MIRABELLIER, A 31, Luxembourg/ Metz/Nancy/Dijon
**Languages spoken:** German and English. **Menu:** 55 Frs
(coffee included). **Restaurant:** Breakfast served from
6:00am. Dinner served from midday until 11:00pm.
**Other points:** open to non-residents, children welcome,
car park, modern decor. **Address:** Aire de Service de
Toul-Dommartin , dans les deux sens.
MR JOEL FRERES
**Telephone:** 83.64.64.01. **Fax:** 83.64.51.37
⊗ Map 17

## CHAUMONT, Haute-Marne, 52000

### BELLEVUE RELAIS ROUTIERS, RN 67, exit Chaumon, towards Saint Dizier
**Menu:** 55 Frs. **Accommodation:** 80 to 150 Frs.
**Restaurant:** Breakfast served from 6:30am. Lunch
served from 12:00pm until 2:30pm. Dinner served from
7:00pm until 9:30pm. Closed Sundays and in September.
**Specialities:** home cooking. **Hotel:** 8 beds; with shower,
bath. **Other points:** bar, open to non-residents, à la carte
menu, children welcome, lounge area, terraces, pets
welcome – check for details, car park, traditional decor.
**Address:** Route Nationale, Brethenay.
MME MICHELINE BOURGOIN
Telephone: 25.32.51.02
⊗ ♈ ⌂ Map 18

### CHEZ JEAN, RN 19
**Restaurant:** Dinner served from 12:00am until midnight.
**Other points:** bar. **Address:** 29, avenue Carnot.
MR JEAN CORROY
**Telephone:** 25.03.06.57
⊗ ♈ Map 18

### LA HALTE DU VIADUC, RN 65
**Languages spoken:** English. **Menu:** 55 Frs (wine
included). **Restaurant:** Breakfast served from 6:30am.
Lunch served from 11:30am until 3:00pm. Dinner served
from 6:30pm until 11:00pm. Closed Saturdays.
**Specialities:** regional menu, home cooking. **Other
points:** bar, open to non-residents, pets welcome – check
for details, car park, modern decor. **Address:** Route de
Paris.
MR SERGE RICHOUX
**Telephone:** 25.03.55.59, 25.32.04.64
⊗ ♈ Map 18

## CHELSEY, Côte-d'Or, 21430

### LES ROUTIERS – CHEZ URSULA ET BERNARD, RN 6, halfway between Saulieu and Arnay le Duc
**Places of interest:** Bergues, Dunkerque, Belgique,
monts de Flandres. **Languages spoken:** German and
English. **Menu:** 61 Frs. **Accommodation:** 90 to 210 Frs.
**Restaurant:** Breakfast served from 5:00am. Lunch
served from midday until 3:00pm. Dinner served from
7:00pm until midnight. Closed Saturdays and 3 weeks in
August. **Specialities:** home cooking. **Hotel:** 5 beds; 3
single rooms, 2 double rooms with shower. **Other
points:** bar, pets welcome – check for details, car park,
traditional decor. **Address:** Route Nationale 6.
MR BERNARD SENTEIN
**Telephone:** 80.84.40.42
⊗ ♈ ⌂ Map 15

## CHEMAUDIN, Doubs, 25320

### LA COCOTTE, RN 73, between Dole and Besançon
**Menu:** 45 to 55 Frs. **Restaurant:** Breakfast served from
6:00am. Lunch served from 11:00am until 3:00pm.
Dinner served from 7:00pm until 11:00pm. Closed
Sundays. **Specialities:** regional menu. **Other points:**
bar, open to non-residents, children welcome, pets
welcome – check for details, car park, modern decor.
**Address:** Lieu dit 'La Cocotte'.
MR CHRISTIAN GROSPERRIN
**Telephone:** 81.58.64.70, 81.58.55.00
⊗ ♈ Map 16

## CHENEVIERES, Meurthe-et-Moselle, 54122

### RELAIS DES ROUTIERS, RN 59, Saint Dié
**Places of interest:** Montagne au pied du Jura, Grotte de

la Glacière, Saut du Doubs, Besançon, Citadelle. **Menu:** 50 Frs. **Restaurant:** Breakfast served from 6:00am. Lunch served from 11:00am until 3:00pm. Dinner served from 6:00pm until 8:30pm. Closed Sundays. **Specialities:** home cooking. **Other points:** bar, open to non-residents, à la carte menu, children welcome, terraces, pets welcome – check for details, car park, modern decor. **Address:** 10 Route Nationale.
MME AGNES REMY
**Telephone:** 83.72.62.75
⊗ ♗ Map 17

## CHENOVE, Côte-d'Or, 21300

### AU BON COIN, RN 74
**Restaurant:** Closed Saturdays, Sundays and August. **Hotel:** 13 beds. **Other points:** bar. **Address:** 54, route de Dijon.
MR MARCEL MARIN
**Telephone:** 80.52.58.17
⊗ ♗ ⌂ ☆ Map 15

## CHESNE (LE), Ardennes, 08390

### LA CHARRUE D'OR, between Châlons sur Marne and Liège
**Languages spoken:** German, English, Italian and Spanish. **Menu:** 59 Frs (wine included) to 134 Frs. **Accommodation:** 140 to 160 Frs. **Restaurant:** Breakfast served from 7:00am. Lunch served from 12:00pm until 2:00pm. Dinner served from 7:00pm until 9:00pm. **Specialities:** regional menu, home cooking. **Hotel:** 7 beds; 7 single rooms. **Other points:** bar, open to non-residents, à la carte menu, children welcome, lounge area, terraces, pets welcome – check for details, car park, traditional decor. **Address:** 2, Grande Rue.
MME SUZANNE FISCHBACH
**Telephone:** 24.30.10.41
⊗ ♗ ⌂ Map 18

## CLAIRVAUX LES LACS, Jura, 39130

### LES ROUTIERS, Genève
**Languages spoken:** English and Italian. **Menu:** 58 Frs. **Restaurant:** Breakfast served from 7:00am. Lunch served from 11:30am until 2:30pm. Dinner served from 7:00pm until 10:00pm. Closed Sundays. **Specialities:** home cooking. **Other points:** open to non-residents, à la carte menu, children welcome, terraces, pets welcome – check for details, car park, traditional decor. **Address:** 4, route de Lons.
MR DENIS PERRIN
**Telephone:** 84.25.85.57
⊗ Map 16

## CLUNY, Saône-et-Loire, 71250

### AUBERGE DU CHEVAL BLANC, RN 980, between Mâcon and Chalon sur Saône
**Menu:** 77 to 185 Frs. **Restaurant:** Lunch served from 11:45am until 2:00pm. Dinner served from 6:45pm until 9:00pm. Closed Fridays and from December to February. **Specialities:** regional menu. **Other points:** open to non-residents, children welcome, pets welcome – check for details, car park, traditional decor. **Address:** 1, rue Porte de Mâcon.
ELVIRE BOUILLIN
**Telephone:** 85.59.01.13. **Fax:** 85.59.13.32
⊗ ⌣ Map 15

## COLIGNY, Marne, 51130

### LE VAL DES MARAIS, Vertus/Coligny
**Menu:** 52 Frs. **Restaurant:** Breakfast served from 6:30am. Lunch served from 12:00pm until 1:30pm. Dinner served from 7:00pm until 8:30pm. **Specialities:** home cooking. **Other points:** bar, open to non-residents, terraces, pets welcome – check for details, traditional decor. **Address:** 61, rue Saint Gond.
MR MICHEL LAGNIÉ
**Telephone:** 26.52.23.15
⊗ ♗ Map 18

## COLLONGES LES PREMIERES, Côte-d'Or, 21110

### A LA BONNE AUBERGE
**Menu:** 53 Frs. **Restaurant:** Breakfast served from 7:00am. Lunch served from 11:00am until 3:00pm. Dinner served from 7:00pm until 9:00pm. Closed Sundays and in August. **Specialities:** home cooking. **Other points:** bar, pets welcome – check for details, car park, traditional decor. **Address:** 8, rue de la Gare.
MR MICHEL GARNIER
**Telephone:** 80.31.32.01
⊗ ♗ Map 15

## COLOMBEY LES BELLES, Meurthe-et-Moselle, 54170

### AUBERGE LORRAINE, RN 74, Neufchateau
**Menu:** 50 to 100 Frs. **Restaurant:** Breakfast served from 7:00am. Lunch served from 11:30am until 2:30pm. Dinner served from 7:00pm until 10:00pm. Closed weekends, in September and between Christmas and New Year. **Specialities:** home cooking. **Other points:** bar, open to non-residents, à la carte menu, children welcome, terraces, pets welcome – check for details, car park. **Address:** 71, rue Carnot.
MR CLAUDE ARNOULD
**Telephone:** 83.52.00.23
⊗ ♗ Map 17

## COMBLANCHIEN, Côte-d'Or, 21700

### AUBERGE DU GUIDON, RN 74, between Beaune and Dijon
**Menu:** 58 Frs. **Accommodation:** 70 to 120 Frs. **Restaurant:** Breakfast served from 6:00am. Lunch served from 11:30am until 3:00pm. Dinner served from

7:00pm until 10:00pm. Closed Saturdays and mid-August. **Specialities:** home cooking. **Hotel:** 8 beds; 2 single rooms, 6 double rooms. **Other points:** bar, open to non-residents, pets welcome – check for details, car park, traditional decor. **Address:** Route Nationale 74.
MR ANDRÉ VAUCHEZ
**Telephone:** 80.62.94.39
⊗ ⏧ ⌂ Map 15

## CONNANTRAY, Marne, 51230

### LA ROUTIERE, RN 4, Nancy
**Menu:** 55 to 95 Frs. **Accommodation:** 54,50 to 90,50 Frs. **Restaurant:** Open 24 hours. **Specialities:** home cooking. **Hotel:** 8 beds; 1 single room, 7 double rooms. **Other points:** bar, open to non-residents, lounge area, pets welcome – check for details, car park. **Address:** Route Nationale 4.
MR MICHEL VILLAIN
**Telephone:** 26.42.42.03
**Fax:** 26.42.02.65
⊗ ⏧ ⌂ Map 18

## CONNANTRE, Marne, 51230

### LA GRAPPE D'OR, RN 4
**Menu:** 52 Frs (drink included). **Accommodation:** 80 to 120 Frs. **Restaurant:** Breakfast served from 6:45am. Lunch served from midday until 2:00pm. Dinner served from 7:00pm until 9:00pm. Closed Saturdays, 15 days in August and 15 days at Christmas. **Specialities:** home cooking. **Hotel:** 8 beds; 5 single rooms, 3 double rooms with shower, private WC. **Other points:** bar, car park. **Address:** Rue de la Gare.
MR PASCAL DUFOUR
**Telephone:** 26.81.04.62
⊗ ⏧ ⌂ Map 18

## CONSENVOYE, Meuse, 55110

### AUBERGE LORRAINE, RD 964, between Verdun and Sedan
**Languages spoken:** English. **Menu:** 49 to 85 Frs. **Accommodation:** 85 to 100 Frs. **Restaurant:** Breakfast served from 7:00am. Lunch served from 11:30am until 2:00pm. Dinner served from 7:00pm until 9:00pm. Closed Saturdays and the 1st fortnight in September. **Specialities:** regional menu, home cooking. **Hotel:** 6 beds; 3 single rooms, 3 double rooms with shower. **Other points:** bar, open to non-residents, à la carte menu, children welcome, terraces, pets welcome – check for details, car park, traditional decor. **Address:** 16, Grande Rue.
MME DENISE POUSSANT
**Telephone:** 29.85.80.19
⊗ ⏧ ⌂ Map 17

## CONTREXEVILLE, Vosges, 88140

### LE BELFORT, between Epinal and Langres

**Restaurant:** Breakfast served from 6:00am. Lunch served from 12:00pm until 1:30pm. Dinner served from 7:00pm until 9:00pm. Closed Saturdays. **Specialities:** home cooking. **Other points:** bar, terraces, car park. **Address:** 587, avenue de la Division Leclerc.
MR ANDRÉ SUNDHAUSER
**Telephone:** 29.08.04.22
⊗ ⏧ Map 17

## COOLE, Marne, 51320

### LES ROUTIERS
**Menu:** 53 Frs. **Restaurant:** Breakfast served from 8:00am. Closed Saturdays and 15 days in July. **Other points:** bar. **Address:** Route Nationale 4.
MR JEAN-MARIE BRISSON
**Telephone:** 26.74.34.79
⊗ ⏧ Map 18

## CORBIGNY, Nièvre, 58800

### LES AMIS DES ROUTIERS, RD 985
**Menu:** 55 Frs. **Restaurant:** Lunch served from midday until 3:30pm. Dinner served from 7:30pm until 9:30pm. Closed Saturdays, public holidays and from 15 August to 8 September. **Specialities:** home cooking. **Other points:** bar, pets welcome – check for details, car park, traditional decor. **Address:** 8, rue de Clamecy.
MME COLETTE PERINI
**Telephone:** 86.20.19.77
⊗ ⏧ Map 15

## COSNE SUR LOIRE, Nièvre, 58200

### LA TASSEE, RN 7, at Nevers, exit south
**Languages spoken:** English. **Restaurant:** Breakfast served from 6:00am. Lunch served from midday until 1:30pm. Dinner served from 8:00pm until 9:30pm. Closed Sundays and in August. **Specialities:** home cooking. **Other points:** bar, open to non-residents, à la carte menu, children welcome, pets welcome – check for details, car park, modern decor. **Address:** Route Nationale 7.
MR MAURICE CHET
**Telephone:** 86.26.11.76
⊗ ⏧ Map 15

### LES 3 COULEURS, RN 7, the main road between Paris and Nevers
**Menu:** 50 to 120 Frs. **Accommodation:** 100 to 180 Frs. **Restaurant:** Breakfast served from 6:30am. Lunch served from midday until 3:00pm. Dinner served from 7:00pm until 8:30pm. Closed the 4th week of December and New Year's Day. **Specialities:** coq au vin, cuisses de grenouilles à la provençale, regional food, home cooking. **Hotel:** 13 beds; 4 single rooms, 9 double rooms with shower. **Other points:** bar, open to non-residents, children welcome, lounge area, pets welcome – check for details, car park, modern decor. **Address:** 21, rue Saint Agnan.

MRS JEAN & PIERRE MORFAUX
Telephone: 86.28.23.50
⊗ 🍷 🏠 🍽 ☆ Map 15

## COURCELLES CHAUSSY, Moselle, 57530

### AUBERGE DE LA GARE, RN 3

**Languages spoken:** German, English and Italian. **Menu:** 58 (coffee included) to 89 Frs. **Accommodation:** 80 to 140 Frs. **Restaurant:** Breakfast served from 6:00am. Lunch served from midday until 2:00pm. Dinner served from 7:00pm until 10:00pm. **Specialities:** regional menu, home cooking. **Hotel:** 12 beds. **Other points:** bar, terraces, pets welcome – check for details, car park, traditional decor. **Address:** Avenue de la Libération.
MR PIERRE PAPALIA
Telephone: 87.64.00.22
⊗ 🍷 🏠 Map 17

## COURSON LES CARRIERES, Yonne, 89560

### LE RELAIS DE COURSON, RN 151, between Auxerre and Clamery

**Languages spoken:** English, Spanish and Portuguese. **Menu:** 57 to 87 Frs. **Restaurant:** Breakfast served from 6:30am. Lunch served from 11:00am until 3:00pm. Dinner served from 6:30pm until midnight. **Specialities:** home cooking. **Other points:** bar, open to non-residents, à la carte menu, lounge area, terraces, pets welcome – check for details, modern decor. **Address:** Route Nationale 151.
MR JOSÉ CARVALHO
Telephone: 86.41.52.58
⊗ 🍷 Map 15

## CRENEY, Aube, 10150

### RESTAURANT DU CENTRE, RD 960, Troyes/Brienne/Saint Dizier

**Menu:** 55 Frs. **Restaurant:** Breakfast served from 6:00am. Lunch served from 11:00am until 2:30pm. Dinner served from 7:00pm until 10:00pm. **Specialities:** home cooking. **Other points:** bar, open to non-residents, children welcome, car park, traditional decor. **Address:** 29, route de Brienne.
MR JACQUES JEANDON
Telephone: 25.81.39.79
⊗ 🍷 Map 18

## CRESANCEY, Haute-Saône, 70100

### AUBERGE DE LA PETITE FRINGALE

**Languages spoken:** English. **Restaurant:** Dinner served from midday until 9:00pm. Closed Mondays. **Other points:** bar, car park. **Address:** Route Départementale 7.

MR JEAN-PAUL LOISEL
Telephone: 84.31.56.08
⊗ 🍷 Map 16

## CREUSOT (LE), Saône-et-Loire, 71200

### LE RELAIS, RN 80

**Menu:** 52 Frs. **Accommodation:** 100 to 170 Frs. **Restaurant:** Lunch served from midday until 2:00pm. Dinner served from 7:00pm until 8:45pm. Closed Saturdays. **Specialities:** home cooking. **Hotel:** 12 beds; 9 single rooms, 3 double rooms. **Other points:** bar, open to non-residents, à la carte menu, car park, modern decor. **Address:** 26, rue de l'Yser.
MR GUY BEAUCLAIR
Telephone: 85.55.03.34
⊗ 🍷 🏠 Map 15

## CUSSY LES FORGES, Yonne, 89420

### LE RELAIS 6, RN 6, exit Avallon towards Lyon

**Languages spoken:** Arabic. **Menu:** 54 to 70 Frs. **Restaurant:** Breakfast served from 5:00am. Closed Sundays. **Specialities:** home cooking. **Other points:** bar, open to non-residents, à la carte menu, terraces, pets welcome – check for details, car park. **Address:** Route Nationale 6.
MR HAMID ADJAOUD
Telephone: 86.33.10.14
⊗ 🍷 Map 15

## DANJOUTIN, Territoire-de-Belfort, 90400

### LE CHALET FLEURI, Danjoutin Centre

**Languages spoken:** English. **Menu:** 48 to 60 Frs. **Restaurant:** Breakfast served from 6:30am. Lunch served from 11:30am until 1:45pm. Dinner served from 7:15pm until 9:30pm. Closed Saturdays and 15 days in August. **Specialities:** home cooking. **Other points:** bar, open to non-residents, terraces, pets welcome – check for details, car park, modern decor. **Address:** 2, rue de Bosmons.
MR MICHEL BÉDA
Telephone: 84.28.56.12
⊗ 🍷 Map 16

## DANNEMOINE, Yonne, 89700

### A LA BONNE AUBERGE, RD 905, the main road between Paris and Genève

**Menu:** 55 to 60 Frs. **Accommodation:** 60 to 100 Frs. **Restaurant:** Breakfast served from 7:00am. Lunch served from 12:00pm until 1:30pm. Dinner served from 7:30pm until 9:00pm. **Specialities:** home cooking. **Hotel:** 13 beds; 9 single rooms, 4 double rooms with shower. **Other points:** bar, open to non-residents, car park, traditional

decor. **Address:** Route Départementale 905.
MME NICOLE VERDIN
**Telephone:** 86.55.54.22
⊗ 𝖸 ⌂ Map 15

## DEVAY, Nièvre, 58300

### L'ETRIER
**Languages spoken:** German. **Restaurant:** Dinner
served from midday until 10:00pm. **Other points:** bar.
**Address:** Route Nationale 81.
MR JEAN-MARC BOUTET
**Telephone:** 86.25.15.65 **Fax:** 86.50.37.77
⊗ 𝖸 Map 15

## DIJON, Côte-d'Or, 21000

### RELAIS DE DIJON COTE D'OR
**Languages spoken:** German and English. **Restaurant:**
Breakfast served from 7:00am. **Specialities:** regional
menu. **Other points:** à la carte menu, children welcome,
lounge area, terraces, pets welcome – check for details,
car park. **Address:** Aire de Service de Dijon-Brognon,
dans les deux sens.
**Telephone:** 80.23.30.20
⊗ Map 15

## DORLISHEIM, Bas-Rhin, 67120

### RESTAURANT DE LA GARE
**Languages spoken:** German. **Accommodation:** 70 to
90 Frs. **Restaurant:** Breakfast served from 6:00am.
Lunch served from midday until 1:30pm. Dinner served
from 7:00pm until 8:30pm. Closed Saturdays and from
15 August to 4 September. **Specialities:** home cooking.
**Hotel:** 7 beds; 3 single rooms, 4 double rooms with
shower. **Other points:** open to non-residents, pets
welcome – check for details, car park, traditional decor.
**Address:** 4, avenue de la Gare.
MME LAURE JOST
**Telephone:** 88.38.14.28
⊗ ⌂ Map 17

## ECROUVES, Meurthe-et-Moselle, 54200

### LE RELAIS MATHY – LES ROUTIERS,
### RD 400, town centre/Saint Mihiel/Ecrouves
**Places of interest:** Langres (10km), fouilles gallo-
romaines d'Andilly (30km), nombreux lacs. **Menu:** 59
to 76 Frs. **Accommodation:** 98 to 156 Frs. **Restaurant:**
Breakfast served from 6:00am. Lunch served from
midday until 2:00pm. Dinner served from 7:00pm until
9:30pm. Closed from Friday 3:00pm to Sunday
10:00am, and 1 week between Christmas and New Year.
**Specialities:** home cooking. **Hotel:** 16 beds; 14 single
rooms, 2 double rooms. **Other points:** bar, open to non-
residents, à la carte menu, children welcome, terraces,
pets welcome – check for details, car park, traditional
decor. **Address:** 825, avenue du 15ème Génie, Toul.

MR PAUL MATHY
**Telephone:** 83.43.04.27
⊗ 𝖸 ⌂ Map 17

## EIX ABAUCOURT, Meuse, 55400

### HOTEL DU COMMERCE – CHEZ ODILE,
### RN 3, between Verdun and Etain
**Languages spoken:** English. **Menu:** 54 to 120 Frs.
**Restaurant:** Breakfast served from 5:00am. Closed
Sundays and in February. **Specialities:** home cooking.
**Hotel:** 9 beds; 5 single rooms, 4 double rooms with
shower, private WC. **Other points:** bar, open to non-
residents, à la carte menu, children welcome, lounge
area, terraces, pets welcome – check for details, car
park, traditional decor. **Address:** Route Nationale 3.
MME MARIE-ODILE VINCENT
**Telephone:** 29.88.31.94
⊗ 𝖸 ⌂ Map 17

## ENSISHEIM, Haut-Rhin, 68190

### LE PETIT SAVOYARD
**Languages spoken:** German. **Menu:** 60 Frs.
**Restaurant:** Closed Wednesdays. **Specialities:** Gambas
flambées, magret et cuisses de canard, foie gras,
cassoulet, home cooking. **Other points:** bar, car park.
**Address:** 42, rue de la 1ère Armée.
MME MARTINE COLON
**Telephone:** 89.81.70.14
⊗ 𝖸 Map 17

## EPERNAY, Marne, 51200

### LES ROUTIERS – CHEZ MADAME
### PRÉJENT, RN 3
**Menu:** 65 to 95 Frs. **Accommodation:** 100 to 165 Frs.
**Restaurant:** Breakfast served from 6:00am. Closed
Saturdays and in January. **Specialities:** regional menu,
home cooking. **Hotel:** 15 beds; 8 single rooms, 7 double
rooms with shower, private WC. **Other points:** bar,
open to non-residents, children welcome, pets welcome
– check for details, car park, modern decor. **Address:**
13, rue Jean-Jacques Rousseau.
MME MARIE-LOUISE PRÉJENT
**Telephone:** 26.55.23.29
⊗ 𝖸 ⌂ Map 18

## EPINAL, Vosges, 88000

### LE RELAIS DE L'ABATTOIR, RN 57
**Restaurant:** Breakfast served from 5:00am. Dinner
served from 7:00pm until midnight. Closed Sundays and
from mid-July to mid-August. **Specialities:** home
cooking. **Other points:** bar. **Address:** 63, rue de Nancy.
MR GÉRARD DIDIER
**Telephone:** 29.82.32.13
⊗ 𝖸 Map 17

## EPINEAU LES VOVES, Yonne, 89400

### RELAIS DES SIX BOULES, RN 6
**Languages spoken:** Arabic and German. **Other points:** bar. **Address:** 2, route de Chambery.
MR AHMED BETROUNE
**Telephone:** 86.91.20.45
⊗ ♀ Map 15

## ETANG SUR ARROUX, Saône-et-Loire, 71190

### HOTEL DE LA GARE, RD 994
**Menu:** 55 Frs. **Accommodation:** 95 to 130 Frs.
**Restaurant:** Lunch served from 11:30am until 1:30pm.
Dinner served from 7:00pm until 8:00pm. Closed
Sundays. **Specialities:** home cooking. **Hotel:** 7 beds;
with shower, private WC. **Other points:** bar, open to
non-residents, terraces, pets welcome – check for details,
car park, modern decor. **Address:** Rue d'Autun.
MR PIERRE BOUTELOUP
**Telephone:** 85.82.23.76
⊗ ♀ ⌂ Map 15

## ETOGES, Marne, 51270

### LE CAVEAU DE L'ANCIENNE FORGE
**Restaurant:** Dinner served from midday until 8:00pm.
Closed Wednesdays. **Other points:** bar. **Address:**
Grande Rue.
SARL LA FORGE
**Telephone:** 26.59.32.79
⊗ ♀ Map 18

## EVANS, Jura, 39700

### RELAIS 73, RN 73
**Menu:** 52 Frs (wine and coffee included). **Restaurant:**
Breakfast served from 5:00am. **Specialities:** home
cooking. **Other points:** bar, open to non-residents, car
park. **Address:** Route Nationale 73.
MME YVETTE ARBEY
**Telephone:** 84.81.37.29. **Fax:** 81.80.34.02
⊗ ♀ Map 16

## FONTAINES, Saône-et-Loire, 71150

### LE RELAIS FLEURI, RN 6
**Menu:** 55 Frs (wine and coffee included). **Restaurant:**
Breakfast served from 6:00am. Lunch served from
11:30am until 2:30pm. Dinner served from 7:00pm until
9:30pm. Closed Saturdays, 15 days in August and 1
week at Christmas. **Specialities:** home cooking. **Other
points:** open to non-residents, pets welcome – check for
details, car park. **Address:** Route Nationale 6, le
Gauchard.
MR CLAUDE ECAILLE
**Telephone:** 85.43.11.69
⊗ Map 15

## FONTVANNES, Aube, 10190

### AUBERGE DE LA VANNE, RN 60, the main road between Troyes and Sens
**Languages spoken:** English. **Menu:** 55 Frs.
**Accommodation:** 80 Frs. **Restaurant:** Breakfast served
from 6:00am. Lunch served from 11:30am until 1:30pm.
Closed Sundays. **Specialities:** home cooking. **Hotel:** 8
beds; with shower, private WC. **Other points:** bar, open to
non-residents, à la carte menu, lounge area, pets welcome –
check for details, car park. **Address:** 1, rue Léandre Denis.
MR MICHEL DUBRULLE
**Telephone:** 25.70.37.60
⊗ ♀ ⌂ Map 18

## FRAIZE, Vosges, 88230

### AUBERGE VOSGIENNE, RN 415, between Saint Dié and Colmar
**Menu:** 55 Frs (wine included) to 120 Frs.
**Accommodation:** 98 to 158 Frs. **Restaurant:** Breakfast
served from 8:00am. Lunch served from midday until
2:00pm. Dinner served from 7:00pm until 9:00pm.
Closed Wednesdays. **Specialities:** home cooking. **Hotel:**
7 beds; 5 single rooms, 2 double rooms. **Other points:**
bar, open to non-residents, à la carte menu, children
welcome, terraces, car park, traditional decor. **Address:**
14, rue du Général Ingold.
MR MICHEL GENSE
**Telephone:** 29.50.30.46
⊗ ♀ ⌂ Map 17

## FRASNE, Doubs, 25560

### L'ARC EN CIEL, between Champagnole and Pontarlier
**Languages spoken:** German, English and Italian. **Menu:**
55 Frs. **Restaurant:** Breakfast served from 8:00am. Lunch
served from midday until 2:00pm. Closed Tuesdays.
**Specialities:** regional menu, home cooking. **Other points:**
bar, children welcome, pets welcome – check for details,
car park, modern decor. **Address:** 98, Grande Rue.
MR CLAUDE GUYON
**Telephone:** 81.49.83.68
⊗ ♀ Map 16

## FROUARD, Meurthe-et-Moselle, 54390

### LA CHARENTAISE, on the old road of Metz
**Menu:** 50 Frs (drink included). **Accommodation:** 70 to
110 Frs. **Restaurant:** Breakfast served from 6:00am.
Lunch served from 11:30am until 3:00pm. Closed
Sundays. **Specialities:** home cooking. **Hotel:** 8 beds; 4
single rooms, 4 double rooms with shower, private WC.
**Other points:** bar, terraces, pets welcome – check for
details, car park. **Address:** 29, rue de l'Embanie.
MME PIERRETTE MATIGNON
**Telephone:** 83.24.36.08
⊗ ♀ ⌂ Map 17

**LA GRANDE CHOPE,** *RN 57, Metz*
**Languages spoken:** Hungarian. **Menu:** 43 Frs.
**Restaurant:** Breakfast served from 7:00am. Lunch served from 11:30am until 2:00pm. Closed Saturdays and in August. **Specialities:** home cooking. **Other points:** bar, open to non-residents, pets welcome – check for details, car park, modern decor. **Address:** 4, rue de la Gare.
MME CHRISTIANE PALLAGI
**Telephone:** 93.49.05.64
⊗ ♉ Map 17

**LA PRAIRIE,** *the main road between Nancy and Metz (via the bridge for Nancy and Frouard)*
**Menu:** 55 Frs (wine included). **Restaurant:** Breakfast served from 7:00am. Lunch served from midday until 2:30pm. Dinner served from 6:30pm until 10:00pm. Closed Saturdays and in August. **Specialities:** home cooking. **Other points:** bar, open to non-residents, terraces, pets welcome – check for details, car park, traditional decor. **Address:** 6, rue de l'Ambanie.
MR BERNARD VAN DER WECKENE
**Telephone:** 83.49.31.02
⊗ ♉ Map 17

**LE RELAIS ROUTIERS – CHEZ VIVIANE,** *RN 57*
**Languages spoken:** German. **Menu:** 49,50 Frs.
**Restaurant:** Lunch served from midday until 2:00pm. Dinner served from 7:00pm until 9:00pm. Closed Mondays. **Other points:** bar, car park. **Address:** 1, rue de la Salle.
MME VIVIANE POIROT
**Telephone:** 83.49.03.52
⊗ ♉ Map 17

## FUMAY, Ardennes, 08170

**HOTEL LION,** *RN 51, near station*
**Menu:** 54 to 100 Frs. **Accommodation:** 55 to 120 Frs.
**Restaurant:** Breakfast served from 8:00am. Lunch served from 12:00pm until 2:00pm. Dinner served from 6:00pm until 9:00pm. Closed Sundays and in September. **Specialities:** couscous, home cooking. **Hotel:** 7 beds; 3 single rooms, 4 double rooms with shower, bath. **Other points:** bar, open to non-residents, à la carte menu, pets welcome – check for details, traditional decor. **Address:** 41, rue de la Céramique.
MME EDITH POTIER
**Telephone:** 24.41.10.27
⊗ ♉ 🏠 ☆ Map 18

## GAMBSHEIM, Bas-Rhin, 67760

**EUROPE RELAIS,** *on the 'Route du Rhin' (1km from the border)*
**Languages spoken:** German, English and Italian.
**Menu:** 38 to 59 (wine included). **Accommodation:** 200 Frs. **Restaurant:** Breakfast served from 6:30am. Lunch served from 11:30am until 3:00pm. Dinner served from 7:00pm until 11:00pm. **Specialities:** regional menu, home cooking. **Hotel:** 22 beds; 11 single rooms, 11 double rooms with shower, bath, private WC, television, telephone. **Other points:** bar, open to non-residents, à la carte menu, children welcome, lounge area, terraces, pets welcome – check for details, car park, modern decor. **Address:** Route du Rhin.
MR MARC HUBER
**Telephone:** 88.96.47.47
⊗ ♉ 🏠 ☆☆ Map 17

## GENELARD, Saône-et-Loire, 71420

**LE PROVENCAL,** *RN 70, between Montceau les Mînes and Digoin*
**Languages spoken:** English. **Menu:** 55 Frs.
**Restaurant:** Breakfast served from 8:00am. Lunch served from 11:30am until 2:00pm. Dinner served from 7:00pm until 9:00pm. **Specialities:** home cooking.
**Other points:** bar, open to non-residents, à la carte menu, children welcome, terraces, pets welcome – check for details, car park, traditional decor. **Address:** Place du Champ de Foire.
MME PASCALE RIZARD
**Telephone:** 85.79.28.90
⊗ ♉ Map 15

## GERMIGNY SUR YONNE, Yonne, 89600

**SARL LE RELAIS DES ROUTIERS,** *RN 5*
**Restaurant:** Closed Sundays. **Hotel:** 9 beds. **Other points:** bar. **Address:** Route de Genève.
MR CORNU
**Telephone:** 86.35.06.39
⊗ ♉ 🏠 Map 15

## GOLBEY, Vosges, 88190

**RELAIS DU PETIT CERF,** *RN 166 and 460*
**Menu:** 62 Frs (wine and coffee included). **Restaurant:** Breakfast served from 7:00am. Lunch served from 11:30am until 3:00pm. Dinner served from 6:00pm until 8:00pm. Closed Sundays, public holidays and in August. **Specialities:** home cooking. **Other points:** bar, pets welcome – check for details, car park, modern decor. **Address:** 63, rue du Général Leclerc.
MR CHRISTIAN KUNTZ
**Telephone:** 29.34.23.25
⊗ ♉ Map 17

## GUEMAR, Haut-Rhin, 68970

**A L'ANGE**
**Languages spoken:** German. **Menu:** 56 to 90 Frs.
**Accommodation:** 140 Frs. **Restaurant:** Breakfast served from 6:30am. Lunch served from 11:45am until 3:00pm. Dinner served from 6:30pm until 10:00pm. Closed Saturdays. **Specialities:** regional menu. **Hotel:** 9

beds. **Other points:** bar, open to non-residents, à la carte menu, terraces, pets welcome – check for details, car park, traditional decor. **Address:** 16, route de Selestat.
MR MICHEL SCHWARIZ
**Telephone:** 89.71.83.03
⊗ ▽ 🏠 Map 17

## GUERIGNY, Nièvre, 58130

*HOTEL DU COMMERCE, RD 977, the main road between Nevers and Auxerre*
**Languages spoken:** German. **Menu:** 58 to 74 Frs.
**Accommodation:** 150 to 210 Frs. **Restaurant:**
Breakfast served from 6:30am. Lunch served from 11:30am until 1:30pm. Dinner served from 7:00pm until 8:30pm. Closed Saturdays and from 20 December to 5 January. **Specialities:** regional menu. **Hotel:** 8 beds; 4 single rooms, 4 double rooms with shower. **Other points:** bar, open to non-residents, children welcome, terraces, pets welcome – check for details, car park, traditional decor. **Address:** 2, Grande Rue.
MR GÉRARD PAGE
**Telephone:** 86.37.32.77
⊗ ▽ 🏠 Map 15

## GUMBRECHTSHOFFEN, Bas-Rhin, 67110

*AU SOLEIL, RN 62 and RD 242, between Niederbronn and Haguenau*
**Languages spoken:** German. **Menu:** 32 to 100 Frs.
**Accommodation:** 130 Frs. **Restaurant:** Breakfast served from 6:00am. Dinner served from 7:00pm until 10:00pm. Closed Sundays and in August. **Specialities:** regional menu, home cooking. **Hotel:** 3 beds; 3 double rooms with bath, telephone. **Other points:** bar, open to non-residents, à la carte menu, lounge area, pets welcome – check for details, car park, traditional decor. **Address:** 30, rue Principale.
MME LILIANE PEIFER
**Telephone:** 88.72.90.77
⊗ ▽ Map 17

## GUMERY, Aube, 10400

*AU RELAIS, RD 439, between Nogent sur Seine and Sens*
**Languages spoken:** English. **Menu:** 52 Frs.
**Accommodation:** 80 to 120 Frs. **Restaurant:** Breakfast served from 6:00am. Lunch served from 11:30am until 2:00pm. Dinner served from 7:00pm until 9:00pm. Closed Sundays and 3 weeks in August. **Specialities:** home cooking. **Hotel:** 5 beds; 3 single rooms, 2 double rooms with shower, bath. **Other points:** bar, open to non-residents, children welcome, terraces, pets welcome – check for details, car park, traditional decor. **Address:** 3, route de Sens.
MME EVELYNE VISSE
**Telephone:** 25.39.16.01
⊗ ▽ 🏠 Map 18

## GUNDERSHOFFEN, Bas-Rhin, 67110

*RESTAURANT COUCOU, between Haguenau and Sarregue*
**Languages spoken:** German and English. **Menu:** 60 Frs (wine included). **Restaurant:** Breakfast served from 6:00am. **Specialities:** regional menu, home cooking. **Other points:** bar, open to non-residents, à la carte menu, children welcome, terraces, pets welcome – check for details, car park, modern decor. **Address:** Route de Bitche.
MR RENÉ ADOLFF
**Telephone:** 88.72.92.02. **Fax:** 88.72.88.82
⊗ ▽ Map 17

## HABSHEIM, Haut-Rhin, 68440

*A LA VILLE DE MULHOUSE, RN 66*
**Languages spoken:** German and English. **Other points:** bar. **Address:** 76, rue du Général de Gaulle.
MME GABRIELLE LEHMANN
**Telephone:** 89.44.31.33
⊗ ▽ Map 17

## HAGONDANGE, Moselle, 57300

*LES ROUTIERS, RN 53, Metz*
**Menu:** 54 Frs (wine included). **Accommodation:** 115 to 165 Frs. **Restaurant:** Breakfast served from 8:00am. Lunch served from 12:00pm until 2:00pm. Closed Saturdays and in August. **Specialities:** home cooking. **Hotel:** 9 beds; 4 single rooms, 5 double rooms with shower, private WC. **Other points:** bar, open to non-residents, traditional decor. **Address:** 36, rue de Mezt.
MME MARTINE BOGNOLO
**Telephone:** 87.71.46.63
⊗ ▽ 🏠 Map 17

## HUTTENHEIM, Bas-Rhin, 67230

*AU JARDIN DES ROSES, RN 83*
**Languages spoken:** German. **Restaurant:** Breakfast served from 4:30am. Lunch served from 11:00am until 2:00pm. Closed Saturdays and in August. **Specialities:** home cooking. **Other points:** bar, open to non-residents, à la carte menu. **Address:** Route Nationale 83.
MR MAURICE SCHNEIDER
**Telephone:** 88.74.41.44
⊗ ▽ Map 17

## HYEVRE PAROISSE, Doubs, 25110

*RELAIS LA CREMAILLERE, RN 83, exit A36 Baume les Dames (10km), Isle sur le Doubs, Clerval (15km)*
**Languages spoken:** German and English. **Menu:** 60 to 180 Frs. **Accommodation:** 230 to 260 Frs. **Restaurant:** Closed Saturdays and in October. **Specialities:** coq au vin, canard à l'orange, fritures, carpes, regional food,

home cooking. **Hotel:** 21 beds; with shower, bath, private WC, television, telephone. **Other points:** bar, open to non-residents, à la carte menu, children welcome, terraces, pets welcome – check for details, car park. **Address:** Baume les Dames.
MR ALFRED ZISS
**Telephone:** 81.84.07.88
⊗ ⵖ 🏠 ⌂ ☆☆☆ Map 16

## IMLING SARREBOURG, Moselle, 57400

### LE RELAIS DE LA FERME, RN 4, the main road between Paris and Strasbourg
**Languages spoken:** German. **Menu:** 42 to 140 Frs.
**Restaurant:** Breakfast served from 5:30am. Lunch served from 11:30am until 2:30pm. Dinner served from 6:30pm until 11:00pm. Closed Fridays and 3 weeks from 15 August. **Specialities:** regional menu. **Other points:** bar, open to non-residents, à la carte menu, children welcome, pets welcome – check for details, car park, traditional decor. **Address:** Route de Sarrebourg.
MR JEAN-LUC STEINER
**Telephone:** 87.23.68.72
⊗ ⵖ Map 17

## IS SUR TILLE, Côte-d'Or, 21120

### CAFE DU MIDI
**Menu:** 54 Frs. **Restaurant:** Breakfast served from 7:00am. Lunch served from 11:30am until 2:30pm.
**Specialities:** home cooking. **Other points:** bar, open to non-residents, pets welcome – check for details, car park. **Address:** 2, place Villeneuve Motet.
MR PHILIPPE CHALOPET
**Telephone:** 80.95.07.51
⊗ ⵖ Map 15

## JUZANVIGNY, Aube, 10500

### CHEZ JACKY ET ROSE, RD 400
**Restaurant:** Dinner served from midday until midnight.
Closed Saturdays and Sundays and August. **Hotel:** 3 beds. **Other points:** bar. **Address:** Brienne le Château.
MR JACQUES DEFLIN
**Telephone:** 25.92.80.57
⊗ ⵖ Map 18

## KOGENHEIM, Bas-Rhin, 67230

### A L'ETOILE, RN 83, between Selestat and Benfeld
**Languages spoken:** German. **Menu:** 35 to 90 Frs.
**Accommodation:** 100 to 150 Frs. **Restaurant:**
Breakfast served from 7:15am. Lunch served from midday until 3:00pm. Dinner served from 7:00pm until midnight. Closed Mondays and 3 weeks in January.
**Specialities:** home cooking. **Hotel:** 9 beds; 5 single rooms, 4 double rooms with shower, bath, private WC.

**Other points:** bar, open to non-residents, à la carte menu, pets welcome – check for details, car park, traditional decor. **Address:** 36, route de Strasbourg.
MR ROBERT RAPP
**Telephone:** 88.74.70.02
⊗ ⵖ 🏠 ☆ Map 17

## LANGRES, Haute-Marne, 52200

### LA BONNE AUBERGE, RN 74, the main road between Chaumont and Dijon
**Menu:** 60 to 85 Frs. **Restaurant:** Breakfast served from 6:00am. Lunch served from midday until 2:00pm.
Dinner served from 7:00pm until 9:30pm. Closed Sundays and 2 weeks over Christmas/New Year.
**Specialities:** home cooking. **Hotel:** 6 beds. **Other points:** bar, open to non-residents, à la carte menu.
**Address:** Faubourg de la Collinière.
SNC BAUMANN/OLIVIER
**Telephone:** 25.87.09.18
⊗ ⵖ 🏠 Map 18

### RELAIS DE LA COLLINIERE, RN 19
**Languages spoken:** Portugese. **Menu:** 55 Frs.
**Accommodation:** 85 to 150 Frs. **Restaurant:** Breakfast served from 5:00am. Lunch served from midday until 2:00pm. Dinner served from 7:00pm until 10:00pm.
Closed Sundays and end December. **Specialities:** couscous; couscous, home cooking. **Hotel:** 8 beds; 5 single rooms, 3 double rooms with shower, private WC.
**Other points:** bar, open to non-residents, terraces, pets welcome – check for details, car park, traditional decor.
**Address:** Faubourg de la Collinière.
MME ELISABETH GUERRA
**Telephone:** 25.87.03.27
⊗ ⵖ 🏠 Map 18

## LAVANS LES DOLE, Jura, 39700

### LE PANORAMIC, RN 73, between Dôle and Besançon
**Languages spoken:** German and Italian. **Menu:** 54 to 80 Frs. **Accommodation:** 120 to 150 Frs. **Restaurant:**
Breakfast served from 6:00am. Lunch served from 11:00am until 2:30pm. Dinner served from 7:00pm until 10:00pm. Closed Sundays. **Specialities:** regional menu, home cooking. **Hotel:** 9 beds; 2 single rooms, 7 double rooms with shower. **Other points:** bar, open to non-residents, children welcome, terraces, pets welcome – check for details, car park. **Address:** Route Nationale 73.
MR JEAN-LUC CONFAIS
**Telephone:** 84.81.21.41
⊗ ⵖ 🏠 Map 16

## LESMENILS, Meurthe-et-Moselle, 54700

### LE ZENIUM
**Languages spoken:** German, English and Italian.
**Menu:** 45 to 170 Frs. **Restaurant:** Breakfast served

from 9:00am. Lunch served from midday until 2:00pm. Dinner served from 7:00pm until 10:00pm. Closed Saturdays. **Other points:** bar, open to non-residents, car park, modern decor. **Address:** Tête de Saint Euchamps.
MR BERNARD STABILE
**Telephone:** 83.82.81.38
⊗ ♀ Map 17

## LESMONT, Aube, 10500

### LE RELAIS DES LACS, RN 60
**Menu:** 53 Frs (coffee included) to 110 Frs. **Restaurant:** Breakfast served from 6:00am. Lunch served from 11:30am until 2:00pm. Dinner served from 7:00pm until 10:00pm. Closed Saturdays and Christmas to New Year. **Specialities:** home cooking. **Other points:** bar, open to non-residents, à la carte menu, children welcome, terraces, pets welcome – check for details, car park, traditional decor. **Address:** Route Nationale 60.
MR JEAN-CLAUDE DENIZOT
**Telephone:** 25.92.45.35
⊗ ♀ Map 18

## LOISY PONT A MOUSSON, Meurthe-et-Moselle, 54700

### RESTAURANT DU RELAIS DE L'OBRION, A 31, Luxembourg/Metz/Nancy
**Languages spoken:** Polish, German and English. **Menu:** 53 Frs. **Restaurant:** Breakfast served from 6:00am. Dinner served from midday until 11:00pm. **Other points:** bar, children welcome, terraces, car park. **Address:** Aire de Service de l'Obrion.
MME JACQUELINE FRERES
**Telephone:** 83.81.18.89. **Fax:** 83.64.51.37
⊗ ♀ Map 17

## LONGEAU, Haute-Marne, 52250

### AUBERGE ROUTIERE – CHEZ PATRICIA, RN 74, motorway A 31, exit Langres south
**Menu:** 49 to 100 Frs. **Accommodation:** 75 to 130 Frs. **Restaurant:** Breakfast served from 5:30am. Closed Saturdays. **Specialities:** home cooking. **Hotel:** 9 beds; 4 single rooms, 5 double rooms. **Other points:** bar, open to non-residents, à la carte menu, children welcome, pets welcome – check for details, traditional decor. **Address:** Route Nationale 74.
MME PATRICIA GODART
**Telephone:** 25.88.42.16
⊗ ♀ ⌂ Map 18

### CAFE DES ROUTIERS, RN 74, between Langres and Dijon, exit Langres south
**Menu:** 35 to 100 Frs. **Accommodation:** 75 to 100 Frs. **Restaurant:** Breakfast served from 6:30am. Lunch served from midday until 2:00pm. Dinner served from

7:00pm until 10:00pm. Closed Fridays. **Specialities:** home cooking. **Hotel:** 7 beds; 4 single rooms, 3 double rooms. **Other points:** bar, open to non-residents, à la carte menu, children welcome, pets welcome – check for details, car park, traditional decor. **Address:** Rue de Champagne.
MME EDWIGE DENIS
**Telephone:** 25.88.40.51
⊗ ♀ ⌂ Map 18

## LOUHANS, Saône-et-Loire, 71500

### LES ROUTIERS, RN 78
**Restaurant:** Lunch served from 11:30am until 2:00pm. Closed Sundays. **Specialities:** home cooking. **Other points:** open to non-residents. **Address:** 19, rue Lucien Guillemaut.
MR MICHEL ALEXANDRE
**Telephone:** 85.75.11.75
⊗ Map 15

## LUDELANGE, Moselle, 57710

### L'ESCALE, RN 52 and 521, between Metz and Longwy
**Languages spoken:** German, English, Spanish and Italian. **Menu:** 60 Frs (wine included). **Restaurant:** Breakfast served from 6:00am. **Specialities:** home cooking. **Other points:** bar, open to non-residents, lounge area, terraces, pets welcome – check for details, car park, modern decor. **Address:** Route Nationale 51.
MR JEAN-CLAUDE NEDELLEC
**Telephone:** 82.91.87.97
⊗ ♀ Map 17

## LUGNY, Saône-et-Loire, 71260

### PORTES DE BOURGOGNE, A 6
**Languages spoken:** English and Italian. **Menu:** 59 Frs. **Restaurant:** Open 24 hours. **Other points:** bar, open to non-residents, à la carte menu, children welcome, terraces, pets welcome – check for details, car park, modern decor. **Address:** A 6 Aire de Saint-Albain La Salle, dans les deux sens.
**Telephone:** 85.33.19.80. **Fax:** 85.33.19.98
⊗ ♀ Map 15

## LUSIGNY SUR BARSE, Aube, 10270

### AUBERGE DES PRAIRIES, RN 19
**Menu:** 55 Frs. **Accommodation:** 80 Frs. **Restaurant:** Dinner served from midday until 10:00pm. **Specialities:** home cooking. **Hotel:** 4 beds; 1 single room, 3 double rooms with shower, private WC. **Other points:** bar, à la carte menu, pets welcome – check for details, car park. **Address:** Route Nationale 19.
MME MONIQUE MIREUX
**Telephone:** 25.41.20.32
⊗ ♀ Map 18

## MAILLY LE CAMP, Aube, 10230

### RESTAURANT DU CENTRE
**Menu:** 59 to 91 Frs. **Accommodation:** 80 to 170 Frs.
**Restaurant:** Breakfast served from 6:30am. Lunch
served from 11:30am until 2:30pm. Dinner served
from 5:00pm until 10:00pm. Closed Fridays.
**Specialities:** couscous, paëlla, home cooking. **Hotel:**
14 beds; 12 single rooms, 2 double rooms with shower,
bath. **Other points:** bar, open to non-residents,
terraces, pets welcome – check for details, car park,
traditional decor. **Address:** 64, rue du Général de
Gaulle.
SNC BARDIVAT-MANTZ
**Telephone:** 25.37.30.08
⊗ ⌕ ⌂ Map 18

## MAISON NEUVE – RIOZ, Haute-
Saône, 70190

### LES ROUTIERS, RN 57, between Vesoul
and Besançon
**Menu:** 50 to 60 Frs. **Accommodation:** 80 to 180 Frs.
**Restaurant:** Breakfast served from 6:30am. Lunch
served from 11:30am until 3:00pm. Dinner served from
7:00pm until 10:00pm. Closed Saturdays, 3 weeks in
August and 2 weeks at Christmas. **Specialities:** home
cooking. **Hotel:** 8 beds; 5 single rooms, 3 double rooms.
**Other points:** bar, open to non-residents, children
welcome, lounge area, terraces, pets welcome – check
for details, car park, traditional decor. **Address:**
Quenoche.
MME CHANTAL CARTIER
**Telephone:** 84.91.80.54
⊗ ⌕ ⌂ Map 16

## MAIZIERES LA GRANDE
PAROISSE, Aube, 10510

### LE RELAIS DE POUSSEY, RN 19
**Languages spoken:** English. **Restaurant:** Closed
Sundays. **Other points:** bar. **Address:** ZI, la Glacière.
MME SYLVAINE GAILLARD
**Telephone:** 25.24.27.96
⊗ ⌕ Map 18

## MENIL SUR BELVITTE, Vosges, 88700

### LES ROUTIERS, RD 435, between
Sarrebourg and Epinal
**Menu:** 45 to 65 Frs. **Restaurant:** Breakfast served from
7:30am. Lunch served from 11:30am until 2:00pm.
Closed Mondays. **Specialities:** home cooking. **Other
points:** bar, open to non-residents, à la carte menu,
children welcome, traditional decor.
MME NELLY NICOLAS-JACQUOT
**Telephone:** 29.65.15.02
⊗ ⌕ Map 17

## MERCUREY, Saône-et-Loire, 71640

### LE MERCUREY, RD 978, on the road for
Autun
**Languages spoken:** English. **Menu:** 54 to 150 Frs.
**Accommodation:** 110 to 150 Frs. **Restaurant:**
Breakfast served from 6:30am. Lunch served from
11:00am until 3:00pm. Dinner served from 6:00pm until
10:00pm. **Specialities:** home cooking. **Hotel:** 8 beds; 2
single rooms, 6 double rooms with shower, bath. **Other
points:** bar, open to non-residents, à la carte menu,
children welcome, pets welcome – check for details, car
park. **Address:** Grande Rue.
MME ROSELINE GOY
**Telephone:** 85.45.13.56
⊗ ⌕ ⌂ ☆ Map 15

## MESGRIGNY, Aube, 10170

### LA BELLE ETOILE, RN 19, Paris
**Languages spoken:** English. **Menu:** 59 Frs.
**Restaurant:** Breakfast served from 4:30am. Lunch
served from 11:30am. Dinner served from 7:00pm until
11:00pm. Closed Saturdays. **Specialities:** home cooking.
**Other points:** bar, open to non-residents, children
welcome, lounge area, terraces, pets welcome – check
for details, car park, traditional decor. **Address:** La Belle
Etoile, Route Nationale 19.
MME SYLVIE SCHMUTZ
**Telephone:** 25.21.15.70
⊗ ⌕ Map 18

## MESSIA SUR SORNE, Jura, 39570

### LA CHARMILLE, RN 83, at the exit of Lons
le Saunier, towards Lyon
**Languages spoken:** English. **Menu:** 50 Frs.
**Restaurant:** Lunch served from midday until 2:00pm.
Closed Sundays. **Specialities:** home cooking. **Other
points:** bar, terraces, pets welcome – check for details,
car park, traditional decor. **Address:** 570, route de Lyon.
MR PATRICK VAUCHER
**Telephone:** 84.24.65.92
⊗ ⌕ Map 16

## MONETEAU, Yonne, 89470

### AU RENDEZ-VOUS DES PECHEURS
**Menu:** 56 Frs. **Accommodation:** 140 Frs. **Restaurant:**
Breakfast served from 7:00am. Lunch served from
midday until midnight. Dinner served from 7:30pm until
midday. Closed Sundays. **Hotel:** 6 beds. **Other points:**
bar, open to non-residents, car park. **Address:** 14, route
d'Auxerre.
MR MICHEL RABUAT
**Telephone:** 86.40.63.32
⊗ ⌕ ⌂ Map 15

## MONTBENOIT, Doubs, 25650

### HOTEL RESTAURANT DES VOYAGEURS, between Besançon and Pontarlier

**Menu:** 45 to 147 Frs. **Accommodation:** 120 to 170 Frs. **Restaurant:** Breakfast served from 7:30am. Lunch served from 11:30am until 1:45pm. Dinner served from 7:00pm until 9:00pm. Closed Tuesdays. **Specialities:** regional menu, home cooking. **Hotel:** 5 beds; with shower. **Other points:** bar, open to non-residents, à la carte menu, children welcome, pets welcome – check for details, traditional decor. **Address:** Place de l'Abbaye.
MR PIERRE MAGNIN-FEYSOT
**Telephone:** 81.38.10.85
⊗ ⦙ ⌂ ☆☆ Map 16

## MOUCHARD, Jura, 39330

### LA TONNELLE – RELAIS ROUTIERS, RN 83

**Menu:** 60 to 110 Frs. **Accommodation:** 100 to 200 Frs. **Restaurant:** Breakfast served from 6:30am. Lunch served from 12:00pm until 1:30pm. Dinner served from 7:30pm until 10:30pm. Closed Saturdays and in August. **Specialities:** regional menu, home cooking. **Hotel:** 12 beds; 6 single rooms, 6 double rooms with shower, bath. **Otherpoints:** bar, open to non-residents, à la carte menu, children welcome, lounge area, terraces, pets welcome – check for details, car park, traditional decor. **Address:** Pagnoz.
MR BERNARD MILLER
**Telephone:** 84.37.81.17
⊗ ⦙ ⌂ Map 16

## MOULINS DES MALADES, Jura, 39700

### AU RENDEZ VOUS DE LA MARINE, RN 73

**Restaurant:** Closed Saturdays and in August. **Specialities:** home cooking. **Other points:** open to non-residents. **Address:** Route Nationale 73.
MLLE JOSETTE BULLET
**Telephone:** 84.71.32.10
⊗ Map 16

## MULHOUSE, Haut-Rhin, 68100

### AUBERGE LEFEBVRE

**Menu:** 55 Frs. **Restaurant:** Breakfast served from 7:00am. Lunch served from 11:00am until 3:00pm. Dinner served from 7:00pm until 11:00pm. Closed Sundays. **Specialities:** home cooking. **Other points:** bar, open to non-residents, traditional decor. **Address:** 82, rue Lefebvre.
MME MONIQUE GUERQUIN
**Telephone:** 89.46.25.25
⊗ ⦙ Map 17

## MYENNES, Nièvre, 58440

### LE RANCH

**Menu:** 50 Frs. **Restaurant:** Breakfast served from 6:00am. **Other points:** bar, car park. **Address:** 68, rue de Paris.
MR ROGER DUFOUR
**Telephone:** 86.28.00.98
⊗ ⦙ Map 15

## NANCY, Meurthe-et-Moselle, 54000

### RESTAURANT DU PORT, RN 4

**Languages spoken:** English and German. **Menu:** 50 Frs. **Restaurant:** Breakfast served from 6:30am. Closed Fridays, public holidays and in August. **Specialities:** regional menu, home cooking. **Other points:** bar, pets welcome – check for details, car park, traditional decor. **Address:** 5, rue Henri Bazin.
MR CLAUDE DOPP
**Telephone:** 83.35.49.85
⊗ ⦙ ⌣ Map 17

## NAVILLY, Saône-et-Loire, 71270

### AU BOIS DE BOULOGNE, RN 73 Bis

**Restaurant:** Closed Wednesdays. **Other points:** bar.
MR ANDRÉ GRAPINET
**Telephone:** 85.49.10.40
⊗ ⦙ Map 15

## NEUVY SAUTOUR, Yonne, 89570

### AU BON COIN – CHEZ GÉRARD, RN 77, between Troyes and Auxerre

**Menu:** 47 Frs. **Restaurant:** Breakfast served from 4:00am. Lunch served from midday until 2:00pm. Dinner served from 7:00pm until 9:00pm. Closed Saturdays and in August. **Specialities:** home cooking. **Other points:** bar, open to non-residents, pets welcome – check for details, car park. **Address:** 29, route de Troyes.
MR GÉRARD CHARPIGNON
**Telephone:** 86.56.35.52
⊗ ⦙ Map 15

## NOCLE MAULAIX (LA), Nièvre, 58250

### HOTEL DE LA POSTE, Autun

**Menu:** 36 to 110 Frs. **Restaurant:** Breakfast served from 7:00am. Lunch served from midday until 1:30pm. Closed Mondays and in September. **Other points:** bar, open to non-residents, à la carte menu.
MR MARCEL SENOTIER
**Telephone:** 86.30.80.32
⊗ ⦙ Map 15

## NOUZONVILLE, Ardennes, 08700

### RESTAURANT DE LA PLACE, RD 1
**Menu:** 45 Frs. **Accommodation:** 60 to 90 Frs.
**Restaurant:** Breakfast served from 7:00am. Lunch
served from midday until 1:30pm. Dinner served from
7:30pm until 8:30pm. Closed Sundays. **Specialities:**
home cooking. **Hotel:** 6 beds; 2 single rooms, 4 double
rooms with shower, private WC. **Other points:** bar,
open to non-residents, pets welcome – check for details,
car park, traditional decor. **Address:** 15, place
Gambetta.
MME ANNIE BOQUILLON
**Telephone:** 24.53.80.43
⊗ ⏰ 🏠 Map 18

## NOVION PORCIEN, Ardennes, 08270

### LE FRANCO BELGE, RN 985, Rocroi
**Menu:** 42 Frs. **Restaurant:** Breakfast served from
7:00am. Lunch served from midday until 2:30pm. Dinner
served from 7:00pm until 9:30pm. Closed Sundays.
**Specialities:** home cooking. **Other points:** bar, open to
non-residents, pets welcome – check for details, car park,
traditional decor. **Address:** Place de la Gare.
MLLE SIMONE BONIFACE
**Telephone:** 24.38.70.06
⊗ ⏰ Map 18

## OGEVILLER, Meurthe-et-Moselle, 54450

### LE RELAIS DE LA VERDURETTE, RN 4,
*the main road between Paris and Strasbourg*
**Languages spoken:** German. **Menu:** 52 Frs. **Restaurant:**
Breakfast served from 7:30am. Closed Saturdays and in
August. **Specialities:** home cooking. **Other points:** bar,
car park. **Address:** 22, route de Strasbourg.
MICHEL ET LYDIE MARTIN
**Telephone:** 83.72.24.65
⊗ ⏰ Map 17

## ORNANS, Doubs, 25290

### LE PROGRES, RD 67, between Besançon
*and Lausanne*
**Languages spoken:** German and English. **Menu:** 35 to
130 Frs. **Accommodation:** 230 to 260 Frs. **Restaurant:**
Breakfast served from 7:00am. Lunch served from
11:30am. Dinner served from 7:00pm until midnight.
Closed Sundays. **Specialities:** truite, terrine maison,
escargots maison, home cooking. **Hotel:** 19 beds; 19
double rooms with shower, private WC, telephone.
**Other points:** bar, open to non-residents, à la carte
menu, children welcome, lounge area, pets welcome –
check for details, car park, traditional decor. **Address:**
11, rue Jacques Gervais.
MR LOUIS PERRIOT-COMTE
**Telephone:** 81.62.16.79. **Fax:** 81.62.19.10
⊗ ⏰ 🏠 🍴 ☆ Map 16

## ORSANS, Doubs, 25300

### LA JOCONDE
**Languages spoken:** English. **Menu:** 52 Frs (wine and
coffee included) to 80 Frs. **Restaurant:** Breakfast served
from 6:00am. **Specialities:** home cooking. **Other
points:** bar, à la carte menu, children welcome, terraces,
pets welcome – check for details, car park, traditional
decor. **Address:** Route Départementale 120.
MME CLAUDINE CACHON
**Telephone:** 81.60.45.27
⊗ ⏰ Map 16

## PERTHES, Haute-Marne, 52100

### CHEZ JEAN
**Menu:** 51, 70 to 66 Frs. **Accommodation:** 62 to 94 Frs.
**Restaurant:** Closed Saturdays and in August. **Hotel:** 26
beds. **Other points:** bar, à la carte menu, children
welcome, pets welcome – check for details, car park.
**Address:** Route Nationale 4.
MME LAURENCE KACZMAREK
**Telephone:** 25.56.40.27
⊗ ⏰ 🏠 Map 18

## PETIT REDERCHING, Moselle, 57410

### AUBERGE DE LA FROHMUHL, RN 62
**Languages spoken:** German and English. **Menu:** 59 to
138 Frs. **Restaurant:** Breakfast served from 7:00am.
Lunch served from 11:30am until 2:00pm. Dinner
served from 6:00pm until 9:00pm. Closed Wednesdays.
**Specialities:** home cooking. **Other points:** bar, open to
non-residents, à la carte menu, children welcome,
terraces, pets welcome – check for details, car park,
traditional decor. **Address:** 33, route de Strasbourg.
MR CHRISTOPHE BACH
**Telephone:** 87.96.43.52
⊗ ⏰ Map 17

### RESTAURANT DE LA GARE, RN 62, near
*the station*
**Languages spoken:** German. **Menu:** 55 to 85 Frs.
**Restaurant:** Breakfast served from 6:00am. Lunch
served from midday u8ntil 2:00pm. Dinner served
from 7:00pm until 8:30pm. Closed Saturdays and
from 14 July to 15 August. **Specialities:** regional
menu, home cooking. **Other points:** bar, open to non-
residents, à la carte menu, terraces, pets welcome –
check for details, car park, modern decor. **Address:** 6,
rue de Strasbourg.
MR BERNARD VOGEL
**Telephone:** 87.09.81.09
⊗ ⏰ Map 17

## PLOMBIERES LES BAINS, Vosges, 88370

### LE STRASBOURGEOIS, RN 57

Menu: 70 Frs. **Accommodation:** 110 to 195 Frs.
**Restaurant:** Breakfast served from 7:00am. Lunch
served from midday until 2:00pm. Dinner served from
7:00pm until 8:30pm. Closed Sundays and in
November. **Specialities:** terrine maison, truite à la
crème, vacherin glacé, regional food, home cooking.
**Hotel:** 13 beds; 6 single rooms, 7 double rooms with
shower, bath, private WC, television, telephone. **Other
points:** bar, open to non-residents, à la carte menu,
children welcome, lounge area, terraces, pets welcome
– check for details, car park, modern decor. **Address:**
3, place Beaumarchais.
MR ALAIN ROBERT
**Telephone:** 29.66.00.70, 29.66.01.73. **Fax:** 29.66.01.06
⊗ ♀ 🏠 ☆ Map 17

## POIX TERRON, Ardennes, 08430

*LE GODILLOT, opposite the chemist*
**Menu:** 54 Frs (drink included). **Accommodation:** 90
Frs per person. **Restaurant:** Breakfast served from
6:30am. Lunch served from 11:30am until 2:00pm.
Dinner served from 7:30pm until 9:00pm. Closed
Fridays and 15 days between Christmas Day and New
Year's Day. **Specialities:** home cooking. **Hotel:** 6 beds;
3 single rooms, 3 double rooms with private WC. **Other
points:** bar, open to non-residents, car park. **Address:**
26, place de la Gare.
MR JOSÉ MICHEL
**Telephone:** 24.35.61.46
⊗ ♀ 🏠 Map 18

## PONT A BINSON, Marne, 51700

*RESTAURNAT DE LA GARE, RN 3,*
*Epernay*
**Languages spoken:** German and English. **Menu:** 55 Frs
(coffee included). **Accommodation:** 140 (half board)
185 Frs (full board) **Restaurant:** Breakfast served from
6:30am. Lunch served from midday until 2:00pm.
Dinner served from 7:00pm until 9:00pm. **Specialities:**
home cooking. **Hotel:** 4 beds; with bath. **Other points:**
bar, open to non-residents, pets welcome – chech for
details, car park, traditional decor. **Address:** 22, rue du
Général Leclerc.
MME VIVIANE DERRIEN
**Telephone:** 26.58.30.41
⊗ ♀ Map 18

## PONTARLIER, Doubs, 25300

*CAFE DE LA LIBERTE*
Menu: 55 Frs. Restaurant: Breakfast served from
7.30am. Closed Sunday and from 15 August to 5
September. Specialities: home cooking. Other points:
bar, children welcome. Address: 36, rue de Salins.
MRS BESAND/PETIT
**Telephone:** 81.39.01.68
⊗ ♀ Map 16

## PONTIGNY, Yonne, 89230

*RELAIS DE PONTIGNY, RN 77, the main*
*road between Auxerre and Troyes*
**Languages spoken:** German, English and Italian. **Menu:**
52 to 95 Frs. **Restaurant:** Breakfast served from 6:00am.
Lunch served from midday until 2:15pm. Dinner served
from 7:00pm until 10:00pm. Closed Sunday and from
mid-December to mid-January. **Specialities:** regional
menu, home cooking. **Hotel:** 8 beds. **Other points:** bar,
open to non-residents, à la carte menu, children welcome.
**Address:** 9, rue Paul Desjardin.
MME CAROLE LEDUCQ
**Telephone:** 86.47.54.48
⊗ ♀ 🏠 Map 15

## POUILLY EN AUXOIS, Côte-d'Or, 21490

*RELAIS DE L'AUXOIS, A 6*
**Languages spoken:** English. **Restaurant:** Breakfast
served from 7:00am. **Specialities:** regional menu. **Other
points:** à la carte menu, children welcome, terraces, pets
welcome – check for details, car park. **Address:** Aire de
Service du Chien Blanc, sens Paris/Lyon.
**Telephone:** 80.90.74.25
⊗ Map 15

*RELAIS DE L'AUXOIS, A 6*
**Languages spoken:** English. **Restaurant:** Open 24
hours. **Specialities:** regional menu. **Other points:**
children welcome, terraces, pets welcome – check for
details, car park. **Address:** Aire de Service des
Lochères, sens Lyon/Paris.
**Telephone:** 80.90.83.28
⊗ Map 15

## PREMERY, Nièvre, 58700

*LE ROUTIER, RD 977, between Clamecy*
*and Nevers*
**Languages spoken:** German and English. **Menu:** 55 Frs.
**Restaurant:** Breakfast served from 6:00am. Lunch
served from midday until 2:30pm. Dinner served from
7:30pm until 9:00pm. **Specialities:** home cooking.
**Hotel:** 2 beds; with shower, bath, private WC, television.
**Other points:** bar, open to non-residents, children
welcome, terraces, pets welcome – check for details, car
park, traditional decor. **Address:** 8, route de Lurcy.
MR JEAN-JACQUES LEMARIÉ
**Telephone:** 86.37.97.59
⊗ ♀ Map 15

## PREZ SOUS LAFAUCHE, Haute-Marne, 52700

*LES 3 VALLEES, the main road between*
*Chaumont and Nancy*
**Menu:** 60 to 150 Frs. **Restaurant:** Open 24 hours.

**Specialities:** home cooking. **Other points:** bar, open to non-residents, à la carte menu, children welcome, car park, traditional decor.
MME ELIANE TROMMENSCHLAGER
**Telephone:** 25.31.57.84
⊗ ♀ Map 18

## PROSNES, Marne, 51400

### RELAIS CONSTANTINE, RD 31, A 4 exit Reims, towards Sainte Menehould
**Menu:** 50 to 100 Frs. **Accommodation:** 90 to 240 Frs.
**Restaurant:** Breakfast served from 6:30am. Lunch served from midday until 1:30pm. Dinner served from 7:00pm until 9:00pm. Closed Saturdays and from 15 to 31 August.
**Specialities:** home cooking. **Hotel:** 3 beds; 1 single room, 2 double rooms with shower, private WC. **Other points:** bar, open to non-residents, à la carte menu, car park, modern decor. **Address:** Lieu dit 'Constantine', Route Nationale.
MR RENÉ ROSELET
**Telephone:** 26.61.70.70
⊗ ♀ Map 18

## RACHECOURT SUR MARNE, Haute-Marne, 52170

### L'AURORE, RN 67, in the middle of the countryside
**Menu:** 50 to 90 Frs. **Accommodation:** 70 to 200 Frs.
**Restaurant:** Breakfast served from 8:00am. Dinner served from 7:00pm until 10:00pm. **Specialities:** home cooking. **Hotel:** 4 beds; 1 single room, 3 double rooms with shower, private WC. **Other points:** bar, à la carte menu, terraces, car park. **Address:** Avenue de Belgique.
MR MARIUS NARAT
**Telephone:** 25.04.41.58
⊗ ♀ Map 18

## REGUISHEIM, Haut-Rhin, 68890

### RESTAURANT A L'ANGE, RD 201, Meyenheim
**Languages spoken:** German. **Menu:** 40 to 60 Frs.
**Restaurant:** Breakfast served from 6:00am. Lunch served from midday until 1:30pm. Dinner served from 7:00pm until 9:30pm. Closed Saturdays and in August.
**Specialities:** home cooking. **Hotel:** 5 beds. **Other points:** bar, open to non-residents, à la carte menu, pets welcome – check for details, car park, traditional decor.
**Address:** 90, Grande Rue.
MR RAYMOND BERTRAND
**Telephone:** 89.81.12.66
⊗ ♀ ⌂ Map 17

## REIMS, Marne, 51400

### RELAIS REIMS / CHAMPAGNE, A 4
**Languages spoken:** German and English. **Restaurant:** Open 24 hours. **Specialities:** regional menu. **Other**

**points:** à la carte menu, children welcome, terraces, pets welcome – check for details, car park. **Address:** Aire de service de Reims, dans les deux sens.
**Telephone:** 26.03.93.57
⊗ Map 18

## REVIN, Ardennes, 08500

### CHEZ ALEX, RN 388
**Restaurant:** Dinner served from midday until 9:00pm.
**Hotel:** 4 beds. **Other points:** bar. **Address:** 6, rue Voltaire.
MME JOSEPHA MAHUT
**Telephone:** 24.40.12.91
⊗ ♀ Map 18

## RIVIERES DE CORPS (LA), Aube, 10300

### LA QUEUE DE LA POELE, RN 60, Sens
**Menu:** 55 to 120 Frs. **Restaurant:** Breakfast served from 6:30am. Lunch served from 11:30am until 2:00pm. Dinner served from 7:00pm until 10:00pm. Closed Sundays and 3 weeks in August. **Specialities:** home cooking. **Other points:** bar, open to non-residents, children welcome, car park, traditional decor. **Address:** Rue Lafontaine.
MR GABY BARBIER
**Telephone:** 25.74.47.94. **Fax:** 25.49.84.01
⊗ ♀ Map 18

## ROCHE VINEUSE (LA), Saône-et-Loire, 71960

### RELAIS ROUTIERS – CHEZ FRANCE, RN 79, between Mâcon and Charolles, via the tourist road
**Restaurant:** Breakfast served from 5:30am. Dinner served from midday until 11:00pm. Closed Saturdays and in August. **Specialities:** home cooking. **Other points:** bar, open to non-residents, children welcome, pets welcome – check for details, car park. **Address:** Place du Chaucher.
MME FRANCE BROUILLON
**Telephone:** 85.37.71.51
⊗ ♀ Map 15

## ROCROI, Ardennes, 08230

### HOTEL DE LA GARE, RN 51 and 377
**Menu:** 50 to 100 Frs. **Accommodation:** 100 to 200 Frs.
**Restaurant:** Breakfast served from 7:00am. Lunch served from midday until 2:00pm. Dinner served from 7:00pm until 9:00pm. **Specialities:** home cooking.
**Hotel:** 10 beds; 1 single room, 9 double rooms with shower, bath, private WC. **Other points:** bar, open to non-residents, à la carte menu, car park, traditional decor. **Address:** 1, avenue du Général Moreau.
SARL MINUCCI
**Telephone:** 24.54.10.32
⊗ ♀ ⌂ Map 18

## RONCHAMP, Haute-Saône, 70250

### LE RELAIS DE LA POMME D'OR, RN 19, between Belfot and Vesoul

**Languages spoken:** German, English and Italian. **Menu:** 50 to 200 Frs. **Accommodation:** 100 to 165 Frs. **Restaurant:** Breakfast served from 6:00am. Lunch served from midday until 2:30pm. Dinner served from 7:00pm until 10:30pm. **Specialities:** regional menu, home cooking. **Hotel:** 25 beds; 5 single rooms, 20 double rooms with shower, bath, private WC, television, telephone. **Other points:** bar, open to non-residents, à la carte menu, children welcome, pets welcome – check for details, car park, traditional decor. **Address:** Rue le Corbusier.

MME LUCETTE CENCI
**Telephone:** 84.20.62.12. **Fax:** 84.63.59.45
⊗ ⍭ 🏠 ☆ Map 16

## ROYE, Haute-Saône, 70200

### LE RELAIS DES ROUTIERS, RN 19, the main road between Paris and Belfort

**Menu:** 40 to 50 Frs. **Restaurant:** Breakfast served from 7:30am. Lunch served from midday until 1:30pm. Closed Sundays. **Specialities:** home cooking. **Other points:** open to non-residents, terraces, pets welcome – check for details, car park. **Address:** 50, rue de la Verrerie.

MME HUGUETTE KUHN
**Telephone:** 84.30.06.48
⊗ Map 16

## RUPT SUR MOSELLE, Vosges, 88360

### L'ETAPE, RN 66, Mulhouse

**Languages spoken:** German. **Menu:** 45 Frs. **Restaurant:** Breakfast served from 6:00am. Lunch served from 11:00am until 1:45pm. Dinner served from 6:00pm until 8:45pm. Closed Sundays. **Specialities:** home cooking. **Other points:** bar, open to non-residents, pets welcome – check for details, car park. **Address:** Lieu dit 'Les Meix', Route Nationale 66.

MME CATHERINE SPATZ
**Telephone:** 29.24.35.17
⊗ ⍭ Map 17

## RYE, Jura, 39230

### CHEZ LUCETTE, RD 468

**Menu:** 55 Frs. **Restaurant:** Lunch served from 11:30am until 2:00pm. Closed Thursdays, the 1st fortnight of August and the 2nd fortnight of December. **Specialities:** home cooking. **Other points:** bar, open to non-residents. **Address:** Lieu dit 'Les Meix', Route Nationale 66.

MME LUCETTE CAMBAZARD
**Telephone:** 84.48.61.60
⊗ ⍭ Map 16

## SAINT AUBIN SUR LOIRE, Saône-et-Loire, 71140

### BAR DE L'AMITIE, RD 979, between Nevers and Mâcon

**Languages spoken:** German, English and Spanish. **Menu:** 45 to 85 Frs. **Restaurant:** Breakfast served from 6:30am. Lunch served from 11:45am until 1:30pm. Dinner served from 7:00pm until 9:00pm. Closed Mondays. **Specialities:** home cooking. **Hotel:** 4 beds; 4 single rooms, with shower, bath. **Other points:** bar, open to non-residents, à la carte menu, children welcome, terraces, pets welcome – check for details, car park. **Address:** Le Bourg.

MR DIDIER GAUMARD-MAISON
**Telephone:** 85.53.91.09
⊗ ⍭ Map 15

## SAINT AVOLD, Moselle, 57740

### RELAIS DE LORRAINE, A 4

**Languages spoken:** German and English. **Restaurant:** Open 24 hours. **Specialities:** regional menu. **Other points:** à la carte menu, children welcome, lounge area, terraces, pets welcome – check for details, car park. **Address:** Aire de Service de Saint-Avold, dans les deux sens.

**Telephone:** 87.92.23.89
⊗ Map 17

## SAINT DENIS LES SENS, Yonne, 89100

### LES CERISIERS, RN 360, A 6, exit Sens

**Languages spoken:** English. **Menu:** 54 Frs. **Restaurant:** Breakfast served from 7:00am. Lunch served from 11:00am until 2:00pm. Dinner served from 7:00pm until 9:00pm. Closed weekends (except reservations, 30 pers. min.) and in August. **Specialities:** home cooking. **Other points:** bar, open to non-residents, children welcome, terraces, pets welcome – check for details, car park, modern decor. **Address:** 1, rue de Paris.

MR MICHEL FERRIERE
**Telephone:** 86.65.28.52
⊗ ⍭ Map 15

## SAINT DIE, Vosges, 88100

### LA CROISETTE, RN 59

**Menu:** 58 Frs. **Restaurant:** Breakfast served from 8:00am. Dinner served from midday until 10:00pm. Closed on New Year's Eve. **Specialities:** home cooking. **Other points:** bar. **Address:** 41, avenue de Verdun.

MR BERNARD ROUMIER
**Telephone:** 29.56.14.37
⊗ ⍭ Map 17

## SAINT DIZIER, Haute-Marne, 52100

### LE MOLIERE, 400m from RN 4

**Languages spoken:** German and English. **Menu:** 53,50 to 90 Frs. **Restaurant:** Breakfast served from 7:30am. Lunch served from 11:30am until 2:30pm. Dinner served from 7:30pm until 11:30pm. Closed Saturdays. **Specialities:** regional menu, home cooking. **Other points:** bar, open to non-residents, à la carte menu, children welcome, pets welcome – check for details, car park. **Address:** 10, rue Molière.
MR GÉRARD DELAPORTE
**Telephone:** 25.56.63.05
⊗ ⌇ ☆☆  Map 18

## SAINT EUSEBE, Saône-et-Loire, 71120

### LE RELAIS DU PONT DES MORANDS, RN 70, between Montceau and le Creusot

**Restaurant:** Breakfast served from 5:30am. Lunch served from 11:45am until 2:30pm. Dinner served from 7:30pm until 10:00pm. Closed Saturdays. **Specialities:** Fruits de mer, home cooking. **Other points:** bar, open to non-residents, children welcome, pets welcome – check for details, car park, modern decor. **Address:** Voie Express.
MR PIERRE DESPREZ
**Telephone:** 85.78.46.45
⊗ ⌇  Map 15

## SAINT HIPPOLYTE, Doubs, 25190

### LE GRAND CLOS, RN 437, Belfort, Pontarlier and Besançon

**Languages spoken:** German. **Menu:** 45 to 80 Frs. **Accommodation:** 95 to 130 Frs. **Restaurant:** Breakfast served from 7:00am. Dinner served from midday until 10:00pm. Closed Saturdays. **Specialities:** home cooking. **Hotel:** 6 beds; 4 single rooms, 2 double rooms with shower, private WC. **Other points:** bar, open to non-residents, à la carte menu, terraces, pets welcome – check for details, car park, traditional decor.
MME MARTINE LEPEME
**Telephone:** 81.96.51.12
⊗ ⌇ ⌂  Map 16

## SAINT LOUP DE VARENNES, Saône-et-Loire, 71240

### LA PETITE AUBERGE, RN 6, the main road between Chalon and Mâcon

**Menu:** 60 Frs. **Restaurant:** Breakfast served from 6:30am. Dinner served from midday until 11:00pm. Closed Sundays and in December. **Specialities:** home cooking. **Other points:** bar, open to non-residents, car park, traditional decor. **Address:** Route Nationale 6.
MME SONIA GAUDILLAT
**Telephone:** 85.44.21.87
⊗ ⌇  Map 15

## SAINT LOUP SUR SEMOUSE, Haute-Saône, 70800

### HOTEL DE LA TERRASSE, RN 64

**Restaurant:** Closed Sundays and from 1 to 15 August. **Hotel:** 4 beds. **Other points:** bar. **Address:** Rue de la Gare.
MR JEAN BALLOT
**Telephone:** 84.49.02.20
⊗ ⌇  Map 16

## SAINT MARC SUR SEINE, Côte-d'Or, 21450

### LE SOLEIL D'OR, RN 71, the main road between Troyes and Dijon

**Languages spoken:** English. **Menu:** 60 Frs (drink included). **Restaurant:** Lunch served from midday until 3:00pm. Dinner served from 7:00pm until 9:00pm. Closed Saturdays. **Specialities:** home cooking. **Hotel:** 7 beds; 2 single rooms, 5 double rooms with shower. **Other points:** bar, children welcome, pets welcome – check for details, car park. **Address:** Rue de la Gare.
MME GENEVIEVE GIRARD
**Telephone:** 80.93.21.42
⊗ ⌇ ⌂  Map 15

## SAINT MIHIEL, Meuse, 55300

### LE RELAIS DES ROUTIERS, RD 964, between Verdun and Commercy

**Menu:** 49 Frs. **Accommodation:** 100 to 110 Frs. **Restaurant:** Breakfast served from 7:00am. Lunch served from midday until 3:00pm. Dinner served from 8:00pm until 11:00pm. Closed Sundays and from 15 to 31 August. **Specialities:** regional menu, home cooking. **Hotel:** 8 beds; 4 single rooms, 4 double rooms with shower. **Other points:** bar, open to non-residents, children welcome, terraces, pets welcome – check for details, car park, traditional decor. **Address:** 19, rue de Verdun.
MR CLAUDE DERVIN
**Telephone:** 29.89.00.44
⊗ ⌇ ⌂  Map 17

## SAINT PHAL, Aube, 10130

### RESTAURANT DU COMMERCE, RN 77, the main road between Auxerre and Troyes

**Languages spoken:** German. **Menu:** 53 to 145 Frs. **Restaurant:** Breakfast served from 8:00am. Lunch served from 11:00am until 1:30pm. Dinner served from 7:00pm until 8:45pm. Closed Mondays and in August. **Specialities:** regional menu. **Other points:** bar, children welcome, pets welcome – check for details, car park, traditional decor.
MR DANIEL GODEFROY
**Telephone:** 25.42.16.39
⊗ ⌇  Map 18

## SAINT PIERRE LE MOUTIER,

Nièvre, 58240

### RELAIS SAINT IMBERT, RN 7, between Moulins and Clermont

**Languages spoken:** German. **Menu:** 55 to 70 Frs.
**Restaurant:** Breakfast served from 5:00am. Lunch
served from midday until 2:30pm. Dinner served from
7:00pm until 10:30pm. Closed Saturdays, 15 days in
June and 15 days in December. **Specialities:** choucroute,
potée, regional food, home cooking. **Other points:** bar,
open to non-residents, à la carte menu, children
welcome, pets welcome – check for details, car park,
traditional decor. **Address:** Route Nationale 7, Saint
Imbert.
MLLE PIA FRESSLE
**Telephone:** 86.38.61.65
⊗ ⵟ Map 15

## SAINT PIERREMONT, Vosges, 88700

### LE RELAIS VOSGIEN, RD 414, between Luneville and Rambervillers

**Languages spoken:** German. **Menu:** 60 to 220 Frs.
**Accommodation:** 210 to 390 Frs. **Restaurant:** Breakfast
served from 7:00am. Lunch served from midday until
2:00pm. Dinner served from 7:00pm until 9:00pm.
Closed Fridays. **Specialities:** home cooking. **Hotel:** 18
beds; 18 double rooms with shower, bath, private WC,
television, telephone. **Other points:** bar, open to non-
residents, à la carte menu, children welcome, lounge
area, terraces, pets welcome – check for details, car park,
traditional decor. **Address:** Rambervilliers.
MME CHRISTIANE THÉNOT-PRÉVOST
**Telephone:** 29.65.02.46. **Fax:** 29.65.02.83
⊗ ⵟ 🏠 ☆☆ Map 17

## SAINT SAUVEUR, Haute-Saône, 70300

### CHEZ MAXIM, RN 57, between Nancy and Besançon

**Languages spoken:** German and English. **Menu:** 48 Frs to
95 Frs. **Accommodation:** 90 to 120 Frs. **Restaurant:**
Breakfast served from 6:30am. Lunch served from midday
until 2:30pm. Dinner served from 7:30pm until 10:30pm.
Closed Sundays and in February. **Specialities:** regional
menu, home cooking. **Hotel:** 5 beds; 3 single rooms, 2
double rooms with shower, bath, private WC. **Other points:**
bar, open to non-residents, children welcome, terraces, pets
welcome – check for details, car park, traditional decor.
**Address:** 10, avenue Georges Clémenceau.
MME COLETTE LACK
**Telephone:** 84.40.02.91. **Fax:** 84.93.65.45
⊗ ⵟ 🏠 Map 16

## SAINT YAN, Saône-et-Loire, 71600

### HOTEL DE LA GARE, RN 70, between Digoin and Roanne

**Menu:** 50 to 125 Frs. **Accommodation:** 75 to 130 Frs.
**Restaurant:** Breakfast served from 7:30am. Lunch
served from midday until 2:00pm. Dinner served from
7:00pm until 9:00pm. Closed Wednesdays and from 15
August to 15 September. **Specialities:** regional menu,
home cooking. **Hotel:** 6 beds; 4 single rooms, 2 double
rooms. **Other points:** bar, open to non-residents, à la
carte menu, children welcome, pets welcome – check for
details, car park, traditional decor. **Address:** 12, rue de
la Gare.
MR PASCAL GERMAIN
**Telephone:** 85.84.97.20
⊗ ⵟ 🏠 Map 15

## SAINTE MARGUERITE, Vosges, 88100

### LE RELAIS DES AMIS, RN 59, take the tunnel road at Sainte Marie Mines

**Accommodation:** 100 to 160 Frs. **Restaurant:**
Breakfast served from 7:00am. Lunch served from
12:00pm until 2:00pm. Dinner served from 7:00pm
until 9:00pm. Closed Saturdays. **Specialities:** home
cooking. **Hotel:** 16 beds; 11 single rooms, 5 double
rooms with shower. **Other points:** bar, open to non-
residents, terraces, pets welcome – check for details,
car park, traditional decor. **Address:** 486, rue
d'Alsace.
MME JOSIANE BONHOMME
**Telephone:** 29.56.17.23
⊗ ⵟ 🏠 ☆ Map 17

## SAINTE MARIE SUR OUCHE,

Côte-d'Or, 21410

### BAR DE LA POSTE, RN 5

**Accommodation:** 80 to 110 Frs. **Restaurant:** Breakfast
served from 6:00am. Closed from 24 December to 1
January. **Hotel:** 5 beds. **Other points:** bar.
MR JACQUES VEAULIN
**Telephone:** 80.23.62.70
⊗ ⵟ 🏠 Map 15

## SALINS LES BAINS, Jura, 39110

### BAR RESTAURANT DES SPORTS

**Menu:** 32 to 65 Frs. **Restaurant:** Breakfast served from
6:00am. Lunch served from 11:00am until 2:00pm.
Dinner served from 7:00pm until 9:00pm. **Specialities:**
regional menu, home cooking. **Other points:** bar, à la
carte menu, children welcome, traditional decor.
**Address:** 107, avenue de la République.
MME LILIANE VACELET
**Telephone:** 84.73.11.18
⊗ ⵟ Map 16

## SARREGUEMINES, Moselle, 57200

### LES ROUTIERS, RN 74, in the town centre

**Languages spoken:** German. **Menu:** 30 to 50 Frs.
**Accommodation:** 50 to 120 Frs. **Restaurant:**

Breakfast served from 5:00am. Lunch served from midday until 3:00pm. Dinner served from 7:00pm until midnight. Closed Sundays and in July or August. **Specialities:** choucroute garnie, regional food. **Hotel:** 11 beds; 1 single room, 10 double rooms with shower, bath. **Other points:** open to non-residents, children welcome, car park, modern decor. **Address:** 19, rue du Bac.
MR CAMILLE FASEL
**Telephone:** 87.98.15.39
⊗ 🏠 Map 17

## SAULIEU, Côte-d'Or, 21210

### AUX POIDS LOURDS, RN 6, Lyon

**Accommodation:** 65 to 95 Frs. **Restaurant:** Breakfast served from 7:00am. Lunch served from midday until 2:00pm. Closed Saturdays and in August. **Specialities:** home cooking. **Hotel:** 5 beds. **Other points:** bar, open to non-residents, terraces, car park, traditional decor. **Address:** 12, rue Courtépée.
MME MICHELE GODET
**Telephone:** 81.64.19.83. **Fax:** 80.64.19.83
⊗ ♈ 🏠 Map 15

## SEDAN, Ardennes, 08200

### CHEZ LOULOUTE, RN 43, Charleville-Mézières

**Menu:** 53 Frs (wine included). **Restaurant:** Breakfast served from 5:30am. **Specialities:** home cooking. **Other points:** bar, open to non-residents, children welcome, pets welcome – check for details, car park, traditional decor. **Address:** 56, avenue de la Marne.
MME THÉRESE VARLOTEAUX
**Telephone:** 24.27.16.62
⊗ ♈ Map 18

## SENAN, Yonne, 89710

### HOTEL DE LA CROIX BLANCHE, RD 955

**Restaurant:** Closed Sundays. **Other points:** bar. **Address:** 16, rue d'Aillant.
MR JEAN-CLAUDE LECOURT
**Telephone:** 86.63.41.31
⊗ ♈ Map 15

## SENNECEY LE GRAND, Saône-et-Loire, 71240

### L'ARCHE DE CHALON LA FERTE, A 6

**Languages spoken:** English and Spanish. **Menu:** 40 to 100 Frs. **Restaurant:** Open 24 hours. **Specialities:** regional menu. **Other points:** bar, open to non-residents, children welcome, terraces, pets welcome – check for details, car park, traditional decor. **Address:** A 6 Aire de la Ferté, sens Paris/Lyon.
MR ANTOINE RIVASSEAU
**Telephone:** 85.44.21.79
⊗ ♈ Map 15

### L'ARCHE DE CHALON SAINT AMBREUIL, A 6

**Languages spoken:** German, English and Spanish. **Menu:** 57 Frs. **Restaurant:** Open 24 hours. **Other points:** open to non-residents, children welcome, pets welcome – check for details, car park. **Address:** Aire de Saint-Ambreuil, sens Lyon/Paris.
MR BRUNO BRENEZ
**Telephone:** 85.44.20.64, 85.44.13.12
⊗ Map 15

## SOMMESSOUS, Marne, 51320

### LE MIRABELLIER

**Languages spoken:** German and English. **Menu:** 53 Frs. **Restaurant:** Breakfast served from 6:00am. Dinner served from midday until 11:00pm. **Other points:** bar, car park. **Address:** Aire de Service de Sommessous.
SARL SG2R
**Telephone:** 26.70.17.04
⊗ ♈ Map 18

## SOUGY SUR LOIRE, Nièvre, 58300

### LE SNACK, RN 81, between Décize (7km) and Nevers (27km)

**Languages spoken:** English. **Menu:** 55 (wine and coffee included) to 80 Frs. **Restaurant:** Breakfast served from 6:00am. Closed Sundays. **Specialities:** home cooking. **Other points:** bar, open to non-residents, à la carte menu, children welcome, terraces, pets welcome – check for details, car park, traditional decor. **Address:** Route Nationale 81, la Mouille.
MR DANIEL CHEVALIER
**Telephone:** 86.50.13.88
⊗ ♈ Map 15

## SOULAINES DHUYS, Aube, 10200

### LE RELAIS DES ROUTIERS, RD 960, between Troyes and Nancy

**Menu:** 45 to 70 Frs. **Restaurant:** Breakfast served from 8:00am. Lunch served from midday until 2:30pm. Dinner served from 7:00pm until 11:00pm. Closed Sundays. **Specialities:** regional menu. **Other points:** bar, open to non-residents, car park, modern decor. **Address:** Route Départementale 960.
MME YVETTE DEMONGEOT
**Telephone:** 25.92.76.10
⊗ ♈ Map 18

## SPINCOURT, Meuse, 55230

### HOTEL RESTAURANT DE LA GARE

**Languages spoken:** German English Spanish Italian. **Menu:** 60 Frs. **Accommodation:** 170 Frs. **Restaurant:** Breakfast served from 10:00am. Closed Tuesdays. **Specialities:** home cooking. **Hotel:** 4 beds; with shower.

Other points: bar, pets welcome – check for details, car park, traditional decor.
MR BRUNO CAMPOLMI
Telephone: 29.85.96.93
⊗ ♈ Map 17

## STENAY, Meuse, 55700

### BAR DES SANGLIERS – LA MANGEOIRE, RD 947, road for Reims
Languages spoken: German. Menu: 58 to 150 Frs. Accommodation: 120 to 150 Frs. Restaurant: Breakfast served from 6:30am. Lunch served from 11:30am until 2:00pm. Dinner served from 7:30pm until 9:00pm. Closed Saturdays and in August. Specialities: home cooking. Hotel: 4 beds; 1 single room, 3 double rooms with shower, bath, private WC. Other points: bar, open to non-residents, à la carte menu, pets welcome – check for details, car park, modern decor. Address: 1, rue Carnot.
MR DANIEL DEMACON
Telephone: 29.80.60.06
⊗ ♈ Map 17

## STRASBOURG, Bas-Rhin, 67000

### AU RHIN FRANCAIS, RN 4, on the border, opposite the bridge of Europe
Languages spoken: German, English, Dutch, Swiss. Menu: 38 to 75 Frs. Accommodation: 70 to 140 Frs. Restaurant: Breakfast served from 8:30am. Closed Saturdays and in August. Specialities: regional menu, home cooking. Hotel: 7 beds; with shower, bath. Other points: bar, open to non-residents, à la carte menu, children welcome, terraces, car park. Address: 83, route du Rhin.
MR MARCEL WENDLING
Telephone: 88.61.29.00, 88.61.40.93
⊗ ♈ ⌂ Map 17

## STRASBOURG MEINAU, Bas-Rhin, 67100

### BRASSERIE DES BATELIERS, RN 4
Places of interest: Parc Barbieux, orgues de Wasquehal. Languages spoken: German and Spanish. Menu: 40 to 120 Frs. Restaurant: Lunch served from 11:30am until 2:30pm. Dinner served from 7:00pm until 10:00pm. Closed Saturdays and 3 weeks between July and October. Specialities: regional menu, home cooking. Other points: open to non-residents, à la carte menu, terraces, pets welcome – check for details, car park, traditional decor. Address: 33, rue de la Plaine de Bouchers, ZI Meinau.
MR JEAN-CLAUDE PICCINELLI
Telephone: 88.39.19.50
⊗ Map 17

## SUIPPES, Marne, 51600

### AU BON COIN, RN 77 and 31, between Sedan and Charleville
Languages spoken: Italian. Menu: 59 to 90 Frs. Restaurant: Breakfast served from 8:00am. Dinner served from 7:00pm until 9:00pm. Specialities: home cooking. Other points: bar, open to non-residents, terraces, pets welcome – check for details, car park, traditional decor. Address: 25, rue de la Libération.
SDF TILOCA
Telephone: 26.70.05.84
⊗ ♈ Map 18

## TALMAY, Côte-d'Or, 21270

### CAFE DE LA PLACE – CHEZ MONIQUE, Pontailler sur Saône
Menu: 60 Frs (wine and coffee included). Restaurant: Breakfast served from 7:00am. Closed the 2nd fortnight in August. Specialities: home cooking. Hotel: 8 beds; 2 single rooms, 6 double rooms. Other points: bar, open to non-residents, children welcome, terraces, pets welcome – check for details, car park, traditional decor.
MME MONIQUE TRUDIN-DEFRANCE
Telephone: 80.36.13.24
⊗ ♈ ⌂ Map 15

## THAON LES VOSGES, Vosges, 88150

### RELAIS ROUTIERS 60 10, RN 57, Epinal
Menu: 50 to 70 Frs. Accommodation: 110 Frs. Restaurant: Breakfast served from 5:00am. Lunch served from 11:45am until 1:30pm. Dinner served from 7:00pm until 8:30pm. Closed Saturdays. Specialities: home cooking. Hotel: 4 beds; with television. Other points: bar, children welcome, pets welcome – check for details, car park, modern decor. Address: 200, rue de Lorraine.
MR ROBERT GEHIN
Telephone: 29.39.21.67
⊗ ♈ Map 17

## TIL CHATEL, Côte-d'Or, 21120

### LE RELAIS DES PEUPLIERS, RN 74, the main road between Dijon and Nancy
Menu: 60 Frs (wine and coffee included). Restaurant: Breakfast served from 7:00am. Lunch served from 11:30am until 2:30pm. Dinner served from 6:30pm until 10:00pm. Closed Sundays. Specialities: home cooking. Other points: bar, open to non-residents, children welcome, lounge area, terraces, pets welcome – check for details, car park, modern decor. Address: Route Nationale 74.
MME JUDITH EZZEDINE
Telephone: 80.95.20.14
⊗ ♈ Map 15

## TORCY, Saône-et-Loire, 71210

### LA SPIAGGIA, RN 80

**Languages spoken:** German, English and Italian.
**Restaurant:** Dinner served from midday until 11:00pm.
**Other points:** bar. **Address:** Route Expresse, Montchanin.
MR SALVATORE LOTITO
**Telephone:** 85.55.35.45
⊗ ♇ Map 15

## TOUR DU MEIX (LA), Jura, 39270

### AUBERGE DU PONT DE LA PYLE, RN 470, between Lons le Saunier and Saint Claude via Orgelet

**Languages spoken:** English and German. **Menu:** 57 to
150 Frs. **Restaurant:** Breakfast served from 8:00am.
Lunch served from midday until 3:00pm. Dinner served
from 7:00pm until 10:00pm. Closed and in October.
**Specialities:** home cooking. **Other points:** bar, open to
non-residents, à la carte menu, children welcome,
terraces, pets welcome – check for details, car park,
traditional decor. **Address:** Route Nationale 470.
MR JACQUES BERGER
**Telephone:** 84.25.41.92, 84.25.42.29
⊗ ♇ 👄 Map 16

## TREMBLOIS LES ROCROI, Ardennes, 08150

### RELAIS ROUTIERS DU PIQUET, RN 43

**Languages spoken:** Spanish and Portugese. **Menu:** 52
Frs. **Restaurant:** Breakfast served from 6:00am. Lunch
served from 11:30am until 2:30pm. Dinner served from
7:00pm until 9:00pm. Closed Saturdays and 1 week
between Christmas Day and New Year's Day.
**Specialities:** home cooking. **Other points:** bar, open to
non-residents, car park. **Address:** Le Piquet.
MR GÉRARD CLÉRICE
**Telephone:** 24.35.13.86
⊗ ♇ Map 18

## TRESNAY, Nièvre, 58240

### LA SCIERIE, RN 7, between Saint Pierre le Moutier and Moulins

**Languages spoken:** English. **Menu:** 55 Frs.
**Restaurant:** Open 24 hours. **Specialities:** home
cooking. **Other points:** bar, open to non-residents, à la
carte menu, lounge area, car park, modern decor.
**Address:** Route Nationale 7.
MR MARTIAL PETTINGER
**Telephone:** 86.38.62.14
⊗ ♇ Map 15

## TRONSANGES, Nièvre, 58400

### L'AUBERGE DU SOLEIL LEVANT, RN 7

**Menu:** 48 to 65 Frs. **Restaurant:** Breakfast served from

6:00am. Lunch served from midday until 2:00pm. Closed
Sundays and mid-September. **Specialities:** home cooking.
**Other points:** bar, open to non-residents, children
welcome, pets welcome – check for details, traditional
decor. **Address:** Route Nationale 7, Barbeloup.
MME RENÉE REICHHARD
**Telephone:** 86.37.84.02
⊗ ♇ Map 15

### SARL DE LA CROIX DU PAPE – CHEZ L'AUVERGNAT, RN 7, Nevers

**Menu:** 57, 50 to 100 Frs. **Accommodation:** 120 to 136
Frs. **Restaurant:** Breakfast served from 5:00am. **Hotel:**
6 beds; 2 single rooms, 4 double rooms with shower,
bath, private WC. **Other points:** bar, open to non-
residents, à la carte menu, children welcome, lounge
area, terraces, pets welcome – check for details, car
park, modern decor. **Address:** Barbeloup.
MME AGNES DUMAINE
**Telephone:** 86.37.84.03
⊗ ♇ 🏠 Map 15

## UCKANGE, Moselle, 57270

### LE PRESSOIR, RD 952

**Restaurant:** Breakfast served from 4:30am. Closed
Saturdays, in August and 15 days at Christmas. **Other
points:** bar. **Address:** 22, rue Jeanne d'Arc.
MR SILVIO PICCIN
**Telephone:** 82.58.20.38
⊗ ♇ Map 17

## UNIENVILLE, Aube, 10140

### CHEZ CHRISTIANE ET MARCEL, RD 46

**Menu:** 50 Frs (drink and coffee included). **Restaurant:**
Breakfast served from 7:30am. Lunch served from
11:30am until 1:30pm. Dinner served from 7:00pm until
8:00pm. **Specialities:** home cooking. **Other points:** bar,
pets welcome – check for details, car park.
MME CHRISTIANE SAGET
**Telephone:** 25.92.70.80
⊗ ♇ Map 18

## VARANGES, Côte-d'Or, 21110

### L'AUBERGE, RN 5

**Restaurant:** Breakfast served from 6:30am. Dinner
served from midday until 10:00pm. **Other points:** bar.
**Address:** Rue Nouvelle.
MR JEAN-PIERRE HOL
**Telephone:** 80.31.30.17
⊗ ♇ Map 15

## VARENNES LE GRAND, Saône-et-Loire, 71240

### HOTEL RESTAURANT DU COMMERCE, RN 6, between Chalon sur Saône and Lyon

Languages spoken: English. Menu: 60 Frs (wine and coffee included) to 80 Frs. Accommodation: 110 to 240 Frs. Restaurant: Breakfast served from 5:00am. Closed Saturdays. Specialities: regional menu, home cooking. Hotel: 14 beds; with shower, private WC, television, telephone. Other points: bar, open to non-residents, à la carte menu, children welcome, lounge area, terraces, pets welcome – check for details, car park. Address: Route Nationale 6.
MR BERTRAND CHAVANIS
Telephone: 85.44.22.34
⊗ 𝟈 ⌂ Map 15

## VARENNES LES MACON, Saône-et-Loire, 71000

### LA HALTE DES ROUTIERS, RN 6, Mâcon south

Accommodation: 70 to 130 Frs. Restaurant: Breakfast served from 5:30am. Dinner served from midday until 11:00pm. Closed Saturdays. Hotel: 24 beds; 18 single rooms, 6 double rooms. Other points: bar, open to non-residents, children welcome, pets welcome – check for details, car park, traditional decor. Address: Route Nationale 6.
MR RENÉ MASSONNEAU
Telephone: 85.34.70.44. Fax: 85.29.29.03
⊗ 𝟈 ⌂ Map 15

## VELAINE EN HAYE, Meurthe-et-Moselle, 54840

### LE MOUTON D'OR

Menu: 57 Frs. Restaurant: Breakfast served from 7:00am. Lunch served from 11:30am until 2:30pm. Dinner served from 7:30pm until 10:00pm. Specialities: regional menu, home cooking. Other points: bar, car park. Address: Route Nationale 4.
MME MARTINE CONTAL
Telephone: 83.23.28.71
⊗ 𝟈 Map 15

### RESTAURANT DU PARC

Menu: 60 to 80 Frs. Restaurant: Breakfast served from 8:30am. Lunch served from 11:30am until 2:00pm. Closed Saturdays. Specialities: regional menu, home cooking. Other points: bar, open to non-residents, à la carte menu, pets welcome – check for details, car park, modern decor. Address: 6, allée des Erables.
MR PATRICK HEBACKER
Telephone: 83.23.28.48
⊗ 𝟈 Map 17

## VENDENHEIM, Bas-Rhin, 67550

### LE RELAIS DE LA MAISON ROUGE, RN 63

Languages spoken: German. Menu: 55 to 125 Frs. Restaurant: Breakfast served from 7:30am. Dinner served from midday until 10:00pm. Closed Tuesdays and

1 week in February. Specialities: regional menu, home cooking. Other points: open to non-residents, à la carte menu, children welcome, terraces, pets welcome – check for details, traditional decor. Address: 2, route de Brumath.
MME GERMAINE MICHIELINI-CHAST
Telephone: 88.69.51.79
⊗ ⌐ Map 17

## VERDUN, Meuse, 55100

### A LA BONNE AUBERGE, RN 3, between the station and the road

Languages spoken: German and English. Menu: 49, 90 to 75 Frs. Accommodation: 65 to 91 Frs. Restaurant: Breakfast served from 5:30am. Dinner served from midday until midnight. Specialities: home cooking. Hotel: 7 beds; 3 single rooms, 4 double rooms. Other points: bar, open to non-residents, à la carte menu, pets welcome – check for details, traditional decor. Address: 11, avenue Garibaldi.
MME YOLANDE GAIOTTI-MORANO
Telephone: 29.86.05.16
⊗ 𝟈 ⌂ Map 17

### CAFÉ ROUTE, A 4

Languages spoken: German and English. Restaurant: Breakfast served from 7:00am. Other points: open to non-residents, à la carte menu, children welcome, lounge area, pets welcome – check for details, car park, modern decor. Address: Aire de Verdun Saint-Nicolas, accessible dans les deux sens.
MR SERGE MONCEAU
Telephone: 29.86.41.18. Fax: 29.86.64.65
⊗ Map 17

## VERMENTON, Yonne, 89270

### LE NOUVEAU RELAIS, RN 6, the main road between Paris and Lyon

Accommodation: 90 Frs. Restaurant: Breakfast served from 6:30am. Closed Sundays and mid-December to mid-January. Specialities: regional menu, home cooking. Hotel: 12 beds. Other points: bar, open to non-residents, à la carte menu, pets welcome – check for details, car park, traditional decor. Address: 74, Route Nationale 6.
MR PIERRE JEAN
Telephone: 86.81.51.51
⊗ 𝟈 ⌂ Map 15

## VILLENEUVE AU CHEMIN, Aube, 10130

### LE PETIT SAINT JEAN, RN 77, between Troyes and Auxerre

Languages spoken: Arabic. Menu: 52 to 60 Frs. Restaurant: Breakfast served from 8:00am. Lunch served from 10:00am until midday. Dinner served from

midday until 10:00pm. **Specialities:** home cooking. **Other points:** bar, open to non-residents, à la carte menu, children welcome, terraces, pets welcome – check for details, car park, traditional decor. **Address:** Route Nationale 77.
MR NAFAA NAIT MOHAND
**Telephone:** 25.42.10.51
⊗ ℉ Map 18

## VILLENEUVE L'ARCHEVEQUE,
Yonne, 89190

### L'ESCALE 60, RN 60, between Sens and Troyes
**Languages spoken:** English. **Menu:** 53 Frs. **Accommodation:** 110 to 170 Frs. **Restaurant:** Breakfast served from 7:00am. Lunch served from 11:30am until 1:30pm. Dinner served from 7:00pm until 9:00pm. Closed Saturdays. **Specialities:** home cooking. **Hotel:** 10 beds; 7 single rooms, 3 double rooms with shower. **Other points:** bar, open to non-residents, à la carte menu, terraces, pets welcome – check for details, car park, modern decor. **Address:** 10, route de Sens.
MR DOMINIQUE BOIRE
**Telephone:** 86.86.74.42
⊗ ℉ 🏠 Map 15

## VILLEVALLIER, Yonne, 89330

### RELAIS 89, RN 89, between Joigny and Sens
**Menu:** from 57 Frs. **Restaurant:** Breakfast served from 6:00am. Closed Saturdays. **Specialities:** home cooking. **Hotel:** 6 beds; 2 single rooms, 4 double rooms. **Other points:** bar, open to non-residents, à la carte menu, children welcome, terraces, pets welcome – check for details, car park, modern decor. **Address:** 9, rue de la République.
MME YVETTE PETIT
**Telephone:** 86.91.11.17
⊗ ℉ 🏠 Map 15

## VILLIERS LOUIS, Yonne, 89760

### LE TALLEYRAND, RN 60
**Languages spoken:** English. **Menu:** 53 to 95 Frs. **Restaurant:** Breakfast served from 5:00am. Lunch served from 10:30am until 3:30pm. Dinner served from 6:30pm until 10:00pm. **Other points:** bar, car park. **Address:** Route Nationale 60, le Petit Villiers.
MR MICHEL VANWYMEERSCH
**Telephone:** 86.88.24.02
⊗ ℉ Map 15

## VITRY EN CHAROLLAIS, Saône-et-Loire, 71600

### TOM BAR, between Paray le Monial and Digoin
**Languages spoken:** Spanish. **Restaurant:** Dinner served from midday until 10:30pm. **Specialities:**

regional menu. **Other points:** bar, open to non-residents, à la carte menu, children welcome, terraces, pets welcome – check for details, car park, traditional decor. **Address:** Route Nationale 79.
MR ANDRÉ BORREGO
**Telephone:** 85.81.02.85
⊗ ℉ Map 15

## VITTEAUX, Côte-d'Or, 21350

### RELAIS DE LA ROUTE BLANCHE, RN 5, Dijon
**Menu:** 50 Frs. **Restaurant:** Breakfast served from 7:00am. Lunch served from midday until 2:30pm. Dinner served from 7:30pm until 9:00pm. Closed Sundays and from mid-August to mid-September. **Specialities:** home cooking. **Other points:** bar, open to non-residents, pets welcome – check for details, car park, traditional decor. **Address:** Rue de Verdun.
MR ROGER LE GALL
**Telephone:** 80.49.60.13
⊗ ℉ Map 15

## VITTONVILLE, Meurthe-et-Moselle, 54700

### L'AIGLE D'OR, RN 57, between Metz and Nancy
**Languages spoken:** Dutch and Italian. **Menu:** 50 to 75 Frs. **Restaurant:** Breakfast served from 5:00am. Dinner served from midday until 11:30pm. Closed Saturdays. **Specialities:** home cooking. **Other points:** bar, open to non-residents, à la carte menu, children welcome, lounge area, terraces, pets welcome – check for details, car park, modern decor. **Address:** Route Nationale 57, Pont à Mousson.
ELIANE ET ERIC LANZI
**Telephone:** 83.81.04.08, 83.82.85.89
⊗ ℉ Map 17

## WASSELONNE, Bas-Rhin, 67310

### AU ROCHER, RN 4, between Saverne and Strasbourg
**Languages spoken:** German and English. **Menu:** 60 to 100 Frs. **Accommodation:** 100 to 250 Frs. **Restaurant:** Breakfast served from 6:30am. Lunch served from 11:30am until 2:30pm. Dinner served from 7:00pm until 9:00pm. Closed Sundays. **Specialities:** home cooking. **Hotel:** 8 beds; with shower, bath, private WC. **Other points:** bar, à la carte menu, children welcome, pets welcome – check for details, car park, traditional decor. **Address:** 18, route de Strasbourg.
MR ANDRÉ HECKER
**Telephone:** 88.87.06.72
⊗ ℉ 🏠 Map 17

## WITRY LES REIMS, Marne, 51420

### RELAIS 51-08, RN 51, between Charleville-Mézière and Reims

Menu: 55 to 150 Frs. **Accommodation:** 100 Frs.
**Restaurant:** Breakfast served from 5:00am. Lunch
served from midday until 2:30pm. Dinner served from
7:00pm until 10:30pm. Closed Saturdays. **Specialities:**
home cooking. **Hotel:** 4 beds; 1 single room, 3 double
rooms with shower. **Other points:** bar, open to non-
residents, à la carte menu, children welcome, terraces,
pets welcome – check for details, car park, traditional
decor. **Address:** 62, avenue de Reims.
MR ROBERT VAN HOUTTE
**Telephone:** 26.97.08.30
⊗ ♟ Map 18

## WITTELSHEIM, Haut-Rhin, 68310

### HOTEL DES VOSGES, RN 83, between Mulhouse and Thann

**Languages spoken:** German and Italian. **Menu:** 50 to
100 Frs. **Accommodation:** 130 to 160 Frs. **Restaurant:**
Breakfast served from 5:00am. Lunch served from
midday until 2:30pm. Dinner served from 7:00pm until
9:00pm. Closed Sundays. **Specialities:** regional menu,
home cooking. **Hotel:** 15 beds; 3 single rooms, 12
double rooms with shower, bath, private WC, telephone.
**Other points:** bar, open to non-residents, à la carte
menu, children welcome, car park, traditional decor.
**Address:** 137, rue de Reiningue.
MR DORIS RIEDLE
**Telephone:** 89.55.10.20
⊗ ♟ 🏠 Map 17

## WOIPPY, Moselle, 57140

### CHARDON-LORRAIN-WOIPPY, RN 412, Metz

**Languages spoken:** German. **Menu:** 50 Frs.
**Restaurant:** Breakfast served from 5:00am. Lunch
served from 11:30am until 2:30pm. Dinner served
from 7:00pm until 8:30pm. Closed Wednesdays and
from 19 December to 7 January. **Specialities:** regional
menu, home cooking. **Hotel:** 3 beds; 2 single rooms,

1 double room. **Other points:** bar, open to non-
residents, lounge area, terraces, pets welcome – check
for details, car park, modern decor. **Address:** 58, rue
de Metz.
MME FRANÇOISE DE CECCO
**Telephone:** 87.30.46.61
⊗ ♟ Map 17

## XONRUPT LONGEMER, Vosges, 88400

### LA PIERRE CHARLEMAGNE – CHEZ DÉDÉ

**Languages spoken:** German and English. **Menu:** 50 to
75 Frs (12th meal free). **Accommodation:** 100 to 140
Frs. **Restaurant:** Breakfast served from 9:00am. Lunch
served from midday until 2:30pm. Dinner served from
7:00pm until 10:00pm. Closed Mondays, 15 days in
October and 15 days in June. **Specialities:** regional
menu. **Hotel:** 6 beds; 3 single rooms, 3 double rooms
with shower, bath, private WC. **Other points:** bar, open
to non-residents, à la carte menu, children welcome, pets
welcome – check for details, car park, traditional decor.
**Address:** Le Saut des Cuves.
MR ANDRÉ CAEL
**Telephone:** 29.63.03.86
⊗ ♟ 🏠 Map 17

## YUTZ, Moselle, 57110

### CHEZ CHANTAL ET NOEL, RN 153, Trêves

**Menu:** 56 Frs. **Restaurant:** Breakfast served from
5:00am. Lunch served from 11:30am until 3:00pm.
Dinner served from 7:00pm until 10:00pm. Closed
Saturdays. **Specialities:** home cooking. **Other points:**
bar, open to non-residents, à la carte menu, children
welcome, pets welcome – check for details, car park,
modern decor. **Address:** 140, Route Nationale.
MR NOEL RUBEILLON
**Telephone:** 82.56.00.28
⊗ ♟ Map 17

# The Loire

## ABSIE (L'), Deux-Sèvres, 79240

### RESTAURANT DE LA POSTE
**Restaurant:** Breakfast served from 8:00am. Closed Sundays. **Other points:** bar. **Address:** 21, rue de la Poste.
MR EUGÈNE BIGNON
**Telephone:** 49.95.90.21
⊗ ♈ Map 7

## AIGURANDE, Indre, 36140

### LE RELAIS DE LA MARCHE, the main road between Paris and Châteauroux
**Languages spoken:** English and Spanish. **Menu:** 55 to 195 Frs. **Accommodation:** 60 to 198 Frs. **Restaurant:** Breakfast served from 7:00am. Lunch served from midday until 2:00pm. Dinner served from 7:00pm until 9:00pm. Closed Saturdays. **Specialities:** regional menu, home cooking. **Hotel:** 7 beds; 6 single rooms, 1 double room with shower, private WC, television, telephone. **Other points:** bar, open to non-residents, à la carte menu, children welcome, lounge area, terraces, pets welcome – check for details, car park. **Address:** Place du Champ de Foire.
MR JEAN-PIERRE CHAMBON
**Telephone:** 54.06.31.58
⊗ ♈ 🏠 ☆☆ Map 6

## AIRVAULT, Deux-Sèvres, 79600

### LES CHENES VERTS, RD 938, between Parthenay and Thouars
**Menu:** 47,50 (wine and coffee included) to 89 Frs. **Accommodation:** 70 to 150 Frs. **Restaurant:** Breakfast served from 6:30am. Lunch served from midday until 2:00pm. Dinner served from 7:00pm until 9:00pm. Closed Saturdays and from 15 September to 15 October. **Specialities:** home cooking. **Hotel:** 10 beds; with shower. **Other points:** bar, open to non-residents, à la carte menu, children welcome, lounge area, terraces, pets welcome – check for details, car park, traditional decor. **Address:** La Maucarrière.
MR ALAIN ROUSSEAU
**Telephone:** 49.69.71.11
⊗ ♈ 🏠 Map 7

## AIX D'ANGILLON (LES), Cher, 18220

### LE PARISIEN, at Bourges head towards Sancerre
**Menu:** 50 to 75 Frs. **Accommodation:** 90 to 140 Frs. **Restaurant:** Breakfast served from 7:00am. Lunch served from midday until 2:00pm. Dinner served from 7:30pm until 8:30pm. Closed Sundays and in August. **Specialities:** home cooking. **Hotel:** 6 beds; 4 single rooms, 2 double rooms. **Other points:** bar, open to non-residents, pets welcome – check for details, traditional decor. **Address:** 20, place du Général de Gaulle.
MR JACQUES BLANCHET
**Telephone:** 48.64.43.62
⊗ ♈ 🏠 Map 6

## ALLOGNY, Cher, 18110

### CAFE RESTAURANT DE LA MAIRIE, RD 944, between Salbris and Bourges
**Languages spoken:** English. **Menu:** 55 Frs. **Restaurant:** Breakfast served from 7:30am. Lunch served from midday until 2:00pm. Dinner served from 7:30pm until 10:00pm. Closed Thursdays. **Specialities:** regional menu, home cooking. **Other points:** bar, open to non-residents, à la carte menu, children welcome, terraces, pets welcome – check for details, car park. **Address:** Place de la Mairie.
MR NOËL HELLEGOUARCH
**Telephone:** 48.64.00.71
⊗ ♈ Map 6

## AMBOISE, Indre-et-Loire, 37400

### LE CHANTECLERC, RD 152, between Tours and Blois
**Menu:** 48 Frs. **Accommodation:** 80 to 120 Frs. **Restaurant:** Breakfast served from 6:30am. Lunch served from midday until 2:00pm. Dinner served from 7:30pm until 9:00pm. Closed Sundays. **Specialities:** auvergnates, home cooking. **Hotel:** 4 beds; 1 single room, 3 double rooms with bath. **Other points:** bar, open to non-residents, terraces, pets welcome – check for details, car park, modern decor. **Address:** 34, avenue de Tours.
MR ERIC BOITELLE
**Telephone:** 47.57.11.94
⊗ ♈ Map 6

## ANGLIERS, Vienne, 86330

### AU MILLE PATTES, RN 147, between Angers and Poitiers

**Languages spoken:** English, Spanish and Portugese.
**Menu:** 52 Frs (wine and coffee included). **Restaurant:**
Breakfast served from 5:00am. **Specialities:** saumon,
sauce Galuche, Provençales, home cooking. **Other points:**
bar, open to non-residents, à la carte menu, children
welcome, terraces, pets welcome – check for details, car
park, modern decor. **Address:** Route Nationale 147.
MME ANNICK ELMON
**Telephone:** 49.22.48.92
⊗ ♀ Map 7

## ARDENTES, Indre, 36120

### CAFE DES SPORTS, the main road between Châteauroux and Montluçon

**Menu:** 55 to 70 Frs. **Accommodation:** 75 to 140 Frs.
**Restaurant:** Breakfast served from 7:00am. Lunch served
from midday until 2:00pm. Dinner served from 7:00pm
until 8:30pm. Closed Saturdays and from 1 to 15 August.
**Specialities:** home cooking. **Hotel:** 5 beds; 2 single rooms,
3 double rooms with shower, bath, private WC. **Other
points:** bar, open to non-residents, children welcome, car
park, traditional decor. **Address:** 21, avenue de Verdun.
MME CÉCILE PASCAUD
**Telephone:** 54.36.21.19
⊗ ♀ 🏠 Map 6

### LE RELAIS DE CLAVIERES

**Accommodation:** 75 to 100 Frs. **Specialities:** home
cooking. **Hotel:** 4 beds; 3 single rooms, 1 double room
with shower. **Other points:** bar, terraces, pets welcome
– check for details, car park. **Address:** Clavières, Route
de Montluçon.
MME PASCALE PORTRAIT
**Telephone:** 54.26.98.46
⊗ ♀ Map 6

## ARGENTON SUR CREUSE, Indre, 36200

### LE RELAIS, RN 20

**Languages spoken:** English and Spanish. **Menu:** 62 to
100 Frs. **Accommodation:** 95 to 140 Frs. **Restaurant:**
Breakfast served from 7:00am. Lunch served from
midday until 2:00pm. Dinner served from 7:00pm until
8:30pm. Closed Sundays and from 15 December to 15
January. **Specialities:** coq au vin, coquilles de crabes,
andouillettes grillées, home cooking. **Hotel:** 6 beds; 4
single rooms, 2 double rooms with shower, bath, private
WC. **Other points:** bar, open to non-residents, à la carte
menu, children welcome, lounge area, terraces, pets
welcome – check for details, car park, traditional decor.
**Address:** 7, rue du Président Fruchon, Saint Marcel.
MME MAURICETTE CALMEL
**Telephone:** 54.24.01.77
⊗ ♀ 🏠 ⟡ Map 6

## ASCOUX, Loiret, 45300

### AUBERGE SAINT ELOI, RN 721

**Accommodation:** 130 Frs. **Restaurant:** Dinner
served from midday until 9:00pm. Closed Sundays.
**Specialities:** home cooking. **Hotel:** 10 beds; 10
single rooms. **Other points:** bar, open to non-
residents, car park, traditional decor. **Address:** 1, rue
de Pithiviers.
SDF ROBILLARD-DAROUX
**Telephone:** 38.33.00.20
⊗ ♀ 🏠 Map 6

## AUBIERS (LES), Deux-Sèvres, 79250

### LE CHEVAL BLANC

**Restaurant:** Breakfast served from 9:00am. Lunch
served from midday until 2:00pm. Closed Saturdays and
in August. **Specialities:** home cooking. **Hotel:** 2 beds;
with shower, private WC. **Other points:** bar, open to
non-residents, car park. **Address:** 9, place Saint Mélaine.
MME MARCELLE SAUER
**Telephone:** 49.65.60.51
⊗ ♀ Map 6

## AUBIGNY SUR NERE, Cher, 18700

### LES ROUTIER, RN 940, the main road between Gien and Vierzon

**Menu:** 48 Frs. **Accommodation:** 80 to 104 Frs.
**Restaurant:** Breakfast served from 7:00am. Lunch
served from 11:00am until 1:30pm. Dinner served from
7:30pm until 9:30pm. Closed Saturdays, in August and 1
week at Christmas. **Specialities:** regional menu. **Hotel:**
9 beds; 9 double rooms with shower. **Other points:** bar,
open to non-residents, pets welcome – check for details,
car park, traditional decor. **Address:** 17, avenue Charles
Lefèbvre.
MR BERNARD OLLIER
**Telephone:** 48.58.01.42
⊗ ♀ 🏠 Map 6

## AUNEAU, Eure-et-Loir, 28700

### AUX TROIS MARCHES, A11 exit Ablis / A10 exit Allainville

**Menu:** 50 Frs. **Accommodation:** 100 to 160 Frs.
**Restaurant:** Breakfast served from 6:00am. Lunch
served from 11:00am until 2:30pm. Dinner served from
7:00pm until 9:00pm. Closed Saturdays, public holidays
and in August. **Specialities:** home cooking. **Hotel:** 8
beds; 1 single room, 7 double rooms. **Other points:** bar,
open to non-residents, children welcome, pets welcome
– check for details, car park, traditional decor. **Address:**
2, rue Emile Labiche.
RÉGINE ET CHRISTIAN SÉTTAOUI-GASNIER
**Telephone:** 37.31.70.49
⊗ ♀ 🏠 Map 6

## AUSSAC VADALLE, Charente, 16560

### *LA BELLE CANTINIERE, RN 10, the main road between Poitiers and Bordeaux*

**Languages spoken:** English and Spanish. **Menu:** 55 Frs. **Restaurant:** Breakfast served from 5:00am. Lunch served from 11:30am until 3:00pm. Dinner served from 7:00pm until 11:00pm. Closed Saturdays. **Specialities:** fruits de mer; fruits de mer, home cooking. **Hotel:** with shower, private WC, television, telephone. **Other points:** bar, open to non-residents, children welcome, terraces, pets welcome – check for details, car park, traditional decor. **Address:** Route Nationale 10.
MME CLAUDY JUDES
**Telephone:** 45.20.66.89. **Fax:** 45.20.71.99
⊗ 🍷 Map 7

## AZAY LE FERRON, Indre, 36290

### *L'UNION*

**Menu:** 50 to 110 Frs. **Restaurant:** Breakfast served from 8:00am. Dinner served from 8:00pm until 9:00pm. Closed Mondays. **Specialities:** home cooking. **Other points:** bar, open to non-residents, à la carte menu, children welcome, pets welcome – check for details, car park, traditional decor. **Address:** Place de l'Eglise.
MR THIERRY AUDOIN
**Telephone:** 54.39.20.88
⊗ 🍷 Map 6

## AZAY LE RIDEAU, Indre-et-Loire, 37190

### *RESTAURANT DE LA GARE, RD 57*

**Languages spoken:** English. **Menu:** 48 to 70 Frs. **Restaurant:** Breakfast served from 7:00am. Lunch served from midday until 2:30pm. Dinner served from 7:00pm until 9:30pm. Closed Sundays. **Specialities:** home cooking. **Other points:** bar, open to non-residents, pets welcome – check for details, car park, traditional decor. **Address:** 59, avenue de la Gare.
MR PATRICK VITEL
**Telephone:** 47.45.40.60
⊗ 🍷 Map 6

## BARBEZIEUX, Charente, 16360

### *LA CAMBROUSSE, RN 10, between Angoulême and Bordeaux*

**Menu:** 57 Frs. **Accommodation:** 90 to 110 Frs. **Restaurant:** Open 24 hours. **Specialities:** home cooking. **Hotel:** 13 beds; 10 single rooms, 3 double rooms with shower, private WC. **Other points:** bar, open to non-residents, car park, traditional decor. **Address:** Le Pont du Noble, la Tatre.
MR JEAN-CLAUDE PICHON
**Telephone:** 45.78.52.83
⊗ 🍷 🏠 Map 7

## BARBEZIEUX SAINT HILAIRE, Charente, 16120

### *RELAIS DE LA BILLETTE, RN 10, 20km south Angoulême/10km north Barbezieux*

**Menu:** 68 to 120 Frs. **Restaurant:** Open 24 hours. **Specialities:** Confit de canard, escalope à la Charentaise, magret de canard, regional food, home cooking. **Other points:** bar, open to non-residents, à la carte menu, pets welcome – check for details, car park, traditional decor. **Address:** Ladiville.
MME DANIELLE HOUDUSSE
**Telephone:** 45.78.57.09, 45.78.58.47. **Fax:** 45.78.35.33
⊗ 🍷 Map 7

## BARMAINVILLE, Eure-et-Loir, 28310

### *RELAIS DES BOISSEAUX, RN 20, the main road between Paris and Orléans*

**Menu:** 55 to 65 Frs. **Restaurant:** Breakfast served from 5:00am. Lunch served from midday until 2:00pm. Dinner served from 7:00pm until 11:00pm. Closed Saturdays and in August. **Specialities:** home cooking. **Other points:** bar, open to non-residents, children welcome, pets welcome – check for details, car park, traditional decor. **Address:** La Poste de Boisseaux.
MME NADINE BAUGER
**Telephone:** 38.39.61.20
⊗ 🍷 Map 6

## BAZOCHE GOUET (LA), Eure-et-Loir, 28330

### *LA BONNE AUBERGE, RD 927, the main road between Chartres and le Mans*

**Menu:** 45 to 75 Frs. **Restaurant:** Breakfast served from 7:00am. Closed Sundays, 15 days in February and 15 days in July. **Specialities:** regional menu, home cooking. **Other points:** bar, open to non-residents, children welcome, car park, traditional decor. **Address:** 54, avenue du Général Leclerc.
MR JEAN-PAUL THIERRY
**Telephone:** 37.49.21.61
⊗ 🍷 Map 6

## BAZOCHES EN DUNOIS, Eure-et-Loir, 28140

### *AU BON ACCUEIL, RN 927, Chartres/Orléans/Châteaudun*

**Menu:** 50 Frs. **Restaurant:** Lunch served from 11:00am until 3:00pm. Closed 1 week in September. **Specialities:** home cooking. **Other points:** bar, open to non-residents, children welcome, pets welcome – check for details, car park, traditional decor. **Address:** 7, rue de l'Eglise.
MME MARIE-CLAUDE BOUCHER
**Telephone:** 37.22.08.30
⊗ 🍷 Map 6

## BEAUNE LA ROLANDE, Loiret, 45340

### HOTEL DE LA GARE, the main road between Orléans and Paris

**Menu:** 55 Frs (wine and coffee included) to 145 Frs. **Accommodation:** 170 to 230 Frs. **Restaurant:** Breakfast served from 7:00am. Lunch served from midday until 3:00pm. Dinner served from 7:00pm until 10:00pm. Closed Tuesdays. **Specialities:** regional menu, home cooking. **Hotel:** 10 beds; 6 single rooms, 4 double rooms. **Other points:** bar, open to non-residents, à la carte menu, children welcome, terraces, pets welcome – check for details, car park, traditional decor. **Address:** 25, gare d'Auxy.
MR THIERRY DEVOUCOUX
**Telephone:** 38.96.70.44
⊗ ♀ ⌂ Map 6

## BEAUVOIR SUR NIORT, Deux-Sèvres, 79360

### L'ETAPE, RN 150, between Saint Jean de Angély and Niort

**Languages spoken:** a little English. **Menu:** 53 Frs (wine and coffee included) and 70 Frs. **Restaurant:** Lunch served from midday until 2:00pm. Dinner served from 7:00pm until 9:00pm. Closed Sundays. **Specialities:** regional menu, home cooking. **Other points:** bar, à la carte menu, terraces, pets welcome – check for details, car park. **Address:** 7, place de l'Hôtel de Ville.
MME ANNICK DUVERNE
**Telephone:** 49.09.70.17
⊗ ♀ Map 7

## BEDENAC, Charente-Maritime, 17210

### ESCAGRILL, RN 10, the main road between Angoulême and Bordeaux

**Languages spoken:** German, English, Spanish and Italian. **Menu:** 57 (wine included) to 105 Frs. **Restaurant:** Breakfast served from 5:00am. Dinner served from midday until midnight. **Specialities:** regional menu, home cooking. **Other points:** bar, open to non-residents, à la carte menu, children welcome, terraces, pets welcome – check for details, car park, modern decor. **Address:** Route Nationale 10.
MME MARYLINE HUDELOT
**Telephone:** 46.04.45.42
⊗ ♀ Map 7

## BEURLAY, Charente-Maritime, 17250

### LE RELAIS D'ARY, RN 137, between Rochefort and Saintes

**Languages spoken:** Spanish. **Menu:** 30 to 60 Frs. **Restaurant:** Breakfast served from 6:30am. Lunch served from 10:00am until 3:00pm. Dinner served from

7:00pm until midnight. Closed Sundays. **Specialities:** home cooking. **Other points:** bar, open to non-residents, à la carte menu, terraces, car park, traditional decor. **Address:** 1, route de Rochefort.
MR YVES MARIAUD
**Telephone:** 46.95.01.39
⊗ ♀ Map 7

## BLANC (LE), Indre, 36300

### LE REFLET DES ILES

**Menu:** 49 to 120 Frs. **Restaurant:** Dinner served from midday until 9:00pm. Closed Mondays. **Other points:** bar, car park. **Address:** Lieu dit 'Visais'.
MR SERGE MARIE
**Telephone:** 54.37.4.33
⊗ ♀ Map 6

## BLERE, Indre-et-Loire, 37150

### LE RELAIS, RN 76, the main road between Tours and Vierzon

**Languages spoken:** English. **Menu:** 58 to 80 Frs. **Restaurant:** Breakfast served from 8:00am. Lunch served from midday until 2:30pm. Dinner served from 7:00pm until 9:30pm. **Specialities:** home cooking. **Other points:** bar, open to non-residents, à la carte menu, children welcome, pets welcome – check for details, car park, modern decor. **Address:** 48, rue de Tours.
MME PAULETTE ROSSIGNOL
**Telephone:** 47.57.92.31
⊗ ♀ Map 6

## BLOIS, Loir-et-Cher, 41000

### BAR DE LA CITE, RD 951, town centre, towards Vendôme

**Menu:** 50 Frs (wine included). **Restaurant:** Breakfast served from 6:00am. Lunch served from midday until 2:00pm. Dinner served from 7:30pm until 9:00pm. Closed Saturdays. **Specialities:** home cooking. **Other points:** bar, open to non-residents, children welcome, lounge area, terraces, pets welcome – check for details, car park, modern decor. **Address:** 55, avenue de Vendôme.
MR DIDIER MOREAU
**Telephone:** 54.43.48.54
⊗ ♀ Map 6

### L'ARCHE DE BLOIS, A 10

**Languages spoken:** English. **Restaurant:** Open 24 hours. **Other points:** open to non-residents, à la carte menu, children welcome, terraces, pets welcome – check for details, car park. **Address:** A 10 Aire de Blois-Villerbon, sens Bordeaux/Paris.
MR VINCENT STAELENS
**Telephone:** 54.46.81.71. **Fax:** 54.46.84.77
⊗ Map 6

## BOIS DE FEUGERE, Eure-et-Loir, 28800

### RELAIS ROUTIER DU BOIS DE FEUGERE, RN 10, between Chartres and Châteaudun

**Languages spoken:** English and German. **Menu:** 52 to 66 Frs. **Restaurant:** Breakfast served from 4:00am. Closed Saturdays. **Specialities:** home cooking. **Other points:** bar, open to non-residents, à la carte menu, children welcome, pets welcome – check for details, car park, traditional decor. **Address:** 26, Route Nationale.
MR ALAIN LAURENT
**Telephone:** 37.96.33.01
⊗ ? Map 6

## BORDS, Charente-Maritime, 17430

### CAFE DU CENTRE, RN 137, between Rochefort and Saintes

**Restaurant:** Breakfast served from 7:00am. **Specialities:** home cooking. **Other points:** bar, open to non-residents, pets welcome – check for details, traditional decor. **Address:** Place de l'Eglise.
MR MARTIAL PERROCHEAU
**Telephone:** 46.83.84.31
⊗ ? Map 7

## BOSSEE, Indre-et-Loire, 37240

### AUX DELICES ANTILLAIS, RD 760, between Chinon and Loches

**Languages spoken:** English and Spanish. **Menu:** 56 Frs (wine included) to 135 Frs. **Restaurant:** Breakfast served from 7:00am. Lunch served from 11:45am until 3:00pm. Dinner served from 7:00pm until 11:00pm. Closed Mondays and in February. **Specialities:** regional menu, home cooking. **Other points:** bar, open to non-residents, à la carte menu, children welcome, terraces, pets welcome – check for details, car park, modern decor. **Address:** Route Départementale 760.
MME NICOLE LE LAIN
**Telephone:** 47.92.88.27
⊗ ? Map 6

## BOULAY LES BARRES, Loiret, 45140

### AUBERGE DE LA ROUTE, RN 155

**Restaurant:** Dinner served from midday until 10:00pm. Closed Saturdays and August. **Hotel:** 5 beds. **Other points:** bar. **Address:** 21, route d'Orléans.
MR JACKY GASNOT
**Telephone:** 38.75.34.90
⊗ ? 🏠 Map 6

## BOURGES, Cher, 18000

### LES AILES, RN 151, Châteauroux

**Languages spoken:** English. **Menu:** 46 to 75 Frs.

**Accommodation:** 100 to 170 Frs. **Restaurant:** Breakfast served from 6:00am. Lunch served from midday until 2:00pm. Dinner served from 7:30pm until 10:00pm. Closed Saturdays, 15 days in August and 8 days before Christmas Day. **Specialities:** home cooking. **Hotel:** 16 beds; 9 single rooms, 7 double rooms. **Other points:** bar, open to non-residents, à la carte menu, pets welcome – check for details, car park. **Address:** 147, avenue Marcel Haegelen.
SARL LES AILES
**Telephone:** 48.21.57.86
⊗ ? 🏠 Map 6

### RELAIS DU BERRY, A 71

**Other points:** à la carte menu, children welcome, terraces, pets welcome – check for details, car park. **Address:** Aire de Service de Farges-Allichamps, dans les deux sens.
Map 6

## BOURRAS, Charente, 16200

### RELAIS DES VIGNES, RN 141, between Cognac and Angoulême

**Menu:** 50 to 53,50 Frs. **Restaurant:** Breakfast served from 7:30am. Lunch served from 11:30am until 2:30pm. Dinner served from 7:30pm until 10:00pm. Closed Sundays and from 15 August to 15 September. **Specialities:** home cooking. **Other points:** bar, open to non-residents, children welcome, terraces, pets welcome – check for details, car park.
MME MONIQUE DELAVOIE
**Telephone:** 45.35.81.62, 45.35.83.16
⊗ ? Map 7

## BRECHES, Indre-et-Loire, 37330

### RESTAURANT ROUTIERS, RD 766, between Angers and Blois

**Menu:** 56,50 Frs. **Restaurant:** Breakfast served from 6:00am. Closed Saturdays and in August. **Specialities:** home cooking. **Other points:** bar, open to non-residents, traditional decor. **Address:** Lieu dit 'Le Bel Air'.
MME ANITA VAILLANT
**Telephone:** 47.24.13.03
⊗ ? Map 6

## BRIARE, Loiret, 45250

### LE RELAIS, RN 7

**Menu:** 55 to 65 Frs. **Accommodation:** 75 to 85 Frs. **Restaurant:** Breakfast served from 5:00am. Closed Saturdays. **Specialities:** home cooking. **Hotel:** 9 beds; 2 single rooms, 7 double rooms with shower. **Other points:** bar, open to non-residents, children welcome, pets welcome – check for details, car park, traditional decor. **Address:** Gare de Chatillon sur Loire.
MR ERIC BOURGOIN
**Telephone:** 38.31.44.42
⊗ ? 🏠 Map 6

## BRIE, Charente, 16590

### L'AUBERGE DES ROUTIERS, RN 141, the main road between Limoges and Bordeaux

**Menu:** 55 to 65 Frs. **Restaurant:** Breakfast served from 4:30am. Closed Saturdays and in August. **Specialities:** home cooking. **Other points:** bar, open to non-residents, children welcome, lounge area, pets welcome – check for details, car park, traditional decor. **Address:** Les Rassats.
SARL DORÉ ET FILS
**Telephone:** 45.65.90.24
⊗ ⲩ Map 7

## BRION PRÈS THOUET, Deux-Sèvres, 79290

### LE RELAIS DE BRION, RD 938, the main road between Saumur and Thouars

**Languages spoken:** German and English. **Menu:** 52 to 90 Frs. **Accommodation:** 100 to 150 Frs. **Restaurant:** Breakfast served from 6:15am. Lunch served from 11:30am until 2:00pm. Dinner served from 7:00pm until 9:00pm. Closed Sundays and the last 3 weeks of August. **Specialities:** home cooking. **Hotel:** 2 beds; 1 single room, 1 double room with shower. **Other points:** bar, open to non-residents, à la carte menu, children welcome, terraces, pets welcome – check for details, car park, traditional decor. **Address:** 39, rue Principale.
MR ALAIN BRUNELEAU
**Telephone:** 49.67.73.34
⊗ ⲩ Map 7

## BRIOUX SUR BOUTONNE, Deux-Sèvres, 79170

### AUBERGE DU CHEVAL BLANC, between Poitiers and Saint Jean d'Angély

**Menu:** 50 Frs (wine included) to 100 Frs. **Restaurant:** Breakfast served from 6:30am. Lunch served from 11:00am until 3:00pm. Dinner served from 6:00pm until 10:00pm. **Specialities:** regional menu, home cooking. **Other points:** bar, open to non-residents, à la carte menu, children welcome, terraces, pets welcome – check for details, car park, traditional decor. **Address:** 23, place du Champ de Foire.
MME PIERRETTE ANDRÉ
**Telephone:** 49.07.52.08
⊗ ⲩ Map 7

## BROU, Eure-et-Loir, 28160

### HOTEL DE LA GARE, RD 955, between Alençon and Orléans

**Menu:** 50 Frs. **Accommodation:** 130 to 148 Frs. **Restaurant:** Breakfast served from 6:00am. Lunch served from 11:00am until 2:00pm. Dinner served from 7:00pm until 9:00pm. Closed Sundays and in December.

**Specialities:** home cooking. **Hotel:** 8 beds; 3 single rooms, 5 double rooms with shower. **Other points:** bar, open to non-residents, children welcome, pets welcome – check for details, car park, traditional decor. **Address:** 76, avenue du Général de Gaulle.
MR ALAIN DUPARC
**Telephone:** 32.44.00.81
⊗ ⲩ 🏠 Map 6

## BUZANCAIS, Indre, 36500

### LE RELAIS DES ROUTIERS, RN 151, between Tours and Châteauroux

**Menu:** 50 to 60 Frs. **Accommodation:** 80 Frs. **Restaurant:** Breakfast served from 6:30am. Lunch served from midday until 1:15pm. Dinner served from 7:30pm until 8:30pm. Closed Sundays and in August. **Specialities:** home cooking. **Hotel:** 9 beds; 5 single rooms, 4 double rooms with shower. **Other points:** bar, open to non-residents, terraces, pets welcome – check for details, car park, traditional decor. **Address:** 15–19, rue des Hervaux.
MME RÉGINE IMBERT
**Telephone:** 54.84.07.37
⊗ ⲩ 🏠 Map 6

## CELLE SAINT AVANT (LA), Indre-et-Loire, 37160

### LA CARAVANE, RN 10, between Poitiers and Tours

**Menu:** 55 (wine included) to 65 Frs. **Accommodation:** 60 to 150 Frs. **Restaurant:** Breakfast served from 5:00am. Lunch served from 11:30am until 3:00pm. Dinner served from 7:00pm until 11:00pm. **Specialities:** home cooking. **Hotel:** 8 beds; 4 single rooms, 4 double rooms. **Other points:** bar, open to non-residents, children welcome, pets welcome – check for details, car park, traditional decor. **Address:** Route Nationale 10.
MR JACKY BAUDOUIN
**Telephone:** 47.65.07.82
⊗ ⲩ 🏠 Map 6

## CELON, Indre, 36200

### LES ROUTIERS, RN 20, the main road between Paris and Toulouse

**Menu:** 60 to 90 Frs. **Restaurant:** Closed Sundays. **Specialities:** regional menu, home cooking. **Other points:** bar, open to non-residents, children welcome, pets welcome – check for details, car park, modern decor.
MR MAURICE DUFOUR
**Telephone:** 54.25.32.08, 54.25.34.18
⊗ ⲩ Map 6

## CHAINGY, Loiret, 45161

### LE RELAIS DE FOURNEAUX

**Languages spoken:** English. **Restaurant:** Closed

Sundays. **Other points:** bar. **Address:** Route Nationale 152.
MR CARLOS DE SOUSA
**Telephone:** 38.80.69.12
⊗ ♉ Map 6

## CHAMPAGNE MOUTON, Charente, 16350

*HOTEL PLAISANCE, RN 740, between Ruffec and Confolens*
**Menu:** 60 to 150 Frs. **Accommodation:** 150 to 200 Frs.
**Restaurant:** Breakfast served from 7:00am. Lunch served from midday until 2:00pm. Dinner served from 7:00pm until 9:00pm. **Specialities:** regional menu, home cooking. **Hotel:** 15 beds; 7 single rooms, 8 double rooms with shower, bath, private WC. **Other points:** bar, open to non-residents, à la carte menu, children welcome, lounge area, terraces, pets welcome – check for details, car park, modern decor. **Address:** Place du Château.
MME DENISE DELHOUME
**Telephone:** 45.31.80.52, 45.31.98.19
⊗ ♉ ⌂ ☆ Map 7

## CHAMPROND EN GATINE, Eure-et-Loir, 28240

*RELAIS DE CHAMPROND, RN 23*
**Restaurant:** Closed Sundays and from 15 to 30 August.
**Other points:** bar. **Address:** 5, Grande Rue.
MR MICHEL JONNIER
**Telephone:** 37.49.82.16
⊗ ♉ Map 6

## CHAPELLE D' ANGILLON (LA), Cher, 18380

*LE RELAIS DES ROUTIERS, RD 30*
**Restaurant:** Closed Saturdays. **Other points:** bar.
**Address:** Route Départementale 30.
MME GEORGETTE CHAMPION
**Telephone:** 48.58.06.36
⊗ ♉ Map 6

## CHAPELLE SAINT LAURENT (LA), Deux-Sèvres, 79430

*CAFE DES SPORTS, RN 748, between Niort and Angers*
**Menu:** from 49,50 Frs. **Restaurant:** Breakfast served from 7:00am. Lunch served from 11:30am until 2:00pm. Dinner served from 7:30pm until 9:00pm. Closed Saturdays. **Specialities:** regional menu, home cooking. **Other points:** bar, open to non-residents, children welcome, pets welcome – check for details, car park, traditional decor. **Address:** 6, route de Bressuire.
LOUISETTE ET ANDRÉ GUÉRIN
**Telephone:** 49.72.05.64
⊗ ♉ Map 7

## CHAPELLE SAINT SEPULCRE (LA), Loiret, 45210

*LA POTENCE, RN 60*
**Restaurant:** Closed Saturdays, Sundays and 15 days in June. **Other points:** bar. **Address:** Route Nationale 60.
MME LILIANE VISIER
**Telephone:** 38.92.03.10
⊗ ♉ Map 6

## CHAPELLE SUR LOIRE (LA), Indre-et-Loire, 37140

*LE RELAIS DE LA MAIRIE, RN 152, the main road between Tours and Saumur*
**Menu:** 50 to 98 Frs. **Accommodation:** 130 to 190 Frs.
**Restaurant:** Breakfast served from 6:00am. Lunch served from midday until 3:00pm. Dinner served from 7:00pm until 10:00pm. **Specialities:** regional menu, home cooking. **Hotel:** 12 beds; with private WC, television, telephone. **Other points:** bar, à la carte menu, children welcome, terraces, car park, traditional decor. **Address:** Place Albert Ruelle.
MR JACQUES JOYEAU
**Telephone:** 47.97.34.07
⊗ ♉ ⌂ Map 6

*LE ZEBRE A CARREAUX, RN 152*
**Languages spoken:** German, English and Flemish.
**Menu:** 45 Frs. **Restaurant:** Breakfast served from 6:00am. **Other points:** bar, car park. **Address:** Le Bourg.
MR RAYMOND NOËL
**Telephone:** 47.97.45.50
⊗ ♉ Map 6

## CHARENTON DU CHER, Cher, 18210

*LA BONNE TABLE, RN 151 Bis*
**Restaurant:** Breakfast served from 6:30am. Dinner served from midday until 10:00pm. Closed Tuesdays and in August. **Specialities:** home cooking. **Other points:** bar, open to non-residents, pets welcome – check for details, car park. **Address:** 36, rue Nationale.
MME ANTOINETTE FRÈGE
**Telephone:** 48.60.72.73
⊗ ♉ Map 6

*LE FAISAN DORE, Châteauroux/ Bourges/Moulin*
**Languages spoken:** Spanish. **Menu:** 56 Frs (wine and coffee included) to 90 Frs. **Restaurant:** Breakfast served from 7:00am. Lunch served from 11:00am until 2:30pm. Dinner served from 7:00pm until 9:00pm. Closed Tuesdays. **Specialities:** home cooking. **Other points:** bar, open to non-residents, à la carte menu, children welcome, terraces, pets welcome – check for details, car park, traditional decor. **Address:** Laugère.
MME CARMEN VILLE
**Telephone:** 48.60.75.38
⊗ ♉ Map 6

## CHARSONVILLE, Loiret, 45130

### LES ROUTIERS, RN 157, the main road between Orléans and le Mans

**Menu:** 44 Frs. **Restaurant:** Breakfast served from 5:00am. Lunch served from 11:45am until 2:15pm. Closed Sundays and in August. **Specialities:** regional menu, home cooking. **Other points:** bar, open to non-residents, pets welcome – check for details, car park, traditional decor. **Address:** 15, rue de la Libération.
MR PATRICK BILLARD
**Telephone:** 38.74.23.00
⊗ ☿ Map 6

## CHARTRES, Eure-et-Loir, 28000

### RELAIS BEAUCERON, A 11 and RN 10, the main road between Chartres and Tours

**Languages spoken:** English and Spanish. **Menu:** 69 to 135 Frs. **Accommodation:** 190 to 220 Frs. **Restaurant:** Breakfast served from 6:00am. Lunch served from 11:45am until 2:30pm. Dinner served from 6:45pm until 10:30pm. Closed Saturdays. **Specialities:** oeufs à la Chartres, côte de boeuf au gris meunier, home cooking. **Hotel:** 30 beds; 30 double rooms with shower, bath, private WC, television, telephone. **Other points:** bar, open to non-residents, à la carte menu, children welcome, lounge area, terraces, pets welcome – check for details, car park, traditional decor. **Address:** Route Nationale 10, Mignières.
MR LICHET
**Telephone:** 37.26.46.21. **Fax:** 37.26.30.64
⊗ ☿ 🏠 🍽 ☆☆ Map 6

### RESTAURANT LE PALMIER, RN 10, 250m from station

**Menu:** 48 to 98 Frs. **Restaurant:** Lunch served from 11:30am until 3:00pm. Dinner served from 7:00pm until 10:00pm. **Specialities:** regional menu, home cooking. **Other points:** bar, open to non-residents, à la carte menu, traditional decor. **Address:** 20, rue Saint Maurice.
MR BOUSSAD NAAR
**Telephone:** 37.21.13.89
⊗ ☿ 🍽 Map 6

## CHATEAU GAILLARD SANTILLY, Eure-et-Loir, 28310

### AU ROUTIER GAILLARD CHEZ LILI, RN 20

**Restaurant:** Dinner served from midday until midnight. Closed Saturday evenings and Sundays. **Other points:** bar. **Address:** 1, rue Charles Péguy.
MME LILIANE BOIDROU
**Telephone:** 37.90.07.03
⊗ ☿ Map 6

### LE RELAIS 20

**Languages spoken:** Spanish, Portugese. **Menu:** 56 Frs. **Restaurant:** Breakfast served from 4:00am. Closed Saturdays. **Other points:** bar, open to non-residents, lounge area, pets welcome – check for details, car park, modern decor. **Address:** 33, rue Charles Pefuy.
MRS DAHMANI FRÈRES
**Telephone:** 37.90.07.33. **Fax:** 37.90.07.33
⊗ ☿ Map 6

## CHATEAU LA VALLIERE, Indre-et-Loire, 37330

### LE GRAND CERF, RD 959, the main road between Tour and Laval, between le Lude and Château la Vallière

**Languages spoken:** English. **Menu:** 54 to 280 Frs. **Accommodation:** 130 to 240 Frs. **Restaurant:** Breakfast served from 7:00am. Lunch served from midday until 2:00pm. Dinner served from 7:00pm until 9:00pm. Closed Saturdays and from 25 October to 15 November. **Specialities:** rillette de la Sarthe, ris de veau, aiguillette de canard, regional food, home cooking. **Hotel:** 24 beds; 24 double rooms with shower, private WC, television, telephone. **Other points:** bar, open to non-residents, à la carte menu, children welcome, terraces, pets welcome – check for details, car park, modern decor. **Address:** La Porerie.
MR JEAN MEUNIER
**Telephone:** 47.24.11.06. **Fax:** 47.24.18.95
⊗ ☿ 🏠 ☆☆ Map 6

## CHATEAUBERNARD, Charente, 16100

### PENSION DU CAMP, between Cognac and Bordeaux

**Languages spoken:** English. **Menu:** 50 to 80 Frs. **Accommodation:** 100 to 175 Frs. **Restaurant:** Breakfast served from 6:00am. Dinner served from 7:00pm until 11:00pm. Closed Fridays. **Specialities:** home cooking. **Hotel:** 3 beds; 3 double rooms with shower. **Other points:** bar, open to non-residents, children welcome, terraces, car park, modern decor. **Address:** Route de Barbezieux.
MR JEAN-LOUIS BRUNO
**Telephone:** 45.82.09.47
⊗ ☿ Map 7

## CHATEAUROUX, Indre, 36000

### BAR DE L AVENUE, RN 20

**Languages spoken:** English. **Restaurant:** Closed Sundays. **Other points:** bar. **Address:** 1, avenue de la Manufacture.
MR LAURENT GUILLOT
**Telephone:** 54.34.09.27
⊗ ☿ Map 6

## CHATELLERAULT, Vienne, 86100

*L'ARCHE DE CHATELLERAULT ANTRAN, A 10*
**Menu:** 59 Frs. **Restaurant:** Open 24 hours. **Other points:** open to non-residents, terraces, pets welcome – check for details, car park, modern decor. **Address:** A 10 Aire d'Antran, accessible dans les deux sens.
**Telephone:** 49.02.72.04
⊗ Map 7

## CHATILLON LE ROI, Loiret, 45480

*LE DAGOBERT, RD 927, between Pithiviers and Toury*
**Menu:** 55 Frs (wine included). **Restaurant:** Breakfast served from 6:30am. Lunch served from 11:30am until midday. Dinner served from 7:00pm until midday. **Specialities:** home cooking. **Other points:** bar, open to non-residents, à la carte menu, children welcome, pets welcome – check for details, car park, traditional decor. **Address:** 41, rue du Château.
MME LÉONE ROULLET
**Telephone:** 38.39.97.12
⊗ 🍸 Map 6

## CHATILLON SUR INDRE, Indre, 36700

*AUBERGE DE LA PROMENADE, RN 143*
**Places of interest:** Limoges, Rocamadour, Pompadour, Oradour sur Glane, vallée de la Dordogne. **Menu:** from 55 Frs. **Accommodation:** 180 to 220 Frs. **Restaurant:** Breakfast served from 7:00am. Lunch served from 11:00am until 2:00pm. Dinner served from 7:00pm until 9:30pm. **Specialities:** home cooking. **Hotel:** 7 beds; 6 single rooms, 1 double room with shower, bath, private WC, telephone. **Other points:** bar, open to non-residents, children welcome, terraces, pets welcome – check for details, car park, traditional decor. **Address:** 88, Rue Grande.
MR PASCAL BOUQUIN
**Telephone:** 54.38.80.79
⊗ 🍸 🏠 ☆ Map 6

*LE RELAIS DU MAIL, RN 143*
**Menu:** 48 Frs. **Accommodation:** 90 to 190 Frs. **Restaurant:** Lunch served from midday until midday. Dinner served from 7:00pm until 9:00pm. Closed 10 days at All Saints' holiday. **Specialities:** home cooking. **Hotel:** 5 beds; with bath. **Other points:** bar, pets welcome – check for details, car park, traditional decor. **Address:** Boulevard du Général Leclerc.
MME HUGUETTE SORET
**Telephone:** 54.38.71.21
⊗ 🍸 🏠 Map 6

## CHATRES SUR CHER, Loir et Cher, 41320

*LES ROUTIERS, RN 76, between Tours and Vierzon*
**Menu:** 55 Frs. **Restaurant:** Breakfast served from 7:00am. Lunch served from midday until 2:00pm. Closed Sundays and the 2nd fortnight of August. **Specialities:** home cooking. **Other points:** bar, children welcome, pets welcome – check for details, car park, traditional decor. **Address:** 60, rue du 11 novembre.
MME GÉRARD COUTAUD
**Telephone:** 54.98.01.93
⊗ 🍸 Map 6

## CHAUNAY BOURG, Vienne, 86510

*LE COMMERCE, RN 10, the main road between Poitiers (40km) and Bordeaux*
**Languages spoken:** English. **Menu:** 55 Frs (wine included) to 98 Frs. **Accommodation:** 120 to 180 Frs. **Restaurant:** Breakfast served from 6:00am. Lunch served from midday until 2:30pm. Dinner served from 7:00pm until 10:30pm. **Specialities:** regional menu, home cooking. **Hotel:** 8 beds; 6 single rooms, 2 double rooms with shower, bath. **Other points:** à la carte menu, children welcome, lounge area, terraces, pets welcome – check for details, car park, traditional decor. **Address:** 60, rue du 11 novembre.
MR LE ROUX PATRICK
**Telephone:** 49.59.02.71
⊗ 🏠 ☆ Map 7

## CHAUVIGNY, Vienne, 86300

*RESTAURANT DU MARCHE, RN 151, the main road between Poitiers and Châteauroux*
**Menu:** 46 to 58 Frs. **Restaurant:** Breakfast served from 7:30am. Lunch served from midday until 2:00pm. Dinner served from 7:30pm until 9:00pm. Closed Thursdays and from 15 September to 15 October. **Specialities:** home cooking. **Other points:** bar, open to non-residents, terraces, pets welcome – check for details, car park, modern decor. **Address:** 8, place du Marché.
MR JOËL TORSAT
**Telephone:** 49.46.32.34
⊗ 🍸 Map 7

## CHICHE, Deux-Sèvres, 79350

*CHEZ JACQUES, RN 149*
**Menu:** 40 to 55 Frs. **Restaurant:** Breakfast served from 7:30am. Closed Wednesdays, 15 days in August and between Christmas Day and New Year's Day. **Specialities:** home cooking. **Other points:** bar, pets welcome – check for details, car park. **Address:** 27, place Saint Martin.
MR JACQUES VINCENT
**Telephone:** 49.72.40.51
⊗ 🍸 Map 7

## CHIERZAC PAR BEDENAC, Charente-Maritime, 17210

*LES ROUTIERS, RN 10*

**Restaurant:** Breakfast served from 7:00am. Closed Saturdays and 1 week in July. **Specialities:** home cooking. **Other points:** bar, pets welcome – check for details.
MR ROBERT LAVILLE
**Telephone:** 46.04.44.24
⊗ ♆ Map 7

## CIVRAY, Vienne, 86400

### LE RELAIS DES USINES, the main road between Niort and Limoges

**Menu:** 50 Frs. **Restaurant:** Breakfast served from 6:45am. Dinner served from 7:00pm until 8:30pm. Closed Saturdays. **Specialities:** regional menu, home cooking. **Other points:** bar, children welcome, pets welcome – check for details, car park, traditional decor.
**Address:** 19, rue Norbert Portejoie.
MME BRIGITTE NICOULAUD
**Telephone:** 49.87.04.33
⊗ ♆ Map 7

## CIVRAY DE TOURAINE, Indre-et-Loire, 37150

### LE MARECHAL, RN 76, the main road between Tours and Vierzon

**Menu:** 55 to 62 Frs. **Restaurant:** Breakfast served from 6:00am. Lunch served from midday until 2:00pm. Dinner served from 7:00pm until 10:00pm. Closed Saturdays and from 25 August to 12 September. **Specialities:** regional menu. **Other points:** bar, open to non-residents, à la carte menu, children welcome, terraces, pets welcome – check for details, car park, traditional decor. **Address:** 1, rue de Bléré.
MR JEAN JAVENEAU
**Telephone:** 47.23.92.16
⊗ ♆ Map 6

## CLION SUR INDRE, Indre, 36700

### AUBERGE DU PIE DE BOURGES

**Restaurant:** Lunch served from 11:00am until 1:30pm. Dinner served from 7:00pm until 9:00pm. **Specialities:** home cooking. **Hotel:** 7 beds. **Other points:** bar.
**Address:** 31, rue Nationale.
MME NICOLE CHAMTON
**Telephone:** 54.38.60.90
⊗ ♆ ⌂ Map 6

## CLOTTE (LA), Charente-Maritime, 17360

### LE SABLIER, RD 910 Bis, between Libourne and Mont Guyon

**Menu:** 55 Frs (wine and coffee included). **Restaurant:** Breakfast served from 7:00am. Lunch served from midday until 2:00pm. Dinner served from 7:00pm until 10:00pm. **Specialities:** home cooking. **Other points:** bar, open to non-residents, terraces, pets welcome – check for details, car park, traditional decor. **Address:**

Route Départementale 910 Bis.
MME SYLVIE HUBERT
**Telephone:** 46.04.72.80
⊗ ♆ Map 7

## CONFOLENS, Charente, 16500

### RELAIS DES CIGOGNES, CD 951, between Gueret and Angoulême

**Places of interest:** Les châteaux, églises romaines, Saint Pourcain sur Sioule, ville viticole, parc zoologique.
**Menu:** 60 to 65 Frs. **Restaurant:** Breakfast served from 6:00am. Lunch served from 11:00am until 3:00pm. Dinner served from 6:00pm until 10:00pm. Closed Mondays. **Specialities:** Cuisses de grenouilles, gambas au whisky, home cooking. **Other points:** bar, open to non-residents, children welcome, pets welcome – check for details, car park, traditional decor. **Address:** Brillac.
MR SAÏD YASSA
**Telephone:** 45.89.45.90
⊗ ♆ Map 7

## CORME ROYAL, Charente-Maritime, 17600

### LES TILLEULS, RD 137, between Marennes and Oléron

**Menu:** 52 to 108 Frs. **Accommodation:** 130 to 160 Frs. **Restaurant:** Breakfast served from 8:00am. Lunch served from midday until 2:00pm. Dinner served from 7:00pm until 9:00pm. **Specialities:** home cooking. **Hotel:** 7 beds; with television, telephone. **Other points:** bar, open to non-residents, à la carte menu, children welcome, car park. **Address:** 1, rue du Grand Pré.
MME ARLETTE MARSAY
**Telephone:** 46.94.72.48
⊗ ♆ ⌂ ☆ Map 7

## CORMENON, Loir-et-Cher, 41170

### AUBERGE DU PARC, RD 921

**Menu:** 48 to 75 Frs. **Restaurant:** Breakfast served from 7:00am. Closed Sundays and the 2nd fortnight of August. **Specialities:** home cooking. **Other points:** bar, children welcome, car park. **Address:** 86, rue de la Poterie.
MR ANDRÉ TOUFFU
**Telephone:** 54.80.92.04
⊗ ♆ Map 6

## CORMERY, Indre-et-Loire, 37320

### RESTAURANT LA CHAUMIERE, RN 143, Tours/Loches/Châteauroux

**Menu:** 48 to 100 Frs. **Accommodation:** 80 Frs (1 bed), 160 Frs (2 beds). **Restaurant:** Breakfast served from 7:30am. Lunch served from 11:55am until 2:15pm. Dinner served from 7:00pm until 8:30pm. Closed Wednesdays after 2.30pm and 15 days in August. **Specialities:** home cooking. **Hotel:** 3 beds; 1 single room, 2 double rooms with shower. **Other points:** bar, children

welcome, terraces, pets welcome – check for details, car park. **Address:** 1, avenue de la Gare, Tauxigny.
MR DOMINIQUE GORON
**Telephone:** 47.43.40.26
⊗ 🍷 Map 6

## COULOMBIERS, Vienne, 86600

### LE RELAIS DE LA PAZIOTERIE, RN 11, between Poitiers and Saintes
**Restaurant:** Breakfast served from 5:00am.
**Specialities:** home cooking. **Other points:** bar, open to non-residents. **Address:** Lusignan.
MME YVONNE BARRUSSEAU
**Telephone:** 49.60.90.59
⊗ 🍷 Map 7

## COURTENAY, Loiret, 45320

### LE RELAIS DES SPORTS, RD 60, between Sens and Montargis
**Languages spoken:** German and English. **Menu:** 54 Frs – Plat du jour 40 Frs. **Accommodation:** 70 to 120 Frs.
**Restaurant:** Breakfast served from 7:30am. Lunch served from midday until 2:00pm. Dinner served from 7:00pm until 9:00pm. Closed Saturdays, from 15 to 30 March and from 15 August to 7 September. **Specialities:** home cooking. **Hotel:** 6 beds; 4 single rooms, 2 double rooms with shower, private WC. **Other points:** bar, open to non-residents, pets welcome – check for details, traditional decor. **Address:** 38, rue de Villeneuve.
MR GÉRARD MARTIN
**Telephone:** 38.97.32.37
⊗ 🍷 🏠 Map 6

## COURVILLE, Eure-et-Loir, 28190

### L'ESCALE ROUTIERE, RN 23
**Menu:** 52 to 61 Frs. **Restaurant:** Open 24 hours.
**Specialities:** home cooking. **Other points:** bar, open to non-residents, pets welcome – check for details, car park, traditional decor. **Address:** 1, rue de la Libération.
SARL LES CHATELETS
**Telephone:** 37.23.21.75
⊗ 🍷 Map 6

## COZES, Charente-Maritime, 17120

### STATION SERVICE SHELL
**Address:** Route de Royan, Grezac.
MR JACQUES GADIOU
**Telephone:** 46.90.84.12
Map 7

## CREVANT-MONTIERCHAUME, Indre, 36130

### AU CHEZ SOI, RN 151, between Châteauroux and Bourges
**Menu:** 45 Frs (drink and coffee included). **Restaurant:** Breakfast served from 11:00am. Lunch served from 11:00am until 3:00pm. Closed Saturdays and in August.
**Specialities:** home cooking. **Other points:** children welcome, pets welcome – check for details. **Address:** Route Nationale 151.
MME YVONNE BELOUIN-FERRÉ
**Telephone:** 54.26.00.19
⊗ Map 6

## CROIX CHAPEAU, Charente-Maritime, 17220

### CAFE DE PARIS, between Surgères and la Rochelle
**Menu:** 50 Frs (wine included). **Restaurant:** Breakfast served from 6:00am. Lunch served from 11:30am until 3:00pm. Dinner served from 6:30pm until midnight.
**Specialities:** home cooking. **Other points:** bar, open to non-residents, pets welcome – check for details, car park, traditional decor. **Address:** 60, avenue de la Libération.
MR CLAUDE BLANCHE
**Telephone:** 46.35.81.20
⊗ 🍷 Map 7

## DAMPIERRE EN CROT, Cher, 18260

### LES TILLEULS, RD 923, between Cosnes en Loire and Aubigny
**Menu:** 48 Frs (wine included) to 130 Frs.
**Accommodation:** 80 Frs. **Restaurant:** Breakfast served from 5:30am. Lunch served from midday until 2:30pm. Dinner served from 6:30pm until 9:00pm. **Specialities:** home cooking. **Hotel:** 5 beds; 4 single rooms, 1 double room. **Other points:** bar, open to non-residents, terraces, pets welcome – check for details, car park, traditional decor. **Address:** Route Départementale 923.
MR ANDRÉ PARIS
**Telephone:** 48.73.81.04
⊗ 🍷 🏠 Map 6

## DARVOY, Loiret, 45150

### LES ROUTIERS, RD 951, approximately 18km from Orléans, towards Gien (right bank of the Loire)
**Menu:** 55 Frs. **Restaurant:** Lunch served from midday until 2:00pm. Closed Saturdays and in August. **Specialities:** home cooking. **Other points:** bar, children welcome, pets welcome – check for details, car park, traditional decor.
**Address:** Lieu dit 'La Place', 4, route d'Orléans.
MME JULIE VINGERDER
**Telephone:** 38.59.71.00
⊗ 🍷 Map 6

## DEOLS, Indre, 36130

### L'ESCALE VILLAGE, RN 20, the main road between Paris and Limoges

**Languages spoken:** English and Spanish. **Menu:** 48 to 130 Frs. **Restaurant:** Open 24 hours. **Other points:** bar, open to non-residents, à la carte menu, children welcome, pets welcome – check for details, car park, modern decor. **Address:** Route Nationale 20.
MR JEAN-CLAUDE SERGENT
**Telephone:** 54.22.03.77. **Fax:** 54.22.56.70
⊗ 🍷 Map 6

### *LE RELAIS DE L'INTER*

**Languages spoken:** English, Spanish and Arabic. **Menu:** 49, 50 to 98,50 Frs. **Restaurant:** Breakfast served from 5:00am. Lunch served from 10:30am until 3:30pm. Dinner served from 6:30pm until 11:30pm. **Specialities:** regional menu, home cooking. **Other points:** bar, open to non-residents, à la carte menu, children welcome, terraces, pets welcome – check for details, car park, modern decor. **Address:** Route d'Issoudun.
MR BOUBEKEUR ABDERRAHMANE
**Telephone:** 54.27.20.07, 54.27.22.88
⊗ 🍷 Map 6

## DIGNY, Eure-et-Loir, 28250

### *AUBERGE DE LA VALLEE, RD 928, le Mans*

**Menu:** 40 to 120 Frs. **Restaurant:** Breakfast served from 6:30am. Lunch served from 11:30am until 2:00pm. Dinner served from 7:00pm until 9:00pm. Closed Wednesdays and 15 days in August. **Specialities:** home cooking. **Other points:** bar, à la carte menu, children welcome, terraces, pets welcome – check for details, car park, traditional decor. **Address:** 35, rue du Maréchal Leclerc.
MR CLAUDE DORE
**Telephone:** 37.29.01.04
⊗ 🍷 Map 6

## DRACHE, Indre-et-Loire, 37800

### *RESTAURANT DE LA PIERRE PERCEE, RN 10, between Châtellerault and Sainte Maure*

**Languages spoken:** German and English. **Menu:** 59 Frs (wine and coffee included). **Restaurant:** Breakfast served from 6:00am. Lunch served from 11:00am until 3:00pm. Dinner served from 6:00pm until 11:00pm. Closed Saturdays and the 1st fortnight in August. **Specialities:** coq au vin, coquilles de crabes, andouillettes grillées, regional food, home cooking. **Other points:** bar, open to non-residents, children welcome, terraces, pets welcome – check for details, car park, traditional decor. **Address:** Route Nationale 10.
MME NADIA KITTEL
**Telephone:** 47.65.08.64
⊗ 🍷 Map 6

## DREUX, Eure-et-Loir, 28100

### *CAFE DE LA POSTE, 7N 12 and 154*

**Restaurant:** Closed Sundays and public holidays. **Other points:** bar. **Address:** 2, rue du Général de Gaulle.
MME THÉRESE SEDAINE
**Telephone:** 37.42.12.00
🍷 Map 6

### *LE MARCEAU, RN 12 and 154, Chartres and le Mans*

**Menu:** 51,50 Frs. **Restaurant:** Breakfast served from 6:30am. Lunch served from midday until 2:00pm. Closed Sundays and in August. **Specialities:** home cooking. **Other points:** bar, open to non-residents, terraces, pets welcome – check for details, car park, modern decor. **Address:** 40–2, avenue du Général Marceau.
MR JEAN-PIERRE PARENT
**Telephone:** 37.46.05.57
⊗ 🍷 Map 6

## EPANNES, Deux-Sèvres, 79270

### *LE RELAIS SUISSE OCEAN, RN 11, la Rochelle, exit 23*

**Menu:** 52 to 130 Frs. **Accommodation:** 98 to 140 Frs. **Restaurant:** Breakfast served from 7:00am. Lunch served from 11:30am until 2:30pm. Dinner served from 7:30pm until 9:00pm. Closed Saturdays and beginning of September. **Specialities:** regional menu, home cooking. **Hotel:** 9 beds; 5 single rooms, 4 double rooms. **Other points:** bar, open to non-residents, à la carte menu, pets welcome – check for details, car park, traditional decor.
MR JACKY GUILLOTEAU
**Telephone:** 49.04.80.01
⊗ 🍷 🏠 Map 7

## EPERNON, Eure-et-Loir, 28230

### *LA GUINGUETTE, RD 306, between Chartres and Rambouillet*

**Menu:** 50 to 90 Frs. **Restaurant:** Breakfast served from 8:00am. Lunch served from 11:30am until 2:00pm. Dinner served from 7:00pm until 9:00pm. **Specialities:** home cooking. **Other points:** bar, open to non-residents, children welcome, pets welcome – check for details, car park, modern decor. **Address:** 47, rue du Grand Pont.
MME GISLAINE DASDORES
**Telephone:** 37.83.51.25
⊗ 🍷 Map 6

## ESVRES SUR INDRE, Indre-et-Loire, 37520

### *LE SAINT MALO, RN 143*

**Languages spoken:** English. **Menu:** 48 Frs.

**Restaurant:** Closed Sundays, in August and at
Christmas. **Specialities:** home cooking. **Other points:**
open to non-residents, à la carte menu, children
welcome, terraces, pets welcome – check for details, car
park, traditional decor. **Address:** La Pommeraie, Route
Nationale 143.
MME MARIE-CLAIRE BOUVARD
**Telephone:** 47.65.77.58
⊗ Map 6

## ETAGNAC, Charente, 16150

### RELAIS D'ETAGNAC, RN 141/948
**Languages spoken:** English. **Hotel:** 10 beds. **Other
points:** bar.
MR LOUIS LABROUSSE
**Telephone:** 45.89.21.38
⊗ ♀ ⌂ Map 7

## FERRIERE (LA), Deux-Sèvres, 79390

### AU BON ACCUEIL, RN 149, the main road
between Poitiers and Nantes
**Menu:** 52 to 58 Frs. **Restaurant:** Breakfast served from
8:30am. Lunch served from midday until 2:00pm.
Dinner served from 7:30pm until 9:00pm. Closed
Thursdays, 15 days in January and 3 weeks end of
August. **Specialities:** home cooking. **Other points:** bar,
open to non-residents, pets welcome – check for details,
car park. **Address:** 10, avenue de Poitiers.
MMES BILHEU-BERGER
**Telephone:** 49.63.03.01
⊗ ♀ Map 7

## FLEURE, Vienne, 86340

### AUX AMIS DE LA ROUTE, RN 147, the
main road between Poitiers and Limoges
**Menu:** 50 to 80 Frs. **Restaurant:** Breakfast served
from 6:00am. Lunch served from midday until
2:30pm. Dinner served from 7:00pm until 10:00pm.
**Specialities:** home cooking. **Other points:** bar, open
to non-residents, à la carte menu, children welcome,
pets welcome – check for details, car park, traditional
decor.
MME MICHELE GUIONNET
**Telephone:** 49.42.60.25
⊗ ♀ Map 7

## FONDETTES, Indre-et-Loire, 37230

### LE BEAU MANOIR, RN 152, the main road
between Angers and Nantes
**Menu:** 51 Frs. **Restaurant:** Breakfast served from
7:00am. Lunch served from midday until 2:00pm.
Dinner served from 7:00pm until 9:30pm. Closed
Saturdays and the 1st fortnight in May. **Specialities:**
home cooking. **Other points:** bar, open to non-residents,
children welcome, terraces, pets welcome – check for

details, car park, traditional decor. **Address:** 6, quai de
la Guignière.
MME EDITH BOURREAU
**Telephone:** 47.42.01.02
⊗ ♀ Map 6

## FONTAINE LE COMTE, Vienne, 86240

### AUBERGE DE LA GARENNE, the main
road between Niort and Bordeaux
**Menu:** 60 to 112 Frs. **Restaurant:** Breakfast served
from 6:00am. Lunch served from 11:30am until 2:00pm.
Dinner served from 7:00pm until 10:00pm. Closed
Sundays and in August. **Specialities:** regional menu,
home cooking. **Other points:** bar, open to non-residents,
à la carte menu, children welcome, terraces, pets
welcome – check for details, car park, traditional decor.
**Address:** Allée des Cerfs.
MME MICHELLE GUÉRIN
**Telephone:** 49.57.01.22
⊗ ♀ Map 7

## FONTAINE SIMON, Eure-et-Loir, 28240

### AU BON COIN, Dreux–Rémalard
**Menu:** 48 Frs. **Restaurant:** Breakfast served from
7:00am. Lunch served from midday until 2:00pm.
Dinner served from 7:00pm until 8:30pm. Closed
Fridays and in August. **Specialities:** home cooking.
**Hotel:** 10 beds; with shower, private WC. **Other points:**
bar, open to non-residents, car park, traditional decor.
**Address:** 1, rue de la Mairie.
MME SERGINE DURAND
**Telephone:** 37.81.84.98
⊗ ♀ ⌂ Map 6

## FONTENAY SUR LOING, Loiret, 45210

### LES 100 BORNES, RN 7, between
Montargis and Dordives
**Menu:** 53 to 90 Frs. **Restaurant:** Open 24 hours.
**Specialities:** home cooking. **Other points:** bar, open to
non-residents, pets welcome – check for details, car
park. **Address:** Route Nationale 7.
MR GUY MARTIN
**Telephone:** 38.95.82.06
⊗ ♀ Map 6

## FORGES, Charente-Maritime, 17290

### CHEZ NENE, RN 137, the main road
between la Rochelle and Angoulême
**Languages spoken:** English. **Menu:** 50 Frs (wine
included). **Restaurant:** Breakfast served from 7:30am.
Lunch served from midday until 2:30pm. Dinner served
from 7:30pm until 9:00pm. Closed Sundays.
**Specialities:** home cooking. **Other points:** bar, open to
non-residents, terraces, pets welcome – check for details,

car park, traditional decor. **Address:** Puydrouard.
MR RENÉ BOURIEAU
**Telephone:** 46.35.07.83
⊗ ♀ Map 7

## FOSSE, Loir-et-Cher, 41330

### BAR DE L'ESPERANCE, RN 153, between Vendôme and le Mans
**Menu:** 53 Frs. **Restaurant:** Breakfast served from 6:30am. Lunch served from 11:30am until 2:30pm. Dinner served from 7:00pm until 9:30pm. Closed Saturdays. **Specialities:** home cooking. **Other points:** bar, open to non-residents, children welcome. **Address:** 7, rue de Saint Sulpice.
MME BRIGITTE CHAUVIN-SALA
**Telephone:** 54.20.01.77
⊗ ♀ Map 6

## FRETEVAL, Loir-et-Cher, 41160

### SARL LE PLESSIS, RN 10, between Vendôme (20km) and Châteaudun (24km)
**Languages spoken:** German, English and Spanish. **Menu:** 54 to 90 Frs. **Restaurant:** Lunch served from midday until 2:00pm. Dinner served from 7:00pm until 10:00pm. Closed Saturdays and between Christmas Day and New Year's Day. **Specialities:** home cooking. **Other points:** bar, open to non-residents, pets welcome – check for details, car park, traditional decor. **Address:** Route Nationale 10.
MME ISABELLE THEBAULT
**Telephone:** 54.82.64.28
⊗ ♀ Map 6

## GERMIGNY DES PRES, Loiret, 45110

### HOTEL DE LA PLACE, RN 60, between Orléans and Montargis
**Menu:** 55 to 150 Frs. **Accommodation:** 100 to 170 Frs. **Restaurant:** Breakfast served from 7:00am. Lunch served from midday until 2:00pm. Dinner served from 8:00pm until 9:30pm. Closed Fridays. **Specialities:** fricassé de pintade, home cooking. **Hotel:** 12 beds; 8 single rooms, 4 double rooms with shower, bath, private WC, telephone. **Other points:** bar, open to non-residents, à la carte menu, children welcome, terraces, pets welcome – check for details, car park, traditional decor. **Address:** 2, route de Châteauneuf.
JACKY ET CHRISTIANE MAILLARD
**Telephone:** 38.58.20.14
⊗ ♀ ⌂ ⊖ Map 6

## GIDY, Loiret, 45520

### LA PORTE DU VAL DE LOIRE, A 10, Orléans
**Restaurant:** Breakfast served from 6:00am. Dinner served from midday until midnight. **Other points:** bar,

children welcome, pets welcome – check for details, car park, modern decor. **Address:** A 10 Aire de Gidy, dans les deux sens.
**Telephone:** 38.73.31.02. **Fax:** 38.81.80.50
⊗ ♀ Map 6

## GIEN, Loiret, 45500

### CAFE DU NORD, RN 140 and CD 952
**Languages spoken:** English. **Restaurant:** Closed Sundays and the 1st fortnight in August. **Other points:** bar. **Address:** 51, place de la Victoire.
MME SUZANNE BOTINEAU
**Telephone:** 38.67.32.98
⊗ ♀ Map 6

### LE RELAIS NORMAND, opposite the pottery
**Languages spoken:** English. **Menu:** 51 Frs. **Accommodation:** 120 to 150 Frs. **Restaurant:** Breakfast served from 5:45am. Lunch served from midday until 2:30pm. Dinner served from 7:30pm until 9:00pm. Closed Saturdays and Sundays. **Specialities:** home cooking. **Hotel:** 12 beds; with shower. **Other points:** bar, open to non-residents, children welcome, terraces, pets welcome – check for details, car park, modern decor. **Address:** 64, place de la Victoire.
MR PIERRE MONTCEAU
**Telephone:** 38.67.28.56, 38.67.51.85
⊗ ♀ ⌂ Map 6

## GIEVRES, Loir-et-Cher, 41130

### SARL RELAIS DE NORAY, RN 76, Vierzon
**Menu:** 52 Frs. **Restaurant:** Breakfast served from 7:00am. Lunch served from 11:00am until 2:00pm. Dinner served from 7:30pm until 10:30pm. Closed Saturdays and in August. **Specialities:** home cooking. **Other points:** bar, open to non-residents, children welcome, terraces, car park, traditional decor. **Address:** Route de Vierzon.
MME CHRISTIANE LAITHIER
**Telephone:** 54.98.64.00
⊗ ♀ Map 6

## HUISSEAU EN BEAUCE, Loir-et-Cher, 41310

### LES PLATANES, RN 10, between Vendôme and Tours
**Menu:** 55 Frs. **Restaurant:** Breakfast served from 6:30am. Lunch served from midday until 3:00pm. Dinner served from 7:00pm until 10:30pm. Closed Saturdays, public holidays and the 1st week in September. **Specialities:** home cooking. **Other points:** bar, open to non-residents, children welcome, pets welcome – check for details, car park. **Address:** Route Nationale 10.
MR HUBERT BRETON
**Telephone:** 54.82.81.46
⊗ ♀ Map 6

## ISDES, Loiret, 45620

### HOTEL DU DAUPHIN, RD 83, between la Motte Beuvron and Sully

**Menu:** 55 to 120 Frs. **Accommodation:** 60 to 120 Frs. **Restaurant:** Breakfast served from 6:30am. Lunch served from 11:30am until 2:00pm. Dinner served from 7:00pm until 8:30pm. Closed Mondays. **Specialities:** regional menu, home cooking. **Hotel:** 11 beds; 9 single rooms, 2 double rooms with shower. **Other points:** bar, open to non-residents, children welcome, terraces, pets welcome – check for details, car park, traditional decor. **Address:** 11, Grande Rue.
MR LUCIEN LAURENT
**Telephone:** 38.29.10.29
⊗ ⍨ ⌂   Map 6

## ISSOUDUN, Indre, 36100

### LE RELAIS DE LA CROIX ROUGE, RN 151

**Languages spoken:** English, German, Italian, Turkish. **Restaurant:** Dinner served from midday until 9:00pm. Closed Saturdays and mid-August. **Hotel:** 5 beds. **Other points:** bar. **Address:** 14, faubourg de la Croix Rouge.
MR CLAUDE GROSYEUX
**Telephone:** 54.21.04.91
⊗ ⍨ ⌂   Map 6

### LE RELAIS ISSOLDUNOIS, RN 151, between Châteauroux (27km) and Bourges (27km)

**Languages spoken:** English and German. **Menu:** from 50 Frs. **Accommodation:** 160 to 230 Frs. **Restaurant:** Breakfast served from 5:30am. Lunch served from 11:45am until 2:30pm. Dinner served from 7:00pm until 10:30pm. **Specialities:** regional menu, home cooking. **Hotel:** 16 beds; 12 single rooms, 4 double rooms with shower, private WC, television, telephone. **Other points:** bar, open to non-residents, à la carte menu, children welcome, terraces, car park, modern decor. **Address:** 8, route de Bourges.
MR HERVÉ DE SA
**Telephone:** 54.03.04.05. **Fax:** 54.03.01.00
⊗ ⍨ ⌂ ☆☆   Map 6

## JARNAC, Charente, 16200

### LES ROUTIERS, RN 141

**Menu:** 50 Frs. **Restaurant:** Breakfast served from 7:00am. Lunch served from midday until 2:00pm. Dinner served from 7:00pm until 10:00pm. Closed Sundays. **Specialities:** home cooking. **Other points:** bar, open to non-residents, children welcome. **Address:** 77, rue Pasteur.
MME MARYSE BOUFFINIE
**Telephone:** 45.81.02.40
⊗ ⍨   Map 7

## LADON, Loiret, 45270

### LE RELAIS DE LADON, RN 60, between Montargis and Orléans

**Menu:** 50 to 70 Frs. **Accommodation:** 72 to 110 Frs. **Restaurant:** Breakfast served from 5:30am. Closed Sundays, from 28 June to 19 July and 15 days after Christmas Day. **Specialities:** home cooking. **Hotel:** 7 beds; 7 double rooms with shower. **Other points:** bar, open to non-residents, terraces, pets welcome – check for details, car park. **Address:** 400, avenue du 24 Novembre.
MR PIERRE GUILLAUMIN
**Telephone:** 38.95.51.32
⊗ ⍨ ⌂   Map 6

## LANDES, Charente-Maritime, 17380

### AUX AMIS DE LA ROUTE, between Saint Jean d'Angély and Surgères

**Menu:** 55 Frs (wine included). **Accommodation:** 90 to 150 Frs. **Restaurant:** Breakfast served from 7:00am. Lunch served from 11:30am until 2:30pm. Dinner served from 6:30pm until 9:30pm. **Specialities:** home cooking. **Hotel:** 4 beds; 4 single rooms. **Other points:** bar, children welcome, pets welcome – check for details, car park, traditional decor. **Address:** Rue d'Aunis.
MR ERIC PRESTAVOINE
**Telephone:** 46.59.73.37
⊗ ⍨   Map 7

## LENCLOITRE, Vienne, 86140

### AU 14 ANNE ANDRE, D 725 and D 757, between Chatellerault and Nantes

**Menu:** 47 to 55 Frs. **Restaurant:** Breakfast served from 7:00am. Lunch served from 11:00am until 3:00pm. Dinner served from 7:00pm until 11:00pm. Closed Sundays. **Specialities:** home cooking. **Other points:** bar, open to non-residents, lounge area, pets welcome – check for details, car park, modern decor. **Address:** 2, place du Champ de Foire.
MR ANDRÉ PERNELLE
**Telephone:** 49.90.71.29
⊗ ⍨   Map 7

## LISSAY LOCHY, Cher, 18340

### AUBERGE DES MAISONS ROUGES, RD 28 and 73, by RN 144

**Menu:** 50 to 100 Frs. **Restaurant:** Breakfast served from 6:00am. Lunch served from midday until 2:00pm. Closed Saturdays. **Specialities:** home cooking. **Other points:** bar, open to non-residents, à la carte menu, terraces, pets welcome – check for details, car park, traditional decor. **Address:** Les Maisons Rouges.
MR ROBERT LEGER
**Telephone:** 48.64.76.07
⊗ ⍨   Map 6

## LOGRON, Eure-et-Loir, 28200

### *AUBERGE SAINT NICOLAS, between Orléans and Alençon*

**Menu:** 48 to 90 Frs. **Restaurant:** Breakfast served from 8:00am. Lunch served from 11:30am until 1:00pm. Dinner served from 7:00pm until 10:00pm. Closed Mondays and 15 days at Christmas. **Specialities:** home cooking. **Other points:** bar, open to non-residents, à la carte menu, children welcome, car park. **Address:** 2, rue des Buissonnots.
MR BRUNO HUBERT
**Telephone:** 37.98.98.02
⊗ 🍷 Map 6

## LORRIS, Loiret, 45260

### *AUBERGE DE LA CROIX ROUGE, RD 961*

**Restaurant:** Breakfast served from 8:00am. Closed Sundays. **Specialities:** home cooking. **Other points:** bar, open to non-residents, à la carte menu, children welcome. **Address:** 28, rue Guillaume.
MME LISIANE BERLIN
**Telephone:** 38.92.47.03
⊗ 🍷 Map 6

## LOULAY, Charente-Maritime, 17330

### *CHEZ JO, RN 150, exit Niort*

**Menu:** 55 to 65 Frs. **Accommodation:** 100 to 145 Frs. **Restaurant:** Breakfast served from 7:30am. Lunch served from midday until 2:00pm. Dinner served from 7:00pm until 8:30pm. Closed Saturday evenings and Sundays (out of season). **Specialities:** home cooking. **Hotel:** 5 beds; 1 single room, 4 double rooms with shower, private WC. **Other points:** bar, open to non-residents, children welcome, terraces, pets welcome – check for details, car park, traditional decor. **Address:** 10, place du Général de Gaulle.
MR GEORGES MAHDID
**Telephone:** 46.33.80.59
⊗ 🍷 🏠 Map 7

## LUNERY, Cher, 18400

### *LE BAR DU CENTRE, RD 27, between Bourges and Chateauneuf en Cher*

**Menu:** 50 Frs (wine and coffee included) to 95 Frs. **Restaurant:** Breakfast served from 6:30am. Lunch served from midday until 2:30pm. Dinner served from 7:00pm until 10:00pm. Closed Tuesdays, 15 days in February and 15 days in September. **Specialities:** home cooking. **Other points:** bar, open to non-residents, à la carte menu, children welcome, pets welcome – check for details, car park, traditional decor. **Address:** 1, place Jacques Georges.
MR MICHEL PORCHERON
**Telephone:** 48.68.98.71
⊗ 🍷 Map 6

## LUSSAC LES CHATEAUX, Vienne, 86320

### *LE CHENE VERT, RN 147, the main road between Poitiers and Limoges*

**Menu:** 53,50 Frs (wine included). **Restaurant:** Breakfast served from 6:30am. Lunch served from midday until 3:00pm. Dinner served from 7:00pm until 10:30pm. Closed Sundays. **Specialities:** home cooking. **Other points:** bar, open to non-residents, children welcome, terraces, pets welcome – check for details, car park, traditional decor. **Address:** 14, route de Limoges.
MME NADIA HOMAERT
**Telephone:** 49.48.40.30
⊗ 🍷 Map 7

## LUTZ EN DUNOIS, Eure-et-Loir, 28200

### *LA RENCONTRE, D 955, the main road between Orléans and Alençon*

**Menu:** 50 Frs. **Accommodation:** 60 Frs. **Restaurant:** Breakfast served from 5:30am. Lunch served from 11:00am until 3:00pm. Dinner served from 7:00pm until 9:30pm. Closed Saturdays and from mid-February to beginning of March. **Specialities:** home cooking. **Hotel:** 5 beds; 4 single rooms, 1 double room with shower, bath. **Other points:** bar, open to non-residents, terraces, pets welcome – check for details, car park, traditional decor.
MR FRANCIS BERRIER
**Telephone:** 37.45.18.08
⊗ 🍷 🏠 Map 6

## MAINVILLIERS, Eure-et-Loir, 28300

### *L'ARCHE DE CHARTRES NORD, A 11*

**Languages spoken:** English. **Menu:** 50 to 80 Frs. **Restaurant:** Open 24 hours. **Other points:** open to non-residents, à la carte menu, children welcome, terraces, pets welcome – check for details, car park, traditional decor. **Address:** A 11 Aire de Gasville, sens le Mans/Rennes.
MR JEAN-JACQUES BIGOT
**Telephone:** 37.31.62.42
⊗ Map 6

### *L'ARCHE DE CHARTRES SUD, A 11*

**Menu:** 59 Frs. **Restaurant:** Breakfast served from 6:00am. **Other points:** open to non-residents, children welcome, terraces, pets welcome – check for details, car park. **Address:** A 11 Aire de Bois Paris, sens Nantes/Paris.
MR PATRICK LAFUENTE
**Telephone:** 37.31.62.41, 37.31.60.12. **Fax:** 37.31.90.51
⊗ Map 6

## MANTHELAN, Indre-et-Loire, 37240

### *LE RELAIS DE LA CROIX VERTE*

Languages spoken: English. Other points: bar, car park. Address: 25, rue Nationale.
MME CHRISTIANE MARTIN
Telephone: 47.92.80.16
⊗ ♟ Map 6

## MARANS, Charente-Maritime, 17230

### LE POINT DU JOUR – CHEZ SYLVIANE ET JOËL, RN 137, the main road between la Rochelle and Bordeaux

Menu: 52 to 75 Frs. Restaurant: Breakfast served from 5:30am. Lunch served from 11:00am until 4:30pm. Dinner served from 7:00pm until 11:30pm. Closed Sundays. Specialities: home cooking. Hotel: 5 beds. Other points: bar, open to non-residents, children welcome, pets welcome – check for details, car park, traditional decor. Address: 2, rue des Moulins.
MME SYLVIANE GÉRARD
Telephone: 46.01.14.54
⊗ ♟ 🏠 Map 7

## MAROLLES, Eure-et-Loir, 28260

### AU RELAIS DE MAROLLES, RN 12

Menu: 55 to 85 Frs. Restaurant: Dinner served from midday until midnight. Closed Saturdays and the 1st fortnight in August. Other points: bar, car park.
Address: 44, rue Georges Bréant.
MME VIVIANE BEAUVAIS
Telephone: 37.43.20.50
⊗ ♟ 🍽 Map 6

## MARVILLE MOUTIERS BRULE, Eure-et-Loir, 28500

### LE RELAIS, between Chartres and Dreux

Menu: 50 Frs. Restaurant: Closed Mondays. Other points: bar, car park, modern decor.
MME RAYMONDE LESCH
Telephone: 37.38.36.20
⊗ ♟ Map 6

## MERY SUR CHER, Cher, 18100

### LE RELAIS BERRY SOLOGNE, RN 76, between Vierzon and Tours

Accommodation: 85 to 145 Frs. Restaurant: Breakfast served from 5:00am. Dinner served from 7:00pm until 11:00pm. Closed Saturdays and 15 days in August. Specialities: home cooking. Hotel: 11 beds; 8 single rooms, 3 double rooms with shower. Other points: open to non-residents, children welcome, pets welcome – check for details, car park, traditional decor. Address: Route Nationale 76.
MR CLAUDE CARRÉ
Telephone: 48.75.20.34
⊗ 🏠 Map 6

## MEZIERES EN BRENNE, Indre, 36290

### CAFE DES SPORTS – CHEZ SYLVIANE, RD 925, at the entrance of Mézières on entering Leblanc

Menu: 50 to 80 Frs. Accommodation: 90 to 220 Frs. Restaurant: Breakfast served from 7:00am. Lunch served from midday until 2:30pm. Dinner served from 7:00pm until 10:00pm. Specialities: home cooking. Hotel: 6 beds; with shower, bath. Other points: bar, open to non-residents, children welcome, terraces, pets welcome – check for details, car park. Address: 11, rue de l'Ouest.
MR HENRI PEUVION
Telephone: 54.38.11.62
⊗ ♟ 🏠 Map 6

## MIGNERES, Loiret, 45490

### LE RELAIS DE MIGNERES, RD 94, between Auxy and Montargis

Menu: 53 Frs (wine and coffee included) to 100 Frs. Accommodation: 80 to 120 Frs. Restaurant: Breakfast served from 6:30am. Lunch served from 11:00am until 2:00pm. Dinner served from 7:30pm until 9:30pm. Closed Sundays. Specialities: regional menu, home cooking. Hotel: 7 beds; 4 single rooms, 3 double rooms with shower. Other points: bar, open to non-residents, children welcome, lounge area, pets welcome – check for details, car park, traditional decor. Address: 3, rue de la Gare.
MR ROMAIN COUSIN
Telephone: 38.87.85.57
⊗ ♟ 🏠 Map 6

## MONNAIE, Indre-et-Loire, 37380

### GRILL DE TOURAINE, A 10

Languages spoken: English, Spanish and Dutch. Menu: 56 to 150 Frs. Restaurant: Breakfast served from 6:00am. Lunch served from 11:00am until 3:00pm. Dinner served from 7:00pm until 11:00pm. Specialities: regional menu. Other points: open to non-residents, à la carte menu, children welcome, terraces, pets welcome – check for details, car park, traditional decor. Address: A 10 Aire de la Longue Vue, sens Paris/Bordeaux.
MR OLIVIER PLOT
Telephone: 47.56.44.94. Fax: 47.56.12.17
⊗ Map 6

### L'ARCHE DE TOURS, A 10, 10km to the north of Tours

Languages spoken: English and Spanish. Menu: 59 Frs. Restaurant: Open 24 hours. Other points: open to non-residents, terraces, pets welcome – check for details, car park. Address: A 10 Air de Tours Val de Loire, accessible des deux sens.
MR CHRISTOPHE OZENNE
Telephone: 47.56.15.49. Fax: 47.56.12.17
⊗ Map 6

### LA BONNE ETAPE
**Menu:** 50 to 85 Frs. **Accommodation:** 130 to 150 Frs.
**Restaurant:** Lunch served from midday until 2:00pm.
Dinner served from 7:00pm until 9:00pm. Closed
Sundays and at Christmas. **Hotel:** 6 beds. **Other points:**
bar, car park. **Address:** 67, rue Nationale.
MME CLAUDETTE THAUVIN
**Telephone:** 47.56.10.64
⊗ ⍭ ⌂ Map 6

## MONTARGIS, Loiret, 45200

### LE PARIS-MONTARGIS
**Languages spoken:** English. **Restaurant:** Closed
Sundays. **Hotel:** 10 beds. **Other points:** bar. **Address:**
221, rue Emile Mangin.
MR DARBIER
**Telephone:** 38.85.63.04, 38.93.91.58
⊗ ⍭ ⌂ Map 6

## MONTBAZON, Indre-et-Loire, 37250

### LA GRANGE BARBIER, RN 10, exit south of Montbazon, towards Poitiers
**Menu:** 52 to 105 Frs. **Accommodation:** 100 to 150
Frs. **Restaurant:** Breakfast served from 7:15am.
Lunch served from midday until 2:00pm. Dinner
served from 7:00pm until 9:30pm. Closed Sundays and
the 2nd fortnight in July. **Specialities:** home cooking.
**Hotel:** 5 beds; 3 single rooms, 2 double rooms with
shower. **Other points:** bar, open to non-residents,
children welcome, terraces, pets welcome – check for
details, car park, traditional decor. **Address:** Route
Nationale 10.
MR WILLIAM LABORDE
**Telephone:** 47.26.01.69
⊗ ⍭ ⌂ Map 6

## MONTILS (LES), Loir-et-Cher, 41120

### LES DEUX ROUES, RN 764, between Blois and Montrichard
**Restaurant:** Breakfast served from 7:00am. Lunch
served from 11:30am until 2:00pm. Dinner served from
7:30pm until 8:30pm. Closed Sundays. **Specialities:**
home cooking. **Other points:** bar, open to non-residents,
car park, traditional decor. **Address:** 28, rue de Bel Air.
MR JEAN-PIERRE LEVAUX
**Telephone:** 54.44.02.40
⊗ ⍭ Map 6

## MONTLANDON, Eure-et-Loir, 28240

### LE RELAIS DE LA PERRUCHE, RN 23
**Menu:** 58 Frs. **Restaurant:** Breakfast served from
4:00am. **Specialities:** home cooking. **Other points:** bar,
open to non-residents, children welcome, terraces, pets
welcome – check for details, car park, modern decor.
**Address:** Route Nationale 23.

MR ANDRÉ BAUDELIN
**Telephone:** 37.37.30.95
⊗ ⍭ Map 6

## MONTMOREAU, Charente, 16190

### LES ROUTIERS, RN 674, the main road between Angoulême and Libourne
**Restaurant:** Breakfast served from 8:00am.
**Specialities:** home cooking. **Hotel:** 6 beds; 1 single
room, 5 double rooms with bath. **Other points:** bar,
children welcome, terraces, modern decor. **Address:** 14,
avenue de l'Angoumois.
MME ERNESTINE FERRIER
**Telephone:** 46.60.21.17
⊗ ⍭ ⌂ Map 7

## MORNAY SUR ALLIER, Cher, 18600

### L'ETAPE DU RIVAGE, RN 76, between Bourges and Moulin
**Menu:** 50 Frs. **Accommodation:** 80 to 140 Frs.
**Restaurant:** Closed Saturdays and in August.
**Specialities:** home cooking. **Hotel:** 4 beds; 1 single
room, 3 double rooms with shower, private WC. **Other
points:** bar, open to non-residents, children welcome,
lounge area, pets welcome – check for details, car park,
traditional decor. **Address:** Le Rivage.
MR CHRISTIAN MORET
**Telephone:** 48.74.59.17
⊗ ⍭ Map 6

### LE RELAIS DE LA ROUTE, RN 76
**Languages spoken:** German and English. **Menu:** 52 to
90 Frs. **Accommodation:** 60 to 90 Frs. **Restaurant:**
Open 24 hours **Specialities:** home cooking. **Hotel:** 5
beds; 2 single rooms, 3 double rooms with private WC.
**Other points:** bar, open to non-residents, pets welcome –
check for details, car park. **Address:** Route Nationale 76.
MME JACQUELINE CHEVROT
**Telephone:** 48.74.53.54
⊗ ⍭ ⌂ Map 6

## MOULISMES, Vienne, 86500

### LA TABLE OUVERTE, RN 147, between Poitiers (50km) and Limoges (70km)
**Menu:** 50 to 110 Frs. **Accommodation:** 110 to 195 Frs.
**Restaurant:** Breakfast served from 6:00am. Lunch
served from midday until 2:30pm. Dinner served from
7:30pm until 9:30pm. Closed Saturdays. **Specialities:**
home cooking. **Hotel:** 7 beds; 7 single rooms with
shower, bath, private WC, telephone. **Other points:** bar,
open to non-residents, à la carte menu, pets welcome –
check for details, car park, traditional decor. **Address:**
Route Nationale 147.
SARL GRANSAGNE-BAUDET
**Telephone:** 49.91.90.68, 49.91.33.21
⊗ ⍭ ⌂ ☆ Map 7

## NAINTRE, Vienne, 86530

*LA HALTE, RN 10, take exit for south Chatellerault on Aquitaine motorway*
Languages spoken: English, Arabic, Spanish, German.
Restaurant: Closed Saturdays. Other points: bar.
Address: Route Nationale 10.
HENNI HOUAS
Telephone: 49.90.09.69
⊗ ⍨ Map 7

## NERE, Charente-Maritime, 17510

*HOTEL RESTAURANT DES 3 PLACES, Matha*
Languages spoken: English. Menu: 52, 50 Frs (wine included) to 79 Frs. Accommodation: 90 to 180 Frs.
Restaurant: Breakfast served from 7:00am. Lunch served from 11:30am until 3:00pm. Dinner served from 7:00pm until 10:00pm. Specialities: home cooking.
Hotel: 9 beds; 4 single rooms, 5 double rooms with shower. Other points: bar, open to non-residents, à la carte menu, children welcome, terraces, car park, modern decor. Address: Le Bourg.
MR CHRISTIAN BILLERACH
Telephone: 46.33.00.13
⊗ ⍨ ⌂ Map 7

## NEUVY, Loir-et-Cher, 41250

*LA CHEMINEE, RD 923, the main road between Paris and Angoulême*
Languages spoken: English, Spanish and Portugese.
Menu: 55 (wine and coffee included) to 140 Frs.
Accommodation: 170 to 260 Frs. Restaurant:
Breakfast served from 7:00am. Lunch served from midday until 2:00pm. Dinner served from 7:00pm until 9:00pm. Closed Wednesdays and 15 days in September.
Specialities: regional menu, home cooking. Hotel: 9 beds; 4 single rooms, 5 double rooms. Other points: bar, open to non-residents, à la carte menu, children welcome, lounge area, terraces, pets welcome – check for details, car park, traditional decor. Address: Le Bourg.
MR PHILIPPE MASCLET
Telephone: 54.46.42.70
⊗ ⍨ ⌂ ⌣ Map 6

## NEUVY BOUIN, Deux-Sèvres, 79300

*BAR DES SPORTS, RD 748, between Bressuire and Niort*
Menu: 50 Frs (wine included). Restaurant: Breakfast served from 7:30am. Lunch served from midday until 2:00pm. Dinner served from 7:00pm until 9:00pm.
Closed 1 week in August. Specialities: home cooking.
Other points: bar, open to non-residents, terraces, pets welcome – check for details, car park, traditional decor.
Address: 20, rue du Commerce.

MR BERNARD BENECHERE
Telephone: 49.63.76.22
⊗ ⍨ Map 7

## NEUVY SAINT SEPULCHRE, Indre, 36230

*LA CHARRETTE, RD 927, between la Châtre and Montluçon*
Languages spoken: Italian, Yugoslavian, Polish, Russian. Menu: 60 to 80 Frs. Accommodation: 140 to 170 Frs. Restaurant: Lunch served from 12:30pm until 2:00pm. Dinner served from 7:00pm until 10:00pm.
Specialities: home cooking. Hotel: 7 beds; 4 single rooms, 3 double rooms with bath. Other points: bar, open to non-residents, à la carte menu, children welcome, lounge area, car park, traditional decor.
Address: 21, place du Champ de Foire.
MR NICOLAS PAVLICEVIC
Telephone: 54.30.84.77
⊗ ⍨ ⌂ Map 6

## NIORT, Deux-Sèvres, 79000

*LE BON ACCUEIL, RN 150, the main road between Niort and Bordeaux*
Menu: 52,50 to 68 Frs. Restaurant: Breakfast served from 6:00am. Lunch served from midday until 2:00pm.
Dinner served from 7:30pm until 10:00pm. Closed Sundays and in August. Specialities: home cooking.
Other points: bar, open to non-residents, car park, modern decor. Address: 424, avenue St Jean d'Angély.
MME THÉRÈSE DENIBAUD
Telephone: 49.79.27.60
⊗ ⍨ Map 7

## NOGENT LE PHAYE, Eure-et-Loir, 28630

*LE RELAIS DU MOULIN ROUGE, RN 10, exit Chartres towards Paris*
Menu: 55 Frs (coffee included). Restaurant: Breakfast served from 5:00am. Lunch served from 11:30am until 2:30pm. Dinner served from 7:00pm until 9:45pm.
Closed Saturdays and in August. Specialities: home cooking. Other points: bar, open to non-residents, pets welcome – check for details, car park, traditional decor.
Address: Le Moulin Rouge, Route Nationale 10.
MR CHRISTIAN BRU
Telephone: 37.31.62.68
⊗ ⍨ Map 6

## NOHANT EN GOUT, Cher, 18390

*RELAIS DU BERRY, RN 151, la Charité sur Loire/Auxerre*
Languages spoken: German, English and Spanish.
Menu: 50 to 110 Frs. Restaurant: Lunch served from 11:00am until 3:30pm. Dinner served from 7:00pm until 11:00pm. Closed Mondays and 15 days in February.

**Specialities:** regional menu, home cooking. **Other points:** bar, à la carte menu, children welcome, terraces, pets welcome – check for details, car park, traditional decor. **Address:** Route Nationale 151.
SARL LIGOT
**Telephone:** 48.30.42.90
⊗ ♀ Map 6

# NOYANT DE TOURAINE, Indre-et-Loire, 37800

### CHEZ MIMI, l'Ile Bouchard, RD 760
**Languages spoken:** English. **Menu:** 50 Frs (wine and coffee included). **Restaurant:** Breakfast served from 5:00am. Closed Saturdays. **Specialities:** home cooking. **Other points:** bar, open to non-residents, children welcome, terraces, pets welcome – check for details, car park, traditional decor. **Address:** Route de Chinon.
MME ANNICK GIRET
**Telephone:** 47.65.82.26
⊗ ♀ Map 6

# ORLEANS, Loiret, 45100

### AUX QUATRE MARCHES, RN 20 and RD 951
**Menu:** 46 to 50 Frs. **Restaurant:** Dinner served from midday until 10:00pm. Closed Saturdays and in August. **Specialities:** home cooking. **Hotel:** 5 beds. **Other points:** bar, pets welcome – check for details, modern decor. **Address:** 163, avenue de Saint Mesmin.
MR PIERRE GUYOT
**Telephone:** 38.66.31.12
⊗ ♀ ⌂ Map 6

# PELLEVOISIN, Indre, 36180

### LE RELAIS DES ROUTIERS 'CHEZ BABETTE ET JOËL', RD 11, between Valancay and Pellevoisin
**Languages spoken:** English and Spanish. **Menu:** 50 Frs. **Accommodation:** 135 Frs. **Restaurant:** Breakfast served from 10:00am. Lunch served from midday until 2:00pm. Dinner served from 7:30pm until 9:30pm. Closed Sundays and in August. **Specialities:** home cooking. **Hotel:** 4 beds; 2 single rooms, 2 double rooms with shower, bath, private WC, telephone. **Other points:** bar, open to non-residents, terraces, car park, traditional decor. **Address:** 30, rue Jean Giraudoux.
MME ELISABETH PETIT
**Telephone:** 54.39.03.78
⊗ ♀ Map 6

# PERRUSSON, Indre-et-Loire, 37600

### LES ROUTIERS, RN 143, the main road between Tours and Châteauroux
**Restaurant:** Breakfast served from 7:00am. Lunch served from midday until 3:00pm. Dinner served from

7:00pm until 10:00pm. Closed Sundays and 15 days in August. **Specialities:** home cooking. **Hotel:** 7 beds; 4 single rooms, 3 double rooms with shower, bath. **Other points:** bar, open to non-residents, à la carte menu, children welcome, pets welcome – check for details, car park. **Address:** 3, rue de l'Indre.
MR KLÉBER LANCHAIS
**Telephone:** 47.59.04.34
⊗ ♀ ⌂ Map 6

# PERUSE (LA), Charente, 16370

### LES ROUTIERS, RN 141, the main road between Limoges and Angoulêmes
**Menu:** 50 to 60 Frs. **Restaurant:** Breakfast served from 5:30am. Lunch served from 11:00am until 2:00pm. Dinner served from 7:00pm until 9:00pm. Closed Sundays. **Specialities:** home cooking. **Other points:** bar, open to non-residents, pets welcome – check for details, traditional decor. **Address:** Route Nationale 141.
MR ANDRÉ TROUSSIEUX
**Telephone:** 45.71.11.73
⊗ ♀ Map 7

# PEZOU, Loir-et-Cher, 41100

### RELAIS D'ARGENTEUIL, RN 10
**Menu:** 60 Frs. **Accommodation:** 88 to 178 Frs. **Restaurant:** Breakfast served from 5:00am. Lunch served from 11:30am until 2:00pm. Dinner served from 6:30pm until 10:30pm. Closed Saturdays, in August and 1 week at end of December. **Specialities:** home cooking. **Hotel:** 6 beds; 2 single rooms, 4 double rooms with shower. **Other points:** bar, open to non-residents, children welcome, pets welcome – check for details, car park, traditional decor. **Address:** Lieu dit 'Fontaine'.
MR PIERRE HAUVILLE
**Telephone:** 54.23.42.47
⊗ ♀ ⌂ Map 6

# PITHIVIERS, Loiret, 45300

### LA PORTE DE BEAUCE, RN 152
**Languages spoken:** English and Polish. **Restaurant:** Breakfast served from 6:30am. Lunch served from midday until 2:00pm. Closed Mondays and in September. **Specialities:** home cooking. **Other points:** bar, open to non-residents, à la carte menu, terraces, pets welcome – check for details, car park, traditional decor, modern decor. **Address:** 6, Mail Ouest.
MR CHRISTIAN COLLARD
**Telephone:** 38.30.02.52
⊗ ♀ Map 6

# POMPAIRE, Deux-Sèvres, 79200

### LA CLE DES CHAMPS, in the commercial centre
**Menu:** 52 to 110 Frs. **Restaurant:** Breakfast served from 7:00am. Lunch served from 11:00am until 3:00pm.

Dinner served from 7:00pm until 9:30pm. Closed
Sundays. **Specialities:** regional menu, home cooking.
**Other points:** bar, open to non-residents, à la carte menu,
children welcome, pets welcome – check for details, car
park, modern decor. **Address:** Route de Saint Maixent.
MME YOLANDE DUBIN
**Telephone:** 49.95.20.75
⊗ ♀ Map 7

## PRESSAC, Vienne, 86460

### LE RELAIS ROUTIER, RN 148, Niort/ Poitiers/Limoges/Gueret
**Menu:** 52 Frs (coffee and wine included). **Restaurant:**
Breakfast served from 5:00am. Lunch served from
10:00am until 4:00pm. Dinner served from 7:00pm until
midnight. Closed Saturdays and from 15 to 30 August.
**Specialities:** home cooking. **Other points:** bar, open to
non-residents, children welcome, terraces, pets welcome
– check for details, car park, traditional decor. **Address:**
Place de l'Eglise.
MME FRANCINE BOUYER
**Telephone:** 49.48.56.99
⊗ ♀ Map 7

## PRUNAY LE GILLON, Eure-et-Loir, 28360

### LA GERBE D'OR, RN 154, between Chartres and Orléans
**Menu:** 55 to 110 Frs. **Accommodation:** 160 to 180 Frs.
**Restaurant:** Breakfast served from 7:00am. Lunch
served from 11:00am until 3:00pm. Dinner served from
6:00pm until 9:30pm. Closed Sundays. **Specialities:**
home cooking. **Hotel:** 5 beds; 4 single rooms, 1 double
room with shower, bath, private WC, telephone. **Other
points:** bar, open to non-residents, à la carte menu,
children welcome, terraces, pets welcome – check for
details, car park, traditional decor. **Address:** Lieu dit
'Fainville', 10, rue du Pavillon.
MR HENRI GOSSET
**Telephone:** 37.25.72.38, 37.25.21.05
⊗ ♀ ⌂ Map 6

## REFFANNES, Deux-Sèvres, 79420

### LE CHEVAL BLANC, RD 938
**Restaurant:** Dinner served from midday until 9:00pm.
Closed Saturdays. **Specialities:** home cooking. **Other
points:** bar, pets welcome – check for details, car park.
**Address:** Avenue de la Grande Auberge, le Bourg.
MR DIDIER CHEVALIER
**Telephone:** 49.70.25.18
⊗ ♀ Map 7

## RHODES, Indre, 36170

### RELAIS ROUTIERS DE RHODES, RN 20, between Limoges and Châteauroux
**Menu:** 54 Frs. **Restaurant:** Breakfast served from

6:00am. Lunch served from midday until midday. Dinner
served from midday until 10:30pm. Closed Saturdays
and in August. **Specialities:** home cooking. **Other
points:** bar, open to non-residents, lounge area, pets
welcome – check for details, car park, traditional decor.
**Address:** Mouhet.
MR JEAN-PIERRE PÉREZ
**Telephone:** 54.47.65.26
⊗ ♀ Map 6

## ROCHECORBON, Indre-et-Loire, 37210

### RELAIS DE PATYS, RN 152, between Tours and Blois
**Languages spoken:** English and Spanish. **Menu:** 49 to
60 Frs. **Accommodation:** 105 to 135 Frs. **Restaurant:**
Breakfast served from 6:30am. Lunch served from
midday until 2:00pm. Dinner served from 7:00pm until
9:00pm. Closed Sundays and in August. **Specialities:**
home cooking. **Hotel:** 4 beds; 2 single rooms, 2 double
rooms. **Other points:** bar, open to non-residents, à la
carte menu, children welcome, lounge area, pets
welcome – check for details, car park, modern decor.
**Address:** 1, rue de Patys.
MR JEAN-MARC NOURRY
**Telephone:** 47.52.61.75
⊗ ♀ Map 6

## ROCHELLE (LA), Charente-Maritime, 17000

### L'AQUARELLE, between la Rochelle and l'Ile de Ré
**Languages spoken:** English and Portugese. **Menu:** 50
Frs (wine included). **Restaurant:** Breakfast served from
7:30am. Lunch served from 11:30am until 2:30pm.
Dinner served from 7:30pm until 9:30pm. Closed
Sundays. **Specialities:** home cooking. **Hotel:** 10 beds; 6
single rooms, 4 double rooms with shower. **Other
points:** bar, open to non-residents, terraces, pets
welcome – check for details, car park. **Address:** 26,
boulevard du Maréchal Lyautey.
MME MURIEL PARENTE
**Telephone:** 46.43.00.27
⊗ ♀ ⌂ ☆ Map 7

### L'OCEANIC, between l'Ile de Ré and la Pallice
**Menu:** 50 to 80 Frs. **Accommodation:** 80 to 120 Frs.
**Restaurant:** Breakfast served from 6:30am. Lunch
served from 11:30am until 2:00pm. Dinner served from
7:30pm until 10:00pm. Closed Saturdays. **Specialities:**
home cooking. **Hotel:** 5 beds; 1 single room, 4 double
rooms with shower, private WC. **Otherpoints:** bar, open
to non-residents, terraces, pets welcome – check for
details, car park, traditional decor. **Address:** Place du
Marché de la Pallice.
MR PHILIPPE ALZIN
**Telephone:** 46.42.62.37
⊗ ♀ ⌂ Map 7

### LE DELMAS BAR

**Restaurant:** Breakfast served from 5:30am. Closed Saturday afternoons, Sundays, 15 days in May and 15 days in September. **Other points:** bar, pets welcome – check for details, car park. **Address:** 32, boulevard Emile Delmas.
MME JEANINE FRANCSON
**Telephone:** 46.42.60.23
♈ Map 7

### LE GOELAND

**Languages spoken:** English and Spanish. **Menu:** 50 Frs. **Restaurant:** Breakfast served from 6:30am. Closed Saturdays. **Specialities:** home cooking. **Hotel:** 6 beds; 6 double rooms with shower, bath, private WC, telephone. **Other points:** bar, open to non-residents, à la carte menu, children welcome, terraces, pets welcome – check for details, car park, traditional decor. **Address:** 15, rue du Docteur Bigois.
MR JACQUES DURANDEAU
**Telephone:** 46.42.05.29
⊗ ♈ 🏠 Map 7

### LES EMBRUNS, *Port de la Pallice, head of the bay*

**Languages spoken:** English. **Menu:** 48 to 120 Frs. **Restaurant:** Breakfast served from 6:00am. Lunch served from 11:30am until 3:00pm. Dinner served from 7:00pm until 9:00pm. Closed Saturdays. **Specialities:** couscous, paëlla, choucroute (every Fridays), regional food, home cooking. **Other points:** bar, open to non-residents, children welcome, pets welcome – check for details, car park, traditional decor. **Address:** 413, avenue Jean Guiton.
RENÉ ET FABIENNE POULTIER
**Telephone:** 46.42.61.88
⊗ ♈ Map 7

## ROCHELLE PALLICE (LA),

Charente-Maritime, 17000

### CHEZ ANNIE

**Menu:** 56 Frs. **Restaurant:** Breakfast served from 6:00am. Lunch served from midday until 3:00pm. Dinner served from 7:00pm until 9:30pm. Closed Sundays and the 1st fortnight in August. **Specialities:** home cooking. **Other points:** bar, pets welcome – check for details, car park, modern decor. **Address:** Rue de l'Ile de Ré.
MME ANNIE BERNELAS
**Telephone:** 46.42.53.61
⊗ ♈ Map 7

## ROMORANTIN LANTHENAY,

Loir-et-Cher, 41200

### LES AUBIERS, *RN 722 and 765, town centre*

**Menu:** 54 to 180 Frs. **Accommodation:** 150 to 200 Frs. **Restaurant:** Breakfast served from 6:30am. Lunch served from midday until 2:00pm. Dinner served from 7:30pm until 9:00pm. **Specialities:** home cooking.

**Hotel:** 19 beds; 14 single rooms, 5 double rooms with shower, bath, private WC, television, telephone. **Other points:** bar, open to non-residents, à la carte menu, children welcome, car park, traditional decor. **Address:** 1, avenue de Blois.
MME BOIVIN
**Telephone:** 54.76.05.59
⊗ ♈ 🏠 ☆ Map 6

### RELAIS DE L'AVENIR, *RN 722 and 765*

**Menu:** 49 to 58 Frs. **Restaurant:** Breakfast served from 7:00am. Lunch served from 11:45am until 2:30pm. Closed Saturdays and 15 days in August. **Specialities:** home cooking. **Other points:** bar, open to non-residents, pets welcome – check for details, traditional decor. **Address:** 44, avenue de Villefranche.
MME JOCELYNE BRETON
**Telephone:** 54.76.14.28
⊗ ♈ Map 6

## RORTHAIS, Deux-Sèvres, 79700

### CHEZ FANFAN, *RN 149, the main road between Poitiers and Nantes*

**Menu:** 49 Frs. **Restaurant:** Breakfast served from 5:30am. Lunch served from 11:30am until 2:30pm. Dinner served from 7:00pm until 10:00pm. Closed Sundays and from 24 December to 7 January. **Specialities:** home cooking. **Other points:** bar, open to non-residents, children welcome, pets welcome – check for details, car park, modern decor. **Address:** 10, place Saint Hilaire.
MR MARIE-FRANÇOISE SIMONNET
**Telephone:** 49.81.44.42
⊗ ♈ Map 7

## ROUILLAC, Charente, 16170

### LA BOULE D'OR, *RN 939, between Angoulême and la Rochelle*

**Languages spoken:** German and English. **Menu:** 53 Frs (wine and coffee included) to 80 Frs. **Accommodation:** 100 to 140 Frs. **Restaurant:** Breakfast served from 6:30am. Lunch served from 11:30am until 3:00pm. Dinner served from 6:30pm until 10:00pm. Closed Sundays and 15 days in August. **Specialities:** home cooking. **Hotel:** 8 beds; 5 single rooms, 3 double rooms with shower. **Other points:** bar, à la carte menu, children welcome, pets welcome – check for details, car park, traditional decor. **Address:** 56, rue du Général de Gaulle.
MME ELISABETH LHERMITE
**Telephone:** 45.96.50.45
⊗ ♈ 🏠 Map 7

## ROUILLE, Vienne, 86480

### CHEZ MARYSE, *RD 950, between Poitiers and Royan*

**Menu:** 60 Frs. **Accommodation:** 120 Frs.

**Restaurant:** Breakfast served from 7:00am. Lunch served from midday until 2:00pm. Dinner served from 7:00pm until 9:00pm. Closed Sundays. **Specialities:** home cooking. **Hotel:** 6 beds; 5 single rooms, 1 double room with shower, private WC. **Other points:** bar, open to non-residents, terraces, pets welcome – check for details, car park, modern decor. **Address:** Le Grand Breuil.
MME MARYSE TELLIER
**Telephone:** 49.43.93.75
⊗ ▽ 🏠 Map 7

## ROUMAZIERES, Charente, 16370

### LES ROUTIERS, RN 141, between Limoges and Angoulême
**Menu:** 48 Frs (wine included). **Restaurant:** Breakfast served from 6:30am. Closed Saturdays and 3 weeks in August. **Specialities:** home cooking. **Other points:** bar, open to non-residents, children welcome, pets welcome – check for details, car park, traditional decor. **Address:** 122, Route Nationale.
MME THÉRESE DEVESNE
**Telephone:** 45.71.10.88
⊗ ▽ Map 7

## ROUMAZIERES LOUBERT,
Charente, 16270

### LES ROUTIERS, RD 951, Confolens, Bellac
**Menu:** 55 to 85 Frs. **Accommodation:** 90 to 110 Frs. **Restaurant:** Breakfast served from 5:30am. Lunch served from 11:00am until 3:00pm. Dinner served from 7:00pm until 11:00pm. Closed Saturdays. **Specialities:** home cooking. **Hotel:** 7 beds; with private WC. **Other points:** open to non-residents, children welcome, terraces, pets welcome – check for details, car park, traditional decor. **Address:** Les 3 Chênes.
MR RAYMOND BISSERIER
**Telephone:** 45.77.71.83
⊗ 🏠 Map 7

## ROYAN, Charente-Maritime, 17200

### L'ESPERANCE
**Menu:** 60 to 80 Frs. **Specialities:** regional menu, home cooking. **Other points:** bar, open to non-residents, à la carte menu, pets welcome – check for details, car park. **Address:** 72, avenue Eléonore d'Aquitaine.
MR GIL ALEXANDRE
**Telephone:** 46.05.01.02
⊗ ▽ Map 7

### LE SYMPATIC, at the entrance of Royan on arrival from Bordeaux
**Menu:** 55 to 70 Frs. **Accommodation:** 140 to 200 Frs. **Restaurant:** Breakfast served from 6:00am. Lunch served from midday until 2:00pm. Dinner served from 7:00pm until 9:00pm. Closed Sundays. **Specialities:**

home cooking. **Hotel:** 15 beds; 5 single rooms, 10 double rooms with shower, private WC. **Other points:** bar, open to non-residents, children welcome, terraces, pets welcome – check for details, car park, traditional decor. **Address:** 30, avenue de la Libération.
MR YVES BOINARD
**Telephone:** 46.05.67.21
⊗ ▽ 🏠 Map 7

## ROZIERES EN BEAUCE, Loiret, 45130

### LA BAGATELLE, RN 157, between Orléans and le Mans
**Menu:** 50 to 70 Frs. **Accommodation:** 120 to 150 Frs. **Restaurant:** Breakfast served from 6:00am. Lunch served from 11:00am until 3:00pm. Dinner served from 6:30pm until 11:00pm. Closed Saturdays. **Specialities:** home cooking. **Hotel:** 4 beds; 2 single rooms, 2 double rooms with shower, private WC. **Other points:** bar, open to non-residents, children welcome, pets welcome – check for details, car park, modern decor. **Address:** 1, rue Bagatelle.
MME SYLVIE BIHEL
**Telephone:** 38.74.22.03
⊗ ▽ 🏠 Map 6

## RUFFEC, Charente, 16700

### LE LANDAIS, RN 10, exit for Ruffec, towards Angoulême
**Menu:** 50 to 80 Frs. **Restaurant:** Breakfast served from 6:30am. Lunch served from midday until 2:30pm. Dinner served from 7:00pm until 9:00pm. Closed Sundays and 15 days in December. **Specialities:** home cooking. **Other points:** bar, open to non-residents, à la carte menu, children welcome, terraces, car park, traditional decor. **Address:** 34, avenue Célestin Sieur.
MR JEAN-MICHEL LAPEGUE
**Telephone:** 45.31.04.16
⊗ ▽ Map 7

### LES ROUTIERS, RN 10, Gare SNCF at Ruffec
**Menu:** 48 Frs. **Restaurant:** Breakfast served from 7:00am. Lunch served from 11:00am until 3:00pm. Dinner served from 7:00pm until 11:00pm. Closed Sundays and 2 weeks in August. **Specialities:** home cooking. **Other points:** bar, open to non-residents, pets welcome – check for details, traditional decor. **Address:** 15, boulevard de Verdun.
MME MARIE-HÉLENE CHINIER
**Telephone:** 45.31.18.09
⊗ ▽ Map 7

### PARIS IRUN – CHEZ BRANGER, RN 10, between Poitier and Angoulême
**Menu:** 60 Frs. **Restaurant:** Breakfast served from 6:00am. Lunch served from midday until 2:00pm.

Closed Sundays and in August. **Specialities:** regional menu, home cooking. **Other points:** bar, open to non-residents, pets welcome – check for details, car park. **Address:** Les Adjots.
MR JACKY SOMMIER
**Telephone:** 45.31.02.44
⊗ ♈ Map 7

## RUFFEC LE CHATEAU, Indre, 36300

### CHEZ P'TIT JEAN, RN 151, between Poitiers and Châteauroux

**Menu:** 50 to 90 Frs. **Accommodation:** 85 Frs. **Restaurant:** Breakfast served from 6:00am. Lunch served from 11:30am until 2:30pm. Dinner served from 7:00pm until 10:00pm. Closed Fridays and 15 days in September. **Specialities:** home cooking. **Hotel:** 4 beds; 4 single rooms. **Other points:** bar, open to non-residents, children welcome, terraces, pets welcome – check for details, car park, traditional decor. **Address:** Route Nationale 151.
MME MICHELINE MARANDON
**Telephone:** 54.37.70.05
⊗ ♈ Map 6

## SAINT AGNANT, Charente-Maritime, 17260

### AU RENDEZ-VOUS DES AMIS

**Languages spoken:** German and English. **Menu:** 58 to 60 Frs. **Restaurant:** Lunch served from 11:30am until 2:00pm. Dinner served from 7:00pm until 10:00pm. Closed Mondays and in October/November. **Other points:** bar, car park. **Address:** Le Pont.
MME MURIEL CHAUTARD
**Telephone:** 46.83.30.36
⊗ ♈ Map 7

## SAINT AIGNAN LE JAILLARD, Loiret, 45600

### LES ROUTIERS SAINT AIGNAN, RD 952, between Sully and Gien

**Menu:** 53 to 120 Frs. **Restaurant:** Breakfast served from 7:30am. Lunch served from midday until 3:00pm. Dinner served from 7:00pm until 10:00pm. Closed Wednesdays, vacation periods in February and 15 days at end of August. **Specialities:** home cooking. **Other points:** bar, open to non-residents, children welcome, terraces, pets welcome – check for details, car park, traditional decor. **Address:** 78, rue Nationale.
MME CLAUDINE GASNIER
**Telephone:** 38.36.38.21
⊗ ♈ Map 6

## SAINT ARNOULT DES BOIS, Eure-et-Loir, 28190

### TY KORN

**Restaurant:** Closed in August. **Hotel:** 5 beds. **Other**

points: bar. **Address:** 40, Grande Rue.
MR DANIEL LE CAM
**Telephone:** 37.22.53.17
⊗ ♈ ⌂ Map 6

## SAINT AUBIN DES BOIS, Eure-et-Loir, 28300

### LA MORICERIE, RN 23, between Chartres and Nogent le Rotrou

**Menu:** 48, 50 to 68, 50 Frs. **Restaurant:** Open 24 hours. **Specialities:** home cooking. **Other points:** bar, open to non-residents, à la carte menu, children welcome, lounge area, terraces, pets welcome – check for details, car park. **Addresse:** Lieu dit 'La Moricerie', Route Nationale 23.
MR DOMINIQUE LIBÉRATORE
**Telephone:** 37.32.81.14
⊗ ♈ Map 6

## SAINT AUGUSTIN SUR MER, Charente-Maritime, 17570

### LA MARINA, between Royan and la Tremblade

**Languages spoken:** English and Spanish. **Menu:** 55 (wine and coffee included) to 110 Frs. **Restaurant:** Breakfast served from 7:00am. Lunch served from 11:30am until 2:00pm. Dinner served from 6:30pm until 10:00pm. Closed 3 weeks in October. **Specialities:** regional menu, home cooking. **Other points:** bar, open to non-residents, à la carte menu, children welcome, terraces, pets welcome – check for details, car park, modern decor. **Address:** Centre Commercial.
MR JACKY DUSSAILLANT
**Telephone:** 46.23.28.22
⊗ ♈ Map 7

## SAINT BENOIT DU SAULT, Indre, 36170

### HOTEL DU COMMERCE – CHEZ MARINETTE, RN 20, between Argenton sur Creuse and le Blanc

**Menu:** 50 to 70 Frs. **Accommodation:** 90 to 150 Frs. **Restaurant:** Breakfast served from 7:00am. Lunch served from midday until 2:00pm. Dinner served from 7:30pm until 9:30pm. **Specialities:** home cooking. **Hotel:** 9 beds; 7 single rooms, 2 double rooms. **Other points:** bar, open to non-residents, children welcome, terraces, pets welcome – check for details, car park, traditional decor. **Address:** Place de l'Enchère.
MME MARINETTE THÉVENOT
**Telephone:** 54.47.54.70
⊗ ♈ ⌂ Map 6

## SAINT EUGENE, Charente-Maritime, 17520

### LES DEUX CHARENTES, RD 731, between Barbezieux and Royan

**Menu:** 53 to 170 Frs. **Restaurant:** Breakfast served from 6:30am. Lunch served from 11:00am until 2:30pm. Dinner served from 7:15pm until 9:00pm. Closed Wednesdays and mid-February. **Specialities:** regional menu, home cooking. **Other points:** bar, à la carte menu, children welcome, terraces, pets welcome – check for details, car park, traditional decor. **Address:** Lieu dit 'La Maison de Bois'.
MME MARCELLE BLANCHARD
**Telephone:** 46.49.13.28
⊗ ♈ ᗧ Map 7

## SAINT FLORENT SUR CHER,

Cher, 18400

### L'IMPREVU, RD 28
**Restaurant:** Closed Sundays and in August. **Other points:** bar. **Address:** 60, rue Jean Jaures.
MR BERNARD RUELLAN
**Telephone:** 48.55.12.00
⊗ ♈ Map 6

## SAINT GENIS DE SAINTONGE,

Charente-Maritime, 17240

### LE RELAIS DE SAINTONGE, RN 137, the main road between Saintes and Bordeaux
**Languages spoken:** English. **Menu:** 60 (wine and coffee included) to 130 Frs. **Accommodation:** 95 to 120 Frs. **Restaurant:** Open 24 hours. **Specialities:** regional menu, home cooking. **Hotel:** 10 beds. **Other points:** bar, open to non-residents, à la carte menu, children welcome, lounge area, terraces, pets welcome – check for details, car park, traditional decor. **Address:** Route Nationale 137.
ROUX SA
**Telephone:** 46.49.00.95
⊗ ♈ 🏠 ☆ Map 7

## SAINT GEORGES SUR EURE,

Eure-et-Loir, 28190

### AU RENDEZ-VOUS DES PECHEURS, RN 23, between Chartres and le Mans
**Languages spoken:** Notion d'English. **Menu:** 50 Frs. **Accommodation:** 130 to 170 Frs. **Restaurant:** Breakfast served from 6:30am. Lunch served from midday until 2:00pm. Dinner served from 7:00pm until 8:30pm. Closed Sundays and between Christmas Day and New Year's Day. **Specialities:** home cooking. **Hotel:** 9 beds; 2 single rooms, 7 double rooms with shower, bath, private WC, television. **Other points:** bar, open to non-residents, à la carte menu, children welcome, terraces, pets welcome – check for details, car park, traditional decor. **Address:** 9, rue Raymond Bataille.
HENRI ET MONIQUE HUBERT
**Telephone:** 37.26.81.90
⊗ ♈ 🏠 Map 6

## SAINT GERMAIN LA GATINE,

Eure-et-Loir, 28300

### LE RELAIS DE SAINT GERMAIN, RN 154, between Dreux and Chartres
**Menu:** 49 Frs. **Restaurant:** Breakfast served from 5:00am. Lunch served from 11:30am until 2:30pm. Dinner served from 7:00pm until 9:00pm. Closed Saturdays. **Specialities:** home cooking. **Other points:** bar, children welcome, pets welcome – check for details, car park, modern decor. **Address:** 1, route de Chartres.
MR PIERRE PICARD
**Telephone:** 37.22.80.31
⊗ ♈ Map 6

## SAINT HILAIRE LA GRAVELLE,

Loir-et-Cher, 41160

### AUBERGE DU LOIR, RD 19, the main road between Orléans and le Mans
**Languages spoken:** English. **Menu:** 57 to 60 Frs. **Accommodation:** 195 Frs. **Restaurant:** Breakfast served from 7:00am. Lunch served from midday until 2:00pm. Dinner served from 7:00pm until 10:00pm. Closed Wednesdays and in September. **Specialities:** home cooking. **Hotel:** 2 beds; 2 single rooms with shower, private WC. **Other points:** bar, open to non-residents, children welcome, terraces, pets welcome – check for details, car park, traditional decor. **Address:** 10, rue Léon Cibié.
MR SYLVAIN PIERDOS
**Telephone:** 54.82.65.00
⊗ ♈ Map 6

## SAINT JEAN D'ANGELY, Charente-Maritime, 17400

### CHEZ VEVETTE, CD 950, between Saint Jean d'Angély and Poitiers
**Menu:** 60 Frs. **Accommodation:** 80 to 120 Frs. **Restaurant:** Dinner served from midday until 8:00pm. Closed Friday evenings, Saturday evenings, Sundays and from 15 August to 1 September. **Specialities:** home cooking. **Hotel:** 5 beds; 4 single rooms, 1 double room. **Other points:** bar. **Address:** Les Eglises d'Argenteuil.
MR JOEL PILLOT
**Telephone:** 46.59.94.21
⊗ ♈ 🏠 Map 7

## SAINT LEGER, Charente-Maritime, 17800

### L'ARCHE DE SAINT LEGER, A 10, 20km after the exit for Saintes, towards Bordeaux
**Languages spoken:** German, English and Spanish. **Menu:** 40 to 80 Frs (cafétéria) and 75 to 120 Frs (grill). **Restaurant:** Breakfast served from 6:00am. Lunch served from 10:30am until 3:00pm. Dinner served from 6:00pm until 11:00pm. Open 24 hours in July and

August. **Specialities:** regional menu. **Other points:** open to non-residents, à la carte menu, children welcome, terraces, pets welcome – check for details, car park. **Address:** A 10 Aire de Saint-Léger, accessible dans les deux sens.
ACCOR
**Telephone:** 46.91.95.30. **Fax:** 46.91.93.82
⊗  Map 7

## SAINT MARTIN DE RE, Charente-Maritime, 17410

*EL PANCHO, Saint Martin, at the pedestrian lights turn left*
**Menu:** 55 Frs. **Restaurant:** Breakfast served from 10:00am. Lunch served from midday until 1:45pm. Dinner served from 7:00pm until 10:00pm. Closed Sundays and beginning of October. **Specialities:** pizza, home cooking. **Other points:** open to non-residents, à la carte menu, pets welcome – check for details, car park, traditional decor. **Address:** Route de la Flotte, Venelle de la Cristallerie.
MME BRIGITTE RAGUENAUD
**Telephone:** 46.09.02.05
⊗  Map 7

## SAINT MAUR, Indre, 36250

*LA BUVETTE DES TERRES NOIRES, RN 20, between Châteauroux south and Limoges*
**Languages spoken:** English. **Menu:** 55 (wine included) to 80 Frs. **Restaurant:** Breakfast served from 7:00am. Lunch served from 11:45am until 2:15pm. Dinner served from 6:45pm until 10:00pm. Closed Sundays and the 2nd fortnight in January. **Specialities:** home cooking. **Otherpoints:** bar, open to non-residents, à la carte menu, children welcome, terraces, pets welcome – check for details, car park, traditional decor. **Address:** Route Nationale 20.
MR FRANCK STEVENOT
**Telephone:** 54.27.00.64
⊗  ♈  Map 6

## SAINT MAURICE SUR FESSARD, Loiret, 45700

*CAFE DE LA GARE*
**Languages spoken:** English and Spanish. **Restaurant:** Closed Saturdays. **Other points:** bar. **Address:** Route Nationale 60.
MME COLETTE JEHL
**Telephone:** 38.97.81.00
⊗  ♈  Map 6

*LE RELAIS DE SAINT MAURICE, RN 60, the main road between Montargis and Orléans*
**Menu:** 57 Frs. **Restaurant:** Breakfast served from

6:30am. Lunch served from midday until 2:00pm. Dinner served from 7:15pm until 9:30pm. Closed Saturdays. **Specialities:** regional menu, home cooking. **Other points:** bar, open to non-residents, terraces, car park, traditional decor. **Address:** Route Nationale 60.
MR PASCAL CROUVISIER
**Telephone:** 38.97.80.59
⊗  ♈  Map 6

## SAINT NICOLAS DE BOURGUEIL, Indre-et-Loire, 37140

*LE RELAIS*
**Menu:** 50 to 75 Frs. **Restaurant:** Breakfast served from 7:00am. Lunch served from 11:30am until 2:30pm. Dinner served from 7:30pm until 9:00pm. Closed Sundays and from 15 to 26 August. **Specialities:** home cooking. **Hotel:** 3 beds; 1 single room, 2 double rooms with shower. **Other points:** bar, à la carte menu, pets welcome – check for details, car park. **Address:** Place de l'Eglise.
MR JOEL JOULIN
**Telephone:** 47.97.75.39
⊗  ♈  Map 6

## SAINT PIERRE DES CORPS, Indre-et-Loire, 37700

*LE GRILLON*
**Menu:** 57 Frs (wine included). **Restaurant:** Breakfast served from 5:30am. Lunch served from midday until 2:00pm. Dinner served from 7:15pm until 9:30pm. Closed Saturdays, Sundays and in July or in August. **Specialities:** home cooking. **Other points:** bar, open to non-residents, car park, modern decor. **Address:** 9, quai de la Loire.
MME JEAN-CLAUDE LATOUR
**Telephone:** 47.44.74.90
⊗  ♈  Map 6

## SAINT SAVINIEN, Charente-Maritime, 17350

*LE SAINT SAVINIEN, RD 18, between Saintes (12km) and Saint Jean d'Angély (10km)*
**Menu:** 60 Frs (wine and coffee included). **Accommodation:** 120 to 210 Frs. **Restaurant:** Breakfast served from 7:30am. Lunch served from midday until 2:00pm. Dinner served from 7:30pm until 10:00pm. Closed Wednesdays. **Specialities:** regional menu, home cooking. **Hotel:** 9 beds; 7 single rooms, 2 double rooms. **Other points:** bar, open to non-residents, à la carte menu, children welcome, pets welcome – check for details, car park, traditional decor. **Address:** 27, rue de Champeroux.
MLLE ELISABETH DIEU
**Telephone:** 46.90.20.33
⊗  ♈  ⌂  Map 7

## SAINT SORNIN, Charente, 16220

### LES ROUTIERS, between la Rochefoucaud and Montbron

**Menu:** 58 Frs. **Restaurant:** Breakfast served from 6:30am. Lunch served from midday until 2:00pm. Dinner served from 7:00pm until 9:00pm. Closed Mondays and 15 days in August. **Specialities:** home cooking. **Other points:** bar, open to non-residents, children welcome, terraces, pets welcome – check for details, car park, traditional decor. **Address:** Le Bourg.
MR THÉRESE DUBOIS
**Telephone:** 45.23.12.83
⊗ ⛾ Map 7

## SAINT SYMPHORIEN, Eure-et-Loir, 28700

### LE RELAIS DES ESSARS, RN 10, between Rambouillet and Chartres

**Languages spoken:** English. **Menu:** 51 Frs.
**Restaurant:** Breakfast served from 6:00am.
**Specialities:** home cooking. **Other points:** bar, open to non-residents, children welcome, terraces, car park, modern decor. **Address:** Route Nationale 10, Essars.
MR ALAIN NAU
**Telephone:** 37.31.18.30
⊗ ⛾ Map 6

## SAINT VICTOR DE BUTHON, Eure-et-Loir, 28240

### CHEZ MIMI, RN 23, between Nogent le Rotrou and Chartres

**Menu:** 55 to 115 Frs. **Restaurant:** Breakfast served from 6:30am. Lunch served from midday until 3:00pm. Dinner served from 7:00pm until 10:30pm. Closed Sundays. **Specialities:** home cooking. **Other points:** bar, open to non-residents, children welcome, pets welcome – check for details, car park. **Address:** Lieu dit 'La Hurie'.
MR FAVERIS
**Telephone:** 37.81.34.60
⊗ ⛾ Map 6

## SAINTE MAURE DE TOURAINE, Indre-et-Loire, 37800

### L'ETOILE DU SUD, RN 10, the main road between Tours and Poitiers

**Languages spoken:** English and Arabic. **Menu:** 50 (wine included) to 80 Frs. **Accommodation:** 100 to 250 Frs. **Restaurant:** Breakfast served from 4:00am. Lunch served from midday until 2:30pm. Dinner served from 7:00pm until 10:30pm. **Specialities:** regional menu, home cooking. **Hotel:** 25 beds; 21 single rooms, 4 double rooms with shower, bath, private WC. **Other points:** bar, open to non-residents, à la carte menu, children welcome, lounge area, terraces, pets welcome –

check for details, car park, modern decor. **Address:** Route Nationale 10.
MR KARIM MEDJAHED
**Telephone:** 47.65.40.61
⊗ ⛾ ⌂ ☆ Map 6

## SAINTES, Charente-Maritime, 17100

### L'OASIS, RN 137, town centre

**Menu:** 45 to 95 Frs. **Restaurant:** Breakfast served from 6:00am. Lunch served from midday until 2:00pm. Dinner served from 7:15pm until 9:15pm. Closed Saturdays, from 3 to 25 August and from 24 to 31 December. **Specialities:** home cooking. **Other points:** bar, open to non-residents, à la carte menu, lounge area, terraces, pets welcome – check for details, car park, traditional decor. **Address:** Route de Rochefort.
MR GUY FUMOLEAU
**Telephone:** 46.93.07.20
⊗ ⛾ Map 7

## SANCERGUES, Cher, 18140

### LE BON LABOUREUR, RN 151, between la Charité sur Loire and Bourges

**Languages spoken:** German and Italian. **Menu:** 56, 50 to 150 Frs. **Accommodation:** 90 to 100 Frs.
**Restaurant:** Breakfast served from 7:30am. Lunch served from 11:45am until 1:45pm. Dinner served from 7:00pm until 8:30pm. Closed Tuesdays and from 5 July to 5 August. **Specialities:** home cooking. **Hotel:** 4 beds; 3 single rooms, 1 double room with shower, private WC, telephone. **Other points:** bar, open to non-residents, children welcome, pets welcome – check for details, car park, traditional decor. **Address:** 54, Grande Rue.
MME MARTINE DUBOIS
**Telephone:** 48.72.76.13
⊗ ⛾ Map 6

## SARGE SUR BRAYE, Loir-et-Cher, 41170

### RELAIS DE MONPLAISIR, RN 157, between le Mans/Orléans and Mondoubleau/Montoire

**Languages spoken:** English, Spanish and Italian.
**Menu:** 51 Frs. **Restaurant:** Breakfast served from 6:00am. Lunch served from 11:30am until 3:00pm. Dinner served from 7:00pm until 10:30pm. Closed Saturdays and in August. **Specialities:** home cooking. **Other points:** bar, open to non-residents, terraces, car park, traditional decor. **Address:** Route Nationale 157.
MR MICHEL MOUJEARD
**Telephone:** 54.72.72.21
⊗ ⛾ Map 6

## SAUJON, Charente-Maritime, 17600

### HOTEL DE LA GARE, RN 150, between Saintes and Royan

Languages spoken: English. **Menu:** 35 to 65 Frs.
**Accommodation:** 140 to 200 Frs. **Restaurant:**
Breakfast served from 7:00am. Lunch served from
midday until 2:00pm. Dinner served from 7:30pm until
9:00pm. Closed Sundays and end of December.
**Specialities:** home cooking. **Hotel:** 12 beds; 6 single
rooms, 6 double rooms with shower, private WC,
television, telephone. **Other points:** bar, open to non-
residents, children welcome, lounge area, terraces, pets
welcome – check for details, car park, traditional decor.
**Address:** 2, rue Clémenceau.
MR MICHEL MELLOT
**Telephone:** 46.02.80.33
⊗ ☖ ☆ Map 7

## SAUZE VAUSSAIS, Deux-Sèvres, 79190

### LE RELAIS DES ROUTIERS, RD 948
**Menu:** 50 Frs. **Restaurant:** Breakfast served from
7:00am. Lunch served from 11:30am until 2:30pm.
Dinner served from 7:00pm until 10:00pm. Closed
Saturdays and in August. **Specialities:** home cooking.
**Other points:** bar, open to non-residents, lounge area,
car park, traditional decor. **Address:** Chaignepain.
MR JOEL QUINTARD
**Telephone:** 49.29.34.61
⊗ ☖ Map 7

## SAZILLY, Indre-et-Loire, 37220

### RELAIS DE LA PROMENADE, RN 760, towards Chiron
**Menu:** 46 Frs. **Restaurant:** Breakfast served from
7:00am. Lunch served from 11:45am until 2:00pm.
Dinner served from 7:00pm until 8:30pm. Closed
Sundays. **Specialities:** home cooking. **Other points:**
bar, open to non-residents, terraces, pets welcome –
check for details, car park, traditional decor. **Address:**
Le Bourg.
MME JOCELYNE BIGOT
**Telephone:** 47.58.55.50
⊗ ☖ Map 6

## SCOURY, Indre, 36300

### LE RELAIS ROUTIERS, RN 151, between Châteauroux and le Blanc
**Menu:** 52 Frs. **Accommodation:** 90 Frs. **Restaurant:**
Breakfast served from 5:30am. Lunch served from
11:00am until 3:00pm. Dinner served from 7:00pm until
10:00pm. Closed Sundays and from 24 December to 2
January. **Specialities:** home cooking. **Hotel:** 5 beds; 4
single rooms, 1 double room with shower, bath, private
WC. **Other points:** bar, open to non-residents, children
welcome, pets welcome – check for details, car park,
traditional decor. **Address:** Le Bourg.
MME ROSELYNE PILET
**Telephone:** 54.37.98.09
⊗ ☖ Map 6

## SECONDIGNY, Deux-Sèvres, 79130

### LES ROUTIERS, RD 949, la Roche sur Yon
Languages spoken: English. **Menu:** 50 to 120 Frs.
**Accommodation:** 100 to 150 Frs. **Restaurant:**
Breakfast served from 7:00am. Lunch served from
11:30am until 2:00pm. Dinner served from 7:00pm until
9:00pm. Closed Mondays, 1 week in February and 1
week in September. **Specialities:** regional menu, home
cooking. **Hotel:** 5 beds; 3 single rooms, 2 double rooms
with shower, private WC, television, telephone. **Other
points:** bar, open to non-residents, à la carte menu,
children welcome, terraces, car park, traditional decor.
**Address:** 43, rue de la Vendée.
MR NOEL DURANCEAU
**Telephone:** 49.95.61.35
⊗ ☖ ☞ Map 7

## SERAZEREUX 'LE PEAGE', Eure-et-Loir, 28170

### AU BON ACCEUIL, RN 154, between Chartres and Dreux
**Menu:** 50 to 85 Frs. **Restaurant:** Breakfast served from
4:30am. Closed Sundays and in August. **Specialities:**
home cooking. **Other points:** bar, open to non-residents,
children welcome, pets welcome – check for details, car
park, modern decor. **Address:** Route Nationale 154.
MME ELIANE HÉRISSON
**Telephone:** 37.65.22.49
⊗ ☖ Map 6

## SERIGNY, Charente-Maritime, 17230

### CHEZ JOHAN, Nantes
**Restaurant:** Dinner served from midday until midnight.
Closed Sundays. **Other points:** bar. **Address:** Route
Nationale 137.
MR JOHAN MERCIER
**Telephone:** 46.01.40.43
⊗ ☖ Map 7

## SOLTERRE, Loiret, 45700

### AUBERGE DE LA ROUTE BLEUE, RN 7, Nevers
Languages spoken: German, English and Italian.
**Menu:** 55 to 90 Frs. **Restaurant:** Breakfast served from
6:00am. Lunch served from midday until 2:00pm.
Dinner served from 7:00pm until 10:00pm. Closed
Tuesdays and mid-August. **Specialities:** ris de veau
normand, escalope cordon bleu, escargots roquefort,
home cooking. **Other points:** bar, open to non-residents,
à la carte menu, terraces, pets welcome – check for
details, car park, traditional decor. **Address:** 32, Route
Nationale 7, la Commodité.
ALBERT ET CHARLES ROCCO
**Telephone:** 38.94.90.04
⊗ ☖ ☞ Map 6

## SOMMIERES DU CLAIN, Vienne, 86160

### *AUBERGE DES 3 PILLIERS*

**Menu:** 45 to 120 Frs. **Accommodation:** 65 Frs. **Restaurant:** Breakfast served from 6:00am. Lunch served from midday until 3:00pm. Dinner served from 7:00pm until 11:00pm. Closed Mondays and 15 days in February. **Specialities:** regional menu, home cooking. **Hotel:** 5 beds; 5 single rooms with shower, bath. **Other points:** bar, open to non-residents, à la carte menu, children welcome, terraces, pets welcome – check for details, car park, traditional decor. **Address:** Place de l'Eglise.

MR MARTIAL RICHARD

**Telephone:** 49.87.70.09

⊗ Ῡ ⌂ Map 7

## SUEVRES, Loir-et-Cher, 41500

### *LE RELAIS DE LA PROVIDENCE, RN 152, between Orléans and Tours*

**Languages spoken:** English and Spanish. **Menu:** 55 to 125 Frs. **Accommodation:** 100 to 180 Frs. **Restaurant:** Breakfast served from 6:00am. Lunch served from midday until 3:00pm. Dinner served from 7:00pm until 10:00pm. Closed Saturdays. **Specialities:** home cooking. **Hotel:** 7 beds; 2 single rooms, 5 double rooms with shower. **Other points:** bar, open to non-residents, à la carte menu, children welcome, pets welcome – check for details, car park, traditional decor. **Address:** 1, place de la Mairie.

MR MICHEL GROSSE

**Telephone:** 54.87.80.88

⊗ Ῡ ⌂ Map 6

## SULLY SUR LOIRE, Loiret, 45600

### *CAFE DE LA GARE – CHEZ LIONEL, Gare/Gendarmerie*

**Menu:** 58, 50 Frs. **Restaurant:** Breakfast served from 6:30am. Closed Saturdays and from 8 to 23 August. **Specialities:** home cooking. **Hotel:** 10 beds; 5 single rooms, 5 double rooms with shower, private WC, television. **Other points:** bar, open to non-residents, children welcome, lounge area, terraces, pets welcome – check for details, car park. **Address:** 47–9, avenue de la Gare.

MR LIONEL FUNTEN

**Telephone:** 38.36.26.11

⊗ Ῡ ⌂ ☆ Map 6

### *LE SAINT GERMAIN – LE CERCLE D'OR, RN 152, on leaving Sully, towards Orléans*

**Menu:** 50 to 102 Frs. **Accommodation:** 130 to 155 Frs. **Restaurant:** Breakfast served from 6:30am. Lunch served from 11:30am until 1:45pm. Dinner served from 7:00pm until 9:00pm. Closed Fridays and the 2nd fortnight in December. **Specialities:** regional menu, home cooking. **Hotel:** 6 beds; with shower. **Other points:** bar, open to non-residents, à la carte menu, children welcome, pets welcome – check for details, car park, traditional decor. **Address:** 2, place Saint Germain.

BERNARD ET PATRICIA SCHWARTZ

**Telephone:** 38.36.27.02

⊗ Ῡ ⌂ Map 6

## SURY AUX BOIS, Loiret, 45530

### *LE RELAIS DU PONT DES BEIGNERS, RN 60, between Orléans and Montargis*

**Menu:** 56 to 67 Frs. **Restaurant:** Breakfast served from 6:00am. Lunch served from 11:30am until 2:30pm. Dinner served from 6:30pm until 10:00pm. Closed Saturdays and from mid-August to mid-September. **Specialities:** home cooking. **Other points:** bar, open to non-residents, à la carte menu, terraces, pets welcome – check for details, car park, traditional decor. **Address:** Pont des Beigners.

MR JEAN-PIERRE GUERU

**Telephone:** 38.55.97.72, 38.55.82.43

⊗ Ῡ Map 6

## SURY ES BOIS, Cher, 18260

### *HOTEL DU LAURIER, RD 926, the main road between Auxerre/Vierzon/Bourges*

**Menu:** 50 to 55 Frs. **Accommodation:** 55 to 100 Frs. **Restaurant:** Breakfast served from 7:00am. Lunch served from 11:30am until 2:30pm. Dinner served from 7:00pm until 8:45pm. Closed Sundays, end of August and at Christmas. **Specialities:** home cooking. **Hotel:** 5 beds; 2 single rooms, 3 double rooms. **Other points:** bar, open to non-residents, pets welcome – check for details, car park, traditional decor. **Address:** Le Bourg.

MR DOMINIQUE LE MERCIER

**Telephone:** 48.73.74.62

⊗ Ῡ ⌂ Map 6

## TAVERS, Loiret, 45190

### *LA PIERRE TOURNANTE, RN 152*

**Restaurant:** Closed Sundays. **Other points:** bar. **Address:** 36, Route Nationale 152.

MR DANIEL LECOQ

**Telephone:** 38.44.92.25

⊗ Ῡ Map 6

## TENDU, Indre, 36200

### *LE RELAIS, RN 20, the main road between Paris and Limoges*

**Menu:** 60 to 140 Frs. **Accommodation:** 120 to 180 Frs. **Restaurant:** Dinner served from midday until 8:00pm. Closed Tuesdays, 1 week end of September/beginning of October and 1 week in winter. **Specialities:** regional menu, home cooking. **Hotel:** 9

beds; 4 single rooms, 5 double rooms with shower.
**Other points:** bar, open to non-residents, à la carte menu, pets welcome – check for details, traditional decor. **Address:** Route Nationale 20.
MR ANDRÉ LUNEAU
**Telephone:** 54.24.14.10
⊗ ⅋ 🏠 Map 6

## THEILLAY, Loir-et-Cher, 41300

### RELAIS DE LA LOGE, RD 41, 13km from Vierzon

**Languages spoken:** English. **Accommodation:** 100 to 150 Frs. **Specialities:** Gibier (in season), home cooking. **Hotel:** 35 beds; 15 single rooms, 20 double rooms with shower, private WC. **Other points:** bar, pets welcome – check for details, car park.
MR GUY PAILLAUD
**Telephone:** 54.83.37.20
⊗ ⅋ 🏠 🍽 ☆ Map 6

## THIVARS, Eure-et-Loir, 28630

### LE RESTAURANT DU STADE, RN 10, 5km from Chartres

**Menu:** 50 to 68 Frs. **Accommodation:** 140 Frs (+ 35 Frs for extra bed). **Restaurant:** Breakfast served from 6:30am. Lunch served from midday until 2:30pm. Dinner served from 7:00pm until 9:30pm. Closed Saturdays. **Specialities:** home cooking. **Hotel:** 8 beds; 4 single rooms, 4 double rooms with shower, private WC. **Other points:** bar, open to non-residents, à la carte menu, pets welcome – check for details, car park, modern decor. **Address:** 15, Route Nationale.
MR PATRICK PETIT
**Telephone:** 37.26.40.05
⊗ ⅋ 🏠 Map 6

## THOU, Loiret, 45420

### AU LIT ON DORT, RD 965

**Restaurant:** Lunch served from 11:30am until 2:30pm. Closed Mondays and in August. **Specialities:** home cooking. **Other points:** open to non-residents, pets welcome – check for details, car park, traditional decor. **Address:** 15, Route Nationale.
MR SOLANGE BERTRAND
**Telephone:** 38.31.62.07
⊗ Map 6

## THOUARS, Deux-Sèvres, 79100

### LE MILLE PATTES, RN 1

**Languages spoken:** English and German. **Other points:** bar. **Address:** 17, route de Launay.
MME MARTINE VALLEAU
**Telephone:** 49.56.36.53
⊗ ⅋ Map 7

## TONNAY CHARENTE, Charente-Maritime, 17430

### L'OASIS, RN 137, 300m from the suspension bridge

**Restaurant:** Breakfast served from 8:00am. Lunch served from midday until 2:00pm. Closed Sundays. **Specialities:** home cooking. **Other points:** bar, open to non-residents, pets welcome – check for details, car park. **Address:** 27, rue de Lattre de Tassigny.
MME GENEVIEVE VACHON
**Telephone:** 46.88.70.84
⊗ ⅋ Map 7

### LES FONTAINES, RN 137, between Nantes and Bordeaux, exit Rochefort

**Menu:** 50 Frs. **Restaurant:** Lunch served from 11:30am until 2:30pm. Dinner served from 7:00pm until 9:00pm. Closed Sundays. **Specialities:** home cooking. **Other points:** bar, children welcome, terraces, pets welcome – check for details, car park, traditional decor. **Address:** 110, avenue d'Aunis.
MR JEAN-PAUL REVELAUD
**Telephone:** 46.83.79.11
⊗ ⅋ Map 7

## TOURY, Eure-et-Loir, 28390

### LE RELAIS DE LA CHAPELLE

**Menu:** 59 Frs. **Restaurant:** Breakfast served from 4:00am. Lunch served from midday until 2:30pm. Dinner served from 7:30pm until 11:00pm. Closed Saturdays, 8 days in May and 8 days at Christmas. **Specialities:** home cooking. **Other points:** bar, terraces, car park, traditional decor. **Address:** 60, avenue de la Chapelle.
MME CLAUDINE COMARLOT
**Telephone:** 37.90.64.96
⊗ ⅋ Map 6

## TOUVERAC, Charente, 16360

### LE RELAIS DE TOUVERAC, RN 10, the main road between Angoulême and Bordeaux

**Languages spoken:** English, Spanish, Portugese. **Menu:** 57 (wine included) to 105 Frs. **Restaurant:** Breakfast served from 5:00am. Lunch served from 11:30am until 3:00pm. Dinner served from 7:00pm until 11:00pm. **Specialities:** regional menu, home cooking. **Other points:** bar, open to non-residents, à la carte menu, children welcome, lounge area, terraces, pets welcome – check for details, car park, modern decor. **Address:** Route Nationale 10.
MME MARYLINE HUDELOT
**Telephone:** 45.78.63.53
⊗ ⅋ Map 7

## TREON, Eure-et-Loir, 28500

### LE RELAIS DE TREON, RN 928, between le Mans and Nogent le Rotrou

**Menu:** 55 Frs. **Restaurant:** Breakfast served from 6:30am. Lunch served from 11:30am until 3:00pm. Dinner served from 7:30pm until 9:00pm. Closed Saturdays, Sundays and in August. **Hotel:** 7 beds. **Other points:** bar, open to non-residents, pets welcome – check for details. **Address:** 20, rue de Châteauneuf.
MME PAULETTE CUVELLIER
**Telephone:** 37.82.62.35
⊗ ⓨ ⌂ Map 6

## TRIMOUILLE (LA), Vienne, 86290

### L'AUBERGE FLEURIE, RN 675, take Blois/Périgueux road

**Menu:** 50 to 80 Frs. **Accommodation:** 90 to 160 Frs. **Restaurant:** Lunch served from midday until 2:00pm. Dinner served from 8:00pm until 9:00pm. Closed Sundays and all evenings from 30 June to 1 September. **Specialities:** moules au vert, médaillon de ris de veau à la Trimouillaise, home cooking. **Hotel:** 5 beds; 2 single rooms, 3 double rooms with shower. **Other points:** bar, open to non-residents, car park, traditional decor. **Address:** 30, rue Octave Bernard.
MME MONIQUE DUFOUR
**Telephone:** 49.91.60.64
⊗ ⓨ ⌂ ⌣ Map 7

## VALENCAY, Indre, 36600

### SARL AUBERGE DU CHATEAU, RN 156

**Menu:** 50 Frs. **Accommodation:** 60 to 110 Frs. **Restaurant:** Breakfast served from 6:00am. Lunch served from 11:30am until 2:30pm. Dinner served from 7:30pm until 10:00pm. Closed Sundays, 15 days in September and 3 weeks in February. **Specialities:** home cooking. **Hotel:** 5 beds; 3 single rooms, 2 double rooms. **Other points:** bar, open to non-residents, pets welcome – check for details, car park, traditional decor. **Address:** 1, route de Blois.
MR VINCENT COULON
**Telephone:** 54.00.02.94
⊗ ⓨ ⌂ Map 6

## VARENNE CHANGY, Loiret, 45290

### HOTEL DU CENTRE

**Menu:** 50 Frs (wine and coffee included) to 100 Frs. **Accommodation:** 130 to 160 Frs. **Restaurant:** Breakfast served from 9:00am. Lunch served from midday until 2:30pm. Dinner served from 7:00pm until 8:30pm. **Specialities:** home cooking. **Hotel:** 7 beds. **Other points:** bar, open to non-residents, pets welcome – check for details, traditional decor. **Address:** 1, Grande Place.
MMES TRAMEÇON ET PÉNALVERT
**Telephone:** 38.94.50.14
⊗ ⓨ ⌂ Map 6

## VATAN, Indre, 36150

### LE CHENE VERT, RN 20

**Accommodation:** 90 to 130 Frs. **Restaurant:** Breakfast served from 7:45am. Lunch served from midday until 2:00pm. Dinner served from 7:30pm until 9:30pm. Closed Saturdays, Sundays and in September. **Specialities:** home cooking. **Hotel:** 6 beds; 4 single rooms, 2 double rooms with shower, bath. **Other points:** bar, open to non-residents, pets welcome – check for details, car park, modern decor. **Address:** 13, avenue de Paris.
MME ANDRÉE LAHAYE
**TELEPHONE:** 54.49.76.56
⊗ ⓨ ⌂ Map 6

## VENDOME, Loir-et-Cher, 41100

### CHEZ MEMERE, RN 10, the main road between Tours and Bordeaux

**Menu:** 60 to 120 Frs. **Accommodation:** 75 to 100 Frs. **Restaurant:** Breakfast served from 7:00am. Lunch served from midday until 2:30pm. Dinner served from 7:30pm until 9:30pm. Closed Mondays and from 20 February to 10 March. **Specialities:** home cooking. **Hotel:** 14 beds. **Other points:** open to non-residents, pets welcome – check for details, car park, traditional decor. **Address:** 127, faubourg Chartrain.
MLLE ANDRÉE TOUCHARD
**Telephone:** 54.77.00.32
⊗ ⌂ Map 6

## VERRUE, Vienne, 86420

### LA BALBINIERE – CHEZ RÉMY ET PAULETTE, RN 147, the main road between Angers and Poitiers

**Menu:** 50 to 85 Frs. **Accommodation:** 110 to 200 Frs. **Restaurant:** Breakfast served from 7:30am. Lunch served from midday until 2:00pm. Dinner served from 7:30pm until 10:00pm. Closed Sundays, the 1st or 2nd week in January and 1 week in May. **Specialities:** home cooking. **Hotel:** 8 beds; with shower, bath. **Other points:** bar, open to non-residents, children welcome, pets welcome – check for details, car park, modern decor. **Address:** La Balbinière.
MME PAULETTE NATIVELLE
**Telephone:** 49.22.84.01
⊗ ⓨ ⌂ Map 7

## VIERZON, Cher, 18100

### AUX MILLE PATTES, RN 76, the main road between Vierzon and Tours

**Menu:** 53 Frs. **Restaurant:** Breakfast served from 7:00am. Closed Sundays. **Specialities:** home cooking. **Other points:** bar, open to non-residents, pets welcome – check for details, traditional decor. **Address:** 85, route de Tours.
MR LUDWIG JAKUBIK
**Telephone:** 48.75.46.38
⊗ ⓨ Map 6

### MODERN'SPORT, *RN 20*

**Restaurant:** Breakfast served from 6:30am. Lunch served from midday until 2:00pm. Dinner served from 7:00pm until 10:00pm. Closed Saturdays and in August. **Specialities:** home cooking. **Other points:** bar, open to non-residents, car park, traditional decor. **Address:** 141, avenue Edouard Vaillant.
MME JEANINE MADELEINE
**Telephone:** 48.75.13.63
⊗ ♈ Map 6

## VILLEDOMER, Indre-et-Loire, 37110

### LES GRANDS VINS DE TOURAINE, *RN 10, between Château-Renault and Monnaie*

**Menu:** 58 to 130 Frs. **Accommodation:** 85 to 190 Frs. **Restaurant:** Breakfast served from 7:00am. Lunch served from 11:30am until 2:00pm. Dinner served from 7:00pm until 10:00pm. Closed Wednesdays and the 2nd fortnight in July. **Specialities:** andouillette et cuisse de lapin au Vouvray, cuisses de grenouille, home cooking. **Hotel:** 4 beds; with shower. **Other points:** bar, open to non-residents, à la carte menu, pets welcome – check for details, car park, modern decor. **Address:** Route Nationale 10, la Grande Vallée.
MR CLAUDE ROMIAN
**Telephone:** 47.55.01.05
⊗ ♈ ⏭ Map 6

## VILLEFRANCOEUR, Loir-et-Cher, 41330

### LE CONCORDE, *RD 957*

**Languages spoken:** Italian. **Restaurant:** Dinner served from midday until 10:00pm. Closed Saturdays and in August. **Other points:** bar. **Address:** Le Breuil.
MME ANDRÉE GEHANNO
**Telephone:** 54.20.12.04
⊗ ♈ Map 6

## VILLEROMAIN, Loir-et-Cher, 41100

### AU BON COIN, *RD 957, between Vendôme and Blois*

**Languages spoken:** English and Spanish. **Menu:** 54 to 150 Frs. **Restaurant:** Breakfast served from 7:30am. Lunch served from 11:30am until 2:30pm. Dinner served from 7:30pm until 9:00pm. Closed Sundays and in February or March. **Specialities:** regional menu, home cooking. **Other points:** bar, à la carte menu, children welcome, pets welcome – check for details, car park, modern decor. **Address:** 13, Grande Rue.
MME ISABELLE RENOUF
**Telephone:** 54.23.81.17
⊗ ♈ Map 6

## VILLIERS AU BOUIN, Indre-et-Loire, 37330

### L'ETAPE, *RD 959, Laval*

**Menu:** 48 Frs (coffee included). **Restaurant:** Breakfast served from 8:00am. Closed Saturdays, in August and from 25 December to beginning of January. **Specialities:** home cooking. **Other points:** bar, open to non-residents, children welcome, pets welcome – check for details, car park, traditional decor. **Address:** 15, rue de la Libération.
MME CHANTAL HAIS
**Telephone:** 47.24.03.76
⊗ ♈ Map 6

## VIVONNE, Vienne, 86370

### LE ROUTIERS, *RN 10, between Poitiers and Angoulême*

**Menu:** 55 to 65 Frs. **Restaurant:** Open 24 hours. **Specialities:** regional menu, home cooking. **Other points:** bar, open to non-residents, children welcome, pets welcome – check for details, car park, modern decor.
MR SERGE JUDES
**Telephone:** 49.43.41.03
⊗ ♈ Map 7

## YMONVILLE, Eure-et-Loir, 28150

### A L'ETOILE, *RN 154*

**Menu:** 90 to 150 Frs. **Accommodation:** 140 to 195 Frs. **Restaurant:** Breakfast served from 7:00am. Lunch served from midday until 1:30pm. Dinner served from 7:30pm until 9:00pm. Closed Mondays, 2 weeks in February and 2 weeks in November. **Specialities:** home cooking. **Hotel:** 10 beds; 10 double rooms with shower, bath. **Other points:** bar, open to non-residents, à la carte menu, children welcome, lounge area, terraces, pets welcome – check for details, car park, modern decor. **Address:** 31, rue du Haut Chemin.
MME THÉRESE BRULÉ
**Telephone:** 37.32.25.67
⊗ ♈ ⌂ ☆ Map 6

### LE RELAIS DE BEAUCE, *RN 154, the main road between Orléans and Chartres*

**Menu:** 58 Frs. **Restaurant:** Breakfast served from 5:30am. Lunch served from 11:30am until 2:30pm. Dinner served from 7:00pm until 10:00pm. Closed Saturdays and in August. **Specialities:** home cooking. **Other points:** bar, open to non-residents, pets welcome – check for details, car park, modern decor. **Address:** Lieu dit 'La Michellerie', Route Nationale 154.
MME MARTINE MILLOCHAU
**Telephone:** 37.32.26.34
⊗ ♈ Map 6

# Central France

## AIXE SUR VIENNE, Haute-Vienne, 87700

### LA CHAUMIERE, RN 21, the main road between Limoges and Périgueux
**Menu:** 55 to 120 Frs. **Accommodation:** 95 to 130 Frs. **Restaurant:** Breakfast served from 7:00am. Lunch served from midday until 2:00pm. Dinner served from 7:00pm until 9:00pm. Closed Wednesdays, Sunday evenings and the 2nd fortnight in August. **Specialities:** regional menu, home cooking. **Hotel:** 5 beds; 3 single rooms, 2 double rooms with shower. **Other points:** bar, open to non-residents, pets welcome – check for details, car park, traditional decor. **Address:** 5, avenue de la Gare.
MR JEAN-LOUIS PÉCHALAT
**Telephone:** 55.70.12.12
⊗ ♀ 🏠 Map 11

## ARFEUILLES, Allier, 03640

### LE RELAIS DES CHEVREAUX, RN 7
**Languages spoken:** English, Spanish. **Menu:** 55 to 60 Frs. **Restaurant:** Open 24 hours. **Specialities:** home cooking. **Other points:** bar, open to non-residents, children welcome, pets welcome – check for details, car park, traditional decor. **Address:** Route Nationale 7, Chatelus.
MR JOSEPH BERNARD
**Telephone:** 70.55.03.80
⊗ ♀ Map 12

## ARGENTAT, Corrèze, 19400

### CHEZ RAYMOND, Tulle
**Menu:** 60 Frs (wine included). **Accommodation:** 100 to 150 Frs. **Restaurant:** Breakfast served from 6:00am. Lunch served from midday until 2:00pm. Dinner served from 7:00pm until 9:00pm. Closed Sundays and in August. **Specialities:** home cooking. **Hotel:** 7 beds; 4 single rooms, 3 double rooms with shower. **Other points:** bar, open to non-residents, children welcome, pets welcome – check for details, car park, modern decor. **Address:** Place du 14 juillet.
MME MONIQUE POUZAUD
**Telephone:** 55.28.01.97
⊗ ♀ 🏠 Map 11

## AUBUSSON, Creuse, 23200

### LE RELAIS VERT ET BLEU, between Montluçon and Ussel
**Menu:** 52 Frs (wine included) to 95 Frs. **Restaurant:** Breakfast served from 7:00am. **Specialities:** regional menu, home cooking. **Other points:** bar, open to non-residents, à la carte menu, children welcome, terraces, pets welcome – check for details, car park, traditional decor. **Address:** ZI du Mont.
MME MURIELLE MAGNAT
**Telephone:** 55.83.85.45
⊗ ♀ Map 11

## AURILLAC, Cantal, 15000

### BAR L'ESCUDILLIER, RN 120, the main road between Tulle and Rodez
**Menu:** 50 Frs (wine and coffee included). **Restaurant:** Breakfast served from 6:00am. Lunch served from 11:00am until 2:00pm. Closed Sundays. **Specialities:** home cooking. **Other points:** car park, modern decor. **Address:** Place du 8 Mai.
MR ROBERT MONTOURCY
**Telephone:** 71.63.79.30
⊗ Map 12

### LE RELAIS DE LA SABLIERE, RN 122, Montauban/Toulouse
**Languages spoken:** English and Spanish. **Menu:** 55 Frs. **Restaurant:** Breakfast served from 7:00am. Lunch served from midday until 1:00pm. Dinner served from 6:30pm until 9:00pm. Closed Sundays and in August. **Specialities:** regional menu, home cooking. **Other points:** bar, open to non-residents, terraces, pets welcome – check for details, car park. **Address:** La Sablière, Route Nationale 122.
MME JEANINE DELORT
**Telephone:** 71.64.51.80
⊗ ♀ Map 12

## BEAUNE LES MINES, Haute-Vienne, 87280

### LA TERRASSE DE BEAUNE, RN 20, exit for Limoges
**Languages spoken:** English. **Menu:** 50 (wine and coffee included) to 110 Frs. **Accommodation:** 140 to

220 Frs. **Restaurant:** Breakfast served from 6:00am. **Specialities:** home cooking. **Hotel:** 9 beds; 9 double rooms with bath, private WC. **Other points:** bar, open to non-residents, à la carte menu, children welcome, terraces, pets welcome – check for details, car park, modern decor.
SOCIÉTÉ HOTELIERE DE LA MAZELLE
**Telephone:** 55.39.90.58
⊗ ∇ ⌂ ⌣ Map 11

## BELLEVUE LA MONTAGNE,
Haute-Loire, 43350

### HOTEL DES VOYAGEURS, RD 906
**Menu:** 50 to 90 Frs. **Accommodation:** 100 Frs. **Restaurant:** Open 24 hours. **Specialities:** home cooking. **Hotel:** 7 beds. **Other points:** bar, open to non-residents, lounge area, terraces, pets welcome – check for details, car park.
MME ODETTE CHAPON
**Telephone:** 77.00.60.15
⊗ ∇ ⌂ Map 12

## BESSAY SUR ALLIER, Allier, 03340

### LE BAR DE LA ROUTE BLEUE, RN 7, between Moulins and Varennes
**Places of interest:** Bagnol de l'Orme (30km). **Languages spoken:** English. **Menu:** 55 Frs (wine included). **Restaurant:** Breakfast served from 6:30am. Lunch served from midday until 2:30pm. Dinner served from 7:00pm until 11:00pm. Closed Saturdays, from 15 to 30 August and from 24 to 31 December. **Specialities:** regional menu, home cooking. **Other points:** bar, open to non-residents, children welcome. **Address:** Rue Charles Louis Philippe.
MR FRANCIS BLANCHE
**Telephone:** 70.43.01.59
⊗ ∇ Map 12

## BORT LES ORGUES, Corrèze, 19110

### LE RELAIS DES ROUTIERS, RN 122
**Hotel:** 5 beds. **Other points:** bar. **Address:** 9, place du Champ de Foire.
MME ANTOINETTE CHEREIX
**Telephone:** 55.72.00.42
⊗ ∇ ⌂ Map 11

## BOURGANEUF, Creuse, 23400

### LA BERGERIE, RN 141, between Limoges and Clermont Ferrand
**Menu:** 51 to 200 Frs. **Restaurant:** Breakfast served from 7:00am. Lunch served from 11:00am until 3:00pm. Dinner served from 7:00pm until 11:00pm. Closed from Monday 4:00pm to Tuesday 7:00am. **Specialities:** home cooking. **Other points:** bar, open to non-residents, children welcome, terraces, pets welcome – check for details, car

park, traditional decor. **Address:** Montboucher.
MME BRIGITTE BELZ
**Telephone:** 55.64.20.18
⊗ ∇ Map 11

## BRIOUDE, Haute-Loire, 43100

### LES ROUTIERS, RN 102, le Puy en Velay
**Menu:** 55 to 70 Frs. **Restaurant:** Breakfast served from 6:00am. Lunch served from midday until 2:00pm. Dinner served from 7:30pm until 9:30pm. Closed Sundays and from 15 to 31 August. **Specialities:** home cooking. **Other points:** bar, open to non-residents, children welcome, pets welcome – check for details, car park, modern decor. **Address:** Route de Clermont.
MR ROGER DEVINS
**Telephone:** 71.50.14.39
⊗ ∇ Map 12

## BRIVE LA GAILLARDE, Corrèze, 19100

### LE NOUVEL HOTEL, RN 89, motorway Paris/Toulouse, exit Brive west
**Restaurant:** Breakfast served from 6:30am. Lunch served from midday until 2:00pm. Dinner served from 7:00pm until 9:30pm. Closed Saturdays and 15 days in August. **Specialities:** home cooking. **Hotel:** 11 beds; 9 single rooms, 2 double rooms with shower, private WC. **Other points:** bar, pets welcome – check for details, car park, modern decor. **Address:** 2, rue Desgenettes.
MR PATRICK LOMEY
**Telephone:** 55.86.01.66
⊗ ∇ ⌂ Map 11

## BRIVES CHARENSAC, Haute-Loire, 43700

### LE RELAIS DU COMMERCE, the main road between Valence and Saint Etienne
**Menu:** 55 to 65 Frs. **Accommodation:** 90 to 130 Frs. **Restaurant:** Breakfast served from 6:00am. Lunch served from 11:30am until 2:00pm. Dinner served from 7:00pm until 9:00pm. **Specialities:** home cooking. **Hotel:** 10 beds; 1 single room, 9 double rooms with shower. **Other points:** bar, open to non-residents, children welcome, car park, traditional decor. **Address:** 2, route de Lyon.
MME ELIE MASSON-FERRET
**Telephone:** 71.09.16.16
⊗ ∇ ⌂ Map 12

## BROUT VERNET, Allier, 03110

### SARL CENTRE ROUTIER, RN 9, between Gannat and Saint Pourcain sur Sioule
**Places of interest:** Cathédrale de Chartres. **Menu:** 57 to 60 Frs. **Accommodation:** 120 to 150 Frs. **Restaurant:**

Breakfast served from 5:30am. Lunch served from midday until 2:30pm. Dinner served from 7:00pm until 11:30pm. Closed Saturdays. **Specialities:** Couscous, paëlla, home cooking. **Hotel:** 9 beds; 6 single rooms, 3 double rooms. **Other points:** bar, children welcome, terraces, pets welcome – check for details, car park, traditional decor. **Address:** Route Nationale 9.
MME GEORGETTE
Roux
**Telephone:** 70.58.24.61
⊗ 🍸 ⌂ Map 12

## CHAMALIERE SUR LOIRE, Haute-Loire, 43800

*LES ROUTIERS, RD 103, between le Puy en Velay and Saint Etienne*
**Menu:** 48 Frs. **Restaurant:** Breakfast served from 7:30am. Lunch served from 11:45am until 2:30pm. Dinner served from 7:00pm until 8:30pm. Closed Wednesdays. **Specialities:** home cooking. **Other points:** bar, open to non-residents, pets welcome – check for details, car park, modern decor. **Address:** Rue Nationale.
MME MARIE-LINE ROURE
**Telephone:** 71.03.42.10
⊗ 🍸 Map 12

## CHAMBORET, Haute-Vienne, 87140

*LA BERGERIE, RN 147, between Limoges and Poitiers*
**Menu:** 55 to 110 Frs. **Restaurant:** Breakfast served from 6:00am. Lunch served from midday until 2:00pm. Dinner served from 7:00pm until 11:00pm. Closed Sundays. **Specialities:** home cooking. **Other points:** open to non-residents, à la carte menu, children welcome, pets welcome – check for details, car park, traditional decor.
SARL ALBENQUE/MOREAU
**Telephone:** 55.53.44.16. **Fax:** 55.53.57.41
⊗ Map 11

## CHAPELAUDE (LA), Allier, 03380

*LE RELAIS DES TARTASSES, RD 143, Châteauroux*
**Places of interest:** La côte de granit rose, Euradom, la planétarium, l'aquarium, le centre ornithologique.
**Menu:** 55 to 100 Frs. **Restaurant:** Breakfast served from 6:30am. Lunch served from midday until 2:00pm. Dinner served from 7:00pm until 10:30pm. **Specialities:** home cooking. **Hotel:** 4 beds; with shower. **Other points:** bar, open to non-residents, children welcome, pets welcome – check for details, car park. **Address:** Huriel
MME COLETTE BOUTILLON
**Telephone:** 70.06.45.06
⊗ 🍸 Map 12

## CHAPELLE D'AUREC (LA), Haute-Loire, 43120

*LE RELAIS DE LA CHAPELLE, RN 88, le Puy*
**Menu:** 55 to 120 Frs. **Accommodation:** 120 to 180 Frs. **Restaurant:** Breakfast served from 6:30am. Lunch served from midday until 2:00pm. Dinner served from 7:30pm until 9:00pm. **Specialities:** home cooking. **Hotel:** 4 beds; with shower, bath, private WC. **Other points:** bar, open to non-residents, à la carte menu, children welcome, lounge area, terraces, pets welcome – check for details, car park, modern decor. **Address:** La Mioulaterre.
MR GABRIEL COLOMBET
**Telephone:** 71.66.53.55
⊗ 🍸 Map 12

## CHATEAUNEUF LA FORET, Haute-Vienne, 87130

*AUX CEPS, RD 979, between Limoges and Tulle*
**Languages spoken:** English. **Accommodation:** 76 to 140 Frs. **Restaurant:** Breakfast served from 7:00am. Lunch served from 11:00am until 3:00pm. Dinner served from 6:30pm until 11:00pm. Closed Tuesdays. **Specialities:** regional menu, home cooking. **Hotel:** 8 beds; 6 single rooms, 2 double rooms with shower. **Other points:** bar, open to non-residents, à la carte menu, children welcome, lounge area, terraces, car park. **Address:** La Veytisou.
MME JOELLE FORESTIER
**Telephone:** 55.69.33.38
⊗ 🍸 ⌂ Map 11

## CHOMETTE (LA), Haute-Loire, 43230

*LE COQ HARDI, RN 102, between Clermont Ferrand and le Puy en Velay*
**Menu:** 50 to 80 Frs. **Accommodation:** 90 Frs. **Restaurant:** Breakfast served from 8:00am. Lunch served from midday until 2:00pm. Dinner served from 8:00pm until 10:00pm. Closed Saturdays and in October. **Specialities:** home cooking. **Hotel:** 2 beds; 1 single room, 1 double room. **Other points:** bar, lounge area. **Address:** Route Nationale 102.
MME MARIE-LOUISE MEYRONNEINC
**Telephone:** 71.76.62.29
⊗ 🍸 Map 12

## CLERMONT FERRAND, Puy-de-Dôme, 63000

*AUVERGNE PYRENEES – LES ROUTIERS, RN 9, town centre*
**Languages spoken:** English and Spanish. **Menu:** 54 to 95 Frs. **Accommodation:** 145 to 270 Frs. **Restaurant:**

Breakfast served from 6:30am. Lunch served from midday until 2:00pm. Dinner served from 7:30pm until 9:00pm. **Specialities:** coq au vin, regional food, home cooking. **Hotel:** 15 beds; 13 single rooms, 2 double rooms with shower, bath, private WC, telephone. **Other points:** bar, open to non-residents, lounge area, terraces, pets welcome – check for details, car park, modern decor. **Address:** 12 bis, place des Carmes.
MME MARIE-LOUISE LABORDE
**Telephone:** 73.92.35.73
⊗ ♀ ⌂ ☆ Map 12

### LE ROUTIER

**Menu:** 43 Frs (wine included). **Restaurant:** Breakfast served from 7:00am. Closed Saturdays. **Specialities:** home cooking. **Other points:** bar, open to non-residents, pets welcome – check for details, car park, traditional decor. **Address:** 12, rue d'Estaing.
MME JOCELYNE SAUSSEAU
**Telephone:** 73.90.15.24
⊗ ♀ Map 12

### RELAIS DES VOLCANS D'AUVERGNE, A 71

**Specialities:** regional menu. **Other points:** à la carte menu, children welcome, terraces, pets welcome – check for details, car park. **Address:** Aire de Service des Volcans, dans les deux sens.
⊗ Map 12

## COSNE D'ALLIER, Allier, 03430

### L'ESCALE, A 74, between Montluçon and Villefranche d'Allier

**Languages spoken:** English and Spanish. **Menu:** 55 Frs (wine and coffee included). **Accommodation:** 100 Frs. **Restaurant:** Breakfast served from 6:45am. Lunch served from 11:00am until 3:30pm. Dinner served from 5:00pm until 10:30pm. **Specialities:** regional menu, home cooking. **Hotel:** 6 beds; 6 single rooms with shower, private WC, television. **Other points:** bar, open to non-residents, à la carte menu, children welcome, terraces, pets welcome – check for details, car park, modern decor. **Address:** 2, place de la Liberté.
MME MARIE-JOSEPH SAUVAT-MAJDOUB
**Telephone:** 70.07.21.10, 70.07.25.82
⊗ ♀ ⌂ Map 12

## COSTAROS, Haute-Loire, 43490

### LES ROUTIERS, RN 88, the main road between le Puy en Velay and Marseille

**Languages spoken:** Spanish. **Menu:** 60 to 90 Frs. **Accommodation:** 90 Frs. **Restaurant:** Breakfast served from 7:00am. Lunch served from midday until 2:30pm. Dinner served from 7:30pm until 9:00pm. Closed Saturdays and from end of December to mid-January. **Specialities:** regional menu. **Hotel:** 17 beds; 14 single rooms, 3 double rooms with shower. **Other points:** bar,

open to non-residents, à la carte menu, terraces, pets welcome – check for details, car park, traditional decor. **Address:** Rue Principale.
MME THÉRÈSE ROSSELLO
**Telephone:** 71.57.16.04
⊗ ♀ ⌂ ☜ Map 12

## COUSSAC BONNEVAL, Haute-Vienne, 87500

### LE GAI COUSSAC, RD 901, between Pompadour and Lubensac

**Menu:** 52 Frs (wine and coffee included) to 120 Frs. **Accommodation:** 90 to 190 Frs. **Restaurant:** Lunch served from midday until 2:00pm. Dinner served from 7:00pm until 10:30pm. **Specialities:** home cooking. **Hotel:** 6 beds; 1 single room, 5 double rooms with shower. **Other points:** bar, open to non-residents, à la carte menu, children welcome, lounge area, pets welcome – check for details, car park, modern decor. **Address:** Avenue du 11 Novembre.
MME COLETTE RENAUDIN
**Telephone:** 55.75.21.59
⊗ ♀ ⌂ Map 11

## CREUZIER LE VIEUX, Allier, 03300

### CHEZ LA MERE RIBOULIN, industrial zone of Vichy Rhue

**Restaurant:** Breakfast served from 5:30am. **Specialities:** Brochet ou sandre de Loire au beurre blanc, home cooking. **Hotel:** 16 beds; 11 single rooms, 5 double rooms with shower. **Other points:** bar, open to non-residents, à la carte menu, terraces, pets welcome – check for details, car park. **Address:** 10, rue des Ailes.
MR MARCEL JOLY
**Telephone:** 70.98.44.88
⊗ ♀ ⌂ ☆ Map 12

## CUSSET, Allier, 03300

### HOTEL DE LA GARE

**Menu:** 50 Frs. **Accommodation:** 80 Frs. **Restaurant:** Breakfast served from 6:30am. Lunch served from midday until 1:30pm. Closed Sundays and in July. **Specialities:** home cooking. **Hotel:** 2 beds; with shower. **Other points:** bar, open to non-residents, car park. **Address:** 1, route de Paris.
MR JEAN LAROQUE
**Telephone:** 70.98.26.10
⊗ ♀ Map 12

### LES MONTAGNARDS, at the exit for Cusset, towards Lapalisse

**Menu:** 50 to 55 Frs. **Restaurant:** Breakfast served from 7:00am. Lunch served from 11:30am until 2:00pm. Closed Sundays and in August. **Specialities:** home cooking. **Other points:** bar, open to non-residents, pets welcome – check for details, car park, traditional decor.

**Address:** 20, rue du Général Raynal.
MR ROGER POL
**Telephone:** 70.98.38.60
⊗ ℞ Map 12

## DEUX CHAISES, Allier, 03240

### LE RELAIS DE L AMITIE, RN 145

**Menu:** 52 Frs. **Restaurant:** Breakfast served from
5:30am. Lunch served from midday until 2:00pm.
Dinner served from 7:30pm until 10:00pm. Closed
Saturdays. **Specialities:** home cooking. **Other points:**
open to non-residents. **Address:** Route Nationale 145,
Le Montet.
MR LOUIS DOUGE
**Telephone:** 70.47.15.64
⊗ Map 12

## DOMPIERRE SUR BESBRE, Allier, 03290

### LE RELAIS DE LA BESBRE, RN 79, between Moulin and Mâcon

**Menu:** 52 to 72 Frs. **Restaurant:** Breakfast served
from 6:00am. Lunch served from midday until 2:00pm.
Dinner served from 7:00pm until 9:00pm. Closed
Saturdays and from mid-September to beginning of
October. **Specialities:** coq au vin, cuisses de
grenouilles à la provençale, home cooking. **Other
points:** bar, open to non-residents, pets welcome –
check for details, car park, traditional decor. **Address:**
207, avenue de la Gare.
MR JEAN-PIERRE MAROSSA
**Telephone:** 70.34.53.69
⊗ ℞ Map 12

## DURDAT LAREQUILLE, Allier, 03310

### RESTAURANT DES SPORTS – CHEZ GÉRARD ET NATHALIE, RN 144, the main road between Montluçon and Clermont Ferrand

**Languages spoken:** English, Spanish and Italian.
**Menu:** 55 Frs. **Restaurant:** Breakfast served from
6:00am. Lunch served from 11:30am until 2:00pm.
Dinner served from 7:00pm until 8:00pm. Closed
Sundays and in August. **Specialities:** home cooking.
**Other points:** bar, open to non-residents, terraces, car
park, modern decor. **Address:** Route Nationale 144.
GÉRARD ET NATHALIE LOMBARDI
**Telephone:** 70.51.07.28
⊗ ℞ Map 12

## EYMOUTIERS, Haute-Vienne, 87120

### LE SAINT PSALMET, CD 940 and 941, the main road between Limoges and Ussel or Gueret and Tulle

**Languages spoken:** English and Spanish. **Menu:** 45

(wine included) to 120 Frs. **Accommodation:** 125 to
180 Frs. **Restaurant:** Breakfast served from 6:00am.
Lunch served from midday until 3:00pm. Dinner served
from 7:00pm until 10:00pm. **Specialities:** regional
menu, home cooking. **Hotel:** 38 beds; 8 single rooms, 30
double rooms with shower, bath, private WC, telephone.
**Other points:** bar, open to non-residents, à la carte
menu, children welcome, lounge area, terraces, pets
welcome – check for details, car park. **Address:** Place
du Champ de Foire.
MR MICHEL LE PETIT
**Telephone:** 55.69.10.06. **Fax:** 55.69.23.92
⊗ ℞ ⌂ ☆☆ Map 11

## GIOU DE MAMOU, Cantal, 15130

### L'ETAPE DE LA MAISON NEUVE, RN 122, between Aurillac and Clermont Ferrand

**Menu:** 52 Frs (wine included) to 65 Frs.
**Accommodation:** 100 to 120 Frs. **Restaurant:**
Breakfast served from 6:30am. Lunch served from
11:30am until 2:30pm. Dinner served from 6:30pm until
10:00pm. Closed Sundays. **Specialities:** regional menu,
home cooking. **Hotel:** 10 beds; 8 single rooms, 2 double
rooms. **Other points:** bar, open to non-residents, à la
carte menu, children welcome, lounge area, terraces,
pets welcome – check for details, car park, traditional
decor. **Address:** Lavaurs.
MME CORINNE MULLER
**Telephone:** 71.64.58.42
⊗ ℞ ⌂ Map 12

## ISSOIRE, Puy-de-Dôme, 63500

### AUBERGE DU CHAPEAU ROUGE, exit aérodrome no 14

**Menu:** 50 Frs. **Restaurant:** Breakfast served from
5:00am. Lunch served from 11:30am until 3:00pm.
Dinner served from 7:00pm until 11:00pm. Closed
Saturdays and in August. **Specialities:** home cooking.
**Other points:** bar, open to non-residents, pets welcome
– check for details, car park, modern decor. **Address:**
Route de Saint Germain.
MR MARC OLIVES
**Telephone:** 73.89.14.74
⊗ ℞ Map 12

## LAPALISSE, Allier, 03120

### LE CHAPON DORE, RN 7, Vichy/Paris/ Moulin

**Menu:** 55 Frs. **Accommodation:** 65 to 180 Frs.
**Restaurant:** Breakfast served from 6:30am. Lunch
served from 11:30am until 2:00pm. Dinner served from
7:00pm until 9:00pm. Closed Sundays. **Specialities:**
home cooking. **Hotel:** 8 beds; 3 single rooms, 5 double
rooms with shower, bath. **Other points:** bar, open to
non-residents, children welcome, terraces, pets welcome
– check for details, car park, traditional decor. **Address:**
1, avenue du 8 Mai 1945.

MR JEAN-LUC LALAUZE
Telephone: 70.99.09.51
⊗ ⵷ 🏠 ☆ Map 12

## LIMOGES, Haute-Vienne, 87000

### CHEZ BICHON, RN 20, the main road between Toulouse and Lyon

**Languages spoken:** English and Spanish. **Menu:** 55 Frs (children under 10 – half price). **Restaurant:** Breakfast served from 6:00am. Lunch served from midday until 2:00pm. Dinner served from 6:00pm until 9:00pm. Closed Saturdays. **Specialities:** home cooking. **Other points:** bar, open to non-residents, pets welcome – check for details, traditional decor. **Address:** 68, avenue du Maréchal, between Lattre de Tassigny.
MR ROLAND HOUARD
Telephone: 55.30.68.83
⊗ ⵷ Map 11

### LES LILAS, RN 21, at Limoges heading from Périgueux

**Menu:** 50 to 68 Frs. **Restaurant:** Dinner served from midday until midnight. **Specialities:** lotte, beignet de gambas, potée Limousine, home cooking. **Other points:** bar, à la carte menu, children welcome, terraces, car park, traditional decor. **Address:** 233, avenue Baudin.
MME GILBERTE BROUSSAS
Telephone: 55.34.35.67
⊗ ⵷ Map 11

## MAGNAC BOURG, Haute-Vienne, 87380

### LE RELAIS PARIS/TOULOUSE, RN 20

**Restaurant:** Dinner served from midday until 1:00am. Closed Wednesdays (out of season). **Other points:** bar.
MR MÉRIADEC
Telephone: 55.00.81.53
⊗ ⵷ Map 11

## MALEMORT, Corrèze, 19360

### CHEZ PAULETTE, RN 89, Brive/Tulle/Clermont Ferrand

**Menu:** 55 to 60 Frs. **Restaurant:** Breakfast served from 7:00am. Lunch served from midday until 2:30pm. Closed Sundays and in August. **Specialities:** home cooking. **Other points:** bar, open to non-residents, car park. **Address:** 2, avenue Pierre et Marie Curie.
MME PAULETTE VERGNE
Telephone: 55.92.28.14
⊗ ⵷ Map 11

## MASSERET, Corrèze, 19510

### HOTEL DES VOYAGEURS, RN 20

**Menu:** 50 to 180 Frs. **Accommodation:** 90 to 170 Frs. **Restaurant:** Breakfast served from 7:00am. Lunch served from midday until 3:00pm. Dinner served from 7:00pm

until 10:00pm. Closed Sundays. **Specialities:** corréziennes, regional food, home cooking. **Hotel:** 6 beds; 2 single rooms, 4 double rooms with shower, private WC. **Other points:** bar, open to non-residents, à la carte menu, children welcome, terraces, pets welcome – check for details, car park, traditional decor. **Address:** Route Nationale 20.
MR MICHEL PONS
Telephone: 55.73.40.11
⊗ ⵷ 🏠 Map 11

## MAURIAC, Cantal, 15200

### LES ROUTIERS – CHEZ BRIGITTE, RD 678, Ussel

**Languages spoken:** English. **Menu:** 68 to 100 Frs. **Accommodation:** 95 to 140 Frs. **Restaurant:** Breakfast served from 7:30am. Lunch served from midday until 1:30pm. Dinner served from 7:00pm until 8:30pm. Closed from Friday 3:00pm to Saturday 6:00pm. **Specialities:** home cooking. **Hotel:** 10 beds; 8 single rooms, 2 double rooms with shower, private WC. **Other points:** bar, open to non-residents, à la carte menu, children welcome, car park, traditional decor. **Address:** 27, rue Saint Mary.
SARL LAROCHE-RONGIER
Telephone: 71.68.00.79
⊗ ⵷ 🏠 ☆ Map 12

## MERINCHAL, Creuse, 23420

### HOTEL DU MIDI, RN 141, the main road between Clermont Ferrand and Limoges

**Languages spoken:** English, Spanish and Portugese. **Menu:** 50 to 146 Frs. **Accommodation:** 110 to 230 Frs. **Restaurant:** Breakfast served from 7:30am. Lunch served from midday until 2:00pm. Dinner served from 7:30pm until 10:30pm. **Specialities:** home cooking. **Hotel:** 10 beds; 8 single rooms, 2 double rooms with shower. **Other points:** bar, open to non-residents, à la carte menu, children welcome, lounge area, terraces, pets welcome – check for details, car park, traditional decor. **Address:** 12, Létrade Gare.
MR JOSÉ BARTOLO
Telephone: 55.67.23.63
⊗ ⵷ 🏠 Map 11

## MONESTIER MERLINE, Corrèze, 19340

### LE RELAIS DU VIEUX CHENE, RN 89, the main road between Bordeaux and Lyon

**Menu:** 55 Frs (wine and coffee included) to 128 Frs. **Restaurant:** Breakfast served from 5:30am. Lunch served from 11:30am until 3:00pm. Dinner served from 6:30pm until midnight. **Specialities:** home cooking. **Other points:** bar, open to non-residents, children welcome **Address:** Route Nationale 89.
MME LEBON ET MR DUMAILLE
Telephone: 55.94.39.89
⊗ ⵷ Map 11

## MONTLUCON, Allier, 03100

### LE CADET ROUSSEL, RN 145, industrial zone of Pasquis

**Languages spoken:** Polish, Russian and Czech. **Menu:** 50 to 60 Frs. **Accommodation:** 75 to 120 Frs. **Restaurant:** Breakfast served from 7:00am. Lunch served from midday until 2:00pm. Dinner served from 7:00pm until 9:30pm. Closed Sundays. **Specialities:** home cooking. **Hotel:** 8 beds; 7 single rooms, 1 double room with shower, private WC, television. **Other points:** bar, open to non-residents, à la carte menu, terraces, car park, modern decor. **Address:** 53, rue de Pasquis.
MR EDOUARD GAWRON
**Telephone:** 70.29.32.27
⊗ ♉ 🏠 Map 12

## MONTMARAULT, Allier, 03390

### RELAIS DE L'ETAPE, RN 145, motorway, 100m from the A 71 exit

**Menu:** 60 Frs (coffee included) to 80 Frs. **Restaurant:** Breakfast served from 5:00am. Closed Saturdays. **Specialities:** terrine maison, rognons de veau au ratafia, soufflé au Marc, home cooking. **Other points:** bar, open to non-residents, à la carte menu, children welcome, terraces, pets welcome – check for details, car park, modern decor. **Address:** Route de Moulins.
MR ROBERT LEGAL
**Telephone:** 70.07.36.03
⊗ ♉ Map 12

## MOULINS, Allier, 03000

### LES TROIS RUBANS, RN 7, Lyon

**Restaurant:** Breakfast served from 6:30am. Dinner served from midday until 8:00pm. Closed Saturdays and in August. **Specialities:** home cooking. **Other points:** bar. **Address:** Route de Paris.
MR PIERRE MOLINIE
**Telephone:** 70.44.08.51
⊗ ♉ Map 12

## NEBOUZAT, Puy-de-Dôme, 63210

### AU RENDEZ-VOUS DES ROUTIERS, RN 89, the main road between Lyon and Bordeaux

**Menu:** 55 to 75 Frs. **Accommodation:** 120 to 150 Frs. **Restaurant:** Breakfast served from 7:00am. Closed Sundays. **Specialities:** regional menu, home cooking. **Hotel:** 10 beds; 7 single rooms, 3 double rooms. **Other points:** bar, open to non-residents, à la carte menu, children welcome, pets welcome – check for details, car park, modern decor.
MR PASCAL MENOT
**Telephone:** 73.87.10.04
⊗ ♉ 🏠 Map 12

## NEUSSARGUES, Cantal, 15170

### AUBERGE DES BRANQUES, RN 122, between Aurillac and Clermont Ferrand

**Menu:** 53 Frs (wine and coffee included) to 70 Frs. **Restaurant:** Breakfast served from 7:00am. Lunch served from midday until 2:30pm. Dinner served from 6:30pm until 10:00pm. Closed Sundays. **Specialities:** home cooking. **Other points:** bar, open to non-residents, children welcome, terraces, pets welcome – check for details, car park. **Address:** Rue du Calvaire MME JEANINE TERRISSE
**Telephone:** 71.20.53.92
⊗ ♉ Map 12

## OBJAT, Corrèze, 19130

### RELAIS DU PARC

**Hotel:** 14 beds. **Other points:** bar. **Address:** 1, avenue Poincaré.
MME MONIQUE RICHARD
**Telephone:** 55.84.11.11
⊗ ♉ 🏠 Map 11

## OLLIERGUES, Puy-de-Dôme, 63880

### LA SAPINIERE, RD 906, between le Puy en Velay and Thiers

**Menu:** 50 Frs (wine and coffee included) to 70 Frs. **Restaurant:** Breakfast served from 7:00am. **Specialities:** home cooking. **Other points:** bar, open to non-residents, children welcome, pets welcome – check for details, car park, traditional decor. **Address:** Route Départementale 906, Giroux Gare.
MR BERNARD SOMMA
**Telephone:** 73.53.56.58
⊗ ♉ Map 12

## PANAZOL, Haute-Vienne, 87350

### LA FREGATE, RN 141, the main road between Limoges and Clermont Ferrand

**Languages spoken:** English and Spanish. **Menu:** 55 (wine included). **Restaurant:** Breakfast served from 8:00am. Closed Sundays. **Specialities:** home cooking. **Other points:** bar, open to non-residents, à la carte menu, terraces, pets welcome – check for details, car park, traditional decor. **Address:** Route de Clermont.
MME RÉGINE DESMARET
**Telephone:** 55.06.25.28
⊗ ♉ Map 11

## PERIGNY, Allier, 03120

### LE RELAIS DE PERIGNY, RN 7, 5km along RN 7 from Lapalisse

**Languages spoken:** English. **Menu:** 51 Frs. **Accommodation:** 100 to 120 Frs. **Restaurant:** Open 24 hours. **Specialities:** regional menu, home cooking.

**Hotel:** 6 beds; 3 single rooms, 3 double rooms. **Other points:** bar, lounge area, car park, traditional decor. **Address:** Le Bourg.
MR PATRICE CARDINAUD
**Telephone:** 70.99.84.57
⊗ ♀ ⌂ ☆  Map 12

## PERTUIS (LE), Haute-Loire, 43260

### LE RELAIS DU COL
**Menu:** 55 to 65 Frs. **Accommodation:** 100 to 200 Frs. **Restaurant:** Breakfast served from 5:00am. Lunch served from midday until 2:30pm. Dinner served from 7:00pm until 10:00pm. Closed Saturdays. **Specialities:** home cooking. **Hotel:** 8 beds. **Other points:** bar, open to non-residents, car park. **Address:** Route Nationale 88.
MME ODILE DIÉTRICH
**Telephone:** 71.57.60.06
⊗ ♀ ⌂  Map 12

## PIERREFITTE, Allier, 03470

### CAFE DE LA MAIRIE, between Moulins and Digoin
**Menu:** 75 Frs. **Restaurant:** Breakfast served from 6:00am. Lunch served from 11:00am until 2:00pm. Dinner served from 7:00pm until 9:00pm. Closed Wednesdays. **Specialities:** regional menu, home cooking. **Other points:** bar, open to non-residents, à la carte menu, children welcome, terraces, pets welcome – check for details, car park, traditional decor. **Address:** Place de l'Eglise.
MR CHRISTIAN TEILLIER
**Telephone:** 70.47.00.87
⊗ ♀  Map 12

## PIERREFITTE SUR LOIRE, Allier, 03470

### STATION TOTAL, RN 79, between Moulins (50km) and Mâcon (100km)
**Languages spoken:** English, German and Italian. **Restaurant:** Open 24 hours. **Specialities:** home cooking. **Other points:** à la carte menu, terraces, pets welcome – check for details, car park, traditional decor. **Address:** Route Nationale 79.
MR MICHEL RAY
**Telephone:** 70.42.91.91
⊗  Map 12

## PINOLS, Haute-Loire, 43300

### HOTEL DES VOYAGEURS, RN 590
**Menu:** 65 to 80 Frs. **Accommodation:** 60 to 75 Frs. **Restaurant:** Breakfast served from 7:00am. Dinner served from 7:00pm until 9:00pm. **Specialities:** home cooking. **Hotel:** 6 beds; 5 single rooms, 1 double room with shower, bath. **Other points:** bar, open to non-residents, children welcome, pets welcome –

check for details, traditional decor.
MME JACQUELINE CORNET
**Telephone:** 71.74.11.42
⊗ ♀ ⌂  Map 12

## PONT DE MENAT, Puy-de-Dôme, 63560

### CHEZ ROGER, RN 144, the main road between Montluçon and Clermont Ferrand
**Menu:** 60 to 140 Frs. **Accommodation:** 100 to 160 Frs. **Restaurant:** Breakfast served from 8:00am. Lunch served from midday until 2:00pm. Dinner served from 5:00pm until 9:00pm. Closed Thursdays and in January. **Specialities:** jambon d'Auvergne et sa garniture, potée auvergnate, truite, regional food, home cooking. **Hotel:** 8 beds; 6 single rooms, 2 double rooms with shower, bath. **Other points:** bar, open to non-residents, à la carte menu, children welcome, terraces, pets welcome – check for details, car park, traditional decor. **Address:** Menat.
MME MARIE PINEL
**Telephone:** 73.85.50.17
⊗ ♀ ⌂ ⌒  Map 12

## PONTAUMUR, Puy-de-Dôme, 63380

### CHEZ LUCETTE, between Pontaumur and Aubusson
**Menu:** 55 to 110 Frs. **Restaurant:** Breakfast served from 6:30am. Lunch served from midday until 2:30pm. Dinner served from 7:30pm until 9:00pm. Closed the 2nd fortnight in August. **Specialities:** home cooking. **Other points:** bar, open to non-residents, à la carte menu, terraces, car park. **Address:** Puy Maury.
MME LUCETTE CONDON
**Telephone:** 73.79.00.40
⊗ ♀  Map 12

## PUY EN VELAY (LE), Haute-Loire, 43000

### LA TAVERNE
**Menu:** 65 to 80 Frs. **Accommodation:** 130 to 180 Frs. **Restaurant:** Breakfast served from 7:00am. Lunch served from midday until 2:00pm. Dinner served from 7:00pm until 9:00pm. Closed in September. **Specialities:** regional menu, home cooking. **Hotel:** 10 beds; 9 single rooms, 1 double room with shower. **Other points:** bar, open to non-residents, traditional decor. **Address:** 50, boulevard Carnot.
MR RENÉ ROLLAND
**Telephone:** 71.09.35.16
⊗ ♀ ⌂ ☆☆  Map 12

## RIOM, Puy-de-Dôme, 63200

### AU STAND, RN 9, Riom south
**Languages spoken:** English. **Menu:** 55 to 75 Frs. **Restaurant:** Breakfast served from 7:00am. Lunch served from 11:30am until 2:00pm. Closed Sundays and in August. **Specialities:** home cooking. **Other points:** bar, open to non-residents, children welcome, pets

welcome – check for details, traditional decor. **Address:** 24, avenue de Clermont.
MME JANINE DASSAUD
**Telephone:** 73.38.04.06
⊗ ⵑ Map 12

### LE CANTALOU, RN 9
**Menu:** 50 Frs. **Restaurant:** Breakfast served from 7:00am. Lunch served from 11:00am until 3:00pm. Closed Sundays and in August. **Specialities:** home cooking. **Other points:** bar, open to non-residents, pets welcome – check for details. **Address:** 12, avenue de Clermont.
MR JEAN-LOUIS THOLONIAS
**Telephone:** 73.38.03.68
⊗ ⵑ Map 12

## RIS, Puy-de-Dôme, 63290

### HOTEL DE LA GARE, CD 906, between Vichy and Thiers
**Menu:** 40 to 50 Frs (wine and coffee included). **Accommodation:** 75 to 150 Frs. **Restaurant:** Breakfast served from 5:30am. Lunch served from 11:30am until 2:30pm. Dinner served from 7:00pm until 9:30pm. Closed from Saturday 2:00pm to Monday 5.30am. **Specialities:** home cooking. **Hotel:** 10 beds. **Other points:** bar, open to non-residents, children welcome, terraces, pets welcome – check for details, car park, traditional decor. **Address:** Gare de Ris.
MR JEAN-CLAUDE VÉDRINES
**Telephone:** 73.94.68.68
⊗ ⵑ 🏠 Map 12

## ROFFIAC, Cantal, 15100

### AUBERGE DE LA VALLEE, RD 826, at Saint Flour head towards Aurillac
**Restaurant:** Closed Saturdays, Sundays and from 15 to 30 August. **Specialities:** regional menu, home cooking. **Other points:** bar.
MR PIERRE FARGES
**Telephone:** 71.60.04.50
⊗ ⵑ Map 12

## SAINT BONNET, Puy-de-Dôme, 63200

### LE BON COIN, RN 143
**Restaurant:** Closed from 15 September to 10 October. **Hotel:** 10 beds. **Other points:** bar. **Address:** 2, rue de la République.
MR JEAN LEVADOUX
**Telephone:** 73.63.31.14
⊗ ⵑ 🏠 Map 12

## SAINT FLOUR, Cantal, 15100

### HOTEL LE PROGRES, RN 9
**Hotel:** 10 beds. **Other points:** bar. **Address:** 61, rue des Lacs.

MR ALAIN MOURGUES
**Telephone:** 71.60.03.06
⊗ ⵑ 🏠 🍽 ☆☆ Map 12

### LES ROUTIERS, RN 9
**Languages spoken:** English and Spanish. **Menu:** 60 to 100 Frs. **Accommodation:** 100 Frs. **Restaurant:** Breakfast served from 7:30am. Lunch served from midday until 4:00pm. Dinner served from 7:00pm until 10:00pm. Closed Mondays and in January/February. **Specialities:** regional menu, home cooking. **Hotel:** 7 beds; 4 single rooms, 3 double rooms with shower. **Other points:** open to non-residents, à la carte menu, pets welcome – check for details, traditional decor. **Address:** 49, place de la Liberté.
MME LILIANE TEISSEDRE
**Telephone:** 71.60.23.00
⊗ 🏠 Map 12

## SAINT GENCE, Haute-Vienne, 87510

### LE CAMPANELLE, between Limoges and Bellegarde
**Menu:** 60 Frs. **Restaurant:** Breakfast served from 8:00am. Lunch served from midday until 2:00pm. Dinner served from 7:00pm until 9:00pm. Closed Saturdays and in August. **Specialities:** home cooking. **Other points:** bar, open to non-residents, car park, traditional decor. **Address:** Campanelle.
MR ALBERT DENARDOU
**Telephone:** 55.48.02.83
⊗ ⵑ Map 11

## SAINT GEORGES D'AURAC, Haute-Loire, 43230

### LES TILLEULS, RN 102
**Restaurant:** Breakfast served from 6:30am. Lunch served from midday until 1:30pm. Dinner served from 7:00pm until 9:00pm. Closed Saturdays. **Hotel:** 9 beds. **Other points:** bar, open to non-residents, terraces. **Address:** Route Nationale 102.
MME BRIGITTE GUILLOT
**Telephone:** 71.77.50.75
⊗ ⵑ 🏠 Map 12

## SAINT JEAN D'HEURS, Puy-de-Dôme, 63190

### MA CAMPAGNE, RN 89, between Clermont Ferrand and Thiers
**Menu:** 55 Frs (wine included) to 90 Frs. **Restaurant:** Breakfast served from 5:30am. Closed Saturdays. **Specialities:** home cooking. **Other points:** bar, open to non-residents, à la carte menu, children welcome, terraces, pets welcome – check for details, car park, traditional decor. **Address:** Route Nationale 89.
MME CHRISTIANE DEWEERT
**Telephone:** 73.73.16.52
⊗ ⵑ Map 12

## SAINT JULIEN CHAPTEUIL,
Haute-Loire, 43260

*AUBERGE DU MEYCAL, RD 15, the main road between le Puy en Velay and Valence*
**Menu:** 50 to 90 Frs. **Accommodation:** 120 to 150 Frs. **Restaurant:** Lunch served from midday until 1:30pm. Dinner served from 7:30pm until 8:30pm. **Specialities:** couscous, truites, omelette Norvégienne, home cooking. **Hotel:** 12 beds; with shower, private WC, telephone. **Other points:** bar, open to non-residents, lounge area, terraces, pets welcome – check for details, car park, traditional decor. **Address:** Boussoulet.
MR RENÉ CHAPUIS
**Telephone:** 71.08.71.03
⊗ ⵖ ⌂ ☆ Map 12

## SAINT JUNIEN, Haute-Vienne, 87200

*L'ETOILE, RN 141, the main road between Angoulêmes and Limoges*
**Languages spoken:** English. **Menu:** 55 to 180 Frs. **Accommodation:** 120 to 220 Frs (overnight stop 170 Frs). **Restaurant:** Breakfast served from 6:30am. Lunch served from 11:00am until 4:00pm. Dinner served from 7:30pm until 10:00pm. Closed Sundays and from 20 December to 6 January. **Specialities:** home cooking. **Hotel:** 10 beds; 2 single rooms, 8 double rooms with shower, private WC. **Other points:** bar, open to non-residents, à la carte menu, terraces, pets welcome – check for details, car park, traditional decor. **Address:** 8, avenue Henri Barbusse.
MR ALAIN NOBLE
**Telephone:** 55.02.15.19. **Fax:** 55.02.92.64
⊗ ⵖ ⌂ Map 11

## SAINT JUST LE MARTEL, Haute-Vienne, 87590

*LE PETIT SALE, RD 141, Clermont Ferrand*
**Menu:** 56 to 150 Frs. **Accommodation:** 140 to 280 Frs. **Restaurant:** Breakfast served from 7:00am. Lunch served from midday until 3:00pm. Dinner served from 7:00pm until 10:00pm. **Specialities:** regional menu. **Hotel:** 10 beds; 4 single rooms, 6 double rooms with shower, bath, private WC, television, telephone. **Other points:** bar, open to non-residents, à la carte menu, car park, traditional decor. **Address:** Les Chabanes.
MR JEAN-PIERRE TEYTI
**Telephone:** 55.09.21.14
⊗ ⵖ ⌂ ⌐ Map 11

## SAINT MATHIEU, Haute-Vienne, 87440

*LA GRANGE DU LAC, RN 699, route of Limoges via Cussac*
**Languages spoken:** English. **Menu:** 50 to 140 Frs. **Accommodation:** 110 to 200 Frs. **Restaurant:** Breakfast served from 8:00am. Lunch served from 11:00am until 3:00pm. Dinner served from 7:00pm until midnight. Closed

Tuesdays. **Specialities:** magret, confits, cèpes, regional food. **Hotel:** 6 beds; with shower, bath. **Other points:** bar, open to non-residents, à la carte menu, children welcome, lounge area, terraces, pets welcome – check for details, car park, traditional decor. **Address:** Lieu dit 'Les Champs'.
MR FRANCK VARACHAUT
**Telephone:** 55.00.35.84
⊗ ⵖ ⌂ Map 11

## SAINT POURCAIN, Allier, 03500

*LE BELVEDERE, RN 9, Moulin*
**Places of interest:** la vieille ville, cathédrale, palais Jacques Coeurs. **Menu:** 55 to 145 Frs. **Restaurant:** Breakfast served from 8:00am. **Specialities:** home cooking. **Other points:** bar, open to non-residents, à la carte menu, children welcome, terraces, pets welcome – check for details, car park, modern decor. **Address:** Les Plachis.
MME JEANNINE LACAUSSADE
**Telephone:** 70.42.09.58
⊗ ⵖ Map 12

## SAINT PRIEST DE GIMEL, Corrèze, 19800

*LE RELAIS CHEZ MOUSTACHE, RN 89*
**Restaurant:** Dinner served from midday until 10:00pm. Closed Saturdays and in August. **Hotel:** 3 beds. **Other points:** bar. **Address:** Gare de Corrèze.
MR JEAN-CLAUDE LAVAL
**Telephone:** 55.21.39.64
⊗ ⵖ Map 11

## SAINT SORNIN LEULAC, Haute-Vienne, 87290

*HOTEL DU CENTRE, RN 145, between la Croisière and Bellac*
**Languages spoken:** English. **Menu:** 50 Frs (wine and coffee included). **Restaurant:** Breakfast served from 7:00am. **Specialities:** home cooking. **Other points:** bar, open to non-residents, children welcome, terraces, pets welcome – check for details, car park, traditional decor. **Address:** Gare de Corrèze.
MR PATRICK GAILLAC
**Telephone:** 55.76.32.54
⊗ ⵖ Map 11

## SAINT VICTURNIEN, Haute-Vienne, 87420

*LE PUIS MALAIS, RN 141, the main road between Limoges and Angoulême*
**Menu:** 56 Frs (wine included) to 130 Frs. **Restaurant:** Breakfast served from 6:00am. **Specialities:** regional menu, home cooking. **Hotel:** 8 beds; 1 single room, 7 double rooms with shower. **Other points:** bar, open to non-residents, terraces, pets welcome – check for details, car park, traditional decor. **Address:** Route Nationale 141, la Malaise.

MR MOUM
**Telephone:** 55.03.87.03
⊗ 🍸 Ⓗ Map 11

## SAINT YORRE, Allier, 03270

### *NOUVEL HOTEL, CD 906, between Thiers and Vichy*

**Languages spoken:** English. **Menu:** 50 to 125 Frs. **Accommodation:** 110 to 150 Frs. **Restaurant:** Breakfast served from 6:30am. Lunch served from 11:45am until 2:30pm. Dinner served from 5:45pm until 9:30pm. Closed Saturdays and in February. **Specialities:** truite normande, home cooking. **Hotel:** 12 beds; 6 single rooms, 6 double rooms with shower, private WC, television. **Other points:** bar, open to non-residents, à la carte menu, children welcome, lounge area, terraces, pets welcome – check for details, car park, modern decor. **Address:** 17, avenue de Vichy.
MR HUBERT CHESNEL
**Telephone:** 70.59.41.97. **Fax:** 70.32.54.34
⊗ 🍸 Ⓗ Map 12

## SAUVIAT SUR VIGE, Haute-Vienne, 87400

### *HOTEL DE LA POSTE, RN 141*

**Accommodation:** 130 to 180 Frs. **Restaurant:** Dinner served from midday until 10:00pm. Closed Wednesdays and in September. **Hotel:** 10 beds; 5 single rooms, 5 double rooms with shower, bath, private WC, telephone. **Other points:** bar, pets welcome – check for details, car park, traditional decor..
MR PIERRE CHASSAGNE
**Telephone:** 55.75.30.12
⊗ 🍸 Ⓗ ☆ Map 11

## SEREILHAC, Haute-Vienne, 87620

### *AUBERGE DES ROUTIERS*

**Languages spoken:** English. **Restaurant:** Dinner served from midday until 11:00pm. **Hotel:** 6 beds. **Other points:** bar. **Address:** Route Nationale 21.
MME DENISE VIGNAUD
**Telephone:** 55.39.10.46
⊗ 🍸 Ⓗ Map 11

## SOUTERRAINE (LA), Creuse, 23300

### *LES ROUTIERS, RN 145, between Limoges and Gueret*

**Menu:** 52 Frs. **Accommodation:** 80 to 130 Frs. **Restaurant:** Breakfast served from 5:00am. Lunch served from midday until 3:00pm. Dinner served from 7:00pm until 11:00pm. Closed Sundays and from 24 December to 2 January. **Specialities:** home cooking. **Hotel:** 15 beds; 12 single rooms, 3 double rooms with shower. **Other points:** bar, open to non-residents, terraces, pets welcome – check for details, car park, traditional decor. **Address:** La Croisière Saint Maurice.
MR RAYMOND BOUTET
**Telephone:** 55.63.77.55
⊗ 🍸 Ⓗ Map 11

## TENCE, Haute-Loire, 43190

### *RESTAURANT DES CARS, RN 88, town centre*

**Menu:** 42 to 70 Frs. **Restaurant:** Breakfast served from 7:00am. Lunch served from 11:30am until 3:00pm. Dinner served from 7:00pm until 9:00pm. **Specialities:** home cooking. **Other points:** bar, open to non-residents, à la carte menu, children welcome, pets welcome – check for details, car park, traditional decor. **Address:** 13, Grande Rue.
MR DAVID BONNET
**Telephone:** 71.59.84.01
⊗ 🍸 Map 12

## TOULON SUR ALLIER, Allier, 03400

### *LE FLAMBEAU, RN 7*

**Menu:** 60 to 80 Frs. **Restaurant:** Breakfast served from 8:00am. Lunch served from 11:00am until 3:00pm. Dinner served from 7:00pm until 11:00pm. Closed Sundays. **Specialities:** home cooking. **Other points:** open to non-residents, à la carte menu, children welcome, car park. **Address:** Route Nationale 7.
SARL LE FLAMBEAU
**Telephone:** 70.20.90.28
⊗ Map 12

### *LE RELAIS FLEURI, RN 7*

**Restaurant:** Closed Sundays and in August. **Other points:** bar. **Address:** Route Nationale 7.
MR BELAIN
**Telephone:** 70.44.47.16
⊗ 🍸 Map 12

## USSEL, Cantal, 15300

### *LE RELAIS DE LA PLANEZE, RD 926, between Murat and Saint Flour*

**Menu:** 50 to 65 Frs. **Restaurant:** Breakfast served from 7:15am. Lunch served from midday until 2:00pm. Closed Sundays, the 1st week in September and 1 week at Christmas. **Specialities:** home cooking. **Other points:** bar, open to non-residents, terraces, pets welcome – check for details, car park, traditional decor. **Address:** Route Départementale 926.
MME GILBERTE ESBRAT
**Telephone:** 71.73.20.52. **Fax:** 71.23.11.99
⊗ 🍸 Map 12

## VARENNES SUR ALLIER, Allier, 03150

### *LA RENAISSANCE, RN 7*

**Languages spoken:** Portugese. **Restaurant:** Dinner served from midday until 9:00pm. **Other points:** bar. **Address:** Bellevue.

MME ROSE GARDEL
**Telephone:** 70.45.62.86
⊗ ☙ Map 12

*LE RELAIS DES TOURISTES, RN 7, Lyon*
**Menu:** 60 to 90 Frs. **Accommodation:** 130 to 200 Frs.
**Restaurant:** Breakfast served from 6:00am. Lunch
served from midday until 2:00pm. Dinner served from
7:30pm until 9:00pm. Closed Saturdays. **Specialities:**
savoyardes, home cooking. **Hotel:** 9 beds; 4 single
rooms, 5 double rooms with shower. **Other points:** bar,
open to non-residents, pets welcome – check for details,
car park, traditional decor. **Address:** 1, rue des Halles.
MR ANDRÉ JUNIET
**Telephone:** 70.45.00.51
⊗ ☙ 🏠 🍴 Map 12

## VERNET LA VARENNE (LE), Puy-de-Dôme, 63580

*HOTEL DU CHATEAU, RD 999, Issoire*
**Languages spoken:** English. **Menu:** 45 to 90 Frs.
**Accommodation:** 70 to 115 Frs. **Restaurant:** Breakfast
served from 7:30am. Lunch served from midday until
2:00pm. Dinner served from 7:30pm until 9:00pm.
Closed Mondays. **Specialities:** regional menu, home
cooking. **Hotel:** 7 beds; 4 single rooms, 3 double rooms
with shower. **Other points:** bar, open to non-residents,
children welcome, terraces, pets welcome – check for
details, car park, traditional decor. **Address:** 1, rue des
Halles Bernard et Denis – SNC.
CHARNAY-MAGAUD
**Telephone:** 73.71.31.79
⊗ ☙ 🏠 Map 12

## VICHY, Allier, 03200

*RELAIS DE LA PASSERELLE, between
Thiers and le Puy en Velay*
**Menu:** 50 Frs. **Accommodation:** 80 to 140 Frs.
**Restaurant:** Breakfast served from 6:30am. Lunch served
from midday until 2:00pm. Dinner served from 7:00pm
until 8:00pm. Closed Sundays and in August. **Specialities:**
home cooking. **Hotel:** 4 beds; 2 single rooms, 2 double
rooms with shower, telephone. **Otherpoints:** bar, open to
non-residents, modern decor. **Address:** 1, rue de Bordeaux.
MR JEAN-PIERRE PESCE
**Telephone:** 70.98.57.70
⊗ ☙ Map 12

## VIEILLE BRIOUDE, Haute-Loire, 43100

*LES GLYCINES, RN 102, between Clermont
Ferrand and le Puy en Velay*
**Languages spoken:** English. **Menu:** 59 to 220 Frs.
**Accommodation:** 195 to 320 Frs. **Restaurant:**
Breakfast served from 7:00am. Lunch served from
midday until 2:00pm. Dinner served from 7:30pm until
9:00pm. Closed from Friday afternoon to Saturday

afternoon and in January. **Specialities:** saumon. **Hotel:**
13 beds; 13 double rooms with shower, bath, private
WC, television, telephone. **Other points:** bar, open to
non-residents, terraces, pets welcome – check for details,
car park, modern decor. **Address:** Avenue de Versailles.
MME VIVIANE CHARDONNAL
**Telephone:** 71.50.91.80
⊗ ☙ 🏠 ☆☆ Map 12

## VOLVIC, Puy-de-Dôme, 63530

*LA NUGERE, RD 941, the main road
between Volvic and Limoges*
**Languages spoken:** German and English. **Menu:** 48
(wine included) to 80 Frs. **Restaurant:** Breakfast served
from 6:00am. **Specialities:** Spécialités périgourdines,
home cooking. **Hotel:** 10 beds; 8 single rooms, 2 double
rooms. **Other points:** bar, open to non-residents, à la
carte menu, children welcome, lounge area, terraces,
pets welcome – check for details, car park, traditional
decor. **Address:** Le Cratère.
MME GENEVIEVE PAYOT
**Telephone:** 73.33.80.50
⊗ ☙ 🏠 Map 12

## VOREY SUR ARZON, Haute-Loire, 43800

*RESTAURANT DE LA BASCULE, RN 103,
between Saint Etienne and le Puy en Velay*
**Languages spoken:** Italian. **Accommodation:** 80 to 100
Frs. **Restaurant:** Breakfast served from 6:30am. Lunch
served from 11:45am until 3:00pm. Dinner served from
7:00pm until 9:30pm. **Specialities:** home cooking.
**Hotel:** 5 beds; 4 single rooms, 1 double room. **Other
points:** bar, open to non-residents, children welcome,
pets welcome – check for details, car park. **Address:**
Place des Moulettes.
MR SERGE HILAIRE
**Telephone:** 71.03.41.67
⊗ ☙ 🏠 Map 12

## YSSINGEAUX, Haute-Loire, 43200

*LA PETITE AUBERGE, RN 88, the main
road between Saint Etienne and le Puy en
Velay*
**Menu:** 53 to 130 Frs. **Accommodation:** 75 to 130 Frs.
**Restaurant:** Breakfast served from 6:00am. Lunch
served from midday until 3:00pm. Dinner served from
7:30pm until 10:00pm. Closed Saturdays. **Specialities:**
regional menu, home cooking. **Hotel:** 5 beds; 3 single
rooms, 2 double rooms. **Other points:** bar, open to non-
residents, à la carte menu, children welcome, terraces,
pets welcome – check for details, car park, traditional
decor. **Address:** Lieu dit 'La Guide'.
MR YVES DREVET
**Telephone:** 71.59.57.75
⊗ ☙ 🏠 Map 12

# South West France

## ABZAC, Gironde, 33230

### LE GAULOIS, RN 84, road for Lyon
**Menu:** 50 to 75 Frs. **Restaurant:** Breakfast served from 5:00am. **Specialities:** regional menu, home cooking. **Other points:** bar, open to non-residents, à la carte menu, children welcome, terraces, pets welcome – check for details, car park. **Address:** Tripoteau.
MR JACQUES LACOUX
**Telephone:** 57.49.07.34
⊗ ♀ Map 8

## AGEN, Lot-et-Garonne, 47310

### RELAIS AGEN PORTE D'AQUITAINE, A 62
**Languages spoken:** English. **Restaurant:** Breakfast served from 7:00am. **Specialities:** regional menu. **Other points:** à la carte menu, children welcome, lounge area, terraces, pets welcome – check for details, car park. **Address:** Aire de Service d'Agen, dans les deux sens.
**Telephone:** 53.68.70.75
⊗ Map 8

## AGUESSAC, Aveyron, 12520

### LE BALLON ROND, the main road between Paris/Clermont Ferrand/Béziers
**Menu:** 55 to 110 Frs. **Accommodation:** 100 to 150 Frs. **Restaurant:** Breakfast served from 7:30am. Lunch served from midday until 3:00pm. Dinner served from 7:00pm until 9:00pm. **Specialities:** regional menu. **Hotel:** 6 beds; 4 single rooms, 2 double rooms. **Other points:** bar, open to non-residents, children welcome, lounge area, pets welcome – check for details, car park, traditional decor. **Address:** Route Nationale 9.
MR GUY PAILHAS
**Telephone:** 65.59.80.18
⊗ ♀ ⌂ Map 9

## AIRE SUR L'ADOUR, Landes, 40800

### LES ROUTIERS, RN 134, Mont de Marsan/Tarbe
**Accommodation:** 100 to 140 Frs. **Restaurant:** Breakfast served from 7:00am. Lunch served from midday until 2:00pm. Dinner served from 7:30pm until 10:00pm. Closed Saturdays. **Specialities:** regional menu, home cooking. **Hotel:** 10 beds; 7 single rooms, 3 double rooms with shower, bath. **Other points:** bar, open to non-residents, à la carte menu, children welcome, terraces, pets welcome – check for details, car park, traditional decor. **Address:** 15, rue du 4 Septembre.
MR JOEL DASTE
**Telephone:** 58.71.63.01. **Fax:** 58.71.63.01
⊗ ♀ ⌂ ☆ Map 8

## ALBAN, Tarn, 81250

### RESTAURANT DU MIDI, RD 999, between Albi and Millau
**Languages spoken:** Spanish. **Menu:** 60 Frs (wine included). **Restaurant:** Lunch served from midday until 2:00pm. Dinner served from 7:00pm until 9:00pm. Closed Tuesdays and the last week in August. **Specialities:** regional menu, home cooking. **Other points:** bar, open to non-residents, children welcome, lounge area, terraces, pets welcome – check for details, car park, traditional decor. **Address:** 9, place des Tilleuls.
MR PATRICK DAURELLE
**Telephone:** 63.55.82.24
⊗ ♀ Map 8

## ALBI, Tarn, 81000

### AUBERGE LANDAISE DE CHEZ MARCEL
**Restaurant:** Closed Sundays. **Other points:** bar. **Address:** Route de Montplaisir, la Rivayrolle.
MR MARCEL GAUZERE
**Telephone:** 63.45.03.11
⊗ ♀ Map 8

### LE RELAIS CATALAN, RD 999, the main road between Albi and Millau
**Languages spoken:** English. **Menu:** 63 Frs. **Accommodation:** 100 to 120 Frs. **Restaurant:** Breakfast served from 4:30am. Lunch served from 11:45am until 3:00pm. Dinner served from 7:00pm until 9:30pm. Closed Saturdays. **Specialities:** home cooking. **Hotel:** 8 beds; 6 single rooms, 2 double rooms. **Other points:** bar, open to non-residents, children welcome, terraces, pets welcome – check for details, car park,

traditional decor. **Address:** Barrière de Montplaisir, route de Millau.
MME VIRGINIE CAMPIN
**Telephone:** 63.60.27.00
⊗ ♀ ⌂ Map 8

### LE RELAIS FLEURI, RN 88, at the entrance to Albi, on leaving Toulouse

**Languages spoken:** Spanish. **Menu:** 55 to 120 Frs.
**Accommodation:** 120 to 150 Frs. **Restaurant:**
Breakfast served from 7:30am. Lunch served from
11:00am until 3:00pm. Dinner served from 7:00pm until
10:00pm. Closed Sundays. **Specialities:** regional menu,
home cooking. **Hotel:** 3 beds; 1 single room, 2 double
rooms with shower, private WC. **Other points:** bar,
open to non-residents, à la carte menu, terraces, pets
welcome – check for details, car park, traditional decor.
**Address:** 25, avenue François Verdier.
MR PÉDRO CASADO
**Telephone:** 63.54.07.09
⊗ ♀ Map 8

## ALBINE, Tarn, 81240

### LA GRILLE

**Menu:** 55 Frs. **Restaurant:** Lunch served from 11:30am
until 3:00pm. Dinner served from 7:00pm until 11:00pm.
**Other points:** bar, car park. **Address:** 1, avenue de la
Ribaute.
MME ODILE MAYER
**Telephone:** 63.98.39.11
⊗ ♀ Map 9

## AMBRES, Tarn, 81500

### AUBERGE DES POMMIERS, RD 87, on the road to Gaillac

**Languages spoken:** English and Spanish. **Menu:** 57 to
160 Frs. **Accommodation:** 100 to 200 Frs. **Restaurant:**
Breakfast served from 7:00am. Lunch served from
midday until 2:00pm. Dinner served from 8:00pm until
9:00pm. Closed Fridays. **Specialities:** home cooking.
**Hotel:** 6 beds; with shower, bath, television. **Other
points:** bar, open to non-residents, lounge area, terraces,
car park. **Address:** Le Grès.
MR ALAIN SORE
**Telephone:** 63.58.05.56
⊗ ♀ ⌂ ☆ Map 9

## AMOU, Landes, 40330

### AU FEU DE BOIS, RD 15, between Dax and Pau

**Menu:** 45 to 130 Frs. **Accommodation:** 100 to 270 Frs.
**Restaurant:** Breakfast served from 8:00am. Lunch
served from midday until 2:30pm. Dinner served from
7:30pm until 9:30pm. Closed Fridays, 3 weeks in
January and 2 weeks in September. **Specialities:**
regional menu. **Hotel:** 16 beds; 8 single rooms, 8 double

rooms with shower, private WC. **Other points:** bar,
open to non-residents, à la carte menu, children
welcome, terraces, pets welcome – check for details, car
park, traditional decor. **Address:** Avenue des Pyrénées.
MR JOEL MARTINET
**Telephone:** 58.89.00.86
⊗ ♀ ⌂ ☆☆ Map 8

## ANGLET, Pyrénées-Atlantiques, 64600

### LES MOUETTES

**Languages spoken:** Italian. **Menu:** 52 Frs (wine and
coffee included). **Accommodation:** 80 to 160 Frs.
**Restaurant:** Breakfast served from 6:30am. Lunch
served from midday until 2:00pm. Dinner served from
7:30pm until 10:30pm. Closed Saturdays and the 2nd
fortnight in August. **Specialities:** home cooking. **Hotel:**
11 beds; 5 single rooms, 6 double rooms with shower,
private WC. **Other points:** bar, open to non-residents,
pets welcome – check for details, car park, traditional
decor. **Address:** 5, avenue de l'Adour.
MR JEAN-CLAUDE MOTTA
**Telephone:** 59.52.46.08
⊗ ♀ ⌂ Map 8

## ANIANE, Hérault, 34150

### LA CLAMOUSE, RN 109, between Gignac and Ganges

**Languages spoken:** Spanish. **Menu:** 78 to 200 Frs.
**Accommodation:** 160 to 300 Frs. **Restaurant:** Lunch
served from midday until 2:00pm. Dinner served from
7:30pm until 9:00pm. **Specialities:** regional menu, home
cooking. **Hotel:** 10 beds; 6 single rooms, 4 double rooms
with shower, bath, private WC. **Other points:** bar, open
to non-residents, à la carte menu, children welcome,
lounge area, car park, modern decor. **Address:** 39,
boulevard Saint Jean.
MME MARIE ROVIRA
**Telephone:** 67.57.49.04
⊗ ♀ ⌂ ☆ Map 10

## ANTONNE ET TRIGONANT, Dordogne, 24420

### LE RELAIS DE LAURIERE, RN 21, between Périgueux and Limoges

**Languages spoken:** English. **Menu:** 58 Frs (wine and
coffee included). **Accommodation:** 80 Frs.
**Restaurant:** Closed Sundays and 2 weeks in August.
**Specialities:** regional menu, home cooking. **Hotel:** 4
beds; 3 single rooms, 1 double room. **Other points:**
bar, open to non-residents, à la carte menu, children
welcome, lounge area, terraces, pets welcome – check
for details, car park, traditional decor. **Address:**
Laurière.
MR JEAN-CLAUDE CONDAMINAS
**Telephone:** 53.06.17.92, 53.06.00.28
⊗ ♀ Map 8

## ARDOISE (L'), Gard, 30290

### LE CHALET
**Languages spoken:** English and Italian. **Menu:** 60 to 80
Frs (wine and coffee included). **Accommodation:** 140 to
170 Frs. **Restaurant:** Breakfast served from 6:30am.
Closed Sundays and 15 days at Christmas/New Year.
**Specialities:** croûte morille, poulet au sang (vin de
Bourgogne). **Hotel:** 7 beds; with shower. **Other points:**
bar, car park. **Address:** 440, route d'Avignon.
MME SYLVIE LAROCHE
**Telephone:** 66.50.22.22
⊗ ⍾ ⌂ Map 10

## ASTAFFORT, Lot-et-Garonne, 47220

### LE RELAIS DES PYRENEES, the main
### road between Agen and Lourdes
**Languages spoken:** Spanish and Italian. **Menu:** 58 Frs.
**Restaurant:** Breakfast served from 5:30am. Lunch
served from 11:30am until 3:00pm. Dinner served from
7:00pm until 9:00pm. Closed Sundays and 10 days end
of August. **Specialities:** regional menu, home cooking.
**Other points:** bar, à la carte menu, terraces, pets
welcome – check for details, car park, traditional decor.
**Address:** Barbonvièle.
MR CLAUDE PARMA
**Telephone:** 53.67.14.57
⊗ ⍾ Map 8

## AUCAMVILLE, Haute-Garonne, 31140

### LE TOIT
**Languages spoken:** Spanish. **Restaurant:** Dinner
served from midday until midnight. **Other points:** bar.
**Address:** 50, chaussée des Mazuries.
MR JEAN-PIERRE LABLANCHE
**Telephone:** 61.70.46.37
⊗ ⍾ Map 9

## AVIGNONET LAURAGAIS, Haute-Garonne, 31290

### LA PERGOLA, RN 113, between
### Villefranche and Castelnaudary
**Languages spoken:** Spanish. **Menu:** 59 to 125 Frs.
**Accommodation:** 120 to 170 Frs. **Restaurant:**
Breakfast served from 7:00am. Lunch served from
midday until 2:30pm. Dinner served from 7:30pm
until 9:30pm. Closed Saturdays and in February
(school holidays). **Specialities:** regional menu, home
cooking. **Hotel:** 3 beds; 1 single room, 2 double
rooms with shower. **Other points:** bar, open to non-
residents, à la carte menu, terraces, pets welcome –
check for details, car park. **Address:** Route
Nationale 113.
MR ETIENNE DATAN
**Telephone:** 61.81.63.54. **Fax:** 61.27.82.76
⊗ ⍾ Map 9

## AZERAT, Dordogne, 24210

### LE RELAIS D'AZERAT, RN 89
**Restaurant:** Closed Saturdays and the 2nd fortnight in
August. **Hotel:** 4 beds.
MME ANNIE DEBORD
**Telephone:** 53.05.21.05
⊗ Map 8

## BACCARETS (LES), Haute-Garonne, 31550

### LA CHAUMIERE, RN 20, the main road
### between Toulouse and Foix
**Menu:** 55 Frs. **Accommodation:** 85 to 115 Frs.
**Restaurant:** Breakfast served from 6:00am. Closed
Sundays and 2 weeks from New Year's Eve.
**Specialities:** home cooking. **Hotel:** 12 beds; 4 single
rooms, 8 double rooms. **Other points:** bar, open to non-
residents, children welcome, pets welcome – check for
details, car park, traditional decor. **Address:** Route
Nationale 20, Cintegabelle.
MR DANIEL LAROCHE
**Telephone:** 61.08.90.70
⊗ ⍾ ⌂ Map 9

## BAGNAC SUR CELE, Lot, 46270

### RELAIS ROUTIERS LA PLANQUETTE, RN 122
**Restaurant:** Dinner served from midday until 10:00pm.
Closed Mondays. **Hotel:** 6 beds. **Other points:** bar, car
park. **Address:** Route d'Aurillac.
MME MICHELINE CLAUDON
**Telephone:** 65.34.93.50
⊗ ⍾ ⌂ Map 9

## BAIGTS EN CHALOSSE, Landes, 40380

### LE CARREFOUR, RD 2, between Dax and
### Saint Sever
**Menu:** 55 to 180 Frs. **Accommodation:** 60 to 70 Frs.
**Restaurant:** Breakfast served from 7:30am. Lunch
served from 12:30pm until 2:00pm. Dinner served from
8:00pm until 10:00pm. Closed Mondays. **Specialities:**
regional menu, home cooking. **Hotel:** 4 beds; 3 single
rooms, 1 double room with shower, bath, private WC.
**Other points:** open to non-residents, à la carte menu,
terraces, pets welcome – check for details, car park,
modern decor. **Address:** Le Carrefour.
MR JEAN BONNOT
**Telephone:** 58.95.63.05
⊗ Map 8

## BALIZAC, Gironde, 33730

### LE RELAIS BASQUE, RD 110/111
**Menu:** 55 to 125 Frs. **Restaurant:** Dinner served from

midday until 9:00pm. Closed Mondays and in October. **Specialities:** regional menu, home cooking. **Other points:** bar, open to non-residents, à la carte menu, children welcome, terraces, pets welcome – check for details, car park, traditional decor.
MME JEANNE DESCLAUX
**Telephone:** 56.25.36.71
⊗ ♀ Map 8

# BARAQUEVILLE, Aveyron, 12160

## LE PALOUS, crossroads Albi/Montauban/Millau/Rodez
**Languages spoken:** English. **Menu:** 50 to 130 Frs. **Accommodation:** 190 to 260 Frs. **Restaurant:** Breakfast served from 6:30am. Lunch served from 11:30am until 2:00pm. Dinner served from 7:30pm until 9:30pm. Closed from 24 December to 2 January. **Specialities:** tripous, magret, confit de canard, foie gras, regional food. **Hotel:** 16 beds; 12 single rooms, 4 double rooms with shower, bath, private WC, television, telephone. **Other points:** bar, open to non-residents, à la carte menu, children welcome, lounge area, terraces, pets welcome – check for details, car park, traditional decor, modern decor. **Address:** 184, avenue du Centre.
CLUZEL, DRUILHE ET PALOUS
**Telephone:** 65.69.01.89. **Fax:** 65.69.10.80
⊗ ♀ 🏠 ☆☆ Map 9

# BASTIDE L'EVEQUE (LA), Aveyron, 12200

## RELAIS DE L'HERMET, RD 911
**Restaurant:** Closed Saturdays. **Other points:** bar, car park. **Address:** Route Départementale 911.
MR YVAN BOURDONCLE
**Telephone:** 65.65.61.41
⊗ ♀ Map 9

# BEAUCHALOT, Haute-Garonne, 31360

## AU BEARNAIS, RN 117, the main road between Toulouse and Bayonne
**Languages spoken:** English and Spanish. **Menu:** 50 to 180 Frs. **Accommodation:** 110 to 160 Frs. **Restaurant:** Breakfast served from 7:00am. Lunch served from midday until 2:00pm. Dinner served from 7:30pm until 9:00pm. Closed Mondays and in September. **Specialities:** garbure Béarnaise, foie gras, confit de canard, civet de chevreuil, regional food, home cooking. **Hotel:** 5 beds; 2 single rooms, 3 double rooms with shower, bath, private WC. **Other points:** bar, open to non-residents, à la carte menu, terraces, pets welcome – check for details, car park, traditional decor. **Address:** Saint Martory.
MR RENÉ FRÉCHOU
**Telephone:** 61.90.23.44
⊗ ♀ 🏠 Map 9

# BELARGA, Hérault, 34230

## LA GAITE, RD 32
**Menu:** 55 Frs. **Accommodation:** 130 Frs. **Restaurant:** Breakfast served from 6:30am. Lunch served from 11:30am. Dinner served from 7:00pm until 11:00pm. **Specialities:** home cooking. **Hotel:** 5 beds; 3 single rooms, 2 double rooms with shower, bath. **Other points:** bar, open to non-residents, children welcome, pets welcome – check for details, car park, traditional decor. **Address:** 34, avenue du Grand Chemin.
MME DANIELLE AUSSEL
**Telephone:** 67.25.00.82
⊗ ♀ 🏠 Map 10

# BELLEGARDE, Gard, 30127

## LOU FELIBRE, RN 113, between Arles and Nîmes
**Languages spoken:** German English Italian Spanish. **Menu:** 55 Frs. **Restaurant:** Breakfast served from 5:00am. Lunch served from midday until 2:30pm. Dinner served from 7:15pm until 10:00pm. Closed public holidays and the 2nd fortnight in August. **Specialities:** regional menu, home cooking. **Other points:** bar, open to non-residents, children welcome, terraces, pets welcome – check for details, car park, modern decor. **Address:** Route Nationale 113.
MME SABELINE RAFFI
**Telephone:** 66.01.15.21
⊗ ♀ Map 10

# BERNOS BEAULAC, Gironde, 33430

## LE RESTORELAIS, on the road to Pau
**Menu:** 53 to 63 Frs (wine included). **Restaurant:** Breakfast served from 5:00am. Closed Saturdays. **Specialities:** regional menu, home cooking. **Other points:** bar, open to non-residents, à la carte menu, children welcome, lounge area, terraces, pets welcome – check for details, car park, traditional decor. **Address:** Bois de Fond.
SARL LAMY-LEFEVRE
**Telephone:** 56.25.45.05
⊗ ♀ Map 8

# BERTHOLENE, Aveyron, 12310

## HOTEL BANCAREL, RN 88, between Rodez and Séverac le Châteaux, on the edge of the forest of Palanges
**Menu:** 52 to 140 Frs. **Accommodation:** 140 to 230 Frs. **Restaurant:** Breakfast served from 7:00am. Lunch served from midday until 2:00pm. Dinner served from 7:00pm until 9:00pm. Closed from 25 September to 20 October. **Specialities:** choux farci à la paysanne, feuilleté roquefort, confit de canard, regional food. **Hotel:** 13 beds; 13 single rooms with shower, bath, private WC. **Other points:** bar, open to non-residents, à

la carte menu, children welcome, terraces, pets welcome
– check for details, car park, traditional decor. **Address:**
Route Nationale 88.
MR JEAN BRUN
**Telephone:** 65.69.62.10. **Fax:** 65.70.72.88
⊗ � 🏠 ⛨ ☆ Map 9

## BESSIERES, Haute-Garonne, 31660

### LE RELAIS BESSIERAIN, RD 630, between Montauban (30km) and Castres (45km)

**Languages spoken:** Spanish and Italian. **Menu:** 52 Frs
(wine and coffee included). **Accommodation:** 120 Frs.
**Restaurant:** Breakfast served from 6:30am.
**Specialities:** home cooking. **Hotel:** 12 beds; 7 single
rooms, 5 double rooms. **Other points:** bar, open to non-
residents, children welcome, terraces, pets welcome –
check for details, car park, traditional decor. **Address:**
18, route de Montauban.
MR ANDRÉ BECCARELLI
**Telephone:** 61.84.00.95
⊗ 托 🏠 Map 9

## BEZIERS, Hérault, 34000

### L'OPPIDUM, RN 113, exit Béziers west (3km)

**Languages spoken:** English. **Menu:** 58 Frs (wine and
coffee included). **Accommodation:** 90 to 160 Frs.
**Restaurant:** Breakfast served from 6:30am. Dinner
served from 7:00pm until 10:00pm. Closed Saturdays.
**Hotel:** 16 beds; 12 single rooms, 4 double rooms with
shower. **Other points:** bar, open to non-residents, pets
welcome – check for details, traditional decor. **Address:**
Route Nationale 113.
MR ALAIN CHERRIER
**Telephone:** 67.28.30.34
⊗ 托 🏠 Map 10

### LE CANTAGAL

**Languages spoken:** English and Spanish. **Restaurant:**
Breakfast served from 6:30am. Closed Saturdays.
**Specialities:** regional menu, home cooking. **Other
points:** bar, open to non-residents, terraces, pets
welcome – check for details, car park, modern decor.
**Address:** Route de Pézenas.
MR CHRISTIAN MOURIER
**Telephone:** 67.31.25.47
⊗ 托 Map 10

## BIARS SUR CERE, Lot, 46130

### CHEZ ALAIN, RN 140

**Restaurant:** Lunch served from midday until 3:00pm.
Dinner served from 7:00pm until 10:30pm. Closed
Sundays and in August. **Specialities:** home cooking.
**Hotel:** 4 beds. **Other points:** bar, open to non-residents,
modern decor. **Address:** 16, avenue de la République.

MR ALAIN CAVALHAC
**Telephone:** 65.38.42.30
⊗ 托 Map 9

## BONLOC, Pyrénées-Atlantiques, 64240

### RELAIS LILIPEAN, RD 21, 3km from Hasparren

**Languages spoken:** German, English and Spanish.
**Menu:** 52 to 125 Frs. **Accommodation:** 100 to 150 Frs.
**Restaurant:** Breakfast served from 9:00am. Lunch
served from 11:00am until 2:00pm. Dinner served from
7:00pm until 10:00pm. Closed one Saturday per
fortnight (out of season) and from 22 December to 3
January. **Specialities:** regional menu, home cooking.
**Hotel:** 4 beds; 4 double rooms with shower, bath. **Other
points:** bar, open to non-residents, à la carte menu,
children welcome, terraces, pets welcome – check for
details, car park, traditional decor.
MR GASTON FOUCHÉ
**Telephone:** 59.29.51.48
⊗ 托 Map 8

## BORDEAUX, Gironde, 33800

### AU BON ACCUEIL, on the quay, towards Bayonne

**Languages spoken:** Spanish, Italian and Portugese.
**Menu:** 46 Frs (wine included) to 90 Frs. **Restaurant:**
Breakfast served from 7:00am. Lunch served from
midday until 3:00pm. Dinner served from 7:30pm until
11:30pm. Closed Sundays and in August. **Specialities:**
home cooking. **Other points:** bar, car park, traditional
decor. **Address:** 12, quai de la Monnaie.
MR FIDEL GONZALEZ
**Telephone:** 56.91.05.26
⊗ 托 Map 8

### B.R.I.R. INTER DES ROUTIERS, RN 10

**Languages spoken:** Portugese, Spanish. **Restaurant:**
Dinner served from midday until 11:00pm. Closed
Saturdays and in August. **Other points:** bar. **Address:**
295, Cours Balguerie Stuttenber.
MR ORLANDO GONÇALVES
**Telephone:** 56.43.15.47
⊗ 托 Map 8

### LE BON COIN, RN 10, after the bridge, Toulouse via the quays

**Languages spoken:** a little English. **Menu:** 52 Frs.
**Restaurant:** Breakfast served from 6:00am. Dinner
served from 7:00pm until midnight. Closed Saturdays
and in August. **Specialities:** home cooking. **Other
points:** bar, open to non-residents, children welcome,
pets welcome – check for details, car park, traditional
decor. **Address:** 142, rue Lucien Faure.
MME SANDRINE NOUTS
**Telephone:** 56.39.40.13
⊗ 托 Map 8

### RELAIS DE BORDEAUX, A 10
**Languages spoken:** English. **Restaurant:** Breakfast served from 7:00am. **Specialities:** regional menu. **Other points:** à la carte menu, children welcome, terraces, pets welcome – check for details, car park. **Address:** Aire de Service de Saugon, sens Bordeaux/Paris.
**Telephone:** 57.42.52.52
⊗ Map 8

### RESTAURANT DE L'UNION, RN 10
**Languages spoken:** English. **Menu:** 50 Frs.
**Restaurant:** Breakfast served from 6:00am. Closed Saturdays and in August. **Specialities:** home cooking. **Other points:** bar, open to non-residents, à la carte menu, pets welcome – check for details, car park, traditional decor. **Address:** 116, rue Lucien Faure.
MR DOMINIQUE DEPEYRIS
**Telephone:** 56.50.05.77
⊗ ♀ Map 8

## BORDEAUX BASTIDE, Gironde, 33800

### LE PORTO, RN 10, on the right bank of the Bordeaux, towards Lormont
**Languages spoken:** Spanish and portuguais. **Menu:** from 55 Frs. **Accommodation:** 100 Frs. **Restaurant:** Breakfast served from 6:30am. Dinner served from 7:00pm until 11:00pm. Closed Saturdays and in August. **Specialities:** Portugaises; Portugaises, home cooking. **Hotel:** 6 beds; 5 single rooms, 1 double room with shower, private WC. **Other points:** bar, open to non-residents, pets welcome – check for details, car park, traditional decor. **Address:** 202, bis quai de Brazza.
MME ROSA-MARIA PEREIRA
**Telephone:** 56.86.15.93
⊗ ♀ ⌂ Map 8

## BOUCOIRAN, Gard, 30190

### LE TAHURE, RN 106, between Ales and Nîmes
**Languages spoken:** Spanish. **Menu:** 55 Frs (wine and coffee included). **Restaurant:** Breakfast served from 4:30am. Lunch served from 11:30am until 3:00pm. Dinner served from 7:00pm until 10:00pm. Closed Saturdays. **Specialities:** home cooking. **Other points:** bar, terraces, pets welcome – check for details, car park, traditional decor.
MR JAK D'AMICO
**Telephone:** 66.83.65.93
⊗ ♀ Map 10

## BRAM, Aude, 11150

### CHEZ ALAIN, RN 113, between Carcassonne and Toulouse
**Languages spoken:** Spanish. **Menu:** 60 Frs.
**Accommodation:** 150 Frs. **Restaurant:** Breakfast served from 5:00am. Lunch served from 11:00am until 3:00pm. Dinner served from 7:00pm until 11:00pm. Closed Saturdays and in August.
**Specialities:** Cassoulet, escargots, tripes, blanquettes, regional food, home cooking. **Hotel:** 10 beds; 6 single rooms, 4 double rooms with shower, private WC, telephone. **Other points:** bar, open to non-residents, à la carte menu, lounge area, terraces, pets welcome – check for details, car park, traditional decor. **Address:** Route Nationale 113.
MR ALAIN ALBECQ
**Telephone:** 68.76.12.75, 68.76.53.16
⊗ ♀ ⌂ Map 10

## BRANTOME, Dordogne, 24310

### LE GERGOVIE, RD 939, between Périgueux and Angoulême
**Languages spoken:** English and Spanish. **Menu:** 55 (wine and coffee included) to 95 Frs. **Restaurant:** Open 24 hours. **Specialities:** regional menu, home cooking.
**Other points:** bar, open to non-residents, à la carte menu, children welcome, terraces, pets welcome – check for details, car park, modern decor. **Address:** Lieu dit 'Sarrazignac'.
MR CLAUDE DISTINGUIN
**Telephone:** 53.46.35.87. **Fax:** 53.05.75.95
⊗ ♀ ⌣ Map 8

## BRESSOLS, Tarn-et-Garonne, 82710

### L'ATHENA
**Languages spoken:** English, German and Italian.
**Menu:** 57 Frs. **Restaurant:** Lunch served from 11:00am until 3:00pm. Dinner served from 5:00pm until midnight. Closed Sundays. **Other points:** bar, car park.
**Address:** Route de Montauban.
MME MARIE-THÉRESE CORREGGIA
**Telephone:** 63.02.18.44
⊗ ♀ Map 9

## BUZIET, Pyrénées-Atlantiques, 64000

### LE BELLEVUE, the main road between Pau and Oloron
**Languages spoken:** Spanish. **Menu:** 60 to 100 Frs.
**Accommodation:** 140 to 200 Frs. **Restaurant:** Breakfast served from 8:30am. Lunch served from midday until 2:30pm. Dinner served from 7:30pm until 9:00pm. Closed Saturdays and 1 week between Christmas Day and New Year's Day. **Specialities:** regional menu, home cooking. **Hotel:** 6 beds; 3 single rooms, 3 double rooms with shower. **Other points:** bar, open to non-residents, à la carte menu, terraces, pets welcome – check for details, car park. **Address:** Belair.
MME MARCELLE LORRY
**Telephone:** 59.21.76.03
⊗ ♀ ⌂ Map 8

## CAHORS PERN, Lot, 46170

*LE RELAIS DES CIGALES, RN 20, the main road between Paris and Toulouse*
**Languages spoken:** English and Spanish. **Menu:** 55 to 120 Frs. **Accommodation:** 150 Frs. **Restaurant:** Breakfast served from 5:00am. Lunch served from midday until 3:00pm. Dinner served from 7:00pm until 11:00pm. Closed Sundays. **Specialities:** Confit d'oie, magrets, cassoulets au confit d'oie, regional food, home cooking. **Hotel:** 12 beds; with shower, private WC, television. **Other points:** bar, open to non-residents, à la carte menu, children welcome, lounge area, terraces, pets welcome – check for details, car park. **Address:** Route Nationale 20, Saint Barthelemy.
MR JOSÉ-MANUEL FERNANDEZ
**Telephone:** 65.21.97.49
⊗ ⵏ ⌂ Map 9

## CALMETTE (LA), Gard, 30190

*LE RELAIS DE L'ESCALETTE, RN 6*
**Languages spoken:** English. **Restaurant:** Dinner served from midday until midnight. **Other points:** bar.
**Address:** Route Nationale 6.
MR GEORGES APOSTOLAKIS
**Telephone:** 66.63.13.63
⊗ ⵏ Map 10

## CAMPAGNAC, Aveyron, 12560

*AU BONSECOURS*
**Restaurant:** Dinner served from midday until 11:00pm. Closed Saturdays. **Other points:** bar.
MME THÉRÉSE VAYSSIE
**Telephone:** 65.47.64.77
⊗ ⵏ Map 9

## CAMPSEGRET, Dordogne, 24140

*LES TAMARIS, RN 21, between Bergerac and Périgueux*
**Languages spoken:** English. **Menu:** 55 to 150 Frs. **Accommodation:** 150 to 180 Frs. **Restaurant:** Breakfast served from 6:00am. Dinner served from 7:00pm until 11:00pm. Closed Sundays. **Specialities:** regional menu, home cooking. **Hotel:** 11 beds; with shower, bath, private WC, television, telephone. **Other points:** bar, open to non-residents, à la carte menu, children welcome, lounge area, terraces, pets welcome – check for details, car park, traditional decor. **Address:** La Croix.
MR ALAIN THOMAS
**Telephone:** 53.24.21.75, 53.58.37.91
⊗ ⵏ ⌂ ⌙ ☆ Map 8

## CARMAUX, Tarn, 81400

*RELAIS SAINTE MARIE*
**Menu:** 50 Frs. **Accommodation:** 60 to 120 Frs.

**Restaurant:** Closed Saturdays. **Specialities:** home cooking. **Hotel:** 7 beds; 7 double rooms with shower, private WC. **Other points:** bar, open to non-residents, car park, modern decor. **Address:** 53, avenue Abli.
MME MARIE-LOUISE BERNIER
**Telephone:** 63.76.53.81
⊗ ⵏ ⌂ Map 9

## CASTELNAU RIVIERE BASSE,
Hautes-Pyrénées, 65700

*LE RELAIS DE MADIRAN, RD 935, the main road between Bordeaux/Tarbes/Lourdes*
**Languages spoken:** Spanish, Italian and Portugese. **Menu:** 55 to 140 Frs. **Restaurant:** Breakfast served from 6:00am. Lunch served from midday until 2:00pm. Dinner served from 8:00pm until 10:00pm. Closed Sundays. **Specialities:** regional menu, home cooking. **Other points:** bar, open to non-residents, à la carte menu, children welcome, terraces, car park, traditional decor. **Address:** Route de Bordeaux.
MR MICHEL DUCASSE
**Telephone:** 62.31.97.99
⊗ ⵏ Map 9

## CASTELSARRASIN, Tarn-et-Garonne, 82100

*CHEZ MAURICE, RN 113, the main road between Toulouse and Bordeaux*
**Menu:** 49 to 80 Frs. **Accommodation:** 95 to 165 Frs. **Restaurant:** Breakfast served from 5:00am. Lunch served from midday until 3:00pm. Dinner served from 7:00pm until 11:00pm. Closed Saturdays and 3 weeks in August. **Specialities:** cassoulet, magrets de canard, confits, regional food, home cooking. **Hotel:** 15 beds; 10 single rooms, 5 double rooms with shower. **Other points:** bar, open to non-residents, à la carte menu, lounge area, terraces, pets welcome – check for details, car park. **Address:** 35, route de Toulouse.
MR JEAN-PIERRE BOISSIER
**Telephone:** 63.32.30.83
⊗ ⵏ ⌂ ☆ Map 9

## CASTETS DES LANDES, Landes, 40260

*LE STUC, RN 10*
**Menu:** 50 Frs. **Restaurant:** Breakfast served from 7:00am. Lunch served from midday until 2:30pm. Closed Sundays and from 15 October to 15 November. **Specialities:** home cooking. **Other points:** bar, traditional decor. **Address:** 35, route de Toulouse.
MME DANIELE CALLEJA
**Telephone:** 58.89.40.62
⊗ ⵏ Map 8

## CASTRES, Tarn, 81100

*AUX AMIS DE LA ROUTE, RN 622, at the exit for Castres, on the road to Béziers*

**Menu:** 55 Frs. **Restaurant:** Lunch served from midday until 3:00pm. Dinner served from 7:00pm until 9:00pm. Closed Sundays. **Specialities:** home cooking. **Hotel:** 8 beds. **Other points:** bar, à la carte menu, terraces, pets welcome – check for details, car park, traditional decor. **Address:** 247, avenue Charles de Gaulle.
MR MICHEL LABESSOUILLE
**Telephone:** 63.35.54.38
⊗ 🍷 🏠 Map 9

## CAUNEILLE, Landes, 40300

### AU HAOU, RN 117
**Restaurant:** Dinner served from midday until 11:00pm. Closed from 20 December to 5 January. **Other points:** bar. **Address:** Route Nationale 117.
MME HENRIETTE LALANNE
**Telephone:** 58.73.04.60
⊗ 🍷 Map 8

## CAUSSADE, Tarn-et-Garonne, 82300

### RELAIS D'AUVERGNE, RN 20, between Montauban and Cahors
**Menu:** 51 to 102 Frs. **Accommodation:** 90 to 135 Frs. **Restaurant:** Breakfast served from 6:00am. Lunch served from 11:30am until 2:00pm. Dinner served from 7:00pm until 9:00pm. Closed Sundays. **Specialities:** cassoulet, grillades, home cooking. **Hotel:** 14 beds; 10 single rooms, 4 double rooms with shower, private WC. **Other points:** bar, open to non-residents, à la carte menu, children welcome, lounge area, pets welcome – check for details, car park, modern decor. **Address:** ZI de Meaux.
MR ANTOINE NOUALHAC
**Telephone:** 63.93.03.89
⊗ 🍷 🏠 Map 9

## CENAC, Dordogne, 24250

### LA PROMENADE, RN 703, Sarlat/Domme
**Menu:** 55 to 150 Frs. **Accommodation:** 120 to 170 Frs. **Restaurant:** Breakfast served from 7:00am. Lunch served from midday until 2:00pm. Dinner served from 7:00pm until 9:00pm. **Specialities:** regional menu. **Hotel:** 4 beds; 2 single rooms, 2 double rooms. **Other points:** bar, open to non-residents, à la carte menu, children welcome, pets welcome – check for details, car park. **Address:** Route Nationale 703.
MR PASCAL THOMAS
**Telephone:** 53.28.36.87
⊗ 🍷 🍽 Map 8

## CHANCELADE, Dordogne, 24650

### LE RELAIS DE LA DILIGENCE, RD 939, between Périgueux and Angoulême
**Languages spoken:** German, English. **Menu:** 50 to 90 Frs. **Restaurant:** Breakfast served from 6:00am. Lunch served from midday until 2:30pm. **Specialities:** home cooking. **Other points:** bar, open to non-residents, à la carte menu, children welcome, terraces, pets welcome – check for details, car park, traditional decor. **Address:** Route d'Angoulême, Champagne.
MME LOUISE GRIMAL
**Telephone:** 53.07.64.31
⊗ 🍷 Map 8

## CHAUDEYRAC, Lozère, 48170

### HOTEL DE FRANCE, RN 88, the main road between Lyon and Toulouse
**Languages spoken:** Spanish. **Menu:** 55 Frs (wine and coffee included) to 120 Frs. **Accommodation:** 180 to 230 Frs. **Restaurant:** Breakfast served from 6:00am. Lunch served from midday until 3:00pm. Dinner served from 6:00pm until 10:00pm. **Specialities:** regional menu, home cooking. **Hotel:** 12 beds; 4 single rooms, 8 double rooms with shower, bath, private WC, telephone. **Other points:** bar, open to non-residents, à la carte menu, children welcome, lounge area, terraces, car park, modern decor. **Address:** Route Nationale 88.
MR YVES TRÉMOULET
**Telephone:** 66.47.91.00. **Fax:** 66.47.93.29
⊗ 🍷 🏠 ☆ Map 10

## CONILHAC LES CORBIERES, Aude, 11200

### L'ONCLE ET LE NEVEU
**Languages spoken:** Spanish. **Restaurant:** Breakfast served from 5:15am. **Specialities:** regional menu, home cooking. **Other points:** bar, open to non-residents, children welcome, pets welcome – check for details, car park, traditional decor. **Address:** Route Nationale 113.
MR FRANCK RAYNAUD
**Telephone:** 68.27.08.05
⊗ 🍷 Map 10

## COQUILLE (LA), Dordogne, 24450

### LES PORTES DU PERIGOR VERT, the main road between Périgueux and Limoges
**Languages spoken:** English. **Menu:** 50 to 125 Frs. **Restaurant:** Breakfast served from 6:00am. Lunch served from 11:00am until 3:00pm. Closed Saturdays and the 2nd fortnight in August. **Specialities:** regional menu, home cooking. **Other points:** bar, open to non-residents, children welcome, terraces, pets welcome – check for details, car park, modern decor. **Address:** Route Nationale 21.
MR DIDIER FONTAINE
**Telephone:** 53.56.83.46
⊗ 🍷 Map 8

## CUQ TOULZA, Tarn, 81470

### LE RELAIS CHEZ ALAIN, RD 621, between Toulouse and Castres
**Languages spoken:** English. **Menu:** 60 to 300 Frs.

**Accommodation:** 120 to 240 Frs. **Restaurant:** Lunch served from 11:00am until 4:00pm. Dinner served from 7:00pm until 11:00pm. **Specialities:** regional menu. **Hotel:** 9 beds; 4 single rooms, 5 double rooms with bath, private WC, telephone. **Other points:** bar, open to non-residents, à la carte menu, children welcome, lounge area, terraces, pets welcome – check for details, car park, traditional decor. **Address:** La Bombardière.
MR ALAIN PRATVIEL
**Telephone:** 63.75.70.36
⊗ ♈ 🏠 ☆☆  Map 9

## CUXAC CABARDES, Aude, 11390

### LA MONTAGNE NOIR – CHEZ JOJO, RD 118, between Carcassonne and Mazamet

**Languages spoken:** German, English and Dutch. **Restaurant:** Lunch served from midday until 2:00pm. **Specialities:** home cooking. **Other points:** bar, open to non-residents, children welcome, terraces, pets welcome – check for details, car park, traditional decor. **Address:** Route Départementale 118.
MR HARRY HOVINGA
**Telephone:** 68.26.50.03
⊗ ♈  Map 10

## DAX, Landes, 40100

### AUBERGE DE LA CHALOSSE, between Pau and Orthez

**Menu:** 52 Frs. **Accommodation:** 90 to 160 Frs. **Restaurant:** Breakfast served from 6:00am. Lunch served from midday until 2:00pm. Dinner served from 8:00pm until 10:00pm. Closed Sundays and in August. **Specialities:** home cooking. **Hotel:** 6 beds; 1 single room, 5 double rooms with shower. **Other points:** bar, terraces, car park, modern decor. **Address:** 157, avenue Georges Clémenceau.
MR CHRISTIAN RICHAUD
**Telephone:** 58.74.23.08
⊗ ♈ 🏠  Map 8

## DECAZEVILLE, Aveyron, 12300

### A L'AUBERGE DE SAINT JULIEN, the main road between Aurillac and Rodez

**Menu:** 45 to 100 Frs. **Restaurant:** Breakfast served from 8:30am. Lunch served from midday until 2:00pm. Closed Mondays. **Specialities:** regional menu. **Other points:** bar, open to non-residents, pets welcome – check for details, car park, traditional decor. **Address:** Route Départementale 963, Saint Julien de Piganiol.
MME YVETTE CARRIERE
**Telephone:** 65.64.05.92, 68.64.06.39. **Fax:** 65.64.05.92
⊗ ♈  Map 9

## DENGUIN, Pyrénées-Atlantiques, 64230

### RELAIS PYRENEES MONTAGNE OCEAN, RN 117, the main road between Bayonne and Pau, 1st restaurant on the left on arrival at Denguin

**Languages spoken:** English and Spanish. **Menu:** 50 to 140 Frs. **Accommodation:** 90 to 130 Frs. **Restaurant:** Breakfast served from 6:00am. Lunch served from midday until 2:30pm. Dinner served from 7:30pm until 10:00pm. Closed Fridays. **Specialities:** regional menu, home cooking. **Hotel:** 14 beds; 4 single rooms, 10 double rooms. **Other points:** bar, open to non-residents, à la carte menu, terraces, pets welcome – check for details, car park, modern decor. **Address:** Route Nationale 117.
MR JEAN-BERNARD BOURGUIGNON
**Telephone:** 59.68.85.15
⊗ ♈ 🏠 ☆  Map 8

## DOUZENS, Aude, 11700

### LES ROUTIERS, RD 113, between Narbonne and Carcassonn

**Languages spoken:** English. **Menu:** 53 to 150 Frs. **Accommodation:** 120 to 200 Frs. **Specialities:** regional menu, home cooking. **Hotel:** 8 beds; 6 single rooms, 2 double rooms with shower, private WC. **Other points:** bar, à la carte menu, children welcome, terraces, pets welcome – check for details, car park, traditional decor. **Address:** Route Départementale 113.
MME MONIQUE HULIN
**Telephone:** 68.79.19.99
⊗ ♈ 🏠  Map 10

## ESCOURCE, Landes, 40210

### AU ROUTIER, RN 10, Sabres, exit 15

**Menu:** 65 to 200 Frs. **Accommodation:** 160 to 300 Frs. **Restaurant:** Breakfast served from 6:30am. Lunch served from midday until 2:30pm. Dinner served from 7:30pm until 10:30pm. Closed Sundays and from 20 December to 7 January. **Specialities:** salade de foie de canard frais, ris de veau madère, magret grillé, regional food. **Hotel:** 15 beds; 6 single rooms, 9 double rooms with shower. **Other points:** bar, open to non-residents, à la carte menu, children welcome, terraces, car park, modern decor. **Address:** Cap de Pin.
MR JEAN-PIERRE FORTINON
**Telephone:** 58.07.20.54
⊗ ♈ 🏠 ⊂⊃  Map 8

## ESPALION, Aveyron, 12500

### RELAIS DES QUATRE ROUTES, RD 920, Clermont Ferrand

**Menu:** 50 to 95 Frs. **Accommodation:** 80 to 130 Frs. **Restaurant:** Breakfast served from 6:30am. Lunch served from midday until 2:00pm. Dinner served from 7:30pm until 10:00pm. Closed Sundays. **Specialities:**

regional menu, home cooking. **Hotel:** 4 beds; 2 single rooms, 2 double rooms with shower, private WC. **Other points:** bar, open to non-residents, children welcome, terraces, car park, modern decor. **Address:** Les Quatre Routes, Route Départementale 920.
MR MICHEL MOLINIER
**Telephone:** 65.44.05.14
⊗ ♀ ☆  Map 9

# FABREGUES, Hérault, 34690

### L'ARCHE DE FABREGUES, A 9, the main road between Barcelone and Montpellier
**Languages spoken:** English and Spanish. **Menu:** 59 Frs. **Accommodation:** 270 to 300 Frs. **Restaurant:** Open 24 hours. **Specialities:** home cooking. **Hotel:** 35 beds; with shower, bath, private WC, television, telephone. **Other points:** open to non-residents, à la carte menu, children welcome, lounge area, terraces, pets welcome – check for details, car park, traditional decor. **Address:** A 9 Aire de Fabrègues, dans les deux sens.
MR FRANÇOIS TILLIET
**Telephone:** 67.85.15.06. **Fax:** 67.85.15.29
⊗ ⌂ ☆☆  Map 10

### RESTAURANT LE 113, RN 113
**Restaurant:** Closed Sundays and in October. **Specialities:** regional menu, home cooking. **Other points:** bar, children welcome.
MME JOSETTE AVIGNON
**Telephone:** 67.85.12.86
⊗ ♀  Map 10

# FARGUETTES (LES), Tarn, 81190

### RELAIS DE LA PLAINE, RN 88, the main road between Albi and Rodez
**Languages spoken:** English. **Menu:** 50 to 115 Frs. **Restaurant:** Breakfast served from 5:00am. Lunch served from 11:00am until 3:00pm. Dinner served from 7:00pm until 10:00pm. Closed Saturdays. **Specialities:** regional menu, home cooking. **Other points:** bar, open to non-residents, à la carte menu, children welcome, terraces, pets welcome – check for details, car park, modern decor. **Address:** Route Nationale 88.
MME MARIE-FRANCE MOUGET
**Telephone:** 63.76.65.89
⊗ ♀  Map 9

# FIRBEIX, Dordogne, 24450

### RELAIS DES SPORTS, RN 21
**Restaurant:** Closed in October. **Other points:** bar. **Address:** Route Nationale 21.
MR RENÉ BEAUBATIT
**Telephone:** 53.52.82.53
⊗ ♀  Map 8

# FITOU, Aude, 11510

### LE RELAIS SAINT ROCH, RN 9, between Narbonne and Perpignan
**Languages spoken:** Spanish. **Menu:** 55 to 95 Frs. **Accommodation:** 80 to 110 Frs. **Restaurant:** Breakfast served from 4:00am. Dinner served from 4:30pm until midnight. **Specialities:** home cooking. **Hotel:** 10 beds; 6 single rooms, 4 double rooms with shower, private WC. **Other points:** bar, open to non-residents, à la carte menu, terraces, pets welcome – check for details, car park, traditional decor. **Address:** 39, Route Nationale 9.
MR ROLAND DURAND
**Telephone:** 68.45.71.75
⊗ ♀ ⌂  Map 10

### RELAIS LE PARADOR, RN 9
**Languages spoken:** German, Spanish and Italian. **Accommodation:** 70 to 170 Frs. **Restaurant:** Dinner served from midday until midnight. **Hotel:** 50 beds. **Other points:** bar. **Address:** Cabanne de Fitou.
MR ROBERT MORHAIN
**Telephone:** 68.45.79.11
⊗ ♀ ⌂ ☆  Map 10

# FLEURANCE, Gers, 32500

### RESTAURANT DU STADE, RN 21
**Menu:** 55 to 140 Frs. **Restaurant:** Breakfast served from 10:00am. Lunch served from midday until 2:00pm. Dinner served from 7:00pm until 9:00pm. Closed Saturdays, from mid-June to mid-July and 1 week at Christmas. **Specialities:** home cooking. **Other points:** bar, open to non-residents, à la carte menu, children welcome, terraces, pets welcome – check for details, car park, traditional decor. **Address:** Place de l'Eglise.
MR ALPHONSE PUJADE
**Telephone:** 62.06.02.23
⊗ ♀  Map 9

# FOIX, Ariége, 09000

### LE SOLEIL D'OR, RN 20
**Menu:** 40 to 65 Frs. **Accommodation:** 80 to 120 Frs. **Restaurant:** Breakfast served from 6:30am. Lunch served from midday until 2:00pm. Dinner served from 8:00pm until 9:00pm. Closed Saturdays. **Specialities:** home cooking. **Hotel:** 7 beds; 4 single rooms, 3 double rooms with shower. **Other points:** bar, open to non-residents, pets welcome – check for details, car park. **Address:** 57, avenue du Général Leclerc.
MR JEAN COUMES
**Telephone:** 61.65.01.33
⊗ ♀ ⌂  Map 9

## FONTCOUVERTE, Tarn, 81430

### CHEZ PAPA

**Languages spoken:** Italian and Arabic. **Menu:** 55 to 140 Frs. **Restaurant:** Breakfast served from 7:00am. **Specialities:** regional menu, home cooking. **Other points:** bar, open to non-residents, à la carte menu, children welcome, car park. **Address:** Route Départementale 999.
MME ANNE-MARIE SCALIA
**Telephone:** 63.55.38.23
⊗ ♀ Map 9

## FUMEL, Lot-et-Garonne, 47500

### BAR ROUTIER DE LA SOIERIE

**Menu:** 50 Frs. **Restaurant:** Breakfast served from 6:00am. Dinner served from 6:00pm until 8:00pm. Closed Sundays. **Specialities:** home cooking. **Other points:** bar, terraces, pets welcome – check for details, car park. **Address:** 88, avenue de l'Usine.
MME LILIANE LAFON
**Telephone:** 53.71.34.22
⊗ ♀ Map 8

## GAGES, Aveyron, 12630

### LE RELAIS DE LA PLAINE, RN 88, 10km from Rodez, the main road between Brive and Méditerranée

**Menu:** 65 to 95 Frs. **Accommodation:** 100 to 180 Frs. **Restaurant:** Breakfast served from 6:00am. Lunch served from midday until 2:00pm. Dinner served from 7:30pm until 9:00pm. Closed weekends (out of season), 2 weeks in November and 1 week from New Year's Eve. **Specialities:** tripous, confit de canard, gésiers, regional food, home cooking. **Hotel:** 22 beds; 14 single rooms, 8 double rooms with shower, bath. **Other points:** bar, open to non-residents, à la carte menu, children welcome, lounge area, terraces, pets welcome – check for details, car park, modern decor.
MME YVONNE DALLO
**Telephone:** 65.42.29.03
⊗ ♀ ⌂ ☆ Map 9

## GAILLAN LESPARRE, Gironde, 33340

### MARIE-FRANCE, RN 215

**Menu:** 55 to 120 Frs. **Restaurant:** Breakfast served from 8:00am. Lunch served from 11:30am until 3:00pm. Dinner served from 7:00pm until 9:00pm. Closed Sundays, the 2nd fortnight in August and 1 week at Christmas. **Specialities:** regional menu. **Other points:** bar, open to non-residents, à la carte menu, children welcome, terraces, pets welcome – check for details, car park. **Address:** Place des Ecoles.
MME MARIE-FRANCE DUPUY
**Telephone:** 56.41.20.53, 56.41.04.45
⊗ ♀ Map 8

## GAN, Pyrénées-Atlantiques, 64290

### AUX PETITS BEARNAIS, between Pau and Gourette

**Menu:** 50 to 80 Frs. **Restaurant:** Breakfast served from 7:00am. Lunch served from midday until 3:00pm. Dinner served from 7:00pm until 11:00pm. **Specialities:** home cooking. **Other points:** bar, open to non-residents, terraces, pets welcome – check for details, car park, modern decor. **Address:** Route de Rebenacq.
MR LAURENT COURTADIOU
**Telephone:** 59.05.51.07
⊗ ♀ Map 8

## GARANOU LUZENAC, Ariége, 09250

### LES ROUTIERS, RN 20, between Toulouse and Andorra

**Languages spoken:** Spanish and Portugese. **Menu:** from 60 Frs. **Accommodation:** 110 to 140 Frs. **Restaurant:** Breakfast served from 8:00am. Lunch served from midday until 2:00pm. Dinner served from 8:00pm until 10:00pm. Closed Sundays and in August. **Specialities:** home cooking. **Hotel:** 9 beds; 6 single rooms, 3 double rooms with shower, private WC, telephone. **Other points:** bar, open to non-residents, children welcome, terraces, pets welcome – check for details, car park, traditional decor. **Address:** Avenue de la Gare.
MME MARIE PIRES
**Telephone:** 61.64.47.13
⊗ ♀ ⌂ Map 9

## GER, Pyrénées-Atlantiques, 64530

### A LA CLE D'OR, RN 117, the main road between Pau (28km) and Tarbes (12km)

**Languages spoken:** Spanish. **Menu:** 52 Frs. **Accommodation:** 75 to 100 Frs. **Restaurant:** Breakfast served from 6:00am. Lunch served from midday until 2:00pm. Closed Saturdays and from 15 August to 5 September. **Specialities:** home cooking. **Hotel:** 4 beds; 2 single rooms, 2 double rooms. **Other points:** bar, car park, modern decor. **Address:** Route Nationale 117.
MR ALAIN COUDERT
**Telephone:** 62.31.50.56
⊗ ♀ Map 8

## GOURDON, Lot, 46300

### HOTEL DE LA MADELEINE, RD 673, between Souillac and Sarlat

**Menu:** 60 Frs (wine included) to 135 Frs. **Accommodation:** 165 to 250 Frs. **Restaurant:** Breakfast served from 7:30am. Lunch served from midday until 3:30pm. Dinner served from 8:00pm until 10:00pm. Closed weekends (out of season) and in October. **Specialities:** regional menu, home cooking. **Hotel:** 13 beds; 10 single rooms, 3 double rooms with shower, bath, private WC, television, telephone. **Other**

points: bar, open to non-residents, à la carte menu, children welcome, lounge area, terraces, pets welcome – check for details, car park, traditional decor. **Address:** Boulevard de la Madeleine.
MR JEAN BARBES
**Telephone:** 61.41.02.63
⊗ ♀ ⌂ Map 9

## GRAMAT, Lot, 46500

*HOTEL DU CENTRE, RN 140, between Brive and Rodez*
**Languages spoken:** English. **Menu:** 80 to 200 Frs. **Accommodation:** 220 to 350 Frs. **Restaurant:** Breakfast served from 7:00am. Lunch served from midday until 2:00pm. Dinner served from 7:30pm until 9:00pm. Closed Saturdays, the 3rd week in November and vacation periods in February. **Specialities:** foie gras, confits de canard, cèpes, tripous, gésiers, cassoulet, regional food, home cooking. **Hotel:** 14 beds; 10 single rooms, 4 double rooms with shower, bath, private WC, television, telephone. **Other points:** bar, open to non-residents, à la carte menu, children welcome, lounge area, terraces, pets welcome – check for details, car park, modern decor. **Address:** Place de la République.
MR ANDRÉ GRIMAL
**Telephone:** 65.38.73.37. **Fax:** 65.38.73.66
⊗ ♀ ⌂ ⛄ ☆☆ Map 9

## GRISOLLES, Tarn-et-Garonne, 82170

*LE RELAIS DE LA GARE*
**Languages spoken:** English. **Menu:** 58 to 130 Frs. **Restaurant:** Lunch served from 11:30am until 3:00pm. Dinner served from 7:15pm until 10:30pm. **Specialities:** regional menu. **Other points:** bar, car park. **Address:** Route Nationale 20.
LAURENCE ET JEAN-GILBERT MORONI
**Telephone:** 63.67.37.63, 63.67.31.83
⊗ ♀ Map 9

## HENDAYE, Pyrénées-Atlantiques, 64700

*RELAIS ROUTIERS – CHEZ MONGOBERT, RN 10, near the Spanish border*
**Languages spoken:** German. **Menu:** 58 Frs. **Restaurant:** Breakfast served from 7:00am. Closed Sundays and in August. **Specialities:** home cooking. **Other points:** bar. **Address:** 11, avenue d'Espagne.
MR ALAIN MONGOBERT
**Telephone:** 59.70.78.95, 59.20.73.00
⊗ ♀ Map 8

## HOSTENS, Gironde, 33125

*AU BON ACCUEIL*
**Restaurant:** Closed Saturdays, Sundays and in August. **Other points:** bar, car park.

SARL AU BON ACCUEIL
**Telephone:** 56.88.50.63
⊗ ♀ Map 8

## HOUEILLES, Lot-et-Garonne, 47420

*AUBERGE DES RELAIS, RD 665, Agen, towards Mont de Marsan, Dax*
**Menu:** 50 Frs (wine included) to 180 Frs. **Restaurant:** Breakfast served from 7:00am. Lunch served from 11:30am until 3:00pm. Dinner served from 7:00pm until 9:00pm. **Specialities:** regional menu, home cooking. **Other points:** bar, open to non-residents, à la carte menu, children welcome, terraces, pets welcome – check for details, car park, traditional decor. **Address:** Au Bourg de Boussés.
MLLE NICOLE GUILLYGOMARCH
**Telephone:** 53.89.11.62
⊗ ♀ Map 9

## ISLE JOURDAIN (L'), Gers, 32600

*L'OLYMPIA – LES ROUTIERS, RN 124, between Toulouse and Auch*
**Menu:** 47 Frs. **Restaurant:** Breakfast served from 9:00am. Lunch served from 11:00am until 2:00pm. Dinner served from 7:00pm until 9:00pm. Closed Mondays and in August. **Specialities:** Plats typiques selon saison, home cooking. **Other points:** bar, open to non-residents, à la carte menu, lounge area, pets welcome – check for details, car park, traditional decor. **Address:** 5, rue de la République.
MR MICHEL AMOUR
**Telephone:** 62.07.01.35
⊗ ♀ Map 9

## ISSANKA, Hérault, 34540

*LE GARRIGOU, RN 113, exit Sète, towards Gigean*
**Languages spoken:** English and Spanish. **Menu:** 60 to 120 Frs. **Accommodation:** 148 Frs. **Restaurant:** Breakfast served from 6:00am. Dinner served from 7:00pm until 11:00pm. Closed Sundays. **Specialities:** seiche à la rouille, poissons divers, regional food, home cooking. **Hotel:** 8 beds; 4 single rooms, 4 double rooms with bath, telephone. **Other points:** open to non-residents, à la carte menu, children welcome, terraces, pets welcome – check for details, car park, modern decor. **Address:** Le Garrigou.
MME DANYELLE HOHMANN
**Telephone:** 67.78.71.30
⊗ ⌂ ☆☆ Map 10

## LABATUT, Landes, 40300

*LA GUINGUETTE, RN 117, between Toulouse and Bayonne*
**Languages spoken:** Pale English and Spanish. **Menu:**

55 to 180 Frs. **Accommodation:** 130 to 250 Frs.
**Restaurant:** Breakfast served from 7:00am. Lunch
served from 11:30am until 2:30pm. Dinner served from
6:30pm until 9:30pm. Closed Sundays. **Specialities:**
regional menu. **Hotel:** 5 beds; 1 single room, 4 double
rooms with shower, bath. **Other points:** bar, open to
non-residents, à la carte menu, children welcome, lounge
area, terraces, pets welcome – check for details, car
park. **Address:** Route Nationale 117.
MR CHRISTIAN BEGU
**Telephone:** 58.98.18.82
⊗ ♀ ⌂ Map 8

## LABRUGUIERE, Tarn, 81290

### LA MARMITTE, RN 621

**Menu:** 58 to 70 Frs. **Accommodation:** 100 Frs.
**Restaurant:** Breakfast served from 7:00am. Closed
Saturdays. **Specialities:** home cooking. **Hotel:** 16 beds;
8 single rooms, 8 double rooms. **Other points:** open to
non-residents, pets welcome – check for details, car
park. **Address:** 35, avenue Henri Simon.
MR RENÉ OZANNE
**Telephone:** 63.50.21.19
⊗ ⌂ Map 9

## LACAUNE, Tarn, 81230

### LE CHALET, RN 81, the main road between Albi and Castres

**Languages spoken:** English and Spanish. **Menu:** 60 to
200 Frs. **Accommodation:** 130 to 160 Frs. **Restaurant:**
Breakfast served from 7:00am. Lunch served from
midday until 2:30pm. Dinner served from 7:30pm until
9:30pm. Closed Sundays and in December. **Specialities:**
paëlla, couscous, cassoulet, home cooking. **Hotel:** 10
beds; 4 single rooms, 6 double rooms with shower, bath.
**Other points:** bar, open to non-residents, à la carte
menu, children welcome, terraces, car park, traditional
decor. **Address:** 14, rue André Theron.
MR JOSEPH DELPINO
**Telephone:** 63.37.08.91
⊗ ♀ ⌂ Map 9

## LAFITTE SUR LOT, Lot-et-Garonne, 47320

### LES AMIS DE LA ROUTE, RD 666, Villeneuve en Lot

**Languages spoken:** English and Spanish. **Restaurant:**
Breakfast served from 7:00am. Lunch served from
midday until 2:00pm. Dinner served from 7:00pm until
10:00pm. Closed Saturdays and in August. **Specialities:**
home cooking. **Other points:** bar, open to non-residents,
pets welcome – check for details, car park. **Address:**
Route de Villeneuve.
MR MAX BRIOT
**Telephone:** 53.84.08.98
⊗ ♀ Map 8

## LAFOX, Lot-et-Garonne, 47270

### LE RELAIS TOULOUSAIN, RN 113, the main road between Bordeaux and Toulouse

**Languages spoken:** Spanish and Italian. **Menu:** 55 to
85 Frs. **Accommodation:** 57 to 100 Frs. **Restaurant:**
Breakfast served from 4:30am. Dinner served from
midday until midnight. Closed Saturdays and 3 weeks in
August. **Specialities:** regional menu, home cooking.
**Hotel:** 27 beds; with shower, bath, private WC,
television, telephone. **Other points:** bar, open to non-
residents, à la carte menu, children welcome, lounge
area, terraces, pets welcome – check for details, car
park, traditional decor. **Address:** Route Nationale 113.
MR RENÉ ANDRÉ
**Telephone:** 53.68.54.83
⊗ ♀ ⌂ ☆ Map 8

## LAGARRIGUE, Tarn, 81090

### RESTAURANT BIGUES, RN 112, between Castres and Mazamet

**Menu:** 60 Frs. **Accommodation:** 120 to 170 Frs.
**Restaurant:** Lunch served from 11:00am until 2:30pm.
Dinner served from 7:00pm until 10:00pm. Closed
Saturdays and the 1st fortnight in August. **Hotel:** 8 beds.
**Other points:** bar, car park, modern decor. **Address:** 2,
avenue de Mazamet.
MME JOSIANE BIGUES
**Telephone:** 63.35.85.19
⊗ ♀ ⌂ Map 9

## LALOUBERE, Hautes-Pyrénées, 65310

### HOTEL DES PYRENEES, RD 135, between Bagnères de Bigorre and la Mongie

**Languages spoken:** English and Spanish. **Menu:** 60
to 80 Frs. **Accommodation:** 110 to 140 Frs.
**Restaurant:** Breakfast served from 7:00am. Lunch
served from midday until 2:00pm. Dinner served from
7:30pm until 9:00pm. Closed Sundays and in August.
**Specialities:** regional menu. **Hotel:** 13 beds; 12 single
rooms, 1 double room with shower, bath, private WC.
**Other points:** bar, open to non-residents, children
welcome, lounge area, pets welcome – check for
details, car park, modern decor. **Address:** 13, rue du
Maréchal Foch.
MME MICHELE CAZAMAYOU
**Telephone:** 62.93.29.62
⊗ ♀ ⌂ ☆ Map 9

## LAMAGISTERE, Tarn-et-Garonne, 82360

### CHEZ BOMPA, RN 113, the main road between Bordeaux and Toulouse

**Languages spoken:** Spanish. **Menu:** 55 to 78 Frs.
**Restaurant:** Breakfast served from 6:00am. Lunch
served from 11:00am until 3:00pm. Dinner served from
6:00pm until 10:00pm. Closed Saturdays and 15 days in

August. **Specialities:** home cooking. **Other points:** bar, open to non-residents, à la carte menu, children welcome, lounge area, terraces, pets welcome – check for details, car park, traditional decor. **Address:** 56, avenue Saint-Michel.
MR GILBERT BOMPA
**Telephone:** 63.39.91.56
⊗ ⵌ Map 9

# LAMONZIE SAINT MARTIN,
Dordogne, 24680

## RELAIS LA POMME D'OR, RD 936,
*Bergerac towards Bordeaux*
**Languages spoken:** English, Spanish. **Menu:** 65 to 160 Frs. **Restaurant:** Breakfast served from 6:00am. Lunch served from midday until 2:30pm. Dinner served from 7:30pm until 9:30pm. Closed Saturdays and in August. **Specialities:** regional menu. **Other points:** bar, open to non-residents, à la carte menu, children welcome, car park.
MR JEAN-LOUIS GONTHIER
**Telephone:** 53.24.04.00
⊗ ⵌ Map 8

# LANGOGNE, Lozère, 48300

## HOTEL DU LUXEMBOURG, RN 88,
*between le Puy en Velay and Mende*
**Languages spoken:** English. **Menu:** 60 to 100 Frs. **Accommodation:** 100 to 200 Frs. **Restaurant:** Breakfast served from 8:00am. Lunch served from midday until 1:30pm. Dinner served from 7:00pm until 8:30pm. Closed in January. **Specialities:** home cooking. **Hotel:** 16 beds; 6 single rooms, 10 double rooms with shower, private WC, television, telephone. **Other points:** bar, open to non-residents, children welcome, lounge area, terraces, pets welcome – check for details, car park, traditional decor. **Address:** Place de la Gare.
MME ADRIENNE CHABALIER
**Telephone:** 66.69.00.11
⊗ ⵌ 🏠 ☆ Map 10

# LANGON, Gironde, 33210

## LE PASSAGER, CD 932, exit for Langon (3km), towards Pau
**Menu:** 56 Frs (wine and coffee included). **Restaurant:** Breakfast served from 5:00am. Lunch served from 11:30am until 2:30pm. Dinner served from 7:30pm until 10:00pm. Closed Saturdays and the 2nd fortnight in August. **Specialities:** home cooking. **Other points:** bar, open to non-residents, lounge area, terraces, pets welcome – check for details, car park, traditional decor. **Address:** Route de Pau, Mazères.
GÉRARD ET NADINE BARCELONA
**Telephone:** 56.63.15.22
⊗ ⵌ Map 8

## RESTAURANT DARLOT, RN 113,
*motorway A62, exit Langon*
**Languages spoken:** English and Spanish. **Menu:** 60 to 200 Frs. **Accommodation:** 110 to 150 Frs. **Restaurant:** Breakfast served from 7:00am. Lunch served from midday until 3:00pm. Dinner served from 7:00pm until 10:00pm. Closed Saturdays and in August. **Specialities:** Civet de lièvre, cèpes à la bordelaise, salmis de palombe, regional food, home cooking. **Hotel:** 11 beds; 5 single rooms, 6 double rooms with shower, private WC, television, telephone. **Other points:** bar, open to non-residents, à la carte menu, children welcome, lounge area, terraces, pets welcome – check for details, car park, traditional decor. **Address:** 10, rue Dotézac
MR JEAN-PAUL DARLOT
**Telephone:** 56.63.01.36
⊗ ⵌ 🏠 🛏 Map 8

# LANNEMEZAN, Hautes-Pyrénées, 65300

## HOSTELLERIE DU CHATEAU, between Auch (70km) and Tarbes (35km)
**Languages spoken:** Spanish. **Menu:** 53 to 95 Frs. **Accommodation:** 80 to 120 Frs. **Restaurant:** Lunch served from 11:30am until 2:30pm. Dinner served from 7:00pm until 9:00pm. Closed Sundays. **Specialities:** regional menu, home cooking. **Hotel:** 7 beds; 1 single room, 6 double rooms. **Other points:** bar, open to non-residents, à la carte menu, children welcome, terraces, pets welcome – check for details, car park, traditional decor. **Address:** 133, place du Château.
MONIQUE ET VIRGINIO VASSILIOU-RODRIGUEZ
**Telephone:** 62.98.06.29
⊗ ⵌ 🏠 Map 9

# LANUEJOULS, Aveyron, 12350

## CHEZ HUGUETTE, between Rodez and Villefranche de Rouergue
**Menu:** 55 to 85 Frs (wine included). **Restaurant:** Breakfast served from 6:00am. Lunch served from midday until 1:30pm. Dinner served from 7:00pm until 9:00pm. Closed Mondays. **Specialities:** home cooking. **Other points:** bar, open to non-residents, terraces, pets welcome – check for details, car park, modern decor. **Address:** 25, avenue du Rouergue.
MME HUGUETTE COUDERC
**Telephone:** 65.81.95.10
⊗ ⵌ Map 9

# LAPALME, Aude, 11480

## LE CALYPSO, A 9
**Languages spoken:** German, English, Spanish and Italian. **Menu:** from 65 Frs. **Restaurant:** Breakfast served from 7:00am. **Specialities:** home cooking. **Other points:** open to non-residents, children welcome, terraces, pets welcome – check for details, car park, modern decor. **Address:** Aire de Lapalme.

MME ROSIE GUIRAUD
**Telephone:** 68.45.65.00. **Fax:** 68.45.65.03
⊗ Map 10

*LE CHANTECLAIR, RN 9, 2km from the*
*exit for Leucate and on arriving at Narbonne*
**Menu:** 55 to 140 Frs. **Accommodation:** 120 to 190 Frs.
**Restaurant:** Breakfast served from 6:00am. Lunch
served from 11:30am until 2:30pm. Dinner served from
7:00pm until 10:00pm. Closed Saturdays. **Specialities:**
regional menu, home cooking. **Hotel:** 7 beds; 3 single
rooms, 4 double rooms with shower. **Other points:** bar,
open to non-residents, à la carte menu, children
welcome, terraces, pets welcome – check for details, car
park, traditional decor. **Address:** Les Cabanes de la
Palme, Route Nationale 9.
MR YVES DEFROMERIE
**Telephone:** 68.48.15.03
⊗ ♈ 🏠 Map 10

## LAPANOUSE DE SEVERAC,
Aveyron, 12150

*LES ROUTIERS, RN 88, centre of the*
*village of Lapanouse*
**Menu:** 48 to 58 Frs. **Accommodation:** 70 to 100 Frs.
**Restaurant:** Breakfast served from 7:30am. Lunch
served from midday until 3:00pm. Dinner served from
7:30pm until 10:00pm. Closed Sundays. **Specialities:**
regional menu, home cooking. **Hotel:** 5 beds; 5 single
rooms with shower, private WC. **Other points:** bar,
open to non-residents, terraces, pets welcome – check
for details, traditional decor. **Address:** Route de Rodez.
MR ROGER ARNAL
**Telephone:** 65.71.60.44
⊗ ♈ 🏠 Map 9

## LARDIN SAINT LAZARE (LE),
Dordogne, 24570

*LE RELAIS SAINT LAZARE, RN 89,*
*between Périgueux (47km) and Brive (20km)*
**Languages spoken:** English and Italian. **Menu:** 55
(wine included) to 65 Frs. **Accommodation:** 120 to 160
Frs. **Restaurant:** Breakfast served from 6:30am. Lunch
served from midday until 2:30pm. Dinner served from
7:00pm until 10:30pm. Closed Sundays. **Specialities:**
home cooking. **Hotel:** 10 beds. **Other points:** bar, open
to non-residents, children welcome, pets welcome –
check for details, car park, traditional decor. **Address:**
Route Nationale 89.
MR ALLEN WESTWOOD
**Telephone:** 53.51.37.45
⊗ ♈ 🏠 Map 8

*LE VEZERE, RN 89, the main road between*
*Périgueux and Brive*
**Menu:** 50 Frs (wine and coffee included) to 100 Frs.
**Accommodation:** 70 to 100 Frs. **Restaurant:** Breakfast

served from 5:00am. Lunch served from midday until
3:00pm. Dinner served from 7:00pm until midnight.
Closed Sundays. **Specialities:** home cooking. **Hotel:** 6
beds. **Other points:** bar, open to non-residents, children
welcome, terraces, pets welcome – check for details, car
park, traditional decor. **Address:** Route Nationale 89.
MME MARIE-CLAIRE SEMPREZ
**Telephone:** 53.51.28.21
⊗ ♈ 🏠 Map 8

## LARUSCADE, Gironde, 33620

*LE CHAT HUANT, RN 10, the main road*
*between Bordeaux and Angoulême*
**Languages spoken:** Spanish and Portugese. **Menu:** 55 Frs
(wine and coffee included). **Restaurant:** Breakfast served
from 6:00am. **Specialities:** home cooking. **Other points:**
bar, open to non-residents, children welcome, terraces, pets
welcome – check for details, car park, traditional decor.
**Address:** Le Chauan, Route Nationale 10.
MR ANGE PORTELA
**Telephone:** 57.68.54.16
⊗ ♈ Map 8

## LAUSSEIGNAN BARBASTE, Lot-et-
Garonne, 47230

*LES PALMIERS, RN 655, the main road*
*between Agen and Bayonne*
**Menu:** 45 to 120 Frs. **Restaurant:** Breakfast served
from 7:00am. Lunch served from midday until 2:00pm.
Dinner served from 7:30pm until 9:15pm. Closed
Saturdays and in January. **Specialities:** regional menu.
**Other points:** bar, open to non-residents, à la carte
menu, children welcome, lounge area, terraces, pets
welcome – check for details, car park, traditional decor.
SNC GINESTE & FILS
**Telephone:** 53.65.55.02, 53.65.64.69.
⊗ ♈ 🖐 Map 8

## LEDENON, Gard, 30210

*LE RELAIS DE LEDENON*
**Languages spoken:** English and Spanish. **Menu:** 60 Frs
(coffee included). **Accommodation:** 100 to 120 Frs.
**Restaurant:** Closed Sundays. **Hotel:** 6 beds. **Other
points:** bar, car park. **Address:** Route Nationale 86.
MR SERGE KASZUBA
**Telephone:** 66.37.34.46
⊗ ♈ 🏠 Map 10

## LIBOURNE, Gironde, 33500

*LE MOULIN BLANC, RN 89, the main road*
*between Libourne and Périgueux*
**Languages spoken:** Spanish and Italian. **Menu:** 60 to
120 Frs. **Accommodation:** 120 to 200 Frs. **Restaurant:**
Breakfast served from 7:30am. Lunch served from
midday until 3:00pm. Dinner served from 7:00pm until

9:30pm. **Specialities:** home cooking. **Hotel:** 10 beds; 6 single rooms, 4 double rooms with shower, private WC. **Other points:** bar, open to non-residents, à la carte menu, children welcome, lounge area, pets welcome – check for details, car park, traditional decor. **Address:** 132, avenue Georges Clémenceau.
MME GENEVIEVE FERNANDEZ
**Telephone:** 57.25.06.27, 57.25.01.61
⊗ ⟡ ⌂ ☆  Map 8

# LIGARDES, Gers, 32100

### *RELAIS CHEZ DUDULE, the main road between Agen and Pau*
**Restaurant:** Breakfast served from 7:30am. **Specialities:** regional menu, home cooking. **Other points:** open to non-residents, terraces, pets welcome – check for details, car park, traditional decor. **Address:** Route d'Agen.
MR FRANCIS DULONG
**Telephone:** 62.28.85.76
⊗  Map 9

# LIPOSTHEY, Landes, 40410

### *CHEZ ALINE, RN 10*
**Menu:** 58 to 150 Frs. **Restaurant:** Breakfast served from 7:30am. Lunch served from midday until 2:00pm. Dinner served from 7:30pm until 9:00pm. Closed Saturdays and from Christmas Day to mid-January. **Specialities:** home cooking. **Other points:** bar, open to non-residents, children welcome, pets welcome – check for details, traditional decor.
MME ALINE GROS
**Telephone:** 58.82.30.30
⊗ ⟡  Map 8

# LODEVE, Hérault, 34700

### *RELAIS DE LA CROIX, RN 9*
**Restaurant:** Closed Sundays. **Hotel:** 6 beds. **Other points:** bar, car park. **Address:** Cartels.
MR JEAN-DENIS ROIG
**Telephone:** 67.44.00.72
⊗ ⟡ ⌂  Map 10

### *RELAIS ESCALETTE, RN 9*
**Languages spoken:** German, English and Italian. **Menu:** 70 to 180 Frs. **Accommodation:** 100 to 170 Frs. **Restaurant:** Breakfast served from 5:00am. Lunch served from midday until 1:30pm. Dinner served from 7:30pm until 10:00pm. **Specialities:** regional menu. **Hotel:** 21 beds; 16 single rooms, 5 double rooms with shower, bath, private WC. **Other points:** bar, open to non-residents, à la carte menu, lounge area, pets welcome – check for details, car park. **Address:** Route Nationale 9.
MR GILBERT CAVALIER
**Telephone:** 67.44.01.14. **Fax:** 67.44.43.93
⊗ ⟡ ⌂  Map 10

# LONS, Pyrénées-Atlantiques, 64149

### *LE MIDI – MINUIT, Pau*
**Menu:** 50 to 100 Frs. **Restaurant:** Breakfast served from 6:30am. Lunch served from 11:30am until 3:00pm. Dinner served from 7:30pm until 11:00pm. Closed Sundays and in August. **Specialities:** regional menu. **Other points:** bar, open to non-residents, à la carte menu, car park, traditional decor. **Address:** Avenue Larregain.
MR CLAUDE PRODOCINI
**Telephone:** 59.32.07.57
⊗ ⟡  Map 8

# LOURDES, Hautes-Pyrénées, 65100

### *LE MALLORY'S*
**Menu:** 50 to 65 Frs. **Restaurant:** Lunch served from midday until 2:30pm. Dinner served from 7:00pm until 10:00pm. **Other points:** bar, car park. **Address:** 21, avenue Alexandre Marqui.
MRS SERGE, DIDIER ET CLAUDE DARRIEUTORT
**Telephone:** 62.94.19.41
⊗ ⟡  Map 9

# LUBBON, Landes, 40240

### *CHEZ MAMY, RD 933, the main road between Périgueux and Bayonne*
**Languages spoken:** Italian. **Menu:** 55 Frs. **Accommodation:** 100 Frs. **Restaurant:** Breakfast served from 5:00am. Lunch served from midday until 3:00pm. Dinner served from 7:00pm until 9:00pm. Closed Saturdays and in October. **Specialities:** regional menu, home cooking. **Hotel:** 9 beds; 9 single rooms with shower. **Other points:** bar, open to non-residents, pets welcome – check for details, car park, traditional decor.
MR LOUIS NICOLETTO
**Telephone:** 58.93.60.47
⊗ ⟡ ⌂  Map 8

# MAGES (LES), Gard, 30960

### *RESTO 104 – CHEZ JO ET NATHALIE, exit Alès, road for Aubenas*
**Menu:** 60 to 80 Frs. **Accommodation:** 100 to 140 Frs. **Restaurant:** Breakfast served from 6:30am. Closed Saturdays and 10 days at New Year. **Specialities:** home cooking. **Hotel:** 16 beds; with shower, telephone. **Other points:** bar, open to non-residents, terraces, pets welcome – check for details, car park, traditional decor.
MR JOSEPH MASTROSIMONE
**Telephone:** 66.25.60.38
⊗ ⟡ ⌂  Map 10

# MAGNANAC, Haute-Garonne, 31340

### *CHEZ FRANCOISE, RN 630, between Montauban and Castres*
**Menu:** 60 Frs. **Restaurant:** Dinner served from midday

until 8:00pm. Closed Fridays, public holidays and the 2nd fortnight in August. **Specialities:** home cooking. **Hotel:** 4 beds; 1 single room, 3 double rooms with shower, private WC. **Other points:** bar, open to non-residents, lounge area, terraces, pets welcome – check for details, car park, traditional decor.
MME FRANÇOISE ROSSI
**Telephone:** 61.09.01.87, 61.09.20.72
⊗ ♀ Map 9

## MARMANDE, Lot-et-Garonne, 47200

### RESTAURANT LE MARINIER, RD 933, Marmande

**Languages spoken:** English, Spanish and Italian. **Menu:** 55 to 85 Frs. **Restaurant:** Breakfast served from 6:00am. Lunch served from midday until 2:00pm. Dinner served from 7:30pm until 10:00pm. Closed Saturdays and from 15 August. **Specialities:** regional menu, home cooking. **Other points:** bar, open to non-residents, children welcome, lounge area, terraces, pets welcome – check for details, car park. **Address:** Pont des Sable, Coussan.
MR ANTOINE FLORES
**Telephone:** 53.93.60.37
⊗ ♀ Map 8

## MARSAN AUBIET, Gers, 32270

### RELAIS 124, RN 124, between Toulouse and Auch

**Languages spoken:** English. **Menu:** 55 Frs (wine included). **Restaurant:** Breakfast served from 7:00am. Lunch served from 11:30am until 3:00pm. Dinner served from 7:00pm until 10:00pm. Closed Saturdays, 1 week in August and 1 week in December. **Other points:** bar, children welcome, terraces, pets welcome – check for details, car park, traditional decor.
MR FERNAND CASTAING
**Telephone:** 62.65.63.43, 62.65.60.80
⊗ ♀ Map 9

## MARSAS, Gironde, 33620

### LE TOURIN, RN 10

**Menu:** 48 Frs (wine included) to 80 Frs. **Restaurant:** Breakfast served from 5:30am. Dinner served from 7:00pm until 10:00pm. **Specialities:** regional menu, home cooking. **Other points:** bar, open to non-residents, à la carte menu, children welcome, terraces, pets welcome – check for details, car park, traditional decor. **Address:** Route de Libourne.
MR DANIEL LECLERC
**Telephone:** 57.68.08.04
⊗ ♀ Map 8

## MARSEILLAN PLAGE, Hérault, 34340

### LE CREOLE, exit Sète, towards Mèze

**Menu:** 50 to 120 Frs. **Restaurant:** Breakfast served from 9:30am. Lunch served from midday until 3:00pm. Dinner served from 7:00pm until 10:00pm. Closed Wednesdays. **Specialities:** regional menu, home cooking. **Other points:** bar, open to non-residents, à la carte menu, children welcome, pets welcome – check for details, car park. **Address:** 5, avenue de la Méditerranée.
MR GILLES LEPINETTE
**Telephone:** 67.21.98.25
⊗ ♀ Map 10

## MARVEJOLS, Lozère, 48100

### HOTEL DE LA PAIX, RN 9

**Languages spoken:** English and Spanish. **Restaurant:** Dinner served from midday until 9:00pm. **Hotel:** 19 beds. **Other points:** bar. **Address:** 2, avenue Brazza.
MR JEAN-JACQUES BOURGUIGNON
**Telephone:** 66.32.10.17. **Fax:** 66.32.34.93
⊗ ♀ ⌂ Map 10

## MASSEUBE, Gers, 32140

### CHEZ YVETTE, RN 129, Lamezan

**Menu:** 50 Frs. **Restaurant:** Breakfast served from 7:00am. Lunch served from 11:30am until 2:00pm. Closed Sundays and in August. **Specialities:** home cooking. **Other points:** children welcome. **Address:** Route Nationale 129.
MME YVETTE BEYRIES
**Telephone:** 62.66.02.14
⊗ Map 9

## MAVALEIX, Dordogne, 24800

### LES JARDINS DE LA TUILIERE, RN 21, the main road between Périgueux and Limoges

**Menu:** 59 Frs to 120 Frs. **Restaurant:** Breakfast served from 6:00am. Lunch served from 11:30am until 3:00pm. Dinner served from 7:00pm until 10:00pm. **Specialities:** regional menu, home cooking. **Other points:** bar, open to non-residents, à la carte menu, terraces, pets welcome – check for details, car park. **Address:** Route Nationale 21.
MME SUZETTE DESCHAMPS
**Telephone:** 53.52.03.85
⊗ ♀ Map 8

## MAZAMET, Tarn, 81200

### CHEZ LOULOU, RN 112 and 118

**Languages spoken:** Spanish. **Restaurant:** Dinner served from midday until 9:00pm. Closed Sundays and in August. **Other points:** bar. **Address:** 21, avenue Charles Sabatic.
MR LOUIS BLAVY
**Telephone:** 63.61.26.16
⊗ ♀ Map 9

## MAZEYROLLES, Dordogne, 24550

### L'AUBERGE D'ANAIS, RD 710, between Fumel and Périgueux

**Languages spoken:** German, English and Spanish. **Menu:** 43 (wine included) to 70 Frs. **Restaurant:** Breakfast served from 7:00am. Lunch served from midday until 3:00pm. Dinner served from 7:30pm until 9:00pm. **Specialities:** home cooking. **Hotel:** 2 beds; 2 single rooms. **Other points:** bar, open to non-residents, children welcome, terraces, pets welcome – check for details, car park. **Address:** Le Got.
MR XAVIER BELBIS
**Telephone:** 53.28.56.87
⊗ ♀ Map 8

## MERCUS GARRABET, Ariége, 09400

### LE CATHARE, RN 20, between Toulouse and Andorra

**Languages spoken:** Spanish. **Menu:** 55 (wine and coffee included) 85 Frs. **Restaurant:** Breakfast served from 7:00am. Lunch served from midday until 3:00pm. Dinner served from 7:00pm until 9:00pm. **Specialities:** regional menu, home cooking. **Other points:** bar, open to non-residents, à la carte menu, children welcome, pets welcome – check for details, car park, traditional decor. **Address:** Route Nationale 20.
MME AMÉLIE CASTELLON
**Telephone:** 61.05.68.09
⊗ ♀ Map 9

## MILLAU LARZAC, Aveyron, 12230

### RELAIS ESPACE, RN 9, the main road between Clermont Ferrand and Béziers

**Languages spoken:** English and Spanish. **Menu:** 40 to 90 Frs. **Accommodation:** 200 Frs. **Restaurant:** Breakfast served from 6:00am. Lunch served from 11:30am until 3:00pm. Dinner served from 6:30pm until 9:30pm. **Specialities:** regional menu, home cooking. **Hotel:** 10 beds; 4 single rooms, 6 double rooms with bath, private WC, television, telephone. **Other points:** bar, open to non-residents, children welcome, lounge area, terraces, pets welcome – check for details, car park, modern decor. **Address:** Aérodrôme Millau-Larzac.
MME GINETTE GINESTE
**Telephone:** 65.62.76.22. **Fax:** 65.62.79.02
⊗ ♀ ⌂ ☆☆ Map 9

## MIMIZAN, Landes, 40200

### HOTEL RESTAURANT DUCOURT, RN 626, between Mimizan Bourg and Mimizan Plage

**Menu:** 55 Frs. **Accommodation:** 120 to 150 Frs. **Restaurant:** Breakfast served from 7:00am. Lunch served from midday until 3:00pm. Dinner served from 7:00pm until 10:00pm. Closed Sundays. **Specialities:** home cooking. **Hotel:** 18 beds; 15 single rooms, 3 double rooms with shower. **Other points:** bar, open to non-residents, à la carte menu, children welcome, terraces, pets welcome – check for details, car park, traditional decor. **Address:** 20, avenue de la Plage.
MME CHRISTINE KANITZER
**Telephone:** 58.82.44.98
⊗ ♀ ⌂ Map 8

## MIRAMONT DE GUYENNE, Lot-et-Garonne, 47800

### LE RELAIS DE GUYENNE, CD 933

**Languages spoken:** Spanish and Italian. **Restaurant:** Dinner served from midday until 10:00pm. Closed Saturdays. **Hotel:** 8 beds. **Other points:** bar, car park. **Address:** Route de Paris, Saint Pardoux Isaac.
MME RAYMONDE RODES
**Telephone:** 53.93.20.76
⊗ ♀ ⌂ ☆☆ Map 8

## MOISSAC, Tarn-et-Garonne, 82200

### RELAIS AUVERGNAT, RN 927

**Languages spoken:** English and Spanish. **Menu:** 50 Frs. **Accommodation:** 100 to 200 Frs. **Restaurant:** Breakfast served from 6:30am. Lunch served from midday until 3:00pm. Dinner served from 7:30pm until 10:00pm. Closed Sundays. **Specialities:** Cassoulet, confit, grillade, regional food, home cooking. **Hotel:** 10 beds; 5 single rooms, 5 double rooms with shower, bath, television. **Other points:** bar, open to non-residents, à la carte menu, children welcome, pets welcome – check for details, car park, traditional decor. **Address:** 31, boulevard Camille Delthil.
MR JACQUES GINISTY
**Telephone:** 63.04.02.58
⊗ ♀ ⌂ ☞ ☆ Map 9

## MONASTIER (LE), Lozère, 48100

### LES AJUSTONS, RN 9, Millau

**Menu:** 56 to 108 Frs. **Accommodation:** 100 and 170 Frs. **Restaurant:** Breakfast served from 7:30am. Lunch served from midday until 2:00pm. Dinner served from 7:30pm until 9:00pm. Closed Saturdays and in January. **Specialities:** home cooking. **Hotel:** 18 beds; with shower, bath, private WC. **Other points:** bar, open to non-residents, à la carte menu, pets welcome – check for details, car park, traditional decor. **Address:** Lieu dit 'Les Ajustons'.
MR GUY GIBELIN
**Telephone:** 66.32.70.35
⊗ ♀ ⌂ ☆ Map 10

## MONDAVEZAN, Haute-Garonne, 31220

### LA FERMIERE, RN 117, the main road between Toulouse and Saint Gaudens, between Cazéres and Martres-Tolosane

**Languages spoken:** Spanish. **Menu:** 56 to 105 Frs.
**Accommodation:** 70 to 150 Frs. **Restaurant:** Breakfast
served from 6:00am. Lunch served from 11:00am until
2:00pm. Dinner served from 7:00pm until 10:00pm.
Closed Sundays and the 2nd fortnight in August.
**Specialities:** regional menu, home cooking. **Hotel:** 21
beds; 15 single rooms, 6 double rooms with shower.
**Other points:** bar, open to non-residents, à la carte
menu, terraces, pets welcome – check for details, car
park. **Address:** Route Nationale 117.
MME ALEXINE FERRAGE
**Telephone:** 61.97.01.52
⊗ ☥ 🏠 ☆ Map 9

## MONT DE MARSAN, Landes, 40000

### BAR DES SPORTS, RN 132
**Languages spoken:** Spanish. **Menu:** 47 to 60 Frs.
**Restaurant:** Lunch served from midday until 2:00pm.
Dinner served from 7:00pm until 9:00pm. Closed Sundays.
**Specialities:** regional menu, home cooking. **Hotel:** 20
beds. **Other points:** bar. **Address:** Place des Arènes.
MME JOSIANE LEDOUX
**Telephone:** 58.75.05.08
⊗ ☥ 🏠 Map 8

## MONTAREN, Gard, 30700

### LES ROUTIERS – CHEZ RÉGINE, RN 981
**Restaurant:** Closed Sundays. **Hotel:** 9 beds. **Other**
points: bar. **Address:** 7, route d'Ales.
MME RÉGINE HANGARD
**Telephone:** 66.22.25.26
⊗ ☥ 🏠 Map 10

## MONTECH, Tarn-et-Garonne, 82700

### RELAIS DE L'AVENUE, RD 928, between
Montauban and Auch
**Menu:** 50 to 100 Frs. **Restaurant:** Breakfast served
from 7:00am. Lunch served from 11:30am until 2:00pm.
Closed Sundays, 1 week from 15 August and from 20
December to 5 January. **Specialities:** regional menu,
home cooking. **Other points:** bar, open to non-residents,
à la carte menu, terraces, car park, modern decor.
**Address:** 7, boulevard Legal.
MR GEORGES TAUPIAC
**Telephone:** 63.64.72.26
⊗ ☥ Map 9

## MONTREAL, Aude, 11290

### LE MALEPERE, RD 119, exit
Castelnaudary, towards Limoux
**Languages spoken:** English and Spanish. **Menu:** 50 to
200 Frs. **Accommodation:** 75 to 170 Frs. **Restaurant:**
Breakfast served from 7:00am. Lunch served from 11:00am
until 2:30pm. Dinner served from 7:00pm until 10:00pm.
Closed Sundays. **Specialities:** regional menu, home
cooking. **Hotel:** 3 beds; 2 single rooms, 1 double room

with shower, bath, private WC, television. **Other points:**
bar, open to non-residents, à la carte menu, children
welcome, lounge area, terraces, pets welcome – check for
details, car park, traditional decor. **Address:** Les Giscarels.
MR GABRIEL FRANÇOIS
**Telephone:** 68.76.29.43
⊗ ☥ Map 10

## MONTREDON DES CORBIERES,
Aude, 11100

### LE STEPHANOIS, RN 113
**Languages spoken:** Spanish. **Restaurant:** Breakfast
served from 4:00am. Lunch served from 11:30am until
2:30pm. Dinner served from 7:00pm until midnight.
Closed Sundays. **Other points:** bar, car park. **Address:**
Route Nationale 113.
MR GILLES PASQUET
**Telephone:** 68.42.08.41. **Fax:** 68.41.37.51
⊗ ☥ Map 10

## MONTVALENT, Lot, 46600

### LA BERGERIE DE POULOT, RN 140,
between Brive and Rodez
**Menu:** 55 (wine included) to 130 Frs. **Restaurant:**
Breakfast served from 6:00am. Lunch served from
11:00am until midday. Dinner served from midday until
10:00pm. **Specialities:** regional menu, home cooking.
**Other points:** open to non-residents, à la carte menu,
children welcome, terraces, pets welcome – check for
details, car park, traditional decor. **Address:** Lieu dit
'Poulot, Route Nationale 140.
MR MARCEL MAGNIER
**Telephone:** 65.37.41.04
⊗ Map 9

## MOULEYDIER, Dordogne, 24520

### RELAIS DU BARRAGE, RD 660, between
Bergerac and Sarlat
**Languages spoken:** English and Spanish. **Menu:** 50 Frs
(wine and coffee included). **Restaurant:** Breakfast
served from 7:00am. Lunch served from midday until
2:00pm. Dinner served from 7:30pm until 11:00pm.
Closed Saturdays. **Specialities:** home cooking. **Other**
points: bar, open to non-residents, children welcome,
lounge area, terraces, pets welcome – check for details,
car park, traditional decor. **Address:** Tuilières.
MR PATRICK DELMAS
**Telephone:** 53.63.47.56
⊗ ☥ Map 8

## MURET, Haute-Garonne, 31600

### LE MARCLAN, between Saint Gaudens and
Tarbes
**Menu:** 52 Frs (coffee included). **Restaurant:** Breakfast
served from 7:00am. Lunch served from 11:30am until

2:30pm. Closed Saturdays. **Specialities:** regional menu, home cooking. **Other points:** open to non-residents, modern decor. **Address:** 22 bis, rue de Marclan, ZI Marclan.
MME RÉGINE SOLER
**Telephone:** 61.56.82.93
⊗  Map 9

## MUSSIDAN, Dordogne, 24400

### LE PERIGORD, RN 89, between Périgueux and Bordeaux, near the church
**Menu:** 50 to 150 Frs. **Accommodation:** 150 to 250 Frs. **Restaurant:** Breakfast served from 7:00am. Lunch served from midday until 2:30pm. Dinner served from 7:30pm until 10:00pm. **Specialities:** regional menu, home cooking. **Hotel:** 6 beds; with shower, bath, private WC. **Other points:** bar, open to non-residents, à la carte menu, children welcome, terraces, pets welcome – check for details, car park, traditional decor. **Address:** 37, avenue Gambetta.
MME ANNIE CALLENS
**Telephone:** 53.81.05.85
⊗ ♈ 🏠 ⌐  Map 8

## NARBONNE, Aude, 11100

### LA CAILLE QUI CHANTE, RN 113, exit south Narbonne, towards Carcassonne
**Languages spoken:** English, Spanish, German. **Accommodation:** 120 to 185 Frs. **Restaurant:** Breakfast served from 4:00am. Lunch served from 11:30am until 2:30pm. Dinner served from 6:30pm until midnight. **Specialities:** regional menu, home cooking. **Hotel:** 20 beds; 13 single rooms, 7 double rooms with shower, bath, private WC, television, telephone. **Other points:** bar, open to non-residents, à la carte menu, children welcome, terraces, pets welcome – check for details, car park. **Address:** Montredon des Corbières.
MR ALAIN GARCIES
**Telephone:** 68.42.04.36. **Fax:** 68.42.42.85
⊗ ♈ 🏠 ☆☆ Map 10

### LE NOVELTY
**Languages spoken:** English, Arabic, Spanish, Italian. **Menu:** 49 to 85 Frs. **Accommodation:** 80 to 175 Frs (with shower on the landing). **Restaurant:** Breakfast served from 7:00am. Lunch served from midday until 2:30pm. Dinner served from 7:30pm until 10:30pm. **Specialities:** regional menu, home cooking. **Hotel:** 21 beds; 4 single rooms, 17 double rooms. **Other points:** bar, open to non-residents, à la carte menu, lounge area, pets welcome – check for details, car park. **Address:** 33, avenue des Pyrénées.
CLAUDE ET LOUIS STRAZZERA
**Telephone:** 68.42.24.28. **Fax:** 68.42.13.37
⊗ ♈ 🏠 Map 10

### RESTAURANT DES 2 MERS, RN 9, exit south Narbonne
**Languages spoken:** English and Italian. **Menu:** 56 to 68 Frs. **Restaurant:** Breakfast served from 6:00am. Dinner served from midday until midnight. Closed Saturdays. **Specialities:** home cooking. **Other points:** bar, open to non-residents, children welcome, terraces, pets welcome – check for details, car park, modern decor. **Address:** Route de la Nautique, Complexe Routier International.
MR FRANCO MATTEI
**Telephone:** 68.41.00.21, 68.41.12.19
⊗ ♈ Map 10

## NEUVIC SUR L'ISLE, Dordogne, 24190

### ESCALE DU BUT, RN 89, between Bordeaux (195km) and Périgueux (30km)
**Languages spoken:** English and Spanish. **Menu:** 53 Frs (wine and coffee included) to 80 Frs. **Restaurant:** Breakfast served from 6:00am. **Specialities:** home cooking. **Other points:** bar, open to non-residents, à la carte menu, children welcome, terraces, pets welcome – check for details, car park, modern decor. **Address:** Route Nationale 89, lieu dit 'Le But'.
MR JEAN-LUC MÉDARD
**Telephone:** 53.81.60.06
⊗ ♈ Map 8

## NICOLE, Lot-et-Garonne, 47190

### LE PLAISANCE, RN 113
**Restaurant:** Dinner served from midday until 10:00pm. Closed Saturdays and in August. **Hotel:** 7 beds. **Other points:** bar. **Address:** Route Nationale 113, Aiguillon.
MR BERNARD LAMBERT
**Telephone:** 53.79.64.07
⊗ ♈ 🏠 Map 8

## NIMES, Gard, 30900

### L'AVONAGE
**Languages spoken:** English and Spanish. **Restaurant:** Dinner served from midday until 9:30pm. Closed Sundays and in October. **Specialities:** regional menu, home cooking. **Other points:** bar, à la carte menu, terraces, pets welcome – check for details, car park, modern decor. **Address:** Route de Générac, camping du domaine de la Bastide.
MR GABRIEL FINIELS
**Telephone:** 66.38.06.99
⊗ ♈ Map 10

## ONET LE CHATEAU, Aveyron, 12850

### LA ROCADE, RN 88, between Sévérac le Château and Millau
**Menu:** 49 to 115 Frs. **Accommodation:** 100 to 170 Frs. **Restaurant:** Breakfast served from 7:00am. Lunch served from midday until 2:00pm. Dinner served from

7:30pm until 8:30pm. Closed Fridays, from 1 to 15 July and from 24 December to 10 January. **Specialities:** confit de canard, civet d'oie, tripoux, grillades au feu de bois, regional food. **Hotel:** 14 beds; 10 single rooms, 4 double rooms with shower, bath, private WC, telephone. **Other points:** bar, open to non-residents, à la carte menu, children welcome, lounge area, terraces, car park. **Address:** La Roquette.
MR FRANCIS GAYRAUD
**Telephone:** 65.67.17.12, 65.67.10.44
⊗ ⥂ ⌂ ⌖ ☆ Map 9

## ORTHEZ, Pyrénées-Atlantiques, 64300

### LE RELAIS DE BAIGTS, RN 117
**Languages spoken:** English and Spanish. **Hotel:** 15 beds. **Other points:** bar.
MME DANIELE AUSTRUY
**Telephone:** 59.65.32.42
⊗ ⥂ ⌂ Map 8

## PAU, Pyrénées-Atlantiques, 64000

### HOTEL DU BOIS LOUIS, RN 117 and 134, SNCF station
**Places of interest:** Donjon Gayette (3km), Vichy (5km) et le centre omnisport (1km). **Menu:** 55 to 120 Frs. **Accommodation:** 85 to 120 Frs. **Restaurant:** Breakfast served from 6:30am. Closed Saturdays and the 1st fortnight in August. **Specialities:** regional menu, home cooking. **Hotel:** 7 beds; 2 single rooms, 5 double rooms with shower, bath. **Other points:** bar, open to non-residents, à la carte menu, children welcome, pets welcome – check for details, car park, traditional decor. **Address:** 18, avenue Gaston Lacoste.
MR JEAN-MARIE BAREILLE
**Telephone:** 59.27.34.98
⊗ ⥂ ⌂ ☆ Map 8

## PAUILLAC, Gironde, 33250

### LE YACHTING, RD 2
**Menu:** 44 to 133 Frs. **Accommodation:** 120 to 280 Frs. **Restaurant:** Lunch served from midday until 2:00pm. Dinner served from 8:00pm until 9:30pm. Closed Saturdays. **Specialities:** home cooking. **Hotel:** 16 beds; 8 single rooms, 8 double rooms with shower, bath, private WC. **Other points:** bar, à la carte menu, children welcome, terraces, pets welcome – check for details, car park, traditional decor. **Address:** 12, port de Plaisance, quai Lèon Ferrier.
MME LOUISETTE PUYFOURCAT-LE FUR
**Telephone:** 56.59.06.43
⊗ ⥂ ⌂ ☆ Map 8

## PERPIGNAN, Pyrénées-Orientales, 66000

### LA CHAUMIERE
**Languages spoken:** English, Italian and Spanish. **Menu:** 60 Frs. **Restaurant:** Breakfast served from

6:30am. Closed Saturdays and from 15 July to 15 August. **Specialities:** home cooking. **Other points:** bar, open to non-residents, terraces, pets welcome – check for details, car park, modern decor. **Address:** Avenue de Bruxelles, ZI Saint Charles.
MR PHILIPPE CHEVALLIER
**Telephone:** 68.56.57.69, 68.56.95.46
⊗ ⥂ Map 10

## PEYRIAC DE MER, Aude, 11440

### PORTE DE CORBIERES, RN 9, opposite the African reserve of Sigean
**Menu:** 50 Frs. **Restaurant:** Lunch served from 11:00am until 3:00pm. Dinner served from 6:00pm until 11:30pm. Closed Sundays. **Specialities:** home cooking. **Other points:** bar, à la carte menu. **Address:** Route Nationale 9.
MME BÉATRICE VINCENT
**Telephone:** 68.48.30.88
⊗ ⥂ Map 10

## PIERREFITTE NESTALAS, Hautes-Pyrénées, 65260

### HOTEL BEL AIR, RN 21, Lourdes/Argelès
**Languages spoken:** Spanish. **Menu:** 45 to 55 Frs. **Accommodation:** 80 to 150 Frs. **Restaurant:** Breakfast served from 7:00am. Lunch served from midday until 2:30pm. Dinner served from 7:30pm until 9:30pm. Closed 1 fortnight in October and 1 fortnight in November. **Specialities:** home cooking. **Hotel:** 11 beds; 8 single rooms, 3 double rooms with shower, bath. **Other points:** bar, open to non-residents, children welcome, lounge area, terraces, pets welcome – check for details, car park, modern decor. **Address:** 5, rue Lavoisier.
MME EUGÉNIE BELLOCQ
**Telephone:** 62.92.75.22
⊗ ⥂ ⌂ Map 9

## PINEUILH, Gironde, 33220

### L'ARBALESTRIER, RD 936, the main road between Bordeaux and Libourne, via Bergerac
**Menu:** 50 to 180 Frs. **Restaurant:** Breakfast served from 7:30am. Lunch served from midday until 2:30pm. Dinner served from 7:30pm until 9:30pm. Closed 1 week in January and 1 week in February. **Specialities:** gratin dauphinois, lotte à l'américaine, regional food, home cooking. **Other points:** bar, open to non-residents, à la carte menu, children welcome, terraces, pets welcome – check for details, car park, traditional decor. **Address:** Route de Bergerac.
MME ANDRÉE TEYSSIER
**Telephone:** 57.48.27.90
⊗ ⥂ Map 8

## PLAISANCE DU GERS, Gers, 32160

### LA PERGOLA, RN 646

**Menu:** 55 to 150 Frs. **Accommodation:** 80 to 230 Frs. **Restaurant:** Breakfast served from 7:00am. Lunch served from midday until 2:00pm. Dinner served from 7:30pm until 9:00pm. Closed Sundays and from 24 December to 3 January. **Specialities:** foie gras, confit, magret, regional food, home cooking. **Hotel:** 10 beds; with shower, bath, television. **Other points:** bar, open to non-residents, à la carte menu, children welcome, terraces, pets welcome – check for details, car park. **Address:** 11, allée des Ormeaux.
MME CHRISTIANE LAGISQUET
**Telephone:** 62.69.30.22
⊗ ♈ 🏠 Map 9

## PORTIRAGNES, Hérault, 34420

### LA VITARELLE, RN 112, between Béziers and Sète

**Languages spoken:** German, English, Spanish and Italian. **Menu:** 55 Frs (wine included) to 198 Frs. **Accommodation:** 100 to 250 Frs. **Restaurant:** Breakfast served from 6:45am. Lunch served from 11:45am until 3:00pm. Dinner served from 6:45pm until 10:00pm. Closed Sundays. **Specialities:** regional menu, home cooking. **Hotel:** 28 beds; 10 single rooms, 18 double rooms with shower, bath, private WC, television, telephone. **Other points:** bar, open to non-residents, à la carte menu, children welcome, lounge area, terraces, pets welcome – check for details, car park. **Address:** La Vitarelle, Route Nationale 112.
MR CHRISTOPHE COMANDINI
**Telephone:** 67.90.88.90
⊗ ♈ 🏠 Map 10

## POUSSAN, Hérault, 34560

### LE 7 SUR SETE

**Languages spoken:** English. **Menu:** 51 Frs. **Restaurant:** Breakfast served from 6:00am. **Other points:** bar. **Address:** Route Nationale 113.
SARL LE 7 SUR SETE
**Telephone:** 67.78.33.29
⊗ ♈ Map 10

### LE LANDRY, RN 113, exit autoroute at Béziers, Landry is 2km

**Languages spoken:** English,Spanish,Italian,German. **Menu:** 55 Frs. **Restaurant:** Dinner served from midday until 10:00pm. Closed Saturdays. **Specialities:** huîtres, moules, sèches rouille, home cooking. **Hotel:** with shower. **Other points:** bar, à la carte menu, terraces, pets welcome – check for details, car park. **Address:** Route Nationale 113.
MR SIAUVAUD
**Telephone:** 67.78.24.74
⊗ ♈ Map 10

## PUJAUT, Gard, 30131

### LES GRAVIERES, RN 580, Bagnols en Ceze

**Menu:** 60 Frs. **Restaurant:** Breakfast served from 6:30am. Lunch served from 12:30pm until 2:30pm. Dinner served from 7:30pm until 10:30pm. Closed Fridays 2:00pm to Saturday mornings. **Specialities:** home cooking. **Other points:** bar, open to non-residents, terraces, pets welcome – check for details, car park, modern decor. **Address:** Les Gravières, route de Bagnols sur Cèze.
MME PATRICIA QUIQUEMELLE
**Telephone:** 90.25.19.70
⊗ ♈ Map 10

## REALMONT, Tarn, 81120

### RESTAURANT LE ROUTIER

**Menu:** 60 to 80 Frs. **Restaurant:** Closed Sundays. **Specialities:** regional menu. **Other points:** bar, à la carte menu, car park. **Address:** 27, boulevard Armengaud.
MR ROGER DAUZATS
**Telephone:** 63.55.65.44
⊗ ♈ Map 9

## REBENACQ, Pyrénées-Atlantiques, 64260

### CHEZ PALU, RD 936, route for Lourdes

**Menu:** 50 to 90 Frs. **Restaurant:** Breakfast served from 7:00am. Lunch served from 10:00am until 3:00pm. Dinner served from 7:00pm until 10:00pm. Closed Mondays. **Specialities:** regional menu, home cooking. **Hotel:** with television. **Other points:** bar, open to non-residents, à la carte menu, children welcome, lounge area, terraces, pets welcome – check for details, car park, traditional decor. **Address:** Place de la Mairie.
MR ALAIN PALU
**Telephone:** 59.05.54.11
⊗ ♈ Map 8

## REMOULINS, Gard, 30210

### LE CALAO, RD 986, exit Remoulins, towards Beaucaire

**Menu:** 50 to 140 Frs. **Accommodation:** 150 to 180 Frs. **Restaurant:** Breakfast served from 6:00am. **Specialities:** regional menu, home cooking. **Hotel:** 5 beds; with shower, private WC, television, telephone. **Other points:** bar, open to non-residents, à la carte menu, children welcome, lounge area, terraces, pets welcome – check for details, car park, traditional decor. **Address:** Route de Beaucaire.
MME BÉATRICE BOUTIN
**Telephone:** 66.37.25.33
⊗ ♈ 🏠 Map 10

### AUBERGE LES PLATANES, RN 86

**Languages spoken:** English and Spanish. **Menu:** 55 to 110 Frs. **Accommodation:** 130 to 350 Frs. **Restaurant:** Dinner served from midday until 10:00pm. **Specialities:**

regional menu. **Hotel:** 35 beds; with shower, bath, private WC, television, telephone. **Other points:** bar, à la carte menu, children welcome, lounge area, terraces, pets welcome – check for details, car park. **Address:** Castillon du Gard, les Croisées.
MR GÉRARD REYNAUD
**Telephone:** 66.37.10.69. **Fax:** 66.37.34.03
⊗ ♈ ⌂ ☞ ☆☆ Map 10

## REOLE (LA), Gironde, 33190

### LE FLAUTAT, RN 113
**Languages spoken:** English. **Menu:** 50 Frs (wine included). **Restaurant:** Breakfast served from 6:00am. Lunch served from 11:00am until 3:00pm. Dinner served from 7:00pm until 10:00pm. Closed Saturdays. **Specialities:** home cooking. **Other points:** bar, open to non-residents, children welcome, pets welcome – check for details, car park, modern decor. **Address:** Le Flaütat, Route Nationale 113.
MR JEAN-PAUL DALDOSS
**Telephone:** 56.71.00.37
⊗ ♈ Map 8

## RIBERAC, Dordogne, 24600

### BAR RESTAURANT LAKANAL, the main road between Angoulême and Agen
**Languages spoken:** English. **Menu:** 50 to 80 Frs. **Restaurant:** Breakfast served from 9:00am. Lunch served from midday until 3:00pm. Dinner served from 5:00pm until 10:00pm. Closed Thursdays. **Specialities:** home cooking. **Other points:** bar, open to non-residents, à la carte menu, children welcome, terraces, pets welcome – check for details, car park, traditional decor. **Address:** 1, avenue Lakanal.
MR JEAN-MARIE LAGARDE
**Telephone:** 53.90.04.77
⊗ ♈ Map 8

## RIEUPEYROUX, Aveyron, 12240

### CHEZ PASCAL, RD 605, between Rodez (38km) and Villefranche de Rouergue (23km)
**Menu:** 60 to 130 Frs. **Accommodation:** 95 to 200 Frs. **Restaurant:** Breakfast served from 7:00am. Lunch served from midday until 2:00pm. Dinner served from 7:00pm until 9:00pm. Closed Sundays and from 1 to 15 October. **Specialities:** Tripous, confits, regional food, home cooking. **Hotel:** 14 beds; 4 single rooms, 10 double rooms with shower, bath, private WC, telephone. **Other points:** bar, open to non-residents, à la carte menu, children welcome, lounge area, terraces, pets welcome – check for details, car park, modern decor. **Address:** Rue de l'Hom.
MR CLAUDE DOU
**Telephone:** 65.65.51.13
⊗ ♈ ⌂ ☆ Map 9

## RIEUTORT DE RANDON, Lozère, 48700

### RELAIS DE LA POSTE, RN 106, between Saint Chely d'Apcher and Mende
**Menu:** 55 to 70 Frs. **Restaurant:** Breakfast served from 6:30am. Lunch served from 11:00am until 2:00pm. Closed Saturdays. **Specialities:** home cooking. **Other points:** bar. **Address:** Place de la Poste.
MME ANNIE MAGNE
**Telephone:** 66.47.34.67
⊗ ♈ Map 10

## RISCLE, Gers, 32400

### RELAIS DE L'AUBERGE, RD 135
**Accommodation:** 65 to 80 Frs. **Restaurant:** Closed Sundays and in October. **Hotel:** 10 beds. **Other points:** bar, pets welcome – check for details, car park. **Address:** Place de la Mairie.
MME ELISABETH PORTES
**Telephone:** 62.69.70.49
⊗ ♈ ⌂ ☆ Map 9

## RIVESALTES, Pyrénées-Orientales, 66600

### RESTAURANT PA AMB OLI, exit Perpignan North, 500m on the left towards Narbonne
**Languages spoken:** English, Catalan and Spanish. **Menu:** 60 Frs (coffee included). **Restaurant:** Open 24 hours. **Specialities:** regional menu, home cooking. **Other points:** bar, open to non-residents, lounge area, terraces, pets welcome – check for details, car park, traditional decor. **Address:** Route Nationale 9.
MME ROSE LLOBELL
**Telephone:** 68.64.63.30
⊗ ♈ Map 10

## RIVIERE (LA), Gironde, 33126

### LA RIVIERE, RD 670, between Libourne and Saint André de Cubzac
**Languages spoken:** Spanish. **Menu:** 50 to 95 Frs. **Restaurant:** Dinner served from midday until 11:00pm. **Specialities:** home cooking. **Other points:** bar, à la carte menu, children welcome, terraces, pets welcome – check for details, car park, traditional decor.
MME JEANINE RASTOUL
**Telephone:** 57.24.94.26
⊗ ♈ Map 9

## ROCAMADOUR, Lot, 46500

### HOTEL DES VOYAGEURS, between Brive and Rodez
**Menu:** 55 to 135 Frs. **Accommodation:** 105 to 200 Frs. **Restaurant:** Breakfast served from 7:00am. Lunch served from midday until 2:00pm. Dinner served from 7:00pm

until 9:00pm. Closed Saturdays and 15 days in October. **Specialities:** home cooking. **Hotel:** 9 beds; 4 single rooms, 5 double rooms with shower, bath, private WC, telephone. **Other points:** bar, open to non-residents, lounge area, terraces, pets welcome – check for details, car park, traditional decor. **Address:** Place de la Gare.
MME SIMONE LASFARGUES
**Telephone:** 65.33.63.19
⊗ ᵧ 🏠 Map 9

## ROCHE CHALAIS (LA), Dordogne, 24490

### CAFE DU MIDI, RD 730
**Languages spoken:** German and English. **Restaurant:** Closed Mondays. **Specialities:** home cooking. **Other points:** bar, pets welcome – check for details, car park. **Address:** 32, avenue du Stade.
MME VIOLETTE RAWYLER
**Telephone:** 53.91.43.65
⊗ ᵧ 🍽 Map 8

## ROQUEFORT DES CORBIERES, Aude, 11540

### RELAIS DES COTES DE ROQUEFORT, RN 9
**Languages spoken:** German and Spanish. **Menu:** 55 to 85 Frs. **Restaurant:** Breakfast served from 7:00am. Lunch served from 11:30am until 3:00pm. Dinner served from 7:00pm until 10:00pm. Closed Sundays. **Other points:** bar, car park. **Address:** Route Nationale 9.
MR RENÉ CARBONNEL
**Telephone:** 68.48.45.51 **Fax:** 68.48.32.88
⊗ ᵧ Map 10

## ROUFFIGNAC DE SIGOULES, Dordogne, 24240

### LA TAVERNE ALSACIENNE, between Marmande and Bergerac
**Languages spoken:** German. **Menu:** 120 Frs. **Restaurant:** Lunch served from 11:30am until 3:00pm. Dinner served from 7:00pm until 11:00pm. **Specialities:** regional menu, home cooking. **Other points:** bar, open to non-residents, à la carte menu, children welcome, lounge area, terraces, pets welcome – check for details, car park, traditional decor. **Address:** La Tabarline.
MME FRANCINE THOMANN
**Telephone:** 53.58.84.13, 53.61.24.93
⊗ ᵧ 🍽 Map 8

## ROUFFILLAC DE CARLUX, Dordogne, 24370

### AUX POISSONS FRAIS, RD 703, between Sarlat and Souillac
**Languages spoken:** English. **Menu:** 70 to 220 Frs. **Accommodation:** 240 to 365 Frs. **Restaurant:**

Breakfast served from 8:00am. Lunch served from 12:30pm until 2:00pm. Dinner served from 7:30pm until 9:00pm. Closed in October. **Specialities:** regional menu, home cooking. **Hotel:** 18 beds; 11 single rooms, 7 double rooms with shower, bath, private WC, television, telephone. **Other points:** bar, open to non-residents, à la carte menu, terraces, pets welcome – check for details, car park, traditional decor.
MR JEAN-NOEL CAYRE
**Telephone:** 53.29.70.24
⊗ ᵧ 🏠 ☆☆ Map 8

## SAINT ANTOINE DE BREUILH, Dordogne, 24230

### CAFE DE FRANCE – LES ROUTIERS, RD 936, between Bergerac (30km) and Libourne (30km)
**Menu:** 50 Frs (wine included). **Restaurant:** Breakfast served from 7:00am. Lunch served from midday until 3:00pm. Dinner served from 7:00pm until 9:00pm. Closed Sundays and 15 days in August. **Specialities:** home cooking. **Other points:** bar, open to non-residents, children welcome, pets welcome – check for details, car park, traditional decor.
MR CHRISTIAN NOBLE
**Telephone:** 53.24.78.97
⊗ ᵧ Map 8

## SAINT AUBIN DE BLAYE, Gironde, 33820

### LE RELAIS DE ROUBISQUE, RN 137, Bordeaux/Saintes/Royan
**Languages spoken:** English and Spanish. **Menu:** 59 Frs (wine and coffee included). **Restaurant:** Breakfast served from 7:00am. Lunch served from 11:30am until 2:30pm. Dinner served from 7:00pm until 10:00pm. Closed Sundays. **Specialities:** Plateau de fruits de mer, regional food, home cooking. **Other points:** bar, open to non-residents, children welcome, terraces, pets welcome – check for details, car park, traditional decor. **Address:** Route Nationale 137.
MR OLIVIER DEVESA
**Telephone:** 57.64.72.62
⊗ ᵧ Map 8

## SAINT CERE, Lot, 46400

### HOTEL RESTAURANT DU QUERCY, between Gramat and Rocamadour
**Menu:** 52 to 180 Frs. **Accommodation:** 130 to 200 Frs. **Restaurant:** Breakfast served from 7:00am. Lunch served from midday until 2:00pm. Dinner served from 7:00pm until 9:00pm. Closed Fridays. **Specialities:** Salade de gésiers, confit de canard forestier, regional food, home cooking. **Hotel:** 10 beds; 6 single rooms, 4 double rooms with shower. **Other points:** bar, open to non-residents, à la carte menu, children welcome,

terraces, pets welcome – check for details, car park, modern decor. **Address:** 21, avenue Anatole de Monzie. MME COLETTE GIBBE
**Telephone:** 65.38.04.83
⊗ ♟ ⌂ Map 9

## SAINT CHELY D'APCHER, Lozère, 48200

*LE BARCELONE, RN 9, Montpellier or Clermont Ferrand*
**Menu:** 52 Frs. **Accommodation:** 90 to 115 Frs. **Restaurant:** Breakfast served from 9:00am. Lunch served from midday until 1:30pm. Dinner served from 7:30pm until 9:00pm. Closed Sundays. **Specialities:** home cooking. **Hotel:** 5 beds; 2 single rooms, 3 double rooms. **Other points:** bar, open to non-residents, pets welcome – check for details, car park. **Address:** 33, avenue de la Gare. MME MONIQUE VITRÉ
**Telephone:** 66.31.01.22
⊗ ♟ ⌂ Map 10

## SAINT FELIX LAURAGAIS, Haute-Garonne, 31540

*LE GRILLON, RN 622*
**Accommodation:** 56 to 60 Frs. **Restaurant:** Dinner served from midday until midnight. Closed Sundays and from 15 to 31 August. **Specialities:** home cooking. **Hotel:** 5 beds; with shower. **Other points:** bar, pets welcome – check for details, car park, modern decor. **Address:** Route de Castelnaudary, Revel. MME ALIETTE BONNES
**Telephone:** 61.27.65.27
⊗ ♟ ⌂ Map 9

## SAINT GEORGES DE MONTCLARD, Dordogne, 24140

*LE BON COIN, RD 21, between Périgueux and Bergerac*
**Menu:** 54 to 110 Frs. **Accommodation:** 100 to 140 Frs. **Restaurant:** Breakfast served from 6:30am. Lunch served from midday until 2:00pm. Dinner served from 7:00pm until 9:00pm. Closed Saturdays. **Specialities:** regional menu, home cooking. **Hotel:** 4 beds; 3 single rooms, 1 double room with shower, private WC. **Other points:** bar, open to non-residents, à la carte menu, pets welcome – check for details, car park, traditional decor. **Address:** Le Bourg. MME CATHERINE MALNATTI
**Telephone:** 53.82.98.47
⊗ ♟ Map 8

## SAINT GERMAIN D'ESTEUIL, Gironde, 33340

*LE RELAIS, RN 215, the main road between Bordeaux and le Verdon*
**Menu:** 55 Frs (wine included). **Restaurant:** Breakfast

served from 7:00am. Closed Sundays. **Specialities:** home cooking. **Other points:** bar, open to non-residents, children welcome, pets welcome – check for details, car park, traditional decor. **Address:** Route Nationale 215. MR ANDRÉ DESTRUEL
**Telephone:** 56.73.06.28
⊗ ♟ Map 8

## SAINT GERMAIN DU BEL AIR, Lot, 46310

*CAFE DE FRANCE, RD 23*
**Restaurant:** Closed Sundays. **Other points:** bar. **Address:** Le Bourg. MME MÉLINA FRANCOUAL
**Telephone:** 65.31.06.99
⊗ ♟ Map 9

## SAINT GILLES, Gard, 30800

*LE MIRADOR, RN 572*
**Languages spoken:** English and Italian. **Restaurant:** Breakfast served from 6:30am. Lunch served from 11:30am until 2:30pm. Dinner served from 7:00pm until 8:30pm. **Specialities:** regional menu, home cooking. **Other points:** bar, open to non-residents, à la carte menu, children welcome, terraces, pets welcome – check for details, car park, modern decor. **Address:** Route de Montpellier, Route Nationale 572. MR ALAIN MARTIN
**Telephone:** 66.87.31.20
⊗ ♟ Map 10

## SAINT JULIEN LES ROSIERS, Gard, 30340

*LE MISTRAL, RD 904*
**Languages spoken:** Spanish. **Accommodation:** 100 to 150 Frs. **Restaurant:** Dinner served from midday until 10:00pm. Closed Wednesdays. **Specialities:** tripous, paëlla, rouille du pêcheur, regional food, home cooking. **Hotel:** 15 beds; 8 single rooms, 7 double rooms with shower. **Other points:** bar, à la carte menu, children welcome, terraces, pets welcome – check for details, car park. **Address:** Route de Saint-Ambraix. MR JOSÉ GARCIA
**Telephone:** 66.86.15.29
⊗ ♟ Map 10

## SAINT LON LES MINES, Landes, 40300

*HOTEL DU FRONTON, CD 6*
**Languages spoken:** Spanish. **Accommodation:** 130 to 160 Frs. **Restaurant:** Closed in February. **Hotel:** 10 beds (8 with WC and 2 with showers); with telephone. **Other points:** bar, pets welcome – check for details, car park. **Address:** Le Bourg. MR DANIEL LAFFITTE
**Telephone:** 58.57.80.45
⊗ ♟ ⌂ ☆ Map 8

## SAINT MARTIAL D'ARTENSET,

Dordogne, 24700

*LA HALTE 24, RN 89, the main road between Périgueux and Bordeaux*
**Languages spoken:** English and Italian. **Menu:** 50 Frs
(wine included). **Restaurant:** Breakfast served from
5:00am. **Specialities:** home cooking. **Other points:**
terraces, pets welcome – check for details, car park,
traditional decor. **Address:** Route Nationale 89.
MME CAROLINE TROUILLET
**Telephone:** 53.81.85.34
⊗ Map 8

## SAINT NAUPHARY, Tarn-et-Garonne, 82370

*LES ROUTIERS, RD 999, between Albi and Castres*
**Languages spoken:** English. **Menu:** 50 Frs (coffee
included) to 62 Frs. **Accommodation:** 80 to 130 Frs.
**Restaurant:** Breakfast served from 7:00am. Lunch
served from midday until 2:00pm. Closed Saturdays and
in August. **Specialities:** home cooking. **Hotel:** 11 beds;
7 single rooms, 4 double rooms with shower, bath,
private WC. **Other points:** bar, open to non-residents,
children welcome, terraces, car park, modern decor.
MR PATRICK MONRUFFET
**Telephone:** 63.67.85.09
⊗ ℉ 🏠 Map 9

## SAINT NAZAIRE, Gard, 30200

*LES TERAILLES, RN 86*
**Restaurant:** Closed Saturdays and in September. **Hotel:**
12 beds. **Other points:** bar. **Address:** Route Nationale 86.
MME MENU
**Telephone:** 66.89.66.14
⊗ ℉ 🏠 ☆ Map 10

## SAINT PAUL CAP DE JOUX, Tarn, 81220

*LES GLYCINES, RN 112, between Lavaur and Castres*
**Menu:** 60 Frs (wine included). **Restaurant:** Closed
Mondays. **Specialities:** home cooking. **Other points:**
bar, open to non-residents, children welcome, terraces,
pets welcome – check for details, car park. **Address:**
Rue Philippe Pinel.
MR CLAUDE PEYRARD
**Telephone:** 63.70.61.37
⊗ ℉ Map 9

## SAINT PAUL DE LOUBRESSAC,

Lot, 46170

*RELAIS DE LA MADELEINE, RN 20,
100m from the RN 20 on RD 83 towards la
Madeleine*
**Languages spoken:** English (Spanish in summer).
**Menu:** 65 to 165 Frs. **Accommodation:** 130 to 230 Frs.
**Restaurant:** Breakfast served from 7:30am. Lunch
served from midday until 1:45pm. Dinner served from
7:30pm until 9:00pm. Closed Saturdays, 8 days at All
Saints' holiday and 15 days at Christmas. **Specialities:**
quercynoise, foie gras, confit, magret, regional food,
home cooking. **Hotel:** 15 beds; 5 single rooms, 10
double rooms with shower, bath, private WC, telephone.
**Other points:** bar, open to non-residents, à la carte
menu, children welcome, terraces, pets welcome – check
for details, car park. **Address:** Route Nationale 20.
MR BERNARD DEVIANNE
**Telephone:** 65.21.98.08
⊗ ℉ 🏠 ⌐ ☆ Map 9

## SAINT PAUL LES DAX, Landes, 40190

*LE VIEUX TACHOIRE, the main road between Bordeaux and Orthez*
**Languages spoken:** English and Spanish. **Menu:** 51 to
100 Frs. **Specialities:** regional menu, home cooking.
**Other points:** bar, open to non-residents, à la carte
menu, children welcome, lounge area, pets welcome –
check for details, car park, modern decor. **Address:**
1049, avenue du Maréchal Foch.
SNC B & C
**Telephone:** 58.91.61.00
⊗ ℉ Map 8

## SAINT PEY D'ARMENS, Gironde, 33330

*RELAIS DE GASCOGNE, RD 936, Bergerac*
**Languages spoken:** English. **Menu:** 53 to 110 Frs.
**Restaurant:** Breakfast served from 6:00am. Lunch
served from 11:30am until 2:30pm. Dinner served from
7:30pm until 10:00pm. Closed Sundays. **Specialities:**
regional menu, home cooking. **Other points:** bar, open to
non-residents, à la carte menu, children welcome, lounge
area, terraces, pets welcome – check for details, car park,
modern decor. **Address:** Route Départementale 936.
MR ERIC SAMSON
**Telephone:** 57.47.15.02
⊗ ℉ Map 8

## SAINT PRIVAT DES VIEUX, Gard, 30340

*L'ESCALE, RD 216, between Alès and Bagnols*
**Languages spoken:** English. **Menu:** 55 to 80 Frs.
**Accommodation:** 90 to 160 Frs. **Restaurant:** Breakfast
served from 5:00am. Lunch served from midday until
2:00pm. Dinner served from 8:00pm until 11:00pm.
**Specialities:** home cooking. **Hotel:** 8 beds; 4 single
rooms, 4 double rooms with shower. **Other points:** bar,
open to non-residents, lounge area, terraces, pets

welcome – check for details, car park. **Address:** 59, route de Bagnols.
MME GINETTE CALCAT
**Telephone:** 66.30.49.76
⊗ ⵐ 🏠 Map 10

## SAINT ROME DE CERNON,
Aveyron, 12490

### CHEZ PIERROT
**Languages spoken:** English and Spanish. **Menu:** 50 to 120 Frs. **Accommodation:** 100 Frs. **Restaurant:** Breakfast served from 8:00am. Lunch served from midday until 3:00pm. **Specialities:** truite au roquefort, écrevisses à l'américaine, regional food, home cooking. **Hotel:** 6 beds; 3 single rooms, 3 double rooms. **Other points:** bar, open to non-residents, à la carte menu, children welcome, terraces, pets welcome – check for details, car park, traditional decor. **Address:** Avenue de Millau.
MR JEAN-PIERRE BOUSQUET
**Telephone:** 65.62.33.56
⊗ ⵐ 🏠 Map 9

## SAINT SULPICE ET CAMEYRAC, Gironde, 33450

### L'ENSOULEIADO, between Libourne and Bordeaux
**Languages spoken:** Spanish. **Menu:** 48 (wine included) to 90 Frs. **Accommodation:** 100 to 140 Frs. **Restaurant:** Breakfast served from 7:30am. Lunch served from 11:00am until 3:00pm. Dinner served from 7:30pm until 10:30pm. Closed Mondays and end of September. **Specialities:** home cooking. **Hotel:** 4 beds; 4 double rooms. **Other points:** bar, open to non-residents, children welcome, terraces, pets welcome – check for details, car park, traditional decor. **Address:** 3, avenue de l'Hôtel de Ville.
MME HÉLENE HUJOL
**Telephone:** 56.30.83.42
⊗ ⵐ Map 8

## SAINT VINCENT DE PAUL, Landes, 40990

### AUX PLATANES, RN 124
**Languages spoken:** Spanish. **Restaurant:** Closed Sundays. **Other points:** bar.
MR ROGER VICENTE
**Telephone:** 58.73.90.13
⊗ ⵐ Map 8

## SAINTE LIVRADE SUR LOT, Lot-et-Garonne, 47110

### AU BON ACCUEIL, RN 111
**Restaurant:** Closed Sundays and from 24 December to 2 January. **Hotel:** 10 beds. **Other points:** bar. **Address:** route de Villeneuve.

MR COUGOUILLE
**Telephone:** 58.01.02.34
⊗ ⵐ 🏠 ☆ Map 8

## SAINTE MARIE DE GOSSE, Landes, 40390

### LE RELAIS ROUTIERS, RN 117, between Bayonne and Pau
**Languages spoken:** English and Spanish. **Menu:** 50 to 120 Frs. **Accommodation:** 120 to 180 Frs. **Restaurant:** Breakfast served from 6:00am. Lunch served from midday until 2:30pm. Dinner served from 7:30pm until 10:00pm. Closed Fridays and in October. **Specialities:** confits, foie gras, poissons régionaux (in season), regional food, home cooking. **Hotel:** 15 beds; 5 single rooms, 10 double rooms with shower, bath, private WC, telephone. **Other points:** bar, open to non-residents, à la carte menu, children welcome, lounge area, terraces, pets welcome – check for details, car park, traditional decor. **Address:** Route Nationale 117.
MR MARC DELOUBE
**Telephone:** 59.56.32.02. **Fax:** 59.56.36.06
⊗ ⵐ 🏠 🍽 ☆ Map 8

## SAINTE MARTHE, Lot-et-Garonne, 47430

### LE RELAIS DU PONT DE L'AVANCE, RN 933, 200m from exit of péage at Marmande
**Menu:** 50 to 70 Frs. **Restaurant:** Breakfast served from 6:00am. Lunch served from 11:00am until 3:00pm. Dinner served from 6:00pm until 10:00pm. Closed Sundays. **Specialities:** home cooking. **Other points:** bar, open to non-residents, children welcome, pets welcome – check for details, car park. **Address:** Route Nationale 933.
MR HERVÉ POUCHET
**Telephone:** 53.20.63.39
⊗ ⵐ Map 8

## SAINTE TERRE, Gironde, 33350

### CHEZ REGIS, the main road between Libourne and Bergérac
**Accommodation:** 100 to 120 Frs. **Restaurant:** Dinner served from 7:00pm until 9:00pm. Closed Mondays and in October and in January. **Specialities:** regional menu. **Hotel:** 6 beds; with shower. **Other points:** bar, à la carte menu, children welcome, terraces, pets welcome – check for details, car park, traditional decor. **Address:** Avenue du Général de Gaulle.
MR JACQUES ASTARIE
**Telephone:** 57.47.16.21
⊗ ⵐ 🏠 🍽 Map 8

## SARLAT, Dordogne, 24200

### CAFETERIA DU PONTET, RN 21, road to Bergerac

**Languages spoken:** English and Spanish. **Restaurant:** Breakfast served from 8:00am. Lunch served from 11:00am until 3:00pm. Dinner served from 7:00pm until 10:00pm. Closed Christmas Eve and Christmas Day, New Year's Eve and New Year's Day. **Specialities:** regional menu, home cooking. **Other points:** bar, terraces, pets welcome – check for details, car park, modern decor. **Address:** Route de Bergerac.
MR JEAN-PIERRE BOUY
**Telephone:** 53.31.05.36, 53.31.05.85
⊗ ☿ Map 8

# SAUVETAT SUR LEDE (LA), Lot-et-
Garonne, 47150

## LA RENAISSANCE, *RD 676, the main road between Limoges and Paris*
**Languages spoken:** English. **Menu:** 58 Frs (wine and coffee included) to 120 Frs. **Accommodation:** 100 to 150 Frs. **Restaurant:** Breakfast served from 8:00am. Lunch served from midday until 3:00pm. Dinner served from 7:00pm until 10:00pm. Closed Mondays.
**Specialities:** home cooking. **Hotel:** 7 beds; with shower, bath, private WC. **Other points:** bar, open to non-residents, à la carte menu, children welcome, lounge area, terraces, pets welcome – check for details, car park, traditional decor. **Address:** Le Bourg.
MR LOUIS LE GALL
**Telephone:** 53.41.94.50
⊗ ☿ ⌂ Map 8

# SAUVETERRE DE GUYENNE,
Gironde, 33540

## HOTEL DE GUYENNE, *on the road to Libourne*
**Languages spoken:** English. **Menu:** 65 to 120 Frs. **Accommodation:** 100 to 160 Frs. **Restaurant:** Lunch served from 11:00am until 3:00pm. Dinner served from 7:00pm until 11:00pm. **Specialities:** escargots à la Bordelaise, magret, foie gras, regional food, home cooking. **Hotel:** 15 beds; 11 single rooms, 4 double rooms with shower, bath, private WC, telephone. **Other points:** bar, open to non-residents, à la carte menu, terraces, pets welcome – check for details, car park.
**Address:** Route de Libourne, Pringis.
MR JEAN-PAUL DALDOSS
**Telephone:** 56.71.54.92
⊗ ☿ ⌂ ☆ Map 8

# SEBAZAC CONCOURES, Aveyron, 12850

## LE LONGCHAMPS, *CD 904*
**Menu:** 50 Frs. **Restaurant:** Breakfast served from 7:15am. Closed Mondays. **Specialities:** regional menu. **Other points:** bar, open to non-residents, children welcome, car park, traditional decor. **Address:** 56, avenue Tabardelle.

MR FRANCIS SAVARIC
**Telephone:** 65.74.93.62
⊗ ☿ Map 9

# SEILH, Haute-Garonne, 31840

## LES ROUTIERS
**Menu:** 55 to 120 Frs. **Restaurant:** Breakfast served from 6:30am. **Other points:** bar, open to non-residents, car park. **Address:** Les Tricheries.
MME NELLY GOUYOU
**Telephone:** 61.59.90.17
⊗ ☿ Map 9

# SERRES CASTET, Pyrénées-Atlantiques, 64121

## LES ROUTIERS, *RN 134, Bordeaux*
**Languages spoken:** Spanish. **Menu:** 50 Frs. **Accommodation:** 60 Frs. **Restaurant:** Breakfast served from 7:00am. Closed Saturdays and in August. **Specialities:** regional menu, home cooking. **Hotel:** 5 beds; with shower, bath. **Other points:** bar, open to non-residents, à la carte menu, children welcome, lounge area, terraces, car park, traditional decor.
MR LÉON SALIS
**Telephone:** 59.33.91.06
⊗ ☿ ⌂ Map 8

# SETE, Hérault, 34200

## LA REGENCE, *RN 108, on the road to Montpellier, at the entrance to the port*
**Languages spoken:** English, Spanish, Italian and Greek. **Menu:** 65 Frs. **Restaurant:** Breakfast served from 8:30am. Lunch served from midday until 3:00pm. Dinner served from 7:00pm until 10:00pm. Closed Sundays. **Specialities:** regional menu. **Other points:** bar, open to non-residents, à la carte menu, children welcome, terraces, pets welcome – check for details, traditional decor. **Address:** 1, place de Lille.
MME SAVITA BARTHE
**Telephone:** 67.74.32.92
⊗ ☿ Map 10

## LE PAVILLON, *RN 108, the harbour*
**Languages spoken:** German and English. **Menu:** 55 Frs. **Restaurant:** Breakfast served from 6:00am. Lunch served from midday until 3:00pm. Dinner served from 7:30pm until 10:00pm. Closed Saturdays. **Specialities:** regional menu, home cooking. **Other points:** bar, open to non-residents, pets welcome – check for details, car park, traditional decor. **Address:** 23, route de Montpellier.
MME MARIE FRANCE PETITFILS
**Telephone:** 67.48.62.53
⊗ ☿

## RESTO ROUTIER – LA PÉNICHE, *RN 108, at the entrance of Sète, on entering Montpellier*

Languages spoken: English and Spanish. Menu: 54 to 89 Frs. Restaurant: Breakfast served from 9:30am. Lunch served from midday until 3:00pm. Dinner served from 7:00pm until 11:00pm. Closed Saturdays. Specialities: regional menu, home cooking. Other points: open to non-residents, children welcome, pets welcome – check for details, car park, modern decor. Address: 1, quai des Moulins.
MME PAQUERETTE DUPUY
Telephone: 67.48.64.13
⊗ Map 10

## SEYCHES, Lot-et-Garonne, 47350

### AU BON ACCUEIL, CD 933, between Marmande and Périgueux
Menu: 48 Frs (wine included). Accommodation: 90 to 120 Frs. Restaurant: Breakfast served from 8:00am. Lunch served from midday until 2:00pm. Dinner served from 7:30pm until 10:00pm. Closed Saturdays. Specialities: home cooking. Hotel: 5 beds; 2 single rooms, 3 double rooms. Other points: bar, open to non-residents, pets welcome – check for details, car park, traditional decor.
MME MARIE LALIETTE
Telephone: 53.83.60.10
⊗ ▽ 🏠 Map 8

## SOUAL, Tarn, 81580

### LA MAIZOU, RN 126
Menu: 58 to 160 Frs. Accommodation: 90 to 140 Frs. Restaurant: Breakfast served from 7:00am. Lunch served from midday until 2:00pm. Dinner served from 7:30pm until 9:30pm. Closed Tuesdays. Specialities: regional menu, home cooking. Hotel: 6 beds; 4 single rooms, 2 double rooms with shower, bath, private WC. Other points: bar, open to non-residents, à la carte menu, children welcome, lounge area, terraces, pets welcome – check for details, car park, traditional decor. Address: 12, Grande Rue.
MR JEAN-MARIE LEMAIRE
Telephone: 63.75.52.24
⊗ ▽ 🏠 Map 9

## SOUMOULOU, Pyrénées-Atlantiques, 64420

### HOTEL RESTAURANT BEARNAIS, RN 64, 20km from Tarbes
Menu: 47, 50 to 60 Frs. Accommodation: 80 to 100 Frs. Restaurant: Breakfast served from 6:00am. Lunch served from 11:00am until 4:00pm. Dinner served from 6:00pm until 10:00pm. Closed Saturdays and 3 weeks in August. Specialities: regional menu, home cooking. Hotel: 6 beds; 3 single rooms, 3 double rooms. Other points: bar, open to non-residents, terraces, pets welcome – check for details, car park, modern decor. Address: 5, rue des Platanes.
MME ANNE-MARIE DELROISE
Telephone: 59.04.60.45
⊗ ▽ 🏠 Map 8

## SOURZAC, Dordogne, 24400

### LES ROUTIERS, RN 89, between Bordeaux and Périgueux
Menu: 45 Frs (wine and coffee included). Restaurant: Breakfast served from 8:00am. Lunch served from 11:30am until 3:00pm. Dinner served from 6:00pm until 9:00pm. Closed Sundays. Specialities: regional menu, home cooking. Other points: bar, open to non-residents, children welcome, pets welcome – check for details, car park, traditional decor. Address: La Gravette.
MME SUZY JOSEPH
Telephone: 53.81.36.99
⊗ ▽ Map 8

## TARBES, Hautes-Pyrénées, 65000

### LE CLAUZIER
Menu: 45 Frs (wine included). Restaurant: Breakfast served from 7:00am. Closed Sundays. Specialities: home cooking. Other points: bar, open to non-residents, children welcome, pets welcome – check for details, car park, traditional decor. Address: 10, place Germain Claverie.
MR JEAN-MARC NOE
Telephone: 62.93.18.57
⊗ ▽ Map 9

### LE RELAIS DES PYRENEES, RN 117, the main road between Bayonne and Toulouse
Languages spoken: Spanish. Menu: 50 to 90 Frs. Restaurant: Breakfast served from 6:30am. Lunch served from 11:45am until 2:15pm. Dinner served from 7:30pm until 9:30pm. Closed Saturdays. Specialities: home cooking. Other points: bar, open to non-residents, à la carte menu, children welcome, lounge area, terraces, pets welcome – check for details, car park, modern decor. Address: Autoport des Pyrénées, Boulevard Kennedy.
MR JEAN-LOUIS PEREZ
Telephone: 62.93.26.06
⊗ ▽ Map 9

### LE VICTOR HUGO, RN 117, opposite the station
Languages spoken: English and Spanish. Menu: 30 to 95 Frs. Accommodation: 65 to 80 Frs (with WC). Restaurant: Breakfast served from 7:00am. Lunch served from 11:00am until 3:00pm. Dinner served from 6:00pm until 9:30pm. Closed Sundays. Specialities: confit de canard maison, magret de canard, gambas flambées, regional food, home cooking. Hotel: 8 beds; 8 double rooms. Other points: bar, open to non-residents, à la carte menu, children welcome, lounge area, pets welcome – check for details, car park. Address: 52, rue Victor Hugo.
MME PATRICIA JOUANLONG
Telephone: 62.93.36.71
⊗ ▽ 🏠 ☆ Map 9

## TEMPLE SUR LOT (LE), Lot-et-Garonne, 47110

### LE VAL DU LOT, RD 911, Villeneuve en Lot/Bordeaux/Agen/Bergerac

**Languages spoken:** English. **Menu:** 47 Frs to 115 Frs. **Accommodation:** 100 to 120 Frs. **Restaurant:** Breakfast served from 7:00am. Lunch served from midday until 2:30pm. Dinner served from 7:00pm until 10:00pm. Closed Saturdays and from 10 August to 10 September. **Specialities:** regional menu, home cooking. **Hotel:** 5 beds; with shower, bath. **Other points:** bar, open to non-residents, à la carte menu, children welcome, lounge area, terraces, pets welcome – check for details, car park, traditional decor. **Address:** Gouneau.
MR LIONEL HUTREL
**Telephone:** 53.84.90.26
⊗ ♀ ⌂ Map 8

## THENON, Dordogne, 24210

### CHEZ SERGE, RN 89, between Brive and Périgueux

**Languages spoken:** English and Spanish. **Menu:** 50 to 90 Frs. **Accommodation:** 80 to 120 Frs. **Restaurant:** Breakfast served from 4:00am. **Specialities:** regional menu, home cooking. **Hotel:** 10 beds; 5 single rooms, 5 double rooms with shower, private WC. **Other points:** bar, open to non-residents, à la carte menu, children welcome, lounge area, terraces, pets welcome – check for details, car park, traditional decor. **Address:** Les Tournissous.
MR SERGE LEYMARIE
**Telephone:** 53.05.20.31
⊗ ♀ ⌂ Map 8

## TOCTOUCAU CESTAS, Gironde, 33610

### RESTAURANT DE LA STATION SCHELL, RN 250, the main road between Bordeaux and Arcachon

**Languages spoken:** English and Spanish. **Menu:** 38 to 120 Frs. **Restaurant:** Breakfast served from 7:00am. **Specialities:** home cooking. **Other points:** bar, open to non-residents, à la carte menu, children welcome, terraces, pets welcome – check for details, car park, traditional decor. **Address:** 101–2, avenue du Maréchal de Tassigny.
MR XAVIER FABRA
**Telephone:** 56.68.03.13
⊗ ♀ Map 8

## TOULOUSE, Haute-Garonne, 31300

### LE PROGRES, RN 124, Auch

**Menu:** 60 to 220 Frs. **Restaurant:** Breakfast served from 7:00am. Lunch served from midday until 2:00pm. Dinner served from 7:00pm until 10:00pm. Closed Sundays and in August. **Specialities:** regional menu. **Other points:** bar, open to non-residents, à la carte menu, traditional decor. **Address:** 185, route de Bayonne.
MR FÉLIX OBER
**Telephone:** 61.49.22.75
⊗ ♀ Map 9

## TREBES, Aude, 11800

### LE RELAIS DES CAPUCINS, RN 113, Narbonne

**Languages spoken:** English and Spanish. **Menu:** 58 Frs (wine included). **Accommodation:** 90 to 130 Frs. **Restaurant:** Breakfast served from 6:00am. Lunch served from 11:30am until 2:00pm. Dinner served from 7:00pm until 10:00pm. Closed Saturdays, 1 week in July and 3 weeks in January. **Specialities:** regional menu, home cooking. **Hotel:** 11 beds. **Other points:** bar, open to non-residents, children welcome, pets welcome – check for details, car park, traditional decor. **Address:** 34, route de Narbonne.
MR GILBERT LAFFONT
**Telephone:** 68.78.70.07
⊗ ♀ ⌂ Map 10

## TRIE SUR BAISE, Hautes-Pyrénées, 65220

### CAFE RESTAURANT DE LA PAIX, RD 632

**Menu:** 50 Frs (wine included). **Restaurant:** Breakfast served from 6:30am. Lunch served from 10:00am until 3:00pm. Dinner served from 7:30pm until 10:00pm. Closed Wednesdays. **Specialities:** home cooking. **Other points:** bar, open to non-residents, children welcome, pets welcome – check for details, car park, traditional decor. **Address:** 37, rue des Monts de Bigorre.
MR JACKY CENAC
**Telephone:** 62.35.61.11
⊗ ♀ Map 9

## VALENCE SUR BAISE, Gers, 32310

### RESTAURANT LADOUCH

**Address:** Place de l'Hôtel de Ville.
MME GINETTE LADOUCH
**Telephone:** 62.28.50.45
Map 9

## VALERGUES, Hérault, 34130

### RELAIS DE VALERGUES, RN 113

**Languages spoken:** Spanish. **Restaurant:** Dinner served from midday until 11:00pm. Closed Sundays and in December. **Other points:** bar, car park. **Address:** Route Nationale 113.
MR CLAUDE BERNABÉ
**Telephone:** 67.86.75.27
⊗ ♀ Map 10

## VENSAC, Gironde, 33590

### RESTAURANT CHEZ NICOLE

**Menu:** 60 to 160 Frs. **Accommodation:** 120 to 180 Frs. **Restaurant:** Breakfast served from 8:00am. Lunch served from midday until 2:00pm. Dinner served from 7:00pm until 9:00pm. **Specialities:** home cooking. **Hotel:** 6 beds; 3 single rooms, 3 double rooms with shower. **Other points:** bar, open to non-residents, à la carte menu, children welcome, terraces, pets welcome – check for details, car park, modern decor. **Address:** 24, Grande Rue.
MME NICOLE FIGEROU
**Telephone:** 56.09.44.05
⊗ ⍾ 🏠 Map 8

## VIC EN BIGORRE, Hautes-Pyrénées, 65500

### LE RANCH, Auch

**Menu:** 55 to 120 Frs. **Restaurant:** Breakfast served from 7:00am. Lunch served from midday until 3:00pm. Dinner served from 8:00pm until 10:00pm. Closed Saturdays and in October. **Specialities:** regional menu, home cooking. **Other points:** bar, open to non-residents, à la carte menu, children welcome, lounge area, terraces, pets welcome – check for details, car park. **Address:** Route de Rabastens de Bigorre.
MR BERNARD GRIFFON
**Telephone:** 62.96.72.32, 62.96.22.84
⊗ ⍾ Map 9

## VIC LA GARDIOLE, Hérault, 34110

### LA RESERVE, RN 112

**Languages spoken:** Spanish. **Restaurant:** Breakfast served from 5:30am. Lunch served from 11:30am until 2:30pm. Closed Sundays. **Other points:** bar, car park. **Address:** Route Nationale 112.
MME CONCEPTION MARTINEZ
**Telephone:** 67.48.14.33
⊗ ⍾ Map 10

## VIC LE FESQ, Gard, 30260

### RELAIS DE LA NOUVELLE, the main road between Nîmes and Montpellier

**Restaurant:** Breakfast served from 6:00am. Lunch served from 11:00am until 2:00pm. Dinner served from 7:00pm until 8:30pm. Closed Saturdays, Sundays and public holidays (out of season). **Specialities:** regional menu, home cooking. **Other points:** bar, open to non-residents, à la carte menu, terraces, pets welcome – check for details, car park, traditional decor. **Address:** La Nouvelle.
MR HUBERT TANI
**Telephone:** 66.77.82.81
⊗ ⍾ Map 10

## VILLEFRANCHE DE ROUERGUE, Aveyron, 12200

### RELAIS DES CABRIERES, RD 926, the main road between Montauban and Toulouse

**Menu:** 45 to 60 Frs. **Restaurant:** Breakfast served from 8:00am. Lunch served from 11:00am until 3:00pm. Closed Sundays. **Specialities:** home cooking. **Other points:** bar, open to non-residents, pets welcome – check for details, car park, traditional decor. **Address:** Route de Montauban.
MR ALAIN TOULOUSE
**Telephone:** 65.81.16.99
⊗ ⍾ Map 9

## VILLENEUVE D'AVEYRON, Aveyron, 12260

### AUBERGE DE LA TOUR – CHEZ ROSY ET FRANCIS

**Menu:** 48 to 120 Frs. **Restaurant:** Breakfast served from 7:00am. Lunch served from 11:30am until 2:00pm. Dinner served from 7:00pm until 8:30pm. Closed Saturdays and 15 days in August. **Specialities:** home cooking. **Other points:** bar, open to non-residents, pets welcome – check for details, car park, traditional decor. **Address:** Faubourg Saint Roch.
MME ROSE-MARY SCUDIER-LAVAL
**Telephone:** 65.81.75.62
⊗ ⍾ Map 9

### L'OREE DU BOIS, RD 922

**Languages spoken:** Spanish. **Menu:** 55 to 120 Frs. **Restaurant:** Breakfast served from 8:00am. Lunch served from midday until 2:00pm. Dinner served from 7:00pm until 9:00pm. Closed Saturdays and in September. **Specialities:** home cooking. **Other points:** bar, open to non-residents, children welcome, pets welcome – check for details. **Address:** Septfonds.
MR MICHEL BOULESQUE
**Telephone:** 65.81.65.77
⊗ ⍾ Map 9

## VILLENEUVE DE RIVIERE, Haute-Garonne, 31800

### L'ESCALE, RN 117, between Toulouse and Irun

**Languages spoken:** Spanish. **Menu:** 50 to 70 Frs. **Accommodation:** 100 to 150 Frs. **Restaurant:** Breakfast served from 5:15am. Lunch served from 11:00am until 2:30pm. Dinner served from 6:30pm until 10:30pm. Closed Sundays. **Specialities:** regional menu, home cooking. **Hotel:** 9 beds; 8 single rooms, 1 double room with shower, television. **Other points:** bar, open to non-residents, à la carte menu, children welcome, terraces, pets welcome – check for details, car park, traditional decor. **Address:** Route Nationale 117.

MR GÉRARD VALENTIN
**Telephone:** 61.89.39.05
⊗ 🍷 🏠 Map 9

# VILLENEUVE SUR LOT, Lot-et-Garonne, 47300

### *RELAIS DE GASCOGNE, RN 21, Agen*
**Languages spoken:** Spanish. **Menu:** 54 to 110 Frs.
**Accommodation:** 90 to 140 Frs. **Restaurant:** Lunch
served from 11:45am until 2:00pm. Dinner served from
7:00pm until 10:00pm. Closed Sundays. **Specialities:**
regional menu. **Hotel:** 8 beds; 2 single rooms, 6 double
rooms with shower. **Other points:** bar, open to non-
residents, à la carte menu, children welcome, pets
welcome – check for details, car park, traditional decor.

**Address:** 31, avenue du Général Leclerc.
MR ALAIN GUIRAUD
**Telephone:** 53.70.06.48, 53.49.14.16
⊗ 🍷 🏠 Map 8

# VILLETELLE, Hérault, 34400

### *BOUQUET RESTAURATION, A 9, between Nîmes and Montpellier*
**Menu:** 60 to 70 Frs. **Restaurant:** Breakfast served from
5:00am. **Other points:** à la carte menu, children
welcome, lounge area, terraces, modern decor. **Address:**
A 9 Aire d'Ambrusson Nord.
BOUQUET SA
⊗ Map 10

# South East France

## ALBENC (L'), Isère, 38470

### AUBERGE DU VERCORS, RN 92, the main road between Grenoble and Valence

**Restaurant:** Breakfast served from 6:30am. Lunch served from midday until 2:00pm. Dinner served from 7:00pm until 9:00pm. Closed Sundays and the 1st week in August. **Specialities:** home cooking. **Other points:** bar, open to non-residents, pets welcome – check for details, car park, modern decor. **Address:** Place Jean Vinay.
MME CLAUDETTE TORRI
**Telephone:** 76.64.75.17
⊗ ⓨ Map 14

## ALBON, Drôme, 26140

### RELAIS DE LA TOUR D'ALBON, RN 7, Exit south Chanas, and then to north Valence

**Accommodation:** 120 to 140 Frs. **Restaurant:** Breakfast served from 5:30am. Lunch served from 11:00am until 3:00pm. Dinner served from 7:00pm until 10:30pm. Closed Sundays. **Specialities:** home cooking. **Hotel:** 13 beds; 9 single rooms, 4 double rooms with shower. **Other points:** bar, open to non-residents, terraces, pets welcome – check for details, car park, modern decor. **Address:** Route Nationale 7.
MR CAMILLE BERTRAND
**Telephone:** 75.03.11.22
⊗ ⓨ 🏠 Map 14

## ALIXAN, Drôme, 26300

### HOTEL ALPES PROVENCE, RN 532, exit north Valence, towards Grenoble

**Languages spoken:** German and English. **Menu:** 55 to 150 Frs. **Accommodation:** 140 to 300 Frs. **Restaurant:** Breakfast served from 6:00am. Lunch served from midday until 2:00pm. Dinner served from 7:30pm until 9:30pm. **Specialities:** regional menu. **Hotel:** 22 beds; 22 double rooms with shower, bath, private WC, television, telephone. **Other points:** bar, open to non-residents, à la carte menu, children welcome, terraces, pets welcome – check for details, car park, traditional decor. **Address:** Aire de Bayanne
MR JEAN-CLAUDE BOCAUD
**Telephone:** 75.47.02.84. **Fax:** 75.47.11.72
⊗ ⓨ 🏠 ☆☆ Map 14

## ALLEX, Drôme, 26400

### LE DAUPHINOIS, RN 7 and D 93, between Fiancey and Crest

**Menu:** 55 to 60 Frs. **Restaurant:** Breakfast served from 6:30am. Lunch served from midday until 1:30pm. Dinner served from 7:00pm until 9:30pm. **Specialities:** home cooking. **Other points:** bar, open to non-residents, terraces, pets welcome – check for details, car park, traditional decor. **Address:** Quartier de la Butte.
MR MARCEL PISANO
**Telephone:** 75.62.61.69
⊗ ⓨ Map 14

## AMBERIEU EN BUGEY, Ain, 01500

### LE RELAIS DU BUGEY HUBERT – CHEZ DENISE, RN 504

**Restaurant:** Dinner served from midday until midnight. Closed Sundays and in August. **Other points:** bar. **Address:** 84, avenue Jules Pellaudin.
MME DENISE HUBERT
**Telephone:** 74.38.10.27
⊗ ⓨ Map 14

## AMPUIS, Rhône, 69420

### AUX PORTES DE PROVENCE, RN 86, Nîmes

**Accommodation:** 80 to 150 Frs. **Restaurant:** Breakfast served from 7:00am. Lunch served from midday until 2:30pm. Dinner served from 7:00pm until 10:00pm. Closed Wednesdays. **Specialities:** home cooking. **Hotel:** 9 beds; 3 single rooms, 6 double rooms with shower, bath. **Other points:** bar, open to non-residents, children welcome, lounge area, pets welcome – check for details, car park. **Address:** Route Nationale 86, les Allées.
MR MAURICE TERPEND
**Telephone:** 74.56.10.31. **Fax:** 74.56.19.10
⊗ ⓨ 🏠 Map 14

## ANDANCETTE, Drôme, 26140

### PIZZERIA DU SOLEIL, RN 7, the main road between Lyon and Valence, exit Chanas

**Menu:** 55 to 130 Frs. **Accommodation:** 100 to 280 Frs. **Restaurant:** Breakfast served from 5:00am. Lunch served from midday until 2:00pm. Dinner served from

7:00pm until 9:30pm. Closed Sundays. **Specialities:** home cooking. **Hotel:** 11 beds; 1 single room, 10 double rooms with shower, bath, private WC. **Other points:** bar, open to non-residents, à la carte menu, terraces, pets welcome – check for details, car park, modern decor. **Address:** Route Nationale 7.
MME MARLAINE SENEZ
**Telephone:** 75.03.11.53
⊗ ⵎ 🏠 Map 14

## APT, Vaucluse, 84400

### LE RELAIS DU LAC, RN 100, the main road between Apt and Avignon
**Languages spoken:** English. **Menu:** 60 Frs.
**Restaurant:** Breakfast served from 7:00am.
**Specialities:** home cooking. **Other points:** bar, open to non-residents, terraces, pets welcome – check for details, car park. **Address:** Route Nationale 100.
MR YVON JEAN
**Telephone:** 90.74.01.10
⊗ ⵎ Map 13

## ARBRESLE (L'), Rhône, 69210

### AUX VOSGIENS, RN 7, opposite the supermarket 'Super U'
**Menu:** 55 Frs. **Restaurant:** Breakfast served from 8:00am. Lunch served from 11:00am until 4:00pm. Closed Saturdays and the 1st fortnight in August. **Specialities:** home cooking. **Other points:** bar, open to non-residents, pets welcome – check for details, car park, traditional decor. **Address:** 49, rue Gabriel Péri.
MME EVELYNE PÉCHARD
**Telephone:** 74.01.00.13
⊗ ⵎ Map 14

### LE RELAIS DES ROUTIERS, RN 7
**Languages spoken:** English and Spanish. **Restaurant:** Closed Saturdays and from 23 December to 8 January. **Other points:** bar. **Address:** 27, route de Paris.
MME MONIQUE GIRAUDIER
**Telephone:** 74.01.07.59
⊗ ⵎ Map 14

### RELAIS DES ROUTIERS, RN 89, towards l'Arbresle via Clermont Ferrand
**Menu:** 55 Frs. **Restaurant:** Breakfast served from 6:00am. Closed Saturdays. **Specialities:** home cooking. **Other points:** bar, pets welcome – check for details. **Address:** 91, rue Gabriel Péri.
MME MARIE-ANTOINETTE DURIX-MICHAUD
**Telephone:** 74.01.05.81
⊗ ⵎ Map 14

## ARCS SUR ARGENS (LES), Var, 83460

### HOTEL DE L'AVENIR
**Menu:** 55 to 73 Frs. **Accommodation:** 80 to 130 Frs.

**Restaurant:** Lunch served from midday until 2:30pm. Dinner served from 7:00pm until 9:30pm. **Hotel:** 9 beds. **Other points:** bar, car park. **Address:** Rue Jean Jaurès.
MME MARIE-JEANNE HORTAL
**Telephone:** 94.73.30.58
⊗ ⵎ 🏠 Map 13

## ARLES, Bouches-de-Rhône, 13200

### LE RELAIS DU PASSAGE A NIVEAU, RN 113
**Languages spoken:** German, English, Spanish, Italian. **Restaurant:** Closed Sundays. **Hotel:** 8 beds. **Other points:** bar. **Address:** Route de Tarascon, 31, avenue de la Libération.
ANTOINE ET LAURENCE PECH-FAURE
**Telephone:** 90.96.06.64
⊗ ⵎ 🏠 Map 13

## ASTET, Ardèche, 07330

### LE RELAIS DE LA SOURCE DE L'ARDECHE
**Menu:** 52 Frs. **Restaurant:** Breakfast served from 6:00am. **Specialities:** home cooking. **Other points:** bar. **Address:** Col de la Chavade.
MME ANNE-MARIE SOULET
**Telephone:** 75.87.20.91
⊗ ⵎ Map 14

## AUBIGNAS, Ardèche, 07400

### CAFE DE LA GARE, RN 102, between Montélimar and le Puy en Velay
**Languages spoken:** English and Spanish. **Accommodation:** 75 to 200 Frs. **Restaurant:** Breakfast served from 6:30am. Closed Sundays. **Specialities:** regional menu, home cooking. **Hotel:** 5 beds; with shower, bath, private WC. **Other points:** bar, open to non-residents, à la carte menu, lounge area, terraces, car park. **Address:** Quartier de la Gare.
MLLE ELISABETH BORNE
**Telephone:** 75.52.43.89
⊗ ⵎ 🏠 Map 14

## AVIGNON, Vaucluse, 84140

### RELAIS D'AVIGNON, RN 7, exit south Avignon
**Menu:** 57 to 150 Frs. **Accommodation:** 145 to 280 Frs. **Restaurant:** Breakfast served from 5:00am. Lunch served from 11:00am until 3:00pm. Dinner served from 7:00pm until midnight. **Specialities:** Toro à la Gardiane, regional food. **Hotel:** 19 beds; 6 single rooms, 13 double rooms with shower, private WC, television, telephone. **Other points:** bar, open to non-residents, à la carte menu, children welcome, lounge area, terraces, modern decor. **Address:** La Petite

Castelette, Montfavet.
MRS DANIEL ET LAURENT SAVRY
**Telephone:** 90.84.18.28. **Fax:** 90.84.17.60
⊗ ⚲ ⌂ ☆☆ Map 13

## BAIX, Ardèche, 07210

### RESTAURANT MA CAMPAGNE
**Menu:** 50 Frs. **Restaurant:** Closed Sundays.
**Specialities:** home cooking. **Other points:** open to non-residents, terraces, pets welcome – check for details, car park, modern decor. **Address:** Quartier des Lilas.
MME NARA ARSAC
**Telephone:** 75.85.80.26
⊗ Map 14

## BALAN LA VALBONNE, Ain, 01360

### LE FRONT DE BANDIERE
**Menu:** 53 Frs. **Accommodation:** 80 to 100 Frs.
**Restaurant:** Lunch served from 11:45am until 3:00pm. Dinner served from 7:45pm until 10:00pm. **Specialities:** couscous, paëlla, choucroute, home cooking. **Hotel:** 10 beds; 5 single rooms, 5 double rooms with shower.
**Other points:** bar, open to non-residents, terraces, pets welcome – check for details, car park, traditional decor.
**Address:** Route de Balan.
MR ANDRÉ VOUSSATIOUK-KOVAL
**Telephone:** 78.06.35.61
⊗ ⚲ ⌂ Map 14

## BARCELONNETTE, Alpes-de-Hautes-Provence, 04400

### LES SEOLANES, le Col de Larche (Italy)
**Languages spoken:** English and Italian. **Menu:** 80 to 120 Frs. **Accommodation:** 100 to 190 Frs. **Restaurant:** Breakfast served from 7:00am. Lunch served from midday until 1:30pm. Closed 1 day per week (out of season) and in January. **Specialities:** home cooking.
**Hotel:** 6 beds; 1 single room, 5 double rooms with shower. **Other points:** bar, open to non-residents, terraces, car park, traditional decor. **Address:** Les Thuiles.
MR HUBERT MAURE
**Telephone:** 92.81.07.37
⊗ ⚲ ⌂ ☆ Map 13

## BARNAS, Ardèche, 07330

### LES ROUTIERS, RN 102
**Menu:** 60 to 115 Frs. **Accommodation:** 120 to 160 Frs.
**Restaurant:** Lunch served from midday until 1:30pm.
Closed Sundays. **Specialities:** home cooking. **Hotel:** 12 beds; 9 single rooms, 3 double rooms with shower.
**Other points:** bar, open to non-residents, terraces, pets welcome – check for details, car park, traditional decor.
**Address:** Route Nationale 102.
MME ROSINE CELLIER
**Telephone:** 75.36.40.78
⊗ ⚲ ⌂ Map 14

## BARQUE (LA), Bouches-de-Rhône, 13710

### LE RELAIS DES 4 CHEMINS
**Menu:** 58 Frs. **Restaurant:** Breakfast served from 4:00am. Lunch served from 11:30am until 2:00pm.
Closed Saturdays. **Specialities:** regional menu, home cooking. **Other points:** bar, open to non-residents, terraces, car park.
MR GIRARDI
**Telephone:** 42.58.60.03
⊗ ⚲ Map 13

## BEAUCROISSANT, Isère, 38140

### LES ROUTIERS DU CHAMP DE FOIRE, RD 159
**Menu:** 55 to 60 Frs. **Restaurant:** Lunch served from 11:00am until 2:30pm. Dinner served from 7:00pm until 9:00pm. Closed Sundays, 15 days in May and 15 days in October. **Specialities:** home cooking. **Other points:** bar, open to non-residents, terraces, pets welcome – check for details, car park, traditional decor. **Address:** Le Bain.
MME MARIE-THÉRESE BLAIN
**Telephone:** 76.91.05.17
⊗ ⚲ Map 14

## BEAUSSET (LE), Var, 83330

### LE RESTAURANT DE L'AERODROME DU CASTELLET, RN 8
**Languages spoken:** English and Portugese.
**Restaurant:** Lunch served from 11:30am until 3:00pm.
Closed Saturdays and in August. **Specialities:** home cooking. **Other points:** bar, open to non-residents, children welcome. **Address:** Route Nationale 8.
MME MARIE-FRANCE GAUTIER
**Telephone:** 94.90.71.48
⊗ ⚲ Map 13

## BELLEVILLE, Rhône, 69220

### RESTAURANT BELLERIVE, RD 37, exit Belleville, towards Chatillon
**Menu:** 54 to 98 Frs. **Restaurant:** Breakfast served from 8:15am. Lunch served from midday until 3:00pm.
Dinner served from 7:00pm until 9:30pm. **Specialities:** fritures de Saône, grenouilles, regional food, home cooking. **Other points:** bar, open to non-residents, terraces, pets welcome – check for details, car park.
**Address:** 6, avenue du Port.
MR LUCIEN PAGES
**Telephone:** 74.66.33.82
⊗ ⚲ Map 14

## BELLEVILLE SUR SAONE, Rhône, 69220

### RELAIS DU BEAUJOLAIS, A 6
**Languages spoken:** English. **Restaurant:** Open 24

hours. **Specialities:** regional menu. **Other points:** à la carte menu, children welcome, terraces, pets welcome – check for details, car park. **Address:** Aire de Service de Taponas, sens Lyon/Paris.
**Telephone:** 74.66.19.80
⊗ Map 14

## BELLEY, Ain, 01300

### RELAIS DE LA GARE, RN 504
**Menu:** 50 Frs (coffee included). **Accommodation:** 80 to 130 Frs. **Restaurant:** Dinner served from midday until 10:00pm. Closed Saturdays and December. **Hotel:** 6 beds. **Other points:** bar. **Address:** Avenue de la Gare.
MME ELISABETH BAVU
**Telephone:** 79.81.06.60
⊗ ♀ ⌂ Map 14

## BELLIGNAT, Ain, 01810

### LA BONNE AUBERGE – LES ROUTIERS, RN 840, exit Saint Martin de la Frene, towards Lyon/Nantua
**Menu:** 55 Frs (wine and coffee included). **Restaurant:** Breakfast served from 6:30am. Lunch served from midday until 1:30pm. Dinner served from 7:30pm until 8:30pm. Closed Sundays and in August. **Specialities:** regional menu, home cooking. **Hotel:** 4 beds; 1 single room, 3 double rooms with shower, private WC, telephone. **Other points:** bar, open to non-residents, children welcome, car park, traditional decor. **Address:** 11, avenue Oyonnax.
MR MICHEL DETOUILLON
**Telephone:** 74.77.24.18
⊗ ♀ Map 14

## BERRE L'ETANG, Bouches-de-Rhône, 13130

### RESTAURANT L'ENTENTE, RN 113, Marseille
**Languages spoken:** German, English. **Menu:** 50 Frs (wine included). **Restaurant:** Breakfast served from 6:30am. Lunch served from 11:00am until 6:00pm. Closed Saturdays, Sundays and in August. **Specialities:** home cooking. **Other points:** pets welcome – check for details, car park, traditional decor. **Address:** Route du Moulin Vieux.
MR DONAT LE GUENNEC
**Telephone:** 42.85.37.44
⊗ Map 13

## BEVENAIS, Isère, 38690

### LE RELAIS DE MI PLAINE, RN 85, the main road between Lyon and Grenoble
**Languages spoken:** English and Spanish. **Menu:** 59 to 75 Frs. **Accommodation:** 130 to 180 Frs. **Restaurant:** Breakfast served from 6:30am. Lunch served from 11:30am until 3:00pm. Dinner served from 7:00pm until

10:00pm. **Specialities:** home cooking. **Hotel:** 10 beds; 7 single rooms, 3 double rooms with shower, private WC, television. **Other points:** bar, open to non-residents, children welcome, lounge area, terraces, pets welcome – check for details, car park, modern decor. **Address:** Mi Plaine, Route Nationale 85.
MR MICHEL FERNANDEZ
**Telephone:** 76.93.21.03
⊗ ♀ ⌂ Map 14

## BLAUSASC, Alpes Maritimes, 06440

### LE RELAIS CAMPAGNARD
**Restaurant:** Dinner served from midday until 9:00pm. Closed Sundays. **Other points:** bar. **Address:** Pointe de Blausasc.
MME MARIE NICOLE NÉGRI
**Telephone:** 93.91.13.14
⊗ ♀ Map 13

## BLYES, Ain, 01150

### AUBERGE DE BLYES, exit Perouge Lagnieu
**Languages spoken:** English. **Menu:** 60 to 138 Frs. **Restaurant:** Breakfast served from 7:00am. Lunch served from 11:30am until 2:30pm. Dinner served from 7:00pm until 9:00pm. Closed Saturdays. **Specialities:** regional menu, home cooking. **Other points:** bar, open to non-residents, à la carte menu, children welcome, lounge area, terraces, pets welcome – check for details, car park, modern decor. **Address:** Lieu dit 'La Plaine de l'Ain'.
MR PATRICE ASTIER
**Telephone:** 74.61.50.15
⊗ ♀ Map 14

## BOEN SUR LIGNON, Loire, 42130

### RELAIS ROUTIERS, RN 89, Clermont Ferrand
**Menu:** 53 Frs. **Accommodation:** 80 Frs. **Restaurant:** Breakfast served from 7:00am. Closed Saturdays and the 1st fortnight in October. **Specialities:** home cooking. **Hotel:** 3 beds; 1 single room, 2 double rooms with shower, bath. **Other points:** bar, open to non-residents, children welcome, pets welcome – check for details, car park, modern decor. **Address:** 83, rue de Lyon.
MME LAURENCE CARTON
**Telephone:** 77.24.44.76
⊗ ♀ Map 14

## BOLLENE, Vaucluse, 84500

### LE RELAIS DE LA CROISIERE, RN 7
**Languages spoken:** English and Spanish. **Accommodation:** 100 to 180 Frs. **Restaurant:** Breakfast served from 4:30am. Closed Sundays. **Hotel:** 15 beds. **Other points:** bar, car park. **Address:** La

Croisière, Route Nationale 7.
MR SERGE BACON
**Telephone:** 90.30.08.53
⊗ ⵟ 🏠 Map 13

## BONSON, Loire, 42160

### RESTAURNT DES SPORTS, RN 198, between Andrézieu and Bouthéon or Saint Just and Saint Rambert

**Languages spoken:** English. **Menu:** 50 to 200 Frs.
**Accommodation:** 90 to 120 Frs. **Restaurant:** Breakfast served from 7:00am. Lunch served from midday until 2:30pm. Dinner served from 7:00pm until 8:30pm. Closed Sundays and in August. **Specialities:** home cooking. **Hotel:** 7 beds; 4 single rooms, 3 double rooms with shower, bath, television. **Other points:** bar, children welcome, pets welcome – check for details, car park. **Address:** 14, avenue de Saint Rambert.
MR ALAIN CHAZELLE
**Telephone:** 77.55.20.12
⊗ ⵟ 🏠 ☆ Map 14

## BORMES LES MIMOSAS, Var, 83230

### LE RELAIS DES 4 SAISONS, RN 98, the main road between Toulon and Saint Tropez

**Languages spoken:** English, Spanish and Italian.
**Menu:** 63 to 85 Frs. **Restaurant:** Breakfast served from 6:90am. Lunch served from 11:30am until 2:30pm. Dinner served from 7:00pm until 10:00pm. **Specialities:** regional menu, home cooking. **Other points:** bar, open to non-residents, à la carte menu, children welcome, terraces. **Address:** 4229, avenue Lou Mistraou.
MR ALDO ALDRIGHETTONI
**Telephone:** 94.71.87.05
⊗ ⵟ Map 13

## BOUC BEL AIR, Bouches-de-Rhône, 13320

### AUBERGE DES MURIERS, RN 8, Aix en Provence

**Menu:** 55 Frs. **Accommodation:** 100 to 140 Frs.
**Restaurant:** Breakfast served from 6:00am. Lunch served from 11:45am until 2:30pm. Dinner served from 7:00pm until 9:00pm. Closed Saturdays. **Specialities:** regional menu, home cooking. **Hotel:** 11 beds; 5 single rooms, 6 double rooms with shower. **Other points:** bar, terraces, pets welcome – check for details, car park, traditional decor. **Address:** Plan Marseillais.
MR FRÉDÉRIC DHILLY
**Telephone:** 42.22.08.04
⊗ ⵟ 🏠 Map 13

### LES ROUTIERS DE LA MALLE, RN 8

**Menu:** 50 Frs. **Restaurant:** Breakfast served from 6:00am. Closed Saturdays. **Specialities:** home cooking. **Other points:** bar, pets welcome – check for details, car park. **Address:** Lieu dit 'La Malle'.

MR JEAN-LOUIS ZANON
**Telephone:** 42.22.08.84
⊗ ⵟ Map 13

## BOUGE CHAMBALUD, Isère, 38150

### LA FONTAINE DU VERNAY, between Chanas and Grenoble

**Languages spoken:** German and English. **Menu:** 68 to 110 Frs. **Accommodation:** 150 Frs. **Restaurant:** Breakfast served from 6:30am. Lunch served from midday until 3:00pm. Dinner served from 7:00pm until 9:00pm. Closed Tuesdays. **Specialities:** regional menu, home cooking. **Hotel:** 6 beds; 2 single rooms, 4 double rooms. **Other points:** bar, open to non-residents, children welcome, terraces, pets welcome – check for details, car park, traditional decor.
MME FRANÇOISE NIVELLE
**Telephone:** 74.84.15.18
⊗ ⵟ 🏠 Map 14

## BOURG DE PEAGE, Drôme, 26300

### RELAIS ROUTIER DU VERCORS, RN 532, between Pizançon and Saint Nazaire in Royan

**Menu:** 60 Frs. **Restaurant:** Breakfast served from 5:00am. Lunch served from 11:45am until 2:00pm. Dinner served from 7:30pm until 10:00pm. Closed Sundays. **Specialities:** home cooking. **Other points:** bar, open to non-residents, pets welcome – check for details, car park, traditional decor. **Address:** L'Ecancière.
**Telephone:** 75.48.83.44
⊗ ⵟ Map 14

## BOURGOIN JALLIEU, Isère, 38300

### RELAIS DE LA MAISON BLANCHE, RN 85, exit Bourgain, towards Grenoble

**Menu:** 60 Frs. **Restaurant:** Breakfast served from 5:00am. Lunch served from 11:15am until 2:00pm. Closed Saturdays, 3 weeks in August and 1 week at Christmas. **Specialities:** home cooking. **Other points:** bar, open to non-residents, à la carte menu, pets welcome – check for details, car park, traditional decor. **Address:** Route Nationale 85, Nivolas Vermelle.
MR ANDRÉ PILOZ
**Telephone:** 74.27.92.86
⊗ ⵟ Map 14

## BREUIL (LE), Rhône, 69620

### CAFE DE L'ESPERANCE, RD 485, between Lyon and Charolles

**Languages spoken:** English and Spanish. **Menu:** 55 to 125 Frs. **Restaurant:** Breakfast served from 6:30am. Lunch served from midday until 1:30pm. Closed Mondays. **Specialities:** home cooking. **Other points:** bar, open to non-residents, children welcome, terraces, pets welcome – check for details, car park, traditional

decor. **Address:** Le Gélicain, Route Départementale 485.
MR MARC THIVIN
**Telephone:** 74.71.64.82
⊗ ♀ Map 14

## BRIANCON, Hautes Alpes, 05100

*LA LANTERNE, RN 94, 2km south of Briançon*
**Languages spoken:** English, Spanish and Italian.
**Menu:** 60 Frs. **Restaurant:** Breakfast served from
8:00am. Lunch served from 11:30am until 2:00pm.
Dinner served from 6:30pm until 9:00pm. Closed from
15 September to 30 May. **Specialities:** home cooking.
**Other points:** bar, open to non-residents, terraces, pets
welcome – check for details, car park, traditional decor.
**Address:** Chamandrin.
MR RENÉ PARISOT
**Telephone:** 92.21.12.33
⊗ ♀ Map 13

## CAMP DU CASTELLET (LE), Var, 83330

*CHEZ MIMI ET BELETTE, RN 8*
**Restaurant:** Breakfast served from 5:30am. Lunch
served from 11:00am until 2:00pm. Dinner served from
7:00pm until 10:00pm. Closed Sundays. **Other points:**
bar, car park. **Address:** Route Nationale 8.
MME ARLETTE AUBRY
**Telephone:** 94.90.70.53
⊗ ♀ Map 13

## CANNES LA BOCCA, Alpes Maritimes, 06150

*CAVE DE LA ROUBINE*
**Menu:** 52 Frs. **Restaurant:** Breakfast served from
7:00am. Dinner served from midday until 10:00pm.
Closed Sundays. **Other points:** bar, terraces, car park.
**Address:** 40, avenue de la Roubine.
MME JEANINE CANTON
**Telephone:** 93.47.77.10
⊗ ♀ Map 13

## CANNET DES MAURES (LE), Var, 83340

*AUBERGE LES QUATRE VENTS, RN 7,*
*exit le Luc, towards Vidaubau*
**Languages spoken:** Italian. **Menu:** 60 Frs (wine and
coffee included). **Restaurant:** Breakfast served from
5:00am. Lunch served from 11:30am until 5:00pm.
Dinner served from 6:30pm until midnight. **Specialities:**
home cooking. **Other points:** bar, open to non-residents,
pets welcome – check for details, car park, traditional
decor. **Address:** Route Nationale 7.
MME ANTONIA SAPPA
**Telephone:** 94.60.96.41
⊗ ♀ Map 13

## CARNOULES, Var, 83660

*CHEZ DOUDOU, RN 97, between Toulon*
*and Nice via le Luc*
**Languages spoken:** Italian. **Menu:** 53 to 170 Frs.
**Accommodation:** 100 Frs. **Restaurant:** Breakfast
served from 6:15am. Lunch served from 11:30am until
2:00pm. Dinner served from 7:30pm until 9:00pm.
Closed Saturdays and 15 days in September.
**Specialities:** home cooking. **Hotel:** 5 beds; 1 single
room, 4 double rooms. **Other points:** bar, open to non-
residents, à la carte menu, children welcome, terraces,
pets welcome – check for details, car park, modern
decor. **Address:** 20, rue Pierre Sémard.
MR ADRIEN PIASCO
**Telephone:** 94.28.33.15
⊗ ♀ ⌂ Map 13

## CARPENTRAS, Vaucluse, 84200

*RESTAURANT DU MARCHE GARE, RN*
*538*
**Languages spoken:** Spanish. **Menu:** 58 Frs (wine
included). **Restaurant:** Breakfast served from 6:00am.
Lunch served from 11:30am until 2:30pm. Dinner served
from 7:00pm until 8:30pm. Closed Sundays. **Specialities:**
home cooking. **Other points:** bar, open to non-residents,
children welcome, pets welcome – check for details, car
park, modern decor. **Address:** Route de Velleron.
MR BERNARD GIL
**Telephone:** 90.63.19.00
⊗ ♀ Map 13

## CAZAN, Bouches-de-Rhône, 13116

*L'ESCALIER, RN 7*
**Restaurant:** Closed Sundays. **Other points:** bar.
**Address:** Route Nationale 7.
MR ALEXANDRE GHIGO
**Telephone:** 90.59.13.15
⊗ ♀ Map 13

## CEIGNES, Ain, 01430

*RELAIS DU BUGEY, A 40*
**Languages spoken:** English. **Restaurant:** Breakfast
served from 7:00am. **Specialities:** regional menu. **Other
points:** à la carte menu, lounge area, terraces, pets
welcome – check for details, car park. **Address:** Aire de
Service de Ceignes, sens Mâcon/Chamonix.
**Telephone:** 74.75.60.06
⌂ Map 14

## CHAMPAGNEUX, Savoie, 73240

*RELAIS DES TROIS PROVINCES –*
*CHEZ NICOLE, RN 516, between Yenne and*
*Saint Genix sur Guiers*
**Menu:** 55 Frs. **Restaurant:** Breakfast served from

6:00am. Lunch served from 11:30am until 2:00pm. Closed Saturdays. **Specialities:** home cooking. **Other points:** bar, open to non-residents, pets welcome – check for details, car park, modern decor. **Address:** La Tuilière.
MME NICOLE CURTILLAT
**Telephone:** 76.31.86.97
⊗ ♀ Map 14

## CHARMES SUR L'HERBASSE,

Drôme, 26260

### RELAIS DU CABARET NEUF, RD 538, Romans

**Menu:** 55 to 115 Frs. **Restaurant:** Breakfast served from 7:00am. Lunch served from midday until 2:00pm. Dinner served from 7:00pm until 8:00pm. Closed Tuesdays and from 15 September to 15 October. **Specialities:** home cooking. **Other points:** bar, open to non-residents, pets welcome – check for details, car park. **Address:** Le Cabaret Neuf.
MR MICHEL DREVETON
**Telephone:** 75.45.65.65
⊗ ♀ Map 14

## CHARVIEU CHAVANIEU, Isère, 38230

### RELAIS DE L'INDUSTRIE

**Menu:** 60 Frs (wine and coffee included). **Restaurant:** Breakfast served from 6:30am. Closed Sundays. **Specialities:** home cooking. **Other points:** bar, open to non-residents. **Address:** Route de Lyon, la Léchère.
MR ELIE MESLATI
**Telephone:** 72.46.04.89
⊗ ♀ Map 14

## CHASSE SUR RHONE, Isère, 38670

### RESTAURANT ROUTIER – CHEZ BABETH, CD 12, the main road between Paris and Marseille, exit Saint Etienne

**Menu:** 57 to 67 Frs. **Restaurant:** Breakfast served from 6:00am. Lunch served from 11:00am until 2:15pm. Dinner served from 7:00pm until 10:00pm. Closed Saturdays. **Specialities:** home cooking. **Other points:** bar, open to non-residents, à la carte menu, pets welcome – check for details, car park, traditional decor. **Address:** 5, rue Pasteur.
MME ELISABETH MAROTTE
**Telephone:** 78.73.10.82
⊗ ♀ Map 14

## CHATEAUNEUF DE GADAGNE,

Vaucluse, 84470

### RESTAURANT DU MARCHE

**Languages spoken:** Spanish. **Menu:** 59 Frs. **Restaurant:** Breakfast served from 6:30am. Closed Sundays. **Other points:** bar, car park. **Address:** Place du Marché.

MR CLAUDE MICHELETTI
**Telephone:** 90.22.41.14
⊗ ♀ Map 13

## CHATEAUNEUF LES MARTIGUES, Bouches-de-Rhône, 13220

### L'OASIS, RN 568, between Martigues and Fos

**Menu:** 55 Frs. **Restaurant:** Breakfast served from 6:00am. Lunch served from 11:00am until 2:00pm. Dinner served from 7:00pm until 9:00pm. Closed Fridays. **Specialities:** home cooking. **Other points:** bar. **Address:** Route Nationale 568.
MR THIERRY DICHARD
**Telephone:** 42.79.88.35
⊗ ♀ Map 13

## CHATTE, Isère, 38160

### LE SIROCCO, RN 92, between Romans and Grenoble

**Menu:** 60 Frs. **Restaurant:** Breakfast served from 6:00am. Lunch served from 11:30am until 2:00pm. Closed Saturdays, from 1 to 15 August and from 23 December to 2 January. **Specialities:** home cooking. **Other points:** bar, open to non-residents, terraces, pets welcome – check for details, car park. **Address:** Quartier Saint Ferreol.
MR MAURICE MOYROUD
**Telephone:** 76.64.43.41. **Fax:** 76.64.45.95
⊗ ♀ Map 14

## CHORGES, Hautes Alpes, 05230

### HOTEL DES ALPES, RN 94, the main road between Gap and Briançon

**Menu:** 55 to 85 Frs. **Accommodation:** 130 to 260 Frs. **Restaurant:** Breakfast served from 7:00am. Lunch served from midday until 1:30pm. Dinner served from 7:30pm until 9:00pm. Closed from 1 October to 10 November. **Specialities:** salade Caturige, gratin Dauphinois, gigot pré-Alpes; regional food, home cooking. **Hotel:** 16 beds; 6 single rooms, 10 double rooms with shower, telephone. **Other points:** bar, à la carte menu, children welcome, lounge area, terraces, pets welcome – check for details, car park, traditional decor. **Address:** Avenue de la Gare.
MR ROGER MAUDUECH
**Telephone:** 92.50.60.08
⊗ ♀ ⌂ ☆ Map 13

## CLUSE (LA), Ain, 01460

### AU PETIT BAR, RN 79 and 84

**Menu:** 55 Frs. **Restaurant:** Breakfast served from 4:00am. Closed Sundays and in August. **Specialities:** home cooking. **Other points:** bar. **Address:** 1, rue du Lyonnais.

MR JEAN DUFOUR
**Telephone:** 74.76.03.57
⊗ ♀ Map 14

## COGOLIN, Var, 83310

### AUBERGE DU GISCLET, RN 98

**Restaurant:** Breakfast served from 8:00am. Closed Sundays. **Specialities:** home cooking. **Other points:** open to non-residents, à la carte menu, children welcome, terraces, car park. **Address:** Route Nationale 98.
MME NICOLE VIALENC
**Telephone:** 94.56.40.39
⊗ Map 13

## CORMORANCHE SUR SAONE, Ain, 01290

### AUBERGE CHEZ LA MERE MARTINET, RN 6, at Crèche sur Saône, 1st left at the lights

**Places of interest:** Facteur cheval, safari de Peaugre, tour d'Albon. Saintes (12km), Saint Jean d'Angely (10km), port miniature, Saint Savinien (site touristique). Port de la Rochelle, l'Ile de Ré, musée maritime, musée des automates. **Languages spoken:** German, English, Spanish. **Menu:** 68 to 220 Frs. **Accommodation:** 180 Frs. **Restaurant:** Lunch served from midday until 2:00pm. Dinner served from 7:30pm until 9:00pm. Closed Tuesdays and from 15 August to 15 September. **Specialities:** saucisson chaud à la Beaujolaise, suprême de volaille, regional food, home cooking. **Hotel:** 7 beds; 7 double rooms with shower, bath, television, telephone. **Other points:** bar, open to non-residents, à la carte menu, children welcome, terraces, pets welcome – check for details, car park, traditional decor. **Address:** Le Bourg.
MME GENEVIEVE MARTINET
**Telephone:** 85.36.20.40. **Fax:** 85.31.77.19
⊗ ♀ ⌂ ⛵ ☆☆ Map 14

## CORPS, Isère, 38970

### RESTAURANT DU TILLEUL, RN 85, between Grenoble and Gap

**Languages spoken:** German and English. **Menu:** 70 to 145 Frs. **Accommodation:** 180 to 310 Frs. **Restaurant:** Breakfast served from 7:00am. Lunch served from midday until 2:00pm. Dinner served from 7:00pm until 9:00pm. Closed in November and the 1st fortnight in December. **Specialities:** gratin Dauphinois, civet de porcelet, poulet aux écrevisses, regional food, home cooking. **Hotel:** 10 beds; 2 single rooms, 8 double rooms with shower, bath, private WC, television, telephone. **Other points:** bar, open to non-residents, à la carte menu, terraces, pets welcome – check for details, car park, modern decor. **Address:** Rue des Fossés.
MR CLAUDE JOURDAN
**Telephone:** 76.30.00.43
⊗ ♀ ⌂ ⛵ ☆☆ Map 14

## COURTHEZON, Vaucluse, 84350

### LE RELAIS DU SOLEIL, RN 7, between Orange and Avignon

**Languages spoken:** English, Spanish and Italian. **Menu:** 56 Frs. **Restaurant:** Breakfast served from 6:00am. Lunch served from 11:30am until 3:30pm. Dinner served from 6:30pm until 10:30pm. Closed Saturdays. **Specialities:** regional menu, home cooking. **Other points:** bar, open to non-residents, terraces, pets welcome – check for details, car park. **Address:** Route Nationale 7.
MME CHANTAL PONZO
**Telephone:** 90.70.74.36
⊗ ♀ Map 13

## COUSTELLET, Vaucluse, 84220

### LE CHEVAL BLANC, RN 100

**Languages spoken:** English and Spanish. **Restaurant:** Lunch served from 11:30am until 2:00pm. Closed Saturdays. **Specialities:** regional menu, home cooking. **Other points:** bar, open to non-residents, pets welcome – check for details, car park. **Address:** Cabrières d'Avignon.
MR YVES RAOUX
**Telephone:** 90.76.92.32
⊗ ♀ Map 13

## CREST, Drôme, 26400

### LE CHAMP DE MARS

**Languages spoken:** German. **Restaurant:** Breakfast served from 6:00am. Lunch served from midday until 2:00pm. Dinner served from 7:00pm until midnight. **Specialities:** home cooking. **Other points:** bar, open to non-residents, modern decor. **Address:** 8, place de la Liberté.
MR BERNARD GENTHON
**Telephone:** 75.40.61.06
⊗ ♀ Map 14

## CROIX VALMER (LA), Var, 83420

### LA CIGALE, RD 559, between la Foux and Cavalaire

**Menu:** 65 Frs. **Restaurant:** Lunch served from midday until 2:30pm. Dinner served from 7:30pm until 9:00pm. Closed Saturdays and from Christmas to New Year. **Specialities:** home cooking. **Other points:** bar, open to non-residents, à la carte menu, children welcome, pets welcome – check for details, car park, modern decor. **Address:** Route Départementale 559.
MR ERIC KORHEL
**Telephone:** 94.79.60.41
⊗ ♀ Map 13

## CRUAS, Ardèche, 07350

### RELAIS ROUTIER, RN 86

**Places of interest:** Loisirs (pêche, chasse, canoë,

piscine, tennis). **Menu:** 50 to 130 Frs. **Restaurant:**
Breakfast served from 6:00am. Lunch served from
10:00am until 5:00pm. Dinner served from 5:00pm until
11:00pm. **Specialities:** home cooking. **Other points:**
bar, open to non-residents, children welcome, pets
welcome – check for details, car park, traditional decor.
**Address:** La Devière.
MME SYLVIE MADEIRA
**Telephone:** 75.51.41.12
⊗ ℡ Map 14

## CUZIEU, Loire, 42330

### RESTAURANT DE LA MAIRIE, RN 82, between Saint Etienne and Roanne
**Menu:** 50 Frs. **Accommodation:** 110 to 160 Frs.
**Restaurant:** Breakfast served from 4:00am. Lunch served
from 11:00am until 3:00pm. Dinner served from 6:00pm
until 11:00pm. Closed Saturdays and in August.
**Specialities:** regional menu, home cooking. **Hotel:** 12 beds;
10 single rooms, 2 double rooms with shower, television.
**Other points:** bar, open to non-residents, children welcome,
pets welcome – check for details, car park, modern decor.
**Address:** Route Nationale 82, le Bourg.
MME JANINE DARD
**Telephone:** 77.54.88.21. **Fax:** 77.54.42.07
⊗ ℡ 🏠 Map 14

## DARDILLY, Rhône, 69570

### AUBERGE POLONAISE: CRACOVIE
**Languages spoken:** English and Polish. **Menu:** 60 Frs.
**Accommodation:** 110 to 130 Frs. **Restaurant:** Lunch
served from 11:30am until 2:00pm. Dinner served from
7:00pm until 9:30pm. Closed Sundays. **Hotel:** 8 beds.
**Other points:** bar, car park. **Address:** 22, Route
Nationale 7.
MR JEAN-JACQUES SADESKI
**Telephone:** 78.48.01.39
⊗ ℡ 🏠 Map 14

### LE CHENE ROND, RN 7, the main road between Lyon and Roanne
**Menu:** 54 Frs. **Restaurant:** Breakfast served from
6:30am. Lunch served from midday until 1:30pm.
Closed Saturdays and in August. **Specialities:** home
cooking. **Hotel:** 6 beds; with bath. **Other points:** bar,
car park. **Address:** 87, Route Nationale 7.
MR EMILE LAGOUTTE
**Telephone:** 78.87.15.48
⊗ ℡ 🏠 Map 14

### LE RELAIS DE LA BASCULE, RN 6, 23km after the toll for Villefranche sur Saône
**Languages spoken:** Italian and Portugese. **Menu:** 60
Frs. **Restaurant:** Breakfast served from 6:00am. Lunch
served from midday until 2:30pm. Dinner served from
7:00pm until 10:00pm. Closed Saturdays and in August.
**Specialities:** home cooking. **Other points:** bar, open to

non-residents, pets welcome – check for details, car
park, traditional decor. **Address:** Porte de Lyon, Route
Nationale 6.
MR ROGER MARTINS
**Telephone:** 78.35.56.30
⊗ ℡ Map 14

## DOMANCY, Haute-Savoie, 74700

### AUBERGE DE L'ETRAZ, RN 205, Mont Blanc
**Languages spoken:** English. **Menu:** 60 Frs.
**Restaurant:** Breakfast served from 9:00am. Dinner
served from 6:00pm until 3:00am. Closed 1 week
between Christmas Day and New Year's Day.
**Specialities:** regional menu. **Other points:** bar, open to
non-residents, à la carte menu, children welcome,
terraces, pets welcome – check for details, car park,
traditional decor. **Address:** L'Etraz, Route Nationale
205.
MME VIVIANE FIVEL-DEMORET
**Telephone:** 50.93.90.86
⊗ ℡ Map 14

## DONZERE, Drôme, 26290

### LA MARGELLE FLEURIE
**Languages spoken:** German and English. **Menu:** 58 to
110 Frs. **Accommodation:** 105 to 150 Frs. **Restaurant:**
Breakfast served from 5:00am. Lunch served from
11:30am until 2:00pm. Dinner served from 7:00pm until
10:00pm. **Specialities:** home cooking. **Hotel:** 9 beds; 7
single rooms, 2 double rooms with shower. **Other
points:** bar, open to non-residents, à la carte menu,
children welcome, terraces, pets welcome – check for
details, car park, modern decor. **Address:** Route
Nationale 7.
MR CLAUDE JEANNAUX
**Telephone:** 75.51.75.11
⊗ ℡ Map 14

### RELAIS DE DONZERE, RN 7
**Languages spoken:** German, Spanish, and Italian.
**Menu:** 60 Frs (wine and coffee included).
**Accommodation:** 85 to 105. **Restaurant:** Closed from
25 December to 1 January. **Specialities:** home cooking.
**Hotel:** 9 beds; 5 single rooms, 4 double rooms with
shower, bath, private WC. **Other points:** bar, open to
non-residents, children welcome, lounge area, terraces,
pets welcome – check for details, car park, traditional
decor. **Address:** Route Nationale 7.
MR JEAN BERTRAND
**Telephone:** 75.51.64.58. **Fax:** 75.51.56.78
⊗ ℡ 🏠 Map 14

### RELAIS LE BOLO, RN 7, exit Montélimar south
**Languages spoken:** English, Spanish and Portugese.
**Menu:** 60 Frs. **Accommodation:** 100 to 180 Frs.

**Restaurant:** Open 24 hours. **Hotel:** 24 beds; with shower, bath, private WC, television. **Other points:** bar, open to non-residents, car park. **Address:** Route Nationale 7.
MR MARTIAL DA FONSECA
**Telephone:** 75.51.61.48, 75.51.55.86
♈ ⌂ ☆ Map 14

## DRAGUIGNAN, Var, 83300

### LE PENALTY
**Menu:** 55 to 65 Frs. **Restaurant:** Breakfast served from 5:30am. Lunch served from midday until 2:00pm. Dinner served from 7:00pm until 8:00pm. Closed Sundays. **Specialities:** regional menu, home cooking. **Other points:** bar, pets welcome – check for details, car park, traditional decor. **Address:** 1, avenue de la 1ère Armée, Quartier Saint Léger.
MR GUY CHABRAND
**Telephone:** 94.68.11.28
⊗ ♈ Map 13

## ECHELLES (LES), Savoie, 73360

### L'ESCAPADE, RN 6, the main road between Lyon and Grenoble
**Menu:** 58 to 85 Frs. **Restaurant:** Breakfast served from 6:30am. Lunch served from midday until 3:00pm. Dinner served from 7:00pm until 10:00pm. Closed Sundays and the 2nd fortnight in August. **Specialities:** home cooking. **Other points:** bar, open to non-residents, à la carte menu, pets welcome – check for details, car park, modern decor. **Address:** Rue Jean-Jacques Rousseau.
MR ALAIN LAURIER
**Telephone:** 79.36.55.99
⊗ ♈ Map 14

## ECULLY, Rhône, 69130

### LES ROUTIERS, RN 7, between Tarare and Roanne, exit Lyon
**Menu:** 47,50 to 75 Frs. **Restaurant:** Breakfast served from 7:00am. Lunch served from 11:30am until 2:00pm. Closed Saturdays and in August. **Specialities:** home cooking. **Other points:** bar, open to non-residents, pets welcome – check for details, traditional decor. **Address:** 30, route de Paris.
MME SYLVIE TAILLANDIER
**Telephone:** 78.34.01.40
⊗ ♈ Map 14

## EYGUIANS, Hautes Alpes, 05300

### HOTEL DE LA GARE, RN 75, exit A 51 Sisteron north of Grenoble, 20km after Sisteron
**Menu:** 60 to 90 Frs. **Accommodation:** 100 to 210 Frs. **Restaurant:** Breakfast served from 6:00am. Lunch served from midday until 2:00pm. Dinner

served from 8:00pm until 9:30pm. Closed Saturdays and in January. **Specialities:** gigot d'agneau de pays, pieds paquets, daube, regional food, home cooking. **Hotel:** 15 beds; 10 single rooms, 5 double rooms with shower, bath, private WC, television, telephone. **Other points:** bar, open to non-residents, à la carte menu, children welcome, terraces, pets welcome – check for details, car park, modern decor. **Address:** 30, route de Paris.
MME MICHELLE ROBERT
**Telephone:** 92.66.20.08
⊗ ♈ ⌂ ☜ ☆ Map 13

## FEISSONS SUR ISERE, Savoie, 73260

### LE RELAIS ROUTIERS, RN 90, between Albertville and Moutiers, exit no 36
**Menu:** 55 Frs. **Restaurant:** Breakfast served from 5:45am. Lunch served from 11:45am until 2:15pm. Closed Saturdays, from 15 to 31 August and between Christmas Day and New Year's Day. **Specialities:** home cooking. **Other points:** bar, open to non-residents, children welcome, terraces, pets welcome – check for details, car park, modern decor.
MR MICHEL RUFFIER
**Telephone:** 79.22.50.97
⊗ ♈ Map 14

## FELINES, Ardèche, 07340

### LE RELAIS DE LA REMISE, RN 82, Annonay/Saint Etienne/le Puy en Velay
**Menu:** 58 to 87 Frs. **Accommodation:** 125 to 140 Frs. **Restaurant:** Breakfast served from 5:30am. Lunch served from 11:30am until 2:30pm. Dinner served from 7:00pm until 9:30pm. Closed Saturdays. **Specialities:** home cooking. **Hotel:** 3 beds; 2 single rooms, 1 double room with shower. **Other points:** bar, open to non-residents, à la carte menu, children welcome, terraces, pets welcome – check for details, car park, traditional decor. **Address:** La Remise.
MR JEAN-JACQUES GOICHOT
**Telephone:** 75.34.82.22
⊗ ♈ Map 14

## FEURS, Loire, 42110

### LE FARFADET, RN 82, between Saint Etienne and Roanne
**Menu:** 50 to 90 Frs. **Restaurant:** Breakfast served from 8:00am. Lunch served from 11:30am until 2:30pm. Dinner served from 7:00pm until 9:30pm. Closed Mondays. **Specialities:** home cooking. **Other points:** bar, open to non-residents, à la carte menu, children welcome, pets welcome – check for details, car park, modern decor. **Address:** 72, rue de Verdun.
MME JEANINE DUBESSET
**Telephone:** 77.26.47.74
⊗ ♈ Map 14

## FIANCEY LIVRON, Drôme, 26250

### ROUVEYROL, RN 7

**Menu:** from 54 Frs. **Accommodation:** 90 to 120 Frs
(with WC). **Restaurant:** Breakfast served from 5:30am.
Lunch served from midday until 2:30pm. Dinner served
from 7:30pm until 11:00pm. Closed Sundays and the
2nd fortnight in the August. **Specialities:** home cooking.
**Hotel:** 13 beds; 5 single rooms, 8 double rooms. **Other
points:** bar, open to non-residents, lounge area, terraces,
pets welcome – check for details, car park. **Address:**
Route Nationale 7.
MR ROLAND ROUVEYROL
**Telephone:** 75.61.62.06
⊗ ⍭ ⌂ Map 14

## FIANCEY LIVRON, Drôme, 26250

### RELAIS DU SUD-EST, RN 7

**Languages spoken:** English. **Menu:** 60 to 83 Frs.
**Accommodation:** 90 to 130 Frs. **Restaurant:** Breakfast
served from 6:30am. Lunch served from 11:30am until
3:00pm. Dinner served from 6:30pm until 10:00pm.
Closed Saturdays. **Specialities:** home cooking. **Hotel:**
10 beds; 8 single rooms, 2 double rooms. **Other points:**
bar, open to non-residents, children welcome, terraces,
pets welcome – check for details, car park, traditional
decor. **Address:** Route Nationale 7.
MR JOSEPH PANDOLFO
**Telephone:** 75.61.61.19
⊗ ⍭ ⌂ Map 14

## FLAVIAC, Ardèche, 07000

### LES ROUTIERS, RN 104, exit Loriol, towards Aubenas

**Menu:** 52 to 80 Frs. **Accommodation:** 110 to 220 Frs.
**Restaurant:** Breakfast served from 6:30am. Dinner
served from midday until 9:00pm. Closed Sundays and
from 15 September to 15 October. **Specialities:** home
cooking. **Hotel:** 8 beds; 5 single rooms, 3 double rooms
with shower, private WC. **Other points:** bar, open to
non-residents, à la carte menu, children welcome, pets
welcome – check for details, car park. **Address:** Place
Emile Crémière.
MR DIDIER GARAYT
**Telephone:** 75.65.77.57
⊗ ⍭ ⌂ Map 14

## FOS SUR MER, Bouches-de-Rhône, 13270

### LE MOULIN, at crossroads Ma Campagne, towards les Plages

**Languages spoken:** English. **Restaurant:** Dinner
served from midday until 10:00pm. **Other points:** bar.
**Address:** Place du Cavaou.
MR JEAN-BERNARD LEFEBVRE
**Telephone:** 42.05.48.38
⊗ ⍭ Map 13

### MA CAMPAGNE, motorway Arles/Marseille

**Languages spoken:** English, Spanish and Italian.
**Menu:** 50 to 98 Frs. **Accommodation:** 100 to 150 Frs.
**Restaurant:** Breakfast served from 6:00am. Lunch
served from 11:00am until 3:00pm. Dinner served from
7:00pm until 10:00pm. Closed Sundays. **Specialities:**
regional menu, home cooking. **Hotel:** 25 beds; 15 single
rooms, 10 double rooms with shower, bath. **Other
points:** bar, open to non-residents, à la carte menu,
children welcome, lounge area, terraces, pets welcome –
check for details, car park, traditional decor. **Address:**
50, avenue Jean Jaurès.
MR BERNARD SILHOL
**Telephone:** 42.05.01.66, 42.05.53.67
⊗ ⍭ ⌂ Map 13

## FOUILLOUSE (LA), Loire, 42480

### LE RELAIS, RN 82

**Menu:** 55 Frs. **Restaurant:** Closed Saturdays, Sundays
and from 14 July to 15 August. **Other points:** bar.
**Address:** Lieu dit 'Les Molineaux'.
MME LOUISE BONNET
**Telephone:** 77.30.13.51
⊗ ⍭ Map 14

## FREJUS, Var, 83600

### LES TROIS CHENES, RN 7, exit Puget-en-Argens, towards Cannes

**Languages spoken:** English and Italian. **Menu:** 60 Frs.
**Accommodation:** 200 to 260 Frs. **Restaurant:** Lunch
served from midday until 2:00pm. Dinner served from
7:00pm until 10:00pm. **Specialities:** bouillabaisse,
paëlla, bourride, regional food, home cooking. **Hotel:** 29
beds; 29 double rooms with shower, bath, private WC,
television. **Other points:** bar, open to non-residents, à la
carte menu, lounge area, terraces, car park, traditional
decor. **Address:** Route de Cannes.
MME MONIQUE LAURENT
**Telephone:** 94.53.20.08
⊗ ⍭ ⌂ ☆ Map 13

## GAP, Hautes Alpes, 05000

### RESTAURANT ALPES/DAUPHINE, RN 85, north Gap

**Languages spoken:** German and English. **Menu:** 58 to
120 Frs. **Restaurant:** Breakfast served from 6:30am.
Lunch served from 11:00am until 3:00pm. Dinner served
from 7:00pm until 9:30pm. Closed Mondays.
**Specialities:** regional menu, home cooking. **Other
points:** bar, open to non-residents, à la carte menu,
children welcome, terraces, pets welcome – check for
details, car park. **Address:** La Descente.
MME MICHELINE ARGELAS
**Telephone:** 92.51.47.15
⊗ ⍭ Map 13

## GENAY, Rhône, 69730

### LA PETITE RIVE, A 46
**Languages spoken:** English. **Menu:** 60 to 115 Frs.
**Accommodation:** 135 Frs. **Restaurant:** Breakfast
served from 6:30am. Lunch served from midday until
2:30pm. Dinner served from 7:00pm until 9:30pm.
**Specialities:** regional menu, home cooking. **Hotel:** 8
beds; 1 single room, 7 double rooms with shower,
private WC, television, telephone. **Other points:** bar,
open to non-residents, à la carte menu, children
welcome, terraces, pets welcome – check for details, car
park, modern decor. **Address:** Zone Industrielle Nord,
Chemin de Halage.
SARL FEGOTOME
**Telephone:** 78.91.34.02
⊗ ♀ ⌂ ☆ Map 14

## GRANGES LES VALENCE, Ardèche, 07500

### LE RELAIS DE CRUSSOL, RN 86, between Valence and la Voulte sur Rhône
**Menu:** 54 Frs. **Restaurant:** Breakfast served from
6:00am. Closed Sundays. **Specialities:** home cooking.
**Other points:** bar, open to non-residents, à la carte menu,
terraces, pets welcome – check for details, car park.
**Address:** Lieu dit 'Les Freydières', Avenue Sadi Carnot.
MR GILBERT BRIDON
**Telephone:** 75.41.40.10
⊗ ♀ Map 14

## GRENOBLE, Isère, 38000

### LE CATALPA, Grenoble Bastille
**Menu:** 59 Frs (wine and coffee included). **Restaurant:**
Breakfast served from 7:00am. Lunch served from
midday until 3:00pm. Dinner served from 7:00pm until
midnight. **Specialities:** regional menu, home cooking.
**Other points:** bar, open to non-residents, terraces, pets
welcome – check for details, car park, modern decor.
**Address:** 8, boulevard de l'Esplanade.
MME DENISE BRISSET
**Telephone:** 76.47.38.03
⊗ ♀ Map 14

## GRIMAUD, Var, 83310

### LE RESTAUROUTE, RN 98, Saint Tropez
**Languages spoken:** English, Italian. **Menu:** 65 Frs.
**Restaurant:** Breakfast served from 6:00am. Lunch
served from midday until 2:00pm. Dinner served from
7:00pm until 9:45pm. Closed Sundays and in December.
**Specialities:** home cooking. **Other points:** bar, open to
non-residents, à la carte menu, children welcome,
terraces, pets welcome – check for details, car park.
**Address:** Route Nationale 98, Saint Pons les Mûrs.
MR BERNARD GENTILE
**Telephone:** 94.56.03.75
⊗ ♀ Map 13

## GUEREINS, Ain, 01090

### LA CROISEE, RD 17, motorway exit Belleville, towards Chatillon sur Chalaronne
**Menu:** 55 to 99 Frs. **Restaurant:** Breakfast served from
6:30am. Closed Tuesdays and 3 weeks in August.
**Specialities:** fruits de mer, homard à l'américaine (sur
commande), home cooking. **Other points:** bar, open to
non-residents, à la carte menu, children welcome, pets
welcome – check for details, car park, modern decor.
**Address:** La Croisée.
MR MICHEL MANAINS
**Telephone:** 74.66.14.93
⊗ ♀ Map 14

## GUILLESTRE, Hautes Alpes, 05600

### HOTEL DE LA GARE, RN 94
**Places of interest:** Pérouges (25km), le parc des oiseaux
de Villars les Dombes (15km), musée du camion à
Villars et automobile de Rochetaillée. **Languages
spoken:** English. **Menu:** 612 to 170 Frs.
**Accommodation:** 140 to 330 Frs. **Restaurant:**
Breakfast served from 7:00am. Lunch served from
midday until 1:45pm. Dinner served from 7:00pm until
9:00pm. Closed Saturdays. **Specialities:** truites aux
morilles, filet de boeuf grillé, côte d'agneau, regional
food. **Hotel:** 30 beds; 2 single rooms, 28 double rooms
with shower, bath, private WC, television. **Other points:**
bar, open to non-residents, à la carte menu, children
welcome, lounge area, terraces, pets welcome – check
for details, car park, modern decor. **Address:**
Montdauphin Gare.
SNC LACOUR
**Telephone:** 92.45.03.08. **Fax:** 92.45.40.09
⊗ ♀ ⌂ ♨ ☆☆ Map 13

## HOPITAL SOUS ROCHEFORT (L'), Loire, 42130

### CHEZ SYLVIANNE ET JEANNOT, RN 89
**Languages spoken:** English. **Restaurant:** Dinner
served from midday until 11:00pm. **Other points:** bar,
car park. **Address:** Route Nationale 89, Boen-sur-
Lignon.
MR JEAN DEVANNE
**Telephone:** 77.24.55.52
⊗ ♀ Map 14

## ISLE D'ABEAU, Isère, 38080

### L'ARCHE DE L'ISLE D'ABEAU, A 43, the main road between Grenoble and Chambéry
**Languages spoken:** English. **Menu:** 59 to 100 Frs.
**Accommodation:** 260 to 330 Frs. **Restaurant:**
Breakfast served from 6:00am. Dinner served from
midday until 11:00pm. **Specialities:** home cooking.
**Hotel:** 33 beds; 33 double rooms with shower, bath,
private WC, television, telephone. **Other points:** open

to non-residents, à la carte menu, children welcome, lounge area, terraces, pets welcome – check for details, car park, modern decor. **Address:** A 43 Aire de l'Isle d'Abeau, dans les deux sens.
**Telephone:** 74.27.10.14. **Fax:** 74.27.01.45
⊗ 🏠 ☆☆ Map 14

## ISLES SUR LA SORGUE (L'),
Vaucluse, 84800

### CHEZ L'ANCHOIS, *between Cavaillon and Carpentras*
**Menu:** 58 to 65 Frs. **Restaurant:** Breakfast served from 6:00am. Lunch served from midday until 3:00pm. Dinner served from 8:00pm until 11:00pm. **Specialities:** home cooking. **Other points:** bar, open to non-residents, à la carte menu, children welcome, terraces, pets welcome – check for details, car park, modern decor. **Address:** Hameau de Vellorgues.
MR LUC SANNA
**Telephone:** 90.38.01.38
⊗ ♀ Map 13

## JARRIE, Isère, 38560

### LE RELAIS DU PONT, *RN 85, between Grenoble and Briançon*
**Languages spoken:** Italian. **Menu:** 48 to 60 Frs. **Restaurant:** Breakfast served from 6:00am. Lunch served from 11:30am until 2:00pm. Dinner served from 7:00pm until 9:00pm. Closed Saturdays. **Specialities:** home cooking. **Other points:** bar, open to non-residents, terraces, pets welcome – check for details, car park, modern decor. **Address:** Champ sur Drac.
MR ANDRÉ NUCCI
**Telephone:** 76.68.85.38
⊗ ♀ Map 14

## JAYAT, Ain, 01340

### LE RELAIS DE JAYAT, *RD 975, between Tournus Bourg and Chalon sur Saône*
**Languages spoken:** English. **Menu:** 62 Frs. **Accommodation:** 95 to 160 Frs. **Restaurant:** Breakfast served from 6:00am. Lunch served from midday until 2:30pm. Dinner served from 7:00pm until 9:30pm. **Specialities:** home cooking. **Hotel:** 10 beds; 7 single rooms, 3 double rooms. **Other points:** bar, open to non-residents, à la carte menu, children welcome, terraces, pets welcome – check for details, car park, modern decor.
MR YVES ROUSSELLE
**Telephone:** 74.30.84.69
⊗ ♀ 🏠 ☆ Map 14

## JOYEUSE, Ardèche, 07260

### LES CEVENNES
**Menu:** 50 to 100 Frs. **Accommodation:** 120 Frs.

**Restaurant:** Breakfast served from 7:00am. Lunch served from midday until 2:00pm. Dinner served from 8:00pm until 10:00pm. **Specialities:** home cooking. **Hotel:** 14 beds; 10 single rooms, 4 double rooms. **Other points:** bar, open to non-residents, à la carte menu, children welcome, terraces, pets welcome – check for details, car park, traditional decor. **Address:** Rosières.
MME COLETTE REYNOUARD
**Telephone:** 75.39.52.07
⊗ ♀ 🏠 ☆ Map 14

## LABEGUDE, Ardèche, 07200

### RELAIS DE LA POSTE, *RN 104*
**Menu:** 55 to 75 Frs. **Accommodation:** 100 to 150 Frs. **Restaurant:** Breakfast served from 6:30am. Lunch served from midday until 1:30pm. Dinner served from 7:00pm until 9:00pm. Closed Sundays and in September. **Specialities:** regional menu, home cooking. **Hotel:** 12 beds; 11 single rooms, 1 double room with shower, private WC. **Other points:** bar, open to non-residents, pets welcome – check for details, car park, traditional decor. **Address:** 64, Route Nationale.
MR MAURICE TEYSSIER
**Telephone:** 75.37.40.25
⊗ ♀ 🏠 Map 14

## LALEVADE D'ARDECHE, Ardèche, 07380

### L'ESCHALLIER, *RN 102, between Aubenas and le Puy en Velay*
**Places of interest:** La Camargue. **Languages spoken:** German and English. **Menu:** 55 (wine and coffee included) to 120 Frs. **Accommodation:** 95 to 190 Frs. **Restaurant:** Breakfast served from 8:00am. Lunch served from 10:30am until 3:00pm. Dinner served from 6:30pm until 9:00pm. Closed Saturdays. **Specialities:** home cooking. **Hotel:** 8 beds; 6 single rooms, 2 double rooms with shower. **Other points:** bar, open to non-residents, à la carte menu, children welcome, terraces, pets welcome – check for details, car park, traditional decor. **Address:** 31, place de la Gare.
MR JOSÉ FERRARO
**Telephone:** 75.94.17.23
⊗ ♀ 🏠 ☆ Map 14

## LAMBESC, Bouches-de-Rhône, 13410

### LE RELAIS DE LA GARE, *RN 7*
**Languages spoken:** Italian. **Restaurant:** Closed Sundays. **Other points:** bar. **Address:** Boulevard des Coopératives.
MME GERMAINE LANSAC
**Telephone:** 42.92.97.60
⊗ ♀ Map 13

## LAMOTTE DU RHONE, Vaucluse, 84840

### LE RELAIS DU RHONE, RN 994, Pont Saint Esprit

**Languages spoken:** German and English. **Menu:** 50 Frs. **Accommodation:** to 50 Frs. **Restaurant:** Breakfast served from 6:00am. Lunch served from midday until 2:00pm. Dinner served from 7:00pm until 9:00pm. Closed from Saturday 3:00pm to Monday 6:00am. **Specialities:** home cooking. **Hotel:** 5 beds; 3 single rooms, 2 double rooms with shower. **Other points:** bar, open to non-residents, terraces, pets welcome – check for details, car park, modern decor. **Address:** Quartier Santi.
MME ELISE RUAT
**Telephone:** 90.30.41.89
⊗ ⛾ ⌂ Map 13

## LANCON DE PROVENCE, Bouches-de-Rhône, 13680

### AUBERGE DU MOULIN, RN 113

**Languages spoken:** Arabic. **Menu:** 55 Frs (wine and coffee included). **Accommodation:** 100 Frs. **Restaurant:** Breakfast served from 5:30am. Closed Sundays. **Specialities:** home cooking. **Hotel:** 6 beds. **Other points:** bar, open to non-residents, à la carte menu, pets welcome – check for details, car park, modern decor. **Address:** Route Nationale 113.
MME JOSIANE CASCIO
**Telephone:** 90.42.71.14
⊗ ⛾ ⌂ Map 13

### LE RELAIS DES FOURCHES, RN 113

**Menu:** 60 to 75 Frs. **Accommodation:** 100 Frs. **Restaurant:** Breakfast served from 6:30am. Closed Sundays. **Specialities:** paëlla, couscous, regional food, home cooking. **Hotel:** 3 beds; 3 double rooms with shower, private WC. **Other points:** bar, open to non-residents, terraces, pets welcome – check for details, car park, traditional decor. **Address:** Quartier des Ferrages, Route Nationale 113.
MR BRUNO CALDERONE
**Telephone:** 90.42.71.21
⊗ ⛾ Map 13

### PORTES DE PROVENCE, A 7

**Restaurant:** Open 24 hours. **Specialities:** home cooking. **Other points:** open to non-residents, à la carte menu, children welcome, terraces, pets welcome – check for details, car park. **Address:** A 7 Aire de Lançon, dans les deux sens.
MR MARCEL PRIOUL
**Telephone:** 90.42.88.88. **Fax:** 90.42.70.82
⊗ Map 13

## LEYMENT, Ain, 01150

### LE RELAIS DE LA GARE, RN 84

**Restaurant:** Closed Tuesdays and from 22 December to 2 January. **Hotel:** 7 beds. **Other points:** bar. **Address:** 34, rue de la Gare.

MR MARCEL BESSIERE
**Telephone:** 74.34.94.30
⊗ ⛾ ⌂ Map 14

## LIGNANE, Bouches-de-Rhône, 13540

### LE RELAIS DE LIGNANE, RN 7, Aix en Provence/Avignon/Salon

**Menu:** 55 to 65 Frs. **Restaurant:** Breakfast served from 6:00am. Lunch served from 11:00am until 2:30pm. Dinner served from 7:00pm until 11:00pm. Closed Sundays and mid-August. **Specialities:** regional menu, home cooking. **Other points:** bar, open to non-residents, terraces, car park, traditional decor. **Address:** Route Nationale 7.
MR CHRISTIAN MONDIN
**Telephone:** 42.92.51.15
⊗ ⛾ ⌣ Map 13

## LIVRON, Drôme, 26250

### AUBERGE RELAIS MACAMP

**Restaurant:** Breakfast served from 6:30am. Closed Sundays and in August. **Specialities:** regional menu, home cooking. **Hotel:** 17 beds; 9 single rooms, 8 double rooms with shower, private WC, television. **Other points:** bar, open to non-residents, children welcome, lounge area, terraces, pets welcome – check for details, car park, traditional decor. **Address:** Route Nationale 7, Fiancey.
MME JOSIANE VOCANSON
**Telephone:** 75.61.73.91
⊗ ⛾ ⌂ Map 14

## LONDE DES MAURES (LA), Var, 83250

### LE PETIT BOIS

**Menu:** 55 Frs. **Restaurant:** Breakfast served from 7:00am. **Other points:** bar. **Address:** Route de Maramar.
MME YVETTE BOUVIER
**Telephone:** 94.66.80.12
⊗ ⛾ Map 13

## LYON, Rhône, 69002

### LES ROUTIERS, via the tunnel under Fourvière, towards Perrache

**Menu:** to 65 Frs (wine included). **Restaurant:** Breakfast served from 7:00am. Lunch served from midday until 3:00pm. Dinner served from 7:30pm until midnight. Closed Saturdays Sundays and in August. **Specialities:** home cooking. **Other points:** bar, open to non-residents, children welcome, pets welcome – check for details, car park, modern decor. **Address:** 21, quai Perrache.
MR PIERRE SALA
**Telephone:** 78.37.75.86
⊗ ⛾ Map 14

## MARCILLY LE CHATEL, Loire, 42130

### *RELAIS DU CHATEL, CD 8, between Montbrison and Boën*

**Menu:** 50 to 72 Frs. **Restaurant:** Breakfast served from 7:00am. Lunch served from 11:30am until 2:00pm. Dinner served from 7:00pm until 9:00pm. Closed the 1st fortnight in September. **Specialities:** home cooking. **Other points:** bar, open to non-residents, à la carte menu, children welcome, terraces, pets welcome – check for details, car park, traditional decor. **Address:** Le Bourg.
MME JOSIANNE BÉAL
**Telephone:** 77.97.44.36
⊗ 🍸 Map 14

## MARSEILLE, Bouches-de-Rhône, 13016

### *BAR DE LA GARE D'ARENC*

**Languages spoken:** English and Italian. **Menu:** 45 Frs. **Restaurant:** Breakfast served from 5:00am. Closed Saturdays. **Other points:** bar, car park. **Address:** 25, rue d'Anthoine.
MR PHILIPPE CHIARAMONTE
**Telephone:** 91.91.23.07
⊗ 🍸 Map 13

### *LE REGALI*

**Menu:** 55 Frs (wine included). **Restaurant:** Breakfast served from 6:00am. Lunch served from 11:30am until 2:30pm. Closed Saturdays, 15 days in August and 15 days at Christmas. **Specialities:** home cooking. **Other points:** bar, open to non-residents, à la carte menu, terraces, pets welcome – check for details, car park. **Address:** 652, chemin du Littoral.
MME ROUECHE
**Telephone:** 91.46.11.64
⊗ 🍸 Map 13

### *LE RELAIS, RN 8, opposite shopping centre*

**Menu:** 53 Frs. **Restaurant:** Breakfast served from 6:00am. Dinner served from midday until 10:00pm. Closed Saturdays and the 2nd fortnight in August. **Other points:** bar, car park. **Address:** 40, quai du Lazaret.
MLLE NATHALIE MASSIAS
**Telephone:** 91.90.93.02
⊗ 🍸 Map 13

### *LE RELAIS DES AMIS, RN 8*

**Menu:** 35 Frs (choose from 8 menus). **Restaurant:** Breakfast served from 5:30am. Dinner served from midday until 9:30pm. Closed Saturdays, public holidays and in August. **Specialities:** regional menu, home cooking. **Other points:** open to non-residents, pets welcome – check for details, car park, traditional decor. **Address:** 110, boulevard de Paris.
MR RAYMOND SERVIERE
**Telephone:** 91.62.60.76
⊗ Map 13

## MEGEVE, Haute-Savoie, 74120

### *CHALET DES FLEURS, RN 212, from Sallanches, 1st buildings on the left on arriving in Mégève*

**Languages spoken:** English. **Menu:** 87 to 150 Frs. **Accommodation:** 130 to 150 Frs. **Restaurant:** Breakfast served from 7:00am. Lunch served from midday until 2:30pm. Dinner served from 7:30pm until 10:00pm. Closed from 15 March to 15 June and from 20 September to 20 December. **Specialities:** truite à la crème et aux amandes, escalope normande garnie, regional food, home cooking. **Hotel:** 20 beds; 4 single rooms, 16 double rooms with shower, bath, private WC, telephone. **Other points:** bar, open to non-residents, à la carte menu, children welcome, lounge area, terraces, pets welcome – check for details, car park, modern decor. **Address:** Pont d'Arbon.
MR GEORGES ROUSSEL
**Telephone:** 50.21.21.46
⊗ 🍸 🏠 ☆☆ Map 14

## MENTON, Alpes Maritimes, 06500

### *RAPID BAR, route for Sainte Agnès*

**Languages spoken:** English and Italian. **Restaurant:** Breakfast served from 7:00am. Lunch served from midday until 2:30pm. **Specialities:** home cooking. **Other points:** bar, terraces, pets welcome – check for details, car park, modern decor. **Address:** 63, avenue Cernuschi.
MR ALEXANDRE PÉRUCCHINI
**Telephone:** 93.35.93.69
⊗ 🍸 Map 13

## MEYTHET, Haute-Savoie, 74960

### *LE RELAIS*

**Accommodation:** 120 to 150 Frs. **Restaurant:** Dinner served from midday until 10:00pm. Closed Sundays, between Christmas Day and New Year's Day and in May. **Hotel:** 17 beds. **Other points:** bar. **Address:** 22, route de Frangy.
MR CLAUDE GALLAY
**Telephone:** 50.22.02.93
⊗ 🍸 🏠 Map 14

## MEYZIEU, Rhône, 69330

### *LE RELAIS DE L'INDUSTRIE, RD 517, Lyon*

**Menu:** 57 Frs. **Restaurant:** Breakfast served from 6:30am. Lunch served from 11:30am until 2:30pm. Dinner served from 7:00pm until 9:30pm. Closed Sundays and in August. **Specialities:** home cooking. **Other points:** bar, open to non-residents, car park, modern decor. **Address:** 104, rue de la République, les Plantées.
MR GÉRARD DUMONT
**Telephone:** 78.31.78.31
⊗ 🍸 Map 14

## MEZEL, Alpes-de-Hautes-Provence, 04270

### HOTEL RESTAURANT DE LA PLACE, RN 85, between Digne and Nice

Places of interest: Jeu de pétanque, loisirs (lac à 800m), mini-golf. Languages spoken: English. Menu: 60 to 105 Frs. Accommodation: 135 to 195 Frs. Restaurant: Breakfast served from 6:30am. Lunch served from midday until 2:00pm. Dinner served from 7:30pm until 9:00pm. Closed Mondays and from 15 December to 15 January. Specialities: home cooking. Hotel: 11 beds; 3 single rooms, 8 double rooms with shower, bath, private WC, television, telephone. Other points: bar, open to non-residents, à la carte menu, children welcome, lounge area, terraces, pets welcome – check for details, car park, traditional decor. Address: Place Victor Arnaux.
MME CHRISTIANE SARRACANIE
Telephone: 92.35.58.10, 92.35.51.05
⊗ ⅋ ⌂ Map 13

## MEZERIAT, Ain, 01660

### RELAIS DE MEZERIAT, RN 79, motorway A 40 exit Mâcon east, towards Bourg

Places of interest: Château de Foix (6km), Montségur (15km). Menu: 68 to 148 Frs. Restaurant: Breakfast served from 6:30am. Lunch served from midday until 2:30pm. Dinner served from 7:00pm until 10:30pm. Closed Sundays and in August. Specialities: grenouilles, poulet à la crème, regional food. Other points: bar, open to non-residents, à la carte menu, children welcome, terraces, pets welcome – check for details, car park, traditional decor. Address: Les Pigots.
MR ALAIN DARBON
Telephone: 74.30.25.87
⊗ ⅋ Map 14

## MIONNAY, Ain, 01390

### LE RELAIS BRESSAN, RN 83, exit les Echets

Menu: 42 to 58 Frs. Restaurant: Breakfast served from 5:00am. Lunch served from 11:00am until 3:00pm. Dinner served from 7:00pm until 8:30pm. Closed Saturdays, 3 weeks in August and 1 week in winter. Specialities: home cooking. Other points: bar, open to non-residents, lounge area, terraces, pets welcome – check for details, car park, traditional decor. Address: Route Nationale 83.
MONIQUE MILLET ET CHRISTIAN DESMARIS
Telephone: 78.91.05.23
⊗ ⅋ Map 14

## MIRABEAU, Vaucluse, 84120

### RELAIS DE LA DILIGENCE, RN 96, Manosque/Sisteron

Languages spoken: English and Italian. Menu: 30 to 55 (wine and coffee included). Accommodation: 80 to 100 Frs. Restaurant: Breakfast served from 5:00am. Specialities: home cooking. Hotel: 5 beds; with shower, private WC, television, telephone. Other points: bar, open to non-residents, children welcome, lounge area, terraces, pets welcome – check for details, car park, traditional decor. Address: Route Nationale 96.
MR ALAIN MICHEL
Telephone: 90.77.00.90
⊗ ⅋ ⌂ Map 13

## MODANE, Savoie, 73500

### LA CROIX DU SUD, RN 6, Fréjus tunnel

Languages spoken: English and Italian. Menu: 60 Frs. Accommodation: 120 Frs. Restaurant: Breakfast served from 7:00am. Lunch served from midday until 2:00pm. Dinner served from 7:00pm until 12:30am. Closed Sundays and in August. Specialities: home cooking. Hotel: 6 beds; 2 single rooms, 4 double rooms with shower, bath. Other points: bar, open to non-residents, children welcome, terraces, pets welcome – check for details, car park. Address: La Praz.
MR BERNARD MESTRALLET
Telephone: 79.05.34.47
⊗ ⅋ ⌂ Map 14

### LE RESTOPORT DU FREJUS, RN 6, 5km before the Fréjus tunnel

Languages spoken: English, Greek and Italian. Menu: 50 to 75 Frs. Restaurant: Breakfast served from 6:30am. Dinner served from midday until midnight. Closed Saturdays. Specialities: regional menu, home cooking. Other points: bar, open to non-residents, lounge area, pets welcome – check for details, car park. Address: Autoport du Fréjus.
MR STAVROS MICHEL STAVRIDIS
Telephone: 79.05.29.98. Fax: 79.05.14.83
⊗ ⅋ Map 14

## MOIDIEU DETOURBE, Isère, 38440

### CHEZ DEDE, RD 502, the main road between Vienne and Grenoble

Menu: 58 Frs. Restaurant: Breakfast served from 5:00am. Lunch served from 11:00am until 2:00pm. Dinner served from 7:00pm until 9:30pm. Closed Saturdays, 15 days in August and 1 week at Christmas. Specialities: home cooking. Other points: bar, open to non-residents, car park.
MR ANDRÉ SEIGLE
Telephone: 74.58.13.02
⊗ ⅋ Map 14

## MOIRANS, Isère, 38430

### LE RELAIS DU VIADUC, RN 85, the main road between Lyon and Grenoble

Menu: 55 Frs. Accommodation: 70 Frs. Restaurant: Breakfast served from 6:00am. Lunch served from

11:30am until 3:00pm. Dinner served from 7:30pm until 10:00pm. Closed Saturdays. **Specialities:** home cooking. **Hotel:** 4 beds; 1 single room, 3 double rooms. **Other points:** bar, open to non-residents, children welcome, terraces, pets welcome – check for details, car park, modern decor. **Address:** 4, route de Grenoble.
MR FERNAND BARRAL-POULAT
**Telephone:** 76.35.31.01
⊗ ♀ Map 14

## MONESTIER DE CLERMONT,

Isère, 38650

*BAR RESTAURANT DU NORD, the main road between Grenoble and Marseille*
**Menu:** 65 to 75 Frs. **Restaurant:** Breakfast served from 6:00am. Lunch served from midday until 2:00pm. Dinner served from 7:00pm until 9:30pm. Closed Sundays. **Specialities:** home cooking. **Other points:** bar, terraces, car park. **Address:** 44, Grande Rue.
MME PAULETTE JACQUET
**Telephone:** 76.34.03.73
⊗ ♀ Map 14

## MONTBRISON, Loire, 42600

*LE RELAIS DE LA GARE, RN 496*
**Menu:** 58 to 100 Frs. **Accommodation:** 99 to 120 Frs. **Restaurant:** Breakfast served from 6:30am. Lunch served from 11:00am until 3:00pm. Dinner served from 7:00pm until 8:00pm. Closed Sundays and in August. **Specialities:** home cooking. **Hotel:** 8 beds; 2 single rooms, 6 double rooms with shower, bath, private WC, telephone. **Other points:** bar, open to non-residents, à la carte menu, children welcome, terraces, pets welcome – check for details, car park. **Address:** 2, place de la Gare.
MR JEAN-PIERRE GAÇON
**Telephone:** 77.58.07.50
⊗ ♀ 🏠 Map 14

## MONTELIMAR, Drôme, 26780

*RELAIS DE MONTELIMAR, A 7*
**Languages spoken:** English. **Restaurant:** Open 24 hours. **Specialities:** regional menu. **Other points:** à la carte menu, children welcome, lounge area, terraces, pets welcome – check for details, car park. **Address:** Aire de Service de Montélimar, dans les deux sens.
**Telephone:** 75.46.60.00
⊗ Map 14

*SODEXAS RELAIS P.L.M., A 7*
**Restaurant:** Open 24 hours. **Other points:** bar, car park. **Address:** Aire de service de Montélimar, Malataverne.
**Telephone:** 75.46.60.00
⊗ ♀ Map 14

## MONTFAVET, Vaucluse, 84140

*RELAIS DE BONPAS, RN 7, between Avignon and Marseille, exit Avignon south*
**Languages spoken:** English and Spanish. **Menu:** 63 to 100 Frs. **Accommodation:** 95 to 120 Frs. **Restaurant:** Breakfast served from 6:00am. Lunch served from 11:30am until 2:30pm. Dinner served from 7:00pm until 11:00pm. **Specialities:** home cooking. **Hotel:** 15 beds; 4 single rooms, 11 double rooms with shower. **Other points:** bar, open to non-residents, à la carte menu, terraces, pets welcome – check for details, car park, modern decor. **Address:** Route Nationale 7.
MR ALAIN LAUGIER
**Telephone:** 90.23.07.01, 90.23.13.92
⊗ ♀ 🏠 ☆ Map 13

## MONTFERRAT, Isère, 38620

*LE PRESSOIR, RN 75, between Bourg en Bresse and Grenoble*
**Menu:** 55 to 120 Frs. **Restaurant:** Breakfast served from 8:00am. Lunch served from midday until 2:30pm. Dinner served from 7:00pm until 9:00pm. Closed Sundays. **Specialities:** regional menu, home cooking. **Other points:** bar, open to non-residents, children welcome, terraces, pets welcome – check for details, car park, modern decor. **Address:** Le Bourg.
MR GÉRARD COFFINHAL
**Telephone:** 76.32.31.82
⊗ ♀ Map 14

## MONTGARDIN, Hautes Alpes, 05230

*LA PLAINE*
**Languages spoken:** English and Italian. **Menu:** 55 Frs. **Accommodation:** 100 to 120 Frs. **Restaurant:** Breakfast served from 4:45am. Lunch served from 11:30am until 2:00pm. Dinner served from 7:00pm until 10:00pm. Closed Sundays. **Specialities:** home cooking. **Hotel:** 8 beds. **Other points:** bar, open to non-residents, car park. **Address:** Route Nationale 94.
MME BRIGITTE MORALES
**Telephone:** 92.50.30.11
⊗ ♀ 🏠 Map 13

## MONTROND LES BAINS, Loire, 42210

*LES OMBRELLES, RN 82, 1.5km after Montrond le Bains, towards Saint Etienne*
**Languages spoken:** English. **Menu:** 55 to 80 Frs. **Restaurant:** Breakfast served from 6:00am. Lunch served from midday until 1:30pm. Dinner served from 7:00pm until 9:30pm. Closed Saturdays, 2 weeks in May and 3 weeks in September. **Specialities:** home cooking. **Other points:** bar, open to non-residents, terraces, pets welcome – check for details, car park, traditional decor. **Address:** Route Nationale 82, Meylieu.

MR LAURENT THOUANT
**Telephone:** 77.54.52.44
⊗ ⟜ Map 14

## MORANCE, Rhône, 69480

### RESTAURANT DE LA MAIRIE, RD 100, Anse/Larbresle/Feurs

**Accommodation:** 120 to 150 Frs. **Restaurant:**
Breakfast served from 7:00am. Lunch served from
11:30am until 2:30pm. Dinner served from 7:00pm until
9:00pm. **Specialities:** home cooking. **Hotel:** 5 beds; 2
single rooms, 3 double rooms. **Other points:** bar, open
to non-residents, children welcome, lounge area,
terraces, pets welcome – check for details, car park,
modern decor. **Address:** Le Bourg.
MR RÉMY DORIER
**Telephone:** 78.43.60.82
⊗ ⟜ ⌂ Map 14

## MORNANT, Rhône, 69440

### LE RELAIS DE BELLEVUE, RD 42, between Brignais and Rive de Gier

**Languages spoken:** Spanish. **Menu:** 55 to 145 Frs.
**Restaurant:** Lunch served from 11:30am until 3:00pm.
Dinner served from 7:00pm until 10:00pm. **Specialities:**
regional menu. **Other points:** bar, à la carte menu, children
welcome, pets welcome – check for details, car park, modern
decor. **Address:** Bellevue, Route Départementale 42.
MR PATRICK COUPARD
**Telephone:** 78.81.22.26
⊗ ⟜ Map 14

## MORNAS, Vaucluse, 84420

### L'ARCHE DE MORNAS, A 7

**Menu:** 60 Frs. **Restaurant:** Open 24 hours. **Other**
points: bar, open to non-residents, children welcome,
terraces, pets welcome – check for details, car park,
traditional decor. **Address:** A 7 Aire de Mornas Village
Ouest, sens Lyon/Marseille.
MR STÉPHANE BRUN
**Telephone:** 90.37.03.09
⊗ ⟜ Map 13

### LA CASCADE, RN 7

**Languages spoken:** Spanish. **Menu:** 60 Frs.
**Restaurant:** Closed Saturdays. **Other points:** bar.
**Address:** Route Nationale 7.
MME JEANNE BRETAGNOLLE
**Telephone:** 90.37.02.67
⊗ ⟜ Map 13

## MUY (LE), Var, 83490

### LA CHAUMIERE, RN 7

**Languages spoken:** Italian. **Menu:** 55 Frs.
**Accommodation:** 110 to 160 Frs. **Restaurant:** Lunch

served from 11:45am until 2:30pm. Dinner served from
7:00pm until 9:30pm. Closed Sundays. **Hotel:** 7 beds.
**Other points:** bar. **Address:** Quartier de la Gare, Route
Nationale 7.
MR CLAUDE BRUNASSO-CATTARELLO
**Telephone:** 94.45.10.81
⊗ ⟜ ⌂ Map 13

## NEAUX, Loire, 42470

### CHEZ GINOU, RN 7, between Lyon and Roanne

**Menu:** 55 Frs. **Restaurant:** Breakfast served from
5:00am. Lunch served from 11:00am until 2:30pm.
Dinner served from 7:00pm until 9:00pm. Closed
Mondays and in August. **Specialities:** home cooking.
**Other points:** bar, open to non-residents, children
welcome, terraces, pets welcome – check for details, car
park, traditional decor. **Address:** Route Nationale 7, la
Croix.
MME GENEVIEVE DUCREUX
**Telephone:** 77.62.70.32
⊗ ⟜ Map 14

## NOVES, Bouches-de-Rhône, 13550

### RELAIS DE LA BASSAQUE, RN 7

**Languages spoken:** Italian. **Restaurant:** Closed
Sundays. **Other points:** bar. **Address:** Route Nationale
7.
MR JOSEPH MASI
**Telephone:** 90.94.26.84
⊗ ⟜ Map 13

## NOYAREY, Isère, 38360

### AU BON ACCUEIL, RN 532, the main road between Grenoble and Valence

**Languages spoken:** German, Spanish and Italian.
**Menu:** 61 to 85 Frs. **Accommodation:** 90 to 140 Frs.
**Restaurant:** Breakfast served from 5:30am. Lunch
served from 11:30am until 2:00pm. Closed Saturdays.
**Specialities:** home cooking. **Hotel:** 11 beds; 5 single
rooms, 6 double rooms with shower. **Other points:** bar,
open to non-residents, children welcome, terraces, pets
welcome – check for details, car park, traditional decor.
**Address:** Rue du Maupas.
MR JEAN-CLAUDE COMPE
**Telephone:** 76.53.95.61
⊗ ⟜ ⌂ Map 14

## ORANGE, Vaucluse, 84100

### LA FINE FOURCHETTE ORANGEOISE, RN 7, exit north

**Languages spoken:** Italian. **Menu:** 50 Frs. **Restaurant:**
Breakfast served from 8:00am. Dinner served from
midday until midnight. Closed Mondays. **Specialities:**
regional menu, home cooking. **Other points:** bar, open

to non-residents, à la carte menu, children welcome, terraces, pets welcome – check for details, car park, modern decor. **Address:** Route Nationale 7, Pont de l'Aygues.
MR JOSEPH DELHORME
**Telephone:** 90.51.76.35
⊗ ⍭ Map 13

## ORGON, Bouches-de-Rhône, 13660

### AU BEC FIN, RN 7, between Aix en Provence and Marseille
**Languages spoken:** Spanish and Italian. **Menu:** 55 Frs. **Restaurant:** Breakfast served from 5:00am. Lunch served from 11:30am until 3:00pm. Dinner served from 7:00pm until 11:00pm. Closed Saturdays. **Specialities:** regional menu, home cooking. **Other points:** bar, open to non-residents, à la carte menu, children welcome, lounge area, terraces, car park, traditional decor. **Address:** Route Nationale 7.
MR MICHEL TOESCA
**Telephone:** 90.73.00.49
⊗ ⍭ Map 13

### LE BELLEVUE, RN 7, the main road between Marseille and Lyon
**Menu:** 55 to 95 Frs. **Restaurant:** Breakfast served from 6:00am. Dinner served from 7:00pm until midnight. **Specialities:** regional menu. **Other points:** bar, open to non-residents, à la carte menu, children welcome, car park, traditional decor. **Address:** Route Nationale 7.
MR JEAN-LOUIS GROS
**Telephone:** 90.73.00.24
⊗ ⍭ Map 13

### RELAIS DES FUMADES, RN 7, between Avignon and Aix en Provence
**Languages spoken:** German and English. **Menu:** 50 to 70 Frs. **Accommodation:** 100 to 150 Frs. **Restaurant:** Breakfast served from 6:00am. Lunch served from midday until 2:00pm. Dinner served from 7:30pm until midnight. **Specialities:** home cooking. **Hotel:** 11 beds; 4 single rooms, 7 double rooms with shower, bath. **Other points:** bar, open to non-residents, lounge area, terraces, pets welcome – check for details, car park, traditional decor. **Address:** Route Nationale 7.
MR JEAN ETCHEVERRY
**Telephone:** 90.73.00.81
⊗ ⍭ 🏠 ☆ Map 13

## ORLIENAS, Rhône, 69530

### BAR RESTAURANT DES 7 CHEMINS, RN 86, the main road between Lyon and Saint Etienne
**Menu:** 55 Frs. **Restaurant:** Breakfast served from 5:30am. Lunch served from midday until 3:00pm. Closed Saturdays. **Specialities:** home cooking. **Other**

points: bar, open to non-residents, children welcome, terraces, pets welcome – check for details, car park, modern decor. **Address:** Lieu dit 'Les 7 Chemins'.
MME ANNIE CHAPELLE
**Telephone:** 78.05.21.54
⊗ ⍭ Map 14

## PACAUDIERE (LA), Loire, 42310

### LE RELAIS DU LAC, RN 7, the main road between Roanne and Paris, via the entrance north 'Pacaudière'
**Menu:** 56 to 90 Frs. **Accommodation:** 60 to 100 Frs. **Restaurant:** Breakfast served from 4:00am. Lunch served from 11:30am until 3:00pm. Dinner served from 7:00pm until midnight. Closed Saturdays and in August. **Specialities:** regional menu, home cooking. **Hotel:** 4 beds; 3 single rooms, 1 double room with shower. **Other points:** bar, open to non-residents, children welcome, pets welcome – check for details, car park, traditional decor. **Address:** Route Nationale 7.
MR MARCEL VERNAY
**Telephone:** 77.64.36.08
⊗ ⍭ Map 14

## PAJAY, Isère, 38260

### MA PETITE AUBERGE, RD 73
**Languages spoken:** German and English. **Menu:** 55 to 120 Frs. **Accommodation:** 80 to 150 Frs. **Restaurant:** Breakfast served from 6:00am. Lunch served from midday until 2:00pm. Dinner served from 7:00pm until 9:00pm. Closed the 1st fortnight in September. **Specialities:** grenouilles, lotte l'américaine, gratin Dauphinois, regional food. **Hotel:** 7 beds; 3 single rooms, 4 double rooms with shower, private WC, television. **Other points:** bar, open to non-residents, à la carte menu, children welcome, lounge area, terraces, pets welcome – check for details, car park, traditional decor. **Address:** La Côte Saint André.
MME HUGUETTE VIVIER
**Telephone:** 74.54.26.06
⊗ ⍭ 🏠 🍽 Map 14

## PARIGNY LE COTEAU, Loire, 42120

### RELAIS LE PARIGNY
**Menu:** 55 Frs. **Accommodation:** 90 to 120 Frs. **Restaurant:** Breakfast served from 6:00am. Lunch served from 11:30am until 2:30pm. Dinner served from 7:00pm until 9:30pm. Closed Saturdays and from 1 to 16 August. **Specialities:** home cooking. **Hotel:** 7 beds; 5 single rooms, 2 double rooms with shower. **Other points:** bar, open to non-residents, children welcome, pets welcome – check for details, car park, traditional decor. **Address:** Route Nationale 7, le Bas de Rhins.
MME CHRISTINE FAVRE
**Telephone:** 77.62.06.18
⊗ ⍭ 🏠 Map 14

## PERTUIS, Vaucluse, 84120

### LE VICTOR HUGO, on the road to Cavaillon

**Languages spoken:** English and Italian. **Menu:** 55 Frs. **Restaurant:** Breakfast served from 6:30am. Lunch served from 11:30am until 3:00pm. Dinner served from 7:00pm until 9:00pm. Closed Saturdays. **Specialities:** home cooking. **Other points:** bar, open to non-residents, children welcome, terraces, pets welcome – check for details, car park, traditional decor. **Address:** 143, boulevard Victor Hugo.
MR JACKY CHALOT
**Telephone:** 90.79.12.29
⊗ ￥ Map 13

## PIOLENC, Vaucluse, 84420

### LE COMMERCE, RN 7

**Languages spoken:** English. **Menu:** 56 to 120 Frs. **Restaurant:** Breakfast served from 7:00am. Lunch served from midday until 2:00pm. Dinner served from 7:00pm until 9:00pm. Closed Wednesdays and in December. **Specialities:** filet de boeuf aux morilles, poulet, écrevisses, home cooking. **Other points:** bar, open to non-residents, à la carte menu, terraces, pets welcome – check for details, car park, modern decor. **Address:** Place Cours Corsin.
MR ROGER SAMBUCINI
**Telephone:** 90.29.60.14. **Fax:** 90.29.60.14
⊗ ￥ ⌣ Map 13

## PONT D'AIN, Ain, 01160

### LE CRISNO

**Menu:** 60 to 150 Frs. **Restaurant:** Breakfast served from 6:00am. Lunch served from 11:30am until 3:30pm. Dinner served from 7:00pm until 11:00pm. **Specialities:** home cooking. **Other points:** open to non-residents, à la carte menu, children welcome, terraces, pets welcome – check for details, car park, modern decor. **Address:** 56, rue Saint Expéry.
MR IVAN PAYÉ
**Telephone:** 74.39.01.22
⊗ Map 14

## PONT DE CHERUY, Isère, 38230

### LES ROUTIERS, RN 517, Loyettes

**Languages spoken:** English. **Menu:** 54 Frs (wine included). **Accommodation:** 100 to 180 Frs. **Restaurant:** Breakfast served from 5:00am. Lunch served from 11:30am until 3:00pm. Dinner served from 7:30pm until 10:00pm. Closed Sundays. **Specialities:** home cooking. **Hotel:** 30 beds; with shower. **Other points:** bar, open to non-residents, lounge area, terraces, car park, modern decor. **Address:** 30, rue Giffard.
MR BERNARD DEMONET
**Telephone:** 78.32.20.02
⊗ ￥ 🏠 Map 14

## PONT TRAMBOUZE, Rhône, 69240

### LA TRAMBOUZE, the main road between le Thyzy and Cours town

**Menu:** 50 Frs. **Restaurant:** Breakfast served from 6:30am. Closed Sundays. **Specialities:** home cooking. **Other points:** bar, terraces, pets welcome – check for details, traditional decor. **Address:** Place Henri Michalot.
MR PASCAL GIDEL
**Telephone:** 74.64.11.30
⊗ ￥ Map 14

## PONTCHARRA, Isère, 38530

### RELAIS DU PONT DE LA GACHE, RN 90, between Grenoble and Chambéry

**Languages spoken:** English and Italian. **Menu:** 60 to 65 Frs. **Restaurant:** Breakfast served from 6:30am. Lunch served from 11:00am until 3:00pm. Dinner served from 7:00pm until 10:00pm. Closed Saturdays and the 2nd fortnight in August. **Specialities:** regional menu, home cooking. **Other points:** open to non-residents, terraces, pets welcome – check for details, car park, modern decor. **Address:** La Gache.
MR JEAN-PIERRE RUBATAT
**Telephone:** 76.97.30.08
⊗ Map 14

## PONTET (LE), Vaucluse, 84130

### LA CROIX VERTE, RN 7, Avignon

**Menu:** 58 to 78 Frs. **Restaurant:** Breakfast served from 6:30am. Lunch served from midday until 2:00pm. Dinner served from 7:30pm until 10:00pm. Closed Sundays. **Specialities:** regional menu, home cooking. **Other points:** bar, open to non-residents, à la carte menu, terraces, pets welcome – check for details, car park **Address:** Route de Lyon.
MR GUY PRAT
**Telephone:** 90.86.39.56
⊗ ￥ Map 13

## PORT DE BOUC, Bouches-de-Rhône, 13110

### RELAIS DE LA GARE

**Languages spoken:** German. **Restaurant:** Breakfast served from 6:30am. Dinner served from midday until 10:00pm. Closed Sundays. **Other points:** bar. **Address:** Quartier de la Gare.
MLLE BRIGITTE STREIFF
**Telephone:** 42.06.43.43
⊗ ￥ Map 13

## POURRIERES, Var, 83910

### SARL LE LORRAINE-PROVENCE, RN 7, between Aix and Saint Maximin

**Menu:** 59 to 70 Frs. **Restaurant:** Breakfast served from

6:00am. Closed Sundays. **Specialities:** home cooking.
**Other points:** bar, open to non-residents, à la carte
menu, children welcome, terraces, pets welcome – check
for details, car park, modern decor. **Address:** Route
Nationale 7.
MR MAGNE
**Telephone:** 94.78.41.28
⊗ ♀ Map 13

## POUZIN (LE), Ardèche, 07250

### LES ROUTIERS, between Liriol and Privas
**Restaurant:** Breakfast served from 7:00am. Lunch
served from midday until 2:00pm. Dinner served from
7:00pm until 8:30pm. Closed Sundays and from 15
August to 15 September. **Specialities:** home cooking.
**Hotel:** 5 beds; 2 single rooms, 3 double rooms. **Other
points:** bar, open to non-residents, children welcome.
**Address:** 64, rue Olivier de Serres.
MME JULIETTE VIALATTE
**Telephone:** 75.63.83.45
⊗ ♀ 🏠 Map 14

## PRIVAS, Ardèche, 07000

### LA RENAISSANCE, RN 104, between
### Pouzin and Aubenas
**Menu:** 50 Frs. **Restaurant:** Breakfast served from
7:30am. Lunch served from 11:15am until 2:00pm.
Dinner served from 7:15pm until 8:30pm. Closed
Sundays and in August. **Specialities:** home cooking.
**Other points:** bar. **Address:** Place du Champ de Mars.
MR JEAN-PIERRE MONTEIL
**Telephone:** 75.64.21.60
⊗ ♀ Map 14

## PUYRICARD, Bouches-de-Rhône, 13540

### LE TOURANGEAU, RN 7
**Languages spoken:** Italian. **Restaurant:** Dinner served
from midday until midnight. Closed Sundays and in
August. **Hotel:** 14 beds. **Other points:** bar. **Address:**
Lieu dit 'La Petite Calale', Route Nationale 7.
MME DANIELLE ROCCIA
**Telephone:** 42.21.60.65
⊗ ♀ 🏠 Map 13

## RAVOIRE (LA), Savoie, 73490

### LA PETITE TARENTAISE, RN 6 and CD
### 21, Albertville, exit la Ravoire
**Menu:** 62 Frs (wine and coffee included). **Restaurant:**
Lunch served from 11:30am until 2:30pm. Dinner served
from 7:00pm until 9:00pm. Closed Sundays.
**Specialities:** home cooking. **Other points:** bar, car park.
**Address:** Route Nationale 6.
MME MARYSE FAURE
**Telephone:** 79.72.92.27
⊗ ♀ Map 14

## REYRIEUX, Ain, 01600

### RESTAURANT DE LA GARE, RD 933,
### between Neuville and Trévoux
**Places of interest:** Montagne bourbonnaise (20km),
Vichy (3km). **Languages spoken:** Spanish and a little
English. **Menu:** 65 Frs (wine and coffee included) –
Sundays 80 to 135 Frs. **Restaurant:** Breakfast served
from 7:00am. Lunch served from 11:00am until 3:30pm.
Dinner served from 7:00pm until 9:00pm. Closed
Sundays and 1 week in April. **Specialities:** couscous,
paëlla, choucroute, potée lorraine, home cooking. **Other
points:** bar, children welcome, terraces, pets welcome –
check for details, car park, traditional decor. **Address:**
Rue de la Gare.
MME YVONNE ORTIZ
**Telephone:** 74.00.03.04
⊗ ♀ Map 14

## RIVE DE GIER – LA MADELEINE, Loire, 42800

### RESTAURANT LE BARBECUE, RN 88, the
### main road between Lyon and Saint Etienne
**Menu:** 55 to 110 Frs. **Restaurant:** Breakfast served
from 7:00am. Lunch served from 11:45am until 2:30pm.
Dinner served from 7:00pm until 9:00pm. Closed
Mondays. **Specialities:** regional menu, home cooking.
**Other points:** bar, open to non-residents, à la carte
menu, children welcome, lounge area, terraces, pets
welcome – check for details, car park, modern decor.
**Address:** 70, rue des Martyrs de la Résistance.
MME MARIE-CLAUDE GONON
**Telephone:** 77.75.59.70
⊗ ♀ Map 14

## ROCHE LA MOLIERE, Loire, 42230

### LE FLORENCE, between Roche la Molière
### and Saint Genest Lerpt
**Menu:** 47 Frs. **Restaurant:** Lunch served from midday
until 2:00pm. Dinner served from 7:00pm until 11:00pm.
Closed Sundays and in August. **Specialities:** home
cooking. **Other points:** à la carte menu. **Address:** 3, rue
des Carrières.
MR MICHEL BRUYAS
**Telephone:** 77.90.58.41
⊗ Map 14

## ROCHEMAURE, Ardèche, 07400

### RELAIS DE LA CONDAMINE, RN 86, the
### main road between Lyon and Marseille
**Menu:** 48 Frs. **Restaurant:** Breakfast served from
6:00am. Lunch served from 11:00am until 2:00pm.
Dinner served from 7:00pm until 8:30pm. Closed
Sundays. **Specialities:** home cooking. **Other points:**
open to non-residents, terraces, pets welcome – check
for details, car park.

MME JOSIANE SICOIT
**Telephone:** 75.52.96.26
⊗ Map 14

## ROCHETAILLEE, Isère, 38520

### HOTEL BELLEDONNE, RD 91, between Briançon and l'Alpe d'Huez
**Menu:** 65 to 110 Frs. **Accommodation:** 110 to 300 Frs. **Restaurant:** Breakfast served from 6:30am. Lunch served from midday until 1:30pm. Dinner served from 7:30pm until 9:00pm. Closed Saturdays. **Specialities:** (sur commande), home cooking. **Hotel:** 21 beds; 21 double rooms with shower, bath. **Other points:** bar, open to non-residents, à la carte menu, terraces, pets welcome – check for details, car park, modern decor.
MME MIREILLE ESPOSITO
**Telephone:** 76.80.07.04
⊗ ℉ ⌂ ⌷ ☆ Map 14

## ROQUE D'ANTHERON (LA), Bouches-de-Rhône, 13640

### AU RELAIS FLEURI, CD 543 and 561, at the intersection of CD 561 and 543
**Languages spoken:** English, German and Italian. **Menu:** 55 to 80 Frs. **Accommodation:** 120 to 150 Frs. **Restaurant:** Breakfast served from 7:00am. Lunch served from midday until 2:00pm. Dinner served from 7:30pm until 10:00pm. **Specialities:** home cooking. **Hotel:** 9 beds; 5 single rooms, 4 double rooms with shower. **Other points:** bar, open to non-residents, à la carte menu, children welcome, terraces, pets welcome – check for details, car park, traditional decor. **Address:** Hameau de Saint-Christophe.
MR GUY AUGUSTE
**Telephone:** 42.50.20.24
⊗ ℉ ⌂ Map 13

## SABLONNIERES, Isère, 38460

### BAR RESTAURANT DE LA PLACE, RD 522 and 517
**Menu:** 55 (75 Frs Sundays). **Restaurant:** Breakfast served from 6:30am. Lunch served from midday until 2:30pm. Dinner served from 7:30pm until 9:00pm. Closed Saturdays and in August. **Specialities:** home cooking. **Other points:** bar.
MME NOELLE MAILLER
**Telephone:** 74.92.80.19
⊗ ℉ Map 14

## SAILLANS, Drôme, 26340

### LE NATIONAL PMU, RN 93, between Dié and Gap
**Menu:** 55 to 80 Frs. **Accommodation:** 100 to 150 Frs. **Restaurant:** Breakfast served from 8:00am. Lunch served from 12:30pm until 2:00pm. Dinner served

from 7:30pm until 8:00pm. Closed Wednesdays and 5 weeks in September/October. **Specialities:** gigot d'agneau, daube provençale, regional food, home cooking. **Hotel:** 6 beds; 2 single rooms, 4 double rooms with shower. **Other points:** bar, open to non-residents, children welcome, terraces, pets welcome – check for details, car park, traditional decor. **Address:** Grande Rue.
MME JEANINE CHAUVET
**Telephone:** 75.21.51.33
⊗ ℉ ⌂ Map 14

## SAINT BONNET LES OULES, Loire, 42330

### LE GORDON
**Menu:** 50 to 100 Frs. **Restaurant:** Breakfast served from 9:00am. Lunch served from midday until 2:00pm. Dinner served from 6:30pm until 9:30pm. **Specialities:** home cooking. **Other points:** bar, children welcome, terraces, pets welcome – check for details, car park, modern decor. **Address:** Lapra.
MME MARIE-THÉRESE MUNIER
**Telephone:** 77.94.93.30
⊗ ℉ Map 14

## SAINT CLAIR DU RHONE, Isère, 38370

### LE RELAIS FLEURI, RN 516
**Languages spoken:** Italian. **Restaurant:** Open 24 hours. **Hotel:** 7 beds. **Other points:** bar, car park. **Address:** 3, rue du Commandant l'Herminier.
MR TONINO TOGNOLONI
**Telephone:** 74.56.43.12
⊗ ℉ ⌂ Map 14

## SAINT CYR DE FAVIERES, Loire, 42132

### RELAIS ALSACIEN, RN 7, the main road between Paris and Lyon
**Restaurant:** Breakfast served from 6:00am. Lunch served from 11:30am until 2:30pm. Dinner served from 7:30pm until 10:00pm. Closed Saturdays and in July. **Specialities:** home cooking. **Other points:** bar, open to non-residents, terraces, pets welcome – check for details, car park, traditional decor.
MR MARCEL TERRIER
**Telephone:** 77.64.81.01
⊗ ℉ Map 14

### RELAIS ROUTIERS LAGOUTTE, RN 7
**Languages spoken:** English. **Menu:** 50 to 130 Frs. **Accommodation:** 75 Frs (per person). **Restaurant:** Breakfast served from 5:30am. Lunch served from midday until 3:00pm. Dinner served from 7:00pm until 10:00pm. Closed Saturdays and in August. **Specialities:** home cooking. **Hotel:** 6 beds; 1 single room, 5 double

rooms. **Other points:** bar, open to non-residents, à la carte menu, terraces, pets welcome – check for details, car park, traditional decor. **Address:** L'Hôpital sur Rhin.
MR YVES JONARD
**Telephone:** 77.64.80.13
⊗ ℣ ⌂ Map 14

# SAINT CYR SUR MENTHON, Ain, 01380

## SARL LE SAINT CYR, RN 79
**Languages spoken:** English. **Menu:** 50 to 55 Frs.
**Restaurant:** Breakfast served from 6:00am. Lunch served from 11:30am until 2:30pm. Dinner served from 7:00pm until 11:00pm. **Address:** Route Nationale 79, le Logis.
MR ALLEK
**Telephone:** 85.36.30.69
⊗ Map 14

# SAINT CYR SUR MER, Var, 83270

## MICKEY RESTO, on the road to Bandol
**Menu:** 45 to 85 Frs. **Restaurant:** Lunch served from midday until midnight. Dinner served from 7:15pm until midnight. Closed Sundays and from 20 December to 3 January. **Specialities:** regional menu, home cooking. **Other points:** open to non-residents, à la carte menu, children welcome, pets welcome – check for details, car park, traditional decor. **Address:** 20, rue d'Arquier.
MR CHRISTIAN REVERBERI
**Telephone:** 94.26.49.98
⊗ Map 13

# SAINT ETIENNE, Loire, 42000

## LE MISTRAL, RN 82, near customs
**Languages spoken:** Spanish. **Menu:** 53 Frs (wine and coffee included). **Restaurant:** Breakfast served from 6:00am. Lunch served from midday until 3:00pm.
Dinner served from 7:30pm until 10:00pm. Closed Saturdays, public holidays and in August. **Specialities:** home cooking. **Other points:** bar, terraces, pets welcome – check for details, car park, traditional decor.
**Address:** 4, rue Jean Neyret.
MME MARTINE GANTE
**Telephone:** 77.32.95.39
⊗ ℣ Map 14

## RELAIS DE L'AUTOROUTE, RN 82, motorway Lyon/Saint Etienne
**Menu:** 57 Frs. **Restaurant:** Breakfast served from 5:30am. Closed Sundays. **Specialities:** home cooking.
**Other points:** bar, children welcome, traditional decor. **Address:** 57, rue des Marandes, Terrenoire.
MME RÉGINE ROUX
**Telephone:** 77.95.63.71
⊗ ℣ Map 14

# SAINT FIRMIN, Hautes Alpes, 05800

## LA TRINITE, RN 85, between Gap and Grenoble
**Menu:** 60 to 150 Frs. **Accommodation:** 130 to 220 Frs.
**Restaurant:** Breakfast served from 6:00am. Lunch served from midday. Dinner served until 11:00pm. **Specialities:** regional menu, home cooking. **Hotel:** 12 beds; 8 single rooms, 4 double rooms with shower, bath, private WC.
**Other points:** bar, open to non-residents, à la carte menu, children welcome, terraces, pets welcome – check for details, car park. **Address:** Route Nationale 85, Route Napoléon.
MR GÉRARD MARLETTA
**Telephone:** 92.55.21.64
⊗ ℣ ⌂ ☆ Map 13

# SAINT GENIX SUR GUIERS, Savoie, 73240

## AUBERGE CAMPAGNARDE, RD 916
**Menu:** 55 to 110 Frs. **Restaurant:** Breakfast served from 7:00am. Lunch served from 11:00am until 3:00pm. Dinner served from 7:00pm until 9:00pm. Closed Saturdays, in September and in October. **Specialities:** home cooking.
**Other points:** bar, open to non-residents, à la carte menu, terraces, pets welcome – check for details, car park, traditional decor. **Address:** Hameau de Joudin.
MME REINE AILLOUD
**Telephone:** 76.31.80.19
⊗ ℣ Map 14

# SAINT GEOIRE EN VALDAINE, Isère, 38620

## AU NENUPHAR, CD 82, between Voiron and le Pont de Beauvoisin
**Languages spoken:** Italian. **Menu:** 60 to 120 Frs.
**Restaurant:** Breakfast served from 6:30am. Lunch served from 11:30am until 2:30pm. Dinner served from 7:00pm until 9:00pm. **Specialities:** home cooking.
**Other points:** open to non-residents, children welcome, pets welcome – check for details, car park, modern decor. **Address:** Lieu dit 'La Combe'.
MR ALAIN GOBATTO
**Telephone:** 76.07.13.91
⊗ Map 14

# SAINT HILAIRE DU ROSIER, Isère, 38840

## LE RELAIS, RN 92, between Grenoble and Valence
**Languages spoken:** German and Spanish. **Menu:** 60 to 98 Frs. **Accommodation:** 160 Frs. **Restaurant:**
Breakfast served from 7:00am. Lunch served from midday until 2:00pm. Dinner served from 7:00pm until 10:00pm. Closed Saturdays and in September.
**Specialities:** regional menu. **Hotel:** 5 beds; with shower,

bath, private WC. **Other points:** bar, open to non-residents, à la carte menu, children welcome, terraces, car park, modern decor.
MR TONY LOPEZ
**Telephone:** 76.64.53.84
⊗ ♀ 🏠 Map 14

## SAINT JEAN DE CHEVELU, Savoie, 73170

### LES QUATRE CHEMINS, RN 504, between Lyon and Chambéry
**Languages spoken:** English. **Menu:** 59 to 78 Frs.
**Accommodation:** 110 to 175 Frs. **Restaurant:** Breakfast served from 4:00am. Lunch served from midday until 2:00pm. Dinner served from 7:00pm until 10:00pm. Closed Saturdays and end of December/beginning of January. **Specialities:** home cooking. **Hotel:** 9 beds; 8 single rooms, 1 double room with bath, private WC. **Other points:** bar, open to non-residents, lounge area, pets welcome – check for details, car park, traditional decor. **Address:** Lieu dit 'Les Quatre Chemins'.
MR JEAN RUBOD
**Telephone:** 79.36.80.06
⊗ ♀ 🏠 Map 14

## SAINT JEAN DE MAURIENNE, Savoie, 73300

### BAR RESTAURANT RELAIS ROUTIERS, RN 6
**Languages spoken:** Italian. **Menu:** 50 to 150 Frs.
**Restaurant:** Breakfast served from 7:00am. Lunch served from 11:30am until 2:00pm. Dinner served from 7:00pm until 10:00pm. Closed Sundays. **Specialities:** home cooking. **Other points:** bar, open to non-residents, children welcome, terraces, pets welcome – check for details, car park, traditional decor. **Address:** Place du Champ de Foire.
MME ANGELE DOMPNIER
**Telephone:** 79.64.12.03
⊗ ♀ 🍵 Map 14

## SAINT JOSEPH DE RIVIERE, Isère, 38134

### LE RELAIS CHAMPETRE, CD 520
**Languages spoken:** German and Italian. **Menu:** 40 to 120 Frs. **Accommodation:** 170 Frs. **Restaurant:** Breakfast served from 6:00am. Lunch served from midday until 2:30pm. Dinner served from 7:00pm until 9:00pm. Closed Saturdays, 10 days at All Saints holiday and 10 days at Christmas. **Specialities:** home cooking. **Hotel:** 7 beds; 7 double rooms with shower, private WC. **Other points:** bar, open to non-residents, à la carte menu, children welcome, terraces, pets welcome – check for details, car park. **Address:** Le Pont Demay.
MME ADELINE MANDRILLON
**Telephone:** 76.55.49.08
⊗ ♀ 🏠 Map 14

## SAINT JUST DE CLAIX, Isère, 38680

### BAR RESTAURANT LE DAUPHINOIS, RN 532, the main road between Valence and Grenoble
**Languages spoken:** German and English. **Menu:** 55 Frs. **Restaurant:** Breakfast served from 6:00am. Lunch served from 11:30am until 3:00pm. Dinner served from 7:00pm until 9:00pm. **Specialities:** home cooking. **Other points:** bar, open to non-residents, children welcome, pets welcome – check for details, car park, modern decor. **Address:** Le Village.
MME ARLETTE DONCQUES
**Telephone:** 75.47.55.25
⊗ ♀ Map 14

## SAINT LAURENT DU VAR, Alpes Maritimes, 06700

### AU COUP DE FUSIL
**Languages spoken:** Italian. **Menu:** 55 to 80 Frs.
**Restaurant:** Breakfast served from 6:30am. Lunch served from 11:30am until 3:00pm. Closed Sundays, public holidays and in August. **Specialities:** regional menu, home cooking. **Other points:** open to non-residents, à la carte menu, pets welcome – check for details, car park, modern decor. **Address:** Boulevard Pierre & Marie Curie, ZI Secteur B.
MR EUGENE BAGI
**Telephone:** 93.31.60.55
⊗ Map 13

### LE RELAIS ROUTIER
**Languages spoken:** German, English and Spanish.
**Menu:** 57 Frs. **Restaurant:** Lunch served from midday until 2:00pm. Dinner served from 7:00pm until 9:30pm. Closed Sundays. **Specialities:** home cooking. **Other points:** bar, car park. **Address:** Allée des Cableurs, ZI Secteur B.
MR CHARLES TORRENTE
**Telephone:** 93.31.26.47
⊗ ♀ Map 13

## SAINT MARCEL DE FELINES, Loire, 42122

### LE REVOULTE, RN 82, between Roanne and Saint Etienne
**Languages spoken:** English. **Menu:** 54 to 105 Frs.
**Restaurant:** Breakfast served from 7:30am. Lunch served from 11:45am until 2:00pm. Dinner served from 7:00pm until 9:00pm. Closed Mondays and in June. **Specialities:** home cooking. **Other points:** bar, open to non-residents, terraces, pets welcome – check for details, car park, modern decor. **Address:** Lieu dit 'Le Revoulte'.
MR DIDIER REY
**Telephone:** 77.64.61.60
⊗ ♀ Map 14

## SAINT MARCEL LES VALENCE,

Drôme, 26320

### LA PRAIRIE, RN 532, between Valence and Romans

**Menu:** 55 to 110 Frs. **Restaurant:** Breakfast served from 7:00am. Closed in August. **Specialities:** regional menu, home cooking. **Other points:** bar, open to non-residents, à la carte menu, children welcome, terraces, pets welcome – check for details, car park. **Address:** 8, rue de la Liberté.
MR MICHEL MONTUSCLAT
**Telephone:** 75.58.70.38
⊗ ⵏ Map 14

## SAINT MARTIN DE CLELLES,

Isère, 38930

### MON REGAL, RN 75

**Restaurant:** Dinner served from midday until 9:00pm. Closed all evenings in November to April. **Specialities:** home cooking. **Other points:** open to non-residents, à la carte menu, children welcome, terraces, car park.
**Address:** Route Nationale 75.
MME MONIQUE FLANDIN
**Telephone:** 76.34.42.84
⊗ Map 14

## SAINT MARTIN DE CRAU, Bouches-

de-Rhône, 13310

### LA CABANE BAMBOU, RN 113, between Salon and Arles

**Languages spoken:** English, Spanish and Italian.
**Restaurant:** Open 24 hours **Specialities:** regional menu.
**Hotel:** 10 beds. **Other points:** bar, à la carte menu, terraces, pets welcome – check for details, car park.
**Address:** Route Nationale 113.
JACQUES GIRAUD & FILS
**Telephone:** 90.58.67.25, 90.50.62.52
⊗ ⵏ ⌂ Map 13

### LE RELAIS DES SPORTS

**Languages spoken:** Spanish and Italian. **Menu:** 50 Frs.
**Restaurant:** Breakfast served from 6:00am. Closed in August. **Other points:** bar, à la carte menu. **Address:** La Dynamite.
MR DANIEL NIVAGGIOLI
**Telephone:** 90.47.05.24
⊗ ⵏ Map 13

### RESTAURANT DE LA GARE, near the station

**Menu:** 52 Frs. **Accommodation:** 100 Frs. **Restaurant:** Breakfast served from 5:30am. Lunch served from 11:30am until 2:30pm. Closed Sundays. **Hotel:** 7 beds. **Other points:** bar, car park. **Address:** Route de la Dynamite.
MR PASCAL SELVA
**Telephone:** 90.47.05.18
⊗ ⵏ ⌂ Map 13

## SAINT PAUL LE JEUNE, Ardèche,

07460

### RELAIS DE CHEYRES, RD 104

**Menu:** 60 to 80 Frs. **Restaurant:** Breakfast served from 8:00am. Closed Sundays. **Specialities:** regional menu, home cooking. **Other points:** bar, open to non-residents, children welcome, terraces, car park, traditional decor.
**Address:** Banne.
MME MARIE-THÉRÉSE VERNEDE
**Telephone:** 75.39.30.09
⊗ ⵏ Map 14

## SAINT PAUL TROIS CHATEAUX,

Drôme, 26130

### HOTEL RESTAURANT DE PROVENCE, RD 59 near A 7, south Montélimar or Bollène

**Menu:** 60 to 150 Frs. **Accommodation:** 65 to 130 Frs.
**Restaurant:** Lunch served from midday until 1:45pm. Dinner served from midday until 9:00pm. Closed Sundays and in February. **Specialities:** home cooking.
**Hotel:** 7 beds; with shower. **Other points:** bar, open to non-residents, à la carte menu, children welcome, lounge area, terraces, pets welcome – check for details, car park, traditional decor. **Address:** 11, avenue Charles de Gaulle.
MME HÉLENE ENTRINGER
**Telephone:** 75.04.72.48
⊗ ⵏ ⌂ Map 14

## SAINT PRIEST EN JAREZ, Loire,

42270

### LE RELAIS FORESIEN

**Languages spoken:** English, Spanish and Italian. **Menu:** 48 to 60 Frs. **Restaurant:** Closed Saturdays. **Other points:** bar. **Address:** 138, avenue Albert Raymond.
MME GERMAINE MONCEL
**Telephone:** 77.74.63.14
⊗ ⵏ Map 14

## SAINT RAPHAEL, Var, 83700

### LE BEL AZUR, RN 98

**Languages spoken:** Italian. **Menu:** 60 to 140 Frs.
**Accommodation:** 200 to 250 Frs. **Restaurant:** Breakfast served from 7:00am. Lunch served from midday until 2:00pm. Dinner served from 7:00pm until 9:30pm. Closed Saturdays and from 24 December to 4 January. **Specialities:** bouillabaisse, aïoli, paëlla, regional food, home cooking. **Hotel:** 20 beds; 3 single rooms, 17 double rooms with television, telephone.
**Other points:** bar, open to non-residents, à la carte menu, children welcome, pets welcome – check for details, car park. **Address:** 247, boulevard de Provence.
MME ROBERT ET NICOLE
MAGNANI/MASTROYANNAKI
**Telephone:** 94.95.14.08
⊗ ⵏ ⌂ ⌁ ☆ Map 13

## SAINT ROMAIN LA MOTTE, Loire, 42640

### *AU BON ACCUEIL, RN 7, the main road between Paris and Roanne*

**Menu:** 60 to 80 Frs. **Accommodation:** 72 to 176 Frs. **Restaurant:** Breakfast served from 5:00am. Lunch served from 11:00am until 3:00pm. Dinner served from 7:00pm until 10:30pm. Closed Saturdays and in September. **Specialities:** home cooking. **Hotel:** 3 beds; 3 double rooms with shower. **Other points:** open to non-residents, pets welcome – check for details, car park, traditional decor. **Address:** Les Baraques, Saint Germain Lespinasse.
MME LUCIENNE GALICHON
**Telephone:** 77.70.12.03
⊗ Map 14

## SAINTE FOY L'ARGENTIERE, Rhône, 69610

### *AUBERGE DE LA PLACE, RN 89, the main road between Lyon and Clermont Ferrand*

**Menu:** 50 Frs. **Restaurant:** Breakfast served from 6:30am. Lunch served from 11:30am until 2:30pm. Closed Saturdays and in August. **Specialities:** home cooking. **Other points:** children welcome, pets welcome – check for details, car park, traditional decor. **Address:** 49, Grande Rue.
MME YVONNE GOUBIER
**Telephone:** 74.70.00.51
⊗ Map 14

## SAINTE FOY LES LYON, Rhône, 69110

### *AU REVEIL MATIN*

**Menu:** 55 to 60 Frs. **Restaurant:** Breakfast served from 6:00am. Lunch served from 11:00am until 3:00pm. Closed Saturdays and in August. **Specialities:** home cooking. **Other points:** bar, open to non-residents, terraces, pets welcome – check for details, car park. **Address:** 66, route de la Libération.
MME MICHELE LELY
**Telephone:** 78.59.03.05
⊗ 🍸 Map 14

## SALAISE SUR SANNE, Isère, 38150

### *RELAIS DE LA SANNE, RN 7, the main road between Lyon and Valence, exit Chanas*

**Languages spoken:** German and English. **Menu:** 62 to 88 Frs. **Restaurant:** Breakfast served from 6:00am. Lunch served from 11:45am until 2:30pm. Dinner served from 7:15pm until 10:30pm. Closed Sundays. **Specialities:** home cooking. **Other points:** bar, open to non-residents, à la carte menu, children welcome, lounge area, terraces, pets welcome – check for details, car park, modern decor. **Address:** Route Nationale 7.
MR MARC GIRAUD
**Telephone:** 74.86.37.91
⊗ 🍸 Map 14

## SALON DE PROVENCE, Bouches-de-Rhône, 13300

### *RESTAURANT LA JAUFFRETTE*

**Menu:** 49 to 60 Frs. **Restaurant:** Closed Saturdays and in August. **Other points:** bar, car park. **Address:** Lieu dit 'La Jauffrette', Route Nationale 113.
MR CLAUDE CACHON
**Telephone:** 90.53.20.19
⊗ 🍸 Map 13

## SARCEY, Rhône, 69490

### *RELAIS DES MARRONNIERS, RN 7, between l'Arbresle and Tarare*

**Languages spoken:** English. **Menu:** 50 to 80 Frs. **Restaurant:** Breakfast served from 6:00am. Lunch served from midday until 1:30pm. Closed Wednesdays. **Specialities:** home cooking. **Other points:** bar, pets welcome – check for details, car park, modern decor. **Address:** Place de l'Eglise.
MR PATRICK PARISI
**Telephone:** 74.26.86.65
⊗ 🍸 Map 14

## SATOLAS ET BONCE, Isère, 38290

### *LE RELAIS DU CHAFFARD, CD 75, between Vienne and Crémieu*

**Menu:** 58 Frs (coffee included). **Restaurant:** Breakfast served from 6:00am. Lunch served from midday until 3:00pm. Dinner served from 7:00pm until 11:00pm. Closed Saturdays. **Specialities:** home cooking. **Other points:** bar, open to non-residents, children welcome, terraces, pets welcome – check for details, car park, traditional decor. **Address:** Chemin Départemental 75.
MR DENIS ZANONI
**Telephone:** 74.94.16.16
⊗ 🍸 Map 14

## SAULCE, Drôme, 26270

### *LE DISQUE BLEU, RN 7 and RD 26, exit motorway Loriol and Montélimar north*

**Menu:** 60 Frs. **Accommodation:** 60 to 80 Frs. **Restaurant:** Dinner served from midday until midnight. Closed Sundays. **Specialities:** home cooking. **Hotel:** 8 beds; 4 single rooms, 4 double rooms. **Other points:** bar, à la carte menu, children welcome, pets welcome – check for details, car park. **Address:** Quartier des Blâches, Cliousclat.
MR JACQUES BRILLO
**Telephone:** 75.63.00.08. **Fax:** 75.63.13.45
⊗ 🍸 🏠 Map 14

## SAUVAGES (LES), Rhône, 69170

### HOTEL SAINT PIERRE, RD 8

**Accommodation:** 80 to 220 Frs. **Restaurant:** Lunch served from midday until 1:30pm. Dinner served from 7:00pm until 8:30pm. Closed Wednesdays, beginning of September and 1 week after Christmas Day. **Specialities:** home cooking. **Hotel:** 7 beds; 6 single rooms, 1 double room with shower, private WC. **Other points:** bar, open to non-residents, car park, traditional decor.
MR JEAN GOUTTENOIRE
**Telephone:** 74.89.10.49
⊗ ♈ ⌂ Map 14

## SAVINES LE LAC, Hautes Alpes, 05160

### LE CHABRIERES

**Languages spoken:** German, English and Italian. **Menu:** 55 to 95 Frs. **Restaurant:** Breakfast served from 4:30am. Dinner served from midday until 11:00pm. Closed Sundays. **Other points:** bar, à la carte menu, car park.
MME NICOLE BERNARD
**Telephone:** 92.44.28.09
⊗ ♈ Map 13

## SENAS, Bouches-de-Rhône, 13560

### L'ETAPE

**Menu:** 54 Frs. **Restaurant:** Breakfast served from 6:00am. Closed Saturdays. **Specialities:** home cooking. **Other points:** open to non-residents, à la carte menu, pets welcome – check for details, car park. **Address:** Route Nationale 7.
SNC VEYRIER FRERES
**Telephone:** 90.59.22.81
⊗ Map 13

## SEYNOD, Haute-Savoie, 74600

### RELAIS SAINTE CATHERINE, RN 201, exit Annecy south, towards Chambéry

**Languages spoken:** German and English. **Menu:** 58 Frs (wine and coffee included) **Accommodation:** 100 to 150 Frs. **Restaurant:** Lunch served from midday until 2:00pm. Dinner served from 7:00pm until 9:00pm. Closed Saturdays, 1 week in July and 15 days in August. **Specialities:** steack aux morilles, fondue savoyarde, regional food, home cooking. **Hotel:** 10 beds; 10 double rooms with shower, bath. **Other points:** bar, open to non-residents, à la carte menu, lounge area, terraces, pets welcome – check for details, car park, modern decor. **Address:** 181, route d'Aix.
MR LUCIEN ZERBOLA
**Telephone:** 50.69.00.86. **Fax:** 50.52.07.49
⊗ ♈ ⌂ ☆ Map 14

## SIGOTTIER, Hautes Alpes, 05700

### PONT LA BARQUE, RN 75

**Languages spoken:** Italian. **Menu:** 60 to 100 Frs. **Restaurant:** Breakfast served from 7:00am. Lunch served from 11:00am until 3:00pm. Dinner served from 7:00pm until 10:00pm. Closed Sundays and from 25 December to 7 January. **Specialities:** home cooking. **Other points:** bar, open to non-residents, à la carte menu, terraces, pets welcome – check for details, car park, traditional decor. **Address:** Pont la Barque.
MR CLAUDE FAIZENDE
**Telephone:** 92.67.04.15
⊗ ♈ Map 13

## SURY LE COMTAL, Loire, 42450

### RESTAURANT DE LA TERRASSE, RD 8, between Saint Etienne and Montbrison

**Menu:** 65 Frs. **Restaurant:** Breakfast served from 7:00am. Lunch served from 11:45am until 3:00pm. Dinner served from 7:00pm until 9:00pm. Closed Sundays and 1 week from 15 August. **Specialities:** home cooking. **Other points:** bar, open to non-residents, children welcome, car park, modern decor. **Address:** Rue Jordan.
MME GEORGETTE COTE
**Telephone:** 77.30.81.38
⊗ ♈ Map 14

## TARARE, Rhône, 69170

### LE PROVENCAL, RN 7, Roanne

**Menu:** 50 Frs. **Restaurant:** Breakfast served from 5:00am. Lunch served from 11:30am until 2:00pm. Dinner served from 7:00pm until 8:00pm. Closed Saturdays. **Specialities:** home cooking. **Other points:** bar. **Address:** 8, avenue Edouard Hérriot.
MR GEORGES BIDOT
**Telephone:** 74.63.33.64
⊗ ♈ Map 14

## TEIL (LE), Ardèche, 07400

### AU BON COIN, RN 86

**Restaurant:** Closed in August. **Other points:** bar. **Address:** 11, rue Henri Barbusse.
MME MARIE GINESTE
**Telephone:** 75.49.02.61
⊗ ♈ Map 14

## TERNAY, Rhône, 69360

### LE GAULOIS, CD 12, exit Chasse en Rhône, towards Saint Synphorien de Ozon

**Languages spoken:** English. **Menu:** 55 to 175 Frs. **Restaurant:** Breakfast served from 6:00am. Lunch served from midday until 2:30pm. Dinner served from 7:00pm until 10:00pm. Closed Sundays and in August. **Specialities:** home cooking. **Other points:** bar, open to non-residents, à la carte menu, children welcome, terraces, pets welcome – check for details, car park, traditional decor. **Address:** 2, rue Saint Nicolas.
MR JEAN-PIERRE COURSAT
**Telephone:** 78.73.07.34
⊗ ♈ Map 14

## THONES, Haute-Savoie, 74230

### L'HERMITAGE, RN 509

**Languages spoken:** English. **Menu:** 60 to 160 Frs.
**Accommodation:** 120 to 200 Frs. **Restaurant:**
Breakfast served from 7:00am. Lunch served from
midday until 2:00pm. Dinner served from 7:00pm until
9:00pm. Closed 1st week of May and from 20 October to
15 November. **Specialities:** regional menu, home
cooking. **Hotel:** 45 beds; 12 single rooms, 33 double
rooms with shower, bath, private WC, television,
telephone. **Other points:** bar, open to non-residents, à la
carte menu, children welcome, lounge area, terraces, car
park, traditional decor. **Address:** Avenue du Vieux Pont.
MR PIERRE BONNET
**Telephone:** 50.02.00.31
⊗ 𝖸 🏠 👝 ☆ Map 14

## TIGNIEU, Isère, 38230

### AUBERGE DES CHARMILLES, RD 18

**Menu:** 52 to 110 Frs – Plat du jour 35 Frs. **Restaurant:**
Breakfast served from 7:00am. Lunch served from midday
until 2:30pm. Closed Sundays. **Specialities:** home cooking.
**Other points:** bar, open to non-residents, à la carte menu,
children welcome. **Address:** 71, route de Bourgoin.
MME JOSIANE RENON
**Telephone:** 78.32.23.57
⊗ 𝖸 Map 14

## TOULON, Var, 83000

### RESTAURANT DE L'ESCAILLON, RN 8, Toulon/Marseille

**Menu:** 58 Frs (¼ carafe wine included). **Restaurant:**
Breakfast served from 6:00am. Lunch served from
midday until 2:00pm. Dinner served from 7:30pm until
9:00pm. Closed the 2nd fortnight in August.
**Specialities:** home cooking. **Other points:** bar, open to
non-residents, pets welcome – check for details, car
park, traditional decor. **Address:** 2, rue Chateaubriand.
MR BERNARD LEMAIRE
**Telephone:** 94.24.21.02
⊗ 𝖸 Map 13

## TOUR DU PIN (LA), Isère, 38110

### CHEZ BABETH, RN 6, between la Tour de la Pin and les Abrets, the main road between Chambéry and Lyon

**Menu:** 58 to 98 Frs. **Restaurant:** Breakfast served from
5:30am. Lunch served from midday until 2:00pm.
Dinner served from 7:00pm until 9:00pm. Closed
Sundays. **Specialities:** home cooking. **Other points:**
bar, open to non-residents, à la carte menu, terraces, car
park, modern decor. **Address:** Saint Didier de la Tour.
MME ELISABETH ROSTAING
**Telephone:** 74.97.15.87
⊗ 𝖸 👝 Map 14

## TRETS, Bouches-de-Rhône, 13530

### L'AERODROME, RN 7

**Languages spoken:** English, Spanish and Italian.
**Menu:** 60 Frs. **Restaurant:** Breakfast served from
5:30am. Closed Saturdays and public holidays and the
following day. **Specialities:** regional menu, home
cooking. **Other points:** bar, lounge area, terraces, pets
welcome – check for details, car park. **Address:** Route
Nationale 7.
MR PASCAL SECLET
**Telephone:** 42.61.48.26, 42.61.49.41
⊗ 𝖸 Map 13

## TULLINS FURES, Isère, 38210

### RESTAURANT DU CENTRE, RN 92, the main road between Grenoble and Valence

**Languages spoken:** English. **Menu:** 50 Frs.
**Restaurant:** Breakfast served from 7:02am. Lunch
served from 8:01pm until 7:01pm. Dinner served from
7:00pm until midnight. Closed Wednesdays.
**Specialities:** sur commande, home cooking. **Other
points:** bar, open to non-residents, children welcome,
pets welcome – check for details, car park, traditional
decor. **Address:** 10, boulevard Michel Perret.
MME MONIQUE DUCLOS
**Telephone:** 76.07.93.08
⊗ 𝖸 Map 14

## VAUX EN BUGEY, Ain, 01150

### LE RAMEQUIN, RN 75, Grenoble

**Restaurant:** Breakfast served from 6:00am. Lunch
served from 11:45am until 2:30pm. Dinner served from
7:15pm until 9:30pm. Closed Saturdays, 15 days in
August and 15 days in December. **Specialities:** home
cooking. **Other points:** bar, open to non-residents,
terraces, pets welcome – check for details, car park.
**Address:** Route Nationale 75.
MME MICHELLE GALLON
**Telephone:** 74.35.95.09, 74.35.95.09
⊗ 𝖸 Map 14

## VENISSIEUX, Rhône, 69200

### LES ROUTIERS, the main road between Saint Etienne and Marseille

**Languages spoken:** Spanish. **Restaurant:** Breakfast
served from 6:00am. Lunch served from 11:30am until
3:00pm. Dinner served from 7:00pm until 9:00pm.
Closed Saturdays and from 14 July to 15 August.
**Specialities:** home cooking. **Other points:** bar, terraces,
car park, modern decor. **Address:** 66, boulevard Joliot
Curie.
MR HERVÉ LIGIER
**Telephone:** 78.76.49.94
⊗ 𝖸 Map 14

## VEYRINS THUELLIN, Isère, 38630

### L'OUSTRAL, RN 75, Bourg Grenoble

**Languages spoken:** English and Italian. **Menu:** 55 to 110 Frs. **Accommodation:** 130 to 170 Frs. **Restaurant:** Breakfast served from 6:30am. Lunch served from midday until 2:30pm. Dinner served from 7:00pm until 10:00pm. Closed from 1 to 15 October. **Specialities:** regional menu, home cooking. **Hotel:** 9 beds; 9 double rooms with shower, bath. **Other points:** bar, open to non-residents, à la carte menu, children welcome, terraces, car park, modern decor. **Address:** Le Bourg.
MR RAYMOND BELINGHERI
**Telephone:** 74.33.94.27
⊗ ⛉ ⌂ ☆ Map 14

## VILLARS SUR VAR, Alpes Maritimes, 06710

### AUBERGE ALP' AZUR, RN 202, the main road between Nice/Digne/Grenoble

**Languages spoken:** English and Italian. **Menu:** 65 to 200 Frs. **Restaurant:** Breakfast served from 6:00am. **Specialities:** regional menu, home cooking. **Other points:** bar, open to non-residents, terraces, pets welcome – check for details, car park. **Address:** Gare de Villars sur Var, Route Nationale 202.
MR MAURICE SÉCULA
**Telephone:** 93.05.75.44
⊗ ⛉ Map 13

## VILLEFRANCHE SUR SAONE, Rhône, 69400

### LE RELAIS CALADOIS, RN 6, Mâcon

**Languages spoken:** English and Spanish. **Menu:** 58 Frs. **Restaurant:** Breakfast served from 5:30am. Lunch served from 11:30am until 2:30pm. Dinner served from 7:00pm until 10:30pm. Closed Saturdays and 15 days in August. **Specialities:** regional menu. **Other points:** bar, open to non-residents, lounge area, terraces, pets welcome – check for details, modern decor. **Address:** 300, rue Joseph Léon Jacquemaire.
MR DENIS GIMARET
**Telephone:** 74.60.69.88
⊗ ⛉ Map 14

## VILLENEUVE, Alpes-de-Hautes-Provence, 04180

### CHEZ ROGER, RN 96, between Aix and Sisteron

**Places of interest:** Pointe de Jobourg, côtes de la Hague. **Menu:** 60 Frs. **Accommodation:** 100 Frs. **Restaurant:** Breakfast served from 5:00am. Closed Sundays, 15 days end of August and 15 days at Christmas. **Specialities:**

home cooking. **Hotel:** 7 beds; 5 single rooms, 2 double rooms with shower, private WC. **Other points:** bar, lounge area, terraces, pets welcome – check for details, car park, traditional decor. **Address:** Route Nationale 96.
PIERRE CURRI
**Telephone:** 92.78.42.47
⊗ ⛉ ⌂ Map 13

## VILLEURBANNE, Rhône, 69100

### CHEZ NICOLE, the main road between Paris and Genève

**Restaurant:** Lunch served from 11:00am until 2:00pm. Closed mid-August. **Specialities:** home cooking. **Other points:** bar, open to non-residents, pets welcome – check for details, car park, modern decor. **Address:** 165, rue Jean Voillot.
MME NICOLE GRASS
**Telephone:** 72.37.52.00
⊗ ⛉ Map 14

## VINEZAC, Ardèche, 07110

### AUBERGE DES COTES, RN 104, between Aubenas and Ales

**Menu:** 65 to 120 Frs. **Restaurant:** Breakfast served from 6:00am. Lunch served from midday until 2:00pm. Dinner served from 7:00pm until 8:00pm. Closed Saturdays and in September. **Specialities:** home cooking. **Hotel:** 3 beds; 3 single rooms with shower. **Other points:** bar, open to non-residents, car park, traditional decor. **Address:** Les Côtes.
MR SERGE ZAGAR
**Telephone:** 75.36.80.10
⊗ ⛉ Map 14

## VIVIERS SUR RHONE, Ardèche, 07220

### LE RELAIS DU VIVARAIS, RN 86, exit motorway for Montélimar north or south

**Places of interest:** Citadelle de Bitche, ligne Maginot, vestiges romains de Bliesbruck, faïencerie de Sarreguemines, musée et fabrique de cristal de Meisenthal. Mulhouse et ses musées, écomusée d'alsace. **Languages spoken:** English. **Menu:** 80 to 150 Frs. **Accommodation:** 100 to 200 Frs. **Restaurant:** Lunch served from midday until 2:00pm. Dinner served from 7:00pm until 9:00pm. Closed Wednesdays and in January. **Specialities:** regional menu, home cooking. **Hotel:** 10 beds; 8 single rooms, 2 double rooms with bath. **Other points:** bar, open to non-residents, children welcome, lounge area, terraces, pets welcome – check for details, car park, traditional decor. **Address:** Lieu dit 'Les Sautelles', Route Nationale 86.
MR ANDRÉ ESPÉRANDIEU
**Telephone:** 75.52.60.41
⊗ ⛉ ⌂ ⭗ ☆ Map 14

**Membership Application Form**
**Britannia Rescue**
**FREEPOST**
**Huddersfield**
**HD1 1WP**

BLOCK LETTERS PLEASE

SURNAME ➤ _____ INITIALS ➤ _____ TITLE (Mr/Mrs/Miss/Ms) ➤ _____

ADDRESS ➤ _____

_____

_____ POSTCODE ➤ _____ TEL NO ➤ _____

Cover commences from midnight of date of our receipt of this application form or later if you specify here ➤

COMPLETE SECTIONS **A** OR **B**, AND **C** TOGETHER WITH METHOD OF PAYMENT DETAILS.

| **A** ANNUAL RATES applicable to 31.12.94 or later review date. | Single Vehicle | ✓ Tick | Two Vehicles | ✓ Tick |
|---|---|---|---|---|
| SUPERSTART | £26.50 | | £53.00 | |
| RESCUE PLUS | £40.00 | | £60.00 | |
| STANDARD | £64.50 | | £81.75 | |
| COMPREHENSIVE | £72.00 | | £108.00 | |
| DELUXE | £88.00 | | £132.00 | |
| Optional extra PERSONAL COVER (with Free Card for Spouse  Please tick ☐ ) | | | £18.00 | |
| JOINING FEE (waived if payment made by Direct Debit or Continuous Credit Card Authority) | | | £10.00 | |
| ENTER TOTAL COST OF TICKED OPTIONS ➤ £ | | | | |

Note: ANNUAL RATE is a single payment, providing 12 months cover.

| **B** MONTHLY PREMIUMS (Direct Debit Only) | Single Vehicle | ✓ Tick | Two Vehicles | ✓ Tick |
|---|---|---|---|---|
| STANDARD | £5.50 | | £8.25 | |
| COMPREHENSIVE | £7.25 | | £10.75 | |
| DELUXE | £8.75 | | £13.25 | |
| Optional extra PERSONAL COVER (with Free Card for Spouse  Please tick ☐ ) | | | £1.80 | |
| ENTER TOTAL COST OF TICKED OPTIONS ➤ £ | | | | |

**Note: MONTHLY PREMIUMS are continuous payments available only by DIRECT DEBIT until cancelled by either party and are subject to amendments from time to time. Members are given prior notice of any change of payment.**

CAR GRILLE BADGE (inc. VAT and P&P) £4.35 payment by cheque only ☐  Additional vehicles – details on request

| **C** 1st CAR DETAILS | Reg No ▼ | Year New ▼ | Make ▼ | Model ▼ |
|---|---|---|---|---|
| | | | | |
| **2nd CAR DETAILS** | Reg No ▼ | Year New ▼ | Make ▼ | Model ▼ |
| | | | | |

The above rates are applicable only to vehicles under 2.5 tonnes/2,540 kilos gross vehicle weight.

I wish to apply for membership of Britannia Rescue and I certify that the vehicle(s) to be covered is/are fully roadworthy and in normal use and is/are insured and kept at my home address here given. I agree to abide by the Terms and Conditions of Britannia Rescue. **ALL MEMBERS MUST SIGN.**

SIGNATURE ➤ _____ DATE ➤ _____

**METHODS OF PAYMENT**

1. TRANSCASH ➤  Complete Transcash forms from the Post Office, make payable to Britannia Recovery Ltd., Girobank Account No 3006980. Please enclose receipt with application form. Standard Transcash fee will be payable.

2. CHEQUE/P.O. ➤  Make payable to Britannia Recovery Ltd.  Cheque/P.O _____

3. CREDIT CARD ➤  Please debit my  ACCESS ☐  VISA ☐  (please tick)

Card No ☐☐☐☐☐☐☐☐☐☐☐☐☐☐☐☐  Card Expiry Date _____

4. CONTINUOUS CREDIT CARD AUTHORITY ➤ Sign here only if you wish to authorise automatic renewal by credit card:

I authorise Britannia Recovery Ltd. until further written notice, to charge my Access/Visa card account with unspecified amounts in respect of my annual Britannia Rescue membership.

SIGNATURE ➤ _____ DATE ➤ _____

5. DIRECT DEBIT ➤  Please complete the direct debit mandate overleaf.

As part of our service, Britannia Rescue will send you information about valuable offers especially negotiated members. If you prefer not to receive this information, please tick here. ☐

269

# DIRECT DEBITING MANDATE

1. NAME OF ACCOUNT HOLDER

2. BANK SORTING CODE

3. BANK ACCOUNT NUMBER

NAME AND FULL POSTAL ADDRESS OF YOUR BANK

4. THE MANAGER

BANK LTD

After signature please return this form to: Britannia Recovery Limited, FREEPOST (No stamp required) Huddersfield HD1 1WP. Instructions cannot be accepted to charge Direct Debits to a Deposit or Savings Account.

Complete the Direct Debiting Mandate by entering:
(1) The name of the Account to be debited; (2) Your bank's Sorting Code; (3)Your Bank Account Number; (4) The name and address of your Bank; and (5) Sign and date the Mandate.

Your Direct Debit Mandate will only be used to collect your Britannia Rescue subscription. Should you wish to cancel your mandate you can do this by notifying your Bank and Britannia Rescue in writing.

Should any error be made by us you may claim reimbursement through your bankers under an indemnity effected by the Company in their favour and lodged with the committee of London Clearing Banks.

OFFICE USE ONLY

I/we authorise you until further notice in writing to charge to my/our account with you unspecified amounts which Britannia Rescue may debit thereto by Direct Debit.

5. SIGNATURE

DATE

WE REGRET THAT NO ALTERATIONS MAY BE MADE TO THE WORDING OF THIS MANDATE.

Index